BIOMES OF THE EARTH

DESERTS

Michael Allaby

Illustrations by
Richard Garratt

CHELSEA HOUSE
PUBLISHERS
An imprint of Infobase Publishing

Deserts

Copyright © 2006 by Michael Allaby

All rights reserved. No part of this book may be reproduced or utilized in any form or by any means, electronic or mechanical, including photocopying, recording, or by any information storage or retrieval systems, without permission in writing from the publisher. For information contact:

Chelsea House
An imprint of Infobase Publishing
132 West 31st Street
New York NY 10001

ISBN-13: 978-0-8160-5320-9
ISBN-10: 0-8160-5320-0

Library of Congress Cataloging-in-Publication Data
Allaby, Michael
  Deserts / author, Michael Allaby; illustrations by Richard Garratt.
      p. cm.—(Biomes of the Earth)
  Includes bibliographical references and index.
  ISBN 0-8160-5320-0
  1. Desert ecology—Juvenile literature. 2. Deserts—Juvenile literature. I. Garratt, Richard, ill.
II. Title. III. Series.
    QH541.5.D4A438 2006
    577.54—dc222005005611

Chelsea House books are available at special discounts when purchased in bulk quantities for businesses, associations, institutions, or sales promotions. Please call our Special Sales Department in New York at (212) 967-8800 or (800) 322-8755.

You can find Chelsea House on the World Wide Web at http://www.chelseahouse.com

Text design by David Strelecky
Cover design by Cathy Rincon
Illustrations by Richard Garratt
Photo research by Elizabeth H. Oakes

Printed in China

CP FOF 10 9 8 7 6 5 4 3 2

This book is printed on acid-free paper.

From Richard Garratt:
To Chantal, who has lightened my darkness

CONTENTS

Preface   ix
Acknowledgments   xiii
Introduction: What is a desert?   xv

CHAPTER 1
GEOGRAPHY OF DESERTS   1
Where deserts are found today   1
How deserts form   4
   Humidity   7
Climate changes of the past   7
Subtropical deserts   10
Deserts of continental interiors   13
West coast deserts   16
Polar deserts   19

CHAPTER 2
GEOLOGY OF DESERTS   23
How continents move   23
   Continental drift and plate tectonics   26
How mountains rise and wear away   29
Desert soils   33
   How soils are classified   35
What is sand?   36
Sand seas and sand dunes   37
   Types of sand dunes   40
Desert pavement and desert varnish   41
Mesas, buttes, and other desert landforms   43
What happens when it rains   45
Wells and oases   47

CHAPTER 3
DESERT CLIMATES 51

Why there are belts of desert throughout the subtropics 51
General circulation of the atmosphere 52
Adiabatic cooling and warming 55
Ocean gyres and boundary currents 56
Monsoons 58
Lapse rates and stability 60
Air masses, fronts, and jet streams 62
Why hot deserts are cold at night 65
Specific heat capacity 66
Why the climates that produce ice sheets are so dry 68
Why Antarctica is colder than the North Pole 69
Why deserts are windy places 73
Dust storms and sandstorms 74
Dust devils and whirlwinds 76
Conservation of angular momentum 79

CHAPTER 4
LIFE IN DESERTS 81

Photosynthesis, respiration, and desert plants 81
C3, C4, and CAM plants 84
Why plants need water 85
Typical plants of subtropical deserts 87
Typical plants of cold deserts 92
Typical animals of hot deserts 93
How heat kills and how animals stay cool 94
The camel: "ship of the desert" 97
How freezing kills and how animals keep warm 99
What happens during estivation and hibernation 102
Scorpions, spiders, and insects 105
Locusts 107
Locust plagues 109
Snakes and lizards 110
Sidewinders 112
Desert mammals 114
Parallel evolution and convergent evolution 116
Desert birds 118

Animals of the Arctic 121
Animals of the Antarctic 124

CHAPTER 5
HISTORY AND THE DESERT 126

When deserts grew crops 126
Desert civilizations 127
The Middle East: birthplace of Western civilization 130
Egypt 132
Peoples of the Sahara and Arabian Deserts 134
Peoples of the Asian deserts 136
Caravans and the Silk Road 138
Peoples of the American desert 140
Peoples of the Arctic 142

CHAPTER 6
DESERT EXPLORATION 145

Explorers in the Far North 145
Fridtjof Nansen 148
Discovering Antarctica 149
Explorers in the deserts of Africa, Arabia, and Asia 151
Ernest Shackleton 152
Roald Amundsen 153
Lawrence of Arabia 156
The Cave of a Thousand Buddhas 158

CHAPTER 7
DESERT INDUSTRIES 159

Oil and modern desert economies 159
Solar energy 161
Minerals, metals, and textiles 163
Solar chimney 164
Tourism 167

CHAPTER 8
THREATS TO DESERTS 171

Depleting the water below ground 171
Waterlogging and salination 173
Porosity and permeability 174

What climate change may mean for deserts   175
Natural climate cycles   178
    El Niño   178
    Milankovitch cycles   182
Overgrazing and desertification   183

CHAPTER 9
MANAGING THE DESERT   **187**
Halting the spread of deserts   187
The end of the nomadic way of life   188
Rainmaking   191
    The discovery of cloud seeding   193
Dams   194
    The Aswān High Dam   196
Diverting rivers   197
Farming oases and making artificial oases   199
Improving irrigation   201
    Qanats   202
Desalination   205
Icebergs to water desert crops?   207
Dry farming   209
Corridor farming   211
New crops for dry climates   213
    Genetic modification   214
Food from the polar regions   217
Conflicts over water resources   219

CONCLUSION   **222**
What future for deserts?   222

SI units and conversions   225
Glossary   228
Bibliography and further reading   239
Index   243

PREFACE

Earth is a remarkable planet. There is nowhere else in our solar system where life can survive in such a great diversity of forms. As far as we can currently tell, our planet is unique. Isolated in the barren emptiness of space, here on Earth we are surrounded by a remarkable range of living things, from the bacteria that inhabit the soil to the great whales that migrate through the oceans, from the giant redwood trees of the Pacific forests to the mosses that grow on urban sidewalks. In a desolate universe, Earth teems with life in a bewildering variety of forms.

One of the most exciting things about the Earth is the rich pattern of plant and animal communities that exists over its surface. The hot, wet conditions of the equatorial regions support dense rain forests with tall canopies occupied by a wealth of animals, some of which may never touch the ground. The cold, bleak conditions of the polar regions, on the other hand, sustain a much lower variety of species of plants and animals, but those that do survive under such harsh conditions have remarkable adaptations to their testing environment. Between these two extremes lie many other types of complex communities, each well suited to the particular conditions of climate prevailing in its region. Scientists call these communities *biomes*.

The different biomes of the world have much in common with one another. Each has a plant component, which is responsible for trapping the energy of the Sun and making it available to the other members of the community. Each has grazing animals, both large and small, that take advantage of the store of energy found within the bodies of plants. Then come the predators, ranging from tiny spiders that feed upon even smaller insects to tigers, eagles, and polar bears that survive by preying upon large animals. All of these living things form a complicated network of feeding interactions, and, at the base of the system, microbes in the soil are ready to consume the energy-rich plant litter or dead animal flesh that remains. The biome, then, is an integrated unit within which each species plays its particular role.

This set of books aims to outline the main features of each of the Earth's major biomes. The biomes covered include the tundra habitats of polar regions and high mountains, the taiga (boreal forest) and temperate forests of somewhat warmer lands, the grasslands of the prairies and the tropical savanna, the deserts of the world's most arid locations, and the tropical forests of the equatorial regions. The wetlands of the world, together with river and lake habitats, do not lie neatly in climatic zones over the surface of the Earth but are scattered over the land. And the oceans are an exception to every rule. Massive in their extent, they form an interconnecting body of water extending down into unexplored depths, gently moved by global currents.

Humans have had an immense impact on the environment of the Earth over the past 10,000 years since the last Ice Age. There is no biome that remains unaffected by the presence of the human species. Indeed, we have created our own biome in the form of agricultural and urban lands, where people dwell in greatest densities. The farms and cities of the Earth have their own distinctive climates and natural history, so they can be regarded as a kind of artificial biome that people have created, and they are considered as a separate biome in this set.

Each biome is the subject of a separate volume. Each richly illustrated book describes the global distribution, the climate, the rocks and soils, the plants and animals, the history, and the environmental problems found within each biome. Together, the set provides students with a sound basis for understanding the wealth of the Earth's biodiversity, the factors that influence it, and the future dangers that face the planet and our species.

Is there any practical value in studying the biomes of the Earth? Perhaps the most compelling reason to understand the way in which biomes function is to enable us to conserve their rich biological resources. The world's productivity is the basis of the human food supply. The world's biodiversity holds a wealth of unknown treasures, sources of drugs and medicines that will help to improve the quality of life. Above all, the world's biomes are a constant source of wonder, excitement, recreation, and inspiration that feed not only our bodies but also our minds and spirits. These books aim to provide the information about biomes that readers need in order to understand their function, draw upon their resources, and, most of all, enjoy their diversity.

ACKNOWLEDGMENTS

Richard Garratt drew all of the diagrams and maps that appear in this book. Richard and I have been working together for many years in a collaboration that succeeds because Richard has a genius for translating the weird electronic squiggles I send him into clear, simple artwork of the highest quality. As always, I am grateful to him for all his hard work. I also wish to thank Elizabeth Oakes for her fine work as a photo researcher.

I must thank Frank K. Darmstadt, Executive Editor, at Chelsea House. Frank shaped this series of books and guided them through all the stages of their development. His encouragement, patience, and good humor have been immensely valuable.

I am especially grateful to Dorothy Cummings, project editor. Her close attention to detail sharpened explanations that had been vague, corrected my mistakes and inconsistencies, and identified places where I repeated myself. And occasionally Dorothy was able to perform the most important service of all: She intervened in time to stop me making a fool of myself. No author could ask for more. This is a much better book than it would have been without her hard work and dedication.

Michael Allaby
Tighnabruaich
Argyll
Scotland
www.michaelallaby.com

INTRODUCTION

What is a desert?

Sand dunes as high as hills stretch into the distance for as far as the eye can see. Above them, the clear sky is pale blue, the Sun small and blazing intensely. A wind drives grains of sand that sting the face, but it is a hot wind that brings no relief from the Sun's scorching rays. Nothing lives in this barren place and nothing could. There is no water. This is a desert.

At least, it is one kind of desert, the kind they show in movies, and the description contains one important mistake. Deserts usually look empty—deserted, in fact—but this does not mean they are uninhabited. During the middle part of the day, when the Sun is high in the sky, animals shelter from the heat. You may see signs of them around dusk and dawn. That is when they seek food. Even during the heat of the day, however, there are traps awaiting any unwary insect or small mammal that should venture abroad. Spiders, scorpions, snakes, and other hunters lie hidden, still, silent, and invisible, but ready to leap or launch a lethal strike at any victim that comes within range.

There are plants too. Plants cannot grow on the sand dunes, because the surface is too unstable for their roots to gain a secure hold, but there are a few shrubs scattered sparsely on the firmer ground. Many more plants lie below ground, waiting as seeds for the occasional rain that will supply enough moisture for them to sprout, grow, flower, and produce seed, all in the brief interval before the ground dries out again.

There are even people living not far away. Groups of them pass this way from time to time. Some ride in trucks, or occasionally on camels, carrying goods to be sold in a market in some distant town. Others walk beside their herds of sheep, goats, cattle, or camels. Their animals have exhausted the pasture in one area and they are on their way to another. The desert is not so deserted as it seems.

Sandy deserts certainly exist, but most deserts are not vast oceans of sand. They are rocky, with a hard surface covered with stones and gravel and outcrops of bare rock. Deserts are windy places and over thousands of years the wind blows away all the dust and sand, exposing the underlying rock and leaving the stones that are too heavy for the wind to lift. In some deserts there are rocks carved by the wind into fantastic shapes. The sand must go somewhere, of course. It piles up to form dunes, but the dunes are constantly shifting as the restless wind ceaselessly rearranges the landscape.

Nor are all deserts hot. Even those that are hot by day are often very cold at night, but some deserts are cold for most of the time. They comprise vast expanses of dry, windswept plains dotted with patches of coarse grasses and tough, thorny shrubs. Deserts of this type are found in the centers of continents, thousands of miles from the ocean. There are also deserts lying beside coasts, where fog is common but rain is extremely rare.

A coastal desert is not far from water, but the ocean might as well be a million miles away, because its waters hardly ever fall on the land. Other deserts are even closer to water that no plant root can absorb.

Most of Antarctica and Greenland are covered by ice that is an average 6,900 feet (2.1 km) thick in Antarctica and up to 10,000 feet (3 km) thick in Greenland. This is a vast amount of water, but it is useless to plants because it is frozen. The polar ice sheets have accumulated slowly over millions of years, from snow that fell but failed to melt. Only a very small amount of snow falls each year, but it is enough to replace the ice that slides into the ocean, drifts away as icebergs, melts, and is lost. Antarctica and Greenland are deserts.

They are all very different: The vast, blistering sand seas, the rocky desert, the cold continental plain, the coastal desert, and the polar ice caps. Yet, different as they are, there is one characteristic they share. All of them have a dry climate.

It is the dry climate that produces a desert, rather than the temperature. Deserts can be hot or they can be cold, but they cannot be wet. All of them are arid wildernesses.

Aridity—dryness—does not result simply from a low average rainfall. Temperature also plays a part. What matters is not the amount of water that falls from the sky, but the amount that is available to plant roots below ground.

As soon as raindrops fall from the base of the cloud that produced them, they enter relatively dry air and begin to evaporate. Some of the water evaporates before even reaching the ground. This is common everywhere in the world. Evaporation continues when the water does reach the ground, so that only a portion of the rain soaks into the ground to the region where plant roots can reach it.

Snow will vaporize in dry air without melting first. This is called *sublimation,* and it removes some of the snow as it falls and also some of the snow lying on the ground. If snow melts after it has fallen, some of the water will evaporate.

Water evaporates when the air is dry. The amount of water vapor that air can hold increases as the temperature rises, so water evaporates faster into warm air than into cold air. As water evaporates, the layer of air next to the water surface becomes very moist. Wind sweeps away this moist air and replaces it with drier air into which more water can evaporate. That is how the wind exerts the drying effect we make use of when we hang laundry outdoors to dry.

Warm temperatures and wind accelerate evaporation. This means that the rate of evaporation varies from place to place. Evaporation removes water before plants can derive benefit from it. A desert will form wherever the amount of water reaching the ground in the course of the year is insufficient to replace the amount that could evaporate over the same period, so that the ground remains dry for most of the time. Plants benefit from occasional heavy rain, but the moisture soon evaporates and, despite being briefly carpeted in flowering plants, the desert remains desert.

CHAPTER 1

GEOGRAPHY OF DESERTS

Where deserts are found today

Cameras mounted on orbiting satellites photograph every part of the Earth at frequent intervals and broadcast the pictures to receiving stations on the ground. Many of the photographs are taken in light at infrared wavelengths. Our eyes cannot detect infrared light, but plants reflect it strongly and it makes them appear red in photographs. Scientists use these false color satellite photographs to measure the areas of the Earth that are covered with vegetation and also those that are not—the deserts and semiarid regions that are almost deserts.

The result is startling. They show that deserts like the Sahara, Arabian, and Gobi Deserts cover approximately one-fifth of the land surface of our planet. When the polar deserts are added the total is close to 30 percent. In addition to these extremely dry deserts, there are also areas that support a little vegetation and receive some rain in most years. They are not quite deserts, but they are dry for most of the year. These areas occupy about 28 percent of the Earth's land surface. When all of these desert and desertlike areas are added together, the total amounts to about 58 percent of the land area of our planet—approximately 33 million square miles (86 million km^2).

As the map on page 2 illustrates, there are deserts in every continent. The Mojave and Sonoran are the principal North American deserts. There is also a large area of semidesert to the west of the Great Salt Lake, Utah, centered on latitude 40°N. The Mojave Desert, in California, lies approximately between latitudes 34°N and 37°N, to the southeast of the Sierra Nevada. The Sonoran Desert, also known as the Yuma Desert and in the north as the Colorado Desert, is the largest North American desert, lying partly in Arizona and California, and partly in Sonora Province, Mexico.

In South America the Atacama Desert, running parallel to the coast of Chile between latitudes 5°S and 30°S, is the world's driest desert. The Patagonian Desert covers all of Argentina to the east of the Andes and south of the Colorado River, at latitude 39°S.

The Sahara is the world's biggest desert. It covers most of Africa north of latitude 15°N. Desert conditions continue eastward through Ethiopia and Sudan, and across the Red Sea, where the Arabian Desert covers the whole of the Arabian Peninsula, and to its north the Syrian Desert covers much of the Middle East. South of the equator, the Kalahari Desert extends from the tropic of Capricorn to about 27°S. To its west, the Kalahari merges into the Namib Desert—almost as dry as the Atacama—that runs along the coast of Namibia.

There are several deserts in central Asia. The largest and most famous is the Gobi, centered on latitude 40°N. To its west there lies the Taklimakan, or Takla Makan, Desert, con-

Location of the world's deserts. Regions of semidesert occupy a much bigger area.

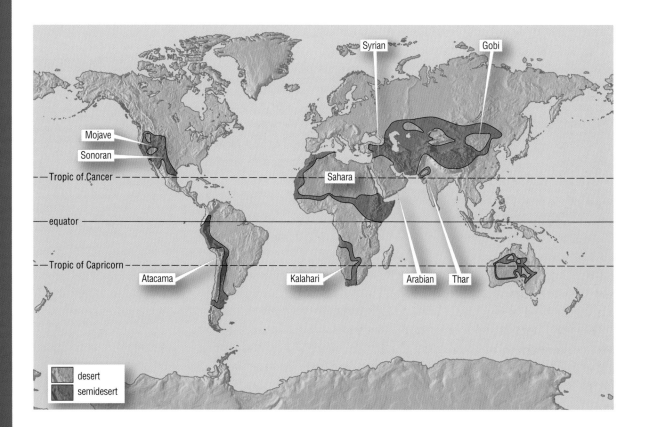

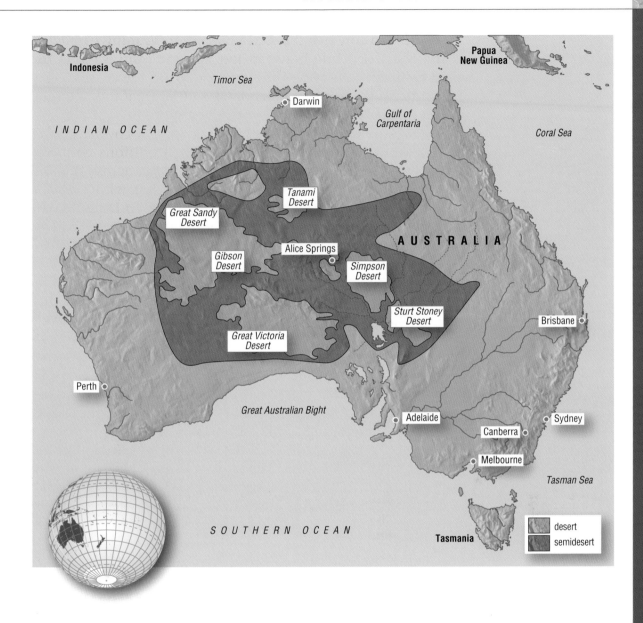

sisting mainly of drifting sand dunes. These deserts are located to the north of the Himalayas. To the south, in India, there is the Thar, or Great Indian, Desert.

Deserts cover a large part of the western side of the Australian interior. The tropic of Capricorn passes through the center of the Australian deserts. There is not one Australian desert, but five. The map shows their locations. The Great Victoria Desert is the largest, stretching across

The five Australian deserts: the Great Sandy, Gibson, Great Victoria, and Simpson Deserts, and the Nullarbor Plain

much of Western Australia and South Australia. To its south, the Nullarbor Plain is also desert, and the Gibson Desert lies to its north. The Simpson Desert is farther to the east, lying to the north of Lake Eyre, a large salt lake and, at about 60 feet (18 m) below sea level, the lowest point in Australia.

How deserts form

Deserts form when the climate becomes warmer or drier. The two are not always the same, because if the temperature rises more water will evaporate from the oceans. There will be more cloud and more rain. So a warmer climate is usually a wetter climate. A fall in temperature will reduce the rate of evaporation. There will be less cloud and less rain. The climates of the world were very much drier during the last Ice Age than they are today.

It sounds, then, as though warmer weather should make deserts shrink, but this is not necessarily the case. Warmer weather increases the rate of evaporation, but if the evaporation rate increases more than the rainfall, then the ground will become drier despite the rainfall having increased. Higher temperatures also reduce the rate at which water vapor condenses. As it grows warmer, the air is able to hold more moisture as water vapor, so although the amount of moisture in the air increases, less cloud forms and rainfall decreases. Deserts are more likely to form if the climate becomes cooler, but they may form if average temperatures increase.

Liquid water (H_2O) consists of groups of water molecules that are held together by *hydrogen bonds* between the hydrogen (H) atoms of one molecule and the oxygen (O) atoms of two adjacent molecules. The illustration on page 5 shows how hydrogen bonds link molecules. The groups of molecules move around and slide past one another, and the individual molecules vibrate. If the temperature rises the molecules have more energy. They vibrate more vigorously and the groups move faster. As the temperature continues to rise, more and more molecules absorb sufficient energy to break free from the hydrogen bonds and escape into the air as separate molecules of water vapor.

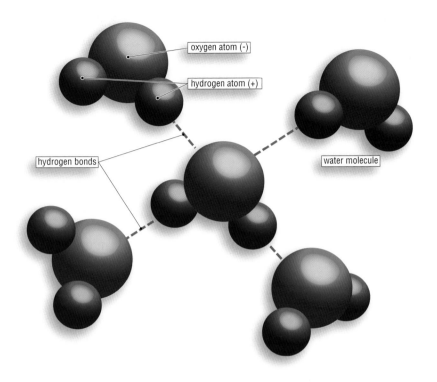

oxygen atom (-)

hydrogen atom (+)

hydrogen bonds

water molecule

Hydrogen bonds. Hydrogen bonds form between the positive charge at the hydrogen end of the water molecule and the negative charge at the oxygen end of adjacent molecules.

While this is happening, molecules of water vapor are also striking the surface of the liquid water and merging into it, so water molecules are both leaving and entering the liquid. If more molecules leave the liquid than enter it, the water evaporates, and the higher the temperature the faster is the rate of evaporation, because the molecules have more energy.

When water evaporates, the air pressure rises because of the water molecules that have entered it, and it increases as more and more water molecules escape into the air. The increase is called the *vapor pressure,* because it is the proportion of the total air pressure that is due to water vapor. Increasing the vapor pressure also means that more molecules are pushed back into the liquid, however. Eventually a point is reached when the number of water molecules entering the liquid is equal to the number leaving. In other words, evaporation and condensation balance. The vapor pressure has then reached the *saturation vapor pressure* and the mixture of air and water vapor is *saturated.*

If the temperature of the air and water rises, the rate of evaporation increases. More water enters the air and the saturation vapor pressure increases. This means that the vapor pressure must reach a higher value before condensation catches up with evaporation, and it is why warm air is able to hold more water vapor than cold air can. The difference is startling. At sea-level pressure and freezing temperature, 32°F (0°C), one pound of dry air can hold 0.27 ounces of water vapor (3.5 g/km). At 86°F (30°C) one pound of air can hold two ounces of water vapor (26.5 g/km), and at 104°F (40°C) it can hold 31.5 ounces (47 g/km). At a temperature of –40°F (–40°C), in contrast, one pound of dry air can hold only 0.008 ounce of water vapor (0.1 g/km).

The amount of water vapor present in the air is known as the *humidity.* This can be measured in several ways, described in the sidebar, but the most widely used measure is *relative humidity* (RH). This is the amount of water vapor expressed as a percentage of the amount needed to saturate the air. As the temperature rises, so does the saturation vapor pressure, and the RH falls. No moisture has been added to the air or removed from it, but the higher saturation vapor pressure means that the air is effectively drier. If the temperature is 32°F (0°C), for example, and the RH is 57 percent, warming the air to 86°F (30°C) will reduce the RH to 7.5 percent. The actual amount of moisture in the air remains the same, but the air has become very much drier.

As the ground dries, plants begin to wilt. At first they will recover if there is a heavy shower of rain, but after a time without water they are beyond hope of recovery. The plants wither and die. Their roots slowly decay, leaving the soil without the countless millions of root fibers that bound soil particles together. The soil loses its structure. Clay soils dry out and crack until the ground is hard as concrete, with deep, narrow fissures. Silt soils turn to dust, sandy soils into fine grains. Dust and grains blow in the wind. They fall on land nearby, coating plants or even burying them, killing those plants and allowing more soil to bake or crumble to dust. This is how the desert spreads.

Humidity

The amount of water vapor air can hold varies according to the temperature. Warm air can hold more than cold air. The amount of water vapor present in the air is called the *humidity* of the air. This is measured in several ways.

The *absolute humidity* is the mass of water vapor present in a unit of volume of air, measured in grams per cubic meter (one gram per cubic meter = 0.046 ounces per cubic yard). Changes in the temperature and pressure alter the volume of air, however, and this changes the amount of water vapor in a unit volume without actually adding or removing any moisture. The concept of absolute humidity takes no account of this, so it is not very useful and is seldom used.

Mixing ratio is more useful. This is a measure of the amount of water vapor in a unit mass of dry air—air with all the water vapor removed. *Specific humidity* is similar to mixing ratio but measures the amount of water vapor in a unit mass of air including the moisture. Both are reported in grams per kilogram. Since the amount of water vapor is always very small, seldom accounting for more than 4 percent of the mass of the air, specific humidity and mixing ratio are almost the same thing.

The most familiar term is *relative humidity*. This is the measurement you read from hygrometers, either directly or after referring to tables—and it is the one you hear in weather forecasts. Relative humidity (RH) is the amount of water vapor in the air expressed as a percentage of the amount needed to saturate the air at that temperature. When the air is saturated the RH is 100 percent (the "percent" is often omitted).

Climate changes of the past

Libya is a vast country. Coastal cities such as Benghazi and Tripoli receive a little rain in winter, but the interior of the country lies inside the Sahara, where it hardly ever rains. The climate was not always so dry, however. In the Tibesti Mountains, on the border between southeastern Libya and Chad (see the map on page 10), there are caves containing wall paintings that were made between 7,000 and 8,000 years ago. The artists were hunters, and their pictures portray the elephants, hippopotamuses, antelope, deer, giraffes, buffalo, and crocodiles that they pursued. Some of the pictures depict people traveling in a type of canoe.

Elephants survived in North Africa until much later. Hannibal (247–183 or 182 B.C.E.), the Carthaginian general who fought against the Romans, used about 38 elephants in one of his campaigns and in 218 B.C.E. they crossed the Alps to invade Italy from the north—though few of them survived the journey. In Hannibal's day, elephants still lived wild in the forests and grasslands of Carthage (modern Algeria), isolated from the main elephant population in the south.

Lake Chad is in the southern Sahara. The map below shows its location. After rain has fallen the lake covers an area of about 10,000 square miles (25,900 km²). But nowhere is it more than 20 feet (6 m) deep, and between rains its area shrinks, sometimes to as little as 4,000 square miles (10,360 km²). About 5,000 years ago, however, Lake Chad was an inland sea, in places more than 150 feet (45 m) deep. The shores of that ancient sea can still be identified and the desert

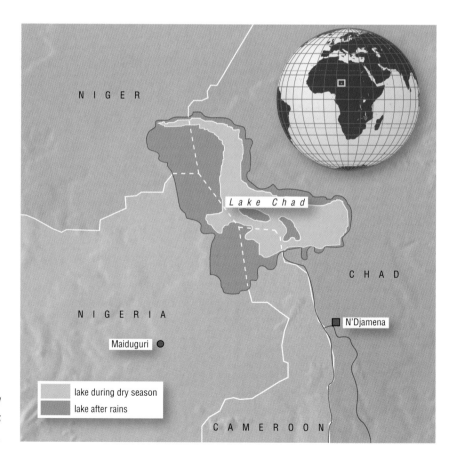

Lake Chad. Situated in the west of Chad, this was once an inland sea.

sands still contain the bones of fish that swam in it. Obviously, the climate was much wetter then.

Changes in climate make deserts appear and vanish, and the Sahara is not the only desert to be affected. A prolonged period of warm, wet weather affecting a large area is known as a *climatic optimum*. The hunters of the Tibesti Mountains lived during what was probably the warmest and longest climatic optimum since the end of the most recent Ice Age. It lasted from about 10,000 to 4,000 years ago and its effects were felt throughout the world. Between 6,000 and 4,400 years ago the rainfall was heavy enough to cause flooding in several ancient cities of the Middle East, including Ur and Nineveh, in modern Iraq. Australia had a much wetter climate than it does today, and about 4,000 years ago farmers were growing melons, dates, wheat, and barley in what is now the Thar Desert, on the border between India and Pakistan, where the annual rainfall was 16–32 inches (400–800 mm). Today the Thar Desert receives five to 10 inches (127–254 mm) a year.

Between about 4,500 and 3,700 years ago, as that optimum was nearing its end, a civilization was flourishing to the west of what is now the Thar Desert, in the Indus Valley, centered on the cities of Mohenjo Daro and Harappa (see the map on page 11). The annual rainfall then was 16–30 inches (400–760 mm). Today it is about 3.5 inches (89 mm).

There was another climatic optimum in Roman times, when North Africa was called the "granary of Rome." Outlines of the fields can still be seen from the air in what is now sandy desert. Rain fell at Alexandria, Egypt, in every month of the year except August. Today no rain falls at Alexandria from the end of April until early in October, and the annual rainfall averages only seven inches (178 mm).

During the Middle Ages, from the 10th to 14th centuries, there was another warm period. That is when the biggest Native American city north of Mexico was built and flourished. Its remains can be seen at the Cahokia Mounds State Park, to the east of St. Louis, Missouri.

Climates are changing constantly. As they change, deserts advance and retreat and, in response, civilizations have risen, flourished, and fallen.

Subtropical deserts

Sahrá is an Arabic word meaning "wilderness" and it gives its name to the Sahara, a wilderness that covers more than 3.5 million square miles (9.1 million km²), making it the biggest of the subtropical deserts. As the map below shows, parts of the Sahara are mountainous. Mount Tousidé in the Tibesti Mountains is an extinct volcano rising to 10,712 feet (3,265 m). Elsewhere there are low-lying basins, but much of the desert is on a plateau 1,300–1,600 feet (395–490 m) above sea level. The desert is conventionally divided into Atlantic, northern, central, southern, and eastern areas. The large Eastern Sahara is further divided into the Libyan and Nubian Deserts. The desert to the east of the Nile River in Egypt is considered part of the Arabian Desert. The Sahara continues to the east as the Arabian Desert, occupying virtually the whole of the Arabian Peninsula and the Syrian Desert, covering much of the Middle East.

As the name suggests, the subtropical deserts are centered on the tropic of Cancer in the Northern Hemisphere and the tropic of Capricorn in the Southern Hemisphere. Due to the way the continents are arranged over the surface of the Earth, there is less land in the Southern Hemisphere than in the Northern, and consequently the southern subtropical deserts occupy a smaller area than do those of the north.

The Sahara

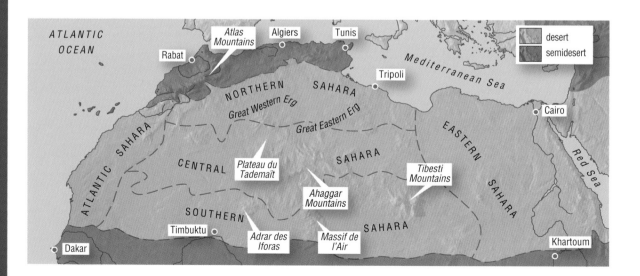

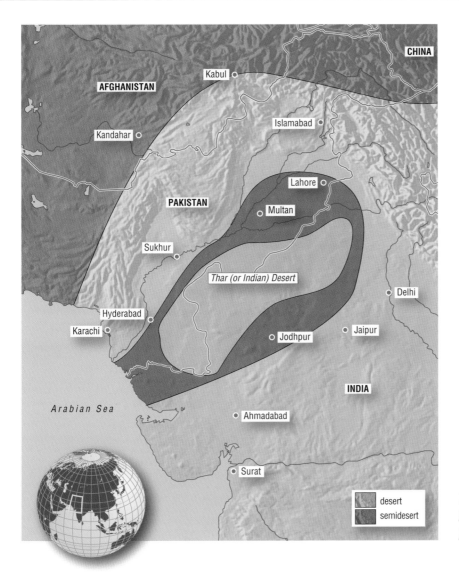

CHINA

AFGHANISTAN

Kabul

Islamabad

Kandahar

PAKISTAN

Lahore

Multan

Sukhur

Thar (or Indian) Desert

Delhi

Hyderabad

Karachi

Jaipur

Jodhpur

INDIA

Arabian Sea

Ahmadabad

Surat

desert
semidesert

Thar, or Great Indian, Desert, in northwestern India

A range of mountains, rising in some places to more than 9,000 feet (2,745 m) above sea level, runs down the western side of Arabia, parallel to the Red Sea coast. The central part of Arabia, to the east of the mountains, is called the *Najd* ("highland"). To the south of the Najd lies the largest sandy desert in the world, called the *Rub' al-Khali,* "the empty quarter," and covering about 230,000 square miles (595,700 km²). The desert to the north of the Najd is called *An Nafud.* The name simply means "desert," but An Nafud is also called the Great Sand Desert. It has fewer watering places than the Rub' al-Khali and is more difficult to cross. *Ad Dahna',* a line of high sand dunes about 50 miles (80 km) wide—sometimes called a sand stream—stretches for about 800 miles (1,290 km) from An Nafud to the Rub' al-Khali, separating the Najd from eastern Arabia.

Extending northward from An Nafud, the Syrian Desert covers western Iraq, eastern Jordan, and southeastern Syria. Its Arabic name is *Badiyat Ash Sham,* which means "arid wasteland." It is a mixture of true desert and poor grassland.

Farther to the east, across the Arabian Sea, the Thar, or Great Indian, Desert covers about half of the Indian state of Rajasthan and part of eastern Pakistan. The map shows its location. The Thar is a sandy desert—*thar* means "sandy waste"—covering about 77,000 square miles (199,430 km²).

The Kalahari Desert, in southern Africa, and the Australian deserts are the subtropical deserts of the Southern Hemisphere. The Kalahari covers about 275,000 square miles (712,250 km²) and the Australian deserts about 1.3 million square miles (3.4 million km²).

The map shows the location of the Kalahari, a desert that is not quite so dry as most subtropical deserts. Its annual rainfall ranges from 10 inches (254 mm) in the south to 25 inches (635 mm) in the north, although the eastern part of the desert receives only about five inches (127 mm) of rain a year. The Australian deserts receive less than 10 inches (254 mm) of rain a year. In both the Kalahari and Australian deserts the rate of evaporation is high enough to ensure that the ground is dry most of the time.

All of the subtropical deserts experience very high temperatures by day, but they can be very cold at night. At Timbuktu, Mali, for example, in the southern Sahara, average summer temperatures reach 110°F (43°C), but temperatures have been known to fall close to freezing on winter nights. In Salah, Algeria, it is even hotter, with July temperatures averaging 113°F (45°C) and sometimes rising to 122°F (50°C), but in winter the temperature at night sometimes falls below freezing. Frost is quite common in winter in many parts of Syria. The hottest place on Earth is El Azizia, Libya, where on September 13, 1922, the temperature rose to 136°F (57.8°C).

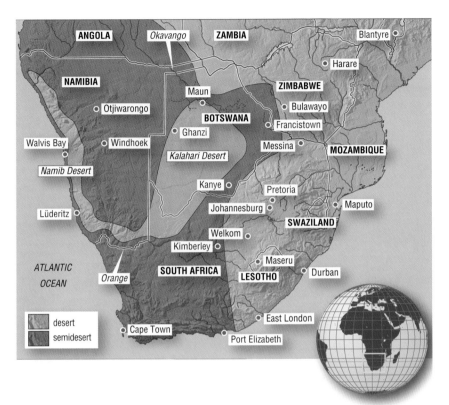

Kalahari Desert, in southern Africa

Deserts of continental interiors

At Ulan Bator (Ulaanbaatar), the capital of Mongolia, the temperature has been known to fall below freezing even in the middle of summer. Ulan Bator is situated on the central Asian steppe grasslands, but it is not far from the northern boundary of the Gobi Desert. There are no published weather records from the mining town of Dalandzadgad in the eastern Gobi, but Jiayuguan, on the southern border of the desert, has a dry climate. Almost no rain falls between October and February, and the average rainfall between March and September is 2.7–3.4 inches (69–86 mm). Winters are cool, with January average daytime temperatures of 27–30°F (from –3°C to –1°C); temperatures at nightfall to about 3–7°F (–16 to –14°C). Summers are warm, but not intensely hot. July is the warmest month in Jiayuguan, with daytime temperatures of 83–86°F (28–30°C). Hohhot, a town close to the eastern boundary of the Gobi, has an average temperature of 9.1°F (–12.7°C) in January and 72.7°F

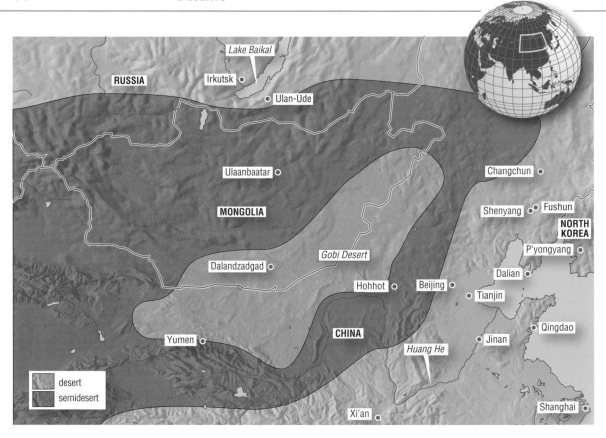

Gobi Desert, in southern Mongolia and the Chinese autonomous region of Inner Mongolia

(22.6°C) in July. The Gobi occupies a plateau, about 3,000 feet (914 m) above sea level in the east and 5,000 feet (1,524 m) in the west, surrounded by mountains. Its surface is mostly bare rock and gravel but with sand dunes in some places.

The total area amounts to about 500,000 square miles (1.3 million km²). Part lies in southern Mongolia and part in the Inner Mongolia Autonomous Region of China. The map above shows its location. Although the center of the Gobi receives only one to two inches (25–50 mm) of rain a year, about three-quarters of the total area supports grass, thornbushes, and other shrubs. Hohhot receives almost 16 inches (406 mm) of rain a year (some falling as snow).

The Gobi is desert and semidesert because of its great distance from the ocean. It is a desert of the type found in the deep interior of large continents outside the Tropics.

West of the Gobi there is another, much drier desert, the Taklimakan, or Takla Makan, covering most of the Tarim Basin, a low-lying area adjoining the Tarim River, in the Xinjiang Uygur Autonomous Region of China. The map below shows its location. It is a sandy desert with large dunes, some as much as 300 feet (91 m) high, covering an area of about 105,000 square miles (272,000 km²).

The climate is very dry. The western part of the desert receives an average of 1.5 inches (38 mm) of rain a year, but in the east the average is only 0.4 inch (10 mm). Sandstorms are common and often last for several days. It is also cool. Although the temperature sometimes rises to 100°F (38°C) the average July temperature is 77°F (25°C). In winter the temperature averages 14–16°F (–10°C) and it sometimes falls to –4°F (–20°C). There is some vegetation around the edges of the Taklimakan, but nothing lives in the inhospitable interior.

Taklimakan Desert, in western China, lies to the west of the Gobi Desert and to the north of Tibet.

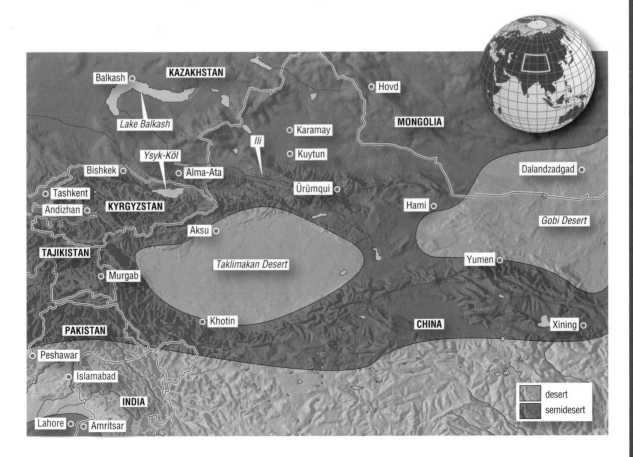

Patagonia is the Southern Hemisphere counterpart of the Gobi and Taklimakan. A desert occupying the interior of a continent, it covers all of Argentina to the east of the Andes and south of the Colorado River, at 39°S. Its total area is about 300,000 square miles (777,000 km²).

Although its climate is wetter than that of the Gobi and Taklimakan, nowhere in Patagonia receives as much as 10 inches (254 mm) of rain a year and little more than five inches (127 mm) a year falls in the central region. Average temperatures in central Patagonia range from 45°F (7°C) in July to 78°F (26°C) in January, but they have been known to rise to 99°F (37°C) in summer and to fall to 3°F (–16°C) in winter.

Patagonia is dry because weather systems arriving from the west lose their moisture as they cross the Andes. The desert lies in the *rain shadow* of the mountains. The Mojave Desert, in North America, is produced in the same way. It covers an area of 15,000 square miles (38,850 km²) to the south and east of the Sierra Nevada (see the map on page 18). The average rainfall is less than five inches (127 mm) a year, but there are woodlands in the mountains and cattle graze in parts of the desert. Summer temperatures often rise above 100°F (38°C). Winter temperatures average about 55°F (13°C) by day, but at night they fall to well below freezing.

West coast deserts

Patagonia is unusual in lying on the eastern side of the continent. Its climate is dry because weather systems approach it from the west. Mild, moist air from the ocean rises to cross the Andes and loses its moisture on the western side of the mountains. By the time the air reaches Patagonia it is able to deliver only a very small amount of rain.

Deserts in the subtropics more often form on the western sides of continents. This is because there the prevailing winds blow toward the equator, bringing cool, dense air that remains close to the ocean surface and prevents moist air from rising and forming clouds. During the day, the land warms up rapidly, but the sea remains cool. Warm air rises over land and cooler air blows in from the sea to replace it. This is a sea breeze, and sea breezes blow on most afternoons

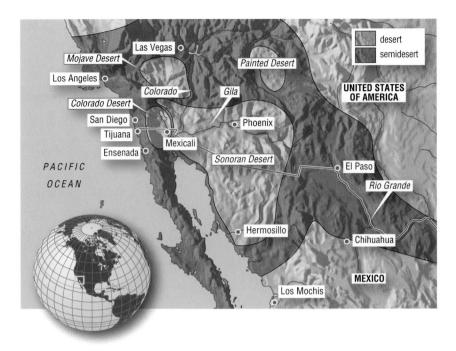

| desert |
| semidesert |

Las Vegas

Mojave Desert

Los Angeles

Painted Desert

Colorado

Gila

Colorado Desert

UNITED STATES
OF AMERICA

San Diego

Phoenix

Tijuana

Mexicali

Ensenada

Sonoran Desert

El Paso

PACIFIC
OCEAN

Rio Grande

Hermosillo

Chihuahua

MEXICO

Los Mochis

North American deserts

in many parts of the subtropics, but the approaching air has to cross cool ocean currents that flow parallel to the western coasts of continents (see "Ocean gyres and boundary currents" on pages 56–58). Contact with the cold water lowers its temperature, so the air tends to subside rather than rising. These climatic conditions produce *west coast deserts.*

The North American deserts, shown on the map above, are produced in this way, by air that has crossed the cool California Current. The Colorado Desert is part of the Sonoran Desert, also called the Yuma Desert and the Desierto de Altar. The Sonoran Desert covers 120,000 square miles (310,800 km²). Most of the area is low-lying. The bed of the Salton Sea, a brackish lake in the Colorado Desert, is 235 feet (72 m) below sea level, but the average elevation in the Sonoran Desert is 1,000 feet (305 m). The annual rainfall ranges from about four inches (102 mm) to more than 10 inches (254 mm) in a few places. Summers are hot, with temperatures that average 90°F (32°C) and can reach 125°F (52°C). Winter days are mild and the nights are cool.

The Atacama, the driest of all west coast deserts, extends for about 600 miles (965 km) parallel to the coast of Chile

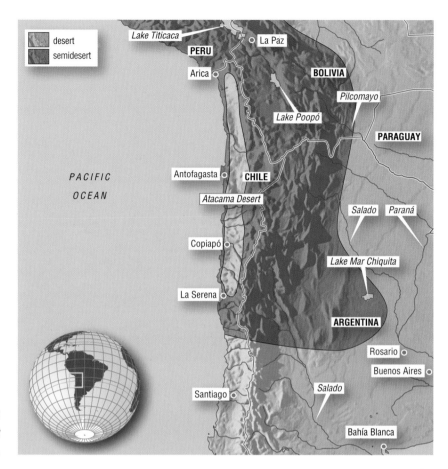

| desert |
| semidesert |

Lake Titicaca
PERU
La Paz
Arica
BOLIVIA
Pilcomayo
Lake Poopó
PARAGUAY
PACIFIC
OCEAN
Antofagasta
CHILE
Atacama Desert
Salado   Paraná
Copiapó
Lake Mar Chiquita
La Serena
ARGENTINA
Rosario
Buenos Aires
Santiago
Salado
Bahía Blanca

Atacama Desert, in Chile. This is the world's driest desert.

and has an area of about 140,000 square miles (363,000 km²). The map above shows its position. Air arriving from the ocean loses some of its moisture when contact with the Peru Current lowers its temperature, and it loses the remainder as it crosses the coastal mountains. Most of the Atacama lies in a depression behind the mountains. Along the coast, the average annual precipitation amounts to about 0.4 inch (10 mm), although it arrives as fog, not rain. Iquique, in the north, received an average of 0.06 inch (1.5 mm) of rain a year over a period of 21 years, including four years when no rain fell at all. Arica received less than 0.03 inch (0.75 mm) a year over 19 years. Despite being so dry, however, the air is very humid (see the sidebar "Humidity" on page 7). Iron corrodes rapidly.

The Atlantic Desert, on the western side of the Sahara, is a west coast desert associated with the cool Canary Current, and there is another west coast desert in southern Africa, associated with the Benguela Current. This is the Namib Desert (shown on the map of the Kalahari Desert on page 13), separated from the Kalahari by hills, except in the south where the two deserts meet, and covering about 19,300 square miles (50,000 km²).

Walvis Bay, on the coast about halfway along the approximately 932-mile (1,500-km) length of the Namib and about 50 miles (80 km) north of the tropic of Capricorn, receives an average of 0.8 inch (20 mm) of rain a year. The average for the desert as a whole is about two inches (51 mm) a year. Low clouds often drift in from the sea at night, bringing fog or light drizzle that clears quickly in the morning. The Namib is a very dry desert but not an especially warm one, despite its latitude. The average temperature at Walvis Bay is 66–75°F (19–24°C) throughout the year. Gravel covers the surface in the northern part of the Namib, but in the south there is a sand sea (see "Sand seas and sand dunes" on pages 37–41) with the highest dunes in the world. Some rise to almost 1,000 feet (305 m).

Polar deserts

As the air temperature falls, more and more water vapor condenses. Eventually the air is so cold that it contains almost no water vapor—it has been "squeezed dry." Greenland (Kalaallit Nunaat) and Antarctica are the coldest places on Earth. Because they are so cold they are also among the driest. They are polar deserts.

A team of German scientists spent the winter of 1930–31 on top of the Greenland ice cap studying weather conditions. They were the first people ever to overwinter on the ice and they recorded an average temperature of –52.9°F (–47.2°C) in February. In July the temperature never rose above 12.8°F (–3°C). Scientific expeditions have returned to the ice cap several times since then and have confirmed these temperatures.

Central Greenland is covered by ice that on average is about 5,000 feet (1,525 m) thick and more than 8,000 feet

(2,440 m) thick at its deepest point. Ice is frozen water, but this abundance of water is misleading. The climate is extremely dry, even for a desert. About three inches (76 mm) of snow falls each year. Snow takes up more space than liquid water because of the pockets of air between ice crystals, and after melting, this amount of snow is equivalent to about 0.3 inch (7.6 mm) of rain. The temperature never rises above freezing, so the snow never melts. Some is lost by sublimation—vaporizing directly into the dry air—but most remains where it lies. Its weight compresses the lower layers into ice and the ice sheet grows slowly thicker. At present it is growing thicker by about 0.8 inch (203 mm) a year. The ice sheet—the "Greenland desert"—covers an area of 708,069 square miles (1,833,898 km²). That is almost the size of Texas, New Mexico, Arizona, California, and Mississippi combined.

Antarctica is much bigger. Its total area is about 4.8 million square miles (12.4 million km²), which is more than half the area of North America. The Antarctic Peninsula and coastal

A typical landscape in Antarctica (Courtesy of Frans Lanting/ Minden Pictures)

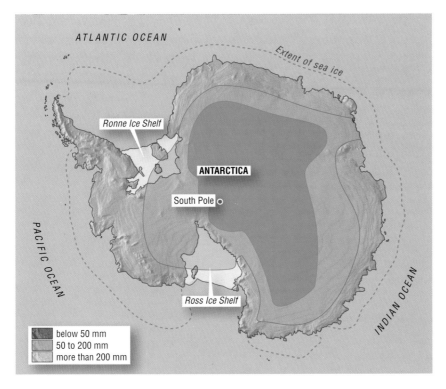

ATLANTIC OCEAN

Extent of sea ice

Ronne Ice Shelf

ANTARCTICA

South Pole

PACIFIC OCEAN

INDIAN OCEAN

Ross Ice Shelf

below 50 mm
50 to 200 mm
more than 200 mm

Precipitation in Antarctica. Most of the interior of the continent receives less than two inches (50 mm) of precipitation a year, measured by melting snow to give the rainfall equivalent.

areas receive the equivalent of more than about eight inches (200 mm) of rain a year. McMurdo station on the coast receives annually an average amount of snow equivalent to eight inches (200 mm) of rainfall. McMurdo has a desert climate, but it is a desert climate with frequent blizzards of snow blown up from the surface by fierce gales. As the map above shows, however, most of the continent receives the equivalent of less than eight inches (200 mm) of rain a year and a substantial area receives less than two inches (50 mm). At the South Pole, the average is little more than one inch (25 mm) a year.

Antarctica has a dry climate for the same reason that Greenland does: its low temperatures. Antarctica is much colder than Greenland, however, and so its air is even drier (see the sidebar "Why Antarctica is colder than the North Pole" on pages 69–70). Although the temperature near the coast reaches 32°F (0°C) for a short time in summer, it is never so warm as this inland. December—midsummer in the Southern Hemisphere—is the warmest month at the

Amundsen-Scott station at the South Pole, when the average temperature rises to –17.5°F (–27.5°C). Winters are much colder. In August, the coldest month, the average temperature is –75.9°F (–60.0°C). The average temperature over the whole year is 56.8°F (–49.3°C).

CHAPTER 2

GEOLOGY OF DESERTS

How continents move

Britain has a cool, wet climate. Its weather systems arrive mainly from the west, so they have crossed the Atlantic Ocean and they bring moist air that produces clouds and rain as it rises to cross the hills. If you explore Britain, however, you may discover some features that do not square with the kind of weather you see and feel around you.

In the first place, there are large coalfields. Most of the mines are closed now, because there is less demand for coal than there used to be, but the mining villages still exist and some mines are now museums. Coal is made from partly decayed plant material. It forms in tropical swamps—but you will find no tropical swamps in Britain.

Visit the south coast of Devon—a popular vacation destination in southwestern England—and you will find distinctive cliffs. Like all coastal cliffs, they are the result of the sea cutting into what were once low hills. They are distinctive because of their brick red color. They are made from a rock called new red sandstone. New red sandstone consists of desert sand that has been cemented together. The Devon hills were once sand dunes. The weather can be very pleasant in Devon, but the climate is not in the least like that of a desert, and inland from the coast you will see fields of crops and gently rolling pastures.

Nevertheless, there is no denying the evidence. British coalfields—and those of North America—were once tropical swamps. South Devon was once a hot desert, like the Sahara.

Climates change, but not to the extent of producing tropical swamps and hot deserts in Britain—an island in the latitude of Labrador. There must be another explanation, and there is. Britain once lay in the Tropics, and at another time it lay deep inside a vast continent, so far from the nearest coast that rain seldom reached it and it was desert. The continents have not always occupied the positions in which we see them today. They move around.

The suspicion that this might be so began as soon as there were reasonably accurate maps of the known world. People noticed that North and South America looked as though they might fit against Greenland, Europe, and Africa if only there were some way to push them all together—or perhaps they were once joined and have since been pushed apart.

More curious facts emerged as scientists gathered information from many parts of the world. There are several plant families that grow naturally in only a few places, but these are places separated by thousands of miles of open ocean. Marsupial mammals, the group that includes kangaroos and opossums, occur in Australia and New Guinea, and also in South and North America, on the opposite side of the Pacific Ocean. There were even more of these strange coincidences among fossil species. Animals move about, so perhaps there was some way they might have crossed oceans, but rocks stay put. Yet there are rock formations in West Africa that continue on the other side of the Atlantic, and rocks in the Highlands of Scotland that match rocks in Canada.

In the early years of the 20th century Alfred Lothar Wegener (1880–1930), a German meteorologist, drew together all of these strands of evidence, and more. He described the conclusions he reached in a short book called *Die Entstehung der Kontinente und Ozeane* (The Origin of the Continents and Oceans), published in 1912, and expanded them in a larger edition of the book published in 1915. Wegener proposed that the continents were once joined together into a single supercontinent that he called Pangaea—the name means "all Earth." Pangaea later broke apart and its fragments slowly moved to their present positions. Wegener thought that the mountains running down the western side of North and South America were due to crumpling of the continent as it was pushed westward, and that the Himalayas also formed by crumpling, due to a collision between India and Asia. He called this process *continental displacement* and maintained that it continues to the pres-

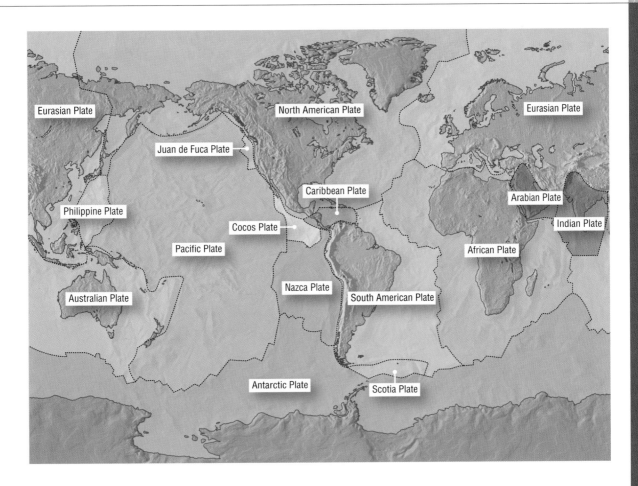

Eurasian Plate

North American Plate

Eurasian Plate

Juan de Fuca Plate

Caribbean Plate

Arabian Plate

Philippine Plate

Indian Plate

Cocos Plate

Pacific Plate

African Plate

Nazca Plate

South American Plate

Australian Plate

Antarctic Plate

Scotia Plate

The major plates that form the Earth's crust

ent day. The name of the process was later changed. We know it as *continental drift.*

His idea found little support, despite the mountain of evidence he found to back it up. The problem was that geologists could think of no way for continents to move. They believed that the rocks forming the continents rested on a solid base and that consequently it was impossible for them to move. It was not until the 1960s, long after Wegener's death, that geologists discovered that the Earth's crust is divided into a number of sections, called *plates,* resting upon a layer of very dense hot rock that is able to flow. The plates are able to move and change their shape, or deform. Deformation is also called *tectonism* and the overall description, including continental drift, is now known as the theory of plate tectonics.

Continental drift and plate tectonics

The Earth is made up of layers, so it comprises a series of spheres, one inside another, as shown in the illustration on page 27. At the center is the solid *inner core,* with a radius of 759 miles (1,221 km) and made from iron, with some nickel and other metals. Surrounding the inner core is the *outer core,* 1,404 miles (2,260 km) thick. It is made from the same metals but is liquid. The outer core is surrounded by the *mantle,* made from rock. The lower mantle is about 1,392 miles (2,240 km) thick and solid. Its upper boundary is about 404 miles (650 km) below the Earth's surface. The upper mantle extends to the base of the *crust,* three to nine miles (5–15 km) below the floor of the oceans and 19–50 miles (30–80 km) below the surface of the continents.

The upper mantle is also made from rock, but it is much less dense than the rock of the lower mantle. Together, the crust and the uppermost part of the upper mantle compose the *lithosphere.* The lithosphere is rigid and brittle, but the part of the upper mantle beneath it, called the *asthenosphere,* is so densely compressed that its material is able to flow—extremely slowly, like a very thick liquid. The lithosphere floats on top of the asthenosphere.

Heat moves through the rigid lithosphere by conduction, but it moves by convection through the asthenosphere. Conduction is the transfer of heat by direct contact between objects at different temperatures, such as when you warm yourself by hugging a hot-water bottle. Convection is the transfer of heat by movement within a fluid—a liquid or gas. In the asthenosphere, material that is heated by contact with the hotter material below rises slowly, cools below the base of the lithosphere, and then sinks back into the mantle. The lithosphere consists of a number of sections, or *plates.* Convection causes movements in the asthenosphere that carry the plates with them, so that the plates move in relation to one another. The movement is slow, averaging about two inches (50 mm) a year. Some plates are diverging, some converging, and some are moving past one another. Continents rest

There are approximately 12 major plates and a number of minor ones. The map shows most of the largest plates. Plates move apart at ridges, where new material rises from beneath the crust and solidifies to make new crust. Where plates of different density converge, the denser plate will sink—be subducted—beneath the less dense. This may scrape sedimentary rock from the lighter plate to form new mountains. Oceanic crust is denser than continental crust, so subduction

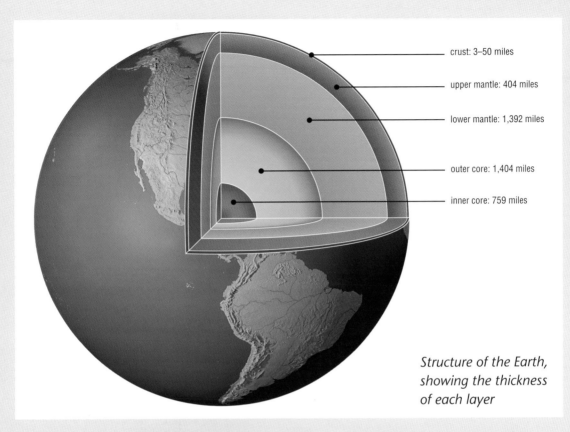

crust: 3–50 miles

upper mantle: 404 miles

lower mantle: 1,392 miles

outer core: 1,404 miles

inner core: 759 miles

Structure of the Earth, showing the thickness of each layer

on plates, so as the plates move, so do the continents. At the same time, oceans open, expand, and then close until the continents on either side meet. The rate of movement is slow, but over many millions of years it drastically alters the map of the world. The maps on page 28 show how the continents and oceans are arranged today and where they were located 65, 135, 180, and 200 million years ago (Ma).

occurs at the margins of continents. Where two continental plates collide, neither plate is subducted; instead the rocks crumple to form high mountains, such as the Himalayas. Plates also move past one another along *transform faults*. All active plate margins are associated with earthquakes and volcanoes.

Scientists now understand the way continents move (see the sidebar on page 26). The theory of plate tectonics explains

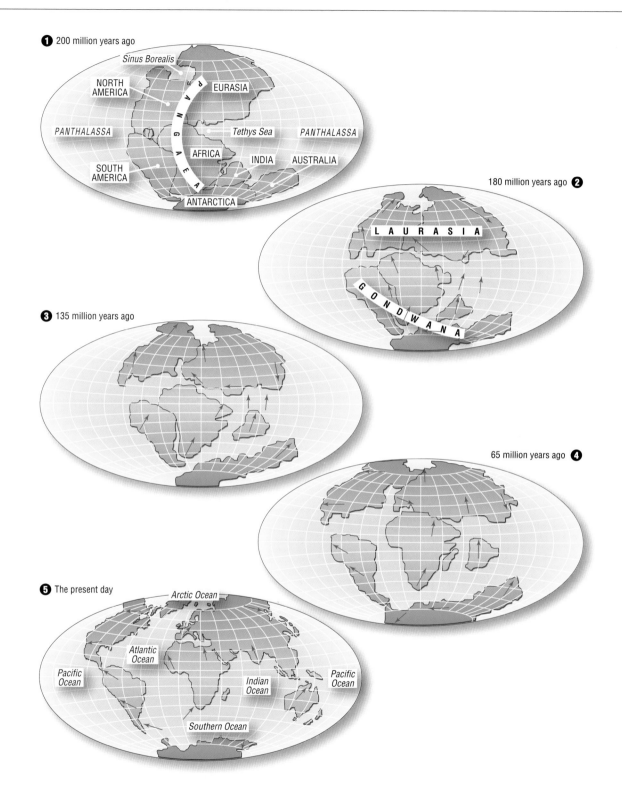

❶ 200 million years ago

Sinus Borealis

NORTH AMERICA

EURASIA

PANTHALASSA

PANGAEA

Tethys Sea

PANTHALASSA

AFRICA

INDIA

AUSTRALIA

SOUTH AMERICA

ANTARCTICA

180 million years ago ❷

LAURASIA

GONDWANA

❸ 135 million years ago

65 million years ago ❹

❺ The present day

Arctic Ocean

Atlantic Ocean

Pacific Ocean

Indian Ocean

Pacific Ocean

Southern Ocean

how it is that about 350 million years ago parts of Britain, Pennsylvania, and many other places were tropical swamps and how, some 250 million years ago, Devon was part of a vast desert.

How mountains rise and wear away

There are fossil seashells high in the Himalayas. It was by studying fossils of fish found in the rocks of the Alps, thousands of feet above sea level and hundreds of miles from the nearest coast, that scientists learned much of what we know about the kinds of fish that lived hundreds of millions of years ago. These mountains and others that formed in the same way are made partly from seafloor sediments that were compressed into sedimentary rock. Mountains such as these are produced when tectonic plates collide.

About 50 million years ago, during the period of the Earth's history known as the Eocene epoch, India, traveling northward on the Indian Plate, crashed into the southern edge of the Eurasian Plate. Continents are made from rocks that are less dense than the rocks forming the ocean floor. Consequently, when two continents collide it is impossible for one plate to sink beneath the other, because both plates are equally buoyant. Instead, the two sections of continental crust crumple upward, usually with one plate riding over the other. This produces very high mountain ranges. The collision between India and Eurasia raised the Himalayas—and the collision is not ended. India is still moving northward at a rate of 1.5–2 inches (4–5 cm) a year and crumpling has shortened the Indian Plate by about 600 miles (1,000 km). As a result, the Himalayas are still rising, though they are probably not growing higher because of rapid erosion.

The Rocky and Andes Mountains, running down the western side of North and South America respectively, grew over a

(opposite page) *Continental drift. The maps show the arrangement of the continents at different times in the past and their arrangement today. The arrows indicate the direction in which the continents have moved and are still moving.*

much longer period, starting about 230 million years ago in the Jurassic period and ending about 100 million years ago, during the Cretaceous (see the table below). These mountains are highly complex and formed in several distinct stages, but the process began when the North and South American Plates started traveling westward, separating from each other and riding over several ocean plates.

Geologic time scale

Eon/ Eonothem	Era/ Erathem	Subera	Period System	Epoch/ Series	Began Ma*
		Quaternary	Pleistogene	Holocene	0.11
				Pleistocene	1.81
Phanerozic	Cenozoic	*Tertiary*	Neogene	Pliocene	5.3
				Miocene	23.03
			Paleogene	Oligocene	33.9
				Eocene	55.8
				Paleocene	65.5
	Mesozoic		Cretaceous	Upper	99.6
				Lower	145.5
			Jurassic	Upper	161.2
				Middle	175.6
				Lower	199.6
			Triassic	Upper	228
				Middle	245
				Lower	251
	Paleozoic	Upper	Permian	Lopingian	260.4
				Guadalupian	270.6
				Cisuralian	299
			Carboniferous	Pennsylvanian	318.1
				Mississippian	359.2
			Devonian	Upper	385.3
				Middle	397.5
				Lower	416
		Lower	Silurian	Pridoli	422.9
				Ludlow	443.7
				Wenlock	428.2
				Llandovery	443.7
			Ordovician	Upper	460.9
				Middle	471.8

Eon/ Eonothem	Era/ Erathem	Subera	Period System	Epoch/ Series	Began Ma*
				Lower	488.3
			Cambrian	Furongian	501
				Middle	513
				Lower	542
Proterozoic	Neoproterozoic		Ediacaran		600
			Cryogenian		850
			Tonian		1000
	Mesoproterozoic	Stenian			1200
			Ectasian		1400
			Calymmian		1600
	Paleoproterozoic	Statherian			1800
			Orosirian		2050
			Rhyacian		2300
			Siderian		2500
Archean	Neoarchean				2800
	Mesoarchean				3200
	Paleoarchean				3600
	Eoarchean				3800
Hadean	Swazian				3900
	Basin Groups				4000
	Cryptic				4567.17

Source: International Union of Geological Sciences, 2004.

Note: *Hadean* is an informal name. The Hadean, Archean, and Proterozoic eons cover the time formerly known as the Precambrian. *Quaternary* is now an informal name and *Tertiary* is likely to become informal in the future, although both continue to be widely used.

*Ma means millions of years ago.

This is the way many mountains form. The process of mountain-building is called an *orogeny*. The Himalayas and Alps result from the *Alpine-Himalayan orogeny* and the mountains of western America from the *Cordilleran orogeny*.

No sooner does a mountain begin to rise than it begins to wear away by *weathering*—a relentless process of *erosion*. Although the Himalayas are still being pushed upward, this does not mean that mountaineers who climb Mount Everest today have to scale a higher peak than those who climbed the mountain several decades ago. Indeed, the opposite may be true, and due to weathering Everest may be a few inches shorter now than it was about 20 years ago.

Snow accumulates in depressions high in the young mountains and its weight compresses the lower layers into ice. Eventually the ice is so thick that it overflows and begins to move down the mountainside as a glacier. Glaciers scour away at the rock beneath them, pushing loose rocks and gravel ahead of them and to the sides. At the same time, water flows into small cracks between rocks and freezes in winter. It expands as it freezes, widening the cracks and breaking off small fragments of rock. Wind blows tiny rock grains against the rock, wearing away the surface. Lower down the mountain, where the temperature is above freezing, rivers carry some of this eroded material down onto the plains and eventually to the sea.

Little by little, the mountains wear away, but while they are being eroded another process is making them rise. Mountains are made from continental rocks, which are less dense than the material of the asthenosphere beneath them

Isostasy. Mountains have roots that extend into the asthenosphere, like the part of an iceberg that lies below the ocean surface. As the upper part of the mountain is worn away by erosion, the mass of the mountain decreases and it rises higher in the asthenosphere.

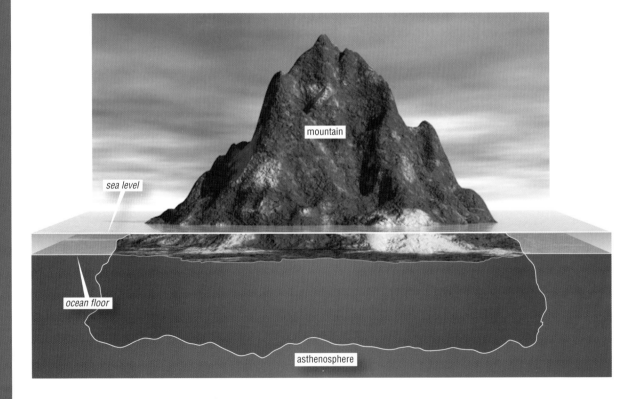

(see the sidebar "Continental drift and plate tectonics" on page 26). Mountains float in the asthenosphere, so that the part we see protruding above the surface is only part of the complete mountain. Below the level of the ocean floor the mountain extends downward, like the part of an iceberg that extends below the surface of the sea. The illustration shows how a mountain floating in the asthenosphere resembles an iceberg floating in the sea. As the exposed part of the mountain erodes, the total mass of the mountain decreases and therefore the mountain rises, to float higher in the underlying rock.

Erosion continues until eventually, after a very long time, the mountains are reduced to low rolling hills. The softer rocks disappear first, but finally even the hardest rock is worn away.

Although the mountains disappear, the rock from which they are made survives. Ground into tiny grains, the mountain rock is carried away by rivers and blown by the wind, until it reaches the sea. There it settles to the bottom as sediment that one day will sink back into the Earth's mantle or be raised above the surface once more to form part of a new range of mountains.

Desert soils

Soil is a mixture of mineral particles and the decomposed remains of plant and animal material, called *humus*. The mineral particles are usually derived from the underlying rock by chemical reactions that dissolve certain compounds present in the rocks, thus weakening the rock and allowing fragments to be detached.

Plant roots absorb some of the compounds released in this way, but the compounds are soluble in water and gradually, as the soil grows older, they are washed to deeper levels. Nutrients that have drained in this way accumulate some distance from the surface until, in a mature soil, there are distinct layers, called *horizons,* extending from the surface all the way down to the bedrock.

Soil formation begins with bare rock and reaches maturity with deep, layered soils that support luxuriant plant life and the animals associated with it. The rate at which soil develops depends on the climate. It happens fastest where summers are warm and winters mild, and where there is abundant rainfall throughout the year. The physical and chemical characteristics of the resulting soil vary according to the composition of the underlying rock—known as the *parent material*—and the type of vegetation that grows in it. There are many possible variations and consequently there are many types of soil. Pedologists—scientists who study soils—classify them in much the same way that biologists classify plants and animals. The sidebar on page 35 outlines the way classification works.

Deserts have a dry climate, so desert soils develop very slowly. Lack of moisture greatly slows the release of mineral compounds from the rock, and the dry climate means that vegetation is sparse. There is less dead plant and animal matter to contribute organic matter and structure to the soil, and decomposition happens more slowly. Dead leaves, plants, animal wastes, and animal bodies tend to dry out rather than decompose.

When rain does fall, it is often torrential. Most of the water runs off across the surface (see "What happens when it rains" on pages 45–47). Rain that does soak into the ground seldom penetrates deeper than about 40 inches (1 m). Calcium carbonate and silicate compounds—oxides of silicon—are washed downward by the rain and tend to accumulate at this *wetting front,* where they may solidify into a hard layer. At about the same level some desert soils have accumulations of clay, salt, or gypsum (calcium sulfate).

Some areas that are deserts today were not always deserts. Much of the northern Sahara was farmed as recently as Roman times. In places like these the soil formed under different climatic conditions and the old soils are preserved. These soils may date from before the last Ice Age, making them more than 75,000 years old.

Lack of water means that there are few plants and the soil contains very little organic matter. Because the land is barren it is natural to assume that the soil is infertile. This is not the case, however. Desert soils are among the most fertile of all soils. This is because there is insufficient rain to wash away the soluble nutrients. Really ancient soils, such as those of

How soils are classified

Farmers have always known that soils vary. There are good soils and poor soils, heavy soils containing a large proportion of clay, sandy soils that dry out rapidly, and light, loamy soils that retain moisture and nutrients. Loam is a mixture of sand, silt, and clay—mineral particles of different sizes. In the latter part of the 19th century Russian scientists were the first to attempt to classify soils. They thought that the differences between soils were due to the nature of the parent material—the underlying rock—and the climate. They divided soils into three broad classes. *Zonal* soils were typical of the climate in which they occur, *intrazonal* soils were less dependent on climate for their characteristics, and *azonal* soils were not the result of climate. Azonal soils include windblown soils and those made from silt deposited by rivers on their floodplains. Individual soil types were placed in one or other of these broad groups. This system remained in use until the 1950s, and some of the Russian names for soils are still widely used, such as Chernozem, Rendzina, Solonchak, and Podzol.

American soil scientists were also working on the problem, and by the 1940s their work was more advanced than that of their Russian colleagues. By 1975 scientists at the United States Department of Agriculture had devised a classification they called "Soil Taxonomy." It divides soils into 10 main groups, called orders. The orders are divided into 47 suborders, and the suborders are divided into groups, subgroups, families, and soil series, with six "phases" in each series. The classification is based on the physical and chemical properties of the various levels, or *horizons*, that make up a vertical cross section, or *profile*, through a soil. These were called "diagnostic horizons."

National classifications are often very effective in describing the soils within their boundaries, but there was a need for an international classification. In 1961 representatives from the Food and Agriculture Organization (FAO) of the United Nations, the United Nations Educational, Scientific, and Cultural Organization (UNESCO), and the International Society of Soil Science (ISS) met to discuss preparing one. The project was completed in 1974 and is known as the FAO-UNESCO Classification. Like the Soil Taxonomy, it was based on diagnostic horizons. It divided soils into 26 major groups, subdivided into 106 soil units. The classification was updated in 1988 and has been amended several times since. It now comprises 30 reference soil groups and 170 possible subunits. The FAO has also produced the World Reference Base (WRB), which allows scientists to interpret the national classification schemes.

tropical rain forests, have lost almost all of their plant nutrients and when farmers clear the forest to grow crops they find that after a few years they have to apply large amounts of fertilizer. All the desert soil needs is moisture. Provide water, and crops will flourish in it.

What is sand?

Think of deserts and the first picture that springs to mind is likely to be one of a landscape covered with sand. Sand is one of the most abundant substances on Earth and an ingredient of most soils. Take a pinch of moist soil and rub it between your thumb and forefinger, and if it feels gritty—and probably it will—the soil contains sand.

Sand grains are tiny fragments of rock. Most sand is made from quartz, which is *silica*—the common name for silicon dioxide (SiO_2). Quartz is an important ingredient of many rocks, especially granite and rocks related to granite. Granite forms when molten rock cools and solidifies. As it cools, the minerals it contains form crystals. Silica forms quartz crystals, which are triangular in cross section. They are hard and it is their sharp edges that make sand grains gritty.

The size of the crystals depends on the rate at which the molten rock cooled. Large crystals grow in rock that cooled slowly. If the rock cooled rapidly the crystals are small, and if it cooled very fast they may be so small they are visible only under a microscope. Pure quartz is clear, like the best quality glass, but impurities transform it into colored versions, some of which are semiprecious stones. Amethyst (purple), cairngorm (dark brown), and citrine (yellow or orange) are varieties of quartz.

Beach sand is a mixture of quartz grains mixed with particles of other minerals and variable amounts of shell fragments. Desert sand is usually made almost entirely from quartz. Sand grains range in size from 0.002 to 0.079 inches (0.05–2 mm). Soils also contain silt and clay. Silt comprises grains that are smaller than 0.000002 inch (0.05 μm), and clay particles are smaller than 0.00000008 inch (0.002 μm). When they are moist, these particles cling to one another, but when they are completely dry, silt turns to fine dust and clay either turns to dust or packs together into a hard mass— bricks are made from clay. (One micrometer (μm) is one millionth of one meter.)

Deserts are often extremely hot by day but very cold at night. This wide range in temperature makes rocks expand and contract repeatedly, shattering them into fragments that are rolled about by the wind until repeated impacts have broken them into small grains. Occasional torrential downpours of rain wash the grains down hillsides and discharge them onto the plains below, where they quickly dry. The smallest and lightest particles travel farthest. Silt and clay tend to accumulate in hollows, as sediments on the beds of temporary lakes. The wind carries some silt particles beyond the desert. Windblown silt forms deposits of a type of soil called *loess*.

Gravel and larger stones are carried for much shorter distances, but each downpour carries them a little farther. After thousands of years they cover extensive areas.

Dry sand is blown away by the incessant wind (see "Dust storms and sandstorms" on pages 74–76). That is why deserts contain large areas of bare rock or boulders that have been worn smooth by the erosive action—sandblasting—of windblown sand.

Airborne sand eventually falls to the ground, and it does so in particular areas because of the direction and strength of the prevailing winds. Just as repeated rainstorms produce surfaces of gravel and stone, the wind deposits sand in areas that grow into vast seas of sand.

Sand seas and sand dunes

For much of the Carboniferous period, 362.5–290 million years ago, the land that now forms the Sahara and Arabian Peninsula lay beneath the sea. Sand covered the seabed. Over time the sediment was compressed and the sand grains cemented together, forming sandstone. The sea retreated but returned about 70 million years ago and deposited more sand. When the land finally arose from the sea much of its surface consisted of sandstone that immediately began to erode. Today sand is abundant.

Sand is so abundant that in places it resembles the sea—a sea of sand, complete with waves. A sand sea in the Sahara is called an *erg* and there are several (see the map on page 10).

One of the largest, the Great Eastern Erg, in Algeria, covers about 74,000 square miles (192,000 km²). The ergs lie in depressions, resembling ocean basins, where sand collects. The Great Eastern and Great Western Ergs are separated by about 60 miles (100 km) of higher ground where the surface is covered by gravel. The Rub' al-Khali (Empty Quarter) of Arabia is also a sand sea.

Level expanses of sand often have a rippled surface, like a beach at low tide. In the desert, of course, the ripples are produced by the wind and not by water. Gradually the wind carries loose sand into places where it piles up into dunes. The world's biggest dunes are found in the Namib Desert (see "West coast deserts" on pages 16–19), but some Saharan dunes are 100 feet (30 m) high.

Sand dunes are hills of windblown sand. Wind has the power to raise sand grains, but usually they fall to the surface again within a short distance. No one is quite sure how a dune begins, but once there is a small pile of sand, the wind blowing up the side of the pile will carry sand toward the top.

Wind accelerates as it blows over the heap. This is because the surface-level air has farther to travel than the air above it, well clear of the surface, but it must arrive on the far side at the same time. As it accelerates, the wind raises sand grains from the upwind side of the heap and carries them up the slope. When the wind reaches the top it slows sharply and no

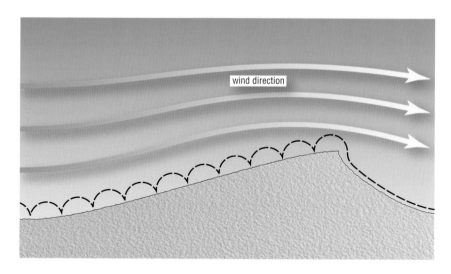

How sand dunes form. The wind blows sand grains up the gentle slope on one side of the dune. At the crest the grains tumble down the steeper side.

wind direction

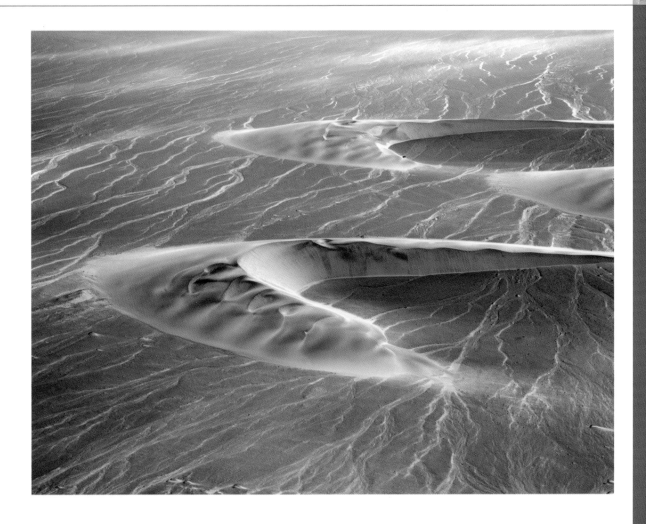

longer has enough energy to carry the sand, so sand falls onto the top of the heap.

There is a limit to how steep the sides of a sand heap can be. Although moist grains will stick together—that is what makes it possible to build sandcastles on the beach—dry sand will not hold together in this way. If you pour dry sand onto the center of a heap of sand, sand grains will run down the sides. The pile will grow higher and wider, but its sides will not grow any steeper. They will never slope at an angle of more than 35°. This is the *angle of repose* for dry sand. Sand is carried up the shallow slope on the upwind side of a dune, but when it is released at the top the grains roll down to give the downwind side a slope of about 35°. The illustration on

Barchan dunes, with their "horns" pointing downwind, in the Skeleton Coast National Park, Namibia (Courtesy of Gerry Ellis/ Minden Pictures)

Types of sand dunes

Sand dunes are built by the wind and it is the wind that gives them their characteristic shapes. The commonest type is the *barchan* dune. It is crescent shaped with the horns of the crescent pointing downwind. Barchan dunes form where the supply of sand is limited and the wind blows mainly from one direction.

Crescent-shaped dunes sometimes develop the other way around, with the horns pointing into the wind. They are then *parabolic* dunes. It is easy to tell whether a crescent-shaped dune is a barchan or parabolic dune. One side of each ridge will slope gently and the other will be much steeper. If the steeper side lies between the horns it is a barchan dune, and if the steeper side lies on the opposite side to the horns it is a parabolic dune.

The more sand that is available, the closer the barchans are to their neighbors. If there is enough sand, barchans may join together to form long, wavy lines of dunes. These are *aklé* dunes.

Alternatively, a plentiful supply of sand may allow the horns of the barchans to grow much longer until the dunes are very long, narrow, wavy *barchanoid ridges.*

If there is abundant sand and the wind nearly always blows from the same direction, long dunes form at right angles to the wind direction. These are *transverse* dunes—and are the type of dune that most commonly forms behind sandy beaches.

Transverse dunes cannot form if the wind direction varies by a few degrees to either side of an average direction. Instead, the sand is heaped into wavy dunes that are aligned with the average wind direction. These are *longitudinal* or *linear* dunes. Sometimes they have very sharp crests. They are then known as *seif* dunes—*seif* is from the Arabic word *sayf,* which means "sword." Some seif dunes are more than 100 miles (160 km) long.

There are places—the northern Sahara is one—where the wind pattern is very complex and no single wind direction predominates. Under these conditions dunes form with ridges aligned in several directions. This produces a *star* or *stellar* dune.

Dunes also develop on the downwind side of large boulders and other obstacles. The wind carries sand around or over the obstacle and drops it on the far side. This produces a *tail* dune, with the tail pointing downwind.

The biggest sand structure of all is called a *draa.* It is a transverse or longitudinal dune that is up to 1,000 feet (300 m) high, with wave crests up to 700 yards (650 m) apart. Draas are about 0.5–3 miles (0.8–5 km) apart and they extend for hundreds of miles. They often have smaller dunes superimposed on them.

Rhourds are a variety of very large star dunes that form where dunes of other types intersect. They are sometimes star-shaped draas.

page 38 shows how this process produces the typical ridge along the top of a sand dune.

Some sand dunes move. Despite their size, they are not landmarks that can guide the traveler. The biggest of them, called *draas,* move up to two inches (5 cm) a year. Dunes vary in shape according to the amount of sand available to build them and to the constancy of the wind direction. Each type of dune has a name (see the sidebar on page 40), but sand dunes are either approximately straight, lying parallel to one another, or crescent shaped.

Desert pavement and desert varnish

You would expect trucks and cars, even tough utility vehicles, to move across the desert slowly, bouncing and lumbering over the rocks and now and again being brought to a standstill with their wheels spinning in loose sand. This is what desert driving is often like, but not always. In some places the traffic moves almost as fast as if it were on a road, each vehicle pursued by a cloud of dust that can be seen for miles but that emphasizes the speed. Speed is possible because over large areas the desert surface is made from half-buried rounded stones that are securely embedded so they do not slide or roll. The surface is almost as good as a road. It is called *desert pavement.*

It takes many thousands of years for the desert to produce such a paved or cobbled surface. There are two ways it can happen. Both result in a stable, solid surface that will bear the weight of trucks.

Torrential streams that flow after rainstorms may transport sand, dust, gravel, and stones of all sizes down steep hillsides, depositing the mixture on a plain at the foot of the hills. Rainstorms do not occur very often and most of the time the streams carry no water at all, but occasional torrents repeated over many thousands of years may spread enough material to cover a substantial area. The deposit arrives on the plain as mud, but the mud quickly dries and then the wind begins to work on it. A light breeze will blow away fine dust, and a wind of more than 12 MPH (19 km/h) will blow sand grains.

Little by little, the wind blows away the dust and sand, leaving behind the stones that are too heavy to shift, until finally all the sand and dust are gone and only the stones remain.

Alternatively, the stones may have been there all the time, mixed with sand and dust to produce a surface with just a few stones scattered about randomly. When it rains, the water washes dust and sand downward. The particles fill small air pockets below ground and work their way around and beneath the stones. From time to time the wind deposits more dust over the surface and the rain then washes the dust below the surface. When the ground dries, the packed dust cracks, making more spaces for windblown dust to fill. Very slowly, the dust and sand are washed beneath the stones, and the stones work their way to the surface. Eventually the stones form a surface layer, like a road pavement, lying above a layer of compacted sand and dust that contains very few stones.

Desert pavement does not consist merely of bare stone, however. Usually the stones have a coating of *rock varnish*—more often known as *desert varnish*. It is found on rocks in many places, but it develops best and is most clearly seen in deserts, where more rocks are exposed and the dry conditions allow time for the varnish to grow, for it grows very slowly.

The thickness of the varnish varies, but it is usually less than about 0.001 inch (30 μm). The varnish is made from clay particles that are cemented firmly to the rock by hydroxides of manganese and iron. Geologists are uncertain about both where the manganese comes from and how the varnish accumulates on the stones. Some scientists think that small changes in acidity trigger chemical reactions that deposit the varnish onto the stones. Others think the process is biological and that bacteria are responsible.

Whatever the cause, desert varnish is found only in hot deserts. Rocks in cooler deserts have a different coating. It is called *silica glaze* and consists of silica (silicon dioxide, SiO_2) mixed with aluminum and iron. Silica glaze is usually up to 0.008 inch (200 μm) thick and makes the rocks shiny and white or orange in color, or sometimes darker. There are rocks covered with silica glaze in the dry valleys of Antarctica—the coldest of all deserts.

There are also rust-colored rocks, both in Antarctica and in hot, extremely dry deserts. The rocks from these diverse areas look similar and all of them are coated with a film containing iron, but the precise composition of the film varies, depending on the conditions.

Mesas, buttes, and other desert landforms

Sandstone and limestone are sedimentary rocks that cover the surface of many deserts. They are made from compressed and cemented material that once lay on the ocean floor where they accumulated as horizontal layers, and in some deserts the rocks retain this orientation. Later, hot, molten, *igneous* rock—from *ignis,* the Latin word for "fire"—rose from below and pushed into the sedimentary layers. When the igneous rock cooled it remained as an intrusion into the sedimentary rock.

Igneous rock, such as granite, is much harder than sedimentary rock, and the forces of erosion that are powerful enough to wear away the sedimentary rock leave the igneous rock exposed. Erosion is ceaseless in the desert. Every wind raises dust and sand particles and dashes them against solid surfaces. This relentless sandblasting wears away the sedimentary rock, at the same time releasing more mineral grains to contribute to further erosion.

Where the sedimentary layers are horizontal, erosion first levels the landscape by wearing away protruding rocks that are more exposed to the wind and its load of sand. This leaves a level plain. But erosion continues, wearing at the surface of the plain, eventually producing structures with names in the languages of the places where they were first seen or of the explorers who described them.

As the sedimentary rock is removed, the igneous intrusions are revealed. Some remain as fragments of the plain, standing like steep-sided, flat-topped hills. A hill of this shape is called a *mesa*—the Spanish word for "plateau."

Further erosion reduces the size of the mesa until all that remains of it is a tower of rock with a flat top. This is called a *butte*—a French word meaning "hill" or "knoll."

A larger igneous intrusion may be left as a steep-sided hill standing alone on the plain. This is an *inselberg*—a German word that means "island mountain."

Sand and wind are the principal agents of erosion, but they are not the only ones. Salt can also sculpt rocks into curious shapes and can make *pedestal rocks*. A pedestal rock is a large rock that stands on top of another rock to which it is connected by only a narrow neck.

Mineral salts, including common salt (sodium chloride) form part of the crystalline structure of many rocks, and each time it rains some of the salt at the rock surface dissolves and the solution seeps into tiny cracks in the rock. The heat and wind quickly evaporate the water and the salts crystallize once more, expanding as they do so and splitting the rock. Salt crystals inside the rock also expand and contract with changes in temperature, but by a much larger amount than the other minerals around them. This also causes rock fractures.

Erosion often wears away one layer of rock more rapidly than the layers above and below it. Sometimes this makes a recess, called an *alcove,* around a section of rock. Rainwater collects in the alcove, salts from the rock dissolve into it, and when the water evaporates the salts crystallize. Grains of salt and sand grains detached by the expansion during crystallization then blow away in the wind. With each repetition of the process the alcove becomes deeper until the rock above it is left standing on a narrow neck. It has become a pedestal rock.

Salt solutions also collect in small depressions on the rock surface. As the salt and sand grains blow away, the depressions deepen to become pits, called *alveoles,* from *alveus,* the Latin word for "cavity." The alveoles grow larger until the rock is honeycombed with holes. These larger holes are *tafoni* (singular *tafone*)—an Italian name that was first used to describe holes of this type in Corsican rocks.

Dissolved salt can also produce a vast, absolutely level salt flat, known variously as a *playa* (Spanish for "beach"), as a *salina* in South America (Spanish for "salt mine"), and as a *sabkha* (Arabic for "salt flat") in Africa. Playas lie in basins surrounded by high ground. At one time, when the climate was moister, lakes or coastal lagoons filled the basins. The water was rich in salts dissolved out of the surrounding rocks and washed into the basins. When the climate became drier the water evaporated, leaving behind the salts. The Bonneville salt flats in Utah, used for attempts to break the world land-speed record, are a playa.

Gypsum (calcium sulfate) and calcite (calcium carbonate) are among the salts found in playas. As they crystallize, surrounded by sand grains, they can form the attractive, flower-like shape called a *desert rose*.

What happens when it rains

Here and there gullies break up the desert surface. Usually about seven feet (2 m) deep and 10 feet (3 m) wide, they are called *arroyos* in North America, *dongas* in Southern Africa,

A cumulonimbus cloud producing a rainstorm over Amboseli National Park, Kenya (Courtesy of Gerry Ellis/ Minden Pictures)

and *wadis* or *ouadis* in the Sahara and Arabia. They are dry river courses, but the rivers that occasionally flow through them are not like the gentle, predictable rivers of temperate lands. Crossing an arroyo is not difficult, but lingering in one to camp or even to picnic can be dangerous. When the river flows it does not begin as you might expect, as a dampness on the bed that increases to a trickle before it is recognizably a river. The bed remains bone dry until, with no warning, a wall of muddy, rock-laden water as high as the banks of the arroyo advances along the stream channel so fast that there may be no time to escape.

It seldom rains in the desert. Clouds quite often cross the sky, but they are too small to deliver rain. Occasionally rain may fall from a larger cloud, but the drops are small. They fall slowly and evaporate in the dry air below the cloud before they can reach the ground. The rain hangs tantalizingly out of reach beneath the cloud like a gray veil, called *virga*.

Only really huge storm clouds are able to produce raindrops that are big enough to reach the ground. A big raindrop falls at about 20 MPH (9 m/s), which means it does not spend very long traveling from the cloud to the ground, so there is less time for it to evaporate. It also means that it falls with considerable force.

Storms are more likely in the mountains than over the plains. Moist air is forced to rise as it crosses mountains, and as it rises its temperature falls (see the sidebar "Adiabatic cooling and warming" on page 55) and its water vapor starts to condense. Under certain conditions this can trigger the formation of large *cumulonimbus* clouds—the clouds that bring violent thunderstorms, heavy rain, and cloudbursts as they begin to disappear (see the sidebar "Lapse rates and stability" on page 60).

Rainwater falling on the bare mountainsides flows away between the rocks along gaps that feed into the arroyos. Far away on the plain, the sky may be clear, with not a cloud in sight, and the storm may be too distant to be seen or heard. The torrent arrives without warning.

That is what makes arroyos dangerous places. Flash floods caused by violent desert storms can cause serious damage if they flow through a town. Floods struck northern Algeria during the period November 9–17, 2001, for example. They killed 750 people and left about 24,000 homeless.

Where the desert surface is sandy, rainwater soaks vertically downward. The combination of surface evaporation and the ease with which the water passes between the sand grains quickly dries the surface. Below ground, the water continues to move downward until it encounters an impermeable layer of clay or rock that checks its progress. Water then fills all the spaces between pebbles, gravel, and sand grains, saturating the material immediately above the impermeable layer. It is then called *groundwater*. The upper boundary of the saturated zone is known as the *water table*.

Groundwater flows, quite slowly, down the gently sloping surface of the impermeable layer. If the water is accessible in useful amounts, the saturated material through which it moves constitutes an *aquifer*.

There are natural depressions below ground in which groundwater accumulates, and water has been held in some of them for a very long time. Groundwater below the surface of the Sahara and under parts of the Australian deserts has been there since before the end of the last Ice Age—more than 10,000 years ago.

Wells and oases

Dig a hole from the surface all the way down past the water table, and the bottom of the hole will fill with water. The hole is then a well, and people can take water from it by lowering a bucket on the end of a rope or, more commonly nowadays, by installing a pump that raises the water to a faucet.

Digging a well is hard work. The hole must be wide enough for at least one and usually more than one person to work. That means it will be up to eight feet (2.4 m) across, and all the excavated material has to be hauled to the surface. As they dig, the workers must secure the sides to prevent them from collapsing. Modern wells are not usually dug by hand, of course, but by drilling machines. Most wells are less than 100 feet (30 m) deep, but some are much deeper.

There are certain places where it is not necessary to use a pump or bucket to raise water from a well. The water rises to the surface without help and flows freely. The first well of this type was sunk in the year 1126 at the town of Lillers, to the west of Lille in northeastern France. In those days that part of France was called Artois. The Latin name for Artois was Artesium, and so the Liller well was called an *artesian* well. Artesian wells are sunk into *confined* aquifers.

Ordinarily, only sand or soil lies between an aquifer and the surface. Such an aquifer is said to be *unconfined*. In some cases, though, a second layer of impermeable material lies above the aquifer. The aquifer is then confined.

Layers of rock and clay seldom lie horizontally. If the two layers confining an aquifer form a hollow, as shown in the illustration below, gravity will force water on the upstream side to sink into the hollow, putting the water in the hollow under pressure. Once the pressure is removed by cutting through the upper impermeable layer, the water held under pressure in the depression will rise to the level of the water to either side of the depression and the well will flow without pumping.

Artesian well. Where an aquifer is confined between two layers of impermeable rock or clay, and these layers form a depression, water will flow without pumping from a well sunk into the center of the depression.

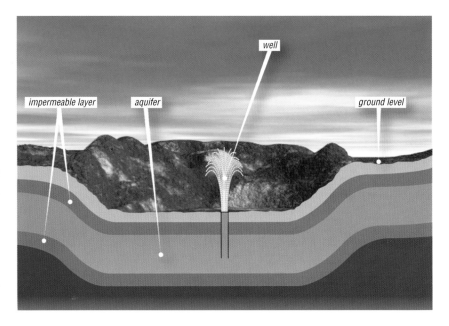

impermeable layer   aquifer   well   ground level

Nowadays Egyptians speak Arabic, but the native Egyptian language is Coptic, now used only in Coptic Christian church services. The Coptic word for "to dwell" is *oueh,* and "to drink" is *saa.* Run the two together and they produce *oasis.* An oasis is a place in the desert where people are able to live because there is water to drink and to sustain crop plants.

Many oases are supplied with water by rivers flowing down from mountains and into the desert. There are oases of this type in the Atacama Desert, fed by rivers from the Andes, and rivers flowing down from the Himalayas and the Karakorum Range feed oases in Asian deserts.

An oasis may also occur for no apparent reason. It is just a place where water lies at the surface or, more usually, just below the surface, within the reach of plant roots and easily accessible. The diagram on page 50 shows how an oasis of

Farms thrive in desert oases. These farms are in Oasis Dakhia, in the Sahara. (Courtesy of Gerry Ellis/Minden Pictures)

lake

aquifer

impermeable layer

Oasis. There is water below the ground in many parts of most deserts. If the bottom of a hollow in the ground surface is lower than the water table, a lake will form, and around the edges of the lake plant roots will be able to reach the moisture below ground.

this kind obtains its water. The water originates in rivers flowing from the mountains, just as it does with the more obvious oases. In this case, though, the water has sunk into the ground and become an aquifer. Erosion has hollowed out the ground, lowering the surface until it lies below the level of the water table. Water then lies on the surface or just below it, for the same reason that water fills the bottom of a well that penetrates the aquifer. In effect, the oasis is a well, but one from which all the overlying material has been removed.

Oases can be large. The Siwa oasis in western Egypt is six miles (10 km) long by four to five miles (6–8 km) wide and its water comes from about 200 springs. The ancient Egyptians knew it as Sekht-am, meaning "palm land."

CHAPTER 3

DESERT CLIMATES

Why there are belts of desert throughout the subtropics

Equatorial regions have a warm, wet climate. Except where they have been cleared, luxuriant forests cover the lowlands and extend up the mountainsides until they reach elevations where the air is too cold for them. Much of the land between the equator and the Tropics experiences this type of climate, but in the subtropics, to either side of the tropics of Cancer and Capricorn, the climate is different. That is where deserts encircle the Earth. In the Northern Hemisphere, the Sahara, Arabian, and Thar, or Great Indian, Deserts lie on or close to the tropic of Cancer, and the Kalahari and Australian Deserts lie on the tropic of Capricorn, in the Southern Hemisphere.

The warm, wet, equatorial climate and the hot, dry climate of the subtropical deserts complement one another. Both result from the fact that the Sun shines more intensely over the equator than it does over any other part of the world. Oddly enough, the deserts are also a consequence of the fact that more ocean than land lies along the equator.

Stand outdoors on a warm day and you will feel the warmth of the Sun shining on your body. You are feeling *radiant heat,* which is electromagnetic radiation similar to visible light, but at a wavelength our eyes cannot see. Air is almost completely transparent to radiation at this wavelength. Sunshine passes through it, barely affecting it. More solid objects, such as our bodies and the surface of land and water, are not transparent to it, however. They absorb the sunshine and it warms them. You cannot feel it, but when the sunshine warms your skin, some of that warmth is transferred to the layer of air touching your skin. As that air grows warmer, it expands and becomes less dense. It then rises away from you and denser, cooler air takes its place. The Sun is

General circulation of the atmosphere

The tropics of Cancer in the north and Capricorn in the south mark the boundaries of the belt around the Earth where the Sun is directly overhead on at least one day in the year. The Arctic and Antarctic Circles mark the boundaries of regions in which the Sun does not rise above the horizon on at least one day of the year and does not sink below the horizon on at least one day in the year.

A beam of sunlight illuminates a much smaller area if the Sun is directly overhead than it does if the Sun is at a low angle in the sky. The amount of energy is the same in both cases, but the energy is spread over a smaller area directly beneath the Sun than it is when the Sun is lower. This is why the Tropics are heated more strongly than any other part of the Earth and the amount of heat falling on the surface decreases with increasing distance from the equator (increasing latitude).

The Sun shines more intensely at the equator than it does anywhere else, but air movements transport some of the warmth away from the equator. Near the equator, the warm surface of the Earth heats the air in contact with it. The warm air rises until it is close to the tropopause, which is the boundary between the lowest layer of the atmosphere (the troposphere) in which air temperature decreases with height, and the layer above (the stratosphere), where the temperature remains constant with increasing height. The height of the tropopause is around 10 miles (16 km), and at this height the air moves away from the equator, some heading north and some south. As it rises, the air cools, so the high-level air moving away from the equator is very cold—about –85°F (–65°C).

This equatorial air subsides around latitude 30°N and S, and as it sinks it warms again. By the time it reaches the surface it is hot and dry, so it warms this region, producing subtropical deserts. At the surface, the air divides. Sometimes called the horse latitudes, this is a region of light, variable winds or no winds at all. Most of the air flows back toward the equator and some flows away from the equator. The air from north and south of the equator meets at the Intertropical Convergence Zone (ITCZ), and this circulation forms a number of vertical cells called *Hadley cells,* after George Hadley (1685–1768), the English meteorologist who first proposed them in 1735.

Over the poles, the air is very cold. It subsides, and when it reaches the surface it flows away from the poles. At about latitude 50–60°N and S, air moving away from the poles meets air moving away from the equator at the polar front. The converging air rises to the tropopause, in these latitudes about seven miles (11 km) above the surface. Some flows back to the poles, forming polar cells, and some flows toward the equator, completing Ferrel cells, discovered in 1856 by the American climatologist William Ferrel (1817–91).

Warm air rises at the equator, sinks to the surface in the subtropics, flows at low level to around latitude 55°, then rises to continue its journey toward the poles. At the same time, cold air subsiding at the poles flows back to the equator. The diagram below shows how this circulation produces three sets of vertical cells in each hemisphere. It is called the "three-cell model" of the atmospheric circulation.

If it were not for this redistribution of heat, weather at the equator would be very much hotter than it is, and weather at the poles would be a great deal colder.

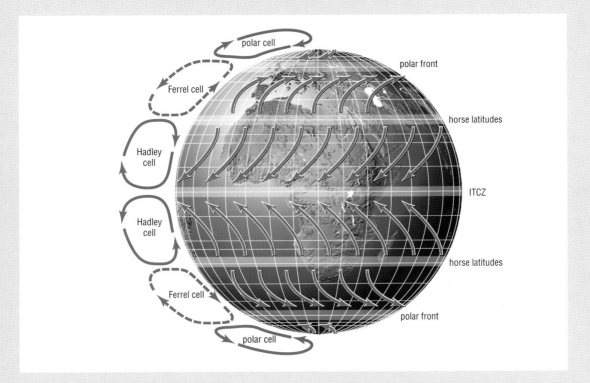

General circulation of the atmosphere. Warm air rises over the equator, moves away from the equator at high altitude, and subsides over the Tropics; there it divides, some flowing back toward the equator and some flowing away from the equator. This forms a series of Hadley cells. Cold air subsides over the poles and flows away from the poles at low level. This forms a series of polar cells. Air rises where Hadley-cell air flowing away from the Tropics meets polar-cell air flowing toward the equator. The air flows toward the equator at high altitude, descending where it meets high-level Hadley-cell air. This forms a series of Ferrel cells.

warming you by radiation and you are warming the air by the process called *convection*. Your body is like a radiator, absorbing warmth and then warming the air with it.

The Earth behaves in exactly the same way—but on a much bigger scale. Its land and water surfaces absorb sunshine, their temperatures rise, and they warm the air in contact with them. The warm air then rises, distributing the Sun's warmth by convection.

It is moist air. Around the equator there is more sea than land for the sunshine to warm, and as the water grows warmer its molecules start to break free and enter the air. Water evaporates and the water vapor rises in the warm air. As it rises, the air grows cooler and the water vapor condenses to form huge clouds. These clouds produce the rain that gives the region its wet climate.

Very high in the sky, the rising air levels off and moves northward and southward, away from the equator. When it reaches the latitudes of the two Tropics, the air meets air moving in the opposite direction, toward the equator. *Convergence*—the meeting of air—makes the air subside all the way to the surface, where some of it flows back toward the equator and the remainder flows away from the equator. This movement of air—rising over the equator, traveling away from the equator, subsiding over the Tropics, and returning to the equator—forms a *convection cell*. It is one part of the overall movement of the atmosphere that transports warmth from the equator to the Poles. The process is called the *general circulation of the atmosphere* (see the sidebar on page 52).

The air moving away from the equator at high altitude is very cold and very dry. It is cold because when air rises its temperature falls. As the air grows colder, its capacity for holding water vapor decreases. That is why clouds form, and it is also why the high-altitude air is so dry: It lost its moisture during its rise.

As it subsides again, the air becomes warmer; this change of temperature is called *adiabatic* (see the sidebar on page 55). The air warms faster as it descends than it cooled when it rose over the equator. This is because rising moist air cools at the *saturated adiabatic lapse rate,* averaging 3°F per 1,000 feet

(6°C/km), but subsiding dry air warms at the *dry adiabatic lapse rate* of 5.4°F for every 1,000 feet (9.8°C/km). By the time the air reaches the surface it is very warm. It is still very

Adiabatic cooling and warming

Air is compressed by the weight of air above it. Imagine a balloon partly inflated with air and made from some weightless substance that totally insulates the air inside. No matter what the temperature outside the balloon, the temperature of the air inside remains the same.

Imagine the balloon is released into the atmosphere. The air inside is squeezed between the weight of air above it, all the way to the top of the atmosphere, and the denser air below it.

Suppose the air inside the balloon is less dense than the air above it. Denser air will push beneath it and the balloon will rise. As it rises, the distance to the top of the atmosphere becomes smaller, so there is less air above to weigh down on the air in the balloon. At the same time, as the balloon moves through air that is less dense, it experiences less pressure from below. This causes the air in the balloon to expand.

When air (or any other gas) expands, its molecules move farther apart. The amount of air remains the same, but it occupies a bigger volume. As they move apart, the molecules must "push" other molecules out of their way. This uses energy, so as the air expands its molecules lose energy. Because they have less energy they move more slowly.

When a moving molecule strikes something, some of its energy is transferred to whatever it strikes, and part of that energy is converted into heat. This raises the temperature of the struck object by an amount related to the number of molecules striking it and their speed.

In expanding air, the molecules are moving farther apart, so a smaller number of them strike an object each second. They are also traveling more slowly, so they strike with less force. This means the temperature of the air decreases. As it expands, air cools.

If the air in the balloon is denser than air below, it will sink. As it sinks, the pressure on the air will increase, its volume will decrease, and its molecules will acquire more energy. Its temperature will increase.

This warming and cooling has nothing to do with the temperature of the air surrounding the balloon. It is called *adiabatic* warming and cooling, from the Greek word *adiabatos,* meaning "impassable," suggesting that the air is enclosed by an imaginary boundary through which heat is unable to pass.

dry, and as its temperature increased, so did its capacity for holding water vapor. Thus the desert air can absorb a large amount of moisture without producing clouds.

Subsiding air produces high atmospheric pressure at the surface, and there are areas of permanent high pressure over the subtropics. Air flows outward from areas of high pressure, in this case as part of the general circulation of the atmosphere, and the outward movement blocks the entry of air from beyond the deserts. Incoming air might bring moisture, and so the high pressure is another factor keeping the subtropical deserts dry.

Ocean gyres and boundary currents

Many deserts lie on the western side of continents. The North American deserts, the Atacama of South America, and the Namib Desert of southern Africa are examples. These west coast deserts (see "West coast deserts" on pages 16–19) are dry because just offshore there is an ocean current carrying cold water. Contact with the cold water lowers the temperature of the layer of air near the surface, and the presence of a surface layer of cool, dense air makes the air highly stable (see the sidebar "Lapse rates and stability" on page 60). No air is rising and therefore no water vapor can condense to form clouds that might produce rain.

Ocean currents are driven by the prevailing winds and in every ocean they follow approximately circular paths, called *gyres*. Gyres turn clockwise in the Northern Hemisphere and counterclockwise in the Southern Hemisphere. Because they flow around the outer rims of ocean basins, the currents that flow close to and parallel to the coasts of continents are known as *boundary currents*. Western boundary currents in both hemispheres carry warm water toward the Poles. They are usually deep, narrow, and fast flowing. Eastern boundary currents carry cool water toward the equator. They are broad, shallow, and slow moving. Deserts occur along western coasts because their climates are influenced by nearby eastern boundary currents.

In the South Pacific, the South Equatorial Current moves from east to west, driven by the southeasterly trade winds. As it approaches Indonesia and Australia, it turns to flow south-ward, passing Australia as the warm East Australian Current. As it leaves the Tropics, the current enters the region where the prevailing winds are from the west and it joins the West Wind Drift, or Antarctic Circumpolar Current. This is the only ocean current that travels uninterrupted all the way around the world. It is able to do so because there is no continent in its path to deflect it.

Although the West Wind Drift travels all around the world, from west to east, at each of the southern continents a part of the current is diverted. In the South Pacific, this section of the current flows northward parallel to the South American coast, as the Peru Current, also called the Humboldt Current. The cold water of the Peru Current produces the stable air that gives the Atacama its extremely dry climate. The Peru Current then comes under the influence of the trade winds and turns to flow westward. It has become the South Equatorial Current once more.

The North Pacific gyre, which produces the North American deserts, begins as the North Equatorial Current, flowing westward. As it approaches Asia, it turns to flow northward, the western boundary current passing Japan as the warm Kuroshio Current. It continues to turn and crosses the ocean eastward as the North Pacific Current. It turns southward as it approaches North America, then flows parallel to the coast as the cool California Current, the eastern boundary current.

In the South Atlantic, the westward-flowing South Equatorial Current turns to flow southward past the South American coast as the warm Brazil Current. It joins the West Wind Drift, and as it approaches Africa part of this eastward-flowing water diverts northward, parallel to the coast, forming an eastern boundary current. This is the cool Benguela Current associated with the Namib Desert, and it rejoins the South Equatorial Current.

The North Atlantic gyre begins as the North Equatorial Current (flowing westward). As it approaches the Caribbean and Central America it becomes the Antilles Current and then the Florida Current, before turning to flow northward from the Gulf of Mexico as the Gulf Stream. The Gulf Stream divides, with one section continuing in a northwesterly

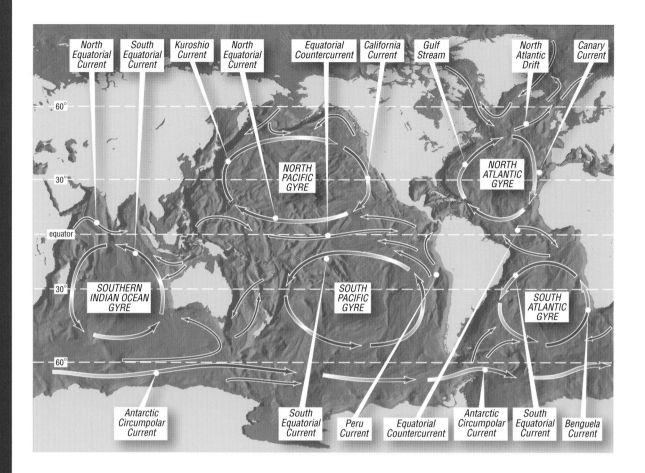

Gyres. The surface currents in all of the oceans follow approximately circular paths, called gyres, but the names of the currents change in different parts of each gyre. The map shows the gyres and some of the names of currents.

direction as the North Atlantic Current, also called the North Atlantic Drift, and the other flowing southward as the cool Canary Current—and bringing dry conditions to the Atlantic Sahara.

The Indian Ocean straddles the equator and it has two, rather more complicated gyres. The southern gyre includes the warm Agulhas Current, which flows along the African coast, and the cool West Australian Current. The map above shows the gyres, with the names of the principal currents.

Monsoons

Despite being in the same latitude as the Sahara, central and southern India and southern Asia are not deserts. They receive very little rain during the winter, but rainfall is heavy in the summer. Their climate is one of seasonal extremes. The Arabic word for "season" is *mausim* and it may have given us the name we use to describe these seasons. We call them the monsoons.

The winter monsoon is dry and the summer monsoon is wet. Between October and May, Bombay (now called Mumbai), India, receives an average 4.1 inches (104 mm) of rain. Between June and September the city receives an average 67.2 inches (1,707 mm). Parts of West Africa, northeastern Brazil, and the interior of the southern United States also experience monsoon seasons—in the United States it is the summer that is dry and the winter that is wet—but nowhere can compare with the extremes of the southern Asian climate.

Monsoons result from the fact that the land warms up and cools much more rapidly than does the ocean (see the sidebar "Specific heat capacity" on page 66). They occur only in tropical and subtropical regions, because they require intense warming of the surface. They also occur only over large continents, because they need a large land area adjacent to an ocean to generate the right atmospheric conditions.

In winter the land cools rapidly. As its temperature falls, the lower layers of air also cool. The air becomes dense, and as the cold air subsides the surface pressure increases. The subsiding air is dry and it flows out from the region of high pressure, producing very dry weather over land. The ocean cools much more slowly and so it remains warmer than the land until late in the winter. Air rises over the ocean, losing its moisture as it does so, and is then drawn over the land at high altitude, where it subsides. Winter is therefore a time of dry winds that blow from the land to the sea. They produce the dry winter monsoon.

In summer the situation reverses. The land warms faster than the ocean. Warm air rises over land, but over the ocean the air is still cold and it subsides. The flow of air reverses, with dry air moving at high altitude from land to sea, and moist air moving at low level from sea to land. The moist air rises as it crosses the coast and high ground inland. This makes it highly unstable (see the sidebar on page 60). Huge clouds form and produce violent storms and torrential rain.

Lapse rates and stability

Air temperature decreases (or lapses) with increasing height. The rate at which it does so is called the *lapse rate.* Although all air contains some water vapor, air that is not saturated with moisture—all of its moisture is present as vapor rather than liquid droplets or ice crystals—is said to be *dry.* When dry air cools adiabatically, it does so at 5.4°F for every 1,000 feet (9.8°C/km) that it rises. This is known as the *dry adiabatic lapse rate* (DALR).

When the temperature of the rising air has fallen sufficiently, its water vapor will start to condense into droplets. Condensation commences at the *dew-point temperature* and the height at which this temperature is reached is called the *lifting condensation level.* Condensation releases *latent heat,* which warms the air. Latent heat is the energy that allows water molecules to break free from each other when liquid water vaporizes or ice melts. It does not change the temperature of the water or ice, which is why it is called *latent,* meaning "hidden." The same amount of latent heat is released, warming the surroundings, when water vapor condenses and when liquid water freezes. Consequently, the rising air then cools at a slower rate, known as the *saturated adiabatic lapse rate* (SALR). The SALR varies, depending on the rate of condensation, but it averages 3°F per 1,000 feet (6°C/km).

The actual rate at which the temperature decreases with height in air that is not rising is called the *environmental lapse rate* (ELR). It is calculated by comparing the surface temperature, the temperature at the tropopause (it is about −85°F; −65°C at the equator), and the height of the tropopause (about 10 miles; 16 km over the equator).

If the ELR is less than both the DALR and SALR, rising air will cool faster than the surrounding air, so it will always be cooler and will tend to subside to a lower height. Such air is said to be *absolutely stable.*

If the ELR is greater than the SALR, air that is rising and cooling at the DALR and later at the SALR will always be warmer than the surrounding air. Consequently, it will continue to rise. The air is then *absolutely unstable.*

If the ELR is less than the DALR but greater than the SALR, rising air will cool faster than the surrounding air while it remains dry but more slowly once it rises above the lifting condensation level. At first it is stable, but above the lifting condensation level it becomes unstable. This air is said to be *conditionally unstable.* It is stable unless a condition (rising above its lifting condensation level) is met, whereupon it becomes unstable. This is shown by the lines in the middle of the diagram on page 61.

Stable air brings settled weather. Unstable air produces heaped clouds of the *cumulus* type. The base of these clouds is at the lifting condensation level, and the cloud tops are at the altitude where the rising air has lost enough water vapor to make it dry once more, so it is cooling at the DALR. If the air is sufficiently unstable, however, the clouds can grow into towering *cumulonimbus* storm clouds. Equatorial air is usually unstable.

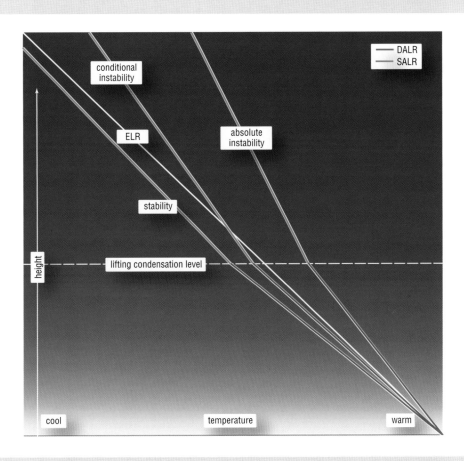

Stability of air. If the environmental lapse rate (ELR) is less than both the dry (DALR) and saturated (SALR) lapse rates, the air is stable. If the ELR is less than both the DALR and the SALR, the air is absolutely unstable. If the ELR is less than the DALR but greater than the SALR, the air is conditionally unstable.

The Indian monsoons are intensified by the influence of the Himalayas and the Tibetan Plateau. Winter temperatures fall very low over central Asia and Tibet. The high pressure this produces does not affect the air to a very great height, but it is fed by air subsiding from the jet stream to the north of the Himalayas (see "Air masses, fronts, and jet streams" below through page 65). Air flowing southward from the Asian high-pressure zone loses any moisture it may carry as it crosses the Himalayas. By the time it reaches India it is extremely dry. Its temperature rises as it descends from the mountains (see the sidebar "Adiabatic cooling and warming" on page 55). The prevailing winds over India are the trade winds, blowing from the northeast. These strengthen the flow of air descending from the mountains.

In spring, as the land heats up, air rises by convection and there are scattered storms. At this time the Intertropical Convergence Zone (ITCZ) is moving northward. The ITCZ is the belt where the northeasterly trade winds of the Northern Hemisphere and southeasterly trade winds of the Southern Hemisphere meet. The ITCZ finally halts along the southern edge of the Himalayas. The winds over India then blow from the southwest, bringing air from the Arabian Sea and the summer monsoon.

Spring is the hot season. Temperatures inland rise above 90°F (32°C). In Jacobabad, Pakistan, the average daytime temperature in May is 111°F (44°C) and it has been known to reach 123°F (51°C). As the ITCZ moves northward, the trade winds slacken and the air becomes still. When the rains arrive they do so suddenly. Clouds have been building for some time until there is a "burst of monsoon," when the skies open and there is a deluge. The monsoon begins in the southeast, reaching southern China early in May, and advances in a northwesterly direction, reaching Pakistan in July.

Air masses, fronts, and jet streams

Air lying over a continent or an ocean acquires fairly uniform characteristics. After a time the temperature, pressure, and humidity at any altitude are much the same everywhere.

This may sound obvious, but it was not until the early 20th century that the implications of this fact were discovered. In 1917 a Norwegian physicist and meteorologist named Vilhelm Bjerknes (1862–1951) left the University of Leipzig, Germany, where he had been a professor, and returned to Norway to establish and become director of the Bergen Geophysical Institute. He gathered together a team of talented scientists, who set up a network of weather stations throughout Norway. The weather stations reported their measurements and observations to Bergen, where Bjerknes and his team assembled them to produce pictures of atmospheric conditions over a large area. The scientists found that the characteristics of air over a large area were often similar everywhere, but that they differed radically from the characteristics of air somewhere else. They called a large, uniform volume of air an *air mass.*

Air masses are given names that describe them. The first division is between continental air (abbreviated as c), which is dry, and maritime air (m), which is moist. These divisions are qualified further according to the latitude in which the air mass formed, as arctic (A), polar (P), tropical (T), and equatorial (E). The names are then combined to give continental arctic (cA), continental polar (cP), continental tropical (cT), maritime arctic (mA), maritime polar (mP), maritime tropical (mT), and maritime equatorial (mE). There is no continental equatorial air, because oceans cover most of the equatorial region.

The Bergen scientists also found that although different air masses move about, they do not mix readily with one another. One air mass is cooler and denser than the air mass adjacent to it and rather than mixing, the warm air rides above the cool air. When Bjerknes and his colleagues made these discoveries it was wartime and the newspapers were full of stories of battles. It seemed to the Norwegian scientists that air masses were a little like opposing armies, and the boundaries where air masses meet and struggle against one another were like fronts, and so that is what they called them. It is the name we still use.

Air masses move, and as they do so their characteristics change. Continental air gathers moisture as it crosses the ocean, for example, and maritime air loses moisture as it crosses a continent. Carried by the prevailing winds, air masses move along tracks that are approximately parallel to the equator, so the changes in air mass characteristics affect the moisture the air carries much more than its temperature. Fronts are named for the air behind them. If the air is warmer after the front has passed it is a warm front. If the air is cooler after it has passed it is a cold front.

Weather maps on TV and in newspapers show the positions of fronts on the surface, using standard symbols to identify them—red semicircles for a warm front and blue triangles for a cold front. Cold fronts travel faster than warm fronts. Consequently, cold air tends to push beneath warm air, raising it from the ground. Once the warm air starts to rise the two fronts begin to merge. They are said to be *occluded* or to form an *occlusion,* symbolized by alternating semicircles and triangles. Eventually the cold air raises all of the warm air clear of the ground. The fronts then disappear, together with any weather associated with them.

In middle latitudes, frontal weather systems often follow one another, traveling from west to east. They are produced along the *polar front.* This is the front between tropical and polar air that forms where the polar and Ferrel cells meet (see the sidebar "General circulation of the atmosphere" on page 52).

Frontal systems move because they are following waves—north-south undulations—traveling along the polar front and the strong wind, or *polar jet stream,* that blows along the top of the front just below the tropopause. A jet stream is a ribbon of wind, 60–300 miles (100–500 km) wide, often blowing at more than 120 MPH (200 km/h) and occasionally at as much as 300 MPH (500 km/h). The jet stream results from the sharp difference in temperature across the polar front. It blows from west to east in both hemispheres. The Northern Hemisphere polar jet stream moves northward in summer and retreats to the south in winter. It is usually located at about 50°N in summer and 40°N in winter, but sometimes it moves farther. Its total range is from 30°N to 70°N. Because the jet stream results from the contrast in temperature between tropical and polar air, it is strongest in winter,

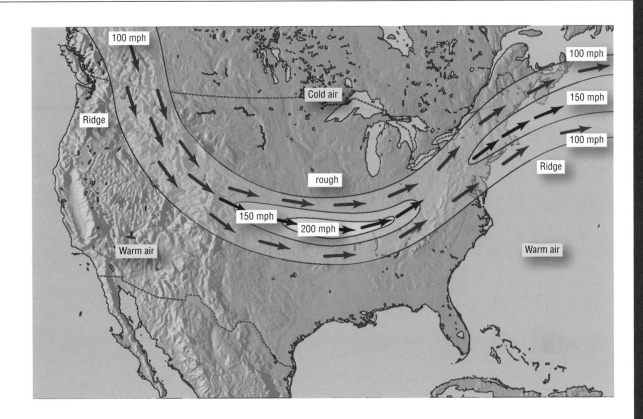

and that is also when the weather systems it produces are most pronounced.

The jet stream follows a wavy course and from time to time the waves grow bigger, extending toward the equator as *troughs* and toward the pole as *ridges,* as shown in the illustration. Troughs bring polar air and low pressure, with cold, wet weather, to regions as far south as Arizona and New Mexico. Ridges carry tropical air, with high pressure and fine warm weather, as far north as Alaska. Ridges and troughs sometimes remain stationary for several days or weeks, producing prolonged spells of fine or wet, hot or cold weather.

Ridges and troughs in the jet stream across North America. A trough is the region where the jet stream projects southward. A ridge is the region where the jet stream projects northward.

Why hot deserts are cold at night

Soon after sunrise the temperature begins to climb. At In Salah, Algeria, however, in the heart of the Sahara where the average rainfall is only 0.7 inch (17 mm) a year, the nights can be cold. In Salah is at latitude 27.2°N, almost in the Tropics, yet between December and February the temperature occasionally falls below freezing at night.

As the morning advances the temperature continues to rise. By mid afternoon it has reached its maximum, and that is hot. Even in the middle of winter—December and January—the temperature at In Salah has been known to reach 88°F (31°C). July is the hottest month, when the average afternoon temperature is 113°F (45°C) and it can rise to 122°F (50°C). At night the temperature drops to an average 83°F (28°C) and sometimes to 73°F (23°C).

Death Valley, at latitude 36.47°N in California's Mojave Desert, experiences even greater extremes of temperature.

Specific heat capacity

When a substance is heated, it absorbs heat energy and its temperature rises. The amount of heat it must absorb in order to raise its temperature by one degree varies from one substance to another, however. The ratio of the heat applied to a substance to the extent of the rise in its temperature is called the *specific heat capacity* for that substance. It is measured in calories per gram per degree Celsius (cal/g/°C) or in the scientific units of joules per gram per kelvin (J/g/K; 1 K = 1°C = 1.8°F). Specific heat capacity varies slightly according to the temperature, so when quoting the specific heat capacity of a substance it is customary to specify the temperature or temperature range to which this refers.

Pure water has a specific heat capacity of 1 cal/g/°C (4,180 J/g/K) at 59°F (15°C). This means that at 59°F (15°C) one gram of water must absorb one calorie of heat in order for its temperature to rise by one degree Celsius (or 0.56 cal to raise its temperature by 1°F). Seawater at 17°C (62.6°F) has a specific heat capacity of 0.94 cal/g/°C (3,930 J/g/K).

The desert surface consists of granite rock and sand. At temperatures between 68°F (20°C) and 212°F (100°C), the specific heat capacity of granite is 0.19–0.20 cal/g/°C (800–840 J/g/K). Within the same temperature range, the specific heat capacity of sand is 0.20 cal/g/°C (800 J/g/K). These values are typical for most types of rock.

Water has a specific heat capacity about five times that of rock. This means that water must absorb five times more heat than rock to produce a similar rise in temperature. It is why water warms up so much more slowly than sand and rock. Visit the beach on a real-

The average maximum temperature in July is 117°F (47°C), but 134°F (57°C) has been recorded. In January the average minimum temperature is 38°F (3°C), but it has been known to drop to 15°F (–9°C).

It comes as no surprise to learn that the Sahara and other subtropical deserts are hot places, especially in summer. The surprise is that the temperature drops so far during the night. Over the course of 24 hours in every month of the year, the average temperature at both In Salah and Death Valley changes by 26–30°F (14–17°C).

Temperatures are always measured in the air well clear of the ground. Air is heated by contact with the ground and so the diurnal change in air temperature reflects a change in the

ly hot day in summer and by lunchtime the sand will be so hot you have to run across it to avoid hurting your bare feet, but when you splash into the water, it is refreshingly cool. The reason for this is the difference in the specific heat capacities of water and sand.

In the desert the rock and sand, with a low specific heat capacity, heat up rapidly. By the middle of the day the ground is extremely hot. Specific heat capacity works both ways, though: Substances that heat quickly also cool down again quickly. The molecular configuration that confers a rapid response to absorbed heat also ensures that the heat cannot be retained for long once the external supply shuts down.

The ground radiates its heat into the sky. If there were clouds, they would absorb much of this heat and reradiate it, effectively trapping heat and keeping the air warm. But the desert sky is cloudless and so the heat is lost into space.

During the day, the desert rock and sand absorb heat from the Sun. Their temperature rises and as it does so they reradiate their energy into the sky, but at the same time they continue to absorb solar radiation. The balance between the energy sand and rock absorb and the energy they radiate allows the surface temperature to rise to a peak in the early afternoon, after which it remains steady. Then, as the Sun sinks toward the horizon, the balance starts to shift. Radiation from the surface remains constant, but less solar energy is absorbed. The surface starts to cool, but slowly at first. Once the Sun sinks below the horizon and darkness falls, there is no more sunshine for the desert to absorb, but its radiation continues. The surface temperature then plummets. Desert nights are cold. Sometimes they are very cold indeed.

temperature of the ground surface. Even in the northern United States, a sandy beach on a summer afternoon can be hot enough to burn your feet. In the Sahara, by about 4 P.M. in summer the temperature of the sand can reach 170°F (77°C).

Desert surfaces are made from rock or sand—and sand is simply weathered rock (see "What is sand?" on pages 36–37). Rock and sand warm up quickly. To put this more technically, they need to absorb only a small quantity of heat before their temperature begins to rise. They are said to have a low *specific heat capacity* (see the sidebar on pages 66–67). Water has a much higher specific heat capacity, so it heats up much more slowly. That is why the sea or lake beside the beach is always a place to cool off, even in the hottest weather. At night the ground loses heat as readily as it absorbed it during the day. It cools rapidly, unlike water, which cools very slowly. That is why the desert is so hot by day and so much cooler, even cold, by about one hour before dawn, when the temperature is at its lowest.

The high specific heat capacity of water moderates the extremes of temperature near the coast. As the land warms up, air above it rises and is replaced by cooler air from over the water. This is a sea or lake breeze, and it blows most strongly in the afternoon, bringing cool air when the temperature over land reaches its maximum. At Algiers, on the coast of the Mediterranean Sea, the average temperature range is 10–15°F (5–8°C)—half that of In Salah. In summer the average temperature at Algiers reaches 84°F (29°C), and even on the coldest night in winter it never falls below freezing.

Why the climates that produce ice sheets are so dry

Both Greenland and Antarctica lie buried beneath ice that is more than one mile (1.6 km) thick, yet despite this abundance of water, both Greenland and the interior of Antarctica have a climate that is more arid than all but the driest deserts. In terms of the precipitation they receive, they are among the driest places in the world.

Why Antarctica is colder than the North Pole

Vostok is the name of a Russian research station in Antarctica, located at about 78.75°S. Qaanaaq is a small town in northern Greenland (Kalaallit Nunaat), at 76.55°N.

They are in comparable latitudes, but they have very different climates. At Vostok, January is the warmest month, when the average temperature is –26°F (–32°C). The coldest month is August, with an average temperature of –90°F (–68°C). At Qaanaaq, the average temperature ranges from a high of 46°F (8°C) in July, the warmest month, to a low of –21°F (–29°C) in February.

Both places are dry, despite all the snow and ice. Qaanaaq has an annual rainfall of 2.5 inches (64 mm). It falls as snow in winter, of course, but in order to standardize measurement it is converted to the equivalent amount of rainfall. Vostok has 0.2 inch (4.5 mm).

The temperature range is similar for both: 64°F (36°C) at Vostok and 67°F (37°C) at Qaanaaq. The difference is that Vostok is much colder than Qaanaaq. This is because Qaanaaq is on the coast, albeit of an ocean that is frozen over for much of the year, and Vostok is in the interior of a large continent. The North Pole is located in the Arctic Ocean and the Arctic Basin is sea, surrounded by Eurasia, North America, and Greenland.

A large ice sheet covers East Antarctica, where Vostok is located. Air subsiding into the permanent Antarctic high-pressure region flows outward as a bitterly cold, extremely dry wind that blows almost incessantly. This combined with its elevation—Vostok is 11,401 feet (3,475 m) above sea level, on top of the thick ice—is what gives Vostok its cold, dry climate.

Antarctica also receives seven percent less solar radiation during its winter than the Arctic does in its winter. That is because the Earth's orbit around the Sun is not circular, but slightly elliptical, and the Sun is not at the center of the orbit. Earth is farthest from the Sun—*aphelion*—on about June 4, in the middle of the Southern Hemisphere winter. It is closest to the Sun—*perihelion*—on about January 4, in the middle of the Northern Hemisphere winter.

Qaanaaq is at sea level, but its altitude is not the principal reason for its warmer climate. It is warmer because of the sea. Ocean currents carry warm water into the Arctic Basin. The sea is frozen for most of the year, but there are gaps in the ice—called *leads*—that appear and disappear. Winds move the ice, piling it up in some places and leaving it thin in others. Heat escapes from the ocean where there are open water surfaces, but ice insulates the areas it covers. The sea temperature never falls below 29°F (–1.6°C); below

(continues)

(continued)

this temperature the water approaches its greatest density and sinks below warmer water that flows in at the surface to replace it. When the air temperature over the water falls below the temperature of the sea surface, heat passes from the water to the air. This warmer air then moves across the ice. Consequently, air temperatures over the entire Arctic Basin are much higher than they would be if there were land rather than sea beneath the ice. The coldest temperature ever recorded over the ice in the Arctic is –58°F (–50°C) and over most of the Basin the average temperature ranges between about 4°F (–20°C) and –40°F (–40°C). On July 21, 1983, the temperature at Vostok fell to –128.6°F (–89.2°C).

The polar regions are dry principally because they are so cold. The amount of water vapor that air can hold depends on the temperature. The warmer the air, the more moisture it can carry. On a bitterly cold winter's day you sometimes hear people say, "It's too cold for snow." They are right. Air that is extremely cold is also extremely dry.

The polar regions are cold because of their high latitude. Even in summer, when the Sun remains above the horizon for 24 hours, producing the "land of the midnight Sun," the Sun remains low in the sky and its warmth is spread thinly over a large area, because of the low angle. In winter there are days when the Sun does not rise above the horizon at all.

The two polar regions are not equally cold, however. Both are in similar latitudes and both receive almost equal amounts of sunshine, but Antarctica is very much colder than Greenland or any other place inside the Arctic Circle. The sidebar on page 69 explains why this is so.

On a bright day in summer, in places sheltered from the wind, the sunshine can feel quite warm, yet it does not warm the ground. Up to 90 percent of the solar radiation is reflected by the snow. If you go outdoors on a sunny day following a fresh fall of snow you may need to protect your eyes from the glare, due to the light being reflected from the white surface. It is not only light that is reflected, however. Heat is also reflected, rather than being absorbed by the ground and warming it. Most surfaces reflect some of the sunlight falling on them. The proportion of the total sunshine a surface reflects is known as the *albedo* of that surface. The table below shows the albedo values for a variety of surfaces. They are percentages of the total sunlight falling on them and usually written as a decimal fraction. For example, fresh snow reflects 75–95 percent of the sunlight falling on it, so it has an albedo of 75–95 percent, which is written as 0.75–0.95. The permanently white surface helps ensure that ice-cold Greenland and Antarctica remain cold.

The air is just as cold and the cold, dense air sits heavily over the surface, producing permanently high atmospheric pressure. Air flows outward, away from centers of high pressure, called *anticyclones*, and, like the subtropical anticyclones that keep the hot deserts dry, air flowing out from the polar anticyclones prevents moister air from entering. The polar regions are dry partly because they lie beneath permanent anticyclones (see the sidebar "General circulation of the atmosphere" on page 52).

They are also dry simply because they are cold. Water molecules consist of two hydrogen atoms (H + H) joined to one

Albedo

Surface	Value
Fresh snow	0.75–0.95
Old snow	0.40–0.70
Cumuliform cloud	0.70–0.90
Stratiform cloud	0.59–0.84
Cirrostratus	0.44–0.50
Sea ice	0.30–0.40
Dry sand	0.35–0.45
Wet sand	0.20–0.30
Desert	0.25–0.30
Meadow	0.10–0.20
Field crops	0.15–0.25
Deciduous forest	0.10–0.20
Coniferous forest	0.05–0.15
Concrete	0.17–0.27
Black road	0.05–0.10

oxygen atom (O), producing H_2O, but the hydrogen atoms are both attached on the same side of the oxygen atom. In liquid water the molecules are linked together by *hydrogen bonds,* which are forces of attraction between the small positive electromagnetic charge on a hydrogen atom of one molecule and the negative charge on the oxygen atom of an adjacent molecule. Water molecules join together in small groups that are constantly breaking apart and forming again and that move freely past one another.

If the water is heated, its molecules absorb energy, making groups of molecules move faster and individual molecules vibrate more vigorously. When a molecule has absorbed enough energy it will vibrate so strongly that it breaks free from the hydrogen bond holding it to its neighbor. As more and more hydrogen bonds break, free molecules escape into the air and the liquid water evaporates.

Water vapor—an invisible gas that is not to be confused with steam, which is a cloud of liquid water droplets—is at the same temperature as the air in which it is dispersed. If the air temperature should fall, the water molecules will possess less energy and move more slowly. If the temperature falls far enough, when two molecules meet, a hydrogen bond may form between them. The water vapor will condense into liquid.

As the temperature continues to fall, more and more water molecules link to one another and clouds form. At temperatures below freezing molecules will form ice crystals. The water droplets and ice crystals then merge with one another to form raindrops or snowflakes, and fall from the cloud. Precipitation—rain and snow—removes water from the air, making the air drier.

Air is said to be *saturated* when it contains as much water vapor as it is capable of holding. Even in warm air this amount is quite small. When the air temperature is 86°F (30°C), one pound of air is able to hold 0.4 ounce (26.5 g/km) of water vapor. On a really hot day, when the temperature is 104°F (40°C), one pound of air can hold only 0.75 ounce (47 g/kg) of water vapor. It is never this warm in Greenland or Antarctica. The midsummer temperature in those places is more likely to be around freezing, and at that temperature one pound of air can hold 0.06 ounce (3.5 g/km) of moisture. At –22°F (–30°C), one pound of air can hold no more than 0.005 ounce (0.3 g/kg) of water vapor.

In fact, the air over Greenland and Antarctica is even drier than these figures suggest, because the surface is covered with ice, not liquid water. Ice will change directly into vapor, but it requires more energy to vaporize ice than it does to evaporate liquid water. Consequently, less water vapor enters the air above an ice surface than enters it from a liquid surface.

Why deserts are windy places

Desert air is seldom still. Trade winds blow across the subtropical deserts. These are the most dependable of all winds, blowing from the northeast in the Northern Hemisphere and from the southeast in the Southern Hemisphere, and they lose any moisture they might be carrying as they cross the hot desert surface. By the time they leave the desert they are very dry and very hot.

Trade winds leaving the Sahara are known as the *harmattan,* a hot, dusty, and often strong wind that blows only during the day. At night it dies down. It blows at all times of year, but in summer the monsoon winds (see "Monsoons" on pages 58–62) blowing in the opposite direction make it weaker and less frequent.

The harmattan is stronger than the trade winds because it is accelerated by the natural flow of air away from the anticyclone centered on the desert. When it arrives in tropical Africa the harmattan is so dry that it turns leaves yellow, hardens leather, and makes wood warp. Its extreme dryness comes as a relief to the inhabitants of the humid Tropics, however. They believe that it brings health benefits by driving away the extremely moist, oppressive air. They call it "The Doctor."

Khamsin is the Arabic word for "fifty." It is also the name of a hot, dry, southeasterly wind that in most years blows across Egypt and Sudan on 50 days in late winter and early spring. It results from the counterclockwise circulation of air around low-pressure systems over Sudan and the northern Sahara, which combine to draw in air from over Arabia. Fortunately, the 50 days are not consecutive and the wind seldom continues for more than three days. The khamsin brings temperatures of more than 100°F (38°C) and so much dust that cars must use their headlights in the middle of the day.

Air flowing away from the subtropical anticyclone produces some of the desert wind. The polar anticyclone also generates winds and, like the harmattan, they are accelerated, though for a different reason.

As well as being the coldest continent, Antarctica is also the highest. The average elevation is 8,200 feet (2,500 m) and the Amundsen-Scott Base, at the South Pole, is 9,301 feet (2,837 m) above sea level. The South Pole is approximately at the center of the continent and it is also near the center of the polar anticyclone. Consequently, air moving away from the anticyclone is also moving downhill as it approaches the coast and sea level. Winds that flow downhill are called *katabatic,* from the Greek word *katabatikos* meaning "going downward." As well as flowing down a pressure gradient, from high to low pressure, the air is also flowing under the force of gravity, which accelerates it. At the South Pole the average wind speed is 14 MPH (22.5 km/h) and there are many calm days. Near the coasts, on the other hand, calm days are rare and winds of more than 50 MPH (80 km/h), with still stronger gusts, are common.

Winds in the subtropical deserts are strongest in the afternoon and during the hottest months. These are when the sand and rock surfaces are hottest. Hot air expands and rises, and denser air replaces it at the surface. This makes the air very turbulent and generates strong, gusty winds.

Low-pressure weather systems also cross the desert from time to time. They bring no rain, of course, or even clouds, but they do bring winds that last for longer and are often stronger than the winds produced by daytime heating.

Dust storms and sandstorms

The Sahara is famed for its sand dunes and sand seas (see "Sand seas and sand dunes" on pages 37–41), but even in the Sahara there is almost no sand over more than two-thirds of the total area. Sand dunes cover no more than about two per-cent of the surface of the Sonoran Desert. Bare rock, stones, and gravel cover the ground. Sand cannot survive in these areas, because as fast as it gathers the wind sweeps it away. The removal of sand and dust by the wind is called *deflation*.

Even a light wind will raise fine dust from the ground, and a wind of 12 MPH (19 km/h)—a breeze strong enough to blow leaves and scraps of paper about—will raise medium-sized sand grains, provided the sand is dry. Deserts are windy places and this wind speed is often exceeded.

Once airborne, desert dust and fine sand can travel a long way. Saharan dust occasionally crosses the Atlantic and is washed to the ground over the United States, and when it is carried northward it has been known to fall over Finland. Desert dust is red and it colors the rain, which is then known as "blood rain." Dust from the Australian deserts sometimes falls as blood rain in New Zealand. The harmattan wind (see "Why deserts are windy places" on pages 73–74) brings relief to people in the hot, humid Tropics, but it also makes them close their doors and windows to keep out the dust.

A strong wind over a large sandy or dusty area will cause a dust storm or sandstorm. A storm of this kind has many local names. It is called a *simoom* in the Sahara, for instance, and *andhis* in the Thar Desert. It is a vast, swirling cloud of sand and dust, driven by the wind. It penetrates clothes and finds its way into houses through the smallest cracks around win-dows and doors. Driven into ears, mouths, noses, and eyes, the dust causes irritation and it can cause eye damage, even blindness. It also reduces visibility, sometimes almost to zero. In March 1998 poor visibility caused by a storm of this kind, driven by a khamsin wind, closed Cairo airport and the Suez Canal.

In July 2003 windblown sand and dust from the Syrian Desert produced the worst sandstorms in living memory in western Afghanistan. They filled wells and canals, destroyed crops, and contaminated the water supply to thousands of people. The storms began on June 5 and continued until the end of August, affecting about 12,000 people living in 57 vil-lages. Up to 20 villages had to be abandoned because they had been completely buried in sand.

China and Mongolia also suffer. Winds from Siberia gather sand and dust in the Taklimakan and Gobi Deserts. In May 1993 one of these storms affected about 425,000 square miles (1.1 million km²) of China, damaging 922,000 acres (373,000 ha) of cropland, killing 12,000 head of livestock, destroying 4,400 houses, and killing 85 people. In 2002 Asian dust storms and sandstorms reached the Korean Peninsula and Japan.

Desert storms on this scale are usually caused by cold fronts (see "Air masses, fronts, and jet streams" on pages 62–65). As it advances, a cold front pushes beneath the warmer air ahead of it. This produces strong turbulence and gusty winds that raise a cloud of dust and sand that advances with the front, like a wall of sand, which is often 3,000 feet (900 m) high. It is impossible to work during a sandstorm and even eating and drinking are difficult, because the sand and dust contaminate food and drink. At its approach, people take shelter and wait until it has passed.

Dust devils and whirlwinds

A sandstorm appears on the horizon as a dark wall towering to a great height. There is time to find shelter before it arrives. Dust devils are much smaller. They give little warning, but they are harmless and short-lived. Whirlwinds are terrifying. They leap from the ground unpredictably and have the power to demolish tents, wrench doors from their hinges, and hurl debris that may injure people nearby.

Dust devils and whirlwinds result from the fact that the desert surface warms unevenly through the day. Every surface reflects some of the Sun's heat. Pale-colored surfaces reflect more than dark surfaces, and dry sand reflects more than bare rock (see the table on page 71). This means that a surface covered with sand heats up more slowly than a bare rock surface, and it does not reach such a high temperature before starting to cool again. At about 6 A.M., as the day begins in the central Sahara, the temperature of the sand surface is about 80°F (27°C) and, depending on their composition, the rock surfaces are at 100–110°F (38–43°C). The sand reaches its maximum temperature of about 145°F (63°C) by noon, but

A dust devil approaches a flock of puna or James' flamingos (Phoenicoparrus jamesi) in Chile (Courtesy of Tui de Roy/ Minden Pictures)

the rock continues warming until about 2 P.M., when its temperature is about 175°F (79°C). By that time the sand has already started to cool, but the rock does not start cooling until about 5 P.M.

In a part of the desert where some of the surface is covered by sand and some by bare rock, by the middle of the afternoon the rock will be markedly warmer than the sand. That is the time of day when dust devils and whirlwinds are most likely.

If there is a wind—and there very often is—it will mix the air so that the difference in surface temperature produces no difference in air temperature. On a calm day, however, such differences do develop. Air over the rock is much warmer than air over the sand. The warm air expands and rises, and cooler air converges from all sides to replace it. Small local winds blow from the sand to the rock.

Converging air does not travel in a straight line. It turns, to the left in the Northern Hemisphere, until it is spiraling horizontally into the area it seeks to fill. Then it joins the rising air, still in a spiral. The rising air over the warm area is then spiraling upward.

If only a small area is heated, the spiraling air will raise a small amount of dust and lightweight material, such as dry leaves and scraps of paper. A larger area will produce a stronger spiral that raises more dust and sand, sometimes to a height of 300 feet (92 m).

The bigger the area of warm ground, the bigger the dust devil will be. That much seems obvious, but it may be less obvious why its winds are also stronger. The strengthening wind is due to a property possessed by all rotating bodies, and air spiraling into a central area is a rotating body. The property is *angular momentum* and it is *conserved.* This means that if one of the components of angular momentum changes, the other components will automatically adjust to ensure that the amount of angular momentum stays the same. The sidebar on page 79 explains this.

The wider the area from which air is drawn toward the center, the greater the outer radius of the spiral and therefore, because the angular momentum of the air is conserved, the stronger the winds will be at the center. On the largest scale, this produces whirlwinds.

A whirlwind develops in the same way as a dust devil, but it can rise to more than 6,500 feet (2 km) as a screaming, twisting funnel of sand and dust that looks very much like a tornado. It is not a tornado. It does not descend from a big, black storm cloud that would provide advance warning, but

Conservation of angular momentum

Imagine a body that is spinning about its own axis. You can measure the mass of the body, the radius of the circle it describes, and the speed of its rotation. Its speed of rotation is known as its *angular velocity* and is measured as the number of degrees through which it turns in a given time. The Earth, for example, completes one revolution in 24 hours. One full turn takes it through 360°, so the Earth's angular velocity is 15° per hour (360 ÷ 24 = 15). Angular velocity is usually expressed in radians per hour or per second. A radian is the angle between two radii of a circle that marks out on the circumference an arc that is equal in length to the radius. Therefore the circumference of a circle is 2 π radians and 1 radian = 57.296°.

Multiply these three values together and the product, called *angular momentum,* is a constant. Call the mass M, the radius R, and the angular velocity V, and $M \times R \times V$ = a constant. M, R, and V are *variables.* They can be altered, but the constant must remain the same.

This is called the *conservation of angular momentum* and it means that if one of the variables changes, one or two of the others must also change in order that the constant remains the same. No one needs to do anything to make this happen; it is entirely automatic.

Dancers and ice skaters make use of the conservation of angular momentum when they perform pirouettes. The dancer starts spinning with her arms fully outstretched. The distance from the center of her body (the axis of her rotation) to her fingertips is the diameter of the circle her body describes; the radius is half of this. Then she slowly draws her arms inward to her body. This reduces her radius of spin. She has reduced one of the three variables and so one or both of the others must increase in order to compensate. Her mass cannot change (she cannot suddenly become heavier) and so the remaining variable, her angular velocity, has to change. It increases as her radius of spin decreases. In other words, she spins faster—but without making any additional effort beyond withdrawing her arms.

rises from the ground on a calm afternoon into a clear, blue sky—with no warning at all. It is weaker than a tornado, with winds that rarely exceed 60 MPH (96 km/h), but that is strong enough to be dangerous.

Whirlwinds are short-lived, but they often occur in "families." They rise suddenly and just as suddenly they die down, but as one dies another rises nearby. During their brief lives they move erratically over the ground. They are made of nothing more substantial than air, of course, made visible by the dust and sand they raise, but these pale, shrieking wraiths have been scaring desert dwellers for thousands of years.

CHAPTER 4

LIFE IN DESERTS

Photosynthesis, respiration, and desert plants

All animals depend on plants for their food, even in the desert. There is no such thing as a vegetarian snake, of course, but snakes eat animals that are vegetarians, and so the snakes depend on plants just as much as a small rodent that feeds on plant seeds. The reason there are few animals to be seen in the desert is not that the desert is too hot, too cold, or too dry for them; animals can adapt to these conditions. It is because plants find it much more difficult to adapt to the lack of water and consequently there are few plants. The lack of plants means there is not much for desert animals to eat.

Plants feed all animals. They occupy this important position because of their ability to manufacture carbohydrates, fats, proteins, and vitamins from raw materials they obtain from the air, the soil, and water. The process that provides the energy for the "plant factory" is called *photosynthesis,* a word derived from two Greek words—*phos,* meaning "light," and *syntithenai* meaning "to put together."

Photosynthesis depends on a pigment called *chlorophyll* contained in bodies called *chloroplasts* in cells just below the surface of leaves and other green parts of plants (such as unripe fruits). Chlorophyll is green and it is what gives plants their green color. Photosynthesis proceeds in two stages. The first stage depends on light, so it is called the *light-dependent* or *light* stage. The second stage does not use light energy and is called the *light-independent* or *dark* stage—although it also takes place in the light.

The light-dependent stage begins when a photon (particle) of light possessing precisely the right amount of energy strikes a chlorophyll molecule. The chlorophyll molecule absorbs the photon, causing an electron (a particle carrying negative charge) in the molecule to break free, leaving the chlorophyll molecule with a positive charge. The electron immediately attaches to a neighboring molecule. The addition of an electron releases an electron from that molecule, which attaches to another molecule, and electrons released in this way then pass from molecule to molecule along an *electron-transport chain* of molecules.

Some of the captured energy is used to convert adenosine diphosphate (ADP) to adenosine triphosphate (ATP) by the addition of phosphate (the reaction is called *phosphorylation*), the electron then returning to the chlorophyll. Converting ADP to ATP absorbs energy; converting ATP to ADP releases the energy. All living organisms use the ADP $\longleftrightarrow$ ATP reaction to transport energy and release it where it is needed.

The remaining energy is used to split a water molecule (H_2O, but it can also be written HOH) into hydrogen bearing a positive charge (H^+) and hydroxyl with a negative charge (OH^-). The H^+ attaches to a molecule of nicotinamide adenine dinucleotide phosphate (NADP), converting it to NADPH. The OH^- passes one electron to the chlorophyll molecule, restoring the neutrality of both chlorophyll and hydroxyl. Hydroxyls then combine to form water ($4OH \rightarrow 2H_2O + O_2\uparrow$). (The upward arrow indicates that the oxygen is released into the air.) This completes the light-dependent stage. Products from the light-dependent stage then trigger the start of the light-independent stage.

Using ATP from the light-dependent stage as a source of energy, the light-independent stage begins by attaching carbon dioxide (CO_2) obtained from the air to ribulose biphosphate (RuBP) in a reaction called *carboxylation* that is catalyzed by the enzyme RuBP carboxylase, or rubisco. In a cycle of reactions carbon is then combined with hydrogen obtained from NADPH; the NADP returns to the light-dependent stage. The cycle ends with the synthesis of molecules of glucose and of RuBP. The entire photosynthetic process is summarized as:

$$6CO_2 + 6H_2O + photon \rightarrow C_6H_{12}O_6 + 6O_2 \uparrow$$

$C_6H_{12}O_6$ is glucose, a simple sugar. Glucose is used as a source of energy, which is released by the process of *respiration,* and for the synthesis of starch and cellulose in plants and glycogen in animals. Glycogen can be converted to glucose to provide fuel for respiration.

Respiration must not be confused with breathing, which is the mechanical action by which animals obtain oxygen and rid their bodies of carbon dioxide. All plants and animals are *aerobic* (air-breathing), but some bacteria are *anaerobic* and use a different respiration process. Aerobic organisms use oxygen to oxidize glucose, a reaction that releases energy. Carbon dioxide and water are by-products of the reaction. This is respiration and it is the direct opposite of photosynthesis:

$$C_6H_{12}O_6 + 6O_2 \rightarrow 6CO_2 + 6H_2O + energy$$

Plants have a problem, however, arising from *photorespiration*. Unlike ordinary respiration, photorespiration wastes energy rather than releasing it. It occurs because the enzyme rubisco can attach itself to oxygen as well as to carbon dioxide. If rubisco attaches to carbon dioxide it catalyzes the carboxylation of RuBP, but if it attaches to oxygen it catalyzes the oxidation of RuBP, triggering a sequence of reactions that end by releasing carbon dioxide but without releasing energy.

Whether rubisco attaches to oxygen or carbon dioxide depends on the relative concentrations of these gases in air. At one time, when the atmospheric concentration of carbon dioxide was higher than it is now, photorespiration may have been unimportant, but today, when the air contains approximately 365 parts per million of carbon dioxide, enough oxygen attaches to rubisco to significantly reduce the efficiency of photosynthesis. Certain groups of plants. known as *C4* and *CAM* plants, have adapted to the low atmospheric concentration of carbon dioxide by modifying the reactions at the start of the light-independent stage (see the sidebar on page 84).

C4 photosynthesis involves more steps than the C3 pathway, and C4 plants use much more energy than C3 plants. Because they avoid photorespiration, however, they use carbon dioxide more efficiently than do C3 plants.

Their improved efficiency gives C4 plants an advantage in dry climates. When water is scarce, plants close their stomata to reduce losses, but with their stomata closed they cannot

C3, C4, and CAM plants

In many plants the light-independent stage of photosynthesis begins with the addition of a molecule of carbon dioxide to a molecule of ribulose biphosphate (RuBP). RuBP is a sugar containing five carbon atoms. Adding a carbon atom produces a six-carbon sugar. This is unstable and breaks into two molecules of 3-phosphoglycerate, a three-carbon sugar. Plants in which photosynthesis uses this reaction are known as *C3 plants.* The efficiency of photosynthesis in C3 plants is often reduced by high rates of photorespiration.

Other plants, mainly tropical and subtropical grasses including corn (maize) and sugarcane, use a different reaction. Carbon dioxide enters *mesophyll* cells lying just below the leaf cells that contain chlorophyll. There the enzyme PEP carboxylase catalyzes a reaction that attaches carbon dioxide to phosphoenolpyruvate, producing the four-carbon compound oxaloacetate, which is then converted to another four-carbon compound. PEP carboxylase has no affinity for oxygen. Plants using this reaction are known as *C4 plants.*

The four-carbon compound leaves the mesophyll cells through passageways called *plasmodesmata* to enter *bundle-sheath cells* that are packed tightly around leaf veins. There the four-carbon compound gives up its carbon dioxide, which combines with rubisco and enters the light-independent stage. Because carbon dioxide accumulates in the bundle-sheath cells its concentration is always high enough to ensure that it wins the competition with oxygen for rubisco, thus preventing photorespiration.

Certain desert plants have evolved a further modification that minimizes the loss of moisture when leaf *stomata* (pores) are open to exchange gases with the air. This modification was first identified in plants belonging to the stonecrop and houseleek family, Crassulaceae, and it is known as *crassulacean acid metabolism,* usually abbreviated to *CAM.*

CAM plants open their stomata at night, when the air is cool and the rate of evaporation is low. Carbon dioxide enters the mesophyll cells and oxygen departs, but little moisture is lost. The carbon dioxide combines with an organic acid and the resulting compound is stored in *vacuoles* (small spaces) inside the mesophyll cells.

Photosynthesis is impossible at night, but at dawn the CAM plants close their stomata and keep them closed until nightfall. During the day they use the carbon dioxide they collected overnight to enter the light-independent stage of photosynthesis.

exchange gases with the air. Carbon dioxide cannot enter leaf cells and oxygen cannot leave them. Consequently, inside the cells where photosynthesis takes place the concentration of oxygen increases, that of carbon dioxide decreases, and the rate of photorespiration rises until sometimes it exceeds the rate of photosynthesis. This is less of a problem for C4 plants than it is for C3 plants. In temperate climates, however, C4 plants are often at a disadvantage compared with C3 plants. Water is usually plentiful in temperate climates and droughts seldom last long, so plants can afford to lose moisture through their open stomata. This favors C3 plants, and because C4 plants use more energy they are often at a disadvantage.

Why plants need water

Photosynthesis, the sequence of chemical reactions by which green plants make sugar, uses carbon dioxide as a source of carbon and water as a source of hydrogen. If a plant had no access to water, photosynthesis would be impossible and the plant would die. Only a small fraction of the water inside a plant is used for photosynthesis; nevertheless, water is an essential raw material for the process that gives a plant the energy it needs to grow, repair its tissues, and reproduce.

Plants also absorb mineral nutrients from the soil. They need relatively large amounts of the elements nitrogen, potassium, phosphorus, sulfur, calcium, magnesium, and iron, and very small amounts of a range of others, including boron, copper, manganese, molybdenum, and zinc. Nitrogen and sulfur are essential ingredients of all proteins, for example. These elements are present in a fertile soil, where they are dissolved in water. They enter plant roots in solution, and this is the only way the plant can obtain them. The plant needs water as a solvent for the mineral nutrients it requires.

Once they have entered the root system, the mineral nutrients must be transported to all the parts of the plant where they are needed—to the leaves, buds, flowers, and fruits, and to every branch, twig, and stem. The nutrients travel along vessels—visible as the veins in leaves—flowing in the form of a solution; they are dissolved in water. The plant needs water to transport nutrients.

The vessels that transport nutrients form *xylem* tissue. Other vessels, comprising *phloem* tissue, transport the sugars made by photosynthesis from the leaves to every part of the plant. The sugars also travel in solution, so the plant needs water to carry sugars to tissues that need the energy they supply.

Plant cells are filled with fluid that is mainly water. The fluid keeps the cell walls rigid, like the air in a tire, and when all the plant cells are rigid so is the whole plant. Plants need water to maintain their rigidity—the scientific term is *turgor.* If they lack water the cells lose their turgor and the plant wilts. Its leaves hang limply, and in nonwoody plants the stem also becomes limp and the plant collapses. Provided it has not been without water for too long, a wilting plant recovers quickly when its roots once more have access to water, but prolonged wilting is fatal.

Plants absorb water through the fine hairs lying just behind the tip of every branch of their roots. Water enters the *root hairs* because the pressure inside the hair is lower than the pressure outside. Inside the root, the water enters the xylem tissue that transports it to the rest of the plant.

Xylem consists of bundles of hollow, approximately cylindrical cells arranged end to end. The cells are dead, but they form continuous tubes leading all the way to the leaves.

Leaves have tiny pores, called *stomata,* through which the gases involved in photosynthesis enter and leave the plant. When the stomata are open for gas exchange, moisture evaporates from inside the mesophyll cells just below the leaf surface. This loss of water is called *transpiration.* As water molecules escape, adjacent molecules cling strongly to depressions in the mesophyll cell walls, and at the same time the mutual attraction of water molecules pulls the water into the shape with the smallest possible surface area. The combined effect is to lower the pressure inside the cell to below the atmospheric pressure, and the difference in pressure causes water to move from the leaf xylem and into the mesophyll cells. Water molecules are drawn through the xylem tissue behind the molecules moving into the mesophyll cells, and this pressure, starting at the stomata, is transferred down through the plant all the way to the root hairs. The pressure is so strong that on a hot day, when the rate of transpiration is high, the sides of the xylem cells are pulled inward and a tree trunk becomes measurably narrower.

Typical plants of subtropical deserts

Cacti, the most famous of all desert plants, cope with the dry conditions in several ways. They dispense with leaves or have only very small leaves. The green swollen structures that are typical of cacti are stems, not leaves. Photosynthesis takes place in the stems and the stems also store water. The bulbous shape of the swollen stems reduces water loss, prevents the plant from overheating, and stores water. This is because the swollen stems have a smaller surface area in relation to their volume than they would have if they were not swollen. The volume of the stem determines the amount of water it can store, and the surface area determines the amount of warmth it can absorb and water it can lose by transpiration.

Naturally, desert animals might like to steal the water and to prevent this most cacti protect themselves with viciously sharp spines. In some species the spines are tiny, barbed, easily detached, and grow in bunches, so that any animal

Spines on a prickly pear cactus (Opuntia species) grow from sunken depressions called areoles. (Courtesy of Fogstock)

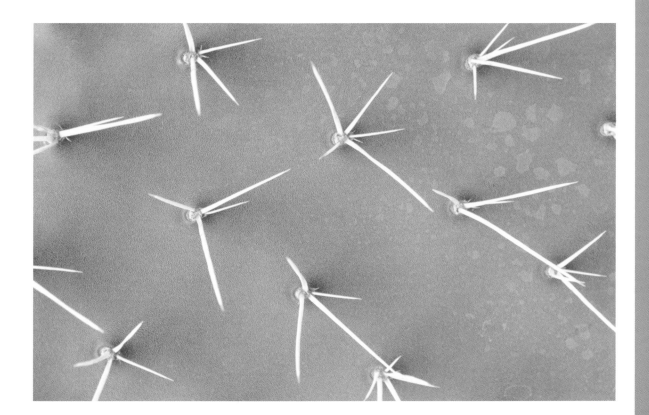

brushing against them has to spend a long time picking them out of its skin. Most cacti have shallow roots, but in larger species these spread a long way horizontally. The roots are adapted to absorb water rapidly just below the ground surface. All cacti are CAM plants (see the sidebar "C3, C4, and CAM plants" on page 84).

The spines of cacti, and also their branches and flowers, grow from sunken cushions called *areoles*. These are set singly on raised lumps called *tubercles* or in rows along ridges or ribs, as in the saguaro or giant cactus (*Carnegiea gigantea*). The biggest of all cacti, the saguaro can grow to a height of 65 feet (20 m) and a diameter of two feet (60 cm). Its flowers are pollinated by birds and insects during the day and by bats at night.

Unrelated plants and animals that live in extreme environments such as deserts often come to resemble one another (see the sidebar "Parallel evolution and convergent evolution" on page 116). There are plants in the African deserts that look almost identical to the cacti of American deserts. They are not cacti, however, but members of the spurge family (Euphorbiaceae). *Euphorbia echinus,* from southern Morocco, grows as bunches of cactuslike, swollen stems up to three feet (90 cm) tall with sharp ridges bearing spines. *E. heterochroma* is similar in appearance, but up to six feet (1.8 m) tall and from East Africa. Abyssinian spurge (*E. abyssinica*) has vertical ridged stems with spines and grows up to 15 feet (4.5 m) tall, and Canary Island spurge (*E. canariensis*) can be 20 feet (6 m) tall. Milk barrel (*E. cereiformis*) from South Africa grows as clusters of ridged stems up to three feet (90 cm) tall and

A saguaro cactus (Carnegiea gigantea) silhouetted against the night sky. (Courtesy of Fogstock)

A barrel cactus (Ferocactus species) growing in the Joshua Tree National Park (Courtesy of Rodolfo Arpia)

up to two inches (5 cm) thick. It resembles *Cereus* cacti so closely that it was given the name *cereiformis,* meaning "cereus shaped." There are differences between euphorbias and cacti, of course. Unlike cacti, euphorbias produce a very poisonous sap. Euphorbias bear their spines in pairs, whereas cacti bear theirs either singly or in bunches. While cacti are CAM plants, euphorbias are C3 plants (see the sidebar "C3, C4, and CAM plants" on page 84).

Thorn trees (1,200 *Acacia* species), known in Australia as wattles, also bear spines. Australia has the largest number of species, but thorn trees also grow in the African and Asian deserts, and the bullhorn acacia (*A. cornigera*) is found in Central America. Its thorns are swollen at the base, and each thorn houses a colony of ants that protect the tree in return for food supplied by the plant.

Many agaves (family Agavaceae) look like cacti. They have thick leaves, up to 10 feet (3 m) long in some species, with prickles along the edges. Agaves grow in many parts of the world, but the century plant (*Agave americana*) is American. Its name refers to the mistaken belief that the plant flowers only once in every century. In fact it flowers every 10–20 years.

Yuccas also belong to the agave family, and all 30 species are American. Some yuccas are the size of small trees. The biggest of them all is the Joshua tree (*Yucca brevifolia*) of the Mojave Desert, which can grow to 35 feet (10.7 m).

Creosote bushes (*Larrea divaricata tridentata*) are the most abundant plants over large areas of the North and Central American deserts. These are shrubs up to five feet (1.5 m) tall, which can survive for a year without rain. Their leaves smell of creosote, hence the name.

Joshua trees (Yucca brevifolia) (Courtesy of Fogstock)

All of these are perennial plants, always present in the desert and able to survive for long periods without water. Cacti, euphorbias, agaves, and yuccas store water in their succulent (moisture-conserving) leaves. Thorn trees and creosote bushes have tiny leaves to minimize water loss and remain dormant between rains. Other plants survive as seeds that germinate when they are moistened.

Tumbleweeds are the most famous of these. There are several unrelated species, and tumble grass (*Schedonardus paniculatus*) is typical. The plant dies after producing seeds. As it withers, it curls up into a ball with the seeds on the inside. The wind blows the ball along, scattering seeds as it goes.

Many other plants survive as seeds in the ground. Following rain, the seeds germinate and the plants grow, flower, and set seeds before the ground dries out. Evening primrose (*Oenothera* species) of California produces seeds that can wait 50 years or more for conditions that allow them to germinate. When it rains the desert blooms, but within a few weeks the flowers are gone, the plants have died, and the desert appears barren as a new crop of seeds awaits the next rain.

Camel thorn (Alhagi maurorum) *seen here in the Namib-Naukluft National Park, Namibia, has branches that exude a sap that hardens into lumps called manna.* (Courtesy of Gerry Ellis/Minden Pictures)

Typical plants of cold deserts

Gobi is a Mongolian word that means "waterless place." Although it is a desert, however, the Gobi is not devoid of plants. Succulent grasses grow in the warmer areas, especially *Echinochloa* species, a type of millet. Elsewhere on the Gobi plateau there are feather grasses (*Stipa* species), with blades folded into tubes, so the stomata are on the inside. This minimizes the loss of water by transpiration and is an adaptation to dry conditions. These include Gobi feather grass (*S. glareosa*) and timuriya (*S. villosa*). Around the desert margins there are snakeweeds (*Cleistogenes* species), including Dzungarian bridlegrass (*C. soongorica*).

There are also shrubs. In places the soils are salty, so many of the woody plants are *halophytes* (tolerant of salt) as well as *xerophytes* (tolerant of drought). Yellow khotir, also called yellowwood beancaper (*Zygophyllum xanthophyllum*), has edible flower buds that are used as a substitute for capers. The nitre bush (*Nitraria sibirica*), a member of the same family (Zygophyllaceae), has a fruit that some animals eat because it is rich in salt. Tamarisks are shrubs or small trees that often grow on sandy soils near coasts. Dzungarian reaumuria (*Reaumuria soongorica*), a member of the tamarisk family (Tamaricaceae), is a small halophytic shrub found in the low-lying Dzungaria basin of northwestern China. Yellow ephedra (*Ephedra prezewalskii*) is a xerophytic shrub or small tree.

Winter fat (*Krascheninnikovia lanata*), a member of the sugar beet family (Chenopodiaceae), also grows in North America where it is known as white sage. It is a small bush that is covered with a dense mat of pale-colored hairs. Gobi kumarchik (*Agriophyllum gobicum*) belongs to the same family, but is an annual herb with seeds that are an important Mongolian food.

Saxaul (*Haloxylon ammodendron*) is a shrub about 10 feet (3 m) tall that grows in the sandy parts of the desert where the sand is stable. In many of the less arid places saxaul plants grow so close together they form "forests" that bind the soil together and prevent erosion. There are also peashrubs (*Caragana bungei* and *C. leucocephala*), small shrubs that are the dominant plants over large areas.

In contrast, the Taklimakan Desert of western China is extremely dry and plants are very few and far between. In depressions, where there is groundwater within 10–15 feet (3–4.5 m) of the surface, there are sparse thickets of tamarisk shrubs and nitre bushes, but over most of the desert the shifting sands make it impossible for plants to gain a secure anchorage. There are more plants near the edges of the desert.

Patagonia, in southern South America, has a much richer plant life. There are forests along the western border. On the tableland to the east of the mountains the plants are xerophytic, adapted to the combination of low rainfall and constant drying winds. Few plants grow in the driest areas, but there are wetter areas completely covered by plants. In the desert proper, where plants cover up to 15 percent of the ground surface, there are halophytes such as saltbushes (*Atriplex* species) and other members of the sugar beet family (Chenopodiaceae).

In the moister areas, where almost half the ground is covered in plants, the predominant species are cushion plants, often growing between rocks, and dwarf shrubs. Cushion plants are typically one to four inches (2–10 cm) high, most with tiny but bright flowers. Many are widely cultivated as alpines, including *Benthamiella, Brachyclados,* and *Nassauvia* species. Among the shrubs and cushion plants there are tufts of feather grass (*Stipa* species) and meadow grass (*Poa* species).

Where the desert merges into the pampas grassland, shrubs cover more than half the ground. They include *Chuquiraga* species, up to 20 inches (50 cm) tall, and *Berberis* species, which grow as small trees up to 10 feet (3 m) tall.

Typical animals of hot deserts

Loose desert sand moves like a liquid and there are animals that swim through it as though they were in the sea. Some lizards swim through the sand (see "Snakes and lizards" on pages 110–114) and so do the golden moles that are found in southern Africa and nowhere else.

All moles have poor eyesight, but golden moles are really blind. Skin covers their eyes and fur covers the outside of their ears. This does not make them deaf, however, because the bones of the inner ear are very large and highly sensitive to vibrations. Golden moles are not closely related to other moles, despite resembling them and living in a similar fashion. They swim just below the surface of the sand foraging for insects, and they will eat any legless lizard that comes their way. Grant's golden mole (*Eremitalpa granti*) swims up to three miles (5 km) a night in search of food.

Desert hedgehogs (*Paraechinus aethiopicus*) of the Sahara and both Brandt's hedgehog (*P. hypomelas*) and the long-eared hedgehog (*Hemiechinus auritus*) of the Central Asian deserts feed mainly on invertebrate animals such as insects, but they will sometimes eat an animal the size of a mouse. These hedgehogs have large ears that work like radiators to keep their owners cool. Blood flowing through them comes very close to the surface and loses heat to the air before returning to the heart. Big ears are a common adaptation to life in the hot desert. Jackrabbits, which are really hares (*Lepus* species) rather than rabbits, also have large ears, and so does the caracal or caracal lynx (*Felis caracal*), a cat up to 2.5 feet (75 cm) not counting the long tail, which hunts it. The biggest ears of all, however, belong to the fennec fox (*Vulpes zerda*) of North Africa, Sinai, and Arabia. It is the smallest of all the foxes. A full-grown adult weighs only 2–3.3 pounds (0.8–1.5 kg). Fennec foxes spend the day in burrows in the sand, emerging at night to hunt for mice, birds, lizards, and insects.

Ears are meant for hearing, of course, and desert animals with big ears have acute hearing. Many predators hunt by night, locating their prey by the slightest sound. Prey species rely on their hearing to detect the approach of a hunter.

How heat kills and how animals stay cool

If your body temperature rises just a few degrees above 98.6°F (37°C) you will become ill and feverish. If it rises above 109°F (43°C) and remains there for more than a few minutes you will suffer brain damage. A high temperature can kill. People are not unique in this respect. No vertebrate animal can tolerate too high a body temperature. In mammals and birds the temperature inside the body, known as the *core temperature,* is between approximately 97°F and 104°F (36–40°C). Birds have a higher core temperature than mammals.

The reason animals tolerate only a limited range of body temperatures is partly chemical. All the functions of a living body, such as respiration, digestion, and muscular activity, involve chemical reactions that are catalyzed by enzymes. The speed with which these reactions take place increases as the temperature rises, approximately doubling for every 18°F (10°C) rise in temperature, but there is a temperature above which they slow down. This means there is an optimum temperature—about 104°F (40°C)—at which enzymes work best, and the optimum temperature for enzymatic reactions determines the normal body temperature. The core temperature remains below the optimum enzyme temperature in most species because at temperatures only slightly above the optimum, the chemical bonds holding enzymes together begin to break and the enzymes degrade. When that happens, ordinary bodily functions start to fail. Survival in the hot desert depends on being able to stay cool.

Reptiles, such as snakes and lizards (see pages 110–114), keep cool by finding shade or burrowing below ground during the heat of the day. Their body temperature falls at night, and just as there is a temperature above which enzymatic reactions slow down there is also a temperature below which they are very slow. When its body is cold a snake or lizard can barely move its muscles. It must start each day by warming up, which it does by basking in the morning sunshine. Animals that bask in the sunshine to raise their core temperature and seek shade to lower it are called *ectotherms. Ectos* is the Greek word for "outside," and an ectotherm regulates its core temperature by external means.

Mammals and birds are *endotherms—endos* is the Greek word for "within." They regulate their core temperature internally, by such means as sweating, panting, shivering, and constricting or dilating blood vessels just below the skin. In reality it is not quite so simple, because endotherms also seek shade and bask in the sunshine—and people wear different clothes in hot and cold weather. Small desert rodents, for example, retreat to a burrow when it is too hot for them. Lying in its burrow, the rodent ceases to move. Its breathing and heartbeat slow, its temperature falls, and the animal falls into a torpor—a kind of deep sleep. A few hours later, when it is cooler above ground, the rodent rouses itself and resumes the search for food.

Endotherms can be active at night and first thing in the morning, and they can live in cold climates, but they pay a price for this flexibility. Endothermy uses energy, so an endotherm must eat more than an ectotherm of similar size. A person uses 30 times more food energy than an alligator of about the same size.

Sweating and panting cool the body by allowing moisture to evaporate from the surface. Rodents do not sweat, but instead they lick their fur, which has the same effect. Evaporation is an efficient way to lose surplus heat, but only if the lost moisture can be replaced quickly. An animal that keeps cool in this way but is unable to drink water to compensate will soon begin to suffer from dehydration.

The water that is lost is taken from the fluid surrounding cells. Only pure water is lost and, consequently, the salts dissolved in the body fluid become more concentrated. When the solution surrounding cells is stronger than the solution inside cells, water flows out of the cells, through the cell walls, to reduce the difference in concentration. This increases the concentration inside the cells. At first the effect is to accelerate cellular activity, because in a more concentrated solution molecules will collide more frequently with the active sites on enzyme molecules to which they bond. Eventually, however, all the active sites will be occupied; the cell will be unable to manufacture more enzymes; and cellular function will be disrupted. Cells will then start to die. People suffering severe dehydration become very confused and lose bodily coordination.

In most mammals, including humans, dehydration also thickens the blood, because blood plasma crosses the walls of blood vessels to replace fluid lost by sweating or panting. As the blood thickens, the heart has to pump harder to circulate it and eventually the circulation slows. The most important mechanism by which endotherms lose heat involves dilating blood vessels in the skin. Warm blood flowing close to the surface loses heat and returns to the heart at a lower temperature. If the circulation slows, however, this process also slows and the core temperature then rises rapidly and uncontrollably. Death follows swiftly when the animal has lost

The camel: "ship of the desert"

The dromedary, or single-hump camel (*Camelus dromedarius*), has been known to go 17 days without drinking in summer. In winter some camels do not drink at all and after two months without drinking they may still refuse water. When it does drink, however, a camel can swallow 27 gallons (103 l) of water in 10 minutes.

A camel survives for so long without drinking by using water very efficiently. Its kidneys extract much of the water from its urine, allowing the animal to excrete as little as one quart (1.14 l) of water a day.

Many animals, including humans, keep cool by sweating. But a camel does not sweat until its body temperature exceeds 105°F (40.5°C). If it has no access to water, at night its body temperature falls, sometimes as low as 93°F (34°C). Consequently, it takes several hours for its temperature to rise during the day. Its temperature varies much less in winter and in summer if water is available.

A camel's body warms very slowly because its thick coat traps a layer of air next to its skin. The outer part of the coat absorbs heat, preventing it from reaching the skin, and when the camel does sweat its perspiration evaporates into the layer of air by the heat of the skin, not the heat of the Sun.

The camel's hump is made of fat and is a food store. Over the rest of its body the layer of fat beneath the skin is very thin. The hump provides insulation from the Sun, and the thin layer of fat elsewhere allows heat to escape from the body.

When a camel loses body fluid it does so from its saliva and moisture in its lungs, and not from its blood, replacing the lost water from other body fluids and fluids in its tissues. This allows the volume of blood to remain constant, avoiding explosive heat death, but the loss of other fluids makes the animal thinner. It can lose up to 25 percent of its body weight through fluid loss while remaining perfectly healthy—despite being so emaciated its ribs are clearly visible—and continuing to eat even though it cannot drink. When it drinks its body fills out again at once.

A camel's hind legs are attached to its pelvis only at the top of the femur (thigh bone); in most animals they are attached by muscles extending all the way to the knee. This

(continues)

(continued)

mode of attachment gives a camel its long-legged look, but it also allows it to tuck its hind legs completely beneath its body when it lies down, thus reducing the area of body surface that is exposed to the heat. When camels lie down they usually lie close together, so they shade each other, and they all face the Sun to minimize the area of their bodies exposed to direct sunlight. As the Sun moves during the day, the camels change their positions to follow it.

A camel has very broad feet. These spread the weight of its body and help prevent the camel from sinking into soft sand. It has long eyelashes and each row of lashes is double. These help keep sand out of its eyes. Long hairs also protect its ears, and it is able to close its nostrils. These are all adaptations that equip the camel for life in the desert.

"Ships of the desert" (Camelus dromedarius) *at Oasis Dakhia, in the Egyptian desert* (Courtesy of Gerry Ellis/Minden Pictures)

between 10 percent and 20 percent (about 12 percent in humans) of the water in its body. This is known as *explosive heat death.*

Some animals are better adapted to life in a hot climate than others, and the camel is probably the most highly equipped of all (see the sidebar on pages 97–98). It avoids explosive heat death and is renowned for its ability to go for long periods without water. A camel can walk 25 miles (40 km) a day carrying a load of 500 pounds (227 kg) and can carry a rider more than 100 miles (160 km) in a day at a steady speed of about 10 MPH (16 km/h). Not for nothing is the camel called "the ship of the desert."

How freezing kills and how animals keep warm

Walk into a room where the temperature is 84°F (29°C) and it will feel warm. It would not be long, however, before a person who was naked and remained motionless in such a room began to feel cold. It may seem warm to someone who is fully clothed, but 84°F (29°C) is 14.6°F (8°C) lower than the normal core temperature of a human body, 98.6°F (37°C).

No animal likes to feel cold. Cold can kill. In an environment at 84°F (29°C) a motionless, bare human body would not sweat at all. If the air temperature slowly fell from 84°F (29°C), blood vessels in the skin would constrict to reduce heat loss from inside the body, making the person look pale. Goose bumps would appear, caused by the contraction of skin muscles. If humans had more body hair, this contraction would make it rise to trap a layer of air next to the skin as thermal insulation. Soon after this the person would begin to shiver uncontrollably.

When the air temperature fell below the *low critical temperature* of about 79°F (26°C) these mechanisms would no longer be sufficient to maintain the core temperature. Cell respiration would then accelerate to drive the body's metabolism faster, "burning" carbon to release energy and consuming more oxygen to fuel the oxidation reaction. Respiration would continue to accelerate as the temperature fell lower, but a point would be reached beyond which the chemical reactions involved in respiration began to fail. The person would then become confused, feel dizzy, and suffer from cramps. If the person's core temperature fell below the *low lethal temperature* of about 90°F (32°C) he or she would die.

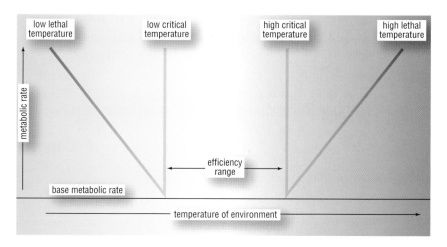

Temperature and metabolic rate. There is a temperature range within which a particular animal functions most efficiently. Outside this range, beyond the low or high critical temperature, the animal's metabolic rate increases to raise or lower the core body temperature. Eventually this proves impossible, and when its core temperature reaches the low or high lethal temperature, the animal dies.

All animals have a range of temperatures within which their bodies function most efficiently, and they will die if their body temperature exceeds or falls below certain limits of tolerance. The diagram above shows the relationship between temperature and metabolic rate.

Frostbite occurs when tissues cool to below freezing. Blood vessels in the skin constrict to reduce heat loss and the tissue begins to freeze. Ice crystals form in the fluid between cells, increasing the salt concentration in the fluid. This draws water out of surrounding cells, causing cell dehydration and eventual death. It can also cause the breakdown of proteins.

Low critical temperatures vary from one species to another, reflecting the climate to which each is adapted. The low critical temperature for rodents living in hot deserts, such as the Sahara, is about 88°F (31°C). For the arctic fox (*Alopex lagopus*) it is –40°F (–40°C). This does not mean, however, that the arctic fox can tolerate temperatures much lower than –40°F (– 40°C). At this temperature the amount of energy the fox needs to generate by respiration is close to the maximum possible. Even if there were a limitless supply of food, the fox simply could not digest it fast enough to generate the necessary warmth. Therefore the gap between the low critical and low lethal temperatures is narrow.

The fox, like all the big animals of cold climates, relies on insulation to keep out the cold, just as Inuit people, fully at home in subzero temperatures, wear thick, windproof clothes. Marine mammals, such as seals, dolphins, and whales, have a thick layer of fat, called *blubber,* just below the skin that doubles as insulation and a store of energy-rich food. Land animals, such as the fox and polar bear (*Ursus maritimus*), have thick coats. Small animals, such as rodents, are not big enough to have really thick coats, and a small animal has a much greater surface area in proportion to its volume than a bigger animal has. Heat is lost through the body surface, so the greater the surface area the more heat an animal loses. Small animals lose body heat readily, and the only way they can survive the winter cold is to hibernate (see "What happens during estivation and hibernation" on pages 102–105).

Animals living in cold climates often have small ears. These reduce heat loss in the same way that the big ears of animals in hot climates maximize heat loss to help them keep cool (see "Typical animals of hot deserts" on page 93–94).

Arctic insulation is extremely effective. The fact that the low critical temperature for the arctic fox is so low shows that it is not until the temperature falls to –40°F (–40°C) that the fox begins to feel cold. Its body fat and thick fur keep it warm.

That is not quite the whole story, however. The fox's nose is naked, and the fur is much thinner on the lower part of its legs and its paws than elsewhere on its body. Practically speaking, it must not mind its feet being cold. If its feet were at its core temperature they would melt the snow and ice the fox stood on, which might be dangerous. But if its feet and nose are almost at freezing temperature, how does the fox avoid transporting cold blood from them into its body and reducing its core temperature? The bodies of arctic birds raise this question even more dramatically: There are no feathers at all covering their lower legs and feet.

The solution lies in *countercurrent exchange.* Close to where a bodily extremity, such as a leg, joins the main part of the body, arteries and veins run side by side and very close together, forming a network of small blood vessels called the *rete mirabile* or "wonderful net." This configuration permits heat exchange. Warm blood from the heart flowing through the arteries toward the extremity warms the cold blood flowing in the opposite direction through the veins. The blood approaching the heart is made warmer than it would otherwise be, greatly reducing the amount of energy the animal must expend in maintaining its core temperature. At the same time, blood flowing toward the extremity is chilled, so the extremity remains cool. When the air temperature is –22°F (–30°C), an arctic fox's paws are at about 32°F (0°C), its ankles at 57°F (14°C), and its nose at 41°F (5°C). Its shoulder muscles are at 99°F (37°C), however, and its chest muscles are at 95°F (35°C). The wonderful net allows animals to live comfortably in temperatures that are far below freezing.

What happens during estivation and hibernation

When the heat becomes unendurable, most desert animals seek shade. Some find shelter beneath rocks while others retreat into their burrows and there they wait until the cool of the evening. While waiting, these animals fall into a deep sleep. This way of escaping the heat for part of the day is called *diurnation.*

The Mojave ground squirrel (*Spermophilus mohavensis*) has a burrow, but when it retreats to its burrow it stays there—by night as well as by day. It lives only on the western side of the Mojave Desert in California and is rare because of disturbance to its habitat, but even allowing for its rarity not many people have ever seen it. That is because not only does it sleep through the heat of the desert summer, it also sleeps through the winter. It emerges above ground in February and disappears in August. If food is scarce it may go back to sleep as early as April.

There is a great deal this small squirrel must do while it is active. It must mate, and males travel up to one mile (1.6 km) a day in search of mates. That is a long way for an animal measuring about nine inches (23 cm) in length, including its tail. The young are born in March, weaned in May, and soon after that are independent. While all this is happening, the squirrel must eat voraciously, almost doubling its weight before the searing heat shrivels all the food plants and it is time to sleep once more.

Its long sleep is no ordinary sleep. As it dozes off, the squirrel's body temperature falls until it is only a degree or two higher than the air temperature in its cool burrow. All its bodily functions slow down. Its breathing and heartbeat slow and occasionally its breathing stops altogether for a time. In this condition, with its body's needs reduced to an absolute minimum, the fat its body stored in spring and early summer provides enough energy—with a wide safety margin—to sustain the squirrel until the first leaf buds open the following spring. Then, when its body senses the lengthening days and rising temperature, its breathing accelerates. After 15–20 minutes of fast breathing its muscles have enough oxygen to become active. The squirrel starts shivering. Shivering generates body heat and about half an hour later the squirrel is awake, alert, and active.

Animals that become dormant during hot weather are said to be *estivating,* from the Latin *aestus,* meaning "heat," and the Mojave ground squirrel is not the only desert species to avoid the heat in this way. Many ground squirrels and all desert frogs and toads do so. Frogs and toads absorb oxygen and release carbon dioxide through their skins. This is called *cutaneous respiration* and it means that frogs and toads have highly permeable skins that lose water readily. Estivation allows them to survive for long periods below ground where the air is moist and there is no risk of desiccation. Couch's spadefoot toad (*Scaphiopus couchii*) of the North American deserts remains dormant for 10 or 11 months of the year and arouses itself only when it hears the sound of falling rain.

An animal that survives cold weather by becoming dormant is said to be *hibernating—hibernus* is the Latin word for "wintry." Many mammals hibernate, and so does the common poorwill (*Phalaenoptilus nuttallii*) of southern California. It is the only bird that is known to hibernate for any length of time. The Hopi Indians call it *hölchoko*—"sleeping one." While it is hibernating the poorwill's temperature, normally about 104°F (40°C), falls to about 65°F (18°C).

Only small animals are able to hibernate, and these include many species found in continental deserts where winters are cold. The arctic ground squirrel (*Spermophilus undulatus*) hibernates. A close relative of the Mojave ground squirrel, this animal occurs in the North American and Eurasian arctic and is known in Russia as the long-tailed souslik.

Marmots (*Marmota* species), which are also squirrels, are the largest animals to hibernate. The bigger an animal is, the longer it takes for it to enter hibernation and awaken from it and the greater the amount of energy that is needed for arousal. This is because the body of a small animal has a large surface area in relation to its volume and therefore loses heat rapidly, and its small size also allows it to warm up rapidly. A marmot weighs an average 11 pounds (5 kg) and this is probably the upper limit for the size of a true hibernator.

Although many people believe that bears hibernate, in fact their long winter rest is not true hibernation. A bear's normal body temperature averages 100°F (38°C). During its winter rest its temperature falls only to about 93°F (34°C) and is rarely lower than 88°F (31°C). In contrast, the arctic ground squirrel's normal body temperature of 100°F (38°C) falls to within a degree or two of freezing during its hibernation. If a bear weighing 440 pounds (200 kg) were to hibernate, allowing its temperature to fall to 40°F (4°C), raising its temperature to 100°F (38°C) would take several days and require as much energy as the bear uses in approximately 3.5 days of ordinary activity. It would be impossible for the bear to eat sufficient food prior to hibernation for it to lay down a layer of body fat thick enough to sustain it through the winter and then allow it to revive.

There is an additional risk. If its body temperature falls below a certain danger threshold a hibernating animal needs to arouse itself. It wakes, warms itself by shivering and moving about, and then eats food from its winter store to replace the energy this activity used. Small animals wake several times during the winter. Under these circumstances it is unlikely that an animal the size of a bear could arouse itself quickly enough to prevent its temperature falling so low as to cause serious harm, and it could not possibly replace the energy this used by snacking from its winter hoard. Only small animals are able to hibernate.

Scorpions, spiders, and insects

Most people are scared of scorpions. The raised tail—in fact the *postabdomen* and not really a tail—with its fearsome sting has earned the scorpion a bad reputation that is partly warranted. All scorpions sting, but they do so in order to subdue their insect prey before eating it. Most of the 700 or so species deliver a sting that is extremely painful to people but one from which they make a full recovery.

There are exceptions, however. *Androctonus* species are very dangerous, and the fat-tailed scorpion (*A. australis*) of Old World deserts is possibly the worst of all. Up to four inches (10 cm) long and with extremely potent venom, it can deliver a lethal sting. It hides under rocks and crevices but also in cracks in the stone and brick walls of houses.

American scorpions are less dangerous. The striped scorpion (*Centruroides vittatus*) is the one people encounter most often. It is about 2.5 inches (6.4 cm) long and hides in cool, damp places. Its sting is very painful but is fatal only to persons allergic to the venom. The related and slightly larger— three inches (7.5 cm) long—bark scorpion (*C. sculpturatus*) is the only American species with a sting that can kill. Children, elderly persons, and those with respiratory illnesses are especially vulnerable. Unlike most scorpions, the bark scorpion never digs burrows, but lives entirely in trees. The desert hairy scorpion (*Hadrurus arizonensis*) is the biggest American species. It is 3.75 inches (9.5 cm) long and lives among rocks.

Despite their reputation, scorpions will sting only if they are handled or touched. Then they grip their molester with their claws, just as they would grip prey, and sting repeatedly. If a scorpion grabs you, tear it away immediately.

All scorpions are nocturnal. That is why they are seldom seen but pose a risk to people out after dark in bare feet or wearing sandals. Their eyesight is poor, but they are able to detect vibrations in the air or ground and are quick to attack once they have located prey.

Wind scorpions are more visible, because they are active by day. They have many names, including sun spiders, false spiders, camel spiders, and jerrymanders. Solitary hunters, they look like balls of thistledown as they race across the desert sand in pursuit of prey. Some have bodies no more than 0.6–0.8 inch (1.5–2.0 cm) long, and the largest are about 2.75 inches (7 cm) long or six inches (15 cm) when the legs are included. They hunt insects, scorpions, spiders, small reptiles, mammals up to the size of a mouse, and each other—they are highly antisocial. They will also eat carrion.

Despite their names, they are neither scorpions nor spiders, although they do possess eight legs and large *chelicerae,* which serve as claws, as well as long *pedipalps,* which look like legs but are appendages used for examining and manipulating objects. They are solifugids (order Solifugae), organisms related to spiders and scorpions but distinct from them. There are about 900 species of solifugids found mainly in hot deserts throughout the world. Some species are nocturnal. These are usually larger and less brightly colored than the solifugids that are active by day.

Wolf spiders really are spiders. They hunt by running their prey down and overpowering it. They have keen eyesight—with two large eyes and four smaller ones below them—and can detect the slightest movement that might betray a potential victim. There are also jumping spiders in the desert. They stalk their prey and jump on it as soon as they are within range.

Tiger beetles (family Cicindelidae) are about one inch (2.5 cm) long and often brightly colored. Active by day, they chase their prey, but their larvae use a different hunting strategy. The larva digs a vertical burrow where it waits. When an insect comes within its reach it grabs its victim and holds tight until the prey is subdued.

Ant lions (family Myrmeleontidae) and worm lions (family Rhagionidae) dig pitfall traps. An ant lion digs a conical pit in the sand and waits at the bottom, buried except for its *mandibles*—mouthparts it uses to seize food. When an insect, commonly an ant, reaches the edge of the pit the ant lion throws sand, triggering a landslide that carries the victim into the pit and to the waiting mandibles.

Insects are plentiful in all deserts. Each shower of rain brings forth butterflies and moths. Every plant harbors vegetarian flies and beetles. The abundance of edible insects means there is ample food for the hunters.

Darkling beetles (family Tenebrionidae) have few enemies, however, despite being active by day. They respond to threats either by releasing a highly offensive smell or by pretending to be dead. Most predators will leave a dead beetle alone.

Locusts

There are venomous snakes that lie hidden beneath the sand, poised to strike. There are deadly scorpions lurking in dark crevices, solifugids that bite, and insects that sting. Yet none of these can inspire the dread conveyed by the name of a particular kind of big grasshopper: locust.

Locusts are grasshoppers. Most of the time they avoid each other and are harmless, but when food is abundant they congregate into vast swarms that devour farm crops. (Courtesy of Rafal Zdeb)

Locusts are strict vegetarians. They do not bite or sting. They transmit no diseases to people. Yet they regularly kill thousands and have been doing so throughout history (see the sidebar on page 109). An adult locust is about two inches (5 cm) long with a wingspan of about four inches (10 cm), and it weighs approximately 0.07 ounces (2 g). The weight is important, because that is roughly the amount of food it eats every day. The amount is small, but one ton of locusts eat as much food each day as 2,500 people, and a locust swarm contains many tons of insects. In 2004 locust swarms swept across large areas of Queensland and parts of New South Wales, Australia, and also devastated food crops in Mauritania and Western Sahara in Africa. A locust invasion of Madagascar began in 1939 and it was 1957 before the swarms disappeared.

Locusts are among at least 10,000 species of short-horned grasshoppers (family Acrididae). All of them feed on leaves, but only about 12 species periodically form swarms. Swarming involves a dramatic change in the insects' behavior and appearance, and it is this ability to change that distinguishes locusts from other grasshoppers. The change is so great that it was not until 1921 that the Russian entomologist Boris P. Uvarov (1889–1970) recognized that what until then had been thought of as two distinct species were in fact two forms of the same species.

Species of locusts occur in various parts of Africa, the Near East, Asia, and Australia. All of them are highly destructive. The South American locust (*Schistocerca paranensis*) is the most serious locust pest of Central and South America, and between 1874 and 1877 swarms of Rocky Mountain locusts (*Melanoplus spretus*) covered 125,000 square miles (324,000 km^2) of the United States to a height of 5,000 feet (1,525 m). During that outbreak, some people tried to protect their crops by covering them with blankets. The locusts ate the blankets and then devoured the crops. The Rocky Mountain locust became extinct soon afterward and the last known specimen was found in 1902 in Canada. Scientists believe that farmers inadvertently destroyed them by plowing the areas where the locusts laid their eggs.

The most destructive species of all, and the likely culprit in most of the great plagues of history, is known simply as the desert locust (*Schistocerca gregaria*). It lives in the deserts and dry grasslands of Africa and Asia, wherever the average annual rainfall is less than eight inches (200 mm). Like all locusts, desert locusts live for most of the time as harmless

Locust plagues

In 1986 swarms of locusts began to move across northern Africa. By 1989, when the swarms finally disappeared, the locusts had devastated crops in approximately 30 countries. In 2004 the rains that ended a prolonged drought triggered a locust plague that swept across eastern Australia.

Along the southern edge of the Sahara, in the region known as the Sahel, 100,000 people died between 1931 and 1932, during an outbreak lasting from 1926 to 1934, because locusts had devoured all the food. There were also severe outbreaks between 1940 and 1948, 1949 and 1963, and 1967 and 1969.

Locust outbreaks are often called plagues and they have occurred in Africa throughout history. The eighth of the plagues of Egypt, described in the Old Testament (Exodus 10:14–15), was a swarm of locusts that, according to the biblical account, darkened the sky for three days. Historians believe this was a real event that took place in about 1470 B.C.E. in the Nile Delta.

More recently, a plague afflicted North Africa, especially Algeria, in 1724 and 1725. Louis de Chénier (1722–96), the French consul in Morocco from 1767 until 1782, was in Rabat in 1779. He described seeing many peasants who had died from starvation, parents selling their children, and women and children running behind camels in the hope of finding grains of undigested barley in their droppings. Morocco suffered again from 1813 to 1815.

Many Greek and Roman authors told of the devastation locust swarms caused in classical times when they moved north from Africa, across the Mediterranean and into southern Europe. Carried by the wind, swarms have crossed the Mediterranean several times. In 1954 a swarm from North Africa was swept all the way to Britain, and in October 1988 a swarm crossed the Atlantic, landing on several Caribbean islands and the South American coast.

During a plague the swarms may cover 11 million square miles (28.5 million km²)—more than one-fifth of the land area of the Earth. Early in 1954, 50 locust swarms invaded Kenya. One of those swarms covered 77 square miles (200 km²) and consisted of an estimated 10 billion locusts.

grasshoppers. They can fly but seldom do so, and although they are often present in large numbers where food is abundant, the gray, brown, or green insects avoid one another. They mate and lay eggs in moist soil below the surface. After about two weeks the eggs hatch and the young, known as *hoppers,* emerge to feed. Hoppers cannot fly, but within two to four months they mature into adults that can fly.

Locusts continue to live in this way until heavy rain is followed by a greatly increased amount of vegetation. Females then lay more eggs to take advantage of the increased abundance of food and the locust population increases. That is when a change comes over the juvenile insects. Their color changes to pink, sometimes with black, yellow, or orange stripes, and they no longer avoid one another. Instead, when two individuals meet they tend to remain together and when pairs meet they also stay together, so that the locusts form bands that steadily increase in size. Insects can grow only by discarding their external skeleton, and after they have molted for the fifth time the locusts are mature and yellow in color. They roost in trees and shrubs at night and feed all day. Before long their food supply is exhausted and that is when they start to migrate, flying by day as an immense swarm that is carried along by the wind and landing wherever there is food. A locust swarm may contain 40 million–80 million insects.

Snakes and lizards

Lizards thrive in deserts. They bask in the morning sunshine until they are warm enough to start looking for food, and when the heat becomes too intense they find shade or bury themselves. Desert lizards eat small animals, the size of the prey depending on the size of the lizard. Most eat insects, but some hunt small mammals and a few eat the eggs of ground-nesting birds. The chuckwalla (*Sauromalus obesus*), found in the southwestern United States, is unusual in being a vegetarian. It is about 16 inches (40 cm) long and has very loose skin that hangs in folds.

Most lizards are fairly small, but the fiercely carnivorous monitor lizards (family Varanidae) are the exception. Gould's monitor, also called the sand monitor (*Varanus gouldi*), lives

Anchieta's desert lizard (Meroles anchietae) *on the side of a sand dune in the Namib-Naukluft National Park, Namibia* (Courtesy of Gerry Ellis/Minden Pictures)

in the Australian deserts. It is about five feet (1.5 m) long and when threatened it rises onto its hind legs, hissing loudly. It is a highly agile lizard that can outrun a man over a short distance. Like all monitors it hunts by day.

The only venomous lizards in the world are two species related to the monitors. The gila monster (*Heloderma suspectum*) inhabits the southwestern United States, and the Mexican beaded lizard (*H. horridum*) is found in western Mexico. Both lizards are about two feet (60 cm) long and they use their venom to subdue prey. Their bite is painful to humans, but rarely fatal.

Many desert predators hunt lizards, and most lizards are small and unarmed. Armor and bluff are their best means of defense. The Texas horned lizard (*Phrynosoma cornutum*) has big horns behind its head, a collar of spikes around its neck, and spines along its back and sides. It looks fierce but is only seven inches (18 cm) long and feeds on ants.

The thorny devil (*Moloch horridus*) of the Australian deserts is about six inches (15 cm) long, moves slowly, and eats ants

Sidewinders

Snakes cross a surface by muscular movements that use their scales to push against small irregularities. This is a highly successful method, but it works only on solid surfaces. A snake travels with difficulty in loose sand, because when it pushes with its scales the sand slides away and the snake barely moves.

A snake finding itself on loose sand moves in a different fashion, by *sidewinding.* Most snakes will use this form of locomotion when they need to do so, but some have specialized in it—although they do not use it to cross solid surfaces.

The most famous sidewinding snake is the sidewinder (*Crotalus cerastes*), a small rattlesnake found in the American deserts. The horned viper (*Cerastes cerastes*), carpet viper (*Echis carinatus*), and desert sidewinding viper (*Bitis peringueyi*) are sidewinders found in African, Middle Eastern, and Indian deserts, respectively. Its potent venom, excellent camouflage, and bad temper make the carpet viper, also known as the saw-scaled viper, possibly the most dangerous snake in the world.

While sidewinding, only two or three sections of the snake's body press against the ground at any time and these press downward, so the sand does not slide away. First, the snake presses with the middle part of its body to raise the forward part upward and throw it to the side. It then presses with the upper and lower parts of its body to throw a loop of its body to behind the head and bring the rest of its body behind it. Repeating this sequence (illustrated in the drawing on page 113) carries the snake across the sand at an angle of about 45° to the line of its body and leaves behind a distinctive set of J-shaped depressions in the surface.

and termites. Its appearance is terrifying. Its entire body is covered in modified scales that look like spines, with a really big spike over each eye. The princely mastigure (*Uromastyx princeps*) has a thick tail covered in spines that it lashes furiously at any animal threatening it. This lizard is about nine inches (23 cm) long and lives in the Eastern Sahara. If its spines fail to deter an attacker the armadillo lizard (*Cordylus cataphractus*) of Southern Africa rolls into a tight ball with its tail in its mouth.

Most skinks (family Scincidae) have very short legs and some are legless, yet these lizards move through desert sand

Sidewinding works only for small snakes. The desert sidewinding viper is only about 10 inches (25 cm) long and the sidewinder and carpet viper are both up to 30 inches (75 cm) long.

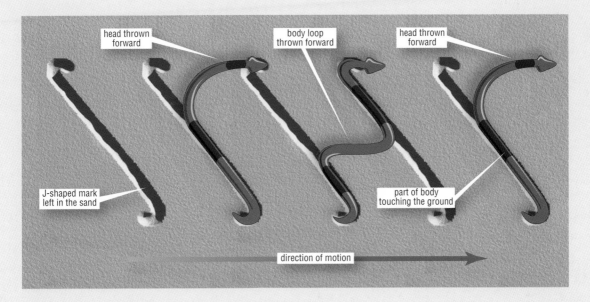

Sidewinding. The dark areas show the parts of its body that the snake presses against the ground for support as it throws its head forward, followed by a loop of its body and then the remainder of its body. The snake leaves a characteristic pattern of marks in the sand.

with such a smooth swimming motion that one species, *Scincus philbyi* of the Arabian Desert, is known as the sandfish. It has strong legs and can walk over the sand surface, but it hunts for millipedes and other small invertebrates just below the surface, swimming through the sand like a fish.

Snakes also thrive in the desert. Most shelter beneath overhanging rocks or in crevices, and some live in burrows. There are also snakes that lie in wait for prey, buried in the sand with just their eyes and nostrils showing. McMahon's viper (*Eristocophis macmahonii*) of the Sahara and Middle East is one of these. A small, highly venomous snake, about 30 inches (75 cm) long, it sweeps its body from side to side, sinking vertically until only its shape in the sand betrays its presence. There it waits for any passing lizard or small mammal that comes within its striking distance. It is easy to step on a snake that hides in this way, and this makes them dangerous.

Although there are snakes in sandy desert, they are more likely to be encountered in rocky areas, where there is plenty of shelter and the ground surface is solid. Snakes find it difficult to move across loose sand and usually do so by throwing their bodies in a series of loops, a method called *sidewinding*. Certain species have specialized in this manner of locomotion, making them fully at home in sandy desert (see the sidebar on pages 112–113).

Cobras are among the most feared of all venomous snakes. The Egyptian cobra (*Naja naje*) is up to eight feet (2.5 m) long and inhabits deserts throughout Africa. The most dangerous American snake, the western diamondback rattlesnake (*Crotalus atrox*), also lives in deserts. It can grow to 6.5 feet (2 m). The Mojave (*C. scutulatus*), tiger (*C. tigris*), and sidewinder (*C. cerastes*) rattlesnakes also inhabit American deserts. In addition, there are several nonvenomous species, some of which eat other snakes. As well as hunting small mammals and lizards, the Californian kingsnake (*Lampropeltis getulus californiae*), found in the deserts of the western United States, eats rattlesnakes, copperheads (*Agkistrodon contortix*), and coral snakes (about 40 *Micrurus* and *Micruroides* species) and is immune to their venom. This snake is three to six feet (0.9–1.8 m) long.

Rattlesnakes are pit vipers. Heat-sensitive organs located in pits between their eyes and nostrils allow them to detect a prey animal by the warmth of its body compared with the background. This ability makes them able to hunt in total darkness. Coral snakes, kingsnakes, and the harmless milk snake (*Lampropeltis triangulum*) are also nocturnal.

Desert mammals

Where water is scarce, animals adopt extreme measures to conserve it. These measures are so efficient that certain desert mammals never drink liquid water.

Gerbils are rodents, most of which live in the deserts of Africa and Asia. There are more than 80 species, some resembling mice and some rats, but all of them are very economical in their use of water. They do not sweat, and the species that live in deserts spend the daytime in their burrows, often with the entrance sealed, emerging at night to forage mainly for seeds. These are often moistened by dew and so they contain some water. The gerbils carry them to their cool burrows, where the air is moister than the air above ground, further increasing the moisture content of the food. When the gerbil digests its meal, its kidneys extract almost all of the water from it, so the gerbil excretes only a few drops of urine each day. The efficiency of an animal's kidneys is measured by the concentration of its urine. If human kidneys have an efficiency (or urine concentration) of one, and those of a dromedary (see the sidebar "The camel: ship of the desert" on pages 97–98) have an efficiency of 1.96, those of a gerbil measure 3.85.

The Australian hopping mouse (*Notomys alexis*) has kidneys that are possibly the most efficient of all, measuring 6.55 on the scale, but most small desert animals survive without ever taking a drink. Meriam's kangaroo rat (*Dipodomys merriami*) has kidneys (efficiency 3.25) that can extract the salts from seawater. It lives in Arizona and Death Valley, California, where it feeds on seeds that have absorbed water while being stored below ground, but it does not collect the seeds itself. Meriam's kangaroo rat steals food from the burrows of the bannertail kangaroo rat (*D. spectabilis*).

The kowari (*Dasyuroides byrnei*) is about half the size of a kangaroo rat, but otherwise very similar. It has big ears, a long, bushy tail, and hind legs that are longer than its front legs. It is not a rodent, however, but a marsupial that inhabits the Australian deserts. Other marsupial mammals of the Australian deserts also resemble rodents, but marsupials and rodents are not closely related. The similarities are superficial between these marsupials and *eutherian* mammals—the group that includes all the native mammals of Africa and Eurasia and most of those of North and South America. They arise through convergent evolution (see the sidebar on page 116).

It is not only small rodents that have no need to drink. The dorcas gazelle (*Gazella dorcas*), native to the deserts from the Sahara to India, also obtains all the moisture its body needs from the food it eats, although it will drink if water is available, and it loses weight on a completely dry diet. The addax

Parallel evolution and convergent evolution

When two species of animals resemble each other and behave in similar ways it is natural to assume they are related. This is often the case. A domestic cat shares many features with a sand cat, for example, and a German shepherd dog bears a close resemblance to a wolf. Domestic cats and sand cats are closely related, and so are domestic dogs and wolves. Saying that two species are related implies that they are descended from a common ancestor.

Sometimes, though, appearances can be deceptive. Kangaroo rats (*Dipodomys* species) of the North American deserts and jerboas (*Jaculus* species) of the Sahara and Arabian Desert look similar and live in the same way, yet they are not closely related. They share a common ancestor, but the evolutionary lines leading to the modern animals diverged 57 million years ago. That ancestor probably had long hind legs and hopped, and both kangaroo rats and jerboas have retained these features because they live under similar conditions. Consequently, they are as alike as their remote ancestors were. This is an example of *parallel evolution:* If two species with a common ancestor separate, but both continue to live in the same way, they may continue to resemble one another.

The kowari (*Dasyuroides byrnei*) might pass for a kangaroo rat, except for being about half the size, and the pygmy planigale (*Planigale maculata*) looks very much like a house mouse (*Mus musculus*), but smaller. They look very similar, but kowaris and pygmy planigales inhabit the Australian deserts and are marsupials, the group of mammals that includes koalas and kangaroos. Mice and rats are *eutherian* mammals, along with cats, dogs, cattle, and most other mammals. Marsupials and eutherians diverged about 100 million years ago, so these apparently similar animals are very distant relations. They resemble one another because they live in almost identical environments, but the similarities are superficial. Desert rodents eat a mainly vegetarian diet, but marsupial "mice" are carnivores.

This is an example of *convergent evolution:* Over many generations, two or more unrelated species that live under similar environmental conditions may evolve to resemble one another.

(*Addax nasomaculatus*) and Arabian oryx (*Oryx leucoryx*) are antelopes that live far from water, the addax in the Sahara and the Arabian oryx in the Arabian Desert. Neither animal needs to drink.

Antelopes are vegetarians. So are rodents, but gerbils will also eat insects and any small animals they can catch, and three species of grasshopper mice (*Onychomys*) are meat eaters, feeding on grasshoppers and other insects, as well as scorpions, lizards, and small mammals. Grasshopper mice live in the deserts and semiarid regions of North and Central America.

Pumas (*Felis concolor*), also called cougars and mountain lions, sometimes venture into North American deserts to hunt. The puma is the only cat to be found in American deserts, but several cat species inhabit the African and Asian deserts. These include lions (*Panthera leo*) in the Sahara and Kalahari Desert and cheetahs (*Acinonyx jubatus*) in deserts from the Sahara eastward to northern India.

There are also several small cats. The sand cat (*Felis margarita*) inhabits deserts from the Sahara to Central Asia, and

Gemsbok (Oryx gazella), a species of antelope found throughout the drier regions of Africa. These animals are resting in a circle, constantly alert for predators approaching from any direction. (Courtesy of Jasen Leathers)

A caracal (Felis caracal) *at rest in the Harnas Wildlife Reserve, Namibia* (Courtesy of Michael and Patricia Fogden/ Minden Pictures)

Pallas's cat (*F. manul*) is found from Iran to western China. Both cats are slightly bigger than a domestic cat and both hunt only at night. The caracal, or caracal lynx (*F. caracal*), usually hunts in twilight, but it hunts by day in winter and by night in very hot weather. Larger and heavier than either the sand cat or Pallas's cat, the caracal resembles a small, long-legged puma with large, pointed ears ending in prominent tufts of dark hair. It pursues prey up to the size of a young deer in dry, open country and deserts from Africa to India.

Desert birds

Birds have several advantages over mammals when it comes to living in the desert. In the first place, their core body temperature is higher, at about 104°F (40°C), so they are troubled by the heat for fewer hours each day. Most birds fly, which takes them into air that is much cooler than the air close to the ground, and because they are moving through the air they experience wind chill. Finally, birds can fly to distant sources of water that are far beyond the reach of mammals.

Mourning doves (*Zenaida macroura*) fly 40 miles (64 km) or more across the North American desert every morning to water holes where they congregate in large numbers. When the birds have drunk their fill they separate to forage for food or return to their young, waiting secure in nests that are constructed in cactus plants and protected by spines. The young cannot make the journey to the water hole and so their parents must carry liquid to them. Mourning doves are pigeons and all pigeons, male as well as female, regurgitate a liquid called *pigeon milk* to feed their young. Pigeon milk is nutritious, but 65–81 percent of it by weight is water, and the young continue to receive it almost until they have all of their adult feathers, even though by this time their parents are bringing them solid food.

Sandgrouse (family Pteroclididae), which are small, ground-nesting birds of the African and Asian deserts, carry water differently. Each morning the adult female sets off for the nearest water hole, up to 20 miles (32 km) distant. When she returns to the nest the male departs. On arriving at the water hole he rubs his belly on the dry, sandy ground to remove the natural oils in his feathers, then walks into the water to drink. The feathers on his belly are modified to act like a sponge, soaking water while he is drinking. When he has drunk his fill the sandgrouse flies back to the nest. Some of the water evaporates from his "sponge" during the flight, but enough remains to satisfy the needs of the young. When they are satisfied he rubs his belly on the ground to dry the feathers, and then all the family starts looking for food.

Pigeons and sandgrouse eat very dry food and so they need water. Meat-eating birds obtain water from their food. Not all of them are airborne hunters. The greater and lesser roadrunners (*Geococcyx californicus* and *G. velox* respectively) of North America are long-tailed members of the cuckoo family (Cuculidae) that hunt by running at up to 15 MPH (24 km/h) and stopping abruptly when they spot prey. They will eat insects, scorpions, lizards, small mammals, birds, and snakes, even rattlesnakes.

Roadrunners have another curious talent, and in this respect they resemble reptiles. Desert nights can be very cold and daytime temperatures are high. Most birds cope with the low temperatures by increasing the rate at which they use energy to keep warm, but the roadrunner is different. It allows its core temperature to fall. By dawn the roadrunner is too cold to be very active, so it begins the day by basking in the sunshine, helped by a patch of dark feathers on its back that it can raise. The dark color of the feathers absorbs warmth, and the raised feathers trap a layer of air.

The secretary bird (*Sagittarius serpentarius*) is a ground-dwelling hunter of the semiarid grasslands and desert edge of Africa south of the Sahara, named for the long feathers at the back of its head, which resemble the quill pens that office clerks once carried behind their ears. It is a bird of prey that flies well and nests in acacia trees, but it hunts on the ground for small animals, including snakes, which it kills by stamping on them.

The greater roadrunner (Geococcyx californianus) *feeds on invertebrate animals and lizards. This bird is in the Bosque del Apache National Wildlife Refuge, New Mexico.* (Courtesy of Gerry Ellis/Minden Pictures)

Other birds of prey hunt from the air. These include three desert falcons—the lanner falcon (*Falco biarmicus*) of Africa and Arabia, the saker falcon (*F. cherrug*) of Central Asia, and the laggar falcon (*F. jugger*) of India. Falcons are no more than 15–20 inches (40–50 cm) long, but they are powerful and highly maneuverable hunters of small birds.

Vultures are the birds many people associate with deserts, but most vultures—including all the American species—avoid deserts. Lappet-faced vultures (*Torgos tracheliotus*) forage over the Sahara, alone or as groups of up to four birds. The lappet-faced is the biggest of the vultures—up to 45 inches (1.1 m) from the tip of its bill to the tip of its tail, with a wingspan of nine feet (2.7 m), and weighing 15 pounds (6.8 kg). The powerful bill of a lappet-faced vulture can rip through the hide of a rhinoceros. Not surprisingly, other vultures leave them in peace while they are feeding. The griffon (*Gyps fulvus*), white-headed (*Trigonoceps occipitalis*), and hooded (*Necrosyrtes monachus*) vultures have ranges that overlap that of the lappet-faced vulture. All of these vultures feed only on carrion, but the Egyptian vulture (*Neophron percnopterus*) also eats vegetable matter, garbage, and small live animals. It is found from Egypt eastward as far as India.

Animals of the Arctic

Lemmings are small rodents, about four inches (10 cm) long with a short tail and longer hair than voles and mice. There are nine species, all but one of which live in the arctic tundra. In winter the arctic or collared lemming (*Dicrostonyx torquatus*) grows a white coat. Other lemmings are uniformly brown through the year, except for the Norway lemming (*Lemmus lemmus*). It has a dark back and pale underside.

Despite the cold, lemmings do not hibernate. Instead they burrow beneath the snow where they are sheltered from the wind, moving freely through the grasses and sedges at the bottom of trenches that separate blocks of ice. Throughout the winter they feed on the plants around them, emerging in spring when the snow starts to melt, flooding their trenches.

All lemming populations fluctuate over a cycle of three or four years. When their numbers reach a maximum the lemmings produce fewer young and many of the young die from stress and hunger, reducing the population to such a low level that it takes three or four years for the population to recover.

It is not true that from time to time Norway lemmings commit mass suicide by leaping over cliffs into the sea, but it is true that they sometimes move in large numbers and may run into the water where many drown. Norway lemmings are quarrelsome animals that usually live alone, but when their numbers increase encounters become unavoidable. Then the older and stronger animals drive out the younger and weaker ones, which move away in all directions until a natural barrier, such as a river or shore, halts their progress. As lemmings continue to arrive, small groups merge into vast crowds of individuals, all of them trying to drive one another away. The resulting stress leads to panic, which sends the lemmings rushing headlong, sometimes into a lake or the sea.

Weasels (*Mustela nivalis*) and stoats (*M. erminea*) hunt lemmings. With their small, slender bodies they are able to follow the rodents through their winter tunnels.

Lemmings are also the principal food for snowy owls (*Nyctea scandiaca*), but these big, white owls must wait until their prey is forced onto the surface. Unlike most owls, snowy owls hunt by day. When the lemming population crashes, the owls move south, sometimes as far as the northern United States.

Ptarmigans (three *Lagopus* species) are the only other birds that remain in the Arctic through the winter. They nest on the ground and feed on berries and other plant material. In fall they shed their brown plumage and grow white feathers that camouflage them against the winter snow.

The arctic fox (*Alopex lagopus*) also grows a white coat in winter; the animal's long, thick fur was once highly prized for making fur coats. These foxes take birds' eggs and ground-nesting birds, but lemmings are their principal food. When the lemming population crashes so does that of the arctic fox.

Tundra wolves (*Canis lupus tundarum*) also hunt in the Arctic. The biggest of all wolves, they will eat eggs, birds, rodents, carrion, and even berries, but they prefer larger prey, especially caribou (*Rangifer tarandus*), known in Europe as reindeer. Caribou undertake long seasonal migrations, always following the same routes that take them northward in spring and south to the shelter of the pine forests in the fall.

Wolves will attack a solitary musk ox (*Ovibos moschatus*), but musk oxen usually live in herds and these are impregnable. When threatened, the musk oxen form a circle, facing outward with their calves inside. They have big, solid horns that are formidable weapons, and the circle turns continually so that the attackers face the horns of the biggest, strongest ox. Any wolf that comes too close will be killed by the horns, and a wolf that penetrates the circle will be trampled to death. Musk oxen feed on grass, leaves, lichens, and other plant material and they will dig through the snow to find it. Their long, thick coats provide such good insulation that snow falling on their backs does not melt.

The polar bear (*Ursus maritimus*) is the biggest and most famous of all the arctic hunters, and the biggest of all land-

A polar bear (Ursus maritimus) *running across the ice at Ellesmere Island, Canada* (Courtesy of Jim Brandenburg/ Minden Pictures)

dwelling carnivores—bigger than a lion or tiger. An adult male is almost 10 feet (3 m) long and weighs 1,400 pounds (635 kg) or more; females are only slightly smaller. A polar bear can run faster than a caribou over a short distance and can kill a musk ox, but polar bears also eat smaller mammals, birds, and some plant material. Seals are their main food, however. Seals are mammals and must surface for air, so the bear waits beside a small area of open water or the breathing hole many seals make in the ice. When the seal appears the bear grabs it and hauls it ashore. Alternatively, a bear will stalk seals that are resting on the ice. It will not attack seals in the water, because although polar bears are strong swimmers, seals can outmaneuver them.

Animals of the Antarctic

No land mammals dwell in Antarctica. The continent is too remote for any to have reached it and too inhospitable to allow any that managed the journey to survive. The only land animals are about 100 species of invertebrates, half of which are parasites of seals or birds—the only permanent residents.

Penguins are the most famous inhabitants and they are superbly adapted to the Antarctic cold. Their small feathers lie in three layers, providing a thick and completely waterproof coat, and most penguins also have a thick layer of insulating fat just below the skin. A few of the 18 species live farther north, but most inhabit Antarctica and the nearby islands and, of course, they are instantly recognizable. They were given the name "penguin" in the 16th century by the first European explorers to encounter them, because they resembled the great auk (*Pinguinus impennis*), a North Atlantic seabird that is now extinct. Penguins range in size from the little blue or fairy penguin (*Eudyptula minor*), 16 inches (41 cm) tall, to the emperor penguin (*Aptenodytes forsteri*), about four feet (1.2 m) tall.

On land, penguins walk with a comical hopping or waddling gait and sometimes they toboggan on their fronts, but in the water they are fast and highly maneuverable. They feed on fish, squid, cuttlefish, and krill.

Krill resemble shrimp, but are only distantly related to them. There are 85 species, but the most abundant in Antarctic water is the whale krill (*Euphausia superba*). It is only about two inches (5 cm) long, but krill occur in such vast numbers that many birds and mammals depend on them, including whales. A blue whale (*Balaenoptera musculus*) eats about four tons (3.6 tonnes) of krill a day. No one knows just how many krill there are, but their population has been estimated as 500 trillion individuals (5 followed by 14 zeros). If the estimate is correct, krill are the most numerous animals on Earth.

There is no large land predator to hunt penguins, but a fearsome hunter awaits them in the ocean. About 10 feet (3 m) long and weighing 770 pounds (300 kg), leopard seals (*Hydrurga leptonyx*) are the largest of all seals. Their bodies are slender, with a long neck, and spotted like a leopard's coat. On land they move slowly and clumsily like all seals, and penguins ignore them, but in the water they are fast, formidable hunters and penguins provide about one-quarter of their diet. Leopard seals also feed on fish, squid, other seals—and krill, of course.

Leopard seals are plentiful, but they are not the most abundant species. Crabeater seals (*Lobodon carcinophagus*) are the most numerous of any seal species, with a population of 15 million–40 million. They are smaller than leopard seals and faster on land, but both leopard seals and killer whales (*Orcinus orca*) hunt them in the water. Crabeaters feed almost entirely on krill.

The Weddell and Ross Seas form deep bays in the Antarctic coast, and the Weddell seal (*Leptonychotes weddelli*) breeds on the permanent ice shelf of the Weddell Sea. It feeds on squid, bottom-dwelling fish, and invertebrate animals and dives up to 1,800 feet (550 m) below the surface in search of food. The Ross seal (*Ommatophoca rossi*), found in the Ross Sea, feeds mainly on squid.

CHAPTER 5

HISTORY AND THE DESERT

When deserts grew crops

Today Tassili-n-Ajjer, Algeria, lies deep inside the Sahara. The nearest city, Tamanrasset, lying a few miles to the south at 22.78°N, 5.50°E, has an average annual rainfall of 1.8 inches (46.7 mm). It is one of the driest places on Earth. Caves at Tassili-n-Ajjer (the name means "Plateau of the Chasms") have paintings on their walls that were made by the people who lived there from about 8000 B.C.E. until 4000 B.C.E. The paintings depict scenes from the everyday life of a people who lived by hunting. Other cave paintings in the same region show a very similar way of life. The hunters pursued buffalo, elephants, rhinoceroses, and hippopotamuses. Hippopotamuses are animals that spend most of their time in water, and in the cave paintings people are seen hunting them in canoes. Clearly, in those days that part of Algeria was not a desert. Until 6000 B.C.E. southern Libya had an average annual rainfall of eight to 16 inches (200–400 mm). Today it rarely rains at all.

As recently as Roman times North Africa was a land of farms producing food for export. It was known as "the granary of Rome," and in some places the outlines of fields are still visible from the air. In about the year 120 C.E., the astronomer, mathematician, and geographer Ptolemy (Claudius Ptolemaeus) recorded that it rained every month except August in the city of Alexandria, where he lived. Alexandria, on the Egyptian coast, now receives an average of seven inches (178 mm) of rain a year.

Climates change over time and, as they do so, deserts appear and disappear—and not only in Africa. Petra, about 16 miles (26 km) northwest of the town of Ma'ān, Jordan, now lies in ruins, but from about 300 B.C.E. until 100 C.E. Petra was a flourishing city and a center for the caravan trade.

Its people had a reliable water supply and were fed from the produce of surrounding farms.

The annual rainfall at Sukkur, Pakistan, averages 3.2 inches (81.5 mm). Sukkur lies in the valley of the Indus River and is on the edge of the Thar Desert. It is not far from the ruins of Mohenjo Daro, a city that flourished from about 2500 B.C.E. until 1700 B.C.E. Farmers grew cereals, dates, and melons there to feed the citizens of Mohenjo Daro, and they may have grown cotton and raised livestock as well.

A few miles to the east of St. Louis, Missouri, Cahokia Mounds State Park contains the remains of the biggest Native American city north of Mexico. When the city was at its peak, between 1050 C.E. and 1250 C.E., its population may have been as high as 40,000 or even 50,000. Farms around the city produced enough food for all of those people. The city was abandoned when the climate changed and the area turned to desert. It is not desert now, because since then the climate has changed again.

Desert civilizations

Mighty empires once prospered in parts of the world that are now barren deserts. The earliest of these lay to the south of modern Baghdad, Iraq, and produced the first written language—Sumerian. The oldest surviving inscriptions written in Sumerian were made in about 3100 B.C.E. The people who made them had arrived about two centuries earlier in the region, which came to be known as Sumer. They were not the earliest inhabitants, however. Sumer was settled between 4500 B.C.E. and 4000 B.C.E. by people who drained the marshes, established industries, and lived in villages set in a landscape that supplied them with all of their food. Clearly the land around them was not a desert. The Sumerians displaced the original inhabitants and developed a civilization based on 12 or more city-states. These eventually fell under the control of Sharrukin, or Sargon, who ruled Akkad, the region to the north of Sumer, from 2334 B.C.E. until 2279 B.C.E. Sumerians invented wheeled vehicles, the potter's wheel, writing, and written laws.

The land lying between the Red Sea and the eastern bank of the Nile River from approximately Aswān south as far as Khartoum is known today as the Nubian Desert, an extension of the Sahara. It was not always so desolate. A stone-age culture had developed there by 6000 B.C.E., and in about 2613 B.C.E. the Egyptians under Pharaoh Snefru raided the region and brought back cattle and prisoners. The Egyptians knew the country as Cush (or Kush) and the Greeks called it Ethiopia, though it lies to the north of modern Ethiopia, in Sudan. It is also called Nubia.

At one time Egypt formed part of the Nubian Empire. The Nubian king Piankhi, who lived around 730 B.C.E., annexed Egypt, styling himself king of Cush and Egypt. Piankhi's successor, Shabaka, also called Sabacon, who ruled from about 719 or 718 B.C.E. to 703 B.C.E. and founded the 25th Egyptian dynasty, is believed to have moved his capital to Memphis, about 14 miles (22 km) south of Cairo. Although the expanding Assyrian Empire drove the Nubians from Egypt in about 650 B.C.E., their own kingdom survived for a further 1,000 years.

In Yemen, in the southwestern corner of the Arabian Peninsula, there once lived a people known as the Sabaeans. Their kingdom was called Saba, and it appears in the Old Testament under the name of Sheba. The first historical mention of the Sabaeans is a record of tribute sent by the king of Saba to the king of Assyria in about 715 B.C.E.

The Sabaeans appear to have been a prosperous people, but little is known about them until the second century C.E., when they joined with Cush to form the kingdom of Aksum. Migrants from Saba had settled in the Tigre region of modern Ethiopia around the town of Aksum (14.08°N, 38.7°E). They traded with Greece, Rome, Cush, and Egypt, and in the third century their descendants conquered Saba. The Aksum Empire had been born, and in 320–350 C.E. it conquered Cush and appropriated that kingdom's considerable wealth. Until about 400 C.E. Aksum was an important meeting point for trade routes between Africa, India, and the Mediterranean. The Aksum Empire began to decline in importance from about 900 C.E.

More recently a large and important empire covered much of West Africa. At its peak in the early 14th century, the Mali empire extended across most of modern Mali, Guinea, Senegal, Gambia, Guinea-Bissau, and Mauritania, and its influence was felt in Sierra Leone, Burkina Faso, Niger, and Algeria. It was not the first West African empire. Until the middle of the 11th century the Ghanaian Empire ruled most of the region. As that empire declined, several short-lived kingdoms competed for its territories, and at the Battle of Kirina in 1235 armies led by Sundiata Keita, king of Kangaba, defeated those of the king of Susu. Both kingdoms then united under Sundiata and the resulting Mali Empire expanded northward to the salt and copper mines of the Sahara. Its capital was at Niani, now a village in northeastern Guinea. Gao, Djenné, and Timbuktu were important commercial centers.

There were rich farmlands on the floodplain of the Niger River, at the heart of the Mali Empire, and there were gold mines nearby. Gold also passed through Mali on its way from mines in countries to the south to Mediterranean ports and from there to Europe, and it was taxed in Mali. By the reign of Mansa Mūsā, from 1307 to perhaps 1337, the empire's wealth was legendary. In 1324–25 Mansa Mūsā made a pilgrimage to Mecca, taking with him 100 camels laden with gold. A pious man, Mansa Mūsā felt obliged to distribute gold to less fortunate fellow Muslims he encountered along the way. He distributed so much gold in Cairo that it caused marked inflation.

Internal strife and rebellion weakened the empire from the second half of the 14th century, and by the 15th century Mali was in decline. The Songhai people, originally from northwestern Nigeria, dominated the surrounding states and had established themselves in Gao by 800, and were themselves dominated by the Mali Empire. As that empire weakened, the Songhai achieved independence, and in 1471 Sonni 'Alī (reigned 1464–92) occupied Djenné. His son, Sonni Baru, was deposed by Muhammad ibn Abī Bakr Ture (also known as Askia Muhammad Touré, reigned 1493–1528), who captured Timbuktu and restored it to its former prosperity. This established the Songhai Empire, which reached the peak of its power and influence in the 15th and 16th centuries. In 1590–91 the Songhai army was defeated by a Moroccan expedition. The Moroccans occupied Gao, Djenné, and Timbuktu, ending the Songhai Empire.

The Middle East: birthplace of Western civilization

Western civilization was born approximately 8,000 years ago on the Anatolian Plain, in southern Turkey. That is where people first discovered the way to select seeds from the best of the plants they liked to eat and to grow more plants from them. At about the same time, people began to capture animals they formerly hunted and breed young animals from them in captivity. They had invented farming and were domesticating a range of food plants and livestock. There is archaeological evidence of farming in Turkey in about 6200 B.C.E.

People who live by gathering plant foods and hunting game move about, living in temporary camps as they follow the migrations of animals between seasonal pastures. Farmers need to live in one place, and as farming spread, villages appeared to accommodate farming communities. The most ancient cities appeared at about this time. This marks the literal beginning of civilization, because our words *civilization* and *citizen* are derived from the Latin *civitas,* which means "city."

One of the most ancient and most famous of these Anatolian cities is called Çatalhüyük (pronounced: chatalHOO-yook). The city consists of rectangular houses made from mud bricks and built without spaces between houses, so people walked across the roofs and entered their homes from above. Inside, the walls were decorated with paintings and the homes were well furnished. The citizens were prosperous. Çatalhüyük was occupied from about 6500 B.C.E. to 5800 B.C.E. and several thousand people lived there.

Knowledge of agriculture spread from Anatolia southward into Egypt (see pages 132–134) and eastward into the lands between the Tigris and Euphrates Rivers in modern Turkey, Syria, and Iraq. As the map on page 131 shows, the region has a crescent shape, and the American historian James

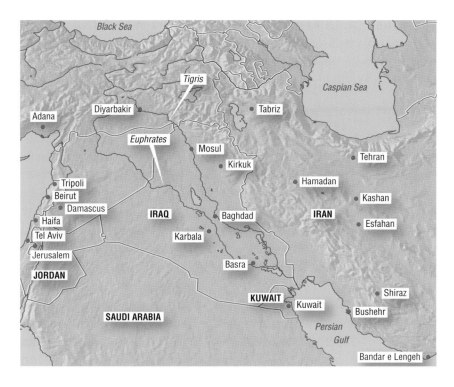

The Fertile Crescent lies between the Tigris and Euphrates Rivers, in what are now Syria and Iraq.

Henry Breasted (1865–1935) gave it the name *Fertile Crescent*, by which it is still often known today. The land between the rivers was more often known by its Greek name of Mesopotamia, "the land between the rivers," from *mesos* (between) and *potamos* (river).

It was in Mesopotamia that the empire of Sumer and Akkad arose, and it is there that the Assyrian and Babylonian Empires flourished from about 1800 B.C.E. The city of Babylon lay close to the modern town of Al Hillah in southern Iraq. Nineveh and Nimrud were two of the most important Assyrian cities. Both lay close to modern Mosul in northern Iraq.

Not far away, the Phoenicians were flourishing at the same time, but they had arrived in Phoenicia—modern Lebanon—in about 3000 B.C.E. Tyre and Sidon (modern Saida) are Phoenician cities mentioned in the Old Testament. From their port of Byblos (modern Jubayl, north of Beirut), the Phoenicians exported paper made from papyrus, and *byblos* became the Greek word for "papyrus." Our word *bible* means "papyrus book." People were living in Byblos by 3000 B.C.E. and the city is inhabited to this day. Byblos-Jubayl has been continuously occupied probably for longer than any other city in the world.

Egypt

Egypt has a desert climate. Cairo receives an average 1.1 inches (28 mm) of rain a year. Yet it is a large, bustling city—by far the biggest city in Africa or the Middle East—and there has been a major city in that area since at least 3100 B.C.E.

Ancient Egypt was originally two countries. Upper Egypt extended from Aswān (24.2°N), where a waterfall known as the First Cataract marks the southern limit of the navigable river, to Cairo. The region from Cairo northward to the Nile Delta and the Mediterranean comprised Lower Egypt. According to tradition, the ancient city, located 14 miles (22.5 km) to the south of modern Cairo, was founded by Menes, the first king of the united kingdoms of Upper and Lower Egypt. The god of the city was Ptah, to whom a vast temple was built. The city was called Memphis, a Greek name derived from Menefer, an alternative name for Pharaoh Pepi I, but the city was also known as Hikupta—"mansion of the soul of Ptah." The Greek version of that name was Aegyptos and they applied it to the entire country.

Memphis was the capital of the Old Kingdom from its founding until about 2258 B.C.E and it remained an important city until Roman times. Its influence declined as that of Alexandria rose, and the Arabs finally destroyed Memphis in the seventh century C.E. The Arab conquerors used much of its stone to build their new city of Al Fustāt, which was the Arab capital of Egypt from 641 until 969, and very little of Memphis now remains.

Farmers were tilling the soil in El Fayyûm, a low-lying area to the southwest of Cairo, long before Memphis was built. They grew wheat and barley for food, cotton and flax for making cloth, and they raised sheep, goats, and pigs. The first farmers arrived in the region in about 4000 B.C.E. and settled because in those days the land was not desert, but grassland. Elephants, rhinoceroses, and giraffes lived there. Farther south a different people were raising livestock near the modern town of Asyūt. By the time knowledge of farming had spread northward to the Nile Delta, in about 3600 B.C.E., however, the climate was becoming drier.

Egypt became home to one of the world's most important civilizations and has thrived ever since. Its success was due to the fact that its farms did not rely directly on the rainfall. Instead, they received their water from the Nile River. Every year, when the snows melt in the distant mountains of Uganda and Ethiopia, the water level rises, first in the Blue Nile flowing from Ethiopia and, as that level starts to subside, then in the White Nile flowing from Uganda. The two rivers meet at Khartoum, and between June and September the combined Nile used to overflow its banks, flooding the land on either side all the way northward to the sea. As well as bringing water, the flood brought fertile soil washed from the Ethiopian hillsides. Today the Aswān High Dam regulates the flow of water and the annual flood no longer occurs.

The flood was never entirely dependable, and when it was late or failed famine was the likely consequence. It was famine that brought down the Old Kingdom in about 2134 B.C.E. and the Middle Kingdom in about 1640 B.C.E.

Fields on either side of the river were on low-lying ground and separated from one another by high banks. Canals leading from the river allowed the floodwater to fill each field. The fields remained under several feet of water for a few weeks, during which the mud settled. Between floods the fields were irrigated by water lifted from the river by a bailing device known as a *shadoof,* or *shaduf,* and poured into the canals. It may have been Egyptian farmers who invented irrigation.

Egyptian farming was highly organized, with a ministry of agriculture overseeing the proper management of the resources. Between them the pharaoh, temples, and wealthy aristocrats owned all of the land, and the farmers were tenants paying a rent that was fixed by law. Seed and oxen for plowing were loaned to the farmers and the loans were repaid from the harvest.

Ordinary people ate mainly bread, beans, and onions. They were the first to use yeast to leaven bread and to bake bread in ovens, rather than on a flat stone over an open fire. They also used yeast to make beer, their staple drink. Wealthier people also enjoyed salads, lentils, peas, and other vegetables and fruit, and also beef, poultry, game, and fish. They loved cakes, some of which were sweetened with honey and fried. The farmers grew grapes, kept bees, and by 1200 B.C.E. were producing olive oil.

Peoples of the Sahara and Arabian Deserts

Deserts are empty and barren, but they have never been entirely uninhabited. People cross them carrying goods for trade, and there are permanent settlements wherever an oasis exists naturally or can be made by sinking a well (see "Oases and wells" on pages 47–51). Traders have meeting places where goods are exchanged and deals done, and towns often grow up in such places.

Tunis, the capital of Tunisia, was once known as Carthage, and in ancient time it was occupied by Phoenicians from what is now Lebanon. The local people, called Numidians, allied themselves with the Phoenicians and so became involved in the Punic Wars between Carthage and Rome, which led to the destruction of Carthage and Roman occupation. The Romans knew the region as Barbary, a name they took from the Greek word *barbaros,* meaning "foreign." A "barbarian" originally meant a person who spoke a foreign language. The Romans gave the name *Berber* to the people living in Barbary, and this is still the name by which outsiders know them, although they prefer to call themselves the Imazighen, or "free men."

Over the succeeding centuries some Berbers became Christians who spoke Latin; others adopted Judaism, and many of their descendants now live in Israel; but most converted to Islam and learned to speak Arabic. Their ancient languages still survive, however, and there are still Berber people who speak no Arabic.

The true desert people are the Tuareg, often called "the blue people" because their men wear blue robes and turbans—although the Regui-Bat, another nomadic tribe, also dress in blue. Most Tuareg live in Niger and Mali, but others are scattered throughout North Africa. The Tuareg are another branch of the Berber people. At one time they lived around oases as peasant farmers, but in the 12th century they were dispersed by Bedouin Arabs and since then they have lived as nomads. They were once feared. No one knew the desert better than they did, and they would appear suddenly, riding horses or camels and heavily armed, to raid travelers. They also traded and exacted taxes from caravans crossing the desert they regarded as their own.

Today the Tuareg live in peace, but modernization has disrupted their way of life. The Tuareg came to dominate desert freight haulage and as recently as the 1940s they owned and operated approximately 30,000 caravans transporting goods across the desert. Camel caravans cannot compete against surfaced roads and diesel trucks, however, and as transport changed the Tuareg lost their means of livelihood.

Farther south, in West Africa, the Fulani were also nomads. They came originally from eastern Sudan, but the expansion of the Ghanaian Empire forced them to move. Eventually they were dispersed across the region between Cameroon and Senegal. They began expanding eastward from Senegal in the 14th century, and by the 16th century they were moving into Hausaland. Many Fulani continued to live a nomadic life but some, especially in Hausaland, settled down in the towns and converted to Islam. In the 1790s Usman dan Fodio, an Islamic cleric living in the state of Gobir, in northern Hausaland, accused the Hausa rulers of being little better than pagans and urged the people to revolt. The uprising of Hausa and Fulani people began in 1804, and by 1808 the rebels had conquered Hausaland and also engulfed Adamwa (northern Cameroon), Nupe, and Yorubaland in the south, and Oyo and the emirate of Ilorin in the northeast. By the end of the 19th century the Fulani Empire had weakened. Its decay made it easier for the British to gain control of what then became Northern Nigeria.

Arab is an Arabic word that means "those who speak clearly"—in other words, in Arabic. Consequently an Arab is anyone whose first language is Arabic. The Arabs came originally from Arabia, and it is probably they who domesticated the

Bedouin people with their camels (Camelus dromedarius), *seen at sunset near Oasis Dakhia, among the sand dunes of the Sahara in Egypt* (Courtesy of Gerry Ellis/Minden Pictures)

dromedary (see the sidebar "The camel: 'ship of the desert' " on pages 97–98), originally for military use.

Severe droughts led to the failure of many farms throughout the Mediterranean region during the fourth century C.E., and people who had been farmers became nomads. The Arabic name for nomads is *badw* (singular *badawi*). The *badw* are the people known in English as Bedouin, and they are the traditionally nomadic people found throughout the desert lands. Most Bedouin speak Badawi, which is their own dialect of Arabic. Bedouin who have adopted a settled way of life on the edge of the desert are known as *fellahin*.

Many Bedouin have now settled down, but some continue to live as nomads, driving their camels, sheep, and goats across the desert from one area of seasonal pasture to another. They live in low, rectangular black tents, the size of the tent reflecting the social position of its owner.

Peoples of the Asian deserts

The Gobi Desert lies partly in Mongolia and partly in the Inner Mongolian Autonomous Region of China. The people of the Gobi are Mongols. Parts of Mongolia are farmed, but the dry climate makes farming precarious, and most of the farmers are descendants of Chinese immigrants. Although nowadays most Mongolians live in towns and villages, the Mongols are traditionally nomads who raise camels, horses, cattle, sheep, and goats. Some also raise yaks (*Bos grunniens*), which are sturdy cattle from Tibet.

Their camels are the two-humped Bactrian camels (*Camelus bactrianus*). People ride camels during very severe winter weather, but they are used mainly as pack animals. Camels also give milk, and their long coats supply the wool that is used to make Mongolian garments and blankets.

Meat and milk are the staple foods. Some of the milk is used to make dried curd and cheese. Mare's milk is fermented to make the national drink, called *airag*. People also drink tea, made in a large bowl with added milk and salt. Mongols do not eat vegetables or fish.

The traditional Mongol dwelling is a circular structure made from wooden poles covered with skins, woven cloth, or more commonly felt. It is known variously as a *ger, yurt,* or *yurta* and is furnished with brightly colored rugs. There is a hearth near the center and a hole in the roof to allow the smoke to escape.

There is never just one ger, but always at least two and sometimes as many as six. These make up the herding camp that is the basis of Mongol society. Families agree to join a herding camp for one year and at the end of the year they decide whether to remain together. A camp must not grow so large that it makes managing the livestock and pastures difficult. Every camp has sheep, managed as a single flock. The families keep other livestock only if there are enough people to look after them and the pasturage will sustain them.

Spring and summer are spent on the pastures. Every morning the livestock are taken out from the camp, returning in the evening. When they have grazed one area of pasture they are taken to the next, starting close to the camp and moving a little farther away each day. When the journey to the pasture becomes inconveniently long it is time for the families to move on. They pack their gers and possessions onto camels and travel to the next site, allowing their animals to make the best possible use of the food and water they find along the way.

Mongolian winters are harsh, and as the weather turns colder the families move to their permanent winter campsites, where the authorities provide fodder and there is shelter for the animals. That is when animals that are unlikely to survive are slaughtered and their meat dried or frozen to provide food during the time when there is no milk.

No one lives in the Taklimakan Desert. It is too dry there for plants to grow, and with no plants, the desert provides nothing for animals to eat.

People live in parts of the Thar Desert, mainly along the northern margin, in the valley of the Indus River. Farming is possible there in the rainy season, and local people have learned to collect and store water and to use it efficiently.

Caravans and the Silk Road

No one should attempt to cross the desert alone. It is extremely dangerous, even today. People who need to cross a desert have always sought companions and experienced guides who will make sure they follow the best route and who will protect them from robbers. A group of people traveling together across a desert is called a *caravan*. A modern caravan might comprise a number of cars, trucks, or buses. A traditional caravan used strings of up to 40 camels linked by ropes. Caravans in the Middle East and North Africa sometimes comprised hundreds or even thousands of camels moving three or four strings abreast. There is safety in numbers, and the more hazardous the route the bigger the caravan.

The camels carried loads of about 350 pounds (160 kg) of goods or of passengers. Passengers rode in *panniers*—large bags or baskets—slung on either side of the animal.

Caravans traveled by day except in extremely hot weather, when they might travel by night, resting at the end of each section of the journey. They moved at a steady two to three MPH (3–5 km/h) and covered 16–40 miles (26–64 km) before stopping to rest. When possible, day caravans rested overnight in a *caravansary*. This was a public facility enclosed by thick, high walls and located, because of its size, outside a town or large village. It offered secure shelter for animals, storage space for goods and supplies, and bedrooms for the travelers. There was a well to supply water and a communal hearth for cooking, but travelers had to provide their own food, bedding, and fodder for their animals. The caravansary remained open from dawn until dusk, when the resident porter closed and locked the only entrance.

Today there are roads across deserts, but the former absence of roads did not mean camel caravans wandered just anywhere. Caravans followed particular routes that were developed to take pilgrims to Mecca and goods from one trading center to another. There were also salt routes. The most important salt routes in the Sahara led to Timbuktu, and there was also a salt route from southern Arabia to the Mediterranean. Routes often went from oasis to oasis. The modern roads often follow the old caravan routes.

The most famous caravan route of all led from China to Alexandria, Egypt, and to Antioch (modern Antakya) in southern Turkey. It is called the Silk Road, and it was once used to transport silk and spices from Asia and gold, silver, precious stones, and woolen cloth from Europe. Although it is no longer used as a trade route, sections of it are now open to tourists. There are plans to restore the entire Silk Road as the Trans-Asian Highway.

When the first Chinese silk cloth reached Europe it was literally worth its weight in gold. No one knew how it was made: The Chinese kept its method of manufacture a closely guarded secret. Demand for this fabulous material was huge, and the Silk Road first opened to export it in about 100 B.C.E.

Smaller trade routes converged on the city of Xi'an (also spelled Sian), where the Silk Road began. From there it went north as far as the Great Wall, then followed the Wall past the Nan Shan Mountains and skirted the southern edge of the Gobi Desert. At the lake of Lop Nur the road divided. One branch passed to the north of Lop Nur and along the northern edge of the Tarim Basin at the center of the Taklimakan Desert, and the other passed to the south of the lake and basin. The road crossed the Pamir and Karakoram Mountains, turned south to Islamabad, Pakistan, then north again to Samarqand, Uzbekistan. It then crossed northern Iran, passed to the south of the Caspian Sea, crossed northern Iraq and Syria, going through Damascus, and finally reached the ports of the eastern Mediterranean. Goods were taken by sea from there to southern Europe.

It is not only goods that travel along roads as important as the Silk Road. Ideas also travel. Information about China, much of it highly unreliable, traveled to Europe. Buddhism traveled northward from India and spread eastward. Nestorian Christianity, a version of Christianity developed in the Near East in the fifth century, traveled to China. And in central Asia, where western and eastern ideas met along the Silk Road, there are Buddhist statues with European faces.

Peoples of the American desert

At some time around 300 B.C.E. people settled in Arizona and lived by hunting game and gathering wild fruits and beans. They also grew corn and dug a canal three miles (5 km) long that carried water from the Gila River to irrigate their fields. Very little is known about where these people came from or why they disappeared. They are known as the Hohokam, a name given to them by the Akimel O'odham (or Pima) people, who may be descended from them and who occupied part of what had been Hohokam territory. The name means "those who have disappeared" in the Akimel O'odham language.

The Akimel O'odham, whose name means "river people," were farmers who settled along the river valleys and used river water to irrigate their crops. Harvests were never reliable, however, and the Akimel O'odham obtained some of their food by hunting and gathering wild plants.

The Hohokam and all of their descendants lived in permanent villages built either from blocks of baked mud called *adobe* or from stone. Dressed stone came into use between 1050 and 1300 C.E. This is stone that has been shaped into squared blocks that fit snugly together to produce a much more solid construction. Using dressed stone, Native Americans built apartment buildings up to four stories high and with up to 1,000 rooms. Rooms on the ground floor often had only one entrance, in the roof, and each upper story was set back from the story below, so that every room had a terrace. The floors between stories were made from a thick layer of adobe laid over rush matting that rested on massive timber beams. Each apartment block was a complete village.

These villages, constructed in and beside the North American desert, are known by the Spanish word for villages—*pueblos*—and their occupants are called Pueblo Indians. Some pueblos were built on ledges and in alcoves along the sides of canyons and mesas (see "Mesas, buttes, and other desert landforms" on pages 43–45). Many pueblos also had underground rooms that were used for important religious ceremonies.

The Anasazi were among the first Pueblo peoples and contemporaries of the Hohokam. Their name means "ancient ones" in the Navajo language. They lived in the Four Corners region to the east of the Wasatch Range, where present-day Utah, Colorado, New Mexico, and Arizona meet. The Anasazi lived by hunting and gathering, and they also cultivated corn and pumpkins.

Part of the Sonoran Desert is known as the Yuma Desert, and it is home to the Yuma people, who once lived along the floodplains of the lower Colorado River. They lived by fishing, hunting, and gathering wild plants, and also by farming. The Yuma farmers had no need for irrigation, because every spring the melting of the snow in the mountains made the river overflow its banks, soaking the fields and leaving behind a deposit of fertile silt.

Farther upstream, the Tohono O'odham—their name means "desert people"—inhabited a much drier area. They relied on farming much less than other Pueblo peoples and lived a partly nomadic life. Heavy summer rains would cause floods, and when these subsided the Tohono O'odham (also called the Papago) planted their seeds in the silt. While their crops of corn, beans, pumpkins, and cotton were growing, the Tohono O'odham lived in villages nearby, but the ground dried after harvesttime and the people moved to other villages in the hills where there was water and game.

The Pueblo Indians still survive, but nowadays most of them live in reservations. The Hopi, one of the best-known groups, live in eastern Arizona on a large reservation surrounded by the Navajo Reservation. The Hopi villages are built on top or at the foot of three mesas, known as the First, Second, and Third Mesas, that project like fingers from the much larger Black Mesa to the north. Oraibi, the unofficial Hopi capital, is built on top of the Third Mesa, about 6,500 feet (1,980 m) above sea level. People have been living in Oraibi since 1100 C.E. and Oraibi may be the oldest continually inhabited settlement in the United States, although the present village is not the original one, which lay at the foot of the Third Mesa.

Peoples of the Arctic

In 1999 an area of 733,400 square miles (1.9 million km^2) in the Northwest Territories of Canada became the self-governing territory of Nunavut, with a population of about 22,000, of which about 17,500 are Inuit. Greenland is also a self-governing Inuit territory, known officially as Kalaallit Nunaat. The Inuit population of Kalaallit Nunaat, accounting for about 85 percent of the total population of 59,000, is descended from Canadian migrants.

Amerindian peoples live in the far north of North America, but the true desert people of the far north are the Inuit—the name means simply "the people." Both Amerindians and Inuit are descended from Asian ancestors, but the two groups are not closely related.

Inuit peoples inhabit the Arctic Regions of Alaska, Canada, Greenland, and Siberia. The Aleuts, living in the Aleutian Islands and western Alaska, are close relatives. The Aleut and Inuit languages are also related, but their speakers have been separated for so long that the languages have diverged and are now about as alike as English and Russian.

Inuit are fully adapted to the arctic climate. Their short and stocky build, with short arms and legs, conserves warmth by reducing the surface area of the body in relation to its volume. The shape of their skulls also minimizes heat loss. Their fingers and toes remain warmer than those of non-Inuit people when exposed to extreme cold, and Inuit people have a high tolerance for pain associated with the cold. Inuit rarely shiver, because their metabolic rate—the speed with which the body generates warmth—is up to 45 percent higher than that of non-Inuit due largely to the Inuit diet. This consists of fish, red meat, and blubber (whale and sea fat) and is very high in fat, calories, and protein. Their diet supplies the Inuit with sufficient vitamins and most minerals, but they do tend to suffer from a deficiency of calcium and an excess of phosphorus. Besides retaining heat due to their physique and diet, Inuit dress in very warm clothes and live and sleep in dwellings that are well insulated, but also well ventilated.

During the winter Inuit communities traditionally spent the winter together. The men caught fish through holes in the sea ice and stalked seals that lay resting on the surface or waited on the ice for them to surface at their breathing holes. In spring the communities dispersed. Some families fished in lakes or rivers, some traveled farther afield in pursuit of seals, and some hunted bowhead whales (*Balaena mysticetus*). They hunted on water in *kayaks*—canoes that carry a single person. The families moved inland in summer, traveling by dogsled and living by hunting large land animals, such as bears and caribou. Animals provided the Inuit with everything they needed. They used bones where other people used wood: to make the framework for houses and boats and to make tools and weapons, such as arrowheads and harpoon heads. Skins were used for clothing, tents, and the outer covering of boats. Seal oil was used as fuel for lighting and heating.

This traditional way of life began to change in North America when European whalers arrived in the 19th century and established trading stations that supplied the Inuit with manufactured goods in exchange for skins, furs, and ivory from walrus tusks. Missionaries opened schools and many Inuit settled in villages. More recently, oil and mining companies have provided jobs for local people and towns have grown up to accommodate them. Most Inuit in Kalaallit Nunaat have permanent houses and live by fishing and sheep farming. Fish processing, handicrafts, fur preparation, and shipbuilding provide additional employment, and in years to come the mining industry may also employ local people. People who hunt now use rifles, snowmobiles, and boats with outboard motors. Inuit life has changed and living conditions have improved in many ways, but not everyone has benefited. Like other Native Americans, some Inuit have found it difficult to adapt to rapid changes and to be accepted into the predominant Western culture.

CHAPTER 6

DESERT EXPLORATION

Explorers in the Far North

English and Dutch merchants were trading extensively with Asia by the 16th century, but the only sea routes involved a long and dangerous journey around the southernmost tip of either Africa or South America. In addition to the storms sailors could expect as they rounded the Cape of Good Hope or Cape Horn, they risked being boarded and having their cargoes seized. Portugal controlled the route around Africa and Spain controlled the route around South America, and naval ships of both countries would attack foreign ships. It was possible to travel overland to Asia, but that journey was even harder.

The merchants sought an alternative route to the north. If ships could sail eastward, around the North Cape of Norway and across the Arctic Ocean, they would reach the Asian ports. This route was called the Northeast Passage. Several attempts were made to find it, but all of them failed. Most reached no farther than the Kola Peninsula and the Barents Sea. It was not until 1778 that the English navigator and scientist James Cook (1728–79) proved that Asia and North America were separate. Cook sailed northward through the Bering Strait as far as Cape Schmidt and could see land on both sides of the Strait. This was progress, but still no one had found the Northeast Passage. The map on page 146 shows the location of these places.

Finally, in 1878–79, an expedition led by the Swedish explorer Baron Nils Adolf Erik Nordenskjöld (1832–1901) found the Northeast Passage. Nordenskjöld sailed eastward in the *Vega* accompanied by three cargo ships. Two of these were bound for the Yenisei River, flowing into the Kara Sea, and the other for the Lena River, flowing into the Laptev Sea. The *Vega* continued to the Chukchi Peninsula at the

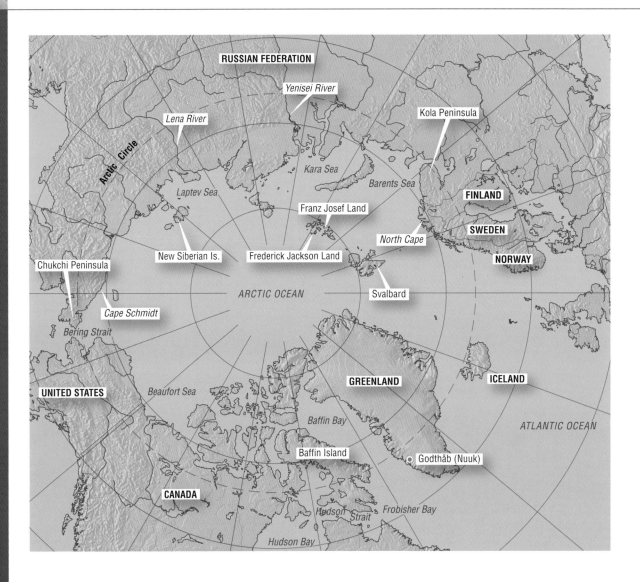

RUSSIAN FEDERATION

Yenisei River

Lena River

Kola Peninsula

Arctic Circle

Kara Sea

Laptev Sea

Barents Sea

FINLAND

Franz Josef Land

SWEDEN

North Cape

NORWAY

New Siberian Is.   Frederick Jackson Land

Chukchi Peninsula

ARCTIC OCEAN

Svalbard

Cape Schmidt

Bering Strait

UNITED STATES   Beaufort Sea

GREENLAND

ICELAND

ATLANTIC OCEAN

Baffin Bay

Baffin Island   Godthåb (Nuuk)

CANADA

Hudson Strait   Frobisher Bay

Hudson Bay

The Arctic. The North Pole lies near the center of the Arctic Ocean, and the Arctic region is mainly covered by sea, surrounded by North America, Greenland, and Eurasia.

northern end of the Bering Strait, where the sea ice forced it to spend the winter.

The alternative to a Northeast Passage was a Northwest Passage, passing to the north of North America. The search for this route also began in the 16th century, and the first expedition to enter the Arctic sailed in 1576, led by the English explorer Sir Martin Frobisher (c. 1539–94). After enduring terrible storms, Frobisher reached Baffin Island and sailed some distance along the inlet that bears his name. This was the first of many attempts, including four made by the

English navigator Henry Hudson (his year of birth is not known), in the course of which Hudson discovered the bay, strait, and river that bear his name. On his last attempt, when he set sail from London on April 17, 1610, in the *Discovery,* Hudson surveyed the eastern shore of Hudson Bay and spent the winter locked in the ice. When the ice began to melt in spring his crew mutinied, and on June 22, 1611, Hudson, his young son, and seven crew members who remained loyal were cast adrift in a small boat. Hudson and his companions were never seen again.

The Northwest Passage was eventually found to exist. The British explorer Commander Sir Robert John le Mesurier McClure (1807–73) traveled the route in 1850–54. McClure commanded HMS *Investigator,* which sailed part of the route before being abandoned. The crew then proceeded on foot before being rescued and returned to Britain.

The *Investigator* was one of four ships composing an official search party that set out in 1848 to search for members of the expedition led by Rear Admiral Sir John Franklin (1786–1847). Franklin had sailed in 1845 to seek the Northwest Passage with HMS *Erebus* and HMS *Terror.* The party disappeared and despite several searches their fate was not discovered until 1859. It was found that Franklin had traveled the Northwest Passage, but it had cost his life and that of his crew. The discovery of the passage is now attributed to both McClure and Franklin. Neither of them sailed the whole of the passage, however. The first person to achieve that was the Norwegian explorer Roald Amundsen (see the sidebar on page 153) in 1906.

Interest in the Northwest Passage became intense between about 1890 and 1910, because there was a widespread belief that the Arctic Ocean was free of ice and it appeared that the ice might be breaking up around the coasts. This did not happen, and the ice thickened again in the early 20th century, but the expeditions it inspired resulted in detailed studies of the coastlines and islands of the Arctic Ocean.

Henry Hudson had attempted to reach the North Pole in 1607, but he was searching for a route to Asia, as were other explorers, and it was not until the late 18th century that adventurers headed for the Pole as a goal in its own right. On

April 6, 1909, Commander Robert Edwin Peary (1856–1920) of the U.S. Navy claimed to have reached the Pole. Hardly had Peary made his claim, however, than Dr. Frederick Albert Cook (1865–1940) challenged it. Cook, a physician who had served as surgeon on one of Peary's earlier expeditions, declared that he had reached the Pole on April 21, 1908—a year before Peary. Cook's evidence that he had reached the Pole at all failed to convince most geographers, and Peary is generally credited with having been the first person to reach the North Pole.

Along with the searches for sea routes and the race to reach the Pole, other expeditions were engaged in scientific studies

Fridtjof Nansen

Fridtjof Nansen (1861–1930) was a Norwegian explorer, scientist, and statesman who won the 1922 Nobel Peace Prize for his humanitarian work with the League of Nations and the International Committee of the Red Cross.

Nansen was born on October 10, 1861, at Store-Fröen, on the outskirts of Christiania (now Oslo). He studied zoology at Christiania University. An avid outdoor sportsman, Nansen was an accomplished skater and skier and developed a strong physique and stamina. He first visited the Arctic in 1882 as a member of the crew of the *Viking,* a sealing ship that sailed close to Greenland. The encounter gave Nansen the idea of crossing the Greenland ice cap. He recruited a party for the trek and set out in August 1888 from the east coast, reaching the west coast almost six weeks later. The group spent the winter at Godthåb (now Nuuk), where Nansen spent his time studying the Inuit people.

This experience led to his most famous expedition. With financial support from the Norwegian government and private subscriptions, a ship called the *Fram* (Forward) was built to Nansen's design and on June 24, 1893, it sailed for eastern Siberia with a crew of 13. Nansen's idea was to allow the ship to be enclosed by sea ice and then to drift with the ice in order to track the direction of the ocean currents. The *Fram* withstood the pressure of the ice and drifted slowly northward.

Nansen left the ship when it reached 84.07°N and headed north by dogsled and kayak accompanied by the Norwegian explorer Frederic Hjalmar Johansen (1867–1923), reaching 86.23°N, the highest latitude anyone had then reached, before making for Franz Josef Land. The two men were forced to spend the winter, from August 1895 of the ocean and its currents. The most famous of these was led by the Norwegian scientist and explorer Fridtjof Nansen (see the sidebar starting on page 148). Nansen believed that the currents carried sea ice from the New Siberian Islands in the Laptev Sea to Svalbard, and he designed a ship, the *Fram,* that would be strong enough to drift with the ice. Nansen's calculations proved correct.

Discovering Antarctica

It is possible that Polynesian sailors glimpsed the icy cliffs of Antarctica long before the first Europeans arrived there, and

until May 1896, on Frederick Jackson Land (Ostrov Dzheksona in Russian), the northernmost island of Franz Josef Land, which Nansen named after the English explorer Frederick George Jackson (1860–1938) whom he met there. Nansen and Johansen built a hut and hunted polar bears and walrus for food and fuel oil. They finally returned to Norway on August 13, 1896. The ice released the *Fram* to the north of Svalbard in 1896, just as Nansen had predicted it would, and the crew returned safely to Norway.

Nansen was also an eminent scientist. In 1896 he was appointed professor of zoology at Kristiania University (the spelling had been changed), but in 1908 this appointment was changed at his request to professor of oceanography. He took part in several scientific cruises, making discoveries about wind-driven ocean currents and the circulation of ocean water.

He took an active part in negotiations over the dissolution of the union between Sweden and Norway, which established Norway as an independent nation, and he became the first Norwegian minister in London. During World War I he headed the Norwegian mission in the United States. Nansen headed the Norwegian delegation to the first assembly of the League of Nations, where one of his tasks was to arrange the repatriation from Russia of almost 430,000 German and Austro-Hungarian prisoners of war. He led the efforts by the Red Cross in 1921 to bring relief to Russia, then stricken by famine, and he proposed a scheme, adopted internationally in 1922, to issue identification documents to refugees. He devoted his Nobel Prize money to furthering international relief work.

Nansen died at his home at Lysaker, near Oslo, on May 13, 1930.

Phoenician ships may have visited the continent as long ago as 1000 B.C.E. Modern exploration did not commence until the 18th century, however.

For centuries European explorers had been sailing ever farther south, and in 1488 the Portuguese navigator Bartolomeu Dias de Novais (c. 1450–1500) became the first European sailor to round the Cape of Good Hope. Ferdinand Magellan (1480–1521), another famous Portuguese explorer, discovered the Magellan Strait, between the southern tip of South America and Tierra del Fuego, in 1520. In 1578 the English sailor Sir Francis Drake (c. 1543–96) discovered the Drake Passage, between Cape Horn and the tip of the Antarctic Peninsula.

The ancient Greeks believed there must be land far to the south to balance the lands in the Northern Hemisphere, and Europeans continued to believe this despite the fact that no one had ever seen this mysterious land. It was shown on maps as *Terra Australis Incognita* ("Unknown Southern Land"), and the European nations were anxious to claim it because they also believed it to be rich in resources and suitable for habitation. Unfortunately, it was also very remote and surrounded by thick sea ice that made it unapproachable.

On January 17, 1772, Captain James Cook (1728–79) became the first sailor to cross the Antarctic Circle (66.5°S), and on January 30, 1774, Cook reached 77.17°S, the closest anyone had ever been to the South Pole. Cook proved that if a large southern continent existed, it lay to the south of latitude 60°S and was a land of perpetual ice and snow. A Russian expedition led by Fabian Gottlieb von Bellingshausen (1778–1852) was the next to cross the Antarctic Circle, but not until 1820. At one point Bellingshausen came within 20 miles (32 km) of the coast.

A French expedition led by Captain Jules-Sébastien-César Dumont d'Urville (1790–1842) sailed with two ships from Toulon in 1837 and mapped the coast of the northern part of the Antarctic Peninsula. Dumont d'Urville named the region Terre Adélie, after his wife. Adélie penguins are also named after her. A United States expedition commanded by Charles Wilkes (1798–1877) explored the coast from 1838 until 1842 and saw land, now called Wilkes Land, several times. The Scottish seaman James Clark Ross (1800–62) was also in the area at that time with HMS *Erebus* and HMS *Terror,* the ships that would later be used in the search for the Northwest Passage (see "Explorers in the Far North" on pages 145–149). Ross found the edge of what came to be called the Ross Ice Shelf, covering much of the Ross Sea. A British seal hunter, James Weddell (1787–1834) had discovered the Weddell Sea, on the opposite side of the Antarctic Peninsula, in 1823.

By the start of the 20th century explorers were starting to venture farther inland. Captain Robert Falcon Scott (1868–1912) led an expedition from 1901 until 1904 that crossed the Ross Ice Shelf. Scott's third lieutenant on that expedition was Ernest Shackleton, destined to become one of the most renowned of all Antarctic explorers (see the sidebar on page 152).

In 1910 Scott left England at the head of an expedition that would attempt to reach the South Pole. They set up a base camp at Cape Evans, on Ross Island, and on October 24, 1911, a party of 12 men headed south, transporting their equipment and supplies on motorized sledges and sledges pulled by ponies and dogs. The motorized sledges broke down and had to be abandoned, and the ponies could not cope with the conditions and had to be shot. When the team reached 83.5°S the dogs could go no farther and they were sent back. From that point the men had to haul the sledges themselves. Five of them—Scott, E. A. Wilson, H. R. Bowers, L. E. G. Oates, and Edgar Evans—reached the Pole on January 18, only to learn that Roald Amundsen (see the sidebar on page 153) had arrived there a month earlier. On the return journey, the party encountered weather that was unusually severe, even for Antarctica. By that time, their supplies of food and fuel were low and all of them perished from cold and exhaustion. Scott, Wilson, and Bowers, the last to die, were only 11 miles (17.7 km) from a depot where they had left stores that would have saved them.

Explorers in the deserts of Africa, Arabia, and Asia

The 15th century was an age of European exploration. That is when ships began venturing north and south and it is also when Europeans first began to visit African shores, although at first they did not travel very far inland.

Ernest Shackleton

Ernest Henry Shackleton (1874–1922) was one of the most famous of Antarctic explorers, greatly admired for his courage, optimism, and ability to inspire confidence and devotion in those he led. Born at Kilkea House in County Kildare, Ireland, on February 15, 1874, he was educated at Dulwich College, London. He entered the merchant navy at the age of 16, sailing from Liverpool in the *Hoghton Tower,* a full-rigged sailing ship bound for Valparaiso via Cape Horn.

Shackleton first traveled to Antarctica as third lieutenant on the 1901–04 expedition led by Captain Robert Falcon Scott (1868–1912). He took part in the sledge crossing of the Ross Ice Shelf and reached latitude 82.28°S, but the journey made him ill and he left Antarctica in March 1903 on a supply ship.

His next journey to the continent was in January 1908 as leader of the British Antarctic *Nimrod* expedition. On that visit Shackleton led a sledge party that came within 97 miles (156 km) of the South Pole, and another party, led by T. W. Edgeworth David, reached the Magnetic South Pole. On their return to London, Shackleton was knighted and made a companion of the Royal Victorian Order.

He set forth again in March 1914 at the head of the British Imperial Trans-Antarctic Expedition. The aim of that expedition was to cross from a base on the Weddell Sea, past the South Pole, to McMurdo Sound on the Ross Sea. It was not to be. Shackleton's ship, the *Endurance,* became trapped in the ice and drifted for 10 months until the ice finally crushed it. Shackleton and his men drifted on ice floes for another five months, finally escaping in boats to Elephant Island, in the South Shetland Islands. From there Shackleton and five companions sailed in an open whaling boat across 800 miles (1,287 km) of the Southern Ocean, through bitter cold and mountainous seas, to South Georgia Island. They then walked across the island—the first people ever to do so—to find help from the whaling station at Stromness, 17 miles (27 km) distant. Shackleton then led four rescue expeditions from South Georgia until finally he was able to rescue his men, all of whom survived. His reputation rests largely on his heroism, determination, and refusal to abandon his men.

His expeditions and the effort needed to raise funds to finance them exhausted him. Shackleton died at Grytviken, South Georgia, on January 5, 1922, while preparing for yet another Antarctic expedition.

Diogo Gomes, a Portuguese explorer who flourished between 1440 and 1482, sailed far up the Gambia River in 1456 and met men from the remote city of Timbuktu, then an important trading center in the Mali Empire (see "Desert civilizations" on pages 127–130). The name Timbuktu and stories about its wealth became a magnet attracting later

Roald Amundsen

One of the greatest of all polar explorers, Roald Engelbregt Gravning Amundsen (1872–1928) was born on July 16, 1872, at Borge, to the south of Christiania (now Oslo), Norway. He began to study medicine, but in 1897 he joined a Belgian Antarctic expedition sailing in the *Belgica*. This was the first expedition ever to spend the winter in Antarctica.

In 1903 Amundsen sailed into arctic waters with a crew of six in the *Gjöa*. Their voyage was the first to navigate the Northwest Passage.

He then planned to drift across the North Pole in Nansen's old ship, the *Fram*, but in 1909 he learned that Robert E. Peary (1856–1920) had reached the Pole. Amundsen continued with his preparations, but when he sailed from Norway in June 1910 only his brother knew that the expedition was heading south rather than north. The *Fram* anchored in the Bay of Whales, on the eastern side of the Ross Sea and close to the edge of the ice shelf, 60 miles (96.5 km) farther south than the Scott camp at Cape Evans. Amundsen began the trek to the Pole on October 19, 1911, accompanied by four men, 52 dogs, and four sledges, and arrived there on December 14. They left the Pole on December 17 and arrived back at their base on January 25, 1912. They were the first people to reach the South Pole.

The success of this expedition brought Amundsen enough money to set up a shipping business, and he built a new ship, the *Maud*, in which he planned to pursue his original plan of crossing the North Pole. He departed in 1918 and sailed the Northeast Passage to the Bering Strait, but there he was forced to abandon the voyage. Instead, he attempted to reach the North Pole by air. He and the American explorer Lincoln Ellsworth (1880–1951) came within 170 miles (273.5 km) of the Pole in 1925, and in 1926 Amundsen crossed the Pole with the Italian explorer Umberto Nobile (1885–1978) in the airship *Norge*, flying from Spitzbergen, Svalbard, to Alaska. The crossing led to a bitter dispute between Amundsen and Nobile over who should be credited with leading the expedition.

In May 1928 Nobile made a second flight in the opposite direction, this time without Amundsen, in the airship *Italia*. He crossed the Pole successfully but crashed at Spitzbergen. Nobile and his crew survived and a major international rescue operation was launched. Amundsen flew from Norway to join in the rescue, but his aircraft crashed into the sea on June 18 and Amundsen was killed.

adventurers, but centuries passed before a European set eyes on the city. The first to do so was a Scottish explorer, Alexander Gordon Laing (1793–1826), who traveled from Tripoli, Libya, was injured in a fight in Tuareg country (see "Peoples of the Sahara and Arabian Desert" on pages 134–136), and entered Timbuktu on August 18, 1826. He stayed there until September 24, then left heading north, but died on September 26, murdered by his guide. René-Auguste Caillé (1799–1838) was the first European to visit Timbuktu and return safely. This French explorer traveled from the West African coast and reached the city on April 20, 1828. He remained there for two weeks before heading north to Morocco and back to France.

Other travelers were exploring the Sahara at about this time. In 1823 a party led by Hugh Clapperton (1788–1827), a Scottish naval officer, reached Lake Chad and continued into what is now Northern Nigeria. The most important scientific study of North and Central Africa took place between 1850 and 1855. James Richardson (1806–51), an English explorer, Heinrich Barth (1821–65), a German geographer, and Adolf Overweg (1822–55), a German geologist and astronomer, traveled southwest from Tripoli into northern Nigeria and around Lake Chad. Richardson led the party, but he died in Nigeria and Barth took command. Overweg died in September 1852 and Barth continued alone, eventually reaching Timbuktu where he remained for six months before returning to Tripoli and from there to London, having covered approximately 10,000 miles (16,000 km). Barth was well equipped for the journey. An accomplished linguist, he spoke fluent Arabic, and he had thoroughly explored the North African coast before attempting to cross the desert.

The first European to study the Tuareg was a French explorer, Henri Duveyrier (1840–92). He met Barth, was inspired by him, and also learned to speak Arabic. He was only 19 years old when in 1859 he embarked on a three-year journey through the northern Sahara, spending much of the time living with the Tuareg. Friedrich Gerhard Rohlfs (1831–96) explored the Atlas Mountains and Morocco in 1862 disguised as an Arab, in 1864 he reached the Fezzan region of central Libya, and in 1865 he crossed the desert from Tripoli to northeastern Nigeria and traveled from there to the West African coast. In 1874 he crossed the Sahara again, this time from Tripoli to Egypt. This colorful German adventurer had joined the French Foreign Legion in 1855 and learned Arabic. In 1885 he was appointed German consul in Zanzibar.

Arabia was much less accessible than the Sahara. The first European expedition was sent by King Frederick V of Denmark and set out in 1762, led by a German surveyor, Carsten Niebuhr (1733–1815). That team explored the coast, but penetrated only a short distance inland. It was 1876 before the next serious attempt was made, this time by an English traveler, Charles Montagu Doughty (1843–1926). He wanted to visit Mecca. Although he never reached that city, he visited several inland towns in the mountainous region of Jabal Shammar and the port of Jidda, not far from Mecca.

The most famous European to be associated with Arabia was not an explorer at all, but an English scholar and soldier. T. E. Lawrence, who became known as Lawrence of Arabia (see the sidebar on pages 156–157), wore Arab dress, spoke fluent Arabic, and fought alongside Arab troops against Turkish forces in World War I. Lawrence was a truly romantic hero, who was not interested in money or social position.

It was Sir Wilfred Thesiger (1910–2003) who did more than anyone else to keep alive the romance of the desert during the latter years of the 20th century. This English soldier, travel writer, and photographer was born in Addis Ababa, Ethiopia, and lived there until he was nine years old. As an adult, he lived with the Bedouin, made several crossings of the Rub'al-Khali—the "Empty Quarter" of the Arabian Desert—and made a special study of the Marsh Arabs of southern Iraq. He also explored Afghanistan and Pakistan.

European exploration of the Asian deserts began in the late 19th century. The Swedish explorer Sven Anders Hedin (1865–1952) spent five years traveling over the Ural and Pamir Mountains, past Lop Nur, and to Beijing along the old Silk Road (see "Caravans and the Silk Road" on pages 138–140). The geographer and geologist Ferdinand Paul Wilhelm, Freiherr von Richthofen (1833–1905), who was

Lawrence of Arabia

Thomas Edward Lawrence (1888–1935) was born on August 15, 1888, at Tremadoc, Caernarfon, Wales. His family moved to Oxford in 1896, and Thomas attended school in that city and completed his education at Jesus College, University of Oxford. He visited Palestine and Syria in 1909 to study the architecture of crusader castles, which was the subject of a thesis he submitted the following year for his degree in modern history. Lawrence then joined several archaeological expeditions to the Middle East.

The last of these expeditions, early in 1914, was to Sinai, and its secondary purpose was to gain military intelligence about preparations for war on the Turkish side of the border with Egypt. Lawrence was still working in Sinai at the outbreak of World War I, but he later moved to the map department of the War Office in London. When Britain and France declared war on Turkey on November 5, 1914, Lawrence was attached to the intelligence staff in Egypt concerned with Arab affairs.

In October 1916 Lawrence accompanied the diplomat Ronald (later Sir Ronald) Storrs (1881–1955) to the Hejaz province of Arabia, where Husain ibn 'Ali, the emir of Mecca, had proclaimed a revolt against the Turks, who occupied parts of Arabia. Storrs held discussions with Husain's son Abdullah and then returned to Egypt, but Lawrence was permitted to visit Abdullah's brother, Faisal, who was leading an army near Medina. Lawrence returned to Cairo, but he was sent back to join Faisal's army as political and liaison officer.

For the remainder of the war Lawrence fought alongside the Arab army, encouraging the soldiers and planning many of its operations. He invariably wore Arab dress, and when Turkish forces captured him in November 1917 they did not know the identity of their prisoner. Lawrence escaped and took part in several other military operations. By the end

born in Upper Silesia (then in Prussia and now in Poland), traveled extensively through China and it was he who coined the name "Silk Road."

The explorer and archaeologist who did more than anyone to rediscover the route of the Silk Road was Sir Aurel Stein. Mark Aurel Stein (1862–1943) was born in Hungary, but he became a British citizen in 1904 and was knighted in 1912. In 1900, 1906, and 1913 Stein went on expeditions through the Xinjiang Uygur autonomous region of China that lasted a total of seven years. He followed the old caravan routes for about 25,000 miles (40,200 km), discovering the Jade Gate of the war Lawrence held the rank of lieutenant colonel and was highly decorated. He was a member of the British delegation to the Paris peace conference in 1919 and an adviser on Arab affairs at the Colonial Office in 1921 and 1922, but then he left government service. "Lawrence of Arabia" had become very famous and he began to write his account of the war.

In August 1922 Lawrence enlisted in the Royal Air Force (RAF), giving his name as John Hume Ross. A newspaper exposed him, however, and in January 1923 he was discharged. In March 1923, using the name T. E. Shaw, to which he changed his name legally in 1927, Lawrence enlisted in the Royal Tank Corps. He transferred to the RAF in 1925 and remained in service until his death on March 19, 1935, following a motorcycling accident.

As well as being a war hero, Lawrence was a distinguished classical scholar and also a skilled mechanic, who was keenly interested in aviation and designed a seagoing motorboat for the RAF. His popularity also rested on his renunciation of his army rank to enlist as an ordinary airman and soldier, his indifference to money, and his sense of fun—but he could be extremely rude to people he despised.

Lawrence published several books, the most famous being *Seven Pillars of Wisdom*. He wrote this over many years and to help with the printing costs in late 1926 he published 200 copies, each bound differently, of an abridged version. These books were sold by subscription but were so beautifully illustrated that they cost much more to produce than subscribers paid for them. To recover the costs Lawrence authorized publication of an even more abridged version called *Revolt in the Desert*. The subscribers' edition appeared in the summer of 1935, soon after Lawrence's death. This was so successful that it prevented publication of the full text, 200 pages longer than the abridged version, which finally appeared in 1997, 75 years after Lawrence finished writing it.

that once stood at the Chinese border and the walls built to prevent nomads from entering China. He carefully excavated ancient sites, discovering ancient cities and—his most famous discovery—the Cave of a Thousand Buddhas (see the sidebar on page 158). In one of the caves Stein found a hoard of approximately 60,000 paper manuscripts and other documents dating from the fifth to 11th centuries that had been walled up in 1015. Written in Chinese, Sanskrit, Tibetan, Uighur, and other languages, they included scriptures, stories, and ballads from Buddhist, Taoist, Zoroastrian, and Nestorian Christian traditions.

The Cave of a Thousand Buddhas

Dunhuang is a small oasis town in northwestern China, on the edge of the Gobi Desert and on the Silk Road. Buddhist monks traveled the Silk Road on their way to China from Central Asia and India, and monks and Buddhist disciples from different parts of Asia met at Dunhuang. Buddhist communities were established there in the third and fourth centuries.

In 366 C.E., a Buddhist monk carved himself a temple inside a cave, and other monks later added to his work until every corner was covered with pictures of the Buddha. It came to be known as "the Cave of a Thousand Buddhas."

In subsequent years Buddhists decorated other caves in the area. Today there are 492 decorated Caves of a Thousand Buddhas, containing religious paintings and sculptures. It is the largest ancient Buddhist site in China, known officially as the Mogao Caves.

The illustrations depict stories from the Buddhist sutras (sacred texts), representations of Buddhas, Boddhisattvas (individuals who have attained enlightenment but choose to continue helping and teaching others rather than enter Nirvana), and other religious figures, as well as portraits of people who have made important donations to the collections. Work on the caves continued until the 12th century, when the site fell into decline until it was rediscovered early in the 20th century.

In 1987 the area was designated a World Heritage Site by the United Nations Educational, Scientific, and Cultural Organization (UNESCO). Many of the caves are open to the public.

CHAPTER 7

DESERT INDUSTRIES

Oil and modern desert economies

Herodotus was a Greek historian who lived in the fifth century B.C.E. The exact years of his birth and death are not known, but what is known is that he was born in Halicarnassus, a Greek city on the Mediterranean coast of Asia Minor (modern Bodrum, Turkey) that was ruled by the Persians. Herodotus was a great admirer of the Persian Empire, and he was also a great traveler. He claimed to have walked the entire length of the Royal Road that ran for about 1,500 miles (2,413 km) from the city of Susa, in the country of Elam near the Zagros Mountains in what is now southwestern Iran, to the coast of the Aegean Sea. What is interesting about his walk is that Herodotus said the road was surfaced with asphalt. Wheeled vehicles, especially horse-drawn chariots, could move rapidly over a hard, smooth surface, and many Assyrian and Persian roads were surfaced in this way.

Asphalt is liquid when hot, but sets hard when it is cold, making it an ideal substance for surfacing roads. It may also have been used almost 6,000 years ago at Mohenjo Daro, in the Indus Valley, to seal the brick walls of a reservoir. In India it was called "earth butter." It was not difficult to obtain asphalt. There are many places where it oozes from the ground. It would be surprising if people had failed to notice that it sets hard when it cools and to conclude that this property might make it useful.

Also known as *pitch* and *bitumen,* asphalt is a petroleum product that remains as a residue after the lighter oils have evaporated. Asphalt was used as mortar, as cement for laying mosaic floors, and as an adhesive for setting jewels and attaching the handles of tools and weapons. Lighter oils were also used widely in the ancient world for lighting and for cleaning clothes. In the Arabic and Persian languages this oil is known as *naft* from which we derive our word *naphtha*.

Petroleum was especially abundant in the United States and in the desert lands of western Asia and Arabia. It was always a valuable natural product, but it was only in the 20th century that it came to dominate the world economy. As demand for oil increased, exploration intensified, and oil was discovered in places where it had not previously been known to exist. Oil was discovered in Libya in the 1950s, in Algeria, Tunisia, Oman, and Nigeria in the 1960s, and in Yemen in the 1980s. Nearly half of the world's known reserves of petroleum are located in the Middle East. North America has the next largest reserves, with approximately 14 percent of the total.

Oil has brought wealth to some desert lands but not to all of them. Economists measure the prosperity of a country by its *gross domestic product,* or GDP. This is the total value of all the goods and services produced in that country in a year, excluding income from investments overseas. The *per capita GDP* is the GDP divided by the size of the population. The per capita GDP does not represent average earnings, but it does make it possible to compare countries of different sizes. The resulting figure is nevertheless misleading, however, because currencies are sometimes overvalued or undervalued in relation to one another. To resolve this, the per capita GDP is often converted to its *purchasing power parity* (PPP) in U.S. dollars. This figure is obtained by spending a given amount of local money on a range of everyday items, such as groceries, rent, and transportation, then finding out what the same goods and services would cost in U.S. dollars. The table on page 161 shows comparable figures for a selection of desert countries, although the PPP is not known for all of them.

The table lists desert countries in descending order of wealth and shows that most oil-producing countries are much richer than countries without oil. The apparently huge discrepancies between the per capita GDP of the United Arab Emirates (UAE), Kuwait, and Qatar and those of the other countries are due mainly to the small size of their populations—3.1 million in the UAE, 2.2 million in Kuwait, and 0.5 million in Qatar. In contrast, the population of Tunisia is 9.7 million. Comparing a country such as Tunisia, which has oil,

Per capita GDP and purchasing power[+]

Country	Per capita GDP (US$)	PPP (US$)
United States	31,910	31,910
Kuwait*	22,110	(not known)
United Arab Emirates*	17,870	(not known)
Qatar*	11,600	(not known)
Bahrain*	7,640	(not known)
Saudi Arabia*	6,900	11,050
Libya*	6,700	(not known)
Mexico*	4,440	8,070
Tunisia*	2,090	5,700
Iran*	1,810	5,520
Jordan	1,630	3,880
Algeria*	1,550	4,840
Egypt	1,380	3,460
Morocco	1,190	3,320
Mongolia	390	1,610
Mauritania	390	1,550
Yemen*	360	730
Nigeria*	260	770
Mali*	240	740
Chad	210	840
Niger	190	740
Ethiopia	100	620

(*oil-producing countries)
[+]figures are for 1999

with one such as Chad, which does not, demonstrates just how economically important oil is to some desert nations.

Solar energy

Not every desert country possesses oil reserves, but there are two things that all the subtropical deserts have in abundance: warm sunshine and empty space. If they can capture the sunshine and put it to work, perhaps their economies will be able to develop without being hindered by the cost of imported fuel.

Some of the devices needed to capture solar energy are familiar and widely used. Solar panels, solar cells, and wind turbines are the best known. *Wind turbines* are driven by the wind, of course, but it is solar energy that produces the differences in air pressure that generate winds, so wind power is derived from solar energy.

Deserts are windy places and therefore suitable for *wind farms*. Wind farms must be large if they are to produce useful amounts of energy, but deserts can provide the space they need.

Unfortunately, wind power is unreliable because, even in the desert, there are times when the wind is too weak to set the blades turning or too fierce, so they have to be shut down to protect them from damage. In practice, a wind turbine spins for less than 40 percent of the time.

Solar panels absorb solar heat and use it to provide hot water or central heating. Their usefulness is limited in high latitudes, where the sunshine is weak for much of the year, but they are very useful in subtropical deserts, where people need hot water and central heating might be welcome on cold desert nights.

Solar cells convert sunlight directly into electricity. They absorb light, not heat, so they work just as well in winter as in summer, but of course they work only during the hours of daylight. If they are to be useful, therefore, they need to generate surplus electricity during the day that can be stored in batteries to provide a supply through the night. Power generated in this way is not cheap, because the cells are made from costly materials and are not very efficient, which means that a large number are required. The price is falling, however. One day it should be possible in desert countries to fit solar panels and cells to commercial premises, apartment buildings, and small factories with low power requirements, making them self-sufficient in solar-heated water and giving enough electrical power to cook and operate electronic equipment.

Solar ponds also use sunshine to heat water, but they do so on a bigger scale than solar panels. A solar pond exploits the fact that salt water is denser than freshwater and the two do not mix readily. The pond has a large surface area and is usually several feet deep. Its bottom and sides are lined with black plastic to absorb radiant heat, and the pond is partly filled with water saturated with salt. Freshwater is then poured in very carefully to form a layer that floats above the denser salt water. Heat from the Sun passes through the water and is absorbed by the plastic. As the temperature of the plastic rises, the salt water in contact with it grows warmer. Convection currents then transport heat throughout the salt water, but they do not penetrate the overlying layer of freshwater, so there is nowhere for the heat to escape. When the temperature reaches approximately 200°F (93°C) salt water is piped to a heat exchanger in a tank of freshwater. It warms the freshwater and then returns to the pond. The freshwater layer has to be replenished from time to time to replace water lost by evaporation, but evaporation losses can be greatly reduced by covering the entire pond with transparent plastic. Warm water from a solar pond can be fed into industrial boilers to raise steam to drive generating turbines, greatly reducing the amount of fuel needed to boil it.

It is possible to use solar heat to generate much higher temperatures using a *solar furnace.* A large, flat mirror called a *heliostat,* driven by a computer-controlled motor, tracks the Sun across the sky, reflecting its image—and also its radiant heat—onto a parabolic mirror. The parabolic mirror reflects the heat to a focal point where there is a target. The arrangement is just like the reflector dish and aerial used to receive satellite TV, only much bigger. The parabolic mirror concentrates the heat, producing temperatures high enough to melt steel. There are experimental solar furnaces in many countries that receive abundant sunshine, but the world's largest is at Odeillo, France. It generates temperatures up to more than 12,600°F (7,000°C).

A *solar chimney* combines the principles of the solar panel and the wind turbine by absorbing solar heat and using it to warm air that spins a generating turbine (see the sidebar on page 164). The structure itself is extremely large and therefore both costly and technologically challenging, but its operating costs are low, and in years to come solar chimneys might provide desert countries with plentiful cheap electricity.

Minerals, metals, and textiles

Economists describe mining and quarrying for industrial minerals and metallic ores as a *primary industry.* A primary industry performs only the first stage in the series of processes culminating in manufactured goods. Each of those stages

Solar chimney

The most ambitious scheme for converting sunshine into electrical power uses air warmed by solar energy to drive several turbines fitted inside a vertical cylinder that is open at both ends. The device looks like a chimney and, like a chimney, it removes warm air. Unlike an ordinary chimney, however, it extracts energy from the rising air.

A circular, transparent roof made from glass or plastic covers a large area of ground. The roof rises gently from the edge, so that the center is higher than the circumference. A cylinder rises vertically from the center of the covered area.

Sunlight warms the air below the transparent roof. The warm air rises up the slope of the underside of the roof and then flows up the chimney, accelerating all the time, and more air is drawn in at ground level to replace it. As it rises up the chimney, the air spins a turbine that generates electrical power.

A solar chimney works throughout the night as well as during the day, because during the night the ground radiates the warmth it absorbed by day, thus warming the air. In some designs, black plastic tubes filled with water cover the ground to enhance this effect. The black plastic absorbs solar heat during the day, heating the water inside the tubes, and the water releases its warmth at night.

In order to work, a solar chimney needs to be very large indeed. An experimental prototype built in 1983 at Manzanares, Spain, worked successfully for several years. Its chimney was 640 feet (195 m) tall and its roof covered an area of about 486,000 square feet (45,250 m²). An operational solar chimney would be at least 3,000 feet (1 km) tall and its roof would cover approximately 40 square miles (104 km²). There are proposals to build solar chimneys in India, South Africa, Australia, and elsewhere. Constructing a chimney as tall as this and a "greenhouse" covering such a large area will be highly challenging from an engineering point of view.

Solar chimneys are very costly to build, because of their size, but their running costs are low, their "fuel" is free, and their lifetimes are very long, so they might generate electricity cheaply. They are not very efficient, however, extracting no more than three percent of the solar energy falling on them. Efficiency can be improved by making the chimney taller to reduce the air pressure at the top, and by increasing the covered area, which increases the air pressure at the bottom of the chimney. Refinements to the design could also reduce energy losses considerably and make solar chimneys much more efficient.

adds to the value of the commodity being processed, and it follows that its value is least at the initial stage of being extracted from the ground. Consequently, primary industries produce large quantities of cheap raw materials. Few nations that depend economically on primary industries are wealthy. In order to increase national prosperity, governments aim to perform as much of the processing and manufacturing as possible within their own borders, so that the added value accrues to local people.

Mineral resources are not distributed evenly. The table below lists desert countries that exploit mineral resources, with the approximate yearly value of their output of metals and nonmetals, in U.S. dollars.

It is not easy to separate figures for metals and nonmetals because countries do not all measure them in the same way. Consequently, for most countries the two are combined, but Bahrain and Libya produce only nonmetals. Some countries, including Chad, Mongolia, and Western Sahara, possess neither oil nor minerals.

Merging the data for metals and nonmetals hides the richness of some of the African reserves. Tunisia has some of the

Mineral output in desert countries (millions of U.S. $ per year)

Country	Metals	Nonmetals	Not differentiated
Bahrain		12.6	
Egypt			51.5
Eritrea			0.5
Ethiopia			54.2
Iran			1,223.2
Jordan			239.3
Libya		599.4	
Mali			81.7
Mauritania			105.9
Morocco			746.5
Namibia			382.8
Niger			62.5
Nigeria			168.6
Oman			44.6
Saudi Arabia			597.9
Sudan			27.4
Tunisia			249.0

(Source: *Britannica Book of the Year, 2005*. Chicago: Encyclopaedia Britannica, Inc.)

largest reserves of phosphate rock in Africa. Phosphate rock is used to make industrial chemicals and fertilizer, which Tunisia exports. Morocco has ores of copper, iron, lead, manganese, and zinc, as well as common salt. Mauritania has ores of copper and titanium, as well as phosphate rock and gypsum. Libya has iron, manganese, and gypsum. Niger is one of the world's most important producers of uranium, and it also possesses high-quality iron ore.

Reserves may exist without being exploited. Mali has copper, iron, manganese, nickel, and bauxite—the most common aluminum ore—but gold is the only metal it exports. Minerals may be located in places that are too remote to be exploited economically. This is because the cost of transport forms a significant proportion of the overall cost; the farther the minerals travel, the higher their price will be. In a highly competitive market, remoteness can make them too expensive. The reserves may also be in places where access is difficult. This also increases the cost of bringing in the heavy machinery used in mining and quarrying and taking out the heavy, bulky rock that is the mineral product.

Desert peoples have always raised sheep and goats. These are kept partly to supply milk and meat, but they also produce wool, and many of the world's finest cloths and carpets are made in desert countries. Iran (formerly Persia), Afghanistan, Turkey, and Bukhara are among the places famous for their carpets.

Carpets are woven or made by knotting colored threads to a woven base. Both techniques, and the resulting products, are well suited to people leading a nomadic life. Looms are easily dismantled and assembled again, wool and dyeing materials are easy to carry, and decorated carpets can transform a tent into a splendid dwelling. In the 16th century European explorers and merchants—often the same individuals—recognized the potential market for Asian carpets and the export trade began. Only the wealthy could afford them and they were much too expensive to be laid on floors. Instead, their owners hung them on walls or over balconies or laid them across chests and tables. They displayed them without risking damage to them.

Persian carpet making reached its peak in the 15th and 16th centuries, and Persian designs and techniques influenced carpet makers in neighboring countries, especially those in Egypt, Turkey, and the Caucasus. Caucasian carpets are still made and exported by nomadic peoples living near the Caspian Sea.

Bokhara, also called Bukhara or Buxoro, is the principal city in Buxoro, province of Uzbekistan, but although it gives its name to Bokhara carpets it is not the place where they are made. Bokhara carpets are made over a wide area of Turkistan. Turkistan is not a country, but an area of more than 1 million square miles (2.6 million km²) in Central Asia bounded by Siberia, Tibet, Afghanistan, India, and Iran. Its name refers to its people, who are Turkic nomads.

The finest woolen garments are made from cashmere, which is a fine soft wool obtained from the Kashmir breed of goats. Iran and Turkey produce some cashmere wool, but most comes from China, Mongolia, and Iran. Only a small amount of cashmere wool is produced, because a Kashmir goat yields no more than one pound (0.5 kg) of wool a year. The demand for it is high, and consequently cashmere is very expensive.

Cashmere was first used to make shawls, which became very fashionable in the late 19th century. Early in the 20th century European factories began making imitation cashmere shawls. These were attractive and much cheaper than the real thing but of poorer quality. Today cashmere is made into sweaters, suits, dresses, and overcoats.

Traditional carpets and garments are luxury items that command high prices, but the supply is limited, and that restricts the contribution their production can make to national economies. Their manufacture can be industrialized, but while increasing the output does not necessarily imply reducing the quality of the product, increasing the supply inevitably lowers the price and, with it, the perceived value. People might come to think the factory-made carpets and garments were only slightly better than equivalent goods made closer to home and sold at lower prices.

Tourism

Deserts are romantic places, full of legends and mystery. They contain ancient cities with magical names such as Timbuktu and Petra—a once-important city that now lies in ruins and abandoned, except by the busloads of tourists that travel to visit it. When Europeans with an adventurous spirit began to travel to new places in the 19th century, the deserts of North Africa and the Middle East attracted them strongly. People today want to vacation in desert lands, so it is no surprise that tourism makes an important contribution to desert economies.

Egypt and North Africa are easily accessible from North American and European airports. Tourists visit Egypt to see the Pyramids, the Sphinx, the Nile, and ancient temples, and while they are in the country they can try riding a camel and explore desert culture. As the table on page 170 shows, tourism earns Egypt $4.3 billion a year.

Visitors to North Africa can examine archaeological remains from the time when this region formed part of the Roman Empire. They can visit the site of Carthage, now a suburb of Tunis, and ports that were built by the Phoenicians. Tunisia earns almost $1.5 billion a year from tourism, and Libya earns $24 million—a figure that is likely to increase in years to come.

Not every country benefits from tourism, however, and the list of tourist destinations could be lengthened. Yemen earns $64 million a year from visitors, but part of Yemen was once the kingdom of Sheba, a fact that might attract more people than it does. Frankincense, the plant resin used in incense, was once exported throughout the Middle East and Mediterranean region from Oman, a country that has been inhabited for at least 10,000 years and that was once the center of an empire extending through much of East Africa. Tourism brings in $120 million a year, but it might bring in more.

Three of the world's major religions originated in the Near East and Arabia, and many of the visitors are pilgrims traveling to sites of religious importance. Pilgrimage is especially important in Saudi Arabia, Israel, and Palestine and might increase if conflicts in the region were resolved.

Now that the more adventurous and wealthy tourists have explored the more accessible parts of the world, they are beginning to look farther afield. It is possible to travel part of the Silk Road (see pages 138–140), with stops at Tashkent, Samarqand, and Bukhara. Mongolia welcomes tourists, offering them the opportunity to meet the descendants of the famed Mongol warriors of old, to join in traditional festivities, and to visit a traditional nomad camp and enter a ger (see "Peoples of the Asian deserts" on pages 136–138).

Polar deserts also attract visitors. Antarctica is extremely remote, but cruise ships visit the Antarctic Peninsula each year, allowing passengers to see icebergs and ice cliffs and enjoy time ashore. The Antarctic Heritage Trust is trying to raise funds to restore huts that were erected and occupied by famous explorers, such as Scott and Amundsen, and that would provide an additional attraction for visitors. In 2001–02 more than 11,500 tourists landed on Antarctica.

Greenland has magnificent scenery and a national park covering 289,500 square miles (750,000 km^2) in the northeast of the country. The number of visitors is controlled, but it increases each year. In 2003 Greenland had 29,712 tourists. The number may seem small, but in January 2004 the population of Greenland was 56,854, so the country receives a large number of tourists in relation to the size of its population.

Tourism brings in foreign currency, but the improvements in travel facilities that make it possible work both ways: They also allow citizens of the tourist destinations to become tourists in their own right, and when they travel they spend money abroad. This means that the income from tourism is partly offset by the money tourism takes out of a country and by the cost of providing facilities for visitors. When account is taken of both figures, the profitability of tourism may be greatly reduced or even reversed. Yemen earns $64 million a year from tourism but loses $83 million a year, and Nigeria earns $200 million but loses $730 million. Mexico has one of the biggest tourist industries. Each year it earns $8.3 billion, mainly from visitors from the United States, but it loses $5.5 billion.

There is a further disadvantage, in that tourism tends to provide low-paid, seasonal jobs, many of them unskilled. If their economies are to develop, the desert nations need modern industries that require highly skilled workers, and educational and training institutions to supply them.

Tourism in desert countries
(million U.S. $ per year)

Country	Income from visitors*	Expenditure*
Algeria	133 (2002)	193 (2000)
Bahrain	741 (2002)	378 (2002)
Burkina Faso	39 (2002)	23 (1994)
Chad	23 (2001)	56 (2001)
Djibouti	4 (1998)	4 (1998)
Egypt	764 (2002)	1,278 (2002)
Eritrea	73 (2002)	—
Ethiopia	77 (2002)	45 (2002)
Iran	1,249 (2002)	2,514 (2002)
Jordan	786 (2002)	416 (2002)
Kuwait	119 (2002)	3,021 (2002)
Libya	75 (2002)	548 (2002)
Mali	71 (2000)	41 (2000)
Mauritania	28 (1999)	55 (1999)
Mexico	8,858 (2002)	6,060 (2002)
Mongolia	167 (2002)	119 (2002)
Morocco	2,046 (2002)	444 (2002)
Namibia	219 (2002)	56 (2002)
Niger	28 (2002)	16 (2002)
Nigeria	263 (2002)	950 (2002)
Oman	242 (2002)	771 (2002)
Qatar	not available	not available
Saudi Arabia	3,420 (2002)	7,356 (2002)
Sudan	62 (2002)	91 (2002)
Syria	1,366 (2002)	610 (2002)
Tunisia	1,422 (2002)	260 (2002)
United Arab Emirates	1,328 (2002)	not available
Yemen	38 (2002)	78 (2002)

*The figure in parentheses is the year to which the amount refers.
(Source: *Britannica Book of the Year, 2005*. Chicago: Encyclopaedia Britannica, Inc.)

CHAPTER 8

THREATS TO DESERTS

Depleting the water below ground

Deserts are dry places where people learn to use water very carefully. Despite their traditional thriftiness, as the populations of desert nations increase so, inevitably, does their demand for water. People need only a small amount of water for drinking, cooking, washing, and hygiene. They need very much more to grow food, and in North Africa and the Middle East crop irrigation accounts for 90 percent of all the water used. It requires about 1,500 tons of water to produce one ton of wheat grain. Industry also uses water. Some, known as *process water,* is incorporated into products and much more is used for cooling. Cooling water is returned to the system, but each time it is used, a proportion is lost by evaporation.

Over the world as a whole, the average amount of water available annually to each person for all uses, including agriculture and industry, is approximately 18,500 gallons (70,000 l), but it is not distributed evenly. In North Africa and the Middle East each person has little more than one-sixth of the global average—an annual 3,200 gallons (12,000 l)—and even that is an average figure that conceals a wide disparity. People in Iran have an average 4,755 gallons (18,000 l) a year, but those living in Jordan and Yemen have less than 530 gallons (2,000 l). The situation is deteriorating. Experts fear that by 2025 the average amount of water available annually to each person throughout the region may be little more than 1,300 gallons (4,900 l).

People take water from rivers, but those living far from any river use wells (see "Wells and oases" on pages 47–50). Wells take water from below ground and in many deserts, especially the Sahara, there is a very large amount of groundwater.

Saharan groundwater is of three types. There are *alluvial aquifers*—reserves lying close to the surface that are filled by water from major rivers, such as the Nile. Along the Mediterranean coast, where the climate is wetter, there are *coastal aquifers* that are filled by rainwater (see "What happens when it rains" on pages 45–47).

Alluvial and coastal aquifers are recharged from rivers and rainfall, respectively, but increased demand for water has raised fears that water is being removed from them faster than it is replenished. In Egypt, water is being removed four times faster than Nile water is entering the aquifer to recharge it, and water is being removed from the coastal aquifer in Libya five times faster than the aquifer is being recharged. There is a risk that some years from now regions dependent on the coastal and alluvial aquifers may face shortages of water unless they find alternative sources such as desalination (see pages 205–207).

By far the biggest aquifer, however, is the *Nubian Sandstone Aquifer* (NSA), which is estimated to hold 89,500 cubic miles (373,000 km³) of water. The NSA covers approximately 770,000 square miles (2 million km²) beneath Egypt, Sudan, Chad, and Libya, and it adjoins the *Continental Intercalaire* aquifer, extending over 48,250 square miles (125,000 km²) from southwestern Algeria to central Libya.

Both the NSA and Continental Intercalaire aquifer contain water they accumulated long ago. Scientists have calculated, for example, that the Continental Intercalaire was intensively recharged between 45,000 and 23,500 years ago but has received little water since. Water in the NSA is much more ancient. These are aquifers holding "fossil" water, and water that is taken from them is not replenished.

Water is being removed from the North African deep aquifers at an estimated rate of 210 gallons (795 l) every second. This rate has increased steadily over the years and is now more than six times what it was in 1950. Abstraction lowers the water table in the vicinity of the well, and the water table is now 65–130 feet (20–40 m) lower than it was in 1950—but only in the area around each well. No one knows whether the water table is falling elsewhere, but the time may come when it is too expensive to deepen the wells sufficiently to maintain the supply of water for irrigation.

People living in and close to the North American deserts are also increasingly concerned about the reliability of their water supply. In the future they may need to increase their reliance on desalination. Other deserts, such as the Namib, Atacama, and Taklimakan, are too dry to support agriculture of any kind, and no one lives in them.

Waterlogging and salination

Ironically, in some areas where farmland is heavily irrigated, the water tables are rising. That is what can happen when the irrigation system is inefficient.

Irrigation water should soak downward at a rate of 0.1–3 inches (2.5–75 mm) per hour. At this rate plant roots are able to absorb the moisture they need, and if irrigation continues over a 24-hour period the soil should be moistened to a depth of two to three feet (60–90 cm). If the water is applied too slowly, much of it will evaporate and be lost before reaching the roots. If it is applied too quickly on a very permeable soil, such as sand or desert gravel (see the sidebar on page 174), much of it will pass straight through the soil and enter the groundwater. Again it will be lost to the plants.

When the water drains away too quickly the soil dries and the crop wilts for lack of water, and so the farmer increases the rate of irrigation. This is unlikely to help, however, and it may make matters worse if the irrigation system pours water through the soil faster than the groundwater flow can remove it. That is when the water table starts to rise. In parts of Egypt and Morocco the water table is rising at up to 10 feet (3 m) a year, and water tables are also rising, though not so fast, in some places in Ethiopia, India, China, and Australia.

No one may notice that the water table is rising, but if it continues to rise it may reach the roots of crop plants. Soil at the surface will still be dry and crops will grow more slowly or even die, but the problem is not too little water, but too much. Soil around the roots is saturated with water and the roots are unable to take in oxygen. Despite the dry

Porosity and permeability

When soil particles pack together, their irregular shapes mean there are small spaces between them. These spaces are called *soil pores,* and the total percentage of the space they occupy—the *pore space*—in a given volume of soil is known as the *porosity* of that soil.

The size and shape of soil particles determines the size of the soil pores, but without necessarily affecting the total amount of pore space. Sand grains are relatively large and usually very angular in shape. They do not fit together neatly, and consequently sand and sandy soils have large pores. Clay, on the other hand, consists of microscopically small, flat-sided particles that lie in sheets, stacked one on top of another with extremely small pores between them. But the difference in size of the particles means that the total pore space may be similar for both soils. In that case, both soils are equally porous.

They are not equally water permeable, however. *Permeability* is a measure of the speed with which water or air is able to move through a soil. Air does not stick to soil particles, so the air-permeability of a soil depends only on the total pore space. Water does stick to soil particles, however, coating each particle with a film approximately one molecule thick that is tightly bound to the surface. If the soil pores are very small the water adhering to particles may reduce their size even more, slowing the movement of water through the soil and therefore reducing the permeability of the soil.

Permeability is classified by the rate at which water moves through the soil. The usual classification is given in the following table.

Class	Rate of movement (inches per hour)	(millimeters per hour)
Slow:		
Very slow	less than 0.05	less than 1.25
Slow	0.05–0.20	1.25–5.08
Moderate:		
Moderately slow	0.20–0.80	5.08–20.32
Moderate	0.80–2.50	20.32–63.50
Moderately rapid	2.50–5.00	63.50–127.00
Rapid:		
Rapid	5.00–10.00	127.00–254.00
Very rapid	more than 10.00	more than 254.00

appearance of the soil, the plants are drowning. This is the effect of *waterlogging* and it can be caused by leaks in the channels and pipes carrying irrigation water.

Irrigation water does not need to be fit for people to drink. It contains a variety of mineral salts, including common salt (sodium chloride), and as it drains through the soil more salts present in the soil dissolve into it. As water evaporates from the soil above the water table, more water is drawn upward to replace it, moving through the pores between soil particles. This water also evaporates, and when water evaporates any substances dissolved in it are left behind, because only pure water enters the air as water vapor. Salt water moves upward, evaporates, and the salts it leaves behind accumulate, making the soil progressively saltier. Each time more water passes through the soil, the salts dissolve in it, and consequently the water above the water table also grows steadily saltier. This is called *salination*.

Water and molecules of nutrients can pass through the walls of plant cells by a process called *osmosis*. If the solution—chemical compounds dissolved in water—is stronger on one side of the cell wall than on the other, water will pass through the wall from the weaker to the stronger solution until the two are at the same strength. If the water surrounding the roots of a plant is saltier than the water inside the roots, water will flow out of the roots by osmosis. This will make the plant wilt and eventually it will die. Salination renders the soil infertile. Plants will not grow in it.

The remedy for waterlogging is to drain off the surplus water. Curing salination is more difficult, more costly, and takes much longer. Water must be poured onto the land and removed by good drains to wash out the salts—taking care that the water does not pollute the groundwater or rivers.

Prevention is better than cure. It involves installing good drainage as part of the irrigation system. Because this increases the cost of the installation, it is tempting to cut corners and rely on natural drainage. That is why both waterlogging and salination are now widespread.

What climate change may mean for deserts

Leave a cup of hot coffee standing on a table and before long it will be cold. The coffee will lose some of its heat in the form of radiation—the warmth you feel when you hold out your hands to a fire. A minute or so in a microwave oven will warm the coffee again. The coffee will absorb microwave radiation and convert it to heat. An object that absorbs all of the radiation falling upon it and then radiates away all the energy it absorbed is known as a *blackbody* and the radiation it emits is *blackbody radiation.*

The Earth is a rather inefficient black body. It absorbs about half of the radiation it receives from the Sun. This warms the surface, and the warm surface then radiates the heat back into space. Radiation travels in waves. The distance between one wave crest and the next is the *wavelength* of the radiation, and the shorter the wavelength the more energy the radiation possesses. The wavelength of blackbody radiation is inversely proportional to the temperature of the black body—the hotter the body, the shorter the wavelength of its radiation. The Sun, which is hot, radiates most intensely at short wavelengths. The Earth, which is much cooler, emits long-wave radiation.

During the day, the Earth absorbs shortwave radiation from the Sun and emits long-wave radiation, but it absorbs radiation faster than it loses it. Consequently, the surface grows steadily warmer. By late afternoon the sunshine has become less intense and the Earth starts to lose radiation faster than it absorbs it. This continues through the night, and the Earth cools, but about an hour before dawn the cooling ceases and the surface begins to absorb radiation from the rising Sun.

On the Moon, which is the same distance as Earth from the Sun, nights are extremely cold and days extremely hot. At noon the average temperature is 230°F (110°C) and by the end of the night the temperature has fallen to –274°F (–170°C). It is the Earth's oceans and atmosphere that prevent temperatures from rising and plummeting as they do on the Moon. The oceans absorb heat and release it very slowly, making summers cooler and winters warmer than they would be on a dry planet, and the atmosphere delays the departure of outgoing radiation. This delay occurs because certain gases, especially water vapor but also carbon dioxide, methane, ozone, and some others, absorb long-wave radiation. The gases then radiate the energy they have absorbed, but during the time it remains trapped in the air, the air temperature is held higher than it would be otherwise. If the air contained none of these gases the average temperature over the whole world would be about −0.4°F (−18°C). The actual average temperature is 59°F (15°C). The warming of the air through the absorption of long-wave radiation is known as the *greenhouse effect* and the gases involved are *greenhouse gases.*

Clearly, without the natural greenhouse effect life on Earth would be very uncomfortable. For one thing, outside the Tropics the lakes and seas would be frozen over all year long. We need the greenhouse effect, but for the last few decades we have been increasing it by releasing greenhouse gases, especially carbon dioxide. The enhanced greenhouse effect is making the average temperature rise, and in years to come the resulting global warming may affect deserts.

There are many uncertainties about the extent of global warming and therefore about its consequences, but the most likely estimate is that by the year 2100 the average temperature will have increased by approximately 2.7°F (1.5°C). The warming is not spread evenly. Most of it is taking place to the north of latitude 30°N, and it is most marked during winter in northwestern North America and northeastern Siberia.

A rise in temperature of 2.7°F (1.5°C) will produce an increase in rainfall, but in middle latitudes probably it will also bring longer periods of settled weather, both wet and dry. The continental deserts, such as the Gobi, may become moister, as may the Northern and Western Sahara. If so, the combination of increased rainfall, slightly warmer temperatures, and increased carbon dioxide—which encourages plant growth—may make it possible to farm areas that are presently too dry and cold for growing crops.

The Asian summer monsoon may become more intense. This could bring rain to the Thar Desert, increasing the amount of vegetation growing there.

In North America, the Sonoran Desert may decrease in area due to increased rainfall, but the Mojave Desert, lying in a rain shadow (see "Deserts of continental interiors" on pages 13–16), is less likely to change. The very dry Atacama Desert will continue to receive air that has crossed the South American continent, and air reaching it from the ocean will continue to cross the cold Peru Current. The Atacama climate is likely to remain unchanged. The Namib Desert, in Africa, is also likely to remain dry, for the same reason. The Australian deserts may shrink a little as the southeasterly trade winds bring rather more rain across the northern part of the country.

Many uncertainties surround the entire issue of global warming, but it seems increasingly probable that the effects during the 21st century will be fairly small. Those effects are likely to include a reduction in the total area of the world's deserts. Deserts will become slightly smaller. This will benefit desert peoples and those living along the semiarid desert edges.

Natural climate cycles

Climates change naturally over periods of decades. There were fears in the 1970s that prolonged drought immediately to the south of the Sahara, in the region called the Sahel, meant that

El Niño

At intervals of between two and seven years, the weather changes across much of the Tropics, and especially in southern Asia and western South America. The weather is drier than usual in Indonesia, Papua New Guinea, eastern Australia, northeastern South America, the Horn of Africa, East Africa and Madagascar, and in the northern part of the Indian subcontinent. It is wetter than usual over the central and eastern tropical Pacific, parts of California and the southeastern United States, eastern Argentina, central Africa, southern India, and Sri Lanka. The phenomenon has been occurring for at least 5,000 years, and there is evidence of it happening 350,000 years ago.

The change is greatest at around Christmas—midsummer in the Southern Hemisphere, of course. That is how it earned its name of *El Niño,* "the boy," specifically the Christ child, in Peru, where its effects are most dramatic. Ordinarily, the western coastal regions of South America have one of the driest climates in the world, but El Niño brings heavy rain. Farm crops flourish, so the Christmas gift of rain means there will be a good harvest. Nowadays, however, many communities rely on fishing and during an El Niño the fish disappear.

Most of the time, the prevailing low-level winds on either side of the equator are the trade winds, blowing from the northeast in the Northern Hemisphere and from the southeast in the Southern Hemisphere. At high altitudes, the winds flow in the opposite direction, from west to east. Air pressure is usually low over the western side of the Pacific, near the desert was advancing. The seasonal summer rains began to fail in the 1960s, and the drought was at its most severe between 1968 and 1973. By the middle of the 1970s, when the outside world began to take note of events in this remote region, approximately 200,000 people and 4 million livestock had starved to death. The tragedy was on such a huge scale that it was easy to believe the Sahara was advancing southward. The drought came to an end, however, and with the return of the rains in the 1980s the vegetation recovered.

Unusual weather in a single year is sometimes associated with a change in the winds and ocean currents in the equatorial South Pacific. The effects of the change usually become apparent in December, and the event is known as *El Niño,* Spanish for "the (boy) child" (see the sidebar starting on page 178).

Indonesia, and high on the eastern side, near South America. This pressure distribution helps drive the trade winds, and the trade winds drive the Equatorial Current, which flows from east to west, carrying warm surface water toward Indonesia, where it accumulates in a *warm pool.* Cool water flows northward parallel to the South American coast as the Peru Current, with many upwellings that bring nutrients close to the surface where they sustain large shoals of fish.

In some years, however, the pressure distribution changes. Pressure rises over the western Pacific and weakens in the east. The trade winds then slacken. They may cease to blow altogether or even reverse direction, so they blow from west to east instead of east to west. This causes the Equatorial Current to weaken or reverse direction. Water then begins to flow out of the warm pool, moving eastward, and the depth of warm water increases off the South American coast, suppressing the upwelling cold water in the Peru Current. Air moving toward South America is warmed and collects a great deal of moisture as it passes over this warm water, bringing heavy rain to the coastal region. This is an El Niño.

In other years the low pressure deepens in the west and the high pressure in the east rises. This accelerates the trade winds and Equatorial Current, increasing the rainfall over southern Asia and the dry conditions along the South American coast. This is called *La Niña.*

The periodic change in pressure distribution is known as the *Southern Oscillation* and the complete cycle is an *El Niño-Southern Oscillation* (ENSO) event.

During the 1990s, northwestern Europe enjoyed a series of mild winters, but in eastern North America many of the winters were unusually severe. This weather pattern resulted from the *North Atlantic Oscillation* (NAO). A region of low atmospheric pressure is semipermanently centered over Iceland, and there is a region of high pressure centered over the Azores (which lie about 800 miles (1,290 km) west of Portugal), sometimes extending to the Caribbean. These are known respectively as the *Icelandic low* and *Azores* (or *Bermuda*) *high*. Air circulates counterclockwise around areas of low pressure and clockwise around areas of high pressure, so between them the Icelandic low and Azores high produce a flow of air from west to east across the North Atlantic. When the difference in pressure is large—pressure is very low over Iceland and high over the Azores—the NAO is said to be high, and when the difference in pressure is small the NAO is said to be low. A high NAO produces mild winters in western Europe and cold winters in eastern North America.

A similar oscillation affects the North Pacific. It is known as the *Pacific Decadal Oscillation* (PDO) and produces alternating warm and cold weather over periods lasting several decades. Scientists now believe that the NAO and PDO are linked to changes in the distribution of pressure over the North Pole and a circle at about 55°N, known as the *Arctic Oscillation.* All three oscillations together produce the *Northern Hemisphere Annular Mode* (*annular* means "ringlike," referring to the fact that the weather patterns circle the globe).

These changes affect the weather over years or tens of years, but there are also changes that happen over longer periods. Average temperatures in many parts of the world, in both the Northern and Southern Hemispheres, began to increase between 600 C.E. and 800 C.E., reaching a peak between 1100 C.E. and 1300 C.E., when some places were warmer than they are today. This was the Medieval Warm Period. It was followed some centuries later by the Little Ice Age, a time of colder weather that lasted from about 1600 until 1850.

The coldest part of the Little Ice Age, from 1645 until 1715, coincided with a time when there were very few sunspots or auroras. Sunspots are dark patches on the surface of the Sun caused by intense magnetic fields. They are strongly linked to the intensity of the *solar wind*—a stream of subatomic particles that pours outward from the Sun. Solar-wind particles cause auroras when they reach the Earth, and the intensity of the solar wind affects the formation of clouds. The stronger the solar wind, the fewer clouds form. Edward Walter Maunder (1851–1928), an English solar astronomer, was the first person to identify this period, and it is known as the *Maunder Minimum.* There have been other minima, before and since the Maunder Minimum, and all of them coincide with periods of cool weather. There have also been sunspot maxima, which coincide with warm weather.

The biggest climatic changes of all are those between an ice age and one of the *interglacials* that occur between one ice age and the next. At present we live in an interglacial called the Holocene, which began approximately 10,000 years ago at the end of the most recent ice age, known as the Wisconsinian. The Wisconsinian was the fourth ice age to affect North America in the last 800,000 years. Their dates and names, together with the dates and names of the interglacials, are listed in the table below.

Scientists believe that the onset and ending of ice ages are triggered by changes in the Earth's orbit about the Sun and in its rotation on its own axis. Milutin Milankovitch (1879–1958), a Serbian astrophysicist, calculated when these

Pleistocene glacials and interglacials in North America

Approximate date ('000 years BP)	Name
10–present	*Holocene*
75–10	Wisconsinian
120–75	*Sangamonian*
170–120	Illinoian
230–170	*Yarmouthian*
480–230	Kansan
600–480	*Aftonian*
800–600	Nebraskan

(Names in italic are those of interglacials. BP means "before present," "present" being 1950.)

astronomical changes occurred over several hundred thousand years and compared their timings with climate changes. The fit was precise, and astronomical changes known as the *Milankovitch cycles* (see the sidebar below) were shown to trigger the sequence of events that cause ice ages and interglacials.

Milankovitch cycles

In 1920 Milutin Milankovitch (1879–1958), a Serbian astrophysicist, proposed an astronomical explanation for why ice ages begin and end when they do. Milankovitch had examined regular changes that occur in the Earth's orbit about the Sun and in Earth's rotation on its own axis. He found there were three changes, or cycles, that periodically alter the amount of sunshine falling on the surface. When the three cycles coincide, an ice age either begins or ends. Most climate scientists now accept the Milankovitch theory. The three cycles affect *orbital stretch, axial tilt,* and *axial wobble.*

Earth follows an elliptical path around the Sun, with the Sun occupying one focus of the ellipse. Orbital *eccentricity* changes over a period of 100,000 years. This means that the ellipse grows longer and then shorter again. When the orbit is at its longest, Earth is approximately 30 percent farther from the Sun at both its closest approach (*perihelion*) and its farthest point (*aphelion*) than it is when the ellipse is short—in fact, almost circular. At these times, the sunlight falling on the Earth is less intense.

Instead of being at right angles to the Sun's rays, Earth's axis is tilted, at present by about 23.45°. Over a period of about 42,000 years the angle of tilt varies from 22.1° to 24.5° and back again. The greater the angle of tilt, called the *obliquity,* the more intense the sunshine falling on high latitudes in summer and the less these latitudes receive in winter.

The Earth's axis wobbles like a toy spinning top, so that without changing the angle of tilt, the axis describes a circle, taking 25,800 years to complete one turn. This alters the dates of midsummer day, midwinter day, and the *equinoxes* (days when there are precisely 12 hours of day and 12 hours of night everywhere). At present, Earth is at perihelion (closest to the Sun) on about July 4 and at aphelion on about January 3. In about 10,000 years from now these dates will be reversed due to the axial wobble. The Northern Hemisphere will then receive more solar radiation in summer and less in winter, and the Southern Hemisphere will receive less radiation in summer and more in winter.

When the orbit is at its most eccentric, the axial tilt is at a minimum, and Earth is at aphelion in June or December, summer temperatures in one or the other hemisphere may be low enough to trigger the onset of an ice age.

All of these changes can affect deserts. During cold periods, less water evaporates from the oceans. Consequently, the rainfall decreases. Cold periods are usually dry and are times when deserts expand. Conversely, warm periods are wet, because higher temperatures mean that more water evaporates and then condenses to form clouds. During warm periods, the deserts contract.

Overgrazing and desertification

Desert vegetation is sparse, but it used to be sufficient to support the livestock owned by nomadic tribes. The nomads are *pastoralists*—people who depend on their livestock and grow no crops—and they used the natural resources very efficiently. They owned sheep, goats, camels, horses, and cattle. Each of these feeds differently from the others, so they could graze an area without competing. As they fed they also trampled the ground and urinated and defecated on it. After a time the plants they had not chewed or nibbled were trampled, fouled, and unfit to eat. At this point, members of the tribe

A fence separating overgrazed pasture on the right from protected land on the left shows the effect of allowing livestock an uncontrolled access to pasture. This scene is in the Chihuahuan Desert, Mexico. (Courtesy of Gerry Ellis/Minden Pictures)

would ride out to find fresh pasture, and when they had done so, the people would pack up their tents and other belongings and move on. The plants they left behind soon recovered, because the animal droppings fertilized them.

Pastoralists had lived in this way for centuries and there was no reason why their way of life could not continue indefinitely, but it was a hard life. Animals were their only form of wealth and were bartered in exchange for grain and for the goods the people could not make themselves. This meant that the animals were too valuable to be killed for food, except on rare occasions, usually to celebrate some important event. When animals fell sick there was no veterinarian to administer modern drugs. If the traditional herbal remedies failed, the sick animals died. Neither were there doctors or hospitals or schools for the children.

Conditions now are much better. Villages have medical centers and schools that are open to the traveling people, and there are veterinary clinics to tend their animals, so sick animals have a much better chance of recovering. There are also larger markets for their animals among wealthy, meat-eating city dwellers. The traders buy animals for money, with which the pastoralists can buy modern luxuries.

Life for the pastoralists has improved greatly, but the improvement has brought change. Better veterinary care and ready markets mean that livestock herds and flocks are bigger, and their composition is different. Nowadays cars, buses, and trucks carry the people and goods that were once transported by camels and horses. There is less need for these animals, so their numbers have fallen. Sheep and goats provide meat and skins, but the greatest demand, and the best price, is for beef. Many herds consist only of cattle.

A herd of cattle utilizes pasture less efficiently than a mixed herd of four or five species. Combined with the increase in livestock numbers, reduced grazing efficiency damages the pasture. Plants are ripped from the ground or trampled to destruction. This is *overgrazing*.

The situation became especially bad in the southern Sahara and the Sahel region bordering the desert, and the pastoralists were not the only people under pressure. Farmers cultivated the better land. During the droughts that occur from time to time, the pastoralists are able to move in search of pasture, but the farmers can only look on as their crops wither. In desperation, they seek to increase the cultivated area by fencing off land that was formerly used by the nomads. This timeless conflict between farmers and pastoralists underlies the biblical story of Cain and Abel and the fights between cowboys and farmers in the Wild West, and during the second half of the 20th century it was reenacted in Africa.

It has always been a conflict the pastoralists lose. In some places farmers allowed the nomads to graze their stock in the fields after the crop had been harvested, but they charged for this. The nomads could ill afford to pay and, in any case, resented paying for the use of land that was once free to them. When the pastoralists found pasture they could use the farmers often sought to enclose it. The nomads were being forced into smaller areas. At the same time, governments were encouraging them to settle down in villages. There they could have permanent houses, proper medical care, regular schooling for their children, and the possibility of paid jobs. It was an attractive offer and many seized the opportunity. They did not abandon their livestock, however. Animals were their most important possessions and so the herds grazed the land around the villages, and when they had destroyed the plants in the immediate vicinity they moved out a little farther.

Again the composition of the herds changed. As the vegetation deteriorates, there comes a point where cattle can no longer survive. Usually they are sold before they die. Sheep desperately nibble the herbs until those, too, are destroyed and most of the sheep have to go. Goats can climb trees and shrubs in search of leaves, shoots, and twigs, so they survive for longest.

Once the vegetation has gone the bare ground becomes indistinguishable from the surrounding desert. Wind blows away the fine soil, leaving the stones, and the windblown soil buries plants some distance away and kills them. That is how the desert spreads. The process is called *desertification*.

People sometimes blame the pastoralists for the spread of deserts. This is very unfair. They are the victims of this tragedy, not its perpetrators, and their goats, which seem to be destroying what little vegetation remains, are survivors of a catastrophe that was not of their making. Once the rains return, overgrazed land will recover provided it is fenced to keep out livestock until the plants are fully established. It is drought that makes deserts expand, and drought is a natural disaster. In time, the villagers whose parents were nomads whose way of life disappeared will find new ways to prosper in the modern world.

CHAPTER 9

MANAGING THE DESERT

Halting the spread of deserts

Estimates by the United Nations Environment Program (UNEP) suggest that one quarter of the land area of the Earth is either desert or threatened by desertification. This does not mean that deserts are expanding into neighboring territory—in fact they are not. UNEP defines desertification as the deterioration of the quality of land in regions with a dry or semi-arid climate.

There are several causes. Poor irrigation leads to waterlogging and salination (see pages 173–175). Overgrazing leaves soil exposed to the wind and vulnerable to erosion (see "Overgrazing and desertification" on pages 183–186). Clearing forest to provide lumber or firewood can also leave land vulnerable to erosion. Growing farm crops year after year without adding fertilizer to replace the nutrients that cropping removes depletes the soil fertility until the land becomes incapable of sustaining crops. The U.S. Bureau of Land Management estimates that 40 percent of the United States is vulnerable to one or other of these types of degradation.

International concern about the extent of the problem and the seriousness of its implications was first expressed in 1973, when nine countries of the Sahel region established a permanent committee to monitor the situation. In August and September 1977 the United Nations Conference on Desertification, held in Nairobi, Kenya, agreed to a plan of action. The issue was raised again at the UN Conference on Environment and Development—the so-called Earth Summit—held in Rio de Janeiro, Brazil, in June 1992. These meetings culminated on June 17, 1994, with the adoption in Paris, France, of the UN Convention to Combat Desertification in Those Countries Experiencing Serious Drought and/or Desertification, Particularly in Africa (UNCCD). The UNCCD was opened for signature in Paris in October 1994 and it came into force on December 26, 1996.

UNCCD aims to improve the efficiency with which the problem of land degradation is addressed. It does this by coordinating the efforts of the rich industrial nations that provide the finances and by encouraging poorer nations that are suffering from desertification to develop and implement practical measures to halt and reverse the deterioration and to help its victims. Numerous countries are now engaged in relevant projects. Many are in Africa, where the problem is most severe, but land degradation is not confined to Africa. It also affects parts of Latin America and the Caribbean as well as Asia, and nations in these regions are also actively seeking to combat land deterioration.

We cannot prevent droughts, but there are ways to reduce their harm and check the spread of deserts. Desert soils suffer badly from erosion, and erosion is preventable. The first step is to ensure that vegetation covers the ground at all times. Friction with the plants slows the wind, reducing its power to blow away fine-grained material, and plant roots bind soil particles together, making them less susceptible to wind erosion.

Maintaining a permanent vegetation cover is possible only if pressure on the land is reduced. People initially destroyed the plants through overgrazing or overcropping because they had no choice if they were to survive. To take pressure off the land to produce crops or pasturage, these people must be given alternatives. Industries can provide nonagricultural jobs, for example, and credit facilities can be developed to allow farmers to invest in the equipment, seeds of improved crop varieties, and chemicals that will increase crop yields without damaging the land.

Once the pressure on the land is eased, other measures can follow. These include more efficient irrigation, new sources of water for farm use, and better farming methods.

The end of the nomadic way of life

Nomads lead insecure lives. They have a detailed knowledge of the land on which they have lived for generations, but they do not own the land or even rent it. They understand the weather and the seasons, and they know where they are most likely to find pasture for their animals. They know the location of all the water holes and oases. But they have no legally enforceable entitlement to the land they use. Individual nomadic groups traditionally enjoyed access to certain resources at particular times of year, but this was by unspoken and unwritten agreement among the groups, and outsiders were not bound by such agreements. The nomads could be evicted from "their" grazing lands by anyone strong enough to expel them—and they often were. Tribal warfare was common.

The wars and famines of the 20th century displaced vast numbers of people, and this made the plight of the nomads still worse. Waves of refugees swept across the lands bordering the deserts. Sometimes nations unable to feed and accommodate so many desperate people closed their borders to them. Frontier fences and border guards prevented the nomads from moving freely between their traditional grazing lands. With the better pasture enclosed to provide farmland and their migration routes obstructed, the nomads found it increasingly difficult to maintain their way of life. Times had changed and the world no longer had room for pastoralists used to wandering freely. Many nomadic groups settled in permanent villages, where people found jobs and grew crops for their own use.

Life was no more secure for the farmers. They did not own the land they farmed. Indeed, the idea of owning land was quite foreign to most desert peoples, and, in any case, they had no money to buy their plots. They fenced the land they worked to protect their crops from wandering livestock, but their fences did not imply ownership. If someone more powerful claimed the land the farmers could be evicted.

Desert farms could be improved. Crops could be irrigated more efficiently (see "Improving irrigation" on pages 201–205); the land could be managed in ways that reduced erosion; and as the soil became more stable and more fertile, crop yields would increase. Making the necessary improvements requires hard work, however, and it is very difficult to persuade people to invest their time and effort in increasing the value of land from which they can be evicted at any time. If they had security of tenure, farmers would see that improvements continued for several years would make their families more prosperous and that their children would enjoy a much better, richer life.

There are new techniques the farmers could introduce. For example, spraying a mixture of oil and synthetic rubber onto sand dunes stabilizes the sand by binding the grains together. The effect is temporary, but it lasts long enough for the farmer to plant tree seedlings through the surface coating. Eucalyptus and acacia species will grow with only six inches (150 mm) of rain a year, and as they grow the tree roots bind the soil more permanently, while the trees themselves shelter the surface from the erosive wind.

It seldom rains in the desert, but when it does the rain can be torrential, sending water rushing along gullies and cascading down hillsides, carrying the soil with it. Stones litter the desert surface, and stone walls built across the slope will absorb some of the energy of the flowing water. As the flow slows down and the water loses energy, soil carried by the torrent will settle onto the ground instead of being lost.

Such measures require work and some of them also cost money. Oil and rubber has to be bought and spraying equipment bought or hired. If they are to improve their land, the farmers must be able to borrow money for investment, but banks and other financial institutions are reluctant to lend money to people with no assets. This is another reason why security of tenure is an essential first step to agricultural improvement and reducing erosion. Farmers must have access to credit facilities.

Not everyone can or should work on the land. Alternative employment, in tourism or light industry, for example, helps the farmers in two ways. Members of farming families who have outside jobs bring extra money into the home, money that can be used to improve the standard of living immediately or invested in farm improvements. At the same time, wage earners belonging to nonfarming families will buy food, as will tourists, providing a local market for farm produce.

The nomadic way of life is fast disappearing, but we should not mourn its passing. Although the nomads were romantic figures, with their flowing robes, camels, horses, and tents, theirs was not a glamorous life. It was hard, sometimes violent, and the risk of famine was always present.

Rainmaking

Deserts are dry, but their skies are not cloudless. White clouds appear fairly often, only to drift tantalizingly past without releasing rain. Life on the ground would be so much easier if only the clouds could be induced to release their moisture.

Controlling the weather is an ancient dream. For countless centuries people have sought to achieve it by flattering, appeasing, or bribing the whimsical and usually bad-tempered gods that were thought to manage the wind and rain. Specialist "rainmakers" would perform rituals, often supported by dances or chants performed by other members of the group afflicted by drought.

Old beliefs die hard, but they often change the language in which they are expressed. According to a story circulated during the U.S. Civil War, every major battle was followed by rain. People supposed that rainfall must have been triggered in some way by the explosions of battle, and in 1891 the Congress authorized the expenditure of $9,000 on attempts to reproduce the effect by firing cannons into clouds. When this failed, kites and balloons were used to carry explosives into clouds, where they were detonated. Eventually, the attempts had to be abandoned. Explosions do not cause rain to fall. What the experimenters did not know was that in the space of about an hour an average summer thunderstorm releases as much energy as burning 7,000 tons (6,356 tonnes) of coal. It takes more than a cannon or 19th-century bomb to manipulate the weather by brute force.

Failure proved no deterrent, however, for there was another problem that might be tackled head-on. Hailstorms can devastate crops, and during the 19th century the belief grew in Europe that an explosion inside a storm cloud would prevent hailstones from forming. Large mortars, called *hail cannons,* were built for the purpose. They fired their bombs upward into the threatening cloud. By 1899 thousands of hail cannons were in use throughout Europe. In the year

1900 alone there were approximately 9.5 million firings of hail cannons in Europe. As late as the 1960s their updated descendants were still being used in Russia, where artillery shells and rockets were fired into clouds.

The cannons did not work, but the theory behind them was believable. An explosion produces large numbers of very small particles. Water vapor condenses onto small particles, so adding many more particles might produce a cloud consisting of droplets that were too small to grow into hailstones. The problem may not have been the theory but only the scale. Perhaps the cannons were not big enough.

Hail cannons have not vanished from the world. Instead, they have grown more powerful. On March 2, 2004, the Nissan company demonstrated one it had installed to protect vehicles in the 140-acre (56-ha) parking lot at its factory near Canton, Missouri. This cannon uses acetylene gas to cause an explosion that is repeated every five to six seconds and that sends repeated shock waves to a height of 50,000 feet (15.25 km). The shock waves are believed to disrupt the formation of hailstones. Several firms are manufacturing hail cannons of this type, and the devices are being used in Ontario, Canada, and Queensland, Australia, as well as in the United States.

The Queensland cannons are being blamed for causing a persistent drought downwind of the area where they are used to protect citrus and grape crops. Growers have been using the cannons since the 1980s, and downwind residents claim that approaching storms appear to divide as the cannons are fired into them, pass on either side of their own land, and then rejoin. The Australians are not alone. Some American farmers oppose programs to suppress hailstorms because they believe these reduce rainfall.

It remains to be seen whether or not modern hail cannons can succeed where earlier models failed. There is less uncertainty about the possibility of persuading clouds to release their moisture as rain or snow. The technique for achieving this, known as *cloud seeding,* was discovered accidentally in 1946 (see the sidebar on page 193), and several U.S. states now have cloud-seeding programs. The evidence suggests that seeding can increase the amount of rain or snow that falls by at least 5 percent and sometimes by more.

The discovery of cloud seeding

When an airplane flying in air below freezing temperature passes through a cloud composed of supercooled droplets—droplets that are liquid despite being a few degrees below freezing temperature—water will freeze on contact with the surfaces of the wings and tail. A layer of ice accumulates, altering the shape of the surface and thereby reducing the amount of lift the wings produce. The weight of the ice may also affect the plane's flight characteristics. This is *aircraft icing* and in the 1940s it became a serious problem in military aircraft.

In 1946 Vincent Joseph Schaefer (1906–93) and Bernard Vonnegut (1914–97) were investigating aircraft icing at the General Electric Research Laboratory in Schenectady, New York. They needed to discover what caused icing, and to do this they used a box containing air at a constant –9.4°F (–23°C) to which Schaefer added crystals of different substances in order to identify those that will cause ice crystals to form. During a spell of very hot weather in July, Schaefer found it difficult to maintain the low temperature inside the box. On July 13 he dropped crushed dry ice (solid carbon dioxide) at –109°F (–78°C) into the box to chill the air. Ice crystals formed instantly and there was a miniature snowstorm. A short time later Vonnegut made a similar snowstorm by burning silver iodide and allowing the smoke to enter the box.

On November 13, 1946, Schaefer started a real snowstorm by dropping six pounds (2.7 kg) of dry ice pellets from an airplane into a cloud over Pittsfield, Massachusetts. Later experiments showed that silver iodide also triggers precipitation, and this method is more convenient to use because it does not have to be kept chilled.

Attempting to induce precipitation by injecting material into supersaturated air—air in which the relative humidity is above 100 percent—is called *cloud seeding.* Silver iodide and dry ice are used when the air temperature is between 5°F (–15°C) and 23°F (–5°C). Different substances are sometimes used at other temperatures.

Seeding clouds can bring rain, but it cannot produce clouds with the potential to release precipitation. Only if the clouds have already formed can the technique make them release their moisture in a particular place. Consequently, cloud seeding is likely to be of only limited value in desert climates—and it carries serious risks. A cloud that releases its moisture in one place cannot also release it in another.

Seeding may produce rain for one farming community only by stealing it from another.

Dams

Farming is possible in some desert regions because there is a river to supply irrigation water to the fields on either side. For almost its entire length, the Indus River, carrying water a distance of approximately 1,800 miles (2,896 km) from the Tibetan highlands to the Arabian Sea, crosses land that receives less than 10 inches (250 mm) of rain a year. The name *Indus* is derived from *sindhu,* the Sanskrit word for "ocean," because this vast river, draining an area of 372,000 square miles (963,500 km²), looked like an ocean to the people who named it. More than 36,000 miles (58,000 km) of canals carry water from the river and its tributaries to irrigate more than 40 million acres (16 million ha) of farmland, and in addition to the canals there are 1 million miles (1.6 million km) of ditches. This is by far the largest irrigation system in the world, and without it the farmlands of Pakistan and northwestern India would be desert.

For centuries, irrigation canals fed by water from the Tigris and Euphrates Rivers sustained farming in the Fertile Crescent of Mesopotamia. Those farms fed the civilizations from which all later Western civilizations developed (see "The Middle East: birthplace of Western civilization" on pages 130–132).

The world's longest river, the Nile, also crosses desert. Rising in the highlands of East Africa, the Nile drains a basin covering 1.1 million square miles (2.85 million km²) and is 4,157 miles (6,689 km) long. For thousands of years, canals on either side of the river carried Nile water into basins below river level. When the river was in flood with meltwater from the distant mountain snows, dikes that remained closed for most of the year were opened, allowing water to flood the basins. As it did so, the water also deposited a layer of fine silt, rich in plant nutrients. The silt was left behind as the flood subsided and the water drained out of the basins, providing a fertile soil into which the crops were sown.

Unfortunately, rivers like the Nile, Tigris, Euphrates, and Indus are not reliable. If the seasonal rains fail the rivers run dry, and if the rains are unusually heavy the rivers overflow and floods destroy the crops. With too much rain or too little the crops fail and famine is likely. Even when the rivers bring water at the right time, the seasonal nature of the climate means the farmers are able to grow only one crop a year.

The Egyptians knew their river well. They invented a device called a *nilometer* that measured the height of the water very accurately. River water flowed through a tunnel into a cistern, the bottom of which was at the same level as the bed of the river. A graduated obelisk at the center of the cistern, or graduations on the side of the cistern, allowed an official to read the height of the water. When the level began to rise steadily at a nilometer station upstream, word was sent to the authorities downstream, ensuring that the dikes to the fields were opened in time to catch the floodwater.

Water can be stored, however, to be released in a controlled fashion throughout the year. A dam wall built across the river's natural valley will trap water in an artificial lake and floodgates in the wall will then regulate the flow.

The first major damming project on the Nile was completed in 1861. It consisted of a series of dams at the head of the Nile Delta, about 12 miles (19 km) north of Cairo. These dams permanently raised the water level upstream, allowing river water to be released into irrigation channels whenever it was needed. This made it possible for farmers to grow two or even three crops a year. In 1901 another dam was added farther downstream, and in 1902 a dam was built near the town of Asyūt, approximately halfway between Cairo and Aswān. Later, two more dams were built upstream of Asyūt, at Isna in 1909 and at Naj' Hammādī in 1930. A much bigger dam was built in 1902 at Aswān, and the largest of all the Nile dams, the Aswān High Dam, was completed in 1970 (see the sidebar on page 196).

The Indus and its tributaries are also dammed. The first dam was the Mangla Dam, on the Jhelum River, an Indus tributary in Pakistan. It was completed in 1967. The Tarbela Dam, also in Pakistan and on the Indus itself, was completed

The Aswān High Dam

Aswān is an Egyptian city located on the eastern bank of the Nile approximately 550 miles (885 km) south of Cairo. The city lies opposite Elephantine Island (also called Jezira Aswān), where there is a restored nilometer. About 3.5 miles (5.6 km) upstream of Aswān an outcrop of granite creates a waterfall known as the *first cataract.* There are an additional five cataracts to the south of the first.

Aswān is an appropriate point at which to dam the Nile. The first Aswān Dam was built in 1902 and subsequently enlarged twice, between 1908 and 1911, and between 1929 and 1934. The dam has four locks to allow ships to pass, and after the second enlargement the granite dam wall was 1.5 miles (2.4 km) long. Behind it a lake extends upstream for 150 miles (240 km). When the river is in flood, surplus water is released through 180 sluices (floodgates) in the wall. A hydroelectric plant inside the dam wall, with an installed capacity of 345 megawatts, came into operation in 1960.

Work on a much bigger dam began at Aswān in 1960. Situated four miles (6.4 km) upstream of the original Aswān Dam, the Aswān High Dam provides year-round irrigation to all the downstream farms bordering the Nile. The High Dam was designed by West German and Soviet engineers. Construction cost $1 billion and was completed in 1970. President Anwar as-Sadat (1918–81) formally inaugurated the dam on January 15, 1971.

When work began the president of Egypt was Gamal Abdel Nasser (1918–70), and the lake behind the Aswān High Dam is known as Lake Nasser. The lake is 310 miles (499 km) long, extending into Sudan for 125 miles (201 km), and an average six miles (9.6 km) wide. Egypt and Sudan share the water in the lake.

The dam wall is rock filled. It is 364 feet (111 m) high, 3,280 feet (1,000 m) thick at the base, and 2.36 miles (3.8 km) long at the crest. The hydroelectric plant inside the wall has an installed capacity of 2.1 gigawatts and supplies almost half of Egypt's electricity.

in the middle 1970s. It is 486 feet (148 m) high and 9,000 feet (2,745 m) long at the crest. The Beas Dam, in India, was completed at about the same time as the Tarbela. It dams the Beas River, an eastern tributary of the Indus, and is 435 feet (133 m) high and 6,400 feet (1,952 m) long.

Dams have also been built across other great rivers. The Karakaya Dam across the Euphrates in Turkey, is 591 feet (180 m) high and 1,293 feet (394 m) long. It was completed in the middle 1980s.

As well as releasing water whenever it is needed, dams also prevent catastrophic flooding, and all large, modern dams contain turbines that use the flow of water to generate electrical power. There are disadvantages, however. Some artificial lakes raise the water table, causing waterlogging and salination (see pages 173–175) in the surrounding land. This has happened with Lake Nasser, behind the Aswān High Dam. Dams trap silt that was formerly deposited on flooded land downstream. Farmers must then buy fertilizer to compensate for the loss of the plant nutrients carried in the silt. Coastal erosion often increases when the silt that once accumulated near the river mouth ceases to arrive. Reducing the flow of water into the sea can allow seawater to penetrate farther inland, as has happened in the Nile Delta. Still, the advantages of controlling these rivers far outweigh the problems. Since 1971 when the Aswān High Dam became operational, Egyptian yields of wheat have increased by 378 percent, of corn by 273 percent, and of rice by 237 percent.

Diverting rivers

Most deserts lie far from a river that could supply water to make them bloom, but in some cases it might be possible to bring water to the desert by diverting the course of a river. It is a hazardous operation, however, and there is much that can go wrong.

In 1905–06 an attempt was made to divert the Colorado River, on the border between California and Arizona, into irrigation channels that would make farming possible in part of the Colorado Desert. Unfortunately, the operation coincided with a spell of very heavy rain and the engineers lost control. The river changed its course and for 16 months water poured into the Salton Trough, a salt-covered basin covering an area of 8,360 square miles (21,652 km²) that was once the bed of a lake. The river was finally returned to its original course, and in 1907 levees were built to control it. The operation left part of the trough flooded, forming the Salton Sea. The Salton Sea has a surface area of 381 square miles (987 km²) and its average depth is 31 feet (9.5 m). It is fed by drainage from agricultural land and by a number of small streams but loses water only by evaporation. Consequently, its water is growing steadily saltier—it is now saltier than seawater. The water is also polluted by sewage, suffers from blooms of algae, and contains bacteria and viruses that have caused serious diseases in fish and birds. Scientists at the Salton Sea Authority are taking steps to improve the sea's condition, but it is a difficult task.

In the 1920s Soviet authorities decided that the Soviet Union should become one of the world's leading exporters of cotton, grown on farms on the dry Kirgiz Steppe, in Kazakhstan—now an independent nation but then part of the Soviet Union. The farms expanded and irrigation canals were installed to serve the cotton fields. Irrigation was necessary, because the average annual rainfall in that region amounts to barely five inches (127 mm). Within a few years, the Soviet Union was one of the three major cotton exporters, after the United States and China. By the 1950s the farms needed more water and so more canals were built to bring water from two rivers, the Syr Dar'ya in Kazakhstan and the Amu Dar'ya in Uzbekistan. The canals were unlined and so much of the water soaked away before reaching the cotton fields. Nevertheless, enough arrived at the farms to maintain production. So much water was removed that the rivers were effectively diverted to the farmlands.

Until they were diverted, the Syr Dar'ya and Amu Dar'ya flowed into the Aral Sea. With a surface area of 23,000 square miles (60,000 km²), the Aral Sea was the fourth largest lake in the world, but diverting the two rivers reduced the amount of water flowing into the sea. Evaporation was high in the desert climate, where winters are cold but average summer temperatures exceed 80°F (27°C), and the Aral Sea steadily began to shrink.

The sea was always shallow. Prior to the river diversion its average depth was 53 feet (16 m), although it was much deeper in some places, and it was dotted with more than a thousand islands. The Aral Sea has now lost 80 percent of the water it once held and become two seas, the Large and Small Aral Seas. If it continues to lose water, by about 2010 it will consist of only three small lakes. Towns that were once seaports are now far from the sea, and salt-caked fishing boats lie incongruously in the desert out of sight of the sea.

As the volume of water decreased, the sea became saltier and salt was deposited on land from where the water had evaporated. Most of the fish died, and the wind blew dry salt across the fields. The irrigation system had been wasteful. Water draining from the unlined channels and excessive amounts applied to the crops combined to raise the water table. This caused salination (see "Waterlogging and salination" on pages 173–175) and salt contaminated drinking water. Cotton farming continued, but yields fell.

Scientists and engineers from many countries are collaborating in schemes to restore the Aral Sea, but it will take a long time. Improving the irrigation system to reduce wastage should eventually allow the water table to fall, and it may then be possible to flush the excess salt from the soil.

One method being considered involves bringing water from two rivers, the Ob' and Irtysh, which flow northward and discharge into the Kara Sea, off the northern coast of Siberia. This idea was first proposed in the 1950s as a means of supplying irrigation water to the deserts of Central Asia. It would involve damming both rivers and constructing a canal to carry the water southward. Environmental scientists objected strongly. They feared that diverting so much water might result in winter ice persisting for much longer on the Kara Sea, leading to a deterioration in the climate over a large area, and that diverting freshwater would result in the Kara Sea becoming saltier. The scheme was eventually abandoned, but in May 2003 it was revived and is now being actively studied.

The experience of the Salton Sea and the Aral Sea suggests that although diverting rivers to irrigate deserts seems a straightforward proposition, the consequences can be disastrous.

Farming oases and making artificial oases

The farmers of the Nile Valley have sustained Egyptian civilization for thousands of years, and most visitors to Egypt explore the Nile and its cities but stray no farther. But most of the land of Egypt lies to the west of the Nile, and despite being in the Sahara parts of it are inhabited—and farmed. The Egyptian government is encouraging development in a western region called the New Valley, which occupies 145,331 square miles (376,505 km²), more than one-third of the total area of Egypt. At present, 150,000 people live there, but numbers are certain to increase in the coming years as the New Valley develops, eventually to rival the Nile Valley in importance.

Oases are often depicted as being small—a pool of water surrounded by grass and palm trees providing an island of tranquillity in the midst of the hostile desert. Oases are cultivated with great care, almost as gardens, and they gave many people their image of paradise. Some oases are like that, but others are much larger and contain large villages, farms, and even factories, as well as gardens. The Al-Hasa oasis in Saudi Arabia, for example, covers 30,000 acres (12,000 ha) and the New Valley, 200–300 miles (322–483 km) to the west of the Nile River, contains even more extensive oases.

The New Valley comprises three large oases, Khārga, Dakhla, and Farafra, as well as several smaller ones. The regional capital is the city of El Khârga, with an industrial quarter, airport, and road and rail links to the cities of the Nile Valley. At the center of El Khârga there is a statue of a woman holding her children. The woman represents Egypt and her children are the oases.

The valley has abundant mineral resources, including marble, limestone, granite, sand suitable for glass making, and phosphate rock, which is the raw material for phosphate fertilizer. It is also a fertile agricultural area. The oases have been inhabited for thousands of years and there are many historical sites and monuments. The farms, covering approximately 520,000 acres (21,000 ha), are watered from more than 1,170 wells that deliver a total of 94.41 million cubic feet (2.6 million m³) of water every day.

The New Valley Project aims to expand the cultivated area by reclaiming 2.18 million acres (882,000 ha) of desert using water carried by a canal from behind the Aswān High Dam on the Nile. The first phase of the project has already begun.

There are oases in most deserts, but some are partly or entirely artificial. Kattakurgan, for example, is a city of almost 60,000 people in Uzbekistan that grew up in the 18th century as a trade and handicraft center built around a natural oasis. Today a modern reservoir holding water from the Zeravshan River supplies the farms and provides recreational facilities. In effect, the oasis has been enlarged using imported water. Most of Uzbekistan is desert, but its rivers provide water for the cities and surrounding farms.

There is often water deep below ground and desert people learned long ago that there are ways to reach it. They built underground watercourses, called *qanats, foggara,* or *qarez,* among other names depending on the language, that guided water into depressions where it surfaced to irrigate fields and supply drinking water (see the sidebar on page 202). No one knows just when the first qanats were constructed, but it may have been thousands of years ago. They were probably invented in Iran, where new ones are still being made. The idea spread both east and west—qanats provided water for some of the oases on caravan routes across the Gobi.

Of course, it would have been easier and safer to dig canals to carry water. That is the way the Roman engineers did it, with *aqueducts,* but the ancient Iranians knew that a canal crossing the hot, windy desert and exposed to the air would lose much of its water by evaporation. An underground canal, on the other hand, would deliver all of its water to the fields that needed it.

Oases have always allowed people to live in the otherwise uninhabitable desert. If ways can be found to bring water into the desert it will most likely be used to create new oases.

Improving irrigation

Southern Israel is shaped like an inverted triangle, bordered on the western side by the Sinai Peninsula and by the Jordan Valley in the east. This region is called the Negev. Nowadays, the name simply means "southland," but it is derived from a Hebrew verb root that means "to dry." The Negev is a dry place, although not all of it is desert. In the north, around Beersheba, the annual rainfall of eight to 12 inches (203–305

Qanats

Qanat is the Arabic and Turkish name for an artificial underground river system that supplies village communities with water for drinking and irrigation. In North Africa the Berbers call them *foggara;* in Pashto (Iranian) they are *qarez.* Similar watercourses are found across the arid regions of Asia as far as western China, and there are the remains of qanats in Spain, built by the Moors. They are most common in central Iran. The technology is very ancient.

Constructing and maintaining a qanat system is labor intensive and very strenuous. Centuries ago slaves performed the work, and when slavery died out many of the watercourses collapsed and were lost. Today local people build and maintain the qanats.

There is often water flowing through an aquifer below the desert surface, and the first step in planning a qanat is to locate the underground water. The aquifer must be at a higher level than the land it will supply, because the water will flow downhill. There must be sufficient water to fill a well to a depth of 6.5 feet (2 m) within about 10 hours, and the flow must be reliable, continuing throughout the year.

Once the aquifer has been located, either by sinking a well into a hillside until it finds water or by noting patches of damp earth at the base of a slope, the next stage is to dig ventilation shafts at intervals along the route of the qanat. The shafts are just wide enough to allow a man to work and are usually 50–70 feet (15–21 m) deep, although some descend more than 150 feet (45 m). Workers then dig out the underground channel. The material they excavate is removed in leather buckets through the ventilation shafts and used to build a mound around the mouth of each shaft to prevent occasional floods from washing earth down into the channel. In places where there is a danger of cave-ins, stonework supports the roofs of channels and the sides of shafts.

A wealthy individual who finances the surveying and construction of a qanat owns the water that flows through it and charges the villagers for its use. If the villagers build the qanat themselves, they own the water.

Once a year the qanat must be cleared of debris that has fallen into it. A contractor may undertake this work, but often the villagers do it themselves. Boys are often used, because they have more room to move about than grown men, but the men go down if there is a risk of a channel or ventilation shaft collapsing.

mm) allows farms to grow cereals without irrigation. Farther south, however, the rainfall averages only three to four inches (76–102 mm) and Eilat, at the southern tip of the triangle, receives only one inch (25 mm) a year. These are averages, however, and the rainfall varies greatly from year to year throughout the Negev. When there is rain it often arrives during intense storms that cause flash flooding but are of little use to farmers, because the rain drains away too rapidly.

During Roman times the Negev was a different place. The climate was probably almost as dry then as it is now, but the southern Negev was covered with prosperous farms supplying grain to the Roman Empire. Farming was possible because a people called the Nabataeans had found a way to conserve water.

The Nabataeans built terraces of fields, each surrounded by a low wall built of stone, in tiers descending the hillsides. Each time it rained, water ran down the upper part of the hillside and soaked into the top tier of terraces until they were thoroughly saturated and water lay on the surface. When the water rose high enough it overflowed the boundary walls onto the terraces below, then onto those below that, until it reached the bottom terraces. Any remaining water then drained into an underground storage tank, for use later. The Nabataeans truly made the desert bloom, but when Arabs invaded the region in the seventh century the system was abandoned and the southern Negev reverted to desert.

Along the dry border between India and Pakistan, not far from the Thar Desert, the monsoon climate (see "Monsoons" on pages 58–62) brings all the year's rain during a short summer period. Bikaner, for example, in Rajasthan State, India, receives an average 11.6 inches (294 mm) of rain a year, but more than half of it falls in July and August. Farmers in this part of the world have developed a technique for conserving water that is similar to the one invented all those years ago by the Nabataeans.

Villagers have built dams of earth across the valleys. During the rainy season, water rushing down the steep hillsides accumulates behind the dams and for a time there is an artificial lake behind each dam. After the rains have ended, the water soaks into the ground, and when there is no more water lying on the surface the farmers plant their crops of wheat and chickpeas. The water that soaks downward joins the groundwater and continues moving slowly downhill to fill wells sunk on the lower ground that provide water for irrigation at other times of the year.

Both the Nabataean and Indian-Pakistani systems do more than conserve water. They also conserve soil and its fertility. Water that roars and tumbles in torrents down the hillsides washes away the soil it crosses. When a stone wall or earth dam checks its progress, the soil it carries settles to the surface as a layer of rich silt.

Terracing can conserve water only in hilly country where the rainfall occurs mainly in short, heavy storms. Elsewhere, farmers must use a different way to improve the efficiency of their irrigation. Many have installed drip or trickle irrigation, a system that works well in hot, dry climates. It is widely used in Israel.

Water is carried along plastic pipes 0.5–1.0 inch (13–25 mm) in diameter with small holes, called *emitters,* at intervals along them. No more than one gallon (3.7 l) of water drips or trickles from each emitter every hour, and it is delivered directly to the soil beside the crop plant. The spacing of the emitters can be varied to suit the crop. A grapevine might need one or two emitters and a fruit tree might have eight, with the delivery pipe laid in a circle around it. Where the climate is very hot and the evaporation rate is high, the pipe is often buried below ground.

Fertilizer is often added to the irrigation water. Drip irrigation allows the amount of fertilizer to be rigorously controlled and the fertilizer is delivered slowly, at a measured rate, directly to the soil around the plant roots. This is a highly efficient way to apply fertilizer.

The disadvantage of drip irrigation is the ease with which the emitters become clogged. Water must be filtered before entering the pipes to minimize the risk, and if a pipe breaks or an emitter clogs, a plant will show signs of distress and may be lost unless the damage is repaired quickly.

This irrigation system can also deposit salts in the soil around the edge of the wetted area. It happens because there is no need to incur the expense of purifying irrigation water to a standard high enough for domestic use. The water contains salts—indeed, it may be fairly salty—and the salts are deposited in the soil as the water evaporates. The soil around the crop plants is kept permanently moist, so salts do not accumulate to harm them, and consequently the problem is not serious.

Desalination

When water evaporates it is only water molecules that enter the air. Substances dissolved in the water are left behind. That is what causes salination (see "Waterlogging and salination" on pages 173–175), but it also suggests that if water is allowed to evaporate and the vapor made to condense into liquid, the condensed water will be pure, its dissolved salts having been removed. The process is called *distillation* and it has been known for thousands of years. Aristotle (384–322 B.C.E.) mentioned it as a way to obtain pure water from seawater, and distillation has been used for centuries to separate chemicals that vaporize at different temperatures. Removing dissolved salts to obtain water that is fit to drink is called *desalination,* and distillation is the most widely used desalination technique, although it is not the only one.

In 1869 the British built a distillation plant at Aden, in Yemen, to provide drinking water for ships calling at the port. Today approximately 75 percent of all desalinated water is produced and used in the Middle East—the distillation plant at Al Jubayl, Saudi Arabia, produces 1.2 billion gallons (4.7 billion l) a year. The United States produces about 10 percent of the world total.

Most desalination plants, including the one at Al Jubayl, use the *multistage flash evaporation* process. Seawater enters along a pipe that passes through a series of chambers, where the pipe is coiled. Water in the pipe is cold, and water vapor inside the chambers condenses onto it and drips into a receptacle to be piped away as freshwater. After it has passed through the final chamber, the seawater pipe passes through a heater where its temperature is increased to about 195°F (90°C). The heated water is then sprayed into the first chamber. The pressure inside the chamber is lower than the pressure inside the pipe and the pressure difference causes the water drops to vaporize instantly. This is *flash evaporation* and it supplies the vapor that condenses onto the cold pipe. The remaining seawater is now a little saltier because of the fresh-water that has been removed from it. It passes into the second chamber where the pressure is lower than it was in the first. Again some of the water vaporizes and is collected. The process is repeated—it is *multistage*—until the residue is concentrated brine. Some desalination plants use the *long-tube vertical distillation process*. The principle is similar, but the chambers are vertical tubes and steam is used to heat and vaporize the salt water.

Freezing also separates water from substances dissolved in it and some desalination plants use this principle. In one version seawater is chilled almost to freezing and sprayed into a chamber where the pressure is low. Some of the water vaporizes instantly, absorbing the latent heat to do so from the water around it (see the sidebar "Lapse rates and stability" on pages 60–61 for an explanation of latent heat). Some of the water freezes, and a mixture of ice and salt water falls to the bottom of the chamber and is piped to a second chamber where the salt water is separated from the ice. The water vapor in the first chamber is then compressed, forcing it to condense as freshwater that is used to wash the remaining brine from the ice and to melt it. The melted ice is collected as freshwater.

Alternatively, in the first chamber, seawater is mixed with a refrigerant substance such as propane or butane that vaporizes at a temperature above 32°F (0°C). The refrigerant vaporizes, absorbing latent heat from the water, some of which freezes. The ice and brine are separated, and the ice is taken to a second chamber where it is washed and from there to a third chamber. The refrigerant is piped out of the top of the chamber and compressed. This makes it condense and raises its temperature. Still in its pipe, the warm refrigerant melts the ice in the third chamber and then returns to the first chamber to be mixed with a new batch of seawater.

Reverse osmosis is an entirely different way to separate salt and water. If a membrane that allows water molecules to pass but not others separates two solutions at different concentrations, water will pass through the membrane from the weaker to the stronger solution until both are at the same concentration. This process is called *osmosis* and it happens because an *osmotic pressure* draws water molecules across the membrane. If sufficient pressure is applied to the stronger solution, however, water will cross the membrane in the opposite direction, from the stronger to the weaker solution. This is reverse osmosis. The process is used to obtain freshwater, but only from water that is less salty than seawater.

Desalination plants require regular maintenance to keep the pipes and surfaces free from the scale that collects on them as water evaporates and minerals are left behind. Removing the freshwater also leaves a residue of brine that is very salty indeed and must be disposed of carefully to avoid causing pollution.

All desalination processes use energy, and consequently desalinated water is expensive. Scientists and engineers are working on ways to use energy more efficiently and reduce the cost of desalination. This is already feasible in small plants. In hot desert countries solar power is sufficient to run simple distillation plants suitable for providing drinking water to households or small communities.

Icebergs to water desert crops?

Freezing separates pure water from any substances dissolved in it. Consequently, icebergs that drift across the oceans in high latitudes consist of freshwater, and they represent a very large amount of water. Each year icebergs entering arctic waters—almost all of them from glaciers along the coast of Greenland—contain about 67 cubic miles (280 km^3) of water. Those entering Antarctic waters contain about 300 cubic miles (1,250 km^3) of water. It is very pure water. So pure, in fact, that a company in St. John's, Newfoundland, sells melted iceberg water in bottles.

With so much solid, pure freshwater available in high latitudes and so many desert communities desperately short of water, it is hardly surprising that the idea of using icebergs has been debated for many years. A single Antarctic iceberg, and by no means a giant, contains in the region of 35 million tons (32 million tonnes) of water. This is enough to supply a city of half a million people for a year.

The obvious way to transport this water would be to attach cables to the iceberg and tow it into a harbor, where it could be broken into pieces, melted, and piped to reservoirs. Unfortunately, there is a problem, because once an iceberg enters warm water it melts rapidly. In the time it would take to tow an iceberg from south of the Antarctic Circle to Australia, 50–80 percent of it would have melted. That means only large icebergs would be of use. In fact, they would need to weigh approximately 350 million tons (318 million tonnes). Towing a block of ice that big would require several very powerful seagoing tugs. The ships would burn a great deal of fuel and, consequently, the water would be very expensive. It would probably be too costly for the poor farmers who need it along the edges of deserts.

There is an alternative. Communities living on densely populated small islands are often short of water because even if the rainfall is plentiful they lack the space to build storage reservoirs. Some of these communities are now supplied with water that is transported from the mainland in huge plastic pouches towed by ships. Icebergs might be transported in much the same way.

Plastic sheeting paid out from a ship would sink under its own weight and would move beneath the chosen iceberg either through the natural movement of sea currents or by being pulled by cables. Tubes along the edges of the sheet would then be inflated, causing the edges to surface and thereby wrapping the underside of the iceberg. More sheeting would then be laid over the top of the iceberg and welded to the lower sheet to make a watertight seal. The iceberg would then be completely enclosed inside a plastic bag and the bag could be towed to wherever the water was needed. There would be no need to hurry, because it would not matter if the ice melted, since it was contained inside a watertight bag. This also means no allowance need be made for losses due to melting and therefore smaller icebergs could be captured. The bag would also prevent contamination of the ice or water by seawater.

The operation would use fuel, so the water would be fairly expensive, but in other respects it would not harm the environment. The plastic could be reused or recycled, and unless all the glaciers and ice sheets melt, which is unlikely in the near future, the supply of icebergs is inexhaustible—icebergs break naturally from the edges of ice sheets and the ends of glaciers. It would be impossible to use icebergs faster than they are produced naturally, because they cannot be removed until they have broken free.

Like the water produced from seawater in desalination plants (see pages 205–207), water from melted icebergs would need to travel from the coast to the regions where it is needed. Transport by pipeline, railroad, or highway would add considerably to the cost, and it might be considered uneconomical to use this source of water to supply people living thousands of miles inland. For those within a few hundred miles, however, icebergs may one day prove a reliable source of clean water for domestic use and for irrigation.

Dry farming

At intervals of about 22 years, the Great Plains of North America suffer drought. Droughts occurred there in the 1950s, 1970s, and 1990s, but the worst droughts of modern times happened in the 1930s. Crops failed, the soil dried to dust, and the wind blew away the soil together with the seeds the farmers had sowed. In the summer of 1934 a cloud of dust three miles (4.8 km) high covered an area of 1.35 million square miles (3.5 million km²). Dust fell on ships 300 miles (480 km) from shore and birds, choked by the dust, fell dead to the ground. The area of the Great Plains affected by this disaster came to be known as the *Dust Bowl.*

Farmers and agricultural scientists learned the lessons of the Dust Bowl years, and when the rains returned farming methods changed. Some areas were left unplowed to allow the natural prairie grasses to return. Droughts are a natural event and the prairie grasses and herbs are able to survive them, their roots binding the soil together and preventing it from blowing away.

The climate of the Great Plains is dry even outside the drought years. Nevertheless, early European explorers found several Native American tribes farming the land successfully without relying on irrigation. When European settlers began farming the land they used the techniques they had learned farther east, where the climate was wetter, and dug irrigation channels to provide the water their crops needed. In the early years they had to work so hard simply to feed themselves that they had no time to experiment with alternative farming methods. Now and then, however, a reservoir would lose its water or channels would break and an irrigation system would fail. Farmers noticed that when this happened the crop was greatly reduced, but it was not lost entirely.

A breakthrough came early in the 1860s when a group of Scandinavian settlers plowed the land close to what is now Bear River City, Utah. The water they used to irrigate their crops was alkaline and the crops failed. With only poisonous water available to them, the farmers did the only thing they could think of. Sagebrush was growing on the land around their farms. They plowed this land, mixing the sagebrush plants into the soil as they did so, sowed their seeds, and hoped for the best. The experiment succeeded and they harvested a good crop. They had devised their own version of what is now known as *dry farming.*

During the subsequent decades of the 19th century, the possibilities of dry farming were explored more deeply at the agricultural colleges that were being established across America. Dry-farming techniques were developed independently in Utah, California, Washington, and Colorado. Following the Dust Bowl years, dry-farming techniques were adopted over an even wider area. Today dry farming is practiced widely in regions where rainfall is sparse and unreliable. It cannot succeed in a true desert, where even a light shower of rain is a rare event, but it does make farming without irrigation possible in climates with less than about 12 inches (305 mm) of rain a year.

Dry farming begins by selecting a crop that tolerates dry conditions—wheat, for example, rather than potatoes. There are several versions of dry farming, but all of them conserve moisture by tilling the soil thoroughly and including a period during which the land lies fallow. Where possible, the land is plowed in the fall and the seed is sown as soon as the soil has been prepared. Once the crop has been harvested the land is left fallow, commonly for three years. An entire field may be left uncultivated, or crops may be grown in widely spaced strips separated by uncultivated strips, with the cropped strips being moved each year. Wild plants grow on the fallow land, and from time to time these are plowed into the soil. The plants gather moisture, and plowing buries their moist tissues before they have time to lose water by transpiration (see "Why plants need water" on pages 85–86). By the end of the fallow period the partly decomposed wild plants will have released sufficient moisture into the soil to sustain the next crop.

Dry farming is not unique to North America, of course. Farmers in many parts of the world have found ways to grow crops in dry climates without irrigation. Using modern crops, adapted to the climatic conditions, traditional methods of dry farming might be developed further to increase food production and the prosperity of agricultural communities living along the edges of the world's deserts.

Corridor farming

Acacia trees belong to the family Fabaceae, the same plant family as peas, beans, peanuts, soybeans, and lentils. They are all legumes. This means their roots exude chemicals that attract *Rhizobium* bacteria. These bacteria penetrate the fine root hairs and exude another chemical that makes the root grow longer and curl around the bacteria. As the bacterial colony and root both continue to grow, a *nodule* develops on the root. Root nodules are clearly visible among the roots. They look like white or gray "lumps" about the size of the head of a map pin. *Rhizobium* bacteria convert atmospheric nitrogen into soluble nitrogen compounds the plant is able to absorb. Nitrogen is a principal component of all proteins, so it is an essential nutrient. If the soil conditions suit them, the bacteria "fix" much more nitrogen than either the bacteria or their host plant can use, and they excrete the surplus into the soil, where it is available to other plants. In this way, legumes improve the fertility of the soil, reducing substantially the amount of fertilizer farmers need to apply in order to grow other crops on the same or adjacent ground.

Trees of any species also shelter the soil and crop plants from the wind. Farmers often plant trees for this purpose, to make shelterbelts. Wind erosion is a serious problem in dry climates, and belts of trees help reduce erosion. If the trees improve soil fertility at the same time they are doubly useful.

The use of trees to shelter and feed the soil forms the basis of a farming system known as *corridor farming* or *alley cropping.* The trees are grown in rows and the farm crop grown in rows between them. The crop is therefore grown in a tree-lined corridor or alley, hence the name. The crop is sown at the start of the rainy season and harvested as soon as it is ready, but the trees are left to continue growing through the dry season. At the end of the dry season the trees are cut down almost to ground level. This technique, known as *coppicing,* encourages many shoots to grow from the stumps. The system simultaneously produces a conventional farm crop, tree leaves that are fed to livestock when the trees are cut down, and also wood that can be used to make small articles or burned as fuel. Far from injuring the tree, coppicing prolongs its life and makes the tree shorter and bushier, thus increasing the number of shoots and leaves it produces and making it a more effective windbreak.

Several combinations of trees and crops are used. In eastern Rajasthan, India, close to the Thar Desert, farmers grow millet in corridors of *Prosopis cineraria* trees, known locally as *khejri* or *jandi.* In the Sahel region and the dry areas of East Africa the apple-ring acacia, also known as winter thorn and camel thorn (*Alhagi maurorum*), grows beside other cereal crops. In some parts of the Middle East mung beans (*Vigna radiata*) are grown beside the umbrella thorn or Israeli babool (*Acacia tortilis*)—this is the tree historians believe may have supplied the wood to make the biblical Ark of the Covenant. *Prosopis* and *Faidherbia* are small leguminous trees closely related to *Acacia.*

Apple-ring acacia is especially useful, because it has the unusual habit of bearing leaves throughout the dry season and shedding them at the start of the rainy season. Animals are able to feed on its leaves and shoots through the dry season when food is scarce. The cut branches of this tree can also be stored without losing their nutritional value for livestock.

Corridor farming was first developed for the humid tropics, where it prevents soil erosion, especially on steep hillsides, but it has also proved highly successful in dry climates. It is a technique that allows farmers to raise plant crops and livestock together. It improves the land, reduces erosion, and increases agricultural output—and therefore contributes to the prosperity of farming communities.

New crops for dry climates

Biologists believe there are approximately 270,000 species of plants. We cultivate only a tiny proportion of all those species. Members of the grass family (Poaceae) provide most of our staple foods. There are about 9,000 grass species, but we use only about two dozen of them—wheat (four species), oats, rye, barley (two species), rice (two species), corn (maize), sugarcane, millet (about 10 species), and sorghum. The bean family (Fabaceae) is even larger, with about 16,400 members. Beans are rich in proteins, making them highly nutritious, but we grow only about two dozen species—beans (about nine species), broad beans, jack beans, peas, asparagus peas, cowpeas, lablab, soybeans, lentils, peanuts, pigeon peas, chickpeas, bambarra groundnut, and alfalfa and clover, which are grown to feed livestock.

Most of these crop plants are difficult to grow in dry climates because they require abundant water, and scientists are exploring alternatives—crops for the desert. So far they have found several. Some are already cultivated locally but could be grown more widely. Others are wild plants that might be domesticated.

Love-lies-bleeding (*Amaranthus caudatus*) is a popular garden plant that is also known as cattail, tumbleweed, and Inca wheat. Its edible seeds are rich in protein, and amaranths are among the few plants (soybean is another) that contain the amino acid lysine, an essential nutrient for humans. Amaranths grow naturally in Central and South America and were cultivated for their seeds until imported cereals displaced them. Prince's feather (*A. hypochondriacus*), native to Mexico, has edible leaves as well as seeds.

Echinochloa species resemble rice and millet and have names like jungle rice, Shama millet, Japanese millet, and paddy-rice mimic weed. As the last name suggests, some are troublesome weeds. Channel millet (*E. turnerana*) is different. It produces highly nutritious seeds and grows well with just one watering, making it potentially valuable as a crop for dry climates. Channel millet grows wild in Australia.

An Andean plant called quinoa, or quinua (*Chenopodium quinoa*), is one of the richest sources of plant protein. Like the amaranths, quinoa was grown for its seeds until imported

Genetic modification

Most physical characteristics of living organisms are determined by the *genes* that are contained in the *chromosomes* present in the nucleus of almost all cells. Genes consist of strings of deoxyribonucleic acid (DNA) arranged in two complementary strands that are wound together in a spiral. When cells divide, the two strands of DNA separate, molecules present in the cell attach themselves to the unpaired strands to reconstitute the spiral pair, and both daughter cells receive a full set of the chromosomes carrying the genes. A chromosome contains many genes joined end to end and interspersed with sections of DNA that carry no genetic information. When plants or animals reproduce, each parent contributes a set of single DNA strands, which combine to produce a paired set in the offspring.

Traditionally, plant breeders develop new varieties by choosing individual plants that possess desirable characteristics and breeding them with members of an existing variety, in the hope of transferring the desirable traits into the resulting offspring. The breeders then cross the offspring with one another or with one of their parents. This process must be repeated many times before the new variety is ready to be grown commercially. Since it involves breeding, obviously it works only among members of the same species.

Breeders also induce *mutations*—genetic changes—to produce entirely new characteristics. They do this by exposing plants to chemicals known to induce mutations or by bombarding them with radiation. It is a hit-or-miss process, but if a useful characteristic appears it can be transferred to other varieties by conventional breeding.

In the 1970s scientists learned how to identify the genes or sets of genes responsible for particular traits, to remove those genes from the cells of one organism, and to insert cereals displaced it, and it is still grown locally in the mountains of Bolivia, Chile, Ecuador, and Peru. Its seeds are enclosed in an outer layer that is extremely bitter. Probably a defense against insects and birds, this feature might make the plant easy to grow with little need for insecticide, and washing removes the bitter flavor.

Buffalo gourds, also known as mock orange and chilicote (*Cucurbita foetidissima*), are rich in oils as well as protein (and their roots have laxative properties). They grow in the dry wastelands of the southwestern United States and Mexico and are highly tolerant of drought. They are also productive. A single plant can produce an average of 60 fruits containing

them into the DNA of another organism. This is called *genetic modification,* or *genetic engineering.*

For example, modern varieties of wheat and rice are much shorter than older varieties. This allows them to support heavier heads of grain without falling over, or *lodging,* when they are battered by wind and rain. These varieties were bred by traditional methods in breeding programs that lasted for many years. The same result could be achieved much more quickly today by identifying the gene that makes particular plants short stemmed, extracting it, and inserting it into plants that produce heavy heads of grain.

As well as being quicker than traditional breeding, genetic modification is much more precise. Traditional breeding transfers thousands of genes from one organism to another. If some of those genes confer undesirable characteristics, further breeding is needed to remove them. Genetic modification manipulates just one or a few genes with known properties.

Genetic modification takes several forms. It may increase or decrease the activity of certain genes without transferring genes from one organism to another. If it does involve transferring genes, the transfer may be between members of the same species or between members of similar but distinct species. It may also involve transferring genes between wholly unrelated organisms. Some crop varieties have been genetically modified by inserting into their DNA a gene from a bacterium, *Bacillus thuringiensis.* This gene causes the cell to produce a substance that is poisonous to insect pests. *Bt plants,* as these are known, produce their own insecticide, rendering them resistant to pest attack. The insecticide has been used for many years, by spraying crops with a *Bt* bacterial culture, but genetic modification does away with the need for spraying and greatly reduces the amount of insecticide entering the environment.

2.5 pounds (1.15 kg) of seeds. In addition to its fruits, the buffalo gourd grows a starchy underground tuber in which it stores water. After two growing seasons the tuber weighs approximately 70 pounds (32 kg) and contains as much starch as 20 potato plants grown in moist, well-drained soil.

Clearly there are many little-known plants that have great potential as crop plants in dry regions. Not all of these are food plants. Vetiver, also known as khus and cuscus (*Vetiveria zizanoides*), is a tropical grass, looking much like pampas grass, which grows in India. Its dried roots give off a pleasant perfume when watered. They are woven into items such as mats and baskets and used in scent making. An immensely tough plant that can survive sunshine, shade, snow, and even immersion in water, vetiver also grows in deserts. Rows of it, planted on hillsides parallel to the contours, would quickly merge to make a screen strong enough to check the movement of soil, thus preventing erosion.

Searching for plants that might thrive in a desert environment is a slow, labor-intensive business with no guarantee of success. An alternative is to modify existing plants to help them tolerate harsh conditions. Many desert soils are salty, some because they are the beds of seas that dried up long ago and others because faulty irrigation systems have led to salination (see "Waterlogging and salination" on pages 173–175). Plants known botanically as *halophytes*—"salt lovers"—flourish in salt soils. If their ability to tolerate salt can be bred into useful crop plants, farming could expand into those saline soils. Some plants survive drought better than others, and if crop plants could acquire those drought-resistant characteristics there would be less need for irrigation on desert farms. That would reduce the cost of crop production.

Plant breeders have been working for many years to produce such crop varieties. Conventional plant breeding is slow, however. The plants must be grown and crossed with one another for many generations in order to establish the desired features securely—so they will not disappear in subsequent generations—in a commercial plant variety. Today techniques of genetic modification (see the sidebar on pages 214–215) greatly reduce the time this takes. At the same time, genetic modification offers still wider opportunities to transfer desirable and heritable traits between plants of different species and even to insert into cultivated plants traits taken from organisms that are not plants at all.

So far, genetic modification has been used principally to develop crops that are more resistant to insect pests and that can be grown with less use of herbicides. In years to come there will be crops that are modified to produce nutritious food on land that today cannot be farmed at all.

Food from the polar regions

Along the northern fringes of North America and Eurasia there is an environment equivalent to the semiarid borders of low-latitude deserts such as the Sahara. The climate is dry and strongly seasonal. The dry season is the long winter, when all of the water is frozen. In summer the ground surface thaws and water is available, but the summer is brief. The vegetation consists of scattered shrubs, just a foot or two (up to 60 cm) tall, growing in hollows where they are sheltered from the drying effect of the incessant wind. There are grasses, sedges, and lichens, but also large expanses of bare rock and gravel. This is the *tundra,* a name derived from *tundara,* the Sami word for a treeless plain where below the surface the ground remains frozen throughout the year. (Sami, or Lapp, is a language spoken in northern Finland, Sweden, and Norway, and on the Kola Peninsula in Russia.) The permanently frozen layer is called *permafrost.*

Traditionally, the people of the tundra lived a seminomadic life very similar to that of the Bedouin and other desert tribes. They owned herds of caribou, known in Europe as reindeer (*Rangifer tarandus*). In summer the herds grazed in the tundra and in winter they migrated southward, to the edges of the *taiga*—the belt of coniferous forest that stretches across northern Canada and Eurasia. Their owners lived in conical tents made from reindeer hides. In southern Greenland there are sheep farmers who live a settled life similar to that of farmers tilling the land around the oases found in deserts far to the south.

The nomadic way of life is slowly breaking down in the far north, just as it is in other parts of the world. The change is due not to droughts and political troubles, as it is along the border of the Sahara, but to the gradual spread of industry and the rapid expansion of modern communications. Mining companies provide employment and attract local people to the settled way of life that it brings. Governments provide schools, hospitals, and other services that encourage people to settle in villages, and modern communications—TV and the Internet—bring people into contact with the wider world and show them alternative ways of life. When young people grow up they leave to seek their fortunes elsewhere.

In the high Arctic, to the north of the tundra, no plants grow on the bare rock and ice, but food is plentiful in the sea. There are fish, seals, walruses, birds, and whales. It is very unlikely that these resources can be exploited more intensively than they are now or that they can be enhanced. The traditional demand for local use is limited, but there is also a much wider demand for fish. Iceland and Greenland are heavily dependent on their fisheries. These were formerly based on cod (*Gadus morhua*) and capelin (*Mallotus villosus*), but like all the other North Atlantic species these have been overexploited, and catches are now restricted to conserve the stocks.

Fishing fleets also visit Antarctic waters. Antarctic cod (*Notothenia coriiceps*), not closely related to the true cod species found only in the Northern Hemisphere, was once abundant but was fished almost to extinction. Icefish (*Chaenocephalus aceratus*), related to the cods, has also been fished very heavily. It is unlikely that the Southern Ocean will yield more food than it does now.

Krill (see "Animals of the Antarctic" on pages 124–125) are extremely abundant around the shores of Antarctica. There are believed to be 66 million–170 million tons (60–155 million tonnes) of *Euphausia superba,* the most numerous species, and in 1972 fishing fleets began hunting them in earnest. By the middle 1970s the fleets, mainly from the Soviet Union and Japan, were catching approximately 550,000 tons (500,000 tonnes) a year. Then the catch began to decrease. Today the annual catch is about 110,000 tons (100,000 tonnes) a year, caught mainly by ships from Japan and Poland.

Catching krill was easy. The animals feed on the algae growing on the underside of the sea ice. Consequently, they are found close to the edge of the ice. The problem was utilizing them. Their shells contain high concentrations of fluorine, making them dangerous to eat unless the shells are removed before the meat is used, and the meat does not keep. Enzymes in the gut of the krill degrade the meat, rendering it unfit to eat. These problems have been overcome in recent years, raising the possibility of expanding the krill fishery, and new uses have been found for the enzymes that degrade the meat. They can now be made into medicines used to treat a number of illnesses, including cancer and gangrene. Krill are also fed to fish raised in fish farms and suitably processed krill is an ingredient in some prepared fish dishes.

Apart from krill, however, it is unlikely that the polar deserts or the seas around them will become a major source of food in years to come.

Conflicts over water resources

Water is a precious commodity to people who live in or near a desert. Without water life cannot continue. Farmers need it to produce food, manufacturing industries need it, and people need it in their homes. It is not surprising that competition for scarce water resources has led to conflict many times in the past or that water and access to it has been used as a weapon of war.

Lebanon, Syria, Israel, and Jordan all depend on water drawn from the Jordan River and its tributaries. In 1951 Jordan announced plans to use water from the Yarmūk River, one of the principal tributaries entering the Jordan from the east, to provide irrigation in the Jordan Valley. This would reduce the amount of water entering the Jordan. Israel responded by draining marshes close to the Israeli-Syrian border, leading to border clashes between Israeli and Syrian troops. In the following years Israel planned a scheme to divert water from the Jordan to irrigate farms in the Negev; Jordan and Syria planned to dam the Jordan near its source, and Israeli forces destroyed the construction site; and in 1969

Israel destroyed a Jordanian canal carrying Jordan water. Access to water resources has since been agreed between Israel, Syria, and Jordan, but it remains one of the most contentious issues standing in the way of a settlement of the conflict between Israel and Palestine.

Egypt depends upon water from the Nile (see "Egypt" on pages 132–134). The Nile has two branches, the Blue Nile and the White Nile, which join at Khartoum, Sudan. The Blue Nile rises in Ethiopia, and in 1978 the Ethiopians proposed to dam the river to provide water for irrigation. This almost led to war, and Egypt continues to threaten Ethiopia with retaliation if that country diverts water from the Blue Nile without discussing the matter first.

Turkey is constructing a series of dams, hydroelectric plants, canals, and irrigation systems as part of its Southeast Anatolia Project. The first stages in the project became operational in 1992. When completed it will divert approximately half of the water flowing through the Euphrates, reducing the amount of water entering Iraq and Syria to less than half its present flow. This also provides Turkey with a powerful weapon. The Turkish government has threatened to cut off the water supply to Syria unless it ends its support for Kurdish rebels operating in southern Turkey.

There have also been fights within countries. In September and October 2002 riots broke out in the states of Karnataka and Tamil Nadu, India, over allocation of water from the Kāveri River which crosses the border between them.

Such disputes are far from new. In about 2500 B.C.E. Urlama, king of the city of Lagash (in Sumer, the land lying between the Euphrates and Tigris), deprived the city of Umma of its water supply by diverting water into ditches. Urlama's son, Il, later cut off the supply to Girsu, another city.

Sometime around 1700 B.C.E., rebels led by Iluma-Ilum declared the independence of Babylon from Sumerian rule. In the resulting fighting the Sumerian king, called Abish or Abi-Eshuh, dammed the Tigris River to block the retreat of the rebels. Babylon was destroyed in 695 B.C.E. The city was then part of the Assyrian Empire and had rebelled. Having razed the city, the Assyrian king, Sennacherib, diverted one of its principal irrigation canals to allow water to wash over the ruins. Babylon recovered and established its own empire, and between 605 B.C.E. and 562 B.C.E. the Babylonian king Nebuchadrezzar used the Euphrates and canals taking water from it to make defensive moats around the huge ramparts of the city.

Water has been a weapon of war and a source of conflict between neighbors for thousands of years, but it has also been the subject of many international treaties. Approximately 3,600 such agreements have been reached between rulers or governments since 805 C.E. Most of those negotiated prior to the early 19th century related to rights of navigation, fishing rights, or boundaries. Some of those agreed since then have dealt with water itself and the right of access to it.

Today the United Nations provides a forum where disputes over water resources can be resolved. Agreements are usually made under the auspices of the UN Environment Program (UNEP), the Food and Agriculture Organization (FAO), or the World Bank. In May 1997 the UN General Assembly adopted the UN Convention on the Law of the Non-navigational Uses of International Watercourses. This is now the principal statement of international law regarding the management of water resources.

The need for agreement has never been more urgent. More than 1.7 billion people, living in more than 80 countries, experience water shortages some or all of the time. Although the size of the global population is stabilizing, the number of people living in many desert lands is likely to continue increasing for some time to come. This will increase the pressure on water supplies. At the same time the fact that 150 of 200 major river systems in the world are shared by two nations and that 50 are shared by 10 shows there is a very real risk of war over water resources.

We must hope that sense and good will prevail and that plans are implemented to use scarce water more efficiently. The world's arid lands may then enjoy peace and prosperity.

CONCLUSION

What future for deserts?

Deserts are barren, inhospitable places. The very word conjures an image of featureless sand dunes stretching beautiful but terrible for as far as the eye can see. Elsewhere the desert surface is made of bare rock and gravel. The wind is incessant, blowing dust that stings as it strikes the skin and sometimes generating dust storms that turn day into night and drive the dust through clothing, through doors and windows, and into every corner. Temperatures range from the scorching heat of midday to the bitter cold of the hours before dawn. And water is the most precious of all commodities. Other deserts are icy wildernesses, no less windy and arid—despite the snow and ice that covers the ground and the screaming blizzards of blown snow that reduce the world to a uniform whiteness.

Yet there is a surprising amount of life in these harshest of environments. No plants grow on the shifting sand of the dunes because their roots can find no anchorage, but there are plants in most other parts of the desert. Some survive as seeds that germinate when it rains, blanketing the desert with green leaves and brilliant flowers and completing their life cycle from seed to seed before the ground dries once more. Other plants store water in their tissues or become dormant during the driest part of the year. There are animals that avoid the excesses of heat and cold and use water so economically that some of them never need to drink. Even in the cold deserts of the Arctic and Antarctica the seas teem with living organisms. Deserts, both hot and cold, are also home to peoples who have found ways to thrive in them.

There is much we can learn from the ways in which plants, animals, and people have adapted to desert life, and the information we acquire will be very useful. If the characteristics that enable desert plants to survive heat, drought, and salt-laden soils could be transferred to crop plants, for example, large expanses of land on the edges of deserts might be cultivated sustainably. That would reduce the risk of soil erosion due to overgrazing and overcultivation. The adaptations developed by desert peoples might help many more people learn to use water more sparingly in those parts of the world where freshwater is in short supply. The physiological adaptations that allow desert animals to remain healthy in extreme conditions might provide medical scientists with information that could be used in treating human patients.

Traditional ways of desert life are disappearing, however, and the day may soon come when the last of the nomadic pastoralists have settled in villages. In the north the Inuit peoples now have permanent homes, although some continue to hunt and fish for food. Villages provide medical centers, schools, shops, and other amenities, and they often attract companies offering jobs. These represent improved living standards and wider opportunities for young people. There may be little time left for us to learn about the old ways from individuals who have lived them.

Desert plants and animals are not threatened, however. If the world is growing warmer, it is possible that some of the low-latitude deserts, such as the Sahara, will shrink in size. This will happen (if it does) because a warmer climate will allow the ITCZ (see "Monsoons" on pages 58–62) to move farther from the equator, bringing the equatorial rains to what are now the margins of deserts. The deserts are unlikely to disappear, however.

Continental and west coast deserts exist because of their locations. No matter what happens to the climate, air will still cross a continent before reaching them, losing its moisture as it does so. Those regions will remain arid.

All predictions of climate change agree that warming will affect the polar regions first and most strongly. Temperatures have already risen in Alaska, Yukon, and northeastern Siberia, and the Antarctic Peninsula is markedly warmer than it was decades ago (although much of the interior of Antarctica is colder). If this trend continues it may reduce the area of polar desert by allowing more species to establish themselves in places that at present are too cold and dry for them.

Deserts are part of our world. Harsh and unforgiving, they nevertheless harbor highly adapted species of plants and animals; desert species have evolved strategies and physiological modifications that enable them to meet the challenges of extreme temperatures and absence of water. At the same time, the deserts remind us of our own dependence on the rain that waters the crops that feed us.

SI UNITS AND CONVERSIONS

UNIT	QUANTITY	SYMBOL	CONVERSION
Base units			
meter	length	m	1 m = 3.2808 feet
kilogram	mass	kg	1 kg = 2.205 pounds
second	time	s	
ampere	electric current	A	
kelvin	thermodynamic temperature	K	1 K = 1°C = 1.8°F
candela	luminous intensity		
mole	amount of substance	cd	mol
Supplementary units			
radian	plane angle	rad	$\pi/2$ rad = 90°
steradian	solid angle	sr	
Derived units			
coulomb	quantity of electricity	C	
cubic meter	volume	m^3	1 m^3 = 1.308 yards^3
farad	capacitance	F	
henry	inductance	H	
hertz	frequency	Hz	
joule	energy	J	1 J = 0.2389 calories
kilogram per cubic meter	density	kg m^{-3}	1 kg m^{-3} = 0.0624 lb. ft.$^{-3}$
lumen	luminous flux	lm	
lux	illuminance	lx	

(continues)

(continued)

UNIT	QUANTITY	SYMBOL	CONVERSION
meter per second	speed	m s^{-1}	1 m s^{-1} = 3.281 ft s^{-1}
meter per second squared	acceleration	m s^{-2}	
mole per cubic meter	concentration	mol m^{-3}	
newton	force	N	1 N = 7.218 lb. force
ohm	electric resistance	Ω	
pascal	pressure	Pa	1 Pa = 0.145 lb. in^{-2}
radian per second	angular velocity	rad s^{-1}	
radian per second squared	angular acceleration	rad s^{-2}	
square meter	area	m^2	1 m^2 = 1.196 yards^2
tesla	magnetic flux density	T	
volt	electromotive force	V	
watt	power	W	1W = 3.412 Btu h^{-1}
weber	magnetic flux	Wb	

Prefixes used with SI units

PREFIX	SYMBOL	VALUE
atto	a	× 10^{-18}
femto	f	× 10^{-15}
pico	p	× 10^{-12}
nano	n	× 10^{-9}
micro	μ	× 10^{-6}
milli	m	× 10^{-3}
centi	c	× 10^{-2}
deci	d	× 10^{-1}
deca	da	× 10
hecto	h	× 10^2
kilo	k	× 10^3
mega	M	× 10^6

PREFIX	SYMBOL	VALUE
giga	G	$\times 10^9$
tera	T	$\times 10^{12}$

Prefixes attached to SI units alter their value.

GLOSSARY

ablation   the removal of snow and ice by melting and by SUBLIMATION

adiabatic   a change in temperature that involves no exchange of heat with an outside source

adobe   clay found in deserts that is used as a building material

aklé dune   a sand dune in the form of a long, wavy ridge at right angles to the wind; the crescent-shaped sections alternately face into the wind (linguoid) and away from the wind (barchanoid)

albedo   the reflectiveness of a surface to light, measured as the percentage of light reflected

alluvial   pertaining to rivers

anabatic   describes a wind that blows up the side of a hill

andhis   *see* SIMOOM

angle of repose   the maximum degree of slope at which a pile of dry, loose grains remains stable; it is typically between 32° and 36°

anticyclone   a region in which the atmospheric pressure is higher than it is in the surrounding air

aphelion   the point in its orbit at which the Earth is farthest from the Sun

aquifer   an underground body of permeable material (such as sand or gravel) lying above a layer of impermeable material (such as rock or clay) that is capable of storing water and through which the GROUNDWATER flows

arroyo (donga, wadi, ouadi)   a dry river valley with steep sides and a flat floor

artesian well   a well that flows without pumping because it taps into water held under pressure in an AQUIFER that is contained by layers of impermeable material above and below

asthenosphere   the upper part of the MANTLE, in which the rocks are slightly plastic and deform under pressure

barchan   a crescent-shaped sand dune that forms where the wind blows mainly from one direction; the crescent faces into the wind with the tails pointing downwind

barchanoid   pertaining to a BARCHAN dune. *See* AKLÉ DUNE.

blackbody   a body that absorbs all of the radiation falling upon it and emits all of its absorbed radiation at a wavelength inversely proportional to its temperature

blubber   a thick layer of fatty tissue lying beneath the skin of whales and seals; it provides thermal insulation

boundary current   an ocean current that flows northward or southward close to the coast of a continent and parallel to it. In the Northern Hemisphere, eastern boundary currents carry cold water southward on the eastern side of ocean basins (not along the eastern coasts of continents), while western boundary currents carry warm water northward on the western side of ocean basins

butte   an isolated, flat-topped hill, made by the erosion of horizontal layers of sedimentary rock

caravan   a group of camels or vehicles crossing a desert together

caravansary   a facility providing secure overnight accommodation for CARAVANS and those traveling with them

carboxylation   a chemical reaction in which a molecule gains a carbon atom

chelicera (pl. chelicerae)   one of the appendages resembling claws possessed by spiders and scorpions

chlorophyll   the pigment present in the leaves and sometimes stems of green plants that gives them their green color. Chlorophyll molecules trap light, thus supplying the energy for PHOTOSYNTHESIS

chloroplast   the structure in plant cells that contains CHLOROPHYLL and in which PHOTOSYNTHESIS takes place

clay   mineral material consisting of particles smaller than 0.00008 inch (0.002 mm) that stack together. A clay soil contains at least 20 percent of clay particles by weight

climatic optimum   a period during which average temperatures are higher than in the preceding and succeeding periods

cloud seeding   dropping particles of solid carbon dioxide, silver iodide, or some other substance into a cloud in order to make rain or snow fall

continental drift   the movement of the continents in relation to one another across the Earth's surface

convection   the transfer of heat by vertical movement within a fluid

core temperature   the temperature inside an animal's body, deep below the surface

countercurrent exchange   the exchange of heat between blood traveling in opposite directions through arteries and veins that lie side by side. This chills blood flowing away from the center of the body and warms blood returning to the heart

crop milk   *see* PIGEON MILK

cutaneous respiration   the exchange of respiratory gases through the skin. Amphibians (such as frogs, toads, salamanders) have skins that allow gas molecules to pass through, and a significant proportion of their RESPIRATION takes place through the skin

cyclone   *see* depression

deflation   the removal of surface material (such as dry soil or sand) by the wind

deposition   the changing of water vapor directly to ice, without passing through a liquid phase

depression (cyclone)   a region along a weather front where the atmospheric pressure is lower than it is in the surrounding air

desalination   the purification of salt water by the removal of salt to render it fit for use in irrigation or to drink

desertification   the deterioration of land until its quality is similar to that of desert

desert pavement (rock pavement)   a thin layer of gravel or small stones that covers the surface of an area of desert

desert rose   a petal-shaped rock, sometimes resembling a rose, that results from chemical reactions in calcite (calcium carbonate) and gypsum (calcium sulfate) minerals

desert varnish   a thin, dark-colored layer of iron and manganese oxides that forms on exposed rock surfaces in hot deserts

dew-point temperature   the temperature at which water vapor condenses to form dew or cloud droplets

diurnation   a period of dormancy into which an animal enters for part of the day

donga   *see* ARROYO

draa   a ridge of sand or chain of sand dunes, more than 1,000 feet (300 m) high, lying some distance from its nearest neighbor, that is found in the Sahara

dry adiabatic lapse rate   *see* LAPSE RATE

eccentricity   the extent to which the orbit of a planet, satellite, or other body departs from a circle

ecliptic   the plane of the Earth's orbit about the Sun

ectotherm an animal that maintains a constant body CORE TEMPERATURE by behavioral means, such as by basking in warm sunshine to warm up and seeking shade to cool down

El Niño a weakening or reversal of the prevailing easterly winds over the tropical South Pacific Ocean that happens at intervals of two to seven years. This weakens the wind-driven surface ocean current, allowing warm water to accumulate off the South American coast and producing weather changes over a large area

endotherm an animal that maintains a constant body CORE TEMPERATURE by physiological means, such as by dilating or contracting blood vessels in the skin, shivering, and sweating

ENSO the full cycle of EL NIÑO and its opposite, La Niña, associated with the SOUTHERN OSCILLATION

equinox March 20–21 and September 22–23, when the noonday Sun is directly overhead at the equator and day and night are of equal length everywhere in the world

estivation a period of dormancy into which an animal enters to escape a period of hot or dry weather

exotherm *see* POIKILOTHERM

false color unnatural color used in some satellite images to enhance the difference between types of surface, such as between vegetation types or between seawater and ice. Vegetation often appears red in false color images

GDP *see* GROSS DOMESTIC PRODUCT

greenhouse effect the absorption and reradiation of long-wave radiation emitted by the Earth's surface by molecules of water vapor, carbon dioxide, ozone, and several other "greenhouse gases," warming the air

gross domestic product (GDP) the value of all the goods and services produced within a country during a specified time (usually one year)

groundwater underground water that flows through an AQUIFER

gyre the approximately circular path followed by the surface currents in all the oceans

halophyte a plant that tolerates salt

harmattan a moderate or strong, hot, dry, dusty wind that blows during the day across West Africa south of the Sahara

heliostat a mirror, driven by a motor so it tracks the Sun, that reflects solar radiation and focuses it onto a small area in order to generate high temperatures

hibernation a state of dormancy into which an animal enters to avoid a period of winter cold

homeotherm   an animal that maintains a constant body CORE TEMPERATURE either by behavioral (an ECTOTHERM) or physiological (an ENDOTHERM) means

humidity   the amount of water vapor present in the air

humus   decomposed plant and animal material in the soil

hydrogen bond   a chemical bond between hydrogen and nitrogen, oxygen, and fluorine. Hydrogen bonds link water molecules in the liquid and solid phases and also occur in a range of other compounds

igneous   describes a rock formed when molten MAGMA cools and solidifies

infrared radiation   electromagnetic radiation with a wavelength from 0.7 μm to 1 mm (1 μm is equal to one millionth of one meter)

inselberg   a steep-sided, isolated hill standing on a plain (the name is German for "island hill")

isostasy   the theory that there is a constant mass of rocks above a certain level below the Earth's surface. If the volume of rock is greater in one place than in another, such as where rocks form a mountain, then that rock and the mountain's roots will be less dense than the thinner, denser crust beneath

jet stream   a winding ribbon of strong wind about 5–10 miles (8–16 km) above Earth's surface. Jet streams are typically thousands of miles long, hundreds of miles wide, and several miles deep

katabatic   describes a cold wind that blows downhill

khamsin   a hot, dry wind that blows in Egypt and Sudan

La Niña   *see* ENSO

lapse rate   the rate at which the air temperature decreases (lapses) with increasing altitude. In unsaturated air the dry *adiabatic* lapse rate is 5.38°F per thousand feet (9.8°C per km); in saturated air the saturated adiabatic lapse rate varies, but it averages 2.75°F per thousand feet (5°C per km)

latent heat   the heat energy that is absorbed or released when a substance changes phase between solid and liquid, liquid and gas, and solid and gas. For water at 32°F (0°C) the latent heat of melting and freezing is 80 cal. per gram (334 joules per gram); of vaporization and condensation 600 cal. per gram (2,501 J per gram); and for SUBLIMATION and DEPOSITION 680 cal. per gram (2,835 J per gram)

leads   areas of open water in a sea otherwise covered with ice

lifting condensation level   the altitude at which the air is at the DEW-POINT TEMPERATURE and water vapor begins to condense to form cloud; the lifting condensation level marks the cloud base

linguoid   *see* AKLÉ DUNE

lithosphere   the uppermost part of the solid Earth, comprising the crust and upper MANTLE

Little Ice Age   a period lasting from the 16th century until the early 20th century during which temperatures throughout the world were lower than they were before or have been since

magma   hot, molten rock from the base of the Earth's crust and the upper part of the MANTLE

mandible   in vertebrate animals, the lower jaw; in birds, strictly the lower jaw and bill but often applied to both upper and lower parts of the bill. In arthropods (such as insects, spiders, scorpions, crustaceans), part of the mouthparts used to seize and cut food items

mantle   that part of the Earth's interior lying between the outer edge of the inner core and the underside of the crust

mesa   a wide, flat-topped hill

mesophyll   the tissue lying just below the surface of a leaf, where PHOTOSYNTHESIS takes place

monsoon   a reversal in wind direction that occurs twice a year over much of the Tropics, producing two seasons with markedly different weather

mushroom rock   *see* PEDESTAL ROCK

nilometer   a device invented in ancient Egypt that monitors the level of water in the Nile River, allowing the seasonal flood to be predicted accurately

oasis   a region in a desert where the WATER TABLE lies close enough to the surface for plant roots to obtain moisture

obliquity   the extent to which the Earth's rotational axis is tilted with respect to the plane of the ECLIPTIC

occlusion   the stage in the life cycle of a frontal weather system at which advancing cold air has pushed beneath warmer air and begun to lift the warm air clear of the surface

orogeny   mountain building

osmosis   the movement of water or some other solvent through a partially permeable membrane from a region of low SOLUTE concentration to a region of high solute concentration until the solutions are at equal concentration on both sides of the membrane

ouadi   *see* ARROYO

parabolic dune   a crescent-shaped sand dune in which the wind blows into the hollow part of the crescent and the tails of the crescent point in the direction from which the wind blows

partial pressure   in a mixture of gases such as air, that part of the total pressure that can be attributed to one of the constituent gases. For example, air consists of approximately 79 percent nitrogen and 21 percent oxygen; if the air pressure is 1,000 millibars (mb) then the partial pressure of oxygen is 210 mb

pastoralist   an individual who leads a seminomadic life herding livestock from one area of seasonal pasture to another, deriving a living from the products of the livestock

pedestal rock (mushroom rock)   an unstable, mushroom-shaped rock most often found in deserts or semiarid regions; it forms through chemical reactions that dissolve minerals from regions in the rock where moisture is retained

pedipalps   in arachnids (such as spiders, scorpions, mites, etc.), appendages at the front of the body used to kill and manipulate prey, and also for defense and digging. Pedipalps are sensitive to touch and chemicals (equivalent to the senses of taste and smell). In arachnids with large CHELICERAE (such as spiders) the pedipalps are also used as walking legs; in those with small chelicerae (such as scorpions) the pedipalps are large and used in hunting

perihelion   the point in the Earth's orbit when it is closest to the Sun

permafrost   permanently frozen ground. To become permafrost the ground must remain frozen throughout a minimum of two winters and the summer between

permeability   the ability of a material to allow water to flow through it

phloem   tissue through which the products of photosynthesis and hormones are transported from the leaves to all parts of a vascular plant

phosphorylation   a chemical reaction in which phosphate (PO_4) is added

photorespiration   a reaction in which rubisco, the enzyme responsible for capturing carbon dioxide during PHOTOSYNTHESIS, instead captures oxygen, triggering a chain of reactions that release carbon dioxide but without releasing any energy

photosynthesis   the sequence of chemical reactions in which green plants and cyanobacteria use sunlight as a source of energy for the manufacture (synthesis) of sugars from hydrogen and carbon, obtained from water and carbon dioxide, respectively. The reactions can be summarized as:

$$6CO_2 + 6H_2O + \textit{light} \rightarrow C_6H_{12}O_6 + 6O_2 \uparrow$$

The upward arrow indicates that oxygen is released into the air; $C_6H_{12}O_6$ is glucose, a simple sugar

pigeon milk (crop milk)   a highly nutritious liquid produced from the lining of the crop in all pigeons (males as well as females) and fed to the chicks

plasmodesmata   passageways in the MESOPHYLL of plants through which the initial four-carbon compound moves in the C4 pathway of PHOTOSYNTHESIS

plate tectonics   the theory holding that the Earth's crust comprises a number of rigid sections, or plates, that move in relation to one another

playa (salina, sabkha)   a low-lying plain with a surface covered by salt formed by the evaporation of a lake

poikilotherm (exotherm)   an animal that is unable to control its body CORE TEMPERATURE, which is therefore equal to the temperature of its surroundings

polar front   the boundary between tropical and polar air

porosity   the percentage of the total volume of a material that consists of spaces between particles

postabdomen   the hind part of the abdomen that a scorpion carries raised over its back; its "sting"

process water   water used during an industrial process that becomes incorporated in the product

purchasing power parity   GROSS DOMESTIC PRODUCT per person, corrected for overvaluation or undervaluation of the local currency by pricing a basket of goods and services first in the local currency and then in U.S. dollars. This yields a fairly true valuation of the local currency against which the GDP is adjusted

qanat   an artificial underground watercourse, built in a desert to collect and transport water for irrigation

rain shadow   the drier climate on the lee (downwind) side of a mountain range caused by the loss of moisture as air approaching the mountains is forced to rise, whereupon its water vapor condenses and falls as rain or snow on the windward slopes. Once past the mountains, the air subsides and contracts, and this compression raises the temperature of the subsiding air, further reducing its RELATIVE HUMIDITY

reg   a stone-covered desert surface, often consisting of rounded pebbles

relative humidity   the amount of water vapor present in air at a particular temperature expressed as the percentage of the water vapor needed to saturate the air at that temperature

respiration   the sequence of chemical reactions in which living cells oxidize carbon in sugar to release energy; the opposite of PHOTOSYNTHESIS. The reactions can be summarized as:

$$C_6H_{12}O_6 + 6CO_2 \rightarrow 6CO_2 + 6H_2O + energy$$

$C_6H_{12}O_6$ is glucose, a simple sugar

reverse osmosis   a method for removing salt from water by applying sufficient pressure to drive water molecules through a partially permeable membrane from the stronger to the weaker solution, the opposite direction to that in OSMOSIS

rock pavement   *see* DESERT PAVEMENT

sabkha   *see* PLAYA

salina   *see* PLAYA

salination   the accumulation of salts in the upper soil, eventually rendering the soil infertile

sand   mineral particles, commonly of quartz (silicon oxide) from 0.002 to 0.079 inches (0.05–2 mm) in size

saturated adiabatic lapse rate   *see* LAPSE RATE

saturation   the condition in which the moisture held by a substance is at a maximum. Saturated air holds as much water vapor as is possible at that temperature; if more water vapor is added an equivalent amount will condense into liquid

saturation vapor pressure   the VAPOR PRESSURE at which water vapor saturates a layer of air at a given temperature lying immediately above an open water surface

seafloor spreading   the theory that the ocean floor is created at ridges where MANTLE material rises to the surface and the crustal rocks move away from the ridges on either side, causing the ocean basin to widen as the seafloor spreads

seif dune   a long sand dune with a wavy crest and an equal angle of slope on both sides; it can extend for hundreds of miles. Seif dunes typically form by the extension of the arms of BARCHAN dunes

silt   mineral particles 0.000000079–0.000002 inch (0.002–0.05 μm) in size

simoom (andhis)   a hot, dry, usually dusty wind that blows in spring and summer across the southeastern Sahara and the Arabian Peninsula

soil horizon   a horizontal layer in a SOIL PROFILE that differs in its mineral or organic composition from the layers above and below it, and from which it can be clearly distinguished visually

soil profile   a vertical section cut through a soil from the surface to the underlying rock

solar cell   a device that converts light energy into electric current

solar chimney   a device for generating electrical power from the upward flow of air heated by sunlight beneath an extensive, transparent canopy and funneled through a tall cylindrical structure (the chimney) containing generating turbines

solar panel   a device that uses solar heat to raise the temperature of water

solar pond   a device for heating water that consists of a pool of salt water with freshwater floating above it. Sunshine passes through the freshwater and heats the black material lining the base and sides of the pond; this heats the salt water

solstice   one of the two dates each year when the noonday Sun is directly overhead at one or other of the Tropics and the difference in length between the hours of daylight and darkness is at its most extreme. The solstices occur on June 21–22 and December 22–23

solute   a substance that is dissolved in another substance (the solvent) to form a solution

solvent   *see* SOLUTE

southern oscillation   a change that occurs periodically in the distribution of surface atmospheric pressure over the equatorial South Pacific Ocean

specific heat capacity   the amount of heat that must be applied to a substance in order to raise its temperature by one degree. It is measured in calories per gram per degree Celsius (cal/g/°C) or in the scientific units of joules per gram per kelvin (J/g/K; $1K = 1°C = 1.8°F$)

star dune   a sand dune consisting of a number of ridges that radiate from a central point. It forms where the wind direction is highly variable

stomata (sing. stoma)   small openings, or pores, on the surface of a plant leaf through which the plant cells exchange gases with the outside air. Stomata can be opened or closed by the expansion or contraction of two guard cells surrounding each stoma

subduction   the movement of one crustal plate beneath another, returning the crustal rock to the Earth's MANTLE

sublimation   the direct change of phase from solid to gas without passing through the liquid phase

supercooling   the chilling of water to below freezing temperature without triggering the formation of ice

supersaturation the condition in which the RELATIVE HUMIDITY of air is greater than 100 percent

tail dune a sand dune that forms as a "tail" pointing downwind on the lee side of a rock or boulder in an area where the wind blows predominantly from one direction

transform fault a boundary between two crustal plates that are moving past each other in opposite directions

transpiration the evaporation of water through leaf STOMATA when these are open for the exchange of gases

turgor rigidity of plant tissues due to water held under pressure in the cells

vapor pressure the PARTIAL PRESSURE exerted on a surface by water vapor present in the air

virga precipitation that falls from the base of a cloud but evaporates before reaching the ground; it is visible as a gray, veil-like extension below the cloud

wadi *see* ARROYO

waterlogging the accumulation of water in a soil until it fills most of the spaces between soil particles

water table the upper margin of the GROUNDWATER; soil is fully saturated below the water table but unsaturated above it

weathering the breaking down of rocks by physical and chemical processes

wetting front in dry climates, the limit to which rainwater penetrates the ground and where substances washed from the upper soil tend to accumulate

xerophyte a plant that tolerates dry conditions

xylem plant tissue through which water entering at the roots is transported to all parts of the plant

BIBLIOGRAPHY AND FURTHER READING

Allaby, Michael. *Floods*. Rev. ed. New York: Facts On File, 2003.

———. *Droughts*. Rev. ed. New York: Facts On File, 2003.

———. *The Facts On File Weather and Climate Handbook*. New York: Facts On File, 2002.

———. *Deserts*. New York: Facts On File, 2001.

Baatar, Shirchin. "The Great 'Gobi' Desert of Legendary Mongolia." Available online. URL: http://baatar.freeyellow.com/. Downloaded on July 29, 2003.

Baird, Rodney R. "Qanat," Ancient Routes. Available online. URL: http://www.ancientroute.com/water/qanat.htm. Downloaded on April 15, 2004.

Baron, Stanley. *The Desert Locust*. London: Eyre Methuen, 1972.

Bathman, Ulrich, Bettina Meyer, and Bettina Fach. "Ecology and ecophysiology of Antarctic krill," Alfred-Wegener-Institut für Polar- und Meeresforschung in der Helmholtz-Gemeinschaft. Available online. URL: http://www.awi-bremerhaven.de/Biomeer/zooplankton-top02-e.html. Downloaded on April 20, 2004.

Bergin, Liz. "The Cave of a Thousand Buddhas," University of Wisconsin-Eau Claire. Available online. URL: http://www.uwec.edu/greider/BMRB/culture/student.work/berginem/. Downloaded on March 11, 2004.

Center for Astrophysical Research in Antarctica. "Virtual Tour—South Pole," Center for Astrophysical Research in Antarctica. Available online. URL: http://astro.uchicago.edu/cara/vtour/pole/. Updated on May 2, 2000.

Cowley, Clive. "The Namib Desert," Clive Cowley's Journey into Namibia: Namibia Guidebook #12. Available online. URL: http://www.orusovo.com/guidebook/content2.htm. Downloaded on July 30, 2003.

Dainer, Joan S. "The Salton Sea," The San Diego State University Center for Inland Waters. Available online. URL: http://www.sci.sdsu.edu/salton/SaltonSeaHomePage.html. Downloaded on April 14, 2004.

Deconinck, Stefan. "Water and Conflict," Waternet. Available online. URL: http://waternet.rug.ac.be/. Updated on February 17, 2004.

Dwyer, Graham. "Cooperating to Combat Dust and Sandstorms in Northeast Asia," Available online. URL: http://www.adb.org/

Documents/Periodicals/ADB_Review/2003/vol35_4/combat_
dust.asp. Downloaded on August 21, 2003.

Earth Summit + 5 Special Session of the General Assembly to
Review and Appraise the Implementation of Agenda 21. "The
United Nations Convention to Combat Desertification: A New
Response to an Age-Old Problem." United Nations. Available
online. URL: http://www.un.org/ecosocdev/geninfo/sustdev/
desert.htm. Downloaded on April 7, 2004.

Foth, H. D. *Fundamentals of Soil Science.* 8th ed. New York: John
Wiley, 1991.

Gecko Productions. "Henties Bay, Namibia: The Namib Desert,"
Henties Bay Municipality: Tourism. Available online. URL:
http://hentiesbay.com/desert.htm. Downloaded on July 30,
2003.

Gleick, Peter H. "Water Conflict Chronology," The World's Water:
Information on the World's Freshwater Resources. Available
online. URL: http://www.worldwater.org/conflict.htm. Updated
on August 13, 2003.

The Hopi Tribe. "Hopi Villages," Available online. URL: http://
www.hopi.nsn.us/Pages/Villages/Hopi_2.htm. Downloaded on
March 9, 2004.

Hubert, Alain, and Michel Brent. "Katabatic Winds: Dreadful
Blizzards," Polar Challenges: Adventure and Research. Available
online. URL: http://www.antarctica.org/UK/Envirn/pag/vents
_cata_UK.htm. Downloaded on August 20, 2003.

Internet Marketing Solutions. "Country: Saudi Arabia," Saudi
Cities: The Saudi Experiences. Available online. URL: http://
saudicities.com/country2.htm. Downloaded on July 28, 2003.

Iziko Museums of Cape Town. "Order Solifugae." *Biodiversity
Explorer.* Iziko Museums of Cape Town. Available online. URL:
http://www.museums.org.za/bio/arachnids/solifugae.htm.
Downloaded on February 26, 2004.

Levy, Sharon. "Last Days of the Locust." *New Scientist,* February 21,
2004, 48–49.

Lutgens, Frederick K., and Edward J. Tarbuck. *The Atmosphere.* 7th
ed. Upper Saddle River, N.J.: Prentice Hall, 1998.

Mesanovic, Mustafa, and Nils Philippsen. "High-Flux Solar
Furnace," Projects: Alternative Energy. Available online. URL:
http://www.=stud=/fhtesslingen.de/projects/alt_energy/sol_
thermal/flux.html. Posted November 29, 1996.

Myers, Joan. "Antarctica Journal," Joan Myers. Available online.
URL: www.joanmyers.com/Journal.htm. Downloaded on August
20, 2003.

Oliver, John E., and John J. Hidore. *Climatology: An Atmospheric
Science.* Upper Saddle River, N.J.: Prentice Hall, 2d ed. 2002.

Rhodes, Barbara. "Umberto Nobile: The North Pole Flights." 90°
North. Available online. URL: http://members.tripod.com/
90north/nobilenorthpole.htm. Downloaded on March 11, 2004.

Schaefer, Jason. "*Centruroides vittatus* (striped scorpion)." University
of Michigan Museum of Zoology: Animal Diversity Web.
Available online. URL: http://animaldiversity.ummz.umich.edu/
site/accounts/information/Centruroides_vittatus.htm.
Downloaded on February 25, 2004.

Schlaich Bergermann und Partner. "The solar chimney—the principle," Schlaich Bergermann und Partner, Structural Consulting
Engineering. Available online. URL: http://www.sbp.de/de/
html/projects/solar/aufwind/pages_auf/principl.htm.
Downloaded on March 15, 2004.

Smith, R. L. "Scorpions," University of Arizona: Urban Integrated
Pest Management. Available online. URL: http://cals.arizona.
edu/urbanipm/scorpions/scorpions.html. Downloaded on May
3, 2005.

South-Pole.com, "Antarctic Explorers: Ernest H. Shackleton,"
South-Pole.com. Available online. URL: http://www.south-
pole.com/p0000097.htm. Downloaded on March 11, 2004.

Spriggs, Amy. "Namib Desert." World Wildlife Fund. Available
online. URL: http://www.worldwildlife.org/wildworld/profiles/
terrestrial/at/at1315_full.html. Downloaded on July 30, 2003.

United Nations General Assembly. "Convention on the Law of the
Non-navigational Uses of International Watercourses," The
Water Page. Available online. URL: http://www.thewaterpage.
com/UN_Convention_97.html. Downloaded on April 21, 2004.

Volk, Sylvia. "Building a Better Qanat," Trivial Pursuits: Page of
Asia. Available online. URL: http://www.iras.ucalgary.ca/~volk/
sylvia/qanat.htm. Updated on April 28, 2000.

Watson, Kathie. "Types of Deserts." U.S. Geological Survey.
Available online. URL: http://pubs.usgs.gov/gip/deserts/types/.
Updated on October 29, 1997.

Whitfield, Roderick, and Seigo Otsuka. "Dunhuang: Caves of the
Singing Sands, Buddhist Art from the Silk Road." Textile and Art
Publications. Available online. URL: http://www.textile-art.
com/dun1.html. Downloaded on March 11, 2004.

Note: *Italic* page numbers refer to illustrations.

A

Abish (king of Sumer) 220
absolute humidity 7
Abyssinian spurge 88
acacia trees 89, 211–213
addax 116–117
adenosine diphosphate (ADP) 82
adenosine triphosphate (ATP) 82
adiabatic process 54–56
adobe 140–141
ADP 82
aerobic organisms 83
Afghanistan 75
Africa
    climate change in 7–9, 126
    climate cycles in 178–179
    dams in 194–195
    early civilizations in 126, 128–130
    exploration of 151–155
    location of deserts in 2
    locusts in 108, 109
    minerals in 165–166
    oil in 160
    people of 134–136
    tourism in 168
    water resources in 171–172
agaves 89–90
agriculture. *See also* irrigation
    before climate change 126–127
    corridor farming 211–213
    discovery of 130
    dry farming 209–211
    in Egypt 132–133

grazing and 184–185
improvements in 189–190
new crops for 213–217
in North America 140, 141
in oases 199–200
spread of 130–133
Agriculture, U.S. Department of (USDA) 35
Agulhas Current 58
air. *See* atmosphere
airag 137
aircraft icing 193
air masses 62–65
air pressure
    in climate cycles 180
    in El Niño 178–179
    evaporation and 5–6
air stability 60–61, *61*
Akimel O'odham people 140
Akkad (region) 127, 131
aklé dunes 40
Aksum Empire 128
albedo 71, *71*
alcoves 44
Aleut people 142
Algeria
    climate change in 126
    locusts in 109
    temperatures in 12, 65–66, 68
alley cropping 212–213
alluvial aquifers 171–172
Alpine-Himalayan orogeny 31
Alps, formation of 31
alveoles 44
amaranths 213–214
Amu Dar'ya (river) 198

Amundsen, Roald 147, 151, 153, 169
anaerobic organisms 83
Anasazi people 141
Anatolian Plain 130
Anchieta's desert lizard *111*
Andes Mountains 29–30
andhis 75
angle of repose 39
angular momentum 78, 79
angular velocity 79
animals xv, 93–125
    in cold environments 99–105
    continental movement and 24
    domesticated 130, 137–138, 166
    in estivation 102–103
    hibernation by 103–105
    in hot environments 93–99
    hunting of 143
    overgrazing by *183*, 183–186
    of polar deserts 121–125, 218–219
Antarctica xvi, *20*
    animals of 124–125
    climate of 21–22, 68–73
    desert varnish in 42–43
    elevation of 74
    exploration of 149–151, 152, 153
    food in 218
    geography of 20–21
    icebergs in 207–208

Antarctica *(continued)*
   precipitation in 21, *21*
   temperatures in 21, 69–70
   tourism in 169
   winds in 74
Antarctic Circumpolar Current
   57
Antarctic cod 218
antelopes 117
anticyclones 71, 73, 74
Antilles Current 57
ant lions 106–107
aphelion 69, 182
apple-ring acacia 212–213
aqueducts 201
aquifers 47
   confined *v.* unconfined 48
   depletion of 171–172
   oases linked to 50
   qanats and 202
Arabian Desert
   European exploration of
      155
   location of 2, 10
   people of 134–136
Arabian oryx 117
Arabic language 135, 136, 154
Arabs 135–136
Aral Sea 198–199
Arctic *146*
   animals of 121–124
   exploration in 145–149,
      153
   food in 218
   icebergs in 207
   people of 142–144
   temperatures in 69–70
   tourism in 169
arctic fox 100–102, 122
arctic ground squirrel 104
arctic lemming 121
Arctic Oscillation 180
areoles 88
aridity
   deserts defined by xvi–xvii
   of polar deserts 68–73
   temperature in xvii, 70
Aristotle (Greek philosopher)
   205
Arizona 140–142

armadillo lizard 112
arroyos 45–47
artesian wells 48, *48*
Asia
   climate change in 9
   European exploration of
      155–158
   location of deserts in 2–3
   oases in 49
   people of 136–138
   tourism in 169
Askia Muhammad Touré 129
asphalt 159
Assyrian Empire 128, 131,
   220–221
asthenosphere 26, *32,* 32–33
Aswān High Dam 195, 196,
   197
Atacama Desert *18*
   climate change in 177
   climate of 18, 57
   geography of 17–18
   location of 2
   oases in 49
   ocean currents and 57
Atlantic Desert 10, 19
atmosphere. *See also* temperature
   adiabatic process in 54–56
   air masses in 62 65
   general circulation of
      52–53, *53,* 54–56
   lapse rates and stability of
      60–61, *61*
ATP 82
auroras 180–181
Australia
   climate change in 9
   climate of 12
   groundwater in 47
   location of deserts in 3,
      3–4
   locusts in 108
   mammals of 115
Australian hopping mouse 115
automobiles 41, 135
axial tilt 182
axial wobble 182
azonal soils 35
Azores high 180

B
Babylon 131, 220–221
Babylonian Empire 131, 221
Bacillus thuringiensis 215
Badawi language 136
bannertail kangaroo rat 115
Barbary (region) 134
barchan dunes *39,* 40
barchanoid ridges 40
bark scorpion 105
barrel cacti *89*
Barth, Heinrich 154
basking 95, 110, 120
beans 213
bears 104–105
Beas Dam 196
Bedouins 135, 136, *136*
beetles 106, 107
Bellingshausen, Fabian Gottlieb
   von 150
Benguela Current 57
Berber people 134, 135
Bergen Geophysical Institute
   63
Bering Strait 145, 146
Bible 131–132
birds 118–121
   core temperature of 95
   hibernation of 103–104
   of polar deserts 122,
      124–125
bitumen 159
Bjerknes, Vilhelm 63
blackbodies 176
blackbody radiation 176
blood 96–97, 101–102
blood rain 75
blubber 101
blue whale 125
body temperature
   of birds 118, 120
   cold and 99–102
   heat and 94–99
   during hibernation
      104–105
Bokhara carpets 167
Bonneville salt flats 45
boundary currents 56–58
Bowers, H. R. 151
Brandt's hedgehog 94

Brazil Current 57
Breasted, James Henry 130–131
breathing
　　during estivation 103
　　v. respiration 83
Britain 23–24, 29
Bt plants 215
Buddhism 140, 157, 158
buffalo gourds 215–216
bullhorn acacia 89
bundle-sheath cells 84
burrows 96, 102
buttes 43
Byblos 131–132

C

cacti 87–89
Cahokia Mounds State Park
　　127
Caillé, René-Auguste 154
Cairo (Egypt) 132
California Current 57
Californian kingsnake 114
camels
　　adaptations of 97–98, 99
　　in caravans 138–139
　　human use of 135–136,
　　　136, 137
camel thorn *91,* 212
CAM plants 83, 84, 88
Canary Current 58
Canary Island spurge 88
Cancer, tropic of 51, 52
cannons, hail 191–192
capelin 218
Capricorn, tropic of 51, 52
caracal lynx 94, 118, *118*
caravans 135, 138–140
caravansary 138–139
carbon dioxide 82, 83–85, 177
carboxylation 82, 83
caribou 123, 217
carpets 166–167
carpet viper 112, 113
Carthage 134, 168
cashmere 167
Çatalhüyük 130
cataracts 196
cats 117–118
cattle 184, 185

Cave of a Thousand Buddhas
　　157, 158
cells 86, 96, 175
century plant 90
C4 plants 83–85
Chad, Lake 7–9, *8*
channel millet 214
cheetah 117
chelicerae 106
Chénier, Louis de 109
China
　　exploration of 155–157
　　sandstorms in 76
　　Silk Road in 139–140,
　　　155–156
chlorophyll 81–82, 84
chloroplasts 81
Christianity 131–132, 140
chromosomes 214
chuckwalla 110
civilizations 127–144
Clapperton, Hugh 154
clay 36–37, 174
climate 51–80. *See also* rainfall;
　　temperature
　　air masses in 62–65
　　atmospheric circulation in
　　　52–56
　　in desert formation 4
　　diversity in xvi
　　of interior deserts 13–16
　　monsoons and 58–62
　　natural cycles in 178–183,
　　　209
　　oceans and 54, 56–58, 176
　　of polar deserts 19–22,
　　　68–73
　　and soil formation 34, 35
　　specific heat capacity and
　　　66–67, 68
　　storms in 74–80
　　of subtropical deserts 12,
　　　51–56
　　of west coast deserts
　　　16–19, 56–58
　　wind in 73–74
climate change
　　agriculture before 126–127
　　effects of 175–178
　　future of 223–224

history of 7–9, 126–127
　　natural cycles of 178–183
climatic optimum 9
clothing 167
clouds *45, 46,* 61, 181
cloud seeding 192–194
coastal aquifers 172
coastal deserts xvi. *See also*
　　west coast deserts
cobras 114
cod 218
cold environments
　　animals in 99–105
　　hibernation in 103–105
cold fronts 64, 76
Colorado Desert 1, 17
Colorado River 197
common poorwill 103–104
condensation 5–6, 60
conduction 26
conservation, of angular
　　momentum 78, 79
continental displacement
　　24–25
continental drift 25–27, *28*
Continental Intercalaire aquifer
　　172
continents
　　deserts in interiors of
　　　13–16
　　movement of 23–29, *28*
convection 26, 54
convection cells 52–53, 54
convergence 54
convergent evolution 116
Cook, Frederick Albert 148
Cook, James 145, 150
coppicing 212
Coptic language 49
coral snakes 114
Cordilleran orogeny 31
core, of Earth 26, *27*
core temperature 95, 99, 118
corridor farming 211–213
Couch's spadefoot toad 103
countercurrent exchange 102
crabeater seal 125
crassulacean acid metabolism.
　　See CAM
creosote bushes 90

Cretaceous period 30
critical temperature, low
    99–101
crust, of Earth 26, *27*
C3 plants 83–85, 89
cumulonimbus clouds *45*, 46,
    61
cumulus clouds 61
Cush (region) 128
cushion plants 93
cutaneous respiration 103

D

Dahna', Ad 12
DALR. *See* dry adiabatic lapse
    rate
dams 194–197, 219–220
darkling beetles 107
David, T. W. Edgeworth 152
death, from extreme tempera-
    tures 97–99
Death Valley 66–67
deflation 75
dehydration 96–98
deoxyribonucleic acid (DNA)
    214–215
desalination 205–207
desertification 185–188
desert locust 109–110
deserts
    aridity defining xvi–xvii
    formation of 4–6
    inhabitants of xv–xvi
    location of 1–4, *2*
    myths about xv–xvi
desert sidewinding viper 112,
    113
Desierto de Altar. *See* Sonoran
    Desert
Devon (Britain) 23, 29
dew-point temperature 60
diagnostic horizons 35
Dias de Novais, Bartolomeu
    150
distillation 205, 206
diurnation 102
DNA 214–215
dongas. *See* arroyos
dorcas gazelle 116
Doughty, Charles Montagu 155

draas 40, 41
Drake, Sir Francis 150
dressed stone 140
drip irrigation 204–205
driving, across deserts 41
dromedary camel 97–98, *98*
droughts
    cycles of 178–179, 209
    and desertification 186,
        188
    plant resistance to 216
dry adiabatic lapse rate (DALR)
    55, 60–61, *61*
dry air 60
dry farming 209–211
dryness. *See* aridity
Dumont d'Urville, Jules-
    Sébastien-César 150
Dust Bowl 209
dust devils 76–78, *77*
dust storms 74–76
Duveyrier, Henri 154
Dzungarian bridlegrass 92
Dzungarian reaumuria 92

E

ears 93–94, 101
Earth
    angular velocity of 79
    area covered by deserts 1
    axis of 182
    layers of 26, *27*
    orbit of 69, 181, 182
    radiation absorbed by 176
    satellite photos of 1
Earth Summit (1994) 187
East Australian Current 57
eccentricity, orbital 182
ectotherms 95
Egypt
    climate change in 126
    conflict over water in 220
    dams in 195, 196, 197
    diet in 133–134
    early civilizations in 126,
        128, 132–134
    locusts in 109
    oases in 49, 50, 199–200
    river management in 195
    tourism in 168

Egyptian cobra 114
Egyptian vulture 121
electron-transport chain 82
elephants 7–8
Ellsworth, Lincoln 153
El Niño 178–179
El Niño–Southern Oscillation
    (ENSO) 179
ELR. *See* environmental lapse
    rate
emitters 204
emperor penguin 124
endotherms 95–99
energy
    for endotherms 96
    in photosynthesis 81–83
    solar 161–163, 164
ENSO. *See* El Niño–Southern
    Oscillation
environmental lapse rate (ELR)
    60, *61*
environmental threats
    171–186
    management of 187–221
enzymes 95
Eocene epoch 29
Equatorial Current 179
ergs 37–38
erosion
    and desertification 185,
        188
    management of 188
    of mountains 31–33
    of rocks 43–44
    by salt 44
    by wind 188, 212
estivation 102–103
Ethiopia 128, 220
Euphorbia echinus 88
Euphorbia heterochroma 88
Euphrates River 196, 220
eutherian mammals 115, 116
Evans, Edgar 151
evaporation xvii
    air temperature and xvii,
        4–6
    body temperature and 96
    in desert formation 4–6
    multistage flash 205–206
evening primrose 91

Everest, Mount 31–32
evolution 116
exploration 145–158
explosive heat death 98–99

F

Faisal (king of Iraq) 156
falcons 121
famines 133
FAO. *See* Food and Agriculture Organization
fat-tailed scorpion 105
faults, transform 27
feather grasses 92, 93
fennec fox 94
Ferrel, William 52
Ferrel cells 52, *53*, 64
Fertile Crescent 131, *131*
fertilizer 204
fish 143, 218–219
flash evaporation 205–206
flooding
    flash 46–47
    management of 190, 197
    on Nile River 133, 194–195
Florida Current 57
flowers 88, 90
foggara 201, 202
Food and Agriculture Organization (FAO) 35, 221
foxes 94, 100–102, 122
Franklin, Sir John 147
Frederick V (king of Denmark) 155
Frobisher, Sir Martin 146
frogs 103
fronts 63–64, 76
frostbite 100
Fulani people 135
fur 101

G

GDP. *See* gross domestic product
gemsbok *117*
genetic modification 214–215, 216–217
geography 1–22

geologic time scale *30–31*
geology 23–50
gerbils 115, 117
gers 137
Ghanaian Empire 129
Gibson Desert *3*, 4
gila monster 111
glaciers 32
global warming 177–178, 223–224
glucose 82–83
glycogen 83
goats 166, 167, 185, 186
Gobi Desert *14*
    climate of 13–14
    geography of 14
    location of 2
    people of 136–138
    plants of 92
    sandstorms in 76
Gobi feather grass 92
Gobi kumarchik 92
gold 129
golden moles 93–94
Gomes, Diogo 152–153
Gould's monitor 110–111
granite 36, 66
Grant's golden mole 94
grasses 92, 213
grasshopper mice 117
grasshoppers 107–110
grazing 183–186
great auk 124
Great Eastern Erg 38
greater roadrunner 119, *120*
Great Indian Desert. *See* Thar Desert
Great Plains 209–210
Great Sand Desert 11–12
Great Victoria Desert *3*, 3–4
Great Western Erg 38
greenhouse effect 177
greenhouse gases 177
Greenland
    climate of 19–20, 68–73
    ice covering xvi, 19–20
    Inuit people in 142, 143
    temperatures in 69–70
    tourism in 169
griffon vulture 121

gross domestic product (GDP) 160, *161*
groundwater
    accumulation of 47, 172
    definition of 47
    depletion of 171–173
    in oases 49–50
    in qanats 201, 202
    wells for 47–48, 171, 202
Gulf Stream 57–58
gullies 45–47
gyres, ocean 56–58, *58*

H

Hadley, George 52
Hadley cells 52, *53*
hail cannons 191–192
hairy scorpion 105
halophytes 92, 93, 216
Hannibal (Carthaginian general) 8
hares 94
harmattan wind 73, 75
Hausa people 135
heat
    and animals 93–99
    in Earth, movement of 26
    and estivation 102–103
    latent 60, 206
    radiant 51–54
heat capacity, specific 66–67, 68
heat death, explosive 98–99
hedgehogs 94
Hedin, Sven Anders 155
heliostats 163
Herodotus (Greek historian) 159
hibernation 103–105
Himalayas
    erosion of 31–32
    formation of 27, 29, 31
    and monsoons 62
hippopotamuses 126
Hohokam people 140
Holocene 181
hooded vulture 121
Hopi people 141–142
hoppers 110
horizons, soil 33, 35

horned viper 112
horse latitudes 52
house mouse 116
Hudson, Henry 147
Humboldt Current. *See* Peru
    Current
humidity 6–7
humus 33
Husain ibn 'Ali 156
hydroelectricity 196, 197
hydrogen bonds 4, *5*, 72

I

ice ages 180, *181*, 181–182
icebergs 207–209
icefish 218
Icelandic low 180
igneous rocks 43–44
Il (king of Lagash) 220
India
    asphalt in 159
    conflict over water in 220
    dams in 194, 195–196
    irrigation in 203–204
    monsoons in 58–62,
        203–204
    movement of plate 29
Indus River 194, 195–196
industries 159–169
Indus Valley 9
infrared light 1
insects 105–110
inselbergs 44
interglacials *181*, 181–182
International Society of Soil
    Science (ISS) 35
Intertropical Convergence Zone
    (ITCZ) 52, 62, 223
intrazonal soils 35
Inuit people 142–144, 223
invertebrates 124
Iraq 127
iron 42–43
irrigation
    amount of water in 171
    dams for 194–197
    improvement of 201–205
    invention of 133
    river diversion for 197–199
    waterlogging from
        173–175

Irtysh River 199
Islam 129
Israel
    conflict over water in
        219–220
    irrigation in 201–203
ISS. *See* International Society of
    Soil Science
ITCZ. *See* intertropical conver-
    gence zone

J

jackrabbits 94
Jackson, Frederick George 149
jandi 212
jerboas 116
jet streams 64–65, *65*
Johansen, Frederic Hjalmar
    148–149
Jordan
    climate change in
        126–127
    conflict over water in
        219–220
Joshua tree 90, *90*
Jurassic period 30

K

Kalaallit Nunaat 142, 143
Kalahari Desert *13*
    location of 2, 12
    rainfall in 12
kangaroo rats 115, 116
Karakaya Dam 196
Kara Sea 199
katabatic winds 74
kayaks 143
khamsin 73–74
khejri 212
kidneys 97, 115
Kirina, Battle of (1235) 129
kowari 115, 116
krill 124–125, 218–219
Kuroshio Current 57
Kush. *See* Cush

L

Lagash 220
laggar falcon 121
Laing, Alexander Gordon 154

landforms 43–45
La Niña 179
lanner falcon 121
lappet-faced vulture 121
lapse rates 60–61
latent heat 60, 206
Lawrence, T. E. (Lawrence of
    Arabia) 155, 156–157
leaves 86, 87, 91
lemmings 121–122
leopard seal 125
lesser roadrunner 119
lethal temperature, low
    99–101
Libya 7, 12
Libyan Desert 10
lifting condensation level 60
limestone 43
linear dunes 40
lion 117
lithosphere 26
little blue penguin 124
Little Ice Age 180
lizards 95, 110–113
loam 35
locusts *107*, 107–110
lodging 215
loess 37
long-eared hedgehog 94
longitudinal dunes 40
love-lies-bleeding 213

M

Madagascar 108
Magellan, Ferdinand 150
Mali Empire 129
mammals 114–118
    core temperature of 95
    heat's impact on 94–99
    hibernation of 103–105
    of polar deserts 121–124,
        125
management, desert 187–221
mandibles 106–107
manganese 42
Mangla Dam 195
mantle, of Earth 26, *27*
marmots 104
marsupials 115, 116
Maunder, Edward Walter 181
Maunder Minimum 181

McClure, Sir Robert John le Mesurier 147
McMahon's viper 113–114
meadow grass 93
Medieval Warm Period 180
Memphis (Egypt) 132
Menes (king of Egypt) 132
Meriam's kangaroo rat 115
mesas 43
mesophyll cells 84, 86
Mesopotamia 131
metabolic rate *100*
metallic ores 163–166, *165*
Mexican beaded lizard 111
mice 116
Middle East
    climate change in 7, 9, 126–127
    conflict over water in 219–221
    desalination in 205
    early civilizations in 126–128, 130–132
    exploration of 155, 156–157
    oil in 159, 160
    textiles in 166–167
    tourism in 168
    water resources in 171
Milankovitch, Milutin 181–182
Milankovitch cycles 182
milk, of camels 137
milk barrel 88–89
milk snake 114
millet 214
mineral nutrients 85–86
minerals 163–166, *165*
mixing ratio 7
Mohenjo Daro 127, 159
Mojave Desert
    animals of 102–103
    climate of 16
    geography of 16
    location of 1
    temperatures in 66–67
Mojave ground squirrel 102–103
Mojave rattlesnake 114
moles 93–94
momentum, angular 78, 79

Mongolia
    people of 136–138
    sandstorms in 76
    temperatures in 13
Mongols 137–138
monitor lizards 110–111
monsoons 58–62
    in irrigation systems 203–204
    wind in 62, 73
Moon, temperatures on 176
Morocco 109
mountains
    erosion of 31–33
    formation of 24, 26, 27, 29–31
    movement of *32*, 32–33
    rainfall in 46
mourning doves 119
Muhammad ibn Abī Bakr Ture 129
mung beans 212
Mūsā (emperor of Mali) 129
musk ox 123
mutations, genetic 214

N

Nabataean people 203
NADP. *See* nicotinamide adenine dinucleotide phosphate
naft 160
Nafud Desert, An 11–12
Najd (Arabia) 11–12
Namib Desert
    climate of 19
    geography of 19
    location of 2
    sand dunes in 38
Nansen, Fridtjof 148–149, 153
NAO. *See* North Atlantic Oscillation
Nasser, Gamal Abdel 196
Nasser, Lake 196, 197
Native Americans 127, 140–144
Nebuchadrezzar (king of Babylonia) 221
Negev region 201–203
Nestorian Christianity 140
New Valley (Egypt) 200

nicotinamide adenine dinucleotide phosphate (NADP) 82
Niebuhr, Carsten 155
Nile River
    conflict over water in 220
    dams on 195, 196
    depletion of 172
    flooding on 133, 194–195
nilometer 195, 196
nitre bush 92, 93
nitrogen 211
Nobile, Umberto 153
nodules, root 211
nomads
    disappearance of 188–191, 217–218, 223
    grazing animals of 183–185
    history of 135–136, 137
Nordenskjöld, Nils Adolf Erik 145–146
North America
    climate change in 9
    dry farming in 209–211
    location of deserts in 1, 17, *17*
    oil in 160
    people of 140–142
North Atlantic Current 58
North Atlantic Oscillation (NAO) 180
Northeast Passage 145–146
North Equatorial Current 57
Northern Hemisphere Annular Mode 180
North Pacific Current 57
North Pole, exploration of 147–149, 153
Northwest Passage 146–147
Norway, air masses in 63
Norway lemming 121, 122
NSA. *See* Nubian Sandstone Aquifer
Nubia (region) 128
Nubian Desert 10, 128
Nubian Empire 128
Nubian Sandstone Aquifer (NSA) 172
Nullarbor Plain *3*, 4
Numidians 134

Nunavut (Canada) 142
nutrients, in plants 85–86

O

oases 49–50
  agriculture in 199–200
  artificial 200–201
  water supply for 49–50, *50*
Oates, L. E. G. 151
obliquity 182
Ob' River 199
occlusion, of fronts 64
ocean currents 56–58, *58*
oceans
  and climate 54, 56–58,
    176
  in monsoons 59
oil industry 159–161
Oraibi (Arizona) 142
orbital stretch 182
orogeny 31
oscillations 179, 180
osmosis 175, 206–207
osmotic pressure 207
ouadis. *See* arroyos
overgrazing *183*, 183–186
Overweg, Adolf 154
owls 122

P

Pacific Decadal Oscillation
  (PDO) 180
Pakistan
  climate change in 127
  dams in 194, 195–196
  monsoons in 62
Pallas's cat 118
Pangaea 24
panniers 138
panting 95, 96
parabolic dunes 40
parallel evolution 116
parent material 34, 35
Patagonian Desert
  climate of 16
  geography of 16
  location of 2
  plants of 93
pavement, desert 41–42

PDO. *See* Pacific Decadal
  Oscillation
Peary, Robert Edwin 148, 153
peashrubs 92
pedestal rocks 44
pedipalps 106
pedology 34
penguins 124–125
PEP carboxylase 84
per capita GDP 160, *161*
perihelion 69, 182
permafrost 217
permeability, soil 174, *174*
Persian carpets 166–167
Persian Empire 159
Peru Current 57, 179
Petra (Jordan) 126–127, 168
petroleum 159–161
phloem tissue 85
Phoenicia 131–132
Phoenicians 131–132, 134
phosphorylation 82
photorespiration 83–85
photosynthesis 81–85, 87
Piankhi (king of Cush) 128
pigeon milk 119
pigeons 119
pilgrimage 168
pitch 159
pit vipers 114
plants xv, 81–93, 222–223
  of cold deserts 92–93
  and erosion 188
  in formation of deserts 6
  photosynthesis in 81–85
  of polar deserts 217
  salination and 175
  in satellite photos 1
  of subtropical deserts
    87–91
  water needs of 85–86
plasmodesmata 84
plates *25*, 25–29
plate tectonics 25–29
playas 44–45
polar bear 101, *123*, 123–124
polar cells 52, *53*, 64
polar deserts 19–22
  animals of 121–125,
    218–219

circulation of atmosphere
    in 52–53
  climate change in 223–224
  climate of 19–22, 68–73
  exploration of 145–151,
    152, 153
  food in 217–219
  people of 142–144
  plants of 217
  tourism in 169
polar front 64
polar jet stream 64–65, *65*
pores, soil 174
pore space 174
PPP. *See* purchasing power parity
precipitation. *See* rainfall; snow
prickly pear cacti *87*
primary industries 163–165
princely mastigure 112
Prince's feather 214
process water 171
profiles, soil 35
Ptah (Egyptian god) 132
ptarmigans 122
Ptolemy (Claudius Ptolemaeus)
  126
Pueblo Indians 141–142
pueblos 141
puma 117
purchasing power parity (PPP)
  160, *161*
pygmy planigale 116

Q

Qaanaaq (Greenland) 69–70
qanats 201, 202
qarez 201, 202
quartz 36
quinoa 214–215

R

radians 79
radiant heat 51–54
radiation 176–177
rainfall
  arroyos during 45–47
  climate change and
    126–127, 177–178
  in desert formation 4

in equatorial regions 54
evaporation of xvii
flash flooding from 46–47
formation of 72
in interior deserts 13–16
irrigation with 203–204
management of 191–194
from monsoons 58–62
in mountains 46
natural cycles of 178–179
in soil formation 34
in subtropical deserts 12
temperature and 4
in west coast deserts
18–19
rainmaking 191–194
rain shadows 16
rattlesnakes 114
reindeer. See caribou
relative humidity (RH) 6, 7
religion
of Berbers 134
in early civilizations 129
Silk Road and 140
and tourism 168
reptiles 95
respiration 82–83, 99, 103
rete mirabile 102
reverse osmosis 206–207
RH. See relative humidity
Rhizobium bacteria 211
rhourds 40
ribulose biphosphate (RuBP)
82, 83, 84
Richardson, James 154
Richthofen, Ferdinand Paul
Wilhelm, Freiherr von
155–156
ridges 65, 65
rivers
dams on 194–197
diversion of 197–199
roadrunners 119–120
roads. See also Silk Road
asphalt 159
desert pavement 41
rocks
in erosion 32, 33
formation of 36
in landforms 43

salt in 44
in sand 36, 37
specific heat capacity of
66–67, 68
temperature of 66–67, 68
varnish on 42–43
in wind storms 76–78
Rocky Mountain locust 108
Rocky Mountains 29–30
rodents 115
cold's impact on 100, 101
diet of 115, 117
heat's impact on 95–96
of polar deserts 121–122
Rohlfs, Friedrich Gerhard
154–155
Roman Empire 134, 168
root hairs 86
roots 85–86, 88, 211
rose, desert 45
Ross, James Clark 150–151
Ross seal 125
Rub' al-Khali 11–12, 38, 155
rubisco 82, 83, 84
RuBP. See ribulose biphosphate

S

Saba (kingdom) 128
Sabacon. See Shabaka
Sabaeans 128
sabkha. See playas
Sadat, Anwar as- 196
saguaro cactus 88, 88
Sahara Desert 10
climate change in 7–9
climate cycles in
178–179
dust blown from 75
exploration of 154–155
geography of 10
groundwater in 47,
171–172
location of 2
locusts in 109
oases in 49
overgrazing in 184–185
people of 134–136
sand dunes in 40, 74–75
sand seas in 37–38
soil formation in 34

temperatures in 12, 65–68,
76–77
winds in 73–74
Sahel (region) 178–179, 184, 187
saker falcon 121
Salah (Algeria) 12, 65–66
salina. See playas
salination 175, 199, 216
SALR. See saturated adiabatic
lapse rate
salt(s)
in animal cells 96
and caravan routes 139
erosion by 44
in irrigation water 175,
204–205
in landforms 44–45
and plants in cold deserts
92
river diversion and
197–198, 199
saltbushes 93
Salton Sea 17, 197–198
salt water desalination
205–207
sand 36–41
composition of 36
in dust devils and whirl-
winds 76–80
formation of 36, 37
movement by wind 37, 38,
38–41, 74–76
porosity of 174
ripples on 38
snakes on 112–113, 113,
114
specific heat capacity of
66–67, 68
temperature of 66–67, 68
sand cat 117–118
sand dunes 38, 38–41
sandfish 113
sandgrouse 119
sand seas 37–38
sandstone 23, 37, 43
sandstorms 74–76
Sargon. See Sharrukin
satellite photographs 1
saturated adiabatic lapse rate
(SALR) 54–55, 60, 61

saturation, of air 72
saturation vapor pressure 5–6
saxaul 92
Schaefer, Vincent Joseph 193
scorpions 105–106
Scott, Robert Falcon 151, 152, 169
seals 124, 125, 143
secretary bird 120
sedimentary rocks 43
seeds 91, 222
seif dunes 40
Sennacherib (king of Assyria) 220–221
Seven Pillars of Wisdom 157
Shabaka (king of Egypt) 128
Shackleton, Ernest Henry 151, 152
shadoof (shaduf) 133
Sharrukin (ruler of Akkad) 127
Sheba (kingdom) 128, 168
sheep 185
shrubs 92–93
sidewinder 112, 114
sidewinding snakes 112–113, 113, 114
silica (silicon dioxide) 36
silica glaze 42
Silk Road 139–140
    exploration of 155–158
    tourism on 169
silt 36–37, 194, 197
simoom 75
Simpson Desert 3, 4
Siwa oasis 50
skinks 112–113
snakes 95, 112–114, 113
snakeweeds 92
Snefru (king of Egypt) 128
snow
    in erosion of mountains 32
    formation of 72
    in polar deserts 20–21
    sublimation of xvii, 20
    sunlight on 70, 71
snowy owl 122
soils 33–36
    classification of 34, 35
    composition of 33
    fertility of 34–36, 211–212

formation of 33–34
permeability of 174, 174
porosity of 174
salination of 175, 199, 216
sand in 36–37
solar cells 162
solar chimneys 163, 164
solar energy 161–163, 164
solar furnaces 163
solar panels 162
solar ponds 162–163
solar wind 181
solifugids 106
Songhai Empire 129–130
Songhai people 129–130
Sonni ʿAlī (Songhai ruler) 129
Sonni Baru (Songhai ruler) 129
Sonoran Desert
    climate of 17
    geography of 17
    location of 1
    people of 141
    sand dunes in 75
South America, location of deserts in 2
South American locust 108
South Equatorial Current 56–57
Southern Oscillation 179
South Pole
    exploration of 151, 152, 153
    snow in 21
    temperatures in 21–22
    winds in 74
Soviet Union, river diversion in 198–199
specific heat capacity 66–67, 68
specific humidity 7
spiders 106
spines
    on cacti 87, 87–88
    on spurges 88–89
spurges 88–89
squirrels 103, 104
stability, of air 60–61, 61
star (stellar) dunes 40
steam, v. water vapor 72
Stein, Sir Mark Aurel 156–157
stems, of cacti 87

stoat 122
stomata 83–85, 86
stones, in desert pavement 41–42
Storrs, Sir Ronald 156
striped scorpion 105
subduction 26–27
sublimation, of snow xvii, 20
subtropical deserts 10–12
    circulation of atmosphere and 52–56
    climate of 12, 51–56
    plants of 87–91
    on west coasts 16
    winds in 73, 74
sugar beet family 92, 93
Sukkur (Pakistan) 127
Sumer 127, 131
Sumerian language 127
Sun
    in climate cycles 180–182
    Earth's orbit around 69, 181, 182
    radiant heat from 51–54
    radiation from 176
    in tropics 52
Sundiata Keita (king of Kangaba) 129
sunlight
    basking in 95
    solar energy from 161–163, 164
    surface reflection of 70–71
sunspots 180–181
swarms, locust 108–110
sweating 95, 96
Syr Dar'ya (river) 198
Syria, conflict over water in 219–220
Syrian Desert
    location of 2, 12
    sandstorms in 75

T

tafoni 44
taiga 217
tail dunes 40
Taklimakan Desert 15
    climate of 15
    geography of 15

location of 2–3, 15
people of 138
plants of 93
sandstorms in 76
tamarisks 92, 93
Tarbela Dam 195–196
Tassili-n-Ajjer (Algeria) 126
tectonism 25
temperature(s). *See also* body
temperature
of air *v.* ground 67–68
and animals 94–102
in aridity xvii, 70
climate change and
176–177
in climate cycles 180
in desert formation 4–6
and desert varnish 42
dew-point 60
in dust devils and whirl-
winds 76–78
and evaporation xvii, 4–6
and humidity 6, 7
in interior deserts 13–16
and metabolic rate *100*
at night *v.* day 65–68
in polar deserts 19–22
in subtropical deserts 12
in west coast deserts 19
terracing 203, 204
Texas horned lizard 111
textiles 166–167
Thar Desert *11*
climate change in 9
geography of 12
location of 3, 12
people of 138
Thesiger, Sir Wilfred 155
thorn trees 89
thorny devil 111–112
threats 171–186
management of 187–221
Tibesti Mountains 7, 9
Tibetan Plateau 62
tiger beetles 106
tiger rattlesnake 114
Timbuktu (Mali) 152–154
timuriya 92
toads 103
Tohono O'odham people 141
tornadoes 78–79

torpor 96
tourism 167–169, *170*
trade winds 62, 73, 178–179
transform faults 27
transpiration 86
transverse dunes 40
trees, in agriculture 211–213
tropopause 52, 60
troughs 65, *65*
Tuareg people 134–135, 154
tubercles 88
tumble grass 91
tumbleweeds 91
tundra 217–218
tundra wolf 122–123
turbines, wind 161–162
turgor 86
Turkey 130, 220
Turkistan 167

U
Ulan Bator (Mongolia) 13
umbrella thorn 212
UNEP. *See* United Nations
Environment Program
UNESCO. *See* United Nations
Educational, Scientific, and
Cultural Organization
United Nations
on conflict over water 221
on desertification 187–188
United Nations Educational,
Scientific, and Cultural
Organization (UNESCO) 35
United Nations Environment
Program (UNEP) 187, 221
Urlama (king of Lagash) 220
USDA. *See* Agriculture, U.S.
Department of
Usman dan Fodio 135
Uvarov, Boris P. 108
Uzbekistan 201

V
vacuoles 84
vapor pressure 5–6
variables 79
varnish, desert 42–43
velocity, angular 79
vetiver 216

virga 46
Vonnegut, Bernard 193
Vostok research station
(Antarctica) 69–70
vultures 121

W
wadis. *See* arroyos
Walvis Bay 19
warm fronts 64
warm pools 179
water. *See also* groundwater
birds' use of 119
and body temperature 96
in cacti 87–88
chemical structure of 4, *5*
conflict over 219–221
desalination of 205–207
humans' use of 171–173
hydrogen bonds in 4, 5,
72
from icebergs 207–209
mammals' use of 114–117
in oases 49–50, *50*
in photosynthesis 82, 85
plant storage of 87, 91
plants' use of 85–86
in solar ponds 162–163
specific heat capacity of
66–67, 68
waterlogging 173–175
water table 47, 172, 173
water vapor 4–6
definition of 72
in humidity 6, 7
temperature and 70, 72–73
wattles 89
wavelength 176
weasel 122
weather. *See* climate
weathering 31–33
Weddell, James 151
Weddell seal 125
Wegener, Alfred Lothar 24–25
wells 47–48, 50, 171, 202
West Australian Current 58
west coast deserts 16–19
climate of 16–19, 56–58
western diamondback rat-
tlesnake 114

West Wind Drift 57
wetting front 34
whale krill 125
whales 125, 143
whirlwinds 76–80
white-headed vulture 121
Wilkes, Charles 150
Wilson, E. A. 151
wilting, in plants 86
wind(s) 73–74
    changes caused by xvi
    deflation by 75
    drying effect of xvii
    in dust devils 76–78
    in El Niño 178–179
    energy from 161–162
    erosion by 188, 212
    and evaporation xvii
    in jet streams 64
    in monsoons 62, 73
    and ocean currents 56–57
    sand moved by 37, *38,* 38–41, 74–76
    in sandstorms 74–76
    in whirlwinds 76–80
wind farms 162
wind scorpions 106
wind turbines 161–162
winter fat 92
Wisconsinian ice age 181
wolf spiders 106
wolves 122–123
wool 166–167
World Bank 221
World War I 156–157
worm lions 106

X

xerophytes 92, 93
xylem tissue 85–86

Y

yellow ephedra 92
yellowwood beancaper 92
yuccas 90
Yuma Desert. *See* Sonoran Desert
Yuma people 141
yurts (yurta) 137

Z

zonal soils 35

PERVASIVE INFORMATION SYSTEMS

Advances in Management Information Systems

Advisory Board

PERVASIVE INFORMATION SYSTEMS

PANOS E. KOUROUTHANASSIS
GEORGE M. GIAGLIS
EDITORS

ADVANCES IN MANAGEMENT
INFORMATION SYSTEMS
VLADIMIR ZWASS SERIES EDITOR

M.E.Sharpe
Armonk, New York
London, England

Library of Congress Cataloging-in-Publication Data

References to the AMIS papers should be as follows:

Biegel, G. and V. Cahill. Requirements for middleware for pervasive information systems. Panos E. Kourouthanassis and George M. Giaglis, eds., *Pervasive Information Systems. Advances in Management Information
Systems*. Volume 10 (Armonk, NY: M.E. Sharpe, 2007), 86–102.

ISBN 978-0-7656-1689-0
ISSN 1554-6152

Printed in the United States of America

The paper in this publication meets the minimum requirements of
American National Standards for Information Sciences
Permanence of Paper for Printed Library Materials,
ANSI Z 39.48-1984.

BM (c)   10   9   8   7   6   5   4   3   2   1

ADVANCES IN MANAGEMENT INFORMATION SYSTEMS

AMIS Vol. 1: Richard Y. Wang, Elizabeth M. Pierce,
Stuart E. Madnick, and Craig W. Fisher
Information Quality
ISBN 978-0-7656-1133-8

AMIS Vol. 2: Sergio deCesare, Mark Lycett, and
    Robert D. Macredie
Development of Component-Based Information Systems
ISBN 978-0-7656-1248-9

AMIS Vol. 3: Jerry Fjermestad and
    Nicholas C. Romano, Jr.
Electronic Customer Relationship Management
ISBN 978-0-7656-1327-1

AMIS Vol. 4: Michael J. Shaw
E-Commerce and the Digital Economy
ISBN 978-0-7656-1150-5

AMIS Vol. 5: Ping Zhang and Dennis Galletta
*Human-Computer Interaction and Management
    Information Systems: Foundations*
ISBN 978-0-7656-1486-5

AMIS Vol. 6: Dennis Galletta and Ping Zhang
*Human-Computer Interaction and Management
    Information Systems: Applications*
ISBN 978-0-7656-1487-2

AMIS Vol. 7: Murugan Anandarajan,
    Thompson S.H. Teo, and Claire A. Simmers
The Internet and Workplace Transformation
ISBN 978-0-7656-1445-2

AMIS Vol. 8: Suzanne Rivard and Benoit A. Aubert
Information Technology Outsourcing
ISBN 978-0-7656-1685-2

AMIS Vol. 9: Varun Grover and M. Lynne Markus
Business Process Transformation
ISBN 978-0-7656-1191-8

AMIS Vol. 10: Panos E. Kourouthanassis and
    George M. Giaglis
Pervasive Information Systems
ISBN 978-0-7656-1689-0

Forthcoming volumes of this series can be found on the series homepage.
www.mesharpe.com/amis.htm

Editor-in-Chief, Vladimir Zwass (zwass@fdu.edu)

CONTENTS

Series Editor's Introduction   vii
    Vladimir Zwass
Preface   xi

1. Toward Pervasiveness: Four Eras of Information Systems Development
    Panos E. Kourouthanassis and George M. Giaglis   3

Part I. Features and Design of Pervasive Information Systems   **27**

2. The Design Challenge of Pervasive Information Systems
    Panos E. Kourouthanassis and George M. Giaglis   29

3. Requirements for Middleware for Pervasive Information Systems
    Gregory Biegel and Vinny Cahill   86

4. A Software Factory for Pervasive Systems Development
    Javier Muñoz and Vicente Pelechano   103

Part II. Applications of Pervasive Information Systems   **127**

5. Domestic Pervasive Information Systems: End-user Programming of Digital Homes
    Victor Callaghan, Jeannette Chin, Victor Zamudio, Graham Clarke,
    Anuroop Shahi, and Michael Gardner   129

6. Corporate Pervasive Information Systems
    Anatole Gershman and Andrew Fano   150

7. Wearable Computing Applications and Challenges
    Cliff Randell   165

8. Pervasive Electronic Services in Health Care
    Ilias Maglogiannis and Stathes Hadjiefthymiades   180

Part III. Properties of Pervasive Information Systems and Their Evaluation   **195**

9. Aesthetic Concerns in Pervasive Information Systems
   Johan Redström   197

10. A Framework for the Evaluation of Pervasive Information Systems
    Jean Scholtz, Mary Theofanos, and Sunny Consolvo   210

Editors and Contributors   233
Series Editor   239
Index   241

SERIES EDITOR'S INTRODUCTION

VLADIMIR ZWASS, EDITOR-IN-CHIEF

Pervasive information systems (PS) are a powerful vision that is being realized right in front of our eyes. It is the vision of the ubiquitous computing technology disappearing into everyday objects, be they eyeglasses, the walls of the rooms we are in, the clothes we wear, or shipping containers. These now "smart" objects, whose location, context, and state can be monitored, instantly processed, and acted upon, may be interconnected with other devices. They can also be provided remotely with the requisite computational power and with access to large distributed databases. Wireless networks afford anywhere-anytime connectivity of mobility as needed. The Internet–Web compound, with its layers of commonly accessible infrastructure and services, turbocharges the capabilities of the individual nodes.

The vision of the power of computer technology disappearing into everyday things was enunciated by Mark Weiser in 1991—and it was a vision of power akin to that of invisible electricity (Weiser, 1991). The World Wide Web that came into everyday use on the Internet substrate some two years later has brought an outpouring of technological creativity, entrepreneurial and intrapreneurial ingenuity, and societal change that have all been underwriting the coming reality of pervasive computing. It has been claimed that, reciprocally, the power of the Internet–Web derives in great part from its embedding in the physical world, rather than from pure virtuality (Zwass, 2002).

The artifacts and concepts of pervasive computing technology are a foundation of pervasive information systems. As all information systems (IS), however, PS are not limited to information technology: they are enabled by it. People and processes are the crucial elements of these systems as well. In many business-oriented systems, we may think of PS as possessing the afferent components, which collect data and direct them toward processing and database servers, and the efferent components that provide information and services to people or control to devices. The afferent capabilities include gathering massive data from globally distributed (or confined to a home), and digitally identifiable, contexts. The efferent capabilities include the personalization and context-dependence of the information and services delivered to the identified users or devices. In some system implementations, much or all of the processing can occur locally within a sensor network, which in turn may be integrated into a larger system.

PS are becoming an important part of our disciplinary concern in the IS field (Lyytinen et al., 2004). Their study will require combining our established research in organizational computing with more intimate involvement in several key technologies. The editors of this volume of *Advances in Management Information Systems* (*AMIS*), Panos E. Kourouthanassis and George M. Giaglis, and the volume's authors contribute worthily to this objective. The editors introduce this area of their research and practice at length and assemble a representative collection of highly interesting articles that present the key aspects of pervasive information systems and several of domains of their application.

Pervasive computing is a fascinating human pursuit. The incarnations are legion. Cell phones are constantly accumulating more capabilities and becoming an essential part of the personal environment. Multiple and various wearable computing devices are emerging. Automobiles carry myriad embedded networked processors and sensors. Tags, sensors, and actuators are becoming ubiquitous. The capabilities here range from passive tags that can only transmit their identification number when energized by a reader to highly capable sensor devices with processing power. In particular, the use of radio frequency identification device (RFID) technology, which allows the ever less expensive tagging and identification of objects or individuals, is spreading (Garfinkel and Rosenberg, 2006). The more powerful active sensors, some three orders of magnitude more expensive than the RFID tags, are being installed in the physical assets of corporations, from pipeline segments to motors, the better to monitor their condition and maintain them proactively (Edwards, 2005). Wireless sensor networks enable new levels of environmental monitoring and enhancement of productivity in manufacturing, agriculture, and transportation (Culler, Estrin, and Srivastava, 2004). Smart building materials can monitor the temperature in all surfaces of a warehouse or perform continuous analysis in real time of the structural integrity of a bridge. With pervasive computing, multimedia personal information management becomes possible in a semi-automatic mode, making its potential for both individual lifestyles and organizational computing worthy of exploration (Teevan, Jones, and Bederson, 2006). Research on the development of the devices and their incorporation into our life proceeds apace (Streitz and Nixon, 2005).

Organizational IS will undergo dramatic change owing to the assimilation of pervasive computing. Supply chains, and logistics in particular, will be profoundly affected by RFID, as new levels and methods of goods tracking, coordination, and control emerge. At this time, it is economical to track only bulked goods, such as containers, pallets, or cases. Retail tagging of individual items is limited today to higher-value items; however, with the costs decreasing, item-level tagging will be progressively introduced (Roussos, 2006). Continuous monitoring of the temperature, humidity, stability, and other parameters of a shipment is possible, which makes for superior—and potentially less expensive—quality control (Betts, 2006). Small businesses are quick to innovate with IS relying on the technology. Here is one example. The designer fashion house Lauren Scott California sews RFID tags made of polyester film into children's clothing, and partners with SmartWear Technologies to integrate these into systems that protect children. The system's database contains the child's medical data for emergencies and the perimeter of the child's whereabouts may be controlled with tag readers (Duvall, 2006).

The diffusion and infusion of technological change of this magnitude takes time. Complementary technologies and societal acceptance need to emerge, and the learning curve has to be traveled (in fact, RFID technology has been available for decades). To provide visibility of supply chains that span many firms and many countries, standards for interoperability are necessary. At this time, the Electronic Product Code (EPC) standard is being introduced, defining six classes of RFID with various capability levels. Much software needs to be written to bridge the gap between the device controllers and enterprise software: this middleware is available only in fragments. There are very significant concerns about privacy and the invasiveness of the technology and of the larger systems behind it. As any infrastructural technology, pervasive computing is vulnerable to technology-based attacks. Technological solutions to these problems are emerging as well. Giving the user control over his or her system identity is possible with systems of identity management (Koch and Möslein, 2005). Some concerns about consumer privacy with regard to item-level tagging may be allayed, for example, with blocker tags (Juels, Rivest, and Szydlo, 2003). But as is well known, technology is always only a part of the solution.

There are momentous implications for organizational competitiveness in general, and for organizational IS in particular. In the environment of inexpensive bandwidth, processing, and storage technologies, the Web-enabled endpoints of information systems will produce immense volumes of data at a relatively low cost. This trend will be reinforced by the ongoing introduction of the next-generation IPv6 Internet protocol. Adopted by several countries and—somewhat slowly—making inroads in the United States, the protocol offers a vastly expanded addressing range and thus enables massive connection of devices to the Internet. The companies that will be able to deploy these data as a source of information for rapid response will gain competitive advantage. Others will lag in the marketplace. The technological means of handling this massive data acquisition are beginning to emerge. More than ever, information systems will be called upon to ward off information overload by processing the data in real time, aggregating and analyzing them, and identifying what makes a difference. For example, stream-processing software for real-time processing of large volumes of event data by storing them exclusively in the main memory is now available as a complement to the traditional databases (Mitchell, 2006). Algorithmic and rule-based absorption of data and information by software means will be necessary to respond to the avalanche of data, in order to reduce the demands on human cognitive faculties. Organizational processes will need to be modified as well.

As we can see, technological, economic, organizational, and societal factors loom large in the gradual move to PS. The editors and authors of this volume are to be thanked for their contribution to our understanding of this encompassing and complex domain.

REFERENCES

Betts, B. 2006. Smart sensors: New standard could save lives and money. *IEEE Spectrum,* 43, 4 (April), 50–53.

Culler, D.; Estrin, D.; and Srivastava, M. 2004. Overview of sensor networks. *Computer,* 37, 8 (August), 41–49.

Duvall, M. 2006. At the seams of RFID. *Baseline,* April, 60–61.

Edwards, J. 2005. Sensors working overtime. *CFO,* August, 25–26.

Garfinkel, S. and Rosenberg, B. 2006. *RFID Applications, Security, and Privacy.* Upper Saddle River, NJ: Addison-Wesley, 2006.

Juels, A.; Rivest, R.I.; and Szydlo, M. 2003. The blocker tag: Selective blocking of RFID tags for consumer privacy. In V. Atluri, *Proceedings of the Tenth ACM Conference on Computer and Communications Security.* Washington, DC: ACM Press, 103–111.

Koch, M. and Möslein, K.M. 2005. Identities management and for e-commerce and collaboration applications. *International Journal of Electronic Commerce,* 9, 3 (Spring), 11–29.

Lyytinen, K.; Yoo Y.; Varshney, U.; Ackerman, M.S.; Davis, G.; Avital, M.; Robey, D.; Sawyer, S.; and Sorensen, C. 2004. Surfing the next wave: Design and implementation challenges of ubiquitous computing environment. *Communications of the AIS,* 13, 697–716.

Mitchell, R.L. 2006. Speed readers. *Computerworld,* June 26, 23–29.

Roussos, G. 2006. Enabling RFID in retail. *Computer,* 39, 3 (March), 25–30.

Streitz, N. and Nixon, P., eds. 2005. The disappearing computer (special section). *Communications of the ACM,* 48, 3 (March), 33–71.

Teevan, J.; Jones, W.; and Bederson, B.B., eds. 2006. Personal information management (special section). *Communications of the ACM,* 49, 1 (January), 40–95.

Weiser, M. 1991. The computer for the twenty-first century. *Scientific American,* September, 94–100.

Zwass, V. 2002. The embedding stage of electronic commerce. In P.B. Lowry, J.O. Cherrington, and R.R. Watson, eds., *The E-Business Handbook.* Boca Raton: St. Lucie Press, 33–43.

PREFACE

We are currently facing the end of traditional personal computer dominance. Information technology artifacts are embedded in more places than just our desktop computers and they provide innovative services in ways unimaginable in the recent past. The home environment has been transformed, key operations such as lighting, inner temperature, the home entertainment system, and so on are controlled automatically (Intille, 2002); supply chain management practices are redefined through the used of radio frequency identification device (RFID) tagging, thus increasing supply chain efficiency and customer value (Karkkainen, 2003; Kourouthanassis and Giaglis, 2004; Pramataris, Doukidis, and Kourouthanassis, 2004; Prater, Frazier, and Reyes, 2005); sensors placed in offices, supermarkets, museums, public spaces, and exhibition environments identify the current location of the user, and provide ad hoc navigation and tailor-made infotainment services when and where needed (Bahl and Padmanabhan, 2000; Davies et al., 2001; Giaglis, Kourouthanassis, and Tsamakos, 2002; Priyantha, Chakraborty, and Balakrishnan, 2000; Want et al., 1992).

More and more, the digital permeates the physical space in a seamless manner. In essence, information technology (IT) is expected to be everywhere and in multiple forms in which it is more noticeable by its absence than its presence. Electronic appliances are being translated to *information* appliances (Norman, 1999); wireless and mobile communication technologies are already widely deployed and integrated in our environment while at the same time their capabilities are increasing; access devices have become small enough, while retaining their processing power, to enable the provision of innovative applications "off the desktop" at the mobile phone or the PDA; new technologies such as WiMAX (Agis et al., 2004; Conti, 2005; Ghosh et al., 2005), ad hoc wireless sensors (Hsin and Liu, 2006; Romer and Mattern, 2003; Tschudin et al., 2005), ZigBee (Egan, 2005; Geer, 2005; Poole, 2004), Bluetooth 2.0 (Zahariadis, 2004), wireless mesh networks (Akyildiz, Wang, and Wang, 2005), 4G networks (Altuntas and Baykal, 2005; Banerjee et al., 2004; Benzaid et al., 2004), and smart-dust microsensors (Boukerche, Chatzigiannakis, and Nikoletseas, 2006; Chivers and Clark, 2004; Cvrcek and Svenda, 2006) promise to create new application domains; even older technologies (such as radio frequency identification) are used under the auspices of a world fully supported and augmented by IT. This notion of an IT-augmented reality is commonly referred to as "pervasive" or "ubiquitous" computing.

Pervasive computing places humans at the center of environments augmented by computing and wireless communications capabilities, gracefully integrated, so that technology recedes into the background of everyday activities. In effect, the vision of an *activated* world is action oriented and follows, rather than dictates, human behavior. This vision of seamless cohabitation of the world by humans and computers was first discussed in Mark Weiser's (1991) article "The Computer of the 21st Century," which stated that "the most profound technologies are those that disappear; they weave themselves into the fabric of everyday life until they are indistinguishable from it."

While from a computer science perspective many see pervasive computing as primarily a systems engineering problem, a pervasive world is also largely defined by applications and services. Such applications present an altogether new set of requirements: they are developed at many different layers of the physical world and may be global, environmental, spatial, localized, ambient, personal, handheld, or wearable; they may be personal or shared; they may consist of multiple components coordinated centrally or built as a distributed and decentralized architecture, autonomous, or unaffiliated; they may vary in their degree of physical interaction as well as their integration with existing information infrastructures; they may show spontaneous behavior; they may generate ambient intelligence to the surrounding environment; and, last, but not least, they may be embedded, mobile, or even ubiquitous. In essence, pervasive computing generates new interdependencies between the physical world and the computing artifacts. The latter should be integrated in the physical environment, continuously monitoring end users actions, and *pre*-acting (rather than *re*-acting) on the end users' wants and needs. Birnbaum (1997) positioned pervasive computing applications and services in the information systems (IS) context, by defining a new class of IS, pervasive information systems (PS), which exploits these novel features.

The consequences of PS for business and society are significant. We are entering an era of unprecedented opportunities for modern industries to redefine their business models by engaging new means to communicate with their value-chain stakeholders and reach their consumers. As a result, the traditional levers of *availability*, *usability*, and *practical functionality* that characterize the design of traditional "desktop" applications and services are also gradually changing; we are witnessing the emergence of new forms of electronic business, namely, "pervasive business" (p-business) and "silent business" (s-business) in which IT lies hidden in the background, but constantly monitors the needs and wants of the end users by being *proactive* and *autonomous*. PS should be able to improve either business performance or user experience through speculative or anticipatory decisions based on past behavioral actions. Moreover, the design of PS should follow a multidisciplinary approach. Successful design and implementation requires the collaboration of hardware and software engineers, human–computer interaction specialists, architects, system developers, end users, and business stakeholders.

PS have received significant attention by IS researchers. This is evident from recent publications in established IS journals and magazines. *Communications of the ACM* has published several dedicated special issues on the topic under different perspectives and terms (e.g., "Personal Information Management" [Teevan, Jones, and Bederson, 2006], "RFID" [Borriello, 2005], and "The Disappearing Computer" [Streitz and Nixon, 2005]). Lyytinen and colleagues (2004) published an article in *Communications of the Association for Information Systems* regarding the design and implementation challenges of PS. Lyytinen and Yoo (2002) proposed a research agenda in *Information Systems Research* for an emerging IS class that they call "nomadic computing." At the same time, new journals, dedicated to the subject of PS, have begun to emerge. Examples include *IEEE Pervasive Computing, Personal and Ubiquitous Computing, ACM Transactions on Sensor Networks (TOSN)*, and *ACM Transactions on Embedded Computing Systems (TECS)*.

This book aims to investigate the PS phenomenon from a multiperspective analytical perspective. Figure P.1 presents the framework for this investigation of the emerging field.

Each examination perspective is supported by a different chapter in the volume. Initially, the volume presents the technology foreground of pervasive systems. The focus is on new forms of *access devices* (emphasizing wearable devices), *software development toolkits*, and also the *middleware infrastructure* that acts as the "glue" in providing innovative pervasive services. Chapter 1, authored by the volume editors, presents the historical evolution of IS, which led to PS. Moreover, it defines PS based on their novel properties compared with "desktop" environments. Chapter 2, by

Figure P.1   **Examination Perspectives of Pervasive Information Systems**

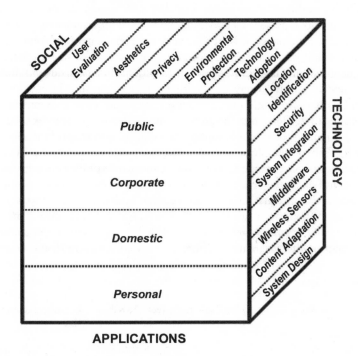

APPLICATIONS

the same authors, presents a holistic research agenda that structures the remainder of the volume. Specifically, the research agenda identifies the current status and design challenges of PS in three layers: technological, application specific, and social. Chapter 3, by Gregory Biegel and Vinny Cahill, proposes a set of specific requirements and research challenges that must be addressed for pervasive middleware to successfully support the development of PS in the future. Chapter 4, by Javier Muñoz and Vicente Pelechano, applies the guidelines and strategies described by software factories and model driven architecture, in order to build a methodological approach for the development of pervasive systems. Moreover, they define PervML, a domain specific modeling language that supports PS development.

The *applications* section of the volume classifies PS into four discrete classes: *personal*, *domestic*, *corporate*, and *public* systems. Each PS type conceals different design objectives as well as end-user requirements. Chapter 5, by Victor Callaghan, Jeannette Chin, Victor Zamudio, Graham Clarke, Anuroop Shahi, and Michael Gardner investigates domestic pervasive systems development. Specifically, the authors describe three approaches that enable home users to configure, program, and command pervasive technology for personal ends based on task computing, pervasive interactive programming, and theoretical work based on agent services. The authors also provide empirical evidence demonstrating the simplicity and usability of these methods. Chapter 6, by Anatole Gershman and Andrew Fano, discusses what it means to conduct commerce in a world where the physical environment is teeming with a variety of technologies capable of providing new classes of services. The authors explore this challenge in the context of a number of examples. Chapter 7, by Cliff Randell, investigates the design challenge of wearable systems. Following a review of the state of the art in the field, the chapter concludes with a set of design requirements for wearable systems. Chapter 8, by Ilias Maglogiannis and Stathes Hadjiefthymiades, investigates an instance of public pervasive systems, pervasive health care systems, by identifying the state of the art, the enabling technologies, and the corresponding challenges for the future.

The last part of the volume addresses certain social issues that are vital for the successful deployment and evaluation of PS. Chapter 9, by Johan Redström, attempts to raise the importance of aesthetics for PS development. He discusses the motivations behind aesthetics, examples of what is being proposed, and a critical discussion of aesthetics prospects for PS design and development. The final chapter, by Jean Scholtz, Mary Theofanos, and Sunny Consolvo, presents an evaluation framework for PS based on metrics and examples from the literature. Moreover, the authors present the results of a case study illustrating the applicability of their framework. Finally, they conclude with a discussion of future needs to enable researchers to share evaluation results.

We believe that this volume will reinforce research in the field of PS by summarizing the existing knowledge and identifying new areas of research for both academics and practitioners. Moreover, we would like to acknowledge that the successful completion of this volume is a credit to all of the authors' excellent contributions. In addition, we would like to extend our gratitude to all reviewers for their assistance and comments on the submitted chapters. Finally, we would like to thank the authors of each chapter who performed considerable reviewing of each other's work.

REFERENCES

Agis, E.; Mitchel, H.; Ovadia, S.; Aissi, S.; Bakshi, S.; Iyer, P.; Kibria, M.; Rogers, C.; and Tsai, J. 2004. Global, interoperable broadband wireless networks: Extending WiMAX technology to mobility. *INTEL Technology Journal,* 8, 3, 173–187.

Akyildiz, I.F.; Wang, X.; and Wang, W. 2005. Wireless mesh networks: A survey. *Computer Networks,* 47, 4, 445–487.

Altuntas, S. and Baykal, B. 2005. Mobile multi-access IP: A proposal for mobile multi-access management in future wireless IP networks. *Computer Networks,* 47, 4, 577–592.

Bahl, P. and Padmanabhan, V. 2000. RADAR: An in-building RF-based user location and tracking system. In *Proceedings of the IEEE Infocom 2000.* Los Alamitos, CA: IEEE CS Press, 775–784.

Banerjee, N.; Wu, W.; Basu, K.; and Das, S.K. 2004. Analysis of SIP-based mobility management in 4G wireless networks. *Computer Communications,* 27, 8, 697–707.

Benzaid, M.; Minet, P.; Al Agha, K.; Adjih, C.; and Allard G. 2004. Integration of Mobile-IP and OLSR for a Universal Mobility. *Wireless Networks,* 10, 4, 377–388.

Birnbaum, J. 1997. Pervasive Information Systems. *Communications of the ACM,* 40, 2, 40–41.

Borriello, G. 2005. RFID: Tagging the world (editorial). *Communications of the ACM,* 48, 9, 34–37.

Boukerche, A.; Chatzigiannakis, I.; and Nikoletseas, S. 2006. A new energy efficient and fault-tolerant protocol for data propagation in smart dust networks using varying transmission range. *Computer Communications,* 29, 4, 477–489.

Chivers, H. and Clark, J.A. 2004. Smart dust, friend or foe? Replacing identity with configuration trust. *Computer Networks,* 46, 5, 723–740.

Conti, J.P. 2005. The long road to WiMAX. *IEE Review,* 51, 10, 38–42.

Cvrcek, D. and Svenda, P. 2006. Smart dust security-key infection revisited. *Electronic Notes in Theoretical Computer Science,* 157, 3, 11–25.

Davies, N.; Cheverst, K.; Mitchell, K.; and Efrat, A. 2001. Using and determining location in a context-sensitive tour guide: The GUIDE experience. *IEEE Computer,* 34, 8, 35–41.

Egan, D. 2005. The emergence of ZigBee in building automation and industrial control. *Computing & Control Engineering,* 16, 2, 14–19.

Geer, D. 2005. Users make a beeline for ZigBee sensor technology. *IEEE Computer,* 38, 12, 16–19.

Ghosh, A.; Wolter, D.R.; Andrews, J.G.; and Chen, R. 2005. Broadband wireless access with WiMax/802.16: Current performance benchmarks and future potential. *IEEE Communications,* 43, 2, 129–136.

Giaglis, G.M.; Kourouthanassis, P.; and Tsamakos, A. 2002. Towards a classification framework for mobile location services. In B.E. Mennecke and T.J. Strader, eds., *Mobile Commerce: Technology, Theory, and Applications.* Hershey, PA: Idea Group, 67–85.

Hsin, C. and Liu, M. 2006. Self-monitoring of wireless sensor networks. *Computer Communications,* 29, 4, 462–476.

Intille, S.S. 2002. Designing a home of the future. *IEEE Pervasive Computing,* 1, 2, 76–82.

Karkkainen, M. 2003. Increasing efficiency in the supply chain for short life goods using RFID tagging. *International Journal of Retail & Distribution Management,* 31, 10, 529–536.

Kourouthanassis, P.E. and Giaglis, G.M. 2004. Shopping in the 21st century: Embedding technology in the retail arena. In G.J. Doukidis and A.P. Vrechopoulos, eds., *Consumer Driven Electronic Transformation: Applying New Technologies to Enthuse Consumers and Transform the Supply Chain.* Berlin: Springer-Verlag.

Lyytinen, K. and Yoo, Y. 2002. The next wave of nomadic computing: A research agenda for information systems research. *Information Systems Research,* 13, 4, 377–388.

Lyytinen, K.; Yoo, Y.; Varshney, U.; Ackerman, M.S.; Davis, G.; Avital, M.; Robey, D.; Sawyer, S.; and Sorensen, C. 2004. Surfing the next wave: Design and implementation challenges of ubiquitous computing environments. *Communications of the Association for Information Systems,* 13, 697–716.

Norman, D.A. 1999. *The Invisible Computer: Why Good Products Can Fail, the Personal Computer Is So Complex, and Information Appliances Are the Solution.* Cambridge, MA: MIT Press.

Poole, I. 2004. What exactly is . . . ZigBee? *Communications Engineer,* 2, 4, 44–45.

Pramataris, K.; Doukidis, G.J.; and Kourouthanassis, P.E. 2004. Towards smarter supply and demand chain collaboration practices enabled by RFID technology. In P. Vervest, E. Van Heck, K. Preiss, and L.F. Pau, eds., *Smart Business Networks.* Berlin: Springer-Verlag, 197–208.

Prater, E.; Frazier, G.V.; and Reyes, P.M. 2005. Future impacts of RFID on e-supply chains in grocery retailing. *Supply Chain Management: An International Journal,* 10, 2, 134–142.

Priyantha, N.B.; Chakraborty, A.; and Balakrishnan, H. 2000. The cricket location-support system. In *Proceedings of the Sixth Annual International Conference on Mobile Computing and Networking (Mobicom 00).* New York: ACM Press, 32–43.

Romer, K. and Mattern, F. 2003. The design space of wireless sensor networks. *IEEE Wireless Communications,* 11, 6, 54–61.

Streitz, N. and Nixon, P. 2005. The disappearing computer (editorial). *Communications Engineer,* 48, 3, 32–35.

Teevan, J.; Jones, W.; and Bederson, B.B. 2006. Personal information management: Editorial. *Communications Engineer,* 49, 1, 40–43.

Tschudin, C.; Gunningberg, P.; Lundgren, H.; and Nordstrom, E. 2005. Lessons from experimental MANET research. *Ad Hoc Networks,* 3, 2, 221–233.

Want, R.; Hopper, A.; Falco, V.; and Gibbons, J. 1992. The active badge location system. *ACM Transactions on Information Systems,* 10, 1, 91–102.

Weiser, M. 1991. The computer of the 21st century. *Scientific American,* 265, 3, 66–75.

Zahariadis, T. 2004. Evolution of the wireless PAN and LAN standards. *Computer Standards & Interfaces,* 26, 3, 175–185.

PERVASIVE
INFORMATION
SYSTEMS

CHAPTER 1

TOWARD PERVASIVENESS

Four Eras of Information Systems Development

PANOS E. KOUROUTHANASSIS AND GEORGE M. GIAGLIS

Abstract: This chapter presents evolutionary perspectives on information systems development, outlined in four interrelated eras. During the first era, information systems were viewed mainly as a strictly technical discipline. Information technology (IT) was used to automate existing manual processes, each application was treated as a separate entity, and the overall purpose of using IT was to increase productivity and efficiency, primarily in an organizational context. At the second stage, the introduction of networking capabilities and personal computers (instead of dummy terminals) created the basis for new and more extensive uses of IT and paved the way for a shift away from technology and toward its actual use. Common applications of the second stage aimed to support professional work, while many systems became highly integrated. The most dominant change introduced in the third era is the World Wide Web, which made it possible to transcend conventional boundaries for using IT. Applications became more integral parts of business strategies while at the same time creating new opportunities to establish alliances and collaboration across organizational and national boundaries. The fourth era transfers information technology to the background. New, "off-the-desktop" applications have emerged intended to assist end users in their everyday activities. User experience has become the critical design factor, outweighing the traditional design objectives of utility and productivity.

Keywords: Pervasive Computing, Information Systems Development, Design

INTRODUCTION

Over the past few years we have witnessed a tendency to move interaction with computers away from the traditional desktop environment. New technologies such as mobile and wireless networks, sensor technologies, and distributed systems allow people to use computational resources while on the move. Moreover, highly specialized computing devices such as digital cameras, microsensors, audio players, and high-quality interactive displays have also started to appear, blurring the distinction between computers and other electronic appliances. These technical advancements have inspired several new research fields that challenge our existing view of computers and how they are used by envisioning new ways of understanding and interacting with them.

This proliferation of computing artifacts into the physical world promises more than spontaneous availability of computational resources to the users; on the contrary, it suggests new paradigms of interaction, inspired by constant access to information and computational capabilities (Abowd and Mynatt, 2000). Today, we question the dominance of the traditional personal computer (PC) as the sole device of access interaction with an information system. The emergence of personal digital assistants, pagers, tablet PCs, mobile phones, appliance devices, and so on provide multiple ways for users to access and interact with an information system.

This shift in the view of information systems is most commonly known as "post-desktop computing" (Press, 1999). The historical evolution of information systems can be decomposed to the following four stages (Birnbaum, 1997):

- They began as laboratory curiosities.
- They were used by a small number of specialists aiming to solve a particular problem.
- They became manufacturable and commonplace, but still required a great deal of specialized training and thus, were used only by a relatively small fraction of the population.
- They will eventually become *pervasive,* viewed as part of the natural world by most people.

This argument is supported by numerous researchers who, over the past few years, have outlined this evolution of information systems (Applegate, McFarlan, and McKenney, 1996; Avison and Fitzgerald, 1988; Lyytinen, 1989; Silver, Markus, and Beath, 1995; Somogyi and Galliers, 2003; Zmud, 1997). This chapter aggregates the main changes that have fundamentally shifted the way we perceive information systems. Initially, we will highlight the historical evolution of the field of information systems, which led to the emergence of a new IS class that we call "pervasive information systems" (PS). Next, PS will be framed against their novel characteristics enabling us to strictly define them. These novel characteristics pave the way for IS researchers to question whether traditional design approaches are capable of addressing the design and implementation of PS. The chapter concludes with some initial thoughts concerning specific areas that require the attention of PS researchers.

INFORMATION SYSTEMS EVOLUTION

The first generation of information systems was viewed mainly as a strictly technical discipline. Information technology (IT) was used to automate existing manual processes, each application was treated as a separate entity, and the overall purpose of using IT was to increase productivity and efficiency mainly in an organizational context. Unsurprisingly, the core efforts of IT professionals focused on devising new means to model information within the organization; thus, database management was the "killer application" (Chen, 1976; Halpin, 2001).

At the second stage, the introduction of networking capabilities and personal computers (instead of terminals) created the basis for new and more extensive uses of IT and paved the way for a shift away from technology and toward its actual *use.* Common applications of the second stage aimed to support professional work, while many systems became highly integrated. Consequently, the design challenge for the second stage has been to *manage* information instead of simply collecting and storing it in a central database (Aiken, Sheng, and Vogel, 1991; Batra, Hoffer, and Bostrom, 1990; Davies and Olson, 1985; Dennis et al., 1988; Drucker, 1991; Gallupe, DeSanctis, and Dickson, 1988; Zwass, 1992). Indicative of this drive toward supporting management rather than clerical operations is the name change that occurred around this time: most data processing departments became management services departments and they were coordinated by management information systems (MIS) managers (Couger, Zawacki, and Oppermann, 1979). Still, most MIS activities of the era were concerned primarily with data management, with little real thought being given to meeting management information needs. We could argue that emphasis was given to *information management* rather than *managing information.* Indeed, key publications of that era highlighted that data and databases represented the core of any MIS effort (Goodhue, Quillard, and Rockart 1988; Senn, 1978).

In the 1980s and the beginning of the 1990s increased attention was paid to identifying pertinent applications of information technology. New application areas, supported by generic types of systems, emerged on the side of data processing systems and MIS. In essence, IS managers realized that the highly intelligent content of MIS applications could be usefully exploited by supporting decision-making processes of higher executives. Thus, the end of the second era of IS evolved concepts such as decision support systems (Kasper, 1996), data warehousing (Chenoweth, Corral, and Demirkan, 2006), executive information systems (Walls, Widmeyer, and El Sawy, 1992), intelligent systems (Gregor and Benbasat, 1999), expert systems (Yoon, Guimaraes, and O'Neal, 1995), and knowledge management systems (Alavi and Leidner, 2001). Management service departments were renamed *information systems* departments with their major task being to make information available to all organizational departments. Issues of interconnectivity, scalability, and reliability of the information system became of paramount importance. Moreover, enterprise resource planning (ERP) systems started to emerge with exponentially increasing installations in mainly large firms (Beatty and Smith, 1987; Hayes, Hunton, and Reck, 2001; Scheer and Habermann, 2000; Sharif, Irani, and Love, 2005).

The most dominant change introduced in the third stage has been global networks and the World Wide Web (WWW), which made it possible to transcend the conventional boundaries of IT use. Applications became more integral parts of business strategies and created new opportunities to establish alliances and collaborations across organizational and country boundaries. Internet computing is considered by many researchers to be a major revolutionary change in computing (Lyytinen and Yoo, 2002a; Walters, 2001) by departing in multiple ways from earlier computing concepts both with respect to what design elements can be manipulated (Isakowitz, Bieber, and Vitali, 1998; Isakowitz, Stohr, and Balasubramanian, 1995) and how an IT service is developed and assembled (Pressman, 1998). For example, Lyytinen and Rose (2003) highlighted that the Internet enables unforeseen flexibility in the design, implementation, distribution, and delivery of IT services that can satisfy previously unexplored user needs. Indeed, the proliferation of the Internet has supported the explosion of several commercial applications that were provided through the new medium. Turban et al. (2006) classified the evolution of these applications in four major phases: presence, e-commerce, collaboration, and integration. Table 1.1 presents the major characteristics of each phase.

The new trend of this era is the "digital firm" (Bauer, 2001), which has been enabled by the developments in electronic commerce and electronic business. New digital relationships are formed through the Internet through interorganizational systems (Allen, 2003; Daniel and White, 2005; Shore, 2006), electronic marketplaces (Albrecht, Dean, and Hansen, 2005; Bakos et al., 2005), Web-enabled auctions (Ba and Pavlou, 2002; Bapna et al., 2004), applications services provision (Currie, Desa, and Khan, 2004; Ma, Pearson, and Tadisina, 2005; Susarla, Barua, and Whinston, 2003), and customer relationship management (Karakostas, Kardaras, and Papathanassiou, 2005), to name a few. Moreover, the Internet produced new business models supporting the operation of organizations depending on the degree of digitalization of their products or services sold, their business processes, or the delivery agent (commonly referred to as "the intermediary" or "online broker" [Oetzel, 2004]). As such, organizations may exist purely online or digitally (Wu, Cook, and Strong, 2005), meaning that they are engaged only in the field of e-business (such as e-bay. com or Amazon.com).

Table 1.1

The Evolution of the Internet over Time

	Time			
	1993–1994	1995–1999	2000–2001 Collaboration and interaction	2001–2005 Integration and services
	Presence	E-commerce		
Emphasis	Eyeballs (human review)	Revue, expansion	Profit	Capabilities, services
Type of transaction	No transaction	B2C, C2C, C2B, G2C, e-CRM	B2B, B2E, supply chain, c-commerce, G2B	Portals, e-learning, m-commerce, l-commerce
Nature	Publish information	Process transaction	Collaborate	Integrate, provide services
Target	Pages	Process transaction	Digital systems	Digital environments
Concentrate on	Web Sites	Web-enabled existing systems, dot-coms	Business transformation and consolidation	Internal and external integration

Source: Turban et al. (2006).

At the same time, organizations realized the strategic importance of information systems. Although some organizations originally regarded IT as a "necessary evil," something that was needed in order to stay in business, most firms saw it as a major source of strategic opportunity, seeking proactively to identify how IT could help them to gain a competitive advantage. Similarly, strategic information systems emerged to support strategy formulation and planning, especially in uncertain or highly competitive environments (Newkirk and Lederer, 2006), such as the airline industry (Buhalis, 2004).

The Internet's emergence has fundamentally changed the ways that many people interact with computers. It has also created a culture that is substantially more amenable to the deployment of emerging computing environments. Indeed, the Internet has created a nearly "ubiquitous" information and communications infrastructure. People can access a huge wealth of knowledge and services from almost any personal computer, mobile device, smart phone, or even personal digital assistant (PDA). Moreover, the Internet has redefined the relationships between users and computers. Nowadays, many users relate not to their computer but rather to their point of presence within the digital world—typically, their homepage, portal, or e-mail service. So, for users who extensively use Internet services and information, the computer that they use to access these services has become largely irrelevant. In addition, many users commonly access the same point in digital space from several different devices (office or home PC, cell phone, PDA, etc.) throughout the course of a typical day. Consequently, for most users, computers themselves are becoming increasingly unimportant—what matters is the view a particular machine provides of the digital world. In this sense, we are moving toward a new era of thinking about computers: computers are gradually "disappearing," while users are free to focus beyond them. Literally, users are primarily interested in having access to any Internet-enabled application irrespective of whether it is provided via a desktop computer, a mobile phone, or an information kiosk located in a public place. Moreover, the generally uniform design of Internet applications has made it possible to minimize the

Figure 1.1 **Information Systems Evolution Eras**

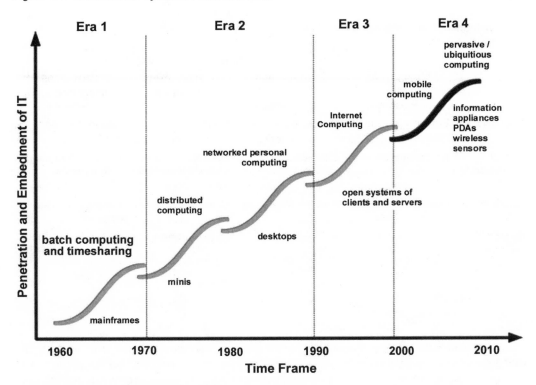

Source: Adapted from Birnbaum (1999).

learning curve for their use. Because people have begun to consider the Internet as a commodity, we argue that Internet applications are becoming pervasive in nature. What gradually changes is the *provision* of these applications through alternate channels and forms.

In parallel, we have moved from personal computers to computerized artifacts. A new generation of information appliances has emerged, offering a means to a particular end; their use seems natural to people. They differ from the small, mobile, general-purpose computers in what they do and in the much smaller learning overhead they impose on the user. Dedicated to a particular task, they are named by that task (e.g., a temperature sensor, a wireless access point), and users think of them in terms of what they do, not how they do it. They have shifted from simple *computing artifacts* to advanced and complicated *information processing artifacts*. This new trend represents the differentiating element of our era. Instead of having information technology in the foreground, triggered, manipulated, and used by humans, we witness that information technology (regardless of whether it consists of computers, small sensors, or other communication means) gradually resides in the background, monitoring the activities of humans, processing and communicating this information to other sources, and intervening should it be required.

Figure 1.1 illustrates the evolution that characterizes the field of information systems. The figure shows the progression of information technology over several decades, spanning the four eras discussed in the previous paragraphs. Interaction paradigms are shown below the S-curves; how the system components are interconnected is shown above. The fourth era marks the latest technology developments in terms of miniaturization of devices and increased processing capability, which ultimately has led to the ability to specialize them according to their function in a volume sufficient for commercial exploitation. It should be noted that the figure reflects the increased embedment of information technology in our everyday life in terms of IT devices (or computerized artifacts) per user/individual. This is the most significant change introduced in the fourth era of information systems. The manifestation of IT artifacts in the physical space enables the provision of new applications and services that target a much wider and more diverse user group. Traditionally, users had to be trained to the functionality of the information system. This training process could be completed either formally or through repeated trial-and-error practice. The vision of "everyday computing" (Norman, 2002) requires that information technology be able to be used, literally, by all people irrespective of their familiarity and past experience with IT. Wireless sensors may sense and process information pertaining to the individual and trigger the system's response based on some dynamic or predefined events. Interactions between the user and the system are expanded beyond the desktop paradigm. Ambient technologies (such as speech or gesture recognition) (Alewine, Ruback, and Deligne, 2004; Sawhney and Schmandt, 2000) promote more natural communication with the emerging class of IS. All of the above have led us to conceptualize and specify a new class of information systems that are commonly called "pervasive IS." The following section presents a short outline of the major landmarks leading to the new IS class.

TOWARD PERVASIVE INFORMATION SYSTEMS

The notion of information technology residing in the background was first discussed by Mark Weiser, former head of the Computer Science Laboratory at Xerox PARC, in his paper "The Computer of the 21st Century" (Weiser, 1991). This paper describes a world of nonintrusive and omnipresent computer technology, a world of "embodied virtuality." Weiser's vision extended the traditional approach of a user interacting with an artificial virtual world (a concept also known as "virtual reality") into a concept where information technology artifacts are integrated seamlessly into the natural world. As a result, Weiser and his colleagues developed a program called *ubiquitous computing*, dedicated to devising new means to make computing an integral, invisible part of people's lives (Weiser, 1991, 1994; Weiser, Gold, and Brown, 1999).

The new program was based on the advances that occurred in two broad areas of computer science, namely, distributed computing and mobile and wireless computing. On the one hand, the introduction of the World Wide Web and the Internet, interconnected computers and enabled them to share resources and capabilities over the new networks almost ubiquitously. Thus, distributed computing paved the way toward pervasiveness by introducing seamless access to remote information resources and communication with fault tolerance, high availability, and increased security (Satyanarayanan, 2001). On the other hand, mobile computing provided "anytime, anywhere" access support, which essentially paved the way for Weiser's "all-time, everywhere" vision (Saha and Mukherjee, 2003).

Mobile computing emerged from the integration of cellular technology with the Web (Saha, Mukherjee, and Bandyopadhyay, 2002), which over the past decade was widely deployed and adopted, primarily in the form of communication through the global system for mobile communications (GSM) (Rahnema, 1993). Furthermore, modern mobile handsets offer increased processing capabilities compared to their predecessors, which today are almost equivalent to a desktop computer of the early 1990s. A typical mobile phone might include such specialized applications as a calendar, games, organizer, and synchronization with a mail program in order to store personal e-mail messages on the mobile phone. Moreover, modern mobile phones tend to have increased storage and contacts capabilities. Combining the aforementioned developments with the gradual decrease in their price, we can argue that mobile phones can be viewed as a commodity by most users; almost everybody has one. To this end, a new class of applications and services emerged: "mobile business" (m-business) or "mobile commerce" (m-commerce), depending on the nature of the transaction involved (Varshney, Vetter, and Kalakota, 2000).

In parallel, recent developments in wireless technologies, namely, wireless local area networks (WLANs) (Burness et al., 2003), Bluetooth (Buttery and Sago, 2003), radio frequency identification devices (RFID) (Borriello, 2005; Prater, Frazier, and Reyes, 2005; Smith and Konsynski, 2003), and worldwide interoperability for microwave access (WiMax) (Agis et al., 2004), introduced a complementary approach to design innovative applications and services capable of providing support for mobile computing in a small area, such as a building, hallway, park, or office. Thus, over recent years the research community has been heavily involved in refining wireless standards in terms of increasing the total quality of service for mobile computing applications, while at the same time identifying new application domains in which the differentiating elements of mobile and wireless technologies could be deployed to enhance a particular application or service (Agrawal, Chari, and Sankar, 2003; Allen, 2003; Gebauer and Shaw, 2004; Stafford and Gillenson, 2003; Varshney, 2003; Varshney and Vetter, 2000). These differentiating elements involve, among others:

- Applications and services that are no longer localized to the strict boundaries set by the desktop computer. Instead, an application or service could be accessed through a mobile phone or a personal digital assistant provided it was connected to a mobile or wireless network.
- With the ability of mobility, location identification that naturally becomes a critical attribute, as it opens the door to a world of applications and services that utilize information related to the geographical position of their users to provide value-adding services to them (Giaglis, Kourouthanassis, and Tsamakos, 2002; Hightower and Biorriello, 2001; Rao and Parikh, 2003). This approach is particularly attractive since physically unobtrusive location techniques that do not rely on explicit user action can be devised. Such location identification techniques can be applied in both indoor and outdoor environments and varied according to accuracy and the method used.
- Applications and services that can be fully personalized to the end users; the mobile phone is a personal device that is not shared with other individuals. Moreover, the subscriber identity module (SIM) in the handset can uniquely identify each individual.

More recent technological developments enable the embedment of computational capabilities in the physical environment. Specifically, the gradual miniaturization of information technology produced concepts such as *wireless ad hoc networks* (Gronkvist, 2006; Yang and Vaidya, 2006) and *wireless sensor networks* (Gao et al., 2005; Hill et al., 2004) capable of providing a fully distributed wireless networking scheme with no dependency on fixed infrastructure nodes, and applicable in several domains, for example, habitat monitoring (Szewczyk et al., 2004). At the same time, established technologies such as WLANs are being refined in terms of capabilities and performance to accommodate the increased needs and requirements of the pervasive environment (Shenoy, 2005; Wool, 2005)

In the following section, we will try to put "order into chaos" regarding the multiplicity of different terminologies and definitions that exist in the literature that characterize the phenomenon of pervasive information systems. To structure our discussion, we provide our own definition to integrate the novel characteristics that these systems incorporate.

DEFINING PERVASIVE INFORMATION SYSTEMS

Introduction

In order to define PS, we have decided to decompose the concept into its distinct elements: the words "pervasive" and "information systems."

The definition of the concept "information system" can be classified into two broad categories or schools of thought: the "hard," functionalist approach, and the "soft," interpretive approach (Checkland and Holwell, 1998). Hard systems thinking assumes that the world contains systems that can be "engineered" to achieve objectives. Soft systems thinking regards the world as problematical and assumes that the process of inquiry into it can be meaningfully organized as a system. In short, the hard approach assumes that organizations are *systems* with *information needs* that information technology can apply, while the soft approach takes a process view of organizations and explores the ways that people in organizations intersubjectively attribute meaning to their world, and hence form a view of what information is relevant (Checkland, 1983; Checkland, 1984).

Information systems rely on information technology in order to support purposeful activities for social units, or collectivities, referred to as "organizations" (Ahituv and Newmann, 1990; Checkland and Holwell, 1998; Zwass, 1992). For the remainder of this chapter, we will use an abstraction of Laudon and Laudon's (2004) definition of an information system. According to the authors, information systems comprise "interrelated (information technology) components, working together to collect, process, store, and disseminate information to support decision making, coordination, control, analysis, and visualisation in an organisation." One might argue how such a broad definition could be expanded in order to encompass the differentiating perspective that characterizes PS. This differentiation derives from the word "pervasive" itself.

The word "pervasive" derives from the verb "pervade," meaning "to become diffused throughout every part of." The verb originates from the Latin word *pervadere,* meaning "to go through."). The word "pervasive" as an adjective characterizes something that is present or noticeable in every part of a thing or place.

This definition implies that pervasive information technology saturates the environment. Thus, to achieve total pervasiveness, information technology no longer superimposes itself on the user. The term "pervasive information systems" was originally introduced by Birnbaum (1997), who defined a PS as "information technology that must transcend in order to be merely manufacturable and commonplace. . . . IT must become intuitively accessible to ordinary people and deliver sufficient value to justify the large investment needed in the supporting infrastructure." Fernandes, Machado, and Carvalho (2004) provided a similar definition, basically stating that pervasive information systems are composed of heterogeneous, mobile, or physically integrated (embedded) devices that are capable of collecting, processing, storing and producing information aimed at contributing to an organization or personal needs in order to achieve a set of well-established objectives.

In recent years, numerous researchers have used the term "pervasive computing system" to define a very similar concept. Table 1.2 presents a sampling of these definitions.

These definitions show that the word "computing" was selected to demonstrate that the novel characteristic of such systems is the deployment of small interconnected artifacts in the physical environment with computing capabilities sufficient for collecting, processing, and communicating contextual information. The following section presents several similar terminologies that are related to PS.

Table 1.2

Various Definitions of the Term "Pervasive Computing System"

Source	Definition
Gupta and Moitra (2004)	An umbrella of IT capabilities working together to provide services to end users characterized by mobility, wireless connectivity, context awareness, implicit inputs including user intent, and proactiveness. These systems generate smart spaces that enhance interactivity among users and devices and employing natural interfaces to support this interaction.
Lyytinen et al. (2004)	Pervasive computing technology refers to an emerging branch of computing devices that are seamlessly embedded in the background to serve preconfigured purposes. These computing devices are designed to blend into people's physical surroundings and are engineered to support work practices and routine activities within and across boundaries. This new breed of computing is based on architecture that is not tied to personal devices but instead embedded into the fabric of life.
Saha and Mukherjee (2003)	A major evolutionary step in work that began in the mid-1970s, when the PC first brought computers closer to people . . . keeping computing separate from our daily life.
Satyanarayanan (2001)	An environment saturated with computing and communication capability, yet so gracefully integrated with users that it becomes a "technology that disappears."
Huang et al. (1999)	Computers "disappeared into the infrastructure" where users use computer-assisted task-specific devices, as opposed to computing devices per se.
Grimm et al. (2001)	A computing infrastructure that seamlessly and ubiquitously aids users in accomplishing their tasks and that renders the actual computing devices and technology largely invisible.
IBM (2004)	Enabling information access anywhere, anytime, on demand.
WhatIs.com (2004)	Pervasive computing is the trend towards increasingly ubiquitous, connected computing devices in the environment, a trend being brought about by a convergence of advanced electronic—and particularly, wireless—technologies and the Internet.
Webopedia (2004)	Pervasive computing combines current network technologies with wireless computing, voice recognition, Internet capability and artificial intelligence, in order to create an environment where the connectivity of devices is embedded in such a way that the connectivity is unobtrusive and always available.
U.S. National Institute of Standards and Technology (2001)	Pervasive computing is a term for the strongly emerging trend toward: numerous, casually accessible, often invisible computing devices, frequently mobile or embedded in the environment, connected to an increasingly ubiquitous network infrastructure, composed of a wired core and wireless edges.

Terminologies Similar to Pervasive Information Systems

The general idea of technology residing in the background of physical space has also been characterized using different, but closely related terminologies. Such terms include *pervasive/ubiquitous computing systems* (Davies and Gellersen, 2002; Stajano, 2002; Stanton, 2001), *sentient computing systems* (Addlesee et al., 2001; Harter et al., 2001; Hopper, 1999; Lopez de Ipina and

Lo, 2001), *nomadic computing systems* (Lyytinen and Yoo, 2002b), *invisible computing systems* (Bohn et al., 2003; Norman, 1999), and *disappearing computing systems* (Cakmakci et al., 2002; Streitz, 2003).

The term *ubiquitous* or *pervasive computing* was coined by Weiser and colleagues at Xerox PARC in the late 1980s. Weiser promoted a new way of thinking about a computer: "one that takes into account the natural human environment and allows the computers themselves to vanish into the background" (Weiser, 1993). The motivating idea is to make computing power available invisibly through the physical environment.

The concept of invisible computing, introduced by Norman (1999), is primarily concerned with how emerging technologies can be best integrated into everyday life. He introduced the notion of information appliances as pivotal to invisible computing. Norman argues that general-purpose personal computers are difficult to use because they are technology-centered products that are inherently complex. Thus, invisible computing facilitates user interaction through information appliances that are small, task-focused devices in place of big, complex, general-purpose personal computers. The idea is to design an information appliance to fit the task so well that the device "becomes a part of the task, feeling like a natural extension of the work, a natural extension of the person."

The term "disappearing computer" was proposed by the European Commission to character-ize European Union-funded research projects that investigate the PS phenomenon. Specifically, the European Commission introduced a research agenda titled "The Disappearing Computer," which aimed to explore how everyday life can be supported and enhanced through the use of col-lections of interacting artifacts collectively forming new people-friendly environments in which the computer as we know it has no role (European Commission, 1999). The agenda was incor-porated into the European Commission's Future and Emerging Technologies program. As a next step, the European Commission deployed "The Disappearing Computer II" program, focused on identifying new technologies that can be diffused in everyday-life objects and settings (European Commission, 2002).

Finally, sentient computing is a collaborative project between AT&T Laboratories and the Uni-versity of Cambridge. Its emphasis is on developing and exploiting technologies to give computers access to the state of their environment. The project began with the development of an ultrasonic indoor location system. The system can provide the locations of tagged objects or people to an accuracy of about 3 centimeters throughout a 10,000 square foot building. The distinguishing feature of sentient computing is its use of sensors and resource status data to maintain a model of the real world that is shared between users and applications. The goal of sentient computing is to make applications more responsive and useful by observing and reacting to the physical world. Research is based on three major themes: developing sensor technology, experimenting with ap-plication devices, and constructing platforms that connect sensors and devices.

Additional terms that are similar to pervasive computing are *calm technology* and *augmented reality*. Calm technology was originally defined by Mark Weiser as alternating between the cen-ter and the periphery of the user's consciousness in order to better convey informational context and to avoid sensory overload (Weiser and Brown, 1995). *Augmented reality* starts from a view similar to Weiser's vision of ubiquitous computing. Augmented reality is a variation of virtual environments, or virtual reality as it is more commonly called. Augmented reality allows the user to see the real world, with virtual objects superimposed upon or merged with the real world, thus supplementing reality, rather than completely replacing it (Azuma, 1995; Barfield, Rosenberg, and Lotens, 1995; Bowskill and Downie, 1995).

Finally, more recently, researchers have also proposed some additional characterizations of pervasive information systems, such as *proactive systems* and *autonomic systems* (Satyanarayanan, 2002). Once again, these terms emphasize specific aspects of the pervasive systems field. Proactive systems, for example, focus on improving performance and user experience through speculative or anticipatory actions of the system itself. One example is ConChat (Ranganathan et al., 2002). The system identifies and communicates the specific situational attributes of one chat partner (such as location and mood) to another chat partner in order to generate rules that automatically translate and refine the phrases that the two partners type to each other. Autonomic systems aim to improve user experience through the system's self-regulation.

Table 1.3 summarizes various scholars' definitions of the aforementioned terms.

As in the case of pervasive computing systems, all of the aforementioned terms rely on a common factor: new computational resources that are embedded in the environment and capable of collecting, processing, and disseminating information when and where desired. Although the primary focus of Weiser's vision was the end user, the initial limitations of technology drove him and his colleagues to focus on *system engineering* issues and the development of proof-of-concept prototypes. The key word in the program was *computing* as a means of embedding computational capabilities in artifacts of our everyday life. The first devices developed from the ubiquitous computing experiments were *tabs*, *pads*, and *boards* (Want and Schilit, 2001; Want et al., 1992, 1995; Weiser, 1993), which corresponded to different sizes of commonsense objects capable of sensing the location of the user in its environment and using this information to modify the behavior of programs running on nearby workstations or even to forward telephone calls arriving at the office PBX to the telephone extension nearest to the intended recipient.

The research community embraced the new research stream and inspired prominent projects during the early 1990s, the most notable being the ParcTab (Want et al., 1995), the Mpad (Kantarjiev et al., 1993), and the Liveboard (Elrod et al., 1992) experiments from the Xerox Palo Alto Research Center, the Active Badge from the Olivetti Research Center (Want et al., 1992), the InfoPad from Berkeley (Truman et al., 1998), and the Active Bat from AT&T Laboratories Cambridge (Harter et al., 2001). All of these projects have benefited from the notable improvements in hardware technology over the past decade, namely, wireless networking, processing capability, storage capacity, and high quality displays (Want et al., 2002).

Synthesis: Reflecting on Pervasive Information Systems

In past years, the academic community considered all of the aforementioned terms as essentially one term and treated them likewise (Gellersen, 1999; Roussos, Gershman, and Kourouthanassis, 2003). Nevertheless, researchers who wanted to describe the notion of technology residing in the background usually selected one of two terms: either "ubiquitous" or "pervasive." In his editorial statement in the first issue of *IEEE Pervasive Computing,* Satyanarayanan (2002) stated that both terms should be used interchangeably and we will follow his recommendation in the remainder of this volume.

We define pervasive information systems as:

> Interconnected technological artifacts diffused in their surrounding environment, which work together to sense, process, store, and communicate information to ubiquitously and unobtrusively support their users' objectives and tasks in a context-aware manner.

This definition takes into account the key differentiating elements that PS introduce. Moreover, it summarizes the viewpoints of all of the scholars investigating this emerging field. At the

Table 1.3

Concepts Similar to Pervasive Information Systems

Definitions of ubiquitous computing systems

Lyytinen and Yoo (2002b)	Computers, embedded in our natural movements and interactions with our environments, both physical and social.
Weiser (2002)	Machines that fit the human environment instead of forcing humans to enter theirs will make using a computer as refreshing as a walk in the woods.
Abowd, Mynatt, and Rodden (2002)	People and environments augmented with computational resources that provide information and services when and where desired.

Definitions of sentient computing systems

Lopez de Ipina and Lo (2001)	Sentient computing aims to make computerized services pervasive in our life, by giving the devices providing such services perception, namely: the capability to see or hear what entities are around them; what these entities are doing; where they are and when something is happening.
Addlesee et al. (2001)	Sentient computing systems are systems that can change their behaviour based on a model of the environment they construct using sensor data.
Harter et al. (2001)	A sentient computing system comprised of a computing platform that collects environmental data, and presents that data in a form suitable for context-aware applications.

Definitions of augmented reality

Newman, Ingram, and Hopper (2001)	Augmented reality both exposes and supplements the user's view of the real world by displaying information using either personal or environment displays in an unobtrusive way.

Definitions of nomadic computing

Lyytinen and Yoo (2002a)	Nomadic computing refers to a heterogeneous assemblage of interconnected technological and organizational elements, which enables physical and social mobility of computing and communication services between organizational actors both within and across organizational borders.

Definitions of ambient intelligence

Aarts and Marzano (2003)	Ambient intelligence refers to electronic environments that are sensitive and responsive to the presence of people, building on advanced networking technologies, which allow robust, ad hoc networks to be formed by a broad range of mobile devices and other objects.

Definitions of disappearing computing

European Commission (1999) Streitz (2003)	Disappearing computer systems aim to support and enhance everyday life through the use of collections of interacting smart artifacts. Together, these artifacts will form new people-friendly environments in which the computer as we know it has no role.

same time, it introduces the main novel characteristics of pervasive information systems: they are composed of *multiple artifacts* instead of only personal computers; they are capable of *perceiving contextual information* instead of simple user inputs; they are *embedded in the environment*; and they *support mobility* instead of stationary services. The following section will briefly discuss these novel characteristics in comparison with the desktop paradigm.

NOVEL CHARACTERISTICS OF PERVASIVE INFORMATION SYSTEMS

The past few years have marked the progress of PS from laboratory, proof-of-concepts examples, to near real-life implementations. In a recent special issue, titled "The Disappearing Computer," *Communications of the ACM* included several articles supporting this argument. For example, Borriello (2005) presented several real-world location-based systems; Bannon et al., (2005) discussed the application of pervasive technologies to enhance the experience of visitors to museums; and Gershman and Fano (2005) discussed several pertinent applications of PS in multiple domains. Apart from purely commercial applications of PS, pervasive technologies are also embedded in multiple activities of our public, everyday life. Indeed, PS examples appear in the entertainment industry (Jegers and Wiberg, 2006), health (Liszka et al., 2004), and even sports (Beetz, Kirchlechner, and Lames, 2005; Michahelles and Schiele, 2005).

These research efforts focus on the applicability of emerging (or *pervasive*) technologies to vertical application domains. Another investigation dimension suggests examining PS from a more horizontal and holistic perspective. Indeed, several current umbrella projects are aimed at further developing pervasive computing technologies and identifying pertinent application areas. One such project is Oxygen, conceptualized and operationalized at Massachusetts Institute of Technology (Rudolph, 2001). The project aims at enabling pervasive, human-centered computing through a combination of specific user and system technologies. The Oxygen vision is to bring an abundance of computation and communication within easy reach of humans through natural perceptual interfaces of speech and vision so computation blends into people's lives enabling them to easily accomplish tasks, and to collaborate, access knowledge, automate routine tasks, and smoothly interact with their environment. The project has developed several technologies in the devices, network, and software layers enabling the system components and its users to interact unobtrusively.

In essence, pervasive information systems introduce new elements in multiple dimensions spanning different IS domains, such as human–computer interaction (HCI) and software engineering, which admonish us to examine them as a new information systems class. In essence, pervasive information systems revisit the way we interact with computers by introducing new input modalities and system capabilities. So far, the interaction paradigm for information systems has been the *desktop*. Thus, the design and implementation of information systems were based on this paradigm. Pervasive information systems extend this paradigm by introducing a set of novel characteristics that may be summarized in the points below:

First, PS always deal with nontraditional computing devices that merge seamlessly into the physical environment. As such, the desktop (in the form of the personal computer) is just "another access device." Consequently, conventional HCI design methods and interaction schemes may not be appropriate for the new IS class since the physical interaction between users and the system will, most certainly, not resemble the prevailing keyboard/mouse/display paradigm followed by information systems that based on the desktop interaction scheme (DIS). On the contrary, PS simulate the way that humans interact with the physical world. Abowd and Mynatt (2000) argue that because humans speak, gesture, and use writing utensils to communicate with other humans and alter physical artifacts, such actions can and should be used as explicit or implicit input to PS. Burkey (2000) argues that the next step in this progression refers to environmental interfaces in which the environment is the interface and the user exists in it. This is fully aligned with PS where, ultimately, every artifact can interact with the system user. Thus, apart from solely physical interactions with the system, PS may also incorporate elements of ambient interactions with devices or objects from physical space (Schur, Decker, and May, 1999). According to the authors, "these interactions should be lauded for their increased learnability and general ease of use." Additionally, they may be used by people with disabilities or IT unfamiliarity for whom the traditional mouse and keyboard are less accessible.

Second, PS support a multitude of *heterogeneous device types* that differ in terms of size, shape (more diverse, ergonomic, and stylistic), and functionality (simple mobile phones, portable laptops, pagers, PDAs, sensors, and so on), providing continuous interaction that moves computing from a *localized tool* to a *constant presence*. In contrast to desktop environments, where the access devices are stationary, PS support *nomadic devices* that may be carried around by users and present *location-based information*. Since these devices are not required to be a fixed part of the pervasive system, PS need to support *spontaneous networking*, implying ad hoc detection and linking of the participating devices into a *temporary pervasive network*. This new type of network may create *dynamic dependencies* among the linked devices, which may eventually lead to a device *swarm (or unpredictable) behavior.*

Third, PS produce a revised viewpoint in the way we perceive system design. "Conventional" system design incorporated more and more of the physical world inside the computer. In this sense, actual system intelligence has been purely cybernetic, comprising software designed to execute predefined tasks and activities efficiently. Moreover, systems were designed in ways that enhanced overall utility and productivity, especially when applied to organizational contexts. In the case of PS, many computerized artifacts (instead of a single computer) monitor and support the user. The system's intelligence no longer resides solely in the computer, but is embedded in the physical world. Thus, each artifact may be specialized to support *a single task* performed in a more efficient way. This task may depend on a geographical location or be triggered by an event such as a user request, a sensor reading change, and so on.

Building on the above, in desktop environments designers typically assume that user profiles are known in advance (Grudin, 1991a, 1991b; Lynch and Gregor, 2004; Poltrock and Grudin, 1994), thus allowing for systematic requirements analysis. In PS, the opposite may be true: it is highly unlikely for the system designer to know in advance the kinds of users who will be interacting with the system. Users may range from those who are vaguely familiar with IT to those who are expert users. In addition, PS users may be *opportunistic* in the sense that they may use the system only sporadically, implying that they may not receive training prior to system use.

Finally, PS introduce the property of *context awareness* as a result of the pervasive artifacts' capability of collecting, processing, and managing environmental or user-related information on a real-time basis. In contrast to desktop computing, where *user action* precedes *system response,* PS promote system *pro-action* based on *environmental stimuli.* This can be accomplished through the deployment of sensors and actuators in the physical world.

Table 1.4 summarizes the differences between the desktop paradigm (DIS) and PS in terms of six dimensions answering the following questions:

- What is the generic profile of a PS user compared with DS? (User)
- What interaction is the user expected to perform? (Task)
- How does the interaction take place? (Medium)

Table 1.4

Differentiating Elements of Desktop Information Systems and Pervasive Information Systems

	Desktop information systems	Pervasive information systems
User	• Committed • Known • Trained	• Opportunistic • Unknown • Untrained
	Role model: office clerk	Role model: citizen
Task	• Generic • Focused on utility and productivity	• Specific • Focused on service delivery and experience
Medium	• Localized • Homogeneous • "Point and click" paradigm	• Constant presence • Heterogeneous • Natural interaction and multimodal paradigm
Space	• Cybernetic	• Physical
Product	• Virtual	• Tangible and virtual
Time	• Reactive	• Proactive

- Where does the interaction take place? (Space)
- What will eventually be designed? (Product)
- When will the system be used? (Time)

CONCLUSIONS

This chapter provided an initial discussion of the novel characteristics that distinguish pervasive information systems from desktop information systems. Specifically, the chapter discussed the evolutionary changes that led to a fourth era of IS, characterized by ultra small-sized IT artifacts with increased computational and storage capabilities, capable of sensing environmental information and communicating it wirelessly. The chapter defined PS and presented their novel features, which led us to conclude that they represent an independent IS class requiring increased research attention.

The applications of physically embedded IT artifacts are as varied as the physical environments in which they will be placed. Want, et al. (2002) observed that the size and weight of those artifacts, their power consumption requirements, and the new interaction modalities that they introduce represent some of the most important challenges for large-scale PS implementations. As the authors state, "these problems transcend individual points on the technology curve, partly because they are somewhat contradictory; a solution in one space greatly confounds that in another." Yet, this is only the tip of the iceberg. The heterogeneity and diversity of pervasive devices and networks and their massive scale of physical and environmental embedment create additional research challenges for system designers. How can we establish a common protocol to support communication among heterogeneous devices? What information will be exchanged (and in what format)? How will a PS discover the participating devices in its application domain? Is it possible to develop a transparent mechanism to support this operation? What about user privacy in an environment capable of perceiving information relevant to each user based on a wireless sensor network? These are just sample questions suggesting that several hardware, software, user interaction, and application-specific research challenges still need to be addressed.

The same applies to specifying an optimal physical architecture for PS development and deployment. Power management, for example, cannot be addressed through changing batteries, or even recharging them, when, possibly, hundreds of devices and sensors are involved. Perhaps this challenge can be met through recent, but still experimental, developments in this field (Amirtharajah et al., 2005; Philipose et al., 2005; Roundy et al., 2005). Moreover, discovery systems aim at supporting device discovery, registration, communication, and quality of service management with PS (Rasheed, Edwards, and Tai, 2002; Zhu et al., 2004). These efforts may raise interoperability in interactive PS environments by standardizing user interface languages or device communication protocols (Lee, Helal, and Lee, 2006; Zucker, Uematsu, and Kamada, 2005). These can be provided through dedicated middleware solutions bridging the gap between the device, networking, and application areas of PS (Cahill et al., 2003; Chan and Perrig, 2003; Gaver et al., 2004; Kordon and Pautet, 2005; Moon et al., 2003).

Technology-related research challenges are the most obvious to pinpoint since PS represent a technology-driven phenomenon. However, blending the physical with the virtual brings forward several additional challenges in both the application of pervasive technologies in new domains and their social acceptability and conformity with existing norms and regulations. PS designers have an unprecedented opportunity to enhance *user experience* by highly differentiating the means by which users interact with an Information System (Abowd, Mynatt, and Rodden, 2002). Using the Internet to browse the exhibits of a museum through hypertext, multimedia, Virtual Reality Modeling Language (VRML), or even avatars (Hemminger, Bolas, and Schiff, 2004; Huang, Chen, and Chung, 2005; Wojciechowski et al., 2004) generates completely different experiences for users than does an actual visit to the museum. Indeed, several studies suggest that PS may augment the experience of visiting museums by providing personalized tour guides, in-museum navigation, and so on (Bellotti et al., 2001; Hsi and Fait, 2005).

At the same time, social and environmental challenges have emerged. Privacy protection in pervasive environments becomes of paramount importance with multiple researchers proposing alternative guidelines, frameworks, or methods aspiring to facilitate PS developers during the design and implementation processes (Brodie et al., 2005; Hengartner and Steenkiste, 2004; Lyytinen et al., 2004; Ohkubo, Suzuki, and Kinoshita, 2005). Moreover, the design of the pervasive information system needs to take into account the existing infrastructure of the physical space. Designers need to devise intelligent ways to place pervasive IT artifacts so that they do not overburden or create cognitive overloads to individuals whether or not they represent actual users of the pervasive system.

Estrin et al. (2002) claim that interconnecting the physical work with pervasive networks requires the PS components to be reusable and evolutionary. They suggest that designers need to identify common building blocks that will facilitate the development of effective and efficient pervasive systems. One such approach is to define taxonomies of PS and applications so that researchers can identify and foster reusable and paramaterizable features.

To summarize, we posit that recent technology developments have made it possible for a vision of PS to emerge and drive researchers to examine them as an independent IS class. Key improvements of PS include wireless networks, wireless sensors, high-performance and low-power processors, new ambient displays, and small-scale and powerful wireless devices. Progress toward integrating these components into large-scale and efficient PS involves many unresolved research issues relating to software development, system architecture, privacy, and managing system complexity. Moving into a pervasive world calls for the information systems community to embrace interdisciplinary approaches to resolve these research challenges. Researchers involved in the field of PS need to examine such disciplines as human–computer interaction, software engineering, operating systems, computer networks, databases, and artificial intelligence to name a few. Moreover, these researchers need to extend their skills beyond the development of effective software algorithms to the manipulation of the physical world in terms of processes, structures, objects, and places.

REFERENCES

Abowd, G.D. and Mynatt, E.D. 2000. Charting past, present, and future research in ubiquitous computing. *ACM Transactions on Computer-Human Interaction, 7*, 1, 29–58.

Abowd, G.D.; Mynatt, E.D.; and Rodden, T. 2002. The human experience. *IEEE Pervasive Computing, 1*, 1, 48–57.

Addlesee, M.; Curwen, R.; Hodges, S.; Newman, J.; Steggles, P.; Ward, A.; and Hopper, A. 2001. Implementing a sentient computing system. *IEEE Computer, 34*, 8, 50–56.

Agis, E.; Mitchel, H.; Ovadia, S.; Aissi, S.; Bakshi, S.; Iyer, P.; Kibria, M.; Rogers, C.; and Tsai, J. 2004. Global, interoperable broadband wireless networks: Extending WiMAX technology to mobility. *Intel Technology Journal, 8*, 3, 173–187.

Agrawal, M.; Chari, K.; and Sankar, R. 2003. Demystifying wireless technologies: Navigating through the wireless technology maze. *Communications of the Association for Information Systems, 12*, 166–182.

Ahituv, N. and Newmann, S. 1990. *Principles of Information Systems for Management.* Dubuque, IA: Wm. C. Brown.

Aiken, M.W.; Sheng, O.R.L.; and Vogel, D.R. 1991. Integrating expert systems with group decision support systems. *ACM Transactions on Information Systems, 9*, 1, 75–95.

Alavi, M. and Leidner, D.E. 2001. Knowledge management and knowledge management systems: Conceptual foundations and research issues. *MIS Quarterly, 25*, 1, 107–136.

Albrecht, C.C.; Dean, D.L.; and Hansen, J.V. 2005. Marketplace and technology standards for B2B e-commerce: Progress, challenges, and the state of the art. *Information and Management, 42*, 6, 865–875.

Alewine, N.; Ruback, H.; and Deligne, S. 2004. Pervasive speech recognition. *IEEE Computer, 3*, 4, 78–81.

Allen, J.P. 2003. The evolution of new mobile applications: A sociotechnical perspective. *International Journal of Electronic Commerce, 8*, 1, 23–36.

Amirtharajah, R.; Collier, J.; Siebert, J.; Zhou, B.; and Chandrakasan, A. 2005. DSPs for energy harvesting sensors: Applications and architectures. *IEEE Pervasive Computing, 4*, 3, 72–79.

Applegate, L.M.; McFarlan, F.W.; and McKenney, J.L. 1996. *Corporate Information Systems Management. Text and Cases.* Chicago: Irwin.

Avison, D.E. and Fitzgerald, G. 1988. Information systems development: Current themes and future directions. *Information and Software Technology, 30*, 8, 458–466.

Azuma, R. 1995. A survey of augmented reality. In *Proceedings of the Computer Graphics Special Interest Group (SIGGRAPH '95)*, 1–38.

Ba, S. and Pavlou, P.A. 2002. Evidence of the effect of trust building technology in electronic markets: Price premiums and buyer behavior. *MIS Quarterly, 26*, 3, 243–268.

Bakos, Y.; Lucas Jr., H.C.; Oh, W.; Simon, G.; Viswanathan, S.; and Weber, B.W. 2005. The impact of e-commerce on competition in the retail brokerage industry. *Information Systems Research, 16*, 4, 352–371.

Bannon, L.; Benford, S.; Bowers, J.; and Heath, C. 2005. Hybrid design creates innovative museum experiences. *Communications of the ACM, 48*, 3, 62–65.

Bapna, R.; Goes, P.; Gupta, A.; and Jin, Y. 2004. User heterogeneity and its impact on electronic auction market design: An empirical exploration. *MIS Quarterly, 28*, 1, 21–43.

Barfield, W.; Rosenberg, C.; and Lotens, W.A. 1995. Augmented-reality displays. In W. Barfield and T.A. Furness III, eds., *Virtual Environments and Advanced Interface Design.* New York: Oxford University Press, 542–575.

Batra, D.; Hoffer, J.A.; and Bostrom, R.P. 1990. A comparison of user performance between the relational and the extended entity relationship models in the discovery phase of database design. *Communications of the ACM, 33*, 2, 126–139.

Bauer, M.J. 2001. *E-Business: The Strategic Impact on Supply Chain and Logistics.* Oak Brook, IL: Council of Logistics Management.

Beatty, S. and Smith, S. 1987. External search effort: An investigation across several product categories. *Journal of Consumer Research,* 14, 83–95.

Beetz, M.; Kirchlechner, B.; and Lames, M. 2005. Computerized real-time analysis of football games. *IEEE Pervasive Computing,* 4, 3, 33–39.

Bellotti, F.; Berta, R.; De Gloria, A.; and Margarone, M. 2001. User testing a hypermedia tour guide. *IEEE Pervasive Computing,* 1, 2, 33–41.

Birnbaum, J. 1997. Pervasive information systems. *Communications of the ACM,* 40, 2, 40–41.

———. 1999. "Physical and the Information Revolution." Keynote presentation during the American Physical Society's Centennial Conference, Atlanta, GA, March 22.

Bohn, J.; Coroama, V.; Langheinrich, M.; Mattern, F.; and Rohs, M. 2003. Disappearing computers everywhere—Living in a world of smart everyday objects. In *Proceedings of the New Media, Technology and Everyday Life in Europe Conference.* Available at http://www.lse.ac.uk/collections/EMTEL/Conference/papers/Bohn.pdf (accessed March 10, 2007).

Borriello, G. 2005. RFID: Tagging the world. *Communications of the ACM,* 48, 9, 34–37.

Bowskill, J. and Downie, J. 1995. Extending the capabilities of the human visual system: An introduction to enhanced reality. *Computer Graphics,* 29, 2, 61–65.

Brodie, C.; Karat, C.M.; Karat, J.; and Feng, J. 2005. Usable security and privacy: A case study of developing privacy management tools. In *Proceedings of the 2005 Symposium on Usable Privacy and Security (SOUPS).* ACM International Conference Proceeding Series, vol. 93. New York: ACM Press, 35–43.

Buhalis, D. 2004. E-airlines: strategic and tactical use of ICTs in the airline industry. *Information and Management,* 41, 7, 805–825.

Burkey, C. 2000. Environmental interfaces: HomeLab. In *Proceedings of the Conference on Human Factors in Computing Systems.* New York: ACM Press, 47–48.

Burness, L.; Higgins, D.; Sago, A.; and Thorpe, P. 2003. Wireless LANs: Present and future. *BT Technology Journal,* 21, 3, 32–47.

Buttery, S. and Sago, A. 2003. Future applications of Bluetooth. *BT Technology Journal,* 21, 3, 48–55.

Cahill, V.; Gray, E.; Seigneur, J.M.; Jensen, C.; Chen, Y.; Shand, B.; Dimmock, N.; Twigg, A.; Bacon, J.; English, C.; Wagealla, W.; Terzis, S.; Nixon, P.; di Marzo Serugendo, J.; Bryce, C.; Carbone, M.; Krukow, K.; and Nielsen, M. 2003. Using trust for secure collaboration in uncertain environments. *IEEE Pervasive Computing,* 2, 3, 53–61.

Cakmakci, O.; Coutaz, J.; Van Laerhoven, K.; and Gellersen, H.-W. 2002. Context awareness in systems with limited resources. In *Proceedings of the Third Workshop on Artificial Intelligence in Mobile Systems (AIMS), ECAI 2002.* Lyon, France, 21–29.

Chan, H. and Perrig, A. 2003. Security and privacy in sensor networks. *IEEE Computer,* 36, 10, 103–105.

Checkland, P. 1983. OR and the systems movement: Mappings and conflicts. *Journal of the Operations Research Society,* 34, 8, 661–675.

———. 1984. Systems theory and information systems. In T. Bemelmans, ed., *Beyond Productivity.* Amsterdam: North-Holland, 9–21.

Checkland, P. and Holwell, S. 1998. *Information, Systems and Information Systems: Making Sense of the Field.* Chichester, UK: Wiley.

Chen, P.P.S. 1976. The entity-relationship model: Toward a unified view. *ACM Transactions on Database Systems,* 1, 1, 9–36.

Chenoweth, T.; Corral, K.; and Demirkan, H. 2006. Seven key interventions for data warehouse success. *Communications of the ACM,* 49, 1, 114–119.

Couger, J.D.; Zawacki, R.A.; and Oppermann, E.B. 1979. Motivation levels of MIS managers versus those of their employees. *MIS Quarterly,* 3, 3, 47–56.

Currie, W.L.; Desa, B.; and Khan, N. 2004. Customer evaluation of application services provisioning in five vertical sectors. *Journal of Information Technology,* 19, 1, 38–58.

Daniel, E.M., and White, A. 2005. The future of inter-organisational system linkages: Findings of an international Delphi study. *European Journal of Information Systems,* 14, 2, 188–203.

Davies, G.B. and Olson, M.H. 1985. *Management Information Systems: Conceptual Foundations.* New York: McGraw-Hill.

Davies, N. and Gellersen, H.W. 2002. Beyond prototypes: Challenges in deploying ubiquitous systems. *IEEE Pervasive Computing,* 1, 1, 26–35.

Dennis, A.; George, J.; Jessup, L.M.; and Nunamaker, J. 1988. Information technology to support electronic meetings. *MIS Quarterly,* 12, 4, 591–624.

Drucker, P.F. 1991. The new productivity challenge. *Harvard Business Review,* 69, 6, 45–53.

Elrod, S.; Bruce, R.; Gold, R.; Goldberg, D.; Halasz, F.; Janssen, W.; Lee, D.; McCall, K.; Pedersen, D.; Pier, K.; Tang, J.; and Welch, B. 1992. Liveboard: A large interactive display supporting group meetings, presentations and remote collaboration. In *Proceedings of the 1992 Conference on Human Factors in Computing Systems (CHI92).* New York: ACM Press, 599–607.

Estrin, D.; Culler, D.; Pister, K.; and Sukhatme, G. 2002. Connecting the physical world with pervasive networks. *IEEE Pervasive Computing,* 1, 1, 59–69.

European Commission. 1999. The disappearing computer. Available at www.disappearing-computer.net (accessed November 24, 2005).

European Commission. 2002. The disappearing computer II. Available at www.cordis.lu/ist/fet/dc2-in.htm. (accessed November 25, 2005).

Fernandes, J.E.; Machado, R.J.; and Carvalho, J.A. 2004. Model-driven methodologies for pervasive information systems development. In *Proceedings of the Fourth International Conference on Application of Concurrency to System Design (ACSD 2004).* IEEE Press, 1–9.

Gallupe, R.; DeSanctis, G.; and Dickson, G. 1988. Computer-based support for group problem-finding: An experimental investigation. *MIS Quarterly,* 12, 2, 277–298.

Gao, Q.; Blow, K.J.; Holding, D.J.; and Marshall, I. 2005. Analysis of energy conservation in sensor networks. *Wireless Networks,* 11, 6, 787–794.

Gaver, W.W.; Bowers, J.; Boucher, A.; Gellerson, H.; Pennington, S.; Schmidt, A.; Steed, A.; Villars, N.; and Walker, B. 2004. The drift table: Designing for ludic engagement. In *Proceedings of the Human Factors in Computing Systems.* Vienna: ACM Press, 885–900.

Gebauer, J. and Shaw, M.J. 2004. Success factors and impacts of mobile business applications: Results from a mobile e-procurement study. *International Journal of Electronic Commerce,* 8, 3, 19–42.

Gellersen, H.W. (ed.) 1999. *Handheld and Ubiquitous Computing: First International Symposium (HUC'99) Proceedings.* Berlin: Springer-Verlag.

Gershman, A. and Fano, A. 2005. Examples of commercial applications of ubiquitous computing. *Communications of the ACM,* 48, 3, 71.

Giaglis, G.M.; Kourouthanassis, P.; and Tsamakos, A. 2002. Toward a classification framework for mobile location services. In B.E. Mennecke and T.J. Strader, eds., *Mobile Commerce: Technology, Theory, and Applications.* Hershey, PA: Idea Group, 67–85.

Goodhue, D.L.; Quillard, J.A.; and Rockart, J.F. 1988. Managing the data resource: A contingency perspective. *MIS Quarterly,* 12, 3, 373–392.

Gregor, S. and Benbasat, I. 1999. Explanations from intelligent systems: Theoretical foundations and implications for practice. *MIS Quarterly,* 23, 4, 497–530.

Gronkvist, J. 2006. Novel assignment strategies for spatial reuse TDMA in wireless ad hoc networks. *Wireless Networks,* 12, 2, 255–265.

Grudin, J. 1991a. Interactive systems: Bridging the gaps between developers and users. *IEEE Computer,* 24, 4, 59–69.

———. 1991b. Systematic sources of suboptimal interface design in large product development organizations. *Human-Computer Interaction,* 6, 2, 47–196.

Gupta, P., and Moitra, D. 2004. Evolving a pervasive IT infrastructure: A technology integration approach. *Personal and Ubiquitous Computing,* 8, 31–41.

Halpin, T.A. 2001. *Information Modeling and Relational Databases.* New York: Morgan Kaufmann.

Harter, A.; Hopper, A.; Steggles, P.; Ward, A.; and Webster, P. 2001. The anatomy of a context-aware application. *Wireless Networks,* 1, 1–16.

Hayes, D.C.; Hunton, J.E.; and Reck, J.L. 2001. Market reaction to ERP implementation announcements. *Journal of Information Systems,* 15, 1, 3–18.

Hemminger, B.; Bolas, G.; and Schiff, D. 2004. Visiting virtual reality museum exhibits. In *Proceedings of the Joint ACM/IEEE Conference on Digital Libraries.* ACM Press, 423.

Hengartner, U. and Steenkiste, P. 2004. Implementing access control to people location information. In *Proceedings of the Ninth ACM Symposium on Access Control Models and Technologies (SACMAT'04).* ACM Press, 11–20

Hightower, J. and Biorriello, G. 2001. Location systems for ubiquitous computing. *IEEE Computer,* 34, 8, 57–66.

Hill, J.; Horton, M.; Kling, R.; and Krishnamurthy, L. 2004. The platforms enabling wireless sensor networks. *Communications of the ACM,* 47, 6, 41–46.

Hopper, A. 1999. *Sentient Computing.* The Royal Society Clifford Paterson Lecture. *Philosophical Transactions of the Royal Society of London,* 358(1773), 2349–2358.

Hsi, S. and Fait, H. 2005. RFID enhances visitors' museum experience at the exploratorium. *Communications of the ACM,* 48, 9, 60–65.

Huang, A.C.; Ling, B.C.; Ponnekanti, S.; and Fox, A. 1999. Pervasive computing: What is it good for? In *Proceedings of the Workshop on Mobile Data Management (MobiDE) in conjunction with ACM MobiCom '99,* ACM Press, 84–91.

Huang, C.R.; Chen, C.S.; and Chung, P.C. 2005. Tangible photorealistic virtual museum. *IEEE Computer Graphics and Applications,* 25, 1, 15–17.

IBM Pervasive Computing Initiative. 2004. Available at www-306.ibm.com/software/pervasive/index.shtml (accessed March 10, 2004).

Isakowitz, T.; Bieber, M.; and Vitali, F. 1998. Web information systems. *Communications of the ACM,* 38, 3, 78–80.

Isakowitz, T.; Stohr, E.A.; and Balasubramanian, P. 1995. RMM: A methodology for structured hypermedia design. *Communications of the ACM,* 38, 8, 34–44.

Jegers, K. and Wiberg, M. 2006. Pervasive gaming in the everyday world. *IEEE Pervasive Computing,* 5, 1, 78–85.

Kantarjiev, C.K.; Demers, A.; Frederick, R.; Krivacic, R.T.; and Weiser, M. 1993. Experiences with X in a wireless environment. In *Proceedings of the USENIX Symposium on Mobile and Location-Independent Computing.* Cambridge, MA: 117–128.

Karakostas, B.; Kardaras, D.; and Papathanassiou, E. 2005. The state of CRM adoption by the financial services in the UK: An empirical investigation. *Information and Management,* 42, 6, 853–863.

Kasper, G.M. 1996. A theory of decision support system design for user calibration. *Information Systems Research,* 7, 2, 215–232.

Kordon, F. and Pautet, L. 2005. Toward next-generation middleware? *IEEE Distributed Systems Online,* 6, 3, 1–6.

Laudon, K.C. and Laudon, J.P. 2004. *Management Information Systems: Managing the Digital Firm,* 9th ed. Upper Saddle River, NJ: Prentice Hall.

Lee, C.; Helal, S.; and Lee, W. 2006. Universal interactions with smart spaces. *IEEE Pervasive Computing,* 5, 1, 16–21.

Liszka, K.J.; Mackin, M.A.; Lichter, M.J.; York, D.W.; Pillai, D.; and Rosenbaum, D.S. 2004. Keeping a beat on the heart. *IEEE Pervasive Computing,* 3, 4, 42–49.

Lopez de Ipina, D. and Lo, S.L. 2001. Sentient computing for everyone. In *Proceedings of the Third IFIP WG 6.1 International Working Conference on Distributed Applications and Interoperable Systems (DAIS '2001.* Deventer: Kluwer, B.V., 41–54.

Lynch, T. and Gregor, S. 2004. User participation in decision support systems development: Influencing system outcomes. *European Journal of Information Systems,* 13, 4, 286–301.

Lyytinen, K. 1989. New challenges of systems development: A vision of the 90's. *Database,* 20, 3, 1–12.

Lyytinen, K. and Rose, G.M. 2003. The disruptive nature of information technology innovations: The case of Internet computing in systems development organizations. *MIS Quarterly,* 27, 4, 557–595.

Lyytinen, K. and Yoo, Y. 2002a. Issues and challenges in ubiquitous computing. *Communications of the ACM,* 45, 12, 63–65.

———. 2002b. The next wave of nomadic computing: A research agenda for information systems research. *Information Systems Research,* 13, 4, 377–388.

Lyytinen, K.; Yoo, Y.; Varshney, U.; Ackerman, M.S.; Davis, G.; Avital, M.; Robey, D.; Sawyer, S.; and Sorensen, C. 2004. Surfing the next wave: Design and implementation challenges of ubiquitous computing environments. *Communications of the Association for Information Systems,* 13, 697–716.

Ma, Q.; Pearson, J.M.; and Tadisina, S. 2005. An exploratory study into factors of service quality for application service providers. *Information and Management,* 42, 8, 1067–1080.

Michahelles, F. and Schiele, B. 2005. Sensing and monitoring professional skiers. *IEEE Pervasive Computing,* 4, 3, 40–46.

Moon, K.D.; Lee, Y.H.; Son, Y.S.; and Kim, C.K. 2003. Universal home network middleware guaranteeing seamless interoperability among the heterogeneous home network middleware. *IEEE Transactions on Consumer Electronics,* 49, 3, 546–553.

Newkirk, H.E. and Lederer, A.L. 2006. The effectiveness of strategic information systems planning under environmental uncertainty. *Information and Management*, 43, 4, 481–501.

Newman, J.; Ingram, D.; and Hopper, A. 2001. Augmented reality in a wide area sentient environment. In *Proceedings of the IEEE and ACM International Symposium on Augmented Reality (ISAR'01)*. Los Alamitos, CA: IEEE Computer Society Press, 77–86.

Norman, D.A. 1999. *The Invisible Computer: Why Good Products Can Fail, the Personal Computer Is So Complex, and Information Appliances Are the Solution*. Cambridge: MIT Press.

———. 2002. *The Design of Everyday Things*. New York: Basic Books.

Oetzel, J.M. 2004. Differentiation advantages in the on-line brokerage industry. *International Journal of Electronic Commerce*, 9, 1, 105–126.

Ohkubo, M.; Suzuki, K.; and Kinoshita, S. 2005. RFID privacy issues and technical challenges. *Communications of the ACM*, 48, 9, 66–71.

Philipose, M.; Smith, J.R.; Jiang, B.; Mamishev, A.; Roy, S.; and Sundara-Rajan, K. 2005. Battery-free wireless identification and sensing. *IEEE Pervasive Computing*, 4, 1, 37–45.

Poltrock, S.E. and Grudin, J. 1994. Organizational obstacles to interface design and development: Two participant observer studies. *IEEE Transactions on Human-Computer Interaction*, 1, 1, 54–80.

Prater, E.; Frazier, G.V.; and Reyes, P.M. 2005. Future impacts of RFID on e-supply chains in grocery retailing. *Supply Chain Management: An International Journal*, 10, 2, 134–142.

Press, L. 1999. The post-PC era. *Communications of the ACM*, 42, 10, 21–24.

Pressman, R. 1998. Can Internet-based applications be engineered? *IEEE Software*, 15, 5, 104–110.

Rahnema, M. 1993. Overview of the GSM system and protocol architecture. *IEEE Communications*, 31, 92–100.

Ranganathan, A.; Campbell, R.H.; Ravi, A.; and Mahajan, A. 2002. ConChat: A context-aware chat program. *IEEE Pervasive Computing*, 1, 3, 51–57.

Rao, B. and Parikh, M.A. 2003. Wireless broadband networks: The U.S. experience. *International Journal of Electronic Commerce*, 8, 1, 37–53.

Rasheed, Y.; Edwards, J.; and Tai, C. 2002. Home interoperability framework for the digital home. *INTEL Technology Journal*, 6, 4, 5–16.

Roundy, S.; Leland, E.S.; Baker, J.; Carleton, E.; Reilly, E.; Lai, E.; Otis, B.; Rabaey, J.M.; Wright, P.K.; and Sundararajan, V. 2005. Improving power output for vibration-based energy scavengers. *IEEE Pervasive Computing*, 4, 1, 28–35.

Roussos, G.; Gershman, A.; and Kourouthanassis, P. 2003. Ubiquitous commerce adjunct proceedings. In *Proceedings of the UbiComp 2003*. ACM Press, 1–3.

Rudolph, L. 2001. Project Oxygen: Pervasive, human-centric computing—An initial experience. In K.R. Dittrich, A. Geppert, and M.D. Norrie, eds., *Proceedings of the Thirteenth International Conference on Advanced Information Systems Engineering*. Springer, 1–12.

Saha, D. and Mukherjee, A. 2003. Pervasive computing: A paradigm for the 21st century. *IEEE Computer*, 36, 3 (March), 25–31.

Saha, D.; Mukherjee, A.; and Bandyopadhyay, S. 2002. *Networking Infrastructure for Pervasive Computing: Enabling Technologies & Systems*. Dordrecht: Kluwer Academic.

Satyanarayanan, M. 2001. Pervasive computing: Visions and challenges. *IEEE Personal Communications*, 8, 4 (August), 10–17.

———. 2002. A catalyst for mobile and ubiquitous computing. *IEEE Pervasive Computing*, 1, 1, 2–5.

Sawhney, N. and Schmandt, C. 2000. Nomadic radio: Speech and audio interaction for contextual messaging in nomadic environments. *ACM Transactions on Computer-Human Interaction*, 7, 3, 353–383.

Scheer, A.W. and Habermann, F. 2000. Enterprise resource planning: Making ERP a success. *Communications of the ACM*, 43, 4, 57–61.

Schur, A.; Decker, S.D.; and May, R. 1999. Design issues for next generation interfaces (NGI). In *Proceedings of the Conference on Human Factors in Computing Systems (CHI'99)*. New York: ACM Press, 130–131.

Senn, J.A. 1978. Essential principles of information systems development. *MIS Quarterly*, 2, 2, 17–26.

Sharif, A.M.; Irani, Z.; and Love, P. 2005. Integrating ERP using EAI: A model for post hoc evaluation. *European Journal of Information Systems*, 14, 2, 162–174.

Shenoy, N. 2005. A framework for seamless roaming across heterogeneous next generation wireless networks. *Wireless Networks*, 11, 6, 757–774.

Shore, B. 2006. Enterprise integration across the globally disbursed service organization. *Communications of the ACM,* 49, 6, 102–106.

Silver, M.S.; Markus, M.L.; and Beath, C.M. 1995. The information technology interaction model: A foundation for the MBA core course. *MIS Quarterly,* 19, 3, 361–390.

Smith, H. and Konsynski, B. 2003. Developments in practice X: Radio frequency identification (RFID)—An Internet for physical objects. *Communications of the Association for Information Systems,* 12, 301–311.

Somogyi, E.K. and Galliers, R.D. 2003. Information technology in business: From data processing to strategic information systems. In R.D. Galliers and D.E. Leidner, eds., *Strategic Information Management: Challenges and Strategies in Managing Information Systems.* Oxford: Butterworth-Heinemann, 3–26.

Stafford, T.F. and Gillenson, M.L. 2003. Mobile commerce: What it is and what it could be. *Communications of the ACM,* 46, 12, 33–34.

Stajano, F. 2002. *Security for Ubiquitous Computing.* New York: Wiley.

Stanton, N.A., ed. 2001. *Ubiquitous Computing: Anytime, Anyplace, Anywhere?* Mahwah, NJ: Lawrence Erlbaum.

Streitz, N.A. 2003. Smart artefacts and the disappearing computer. In *Proceedings of the Smart Objects Conference 2003.* Available at www.minatec.com/grenoble-soc/index.htm (accessed November 10, 2005).

Susarla, A.; Barua, A.; and Whinston, A.B. 2003. Understanding the service component of application service provision: An empirical analysis of satisfaction with ASP services. *MIS Quarterly,* 27, 1, 91–123.

Szewczyk, R.; Osterweil, E.; Polastre, J.; Hamilton, M.; Mainwaring, A.; and Estrin, D. 2004. Habitat monitoring with sensor networks. *Communications of the ACM,* 47, 6, 34–40.

Truman, T.E.; Pering, T.; Doering, R.; and Brodersen, R.W. 1998. The InfoPad multimedia terminal: A portable device for wireless information access. *IEEE Transactions on Computers,* 47, 10, 1073–1087.

Turban, E.; Leidner, D.; McLean, E.; and Wetherbe, J. 2006. *Information Technology for Management: Transforming Organizations in the Digital Economy.* Hoboken, NJ: Wiley.

Varshney, U. 2003. Wireless I: Mobile and wireless information systems: Applications, networks, and research problems. *Communications of the Association for Information Systems,* 12, 155–166.

Varshney, U. and Vetter, R.J. 2000. Emerging mobile and wireless networks. *Communications of the ACM,* 43, 6, 73–81.

Varshney, U.; Vetter, R.J.; and Kalakota, R. 2000. Mobile commerce: A new frontier. *IEEE Computer,* 33, 10, 32–38.

Walls, J.G.; Widmeyer, G.R.; and El Sawy, O.A. 1992. Building an information system design theory for vigilant executive information systems. *Information Systems Research,* 3, 1, 36–59.

Walters, G.J. 2001. Privacy and security: An ethical analysis. *Computers and Society,* 31, 2, 8–23.

Want, R. and Schilit, B.N. 2001. Expanding the horizons of location-aware computing. *IEEE Computer,* 34, 8 (August), 31–34.

Want, R.; Hopper, A.; Falco, V.; and Gibbons, J. 1992. The active badge location system. *ACM Transactions on Information Systems,* 10, 1, 91–102.

Want, R.; Pering, T.; Borriello, G.; and Farkas, K.I. 2002. Disappearing hardware. *IEEE Pervasive Computing,* 1, 1, 36–47.

Want, R.; Schilit, B.N.; Adams, N.I.; Gold, R.; Petersen, K.; Goldberg, D.; Ellis, J.R.; and Weiser, M. 1995. *The PARCTab Ubiquitous Computing Experiment.* Technical report CSL-95-1. Xerox Palo Alto Research Center (March).

Weiser, M. 1991. The computer of the 21st century. *Scientific American,* 265, 3, 66–75.

———. 1993. Some computer science issues in ubiquitous computing. *Communications of the ACM,* 36, 7, 75–84.

———. 1994. The world is not a desktop. *ACM Interactions* (January), 7–8.

Weiser, M., and Brown, J.S. 1995. Designing calm technology. Available at www.ubiq.com/hypertext/weiser/calmtech/calmtech.htm.

Weiser, M.; Gold, R.; and Brown, J.S. 1999. The origins of ubiquitous computing research at PARC in the late 1980s. *IBM Systems Journal,* 38, 4, 693–696.

Wojciechowski, R.; Walczak, K.; White, M.; and Cellary, W. 2004. Building virtual and augmented reality museum exhibitions. In *Proceedings of the Ninth International Conference on 3D Web Technology.* New York: ACM Press, 135–144.

Wool, A. 2005. Lightweight key management for IEEE 802.11 wireless LANs with key refresh and host revocation. *Wireless Networks,* 11, 6, 677–686.

Wu, J.H.; Cook Jr., V.J.; and Strong, E.C. 2005. A two-stage model of the promotional performance of pure online firms. *Information Systems Research,* 16, 4, 334–351.

Yang, X. and Vaidya, N. 2006. Priority scheduling in wireless ad hoc networks. *Wireless Networks,* 12, 3, 273–286.

Yoon, Y.; Guimaraes, T.; and O'Neal, Q. 1995. Exploring the factors associated with expert systems success. *MIS Quarterly,* 19, 1, 83–106.

Zhu, W.; Owen, C.B.; Li, H.; and Lee, J.H. 2004. Personalized in-store e-commerce with the PromoPad: An augmented reality shopping assistant. *eJETA, the Electronic Journal for E-Commerce Tools and Applications,* 1, 3 (February).

Zmud, R. 1997. Editor's comments. *MIS Quarterly,* 21, 2, 21–22.

Zucker, D.F.; Uematsu, M.; and Kamada, T. 2005. Content and Web services converge: A unified user interface. *IEEE Pervasive Computing,* 4, 4, 8–11.

Zwass, V. 1992. *Management Information Systems.* Dubuque, IA: Wm. C. Brown.

PART I

FEATURES AND DESIGN OF PERVASIVE INFORMATION SYSTEMS

THE DESIGN CHALLENGE OF PERVASIVE INFORMATION SYSTEMS

PANOS E. KOUROUTHANASSIS AND GEORGE M. GIAGLIS

Abstract: This chapter provides an integrated research agenda on pervasive information systems. The research agenda refers to a four-layer framework examining technological, social, and application-specific trends and challenges. The chapter presents a systemic view of pervasive information systems in terms of participating components. Specifically, the chapter focuses on the design challenges of pervasive networks, middleware solutions, wireless sensor networks, and pervasive access devices. Moreover, it outlines the importance of context awareness for pervasive systems development. In addition, the chapter provides a four-category classification of the application types that pervasive systems can support: personal, domestic, corporate, and public. The chapter concludes by raising the most important social issues that need to be addressed during pervasive systems design and implementation.

Keywords: Context Awareness, Design, Middleware, Pervasive Computing, Social Challenges

INTRODUCTION

This chapter provides an integrated research agenda on pervasive information systems (PS). Several visionary papers have already been published, each trying to outline some generic properties that PS should incorporate (Abowd and Mynatt, 2000; Huang et al., 1999; Katz, 1994; Lyytinen and Yoo, 2002; Saha and Mukherjee, 2003; Satyanarayanan, 2001; Weiser, 1993). The new paradigm has been called "ubiquitous" or "pervasive" computing. Nevertheless, all of these papers lack a holistic approach. For example, Saha and Mukherjee (2003) focus solely on the hardware and software challenges presented by pervasive computing systems. Weiser (1993) focused on the human aspect of the new class of systems, presenting mainly application scenarios, while Abowd and Mynatt (2000) and Abowd, Mynatt, and Rodden (2002) focused on interaction challenges between users and system components.

PS represent the ultimate form of computing where the physical, the virtual, and the cybernetic blur. Thus, they underlie the interplay between technology, people, and environments. To structure our discussion of PS challenges, we have embodied these dimensions into a four-layer framework:

- The infrastructure layer reflects technological advances that have enabled the provision of pervasive information systems. What *types of technologies* are available for system designers and what are their current *capabilities and limitations*? One could argue that the infrastructure layer incorporates all of the necessary building blocks for pervasive systems design and implementation.

Figure 2.1   **Pervasive Information Systems Layers of Interactivity**

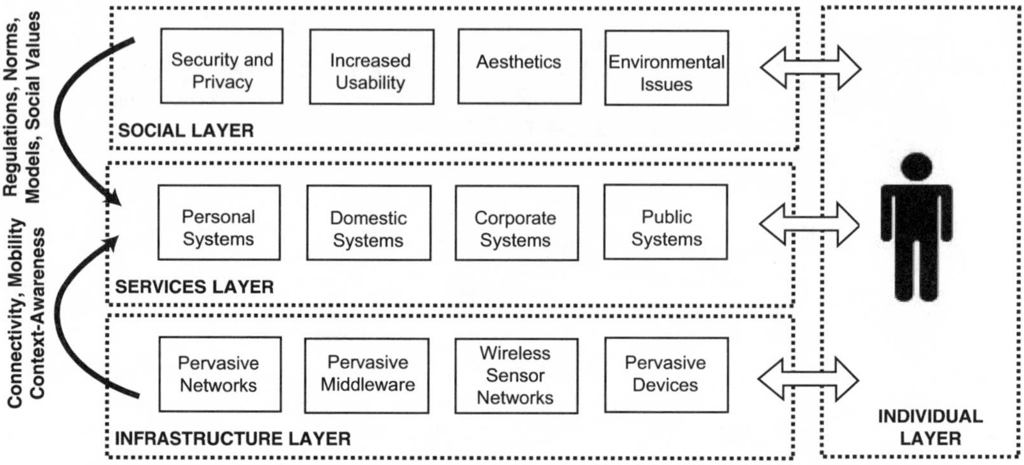

- The services layer reflects the application perspective of pervasive systems. What *types of systems* can we build and what is their *functionality*? This layer integrates the technologies into a value-added system creating new *business and social opportunities.*
- The social layer provides the *restrictions* for the design of pervasive systems through norms, regulations, and social values. Embedding information technology artifacts into the physical space may generate concerns regarding the individual's privacy since actions and behavior may be monitored, enforces rules for their deployment throughout the physical material and the available space, and creates unique requirements for interactivity in addressing a broader spectrum of users.
- Finally, the individual layer reflects the beneficiary of pervasive information systems; the individual who has unique cognitive models, past experiences, needs, and wants.

Figure 2.1 illustrates our examination framework. This framework will be the basis for the presentation of pervasive information systems current status and research challenges. Moreover, it may be used as an initial vehicle to guide the design process of such systems. Indeed, pervasive systems are designed for *particular application domains* each having unique technological, service, and social requirements. Furthermore, the profile of system users in each case may be different. The proposed research framework may help pervasive systems designers to be aware of technological, application-specific, and social concerns and challenges, and to address them early in the design process.

THE INFRASTRUCTURE LAYER

Introduction

The design of a PS is most certainly affected by technological tools and solutions. In effect, these technological trends differentiate PS from the desktop paradigm by introducing new capabilities and functionality for the system designer. Saha and Mukherjee (2003) present a systemic view of PS. In particular, they identify four broad areas that constitute a pervasive environment: devices,

Figure 2.2 **Pervasive Information Systems Components**

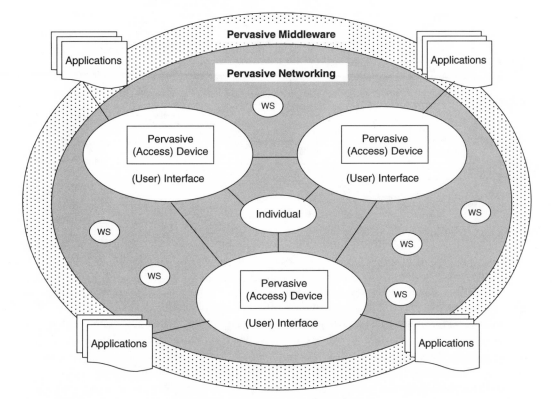

networking, middleware, and applications. Surprisingly, the authors do not include users as a main component of the system. This reflects the technical nature of PS in that most researchers view them solely through their technology perspective.

According to this framework, the functionality of a pervasive system is viewed as the sum of the different applications it supports. An individual may interact with an application through one or more pervasive access devices. Pervasive networks offer the communication conduit that supports this interaction, while pervasive middleware ensures that the system operates as an integrated environment. To collect the information necessary to adjust system behavior, pervasive systems usually integrate wireless sensors, which consist of small devices capable of sensing, processing, and communicating different types of sensory data. Figure 2.2 illustrates the technical components of a pervasive environment. The following sections briefly discuss the current trends and research challenges for each component type.

Pervasive Networks

Pervasive networks represent the backbone infrastructure of any pervasive system and ensures mobility within its boundaries. Streitz (2003) distinguishes mobility in two dimensions:

- Local mobility within the office, home, or other geographically restricted environment.
- Global mobility, achieved by using mobile technologies while traveling or working at different sites.

Figure 2.3 **Categories of Pervasive Networking Technologies**

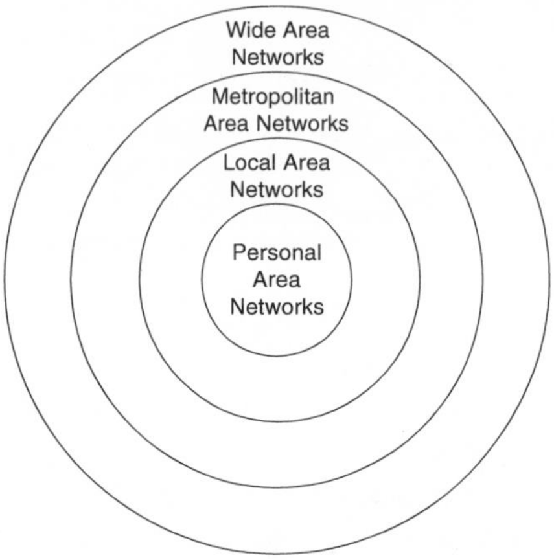

Network Type	Coverage Area	Indicative Enabling Technologies
Personal Area Network (PAN)	Small (a few meters)	IrDA Bluetooth RF-Id
Local Area Network (LAN)	Medium (e.g., a building)	IEEE 802.11 (WiFi) ETSI HiperLAN
Metropolitan Area Network (MAN)	Large (e.g., a city)	IEEE 802.16 (WiMAX)
Wide Area Network (WAN)	Very Large (e.g., a country)	GSM GPRS UMTS

Luff and Heath (1998) follow a similar distinction, referring to micromobility, local mobility, and remote mobility. Micromobility supports interactions that relate to our bodily experience. Local mobility involves interactions between individuals and artifacts within a given space. Finally, remote mobility supports both synchronous and asynchronous communications among people in distant locations. In any case, the degree of mobility for PS is application dependent. For example, an individual performing maintenance operations in a factory using a wearable computer requires very short range coverage while an office clerk who needs wireless access to the corporate data through his personal digital assistant (PDA)/laptop needs wider coverage (on the premises of the company building). For this chapter, we extend the aforementioned classification to include four distinct types of pervasive networks based on their coverage capabilities (see Figure 2.3).

Wireless *personal area networks* (WPANs) connect different devices (sensors, actuators, PDAs, and so on) that a user carries or wears. Thus, their purpose is to connect short-range micronetworks that ensure connectivity between a small number of devices. Ashok and Agrawal (2003) characterize PANs as "on-body networks," mainly because of their ability to support wearable computing applications. The most common PAN wireless technologies are infrared (IrDA) (Ashok and Agrawal, 2003), Bluetooth (Buttery and Sago, 2003), and ZigBee (Schindler, 2004). Other technologies that appear in the literature but are not yet commonly used in research or commercial solutions include BBN Technologies' BodyLAN (based on radio frequencies) (Barfield and Thomas, 2001) and fabric area networks (Hum, 2001). Recently, researchers have paid significant attention to the development of ultra wideband networks (UWB) that are capable of interconnecting several devices at high bandwidth (Cardinali and Lombardo, 2006; Cheok et al., 2004; Irahhauten, Nikookar, and Janssen, 2005; Shi et al., 2005). Moreover, UWB may provide precise positioning of objects with several researchers proposing several promising integrated solutions (Bocquet, Loyez, and Benlarbi-Delai, 2005; Gong, Xu, and Yu, 2004; Takeuchi, Shimizu, and Sanada, 2005).

Wireless *local area networks* (WLANs) are capable of supporting medium-range connections among different devices. They constitute the de facto substitute of wired Ethernet connections, especially in terms of interconnecting indoor environments. The most common WLAN technologies are the IEEE 802.11 family of protocols and the European Telecommunications Standards Institute's HiperLAN2 (Lenzini and Mingozzi, 2001). Developments in the area have specified new protocols (such as IEEE 802.11n or IEEE 802.11e) that promise higher bandwidth, advanced security, and increased quality of service (Abraham, Meylan, and Nanda, 2005; Bianchi, Tinnirello, and Scalia, 2005; Robinson and Randhawa, 2004; Xiao et al., 2001).

Wireless *metropolitan area networks* (WMANs) provide LAN-like services, but over a wider coverage area, such as an entire city. They provide inexpensive broadband access to nomadic or stationary users acting as a replacement for conventional, wired last-mile access systems. Common WMAN technologies are IEEE 802.16 (Hoymann, 2005) and terrestrial trunked radio system (TETRA) (Dunlop, Girma, and Irvine, 1999). Because of the widespread deployment of IEEE 802.11 networks, current research aims at developing hybrid networks that take advantage of the capabilities of both network types (Nielsen and Pullin, 2005; Wong, Chou, and Want, 2005).

Wireless *wide area networks* (WANs) support remote connectivity between individuals and corporate systems through mainly cellular (mobile) networks such as general packet radio service (GPRS) and universal mobile telecommunications systems (UMTS). Similar to the previously described network, current research focuses on developing integration and handover schemes among all network types so that each wireless or mobile device will be capable of identifying and registering with the most appropriate network type based on the application requirements (Choi, Song, and Cho, 2005; Kwon and Zmud, 1987; Salkintzis et al., 2005).

Table 2.1 presents the most commonly used wireless and mobile technologies for each network type. For each technology, we also present its operating frequency, bandwidth, coverage range, security capabilities, and whether it requires a license for deployment (as in the case of mobile networks such as GPRS and UMTS).

A pervasive environment will (most likely) face a proliferation of users, applications, networked devices, and their interactions on a massive scale. As environmental smartness grows, so will the number of devices connected to the environment and the intensity of human–artifact, even artifact–artifact, interactions. Thus, maintaining an adequate *quality of service* (QoS) of the pervasive system is of paramount importance for the system designers, especially in terms of transmitting multimedia content. Researchers have already devised several mechanisms that take into account the characteristics of the wireless medium (irrespective of the protocol involved) in order to ensure acceptable levels of performance for the PS (Davcevski and Janevski, 2005; Deng and Yen, 2005; Ni, 2005; Zhai, Chen, and Fang, 2005).

Likewise, *increased connectivity* is another design challenge of PS. Norman writes, "a distinguishing feature of information appliances is the ability to share information among themselves" (Norman, 1999). In PS, each person is surrounded by hundreds of wirelessly interconnected computers (Weiser, 1993). Through connectivity, a collection of artifacts can act together and produce "new behaviour and new functionality" (European Commission, 1999), making the this term common language for the field, so common that people often forget to justify or even think about reasons for the connections.

Still, increased connectivity may cause new complexity and frustration in PS (Odlyzko, 1999), especially in cases where multiple network connections are available and users should select the most appropriate based on the capabilities of their devices and the desired quality of service. To this end, PS designers should devise new means to handle all of these connections in a way that is unobtrusive to the user (at least to a certain degree). Preferably, the system itself should be able to handle all connections including several technical issues such as traffic management, user interface management, and so on.

The final design challenge for pervasive networks is security. Want and colleagues (2002) distinguish PS based on their locality to *personal* systems and *infrastructure* systems. Personal systems give users access to computing resources, independent of their physical location, at the cost of their having to carry some equipment; infrastructure systems instrument a particular locale. In essence, in-

Table 2.1

Classification of Pervasive Network Technologies

Technology	Operating frequency	Bandwidth	Coverage	Security	License required
Personal area networks					
IrDA	Infrared 850 nm	4 Mbps	<10 meters	High	No
Bluetooth	2.4 GHz	<1 Mbps	<10 meters	Medium	No
ZigBee (802.15.4)	2.4 GHz 868/915 MHz	250 Kbps 20–40 Kbps	<20 meters	Medium	No
Local area networks					
IEEE 802.11b/a/g	2,4 GHz/5GHz	11 Mbps/54Mbps	<100 meters	Low	No
HiperLAN2	5 GHz	32–54 Mbps	<150 meters	High	No
Metropolitan area networks					
IEEE 802.16/IEEE 802.16a (WiMax)	10–66 GHz <11 GHz	120–135 Mbps <70 Mbps	<3 miles <5 miles	High	Unspecified
TETRA	380–400 MHz	28,8 Kbps	Regional	High	Yes
Wide area networks					
GPRS	900/1800/1900 MHz	9.6–144 Kbps	National	High	Yes
UMTS (WCDMA)	5 MHz	<384 Kbps	National (in particular cities)	High	Yes

frastructure systems refer to all computing resources that constantly manifest a particular environment. These infrastructural elements interface with a number of undetermined nomadic devices (users) that enter and exit the system randomly. As such, the pervasive system should be capable of incorporating appropriate policy management mechanisms in order to prevent unauthorized access to the system's resources as well as protect the transmission of sensitive information (where required).

The latter is considered the major vulnerability of pervasive networks. Since information is transmitted wirelessly, the network is prone to eavesdropping. Each networking technology proposes its own encryption protocol intended to secure the wireless infrastructure to the extent possible. For example, IEEE 802.11b/g uses wireless equivalent protocol to encrypt transmissions. A short list of available encryption techniques can be found in Hu, Lee, and Kou (2005).

Wireless Sensor Networks

Wireless sensor networks (WSN) represent the necessary leap toward the PS vision, where the environment anticipates the needs of the system's beneficiaries and acts on their behalf. Pervasive (or smart) sensors are capable of sensing environmental changes. Sensors perform two operations: sensing and actuation. Whatever the sensed quantity (temperature, light intensity), the sensor transforms a particular form of energy (heat, light) into information. Actuation converts the information into action and enables better sensing. Moreover, an actuator may move part of itself, relocate spatially, or move other items in the environment. This enables wireless sensor networks to have a wide range of potential applications, including security and surveillance, control, actuation and maintenance of complex systems, and fine-grain monitoring of indoor and outdoor environments (Cayirci et al., 2003).

The 1990s saw microelectromechanical systems technology transformed from a laboratory curiosity into a source of widespread commercial products. Still, there are many technological hurdles that must be overcome for WSN to become a commodity. Indeed, wireless sensors are resource constrained, they have limited processing, communication, and memory capabilities, and their lifetime depends on the degree of power they consume. Consequently, to efficiently deploy WSN in a PS environment, we need to devise new hardware designs, software applications, and network architectures. The following paragraphs will shed light on some of the most common design challenges of WSN.

A common problem in both sensing and actuation is *uncertainty*. The physical world is a partially observable, dynamic system, and sensors and actuators are physical devices with inherent accuracy and precision limitations. Thus, sensor-measured data are necessarily approximations of actual values. In a large system of distributed nodes, this implies that we need some form of filtering at each node before we can meaningfully use the data. We can also achieve increased accuracy and fault tolerance by redundancy, using sensors with overlapping fields of view. This raises interesting challenges of *sensor placement and fusion*, especially in the context of very large networks. In addition to uncertainty, there is the further problem of *latency* in actuation. For closed loop control, stochastic latency can cause instability and unreliable behavior.

The latest standard from IEEE (1451.4) aims at eradicating any incorrectly transcribed calibration information from sensor data sheets (Betts, 2006). IEEE 1451.4 provides a standard interface and protocol by which a sensor can describe itself over a network. The standard proposes the use of a digital ROM chip embedded in the sensor that stores the sensor's electronic data sheet as well as information identifying the sensor, namely, its type, manufacturer, and a serial number. The sensor transmits this information when it registers to a network system. The operation resembles the way universal serial bus (USB) devices are identified by conventional personal computers.

Power management (and in particular energy harvesting, or scavenging, and conservation) is a major research challenge for the design and deployment of smart sensor nodes. Although each node may be capable of incorporating a small energy source (battery), the limitations in terms of size and weight suggest that pervasive systems designers should evaluate and select alternative sources of power, the most common ones being energy sharing through the network and manipulation of solar (and/or wind) energy. Other researchers propose to design energy-aware software that can identify hardware states that are providing a given service level and select those that are most energy efficient. For instance, in systems with a microprocessor whose energy consumption is greater at high speeds, the software can select the lowest speed possible that still achieves the required task performance (Weiser, 1994). The control software may also be able to modify the quality of service it seeks to deliver (Flinn, 2001). Moreover, to save energy in a multimedia application, the software may reduce the frame rate, or size of an MPEG movie, incrementally resulting in a corresponding loss of fidelity. That operation may be part of the functionality of the pervasive middleware layer. Finally, in a case where a wireless sensor combines multiple radio systems (such as Wi-Fi and Bluetooth) the system may organize wireless hierarchies and instruct the sensor to use the communication model that consumes less power based on network traffic and application requirements (Pering, Ranghunathan, and Want, 2005).

Alternatively, wireless sensor networks may exploit additional or different power sources for storing, and even generating, energy. The major factors affecting the battery life of devices include traffic patterns, passive models such as sleep mode, signal strength, and the transmit/receive duty cycle (Ashok and Agrawal, 2003). Researchers have proposed several alternate solutions that support energy harvesting. For example, they have exploited the human body as an energy source by constructing sneakers that use flexible piezoelectric structures to generate energy (Paradiso and Starner, 2005; Shenck and Paradiso, 2001; Starner, 1996). Similarly, solar energy, thermal gradients, mechanical vibration, ambient radio-frequency power scavenging, and even gravitational fields all represent potential power sources for a pervasive system component (Chandrakasan, 1999; Philipose et al., 2005; Roundy et al., 2005). Future trends propose self-powered sensor microsystems from radioisotope micropower generators (Lal, Duggirala, and Li, 2005) as well as the embedment of power management commands to operating systems for wireless sensor networks (Zeng, Ellis, and Lebeck, 2005).

As discussed in the section on pervasive networks, ensuring *security and privacy* in WSN is a very important design challenge because of the wireless medium's nature. Chan and Perrig (2003) summarized the most important security and privacy considerations and presented several design directions in the following contexts: sensor node compromise, eavesdropping, privacy of sensed data, denial-of-service attacks, and malicious use of commodity networks.

Research in the field of WSN is very active and is producing some very promising results. Chandrakasan (1999) and Hill et al. (2000) propose some alternative architectural directions for the design of sensor networks, while Romer, Kasten, and Mattern (2002) discuss middleware challenges for the integration of WSN by identifying the corresponding research challenges in terms of scope, functionality, and communication. In effect, researchers have proposed several management techniques supporting efficient coordination of wireless sensor networks (Gracanin et al., 2005; Vazquez et al., 2001).

Moreover, the Telecooperation Office of the University of Karlsruhe has developed *Smart-Its*, small-scale embedded devices equipped with sensing, processing, and communication capabilities, which may be attached to everyday objects to let them establish dynamic digital relationships. The best known outcome of this research effort is the *MediaCup* (Beigl, Gellersen, and Schmidt, 2001). Additional examples include the work of Schmidt and Van Laerhoven (2001), who examined smart sensors in the context of creating smart appliances; Gibbons and colleagues (2003) developed IrisNet, an architecture that supports easy deployment of such wide-area sensing services as security services (e.g., monitoring of children or elders), planet-wide observatories (e.g., for near-shore oceanography); Burrell, Brooke, and Beckwith (2004) showcased lessons learned from a real-world sensor network deployment in a vineyard; Szewczyk and colleagues (2004) developed a WSN aiming at delivering to ecologists data on localized environmental conditions at the scale of individual organisms to help settle large-scale land-use issues affecting animals, plants, and people; similarly, Kumagai (2004) presented a WSN that is being used for the study of Leach's storm petrel on Great Duck Island, Maine.

Finally, one of the most well-known projects investigating smart sensors technology is *Smart Dust*, developed at the University of Berkeley (Kahn et al., 1999) and the resulting *MOTES* (Hill et al., 2000), which provides integrated sensing, processing, and communication on a peer-to-peer basis in a very small size (Chatzigiannakis, Nikoletseas, and Spirakis, 2002; Warneke et al., 2001). Smart Dust motes have already been examined as a security mechanism in military applications to detect, classify, and track targets (Arora et al., 2004; Chivers and Clark, 2004), health care (Lubrin, Lawrence, and Navarro, 2005), and as coordination tools supporting telecollaboration in education environments (Chaczko, Ahmad, and Mahadevan, 2005) and control over the lighting systems in buildings (Dubberley, Agogino, and Horvath, 2004). Moreover, it should be noted that commercial versions of the original motes are already available from Crossbow Technology, Inc. and Dust, Inc. at prices of about $50–$100 each. According to the companies, these prices are expected to drop to less than $5 per mote over the next five years.

Pervasive Access Devices

Pervasive access devices constitute the front end of PS and are likely to contain a multitude of different device types that differ in size, shape (more diverse, ergonomic, and stylistic), and functional diversity (mobile phones, laptops, pagers, PDAs, and so on). In essence, pervasive devices dictate the interaction between the user and the pervasive system. Developments in this field reshape the way researchers perceive traditional human–computer interaction techniques and methods, especially due to the fact that pervasive interfaces go beyond the typical displays found on personal computers (PCs), notebooks, PDAs, and even many interactive walls or tables. In particular, over the past few years, many consumer devices have incorporated a multitude of input modalities and sensor capabilities such as accelerometers, multimodal interfaces, global positioning system sensors, and so on. The sensing capabilities are often used to detect human actions, such as gestures, or the relationship among objects (Kidd et al., 1999; Kindberg and Barton, 2001) feeding a specialized application with the respective information.

The most important feature of these devices is their nomadic nature: they move with their users all the time, and accompany them in many types of services. This raises the need to integrate them with other resources as we move around. Hansmann and colleagues (2003) distinguish among four types of devices: information access devices, intelligent appliances, smart controls, and entertainment systems.

A more detailed classification of pervasive devices (taking into account the broad categories specified previously) is as follows:

- *Traditional desktop* devices, such as personal computers (desktops), infokiosks, and so on.
- *Wireless* and *mobile* devices, such as mobile phones, pagers, personal digital assistants, palmtops, tablet PCs, and so on. The MyGROCER pervasive system, uses a tablet PC at-

tached to a shopping cart that enables supermarket consumers to streamline their shopping (Kourouthanassis and Roussos, 2002); handheld devices have been used extensively to enhance the experience of visitors to museums and exhibition environments (Abowd et al., 1997; Bederson, 1995; Bellotti et al., 2001; Bennewitz et al., 2005; Cheverst et al., 2000; Cheverst, 2001; Davies et al., 2001).

- *Smart devices* such as *intelligent appliances* (Roussos, 2003) and *wearable devices* (Hull, Reid, and Geelhoed, 2002).
- *Ambient displays* capable of presenting information and dynamically interacting with their users. Ambient displays usually employ natural-like metaphors that present information without constantly demanding the users' full attention by implicitly making the displays available in the periphery of attention (Streitz et al., 2005). Current technological trends in display technologies range from *autostereotropic 3D displays*, which provide three-dimensional perception without the need for special glasses or other headgear (Dodgson, 2005), *volumetric 3D displays*, which produce volume-filling 3D imagery with voxels (Favalora, 2005; Soltan et al., 1995), and *holographic projections* (Slinger, Cameron, and Stanley, 2005).
- *Everyday life objects* that incorporate sufficient computing capabilities. A notable example is the University of Karlsruhe's MediaCup project (Beigl, Gellersen, and Schmidt, 2001), which enabled coffee cups to sense their physical state and map sensor readings autonomously to a domain-specific model of the cup, providing services such as meeting notifications, warnings if the user picks up a coffee cup that is too hot, and so on. ReachMedia uses radio frequency identification (RFID) tags to everyday objects enabling hands- and eyes-free interaction with relevant information using a unique combination of audio output and gestural input (Feldman et al., 2005). Several prototypes have been implemented attaching RFID tags to fast-moving consumer goods products, allowing supply chain visibility and streamlining (Borriello, 2005).

Table 2.2 aggregates the capabilities and characteristics of pervasive devices. We employ the classification of interaction styles devised by Preece, Rogers, and Sharp (2002) and Preece and colleagues (1994).

A major requirement for participation of a device in a pervasive environment is connectivity. Devices may include one or more connectivity options depending on their functionality. Rasheed, Edwards, and Tai (2002) have classified available connectivity options based on the following:

- Connectivity to the outside world (if required by the pervasive system). This includes both broadcast and broadband access. Broadband access represents Internet connectivity to a wide area network through cable, digital subscriber line (DSL), or wireless local loop (WLL). Broadcast access represents connectivity to external content sources that might be required by the pervasive system.
- Connectivity to the internal network. This includes both wireless local area network options such as 802.11 technologies or Bluetooth, and wired LAN options such as Ethernet, IEEE 13941, or other fixed network connections.

The aforementioned plurality and diversity of pervasive devices poses severe challenges for pervasive information systems designers. In the case of mobile devices (devices that follow the user or are carried around by him/her), the main design challenge is directly related to constraints in terms of physical dimensions. These "physical constraints" limit resources such as battery power,

Table 2.2

Properties and Interaction Styles of Pervasive Devices

Device type	Form factor	Degree of mobility	Interaction style	Interaction duration	Sample application
Desktops	Large	Low	Direct manipulation	Long	Internet browsing
Laptops/tablet PCs	Medium	Medium (transportable)	Direct manipulation	Medium to long	Word-processing
Palmtops/PDAs	Medium/small	Very high	Menus and navigation	Little	Meetings administration
Mobile phones	Small	Very high	Menus and navigation	Medium	Voice communication
Intelligent appliances	Large to very large	Very low	Command entry, natural language	Rare	Television program recording
Infokiosks	Very large	Very low	Menus and navigation, form fills	Very rare	Contextual information provision
Wearables	Medium to small	High	Command entry, menus, and navigation	Medium	Plant operation
Ambient displays	Very large	Low	None*	Rare	Promotional information provision
Everyday-life objects	Small	High	None	Rare	Contextual information sensing

*Implies that the device either passively projects information to the user or senses and communicates contextual information for further processing.

screen size, networking bandwidth, and so forth. A PDA, for example, has relatively little usable screen area and limited battery power; a cell phone has an even smaller screen size but typically a longer battery life and is at least connected to a network; a smart sensor (such as a smart dust mote) requires continuous power supply, thus forcing the pervasive system designer to improvise in order to ensure that sufficient power is available for the mote's operation. Furthermore, applications also experience variability in the availability of resources, which influences the development of applications and their capabilities. Moreover, if the pervasive application follows the user and moves seamlessly between devices, it is implied that applications will have to adapt to changing hardware capabilities (different types of pointing devices, keyboards, network types, and so on) and variability in the available software services (Banavar and Bernstein, 2002).

Pervasive Middleware

One of the most important problems for PS is the management of the multiple computing nodes comprising a large, complex system at both the application and networking levels. The development of pervasive middleware is the most common solution. Pervasive middleware may be considered as the "shell" to interface between the networking kernel and the end-user applications running either on the pervasive devices or on any backbone information systems. Usually, "middleware" is a widely used term to denote a set of generic services above the operating system (Raatikainen, Christensen, and Nakajima, 2002). Typical middleware services include directory, trading, and brokerage services for discovery transactions, and different transparencies such as location transparency and failure transparency. Examples of middleware include the Common Object Request Broker Architecture (CORBA) (CORBA, 2004), the Java 2 Enterprise and Micro Editions, (J2EE and J2ME),[1] the Distributed Common Object Model (DCOM) (Eddon and Eddon, 1998), and the Wireless Application Environment (WAE) (WAPForum, 2001).

According to (Saha and Mukherjee, 2003), pervasive middleware "mediates interactions with the networking kernel on the user's behalf and keeps users immersed in the pervasive computing space." Middleware consists mostly of firmware and software bundles executing in either client–server or peer-to-peer mode. In order to meet the emerging requirements of pervasive systems, various software architectures have been proposed: Sahara,[2] MITA (Asunmaa et al., 2002), M-Echo (Raj, Schwan, and Nathuji, 2005), MICA (Kadous and Sammut, 2005), TOTA (Mamei and Zambonelli, 2005), Allia (Ratsimor et al., 2004), MiddleWhere (Ranganathan et al., 2004), and GAIA (Roman et al., 2002) are just a few examples. These architectures identify an "execution support layer" that encapsulates the functions of middleware for pervasive applications. This execution support layer sustains fast service development and deployment. Additional functions supported by these middleware approaches include adaptability to changes in execution and communication capabilities, efficient use of available communication resources, dynamic configuration of end-user devices as well as robustness, high availability, and rigorous fault-tolerance. The requirements for data and information accessed by pervasive middleware are quite similar. Middleware provides a consistent, reliable, and highly available information base. This implies that all information sources have been registered in a centralized "file system" service. In case a component of the pervasive system requires retrieval (or sending) of data from (to) a particular source, the pervasive middleware locates the appropriate data source and delivers (dispatches) the data accordingly. Raatikainen, Christensen, and Nakajima (2002) have summarized the architectural qualities that a pervasive middleware should incorporate, as follows:

- *Adaptability and modifiability:* The ability of middleware to dynamically cope with changes during the lifetime of a user session. These changes may come from the middleware layer itself (connection quality changes, etc.), from explicit user actions (activating or using new devices), or from the monitored environment (contextual or environmental changes). Moreover, deployed middleware for pervasive information systems must expect the rapid appearance of new devices and services over its lifetime. Thus, middleware components that handle device interaction must be capable of frequent modification.
- *Availability and performance:* The capability of middleware to monitor the system nodes and dynamically reroute user requests in case a particular node fails while at the same time preserving fast response rates.
- *Security:* The ability of middleware to prevent unauthorized access to the pervasive system resources as well as to incorporate adequate security mechanisms to protect the transmission of sensitive information over the networking kernel.

Rasheed and colleagues (2002) extend these qualities to incorporating technical properties as well, including:

- *Device discovery, configuration, management and control.* This property refers to both the administration of the *access devices* and the *participation components* of the pervasive environment. For example, in the case of wireless sensor networks, emphasis should be given to the real-time processing of sensed events, their fusion to obtain a high-level sensor reading, and its communication to another part of the system for processing (and possible reaction). Yao and Gehrke (2002) propose an approach that resembles database management systems where sensor readings are treated as "virtual" relational database tables and processed through a language similar to SQL. Ye, Heidemann, and Estrin (2002) propose an alternative middleware architecture, called "SCADDS" that supports robust and energy-efficient delivery and in-network aggregation of sensor events. Hermann and colleagues (2001) propose DEAPspace, a framework interconnecting pervasive devices over a wireless medium and supporting the development of new proximity-based collective distributed applications.
- *Quality of service (QoS) and policy management.* QoS management is essential for transporting multiple information streams in a pervasive environment especially taking into account the uncertainty surrounding the total number of expected end users. Moreover, pervasive system administrators may want to apply certain usage rules that govern how pervasive system resources are used. The key for both QoS and policy-based network and system management mechanisms is flexibility and ease-of-use. For this to work, all devices must agree on a common framework and associated mechanisms to implement these functions.
- *Overall system management.*
- *Gateway management and control* (in case the pervasive system requires communication with the external world).

A final requirement is that pervasive middleware must manage the user interface that is being displayed to user devices. This is an extremely important requirement due to the high heterogeneity of devices that can participate in a pervasive environment. The middleware should be able to identify the capabilities of the end device (along with the capabilities of its installed browser or microbrowser—in the case of mobile phones and PDAs) and the pervasive network (in terms of traffic management) and to generate the most appropriate user interface.

Pervasive Information Systems and Context Awareness

One of the most important novel characteristics that PS introduce is the notion of context awareness. By understanding the properties of context, pervasive information systems designers will be able to choose what context to use and provide insights into the types of data that need to be supported and the abstractions and mechanisms required to support context-aware computing. In effect, previous definitions of context have either been extensional, that is, an enumeration of examples of context, or simple references to synonyms for context. The following paragraphs aim to shed light on the different interpretations of context in the existing literature.

Schilit, Adams, and Want (1994) were the first to define context as location, the identities of nearby people and objects, and changes to those objects. In a similar definition, Brown, Bovey, and Chen (1997) define context as location, the identities of the people around the user, the time of day, season, temperature, and so on. Ryan, Pascoe, and Morse (1998) define context as the user's location, environment, identity, and time. Dey, Abowd, and Wood (1998) approach context as the user's emotional state, focus of attention, location and orientation, date and time, objects, and people in the user's environment. Other definitions have simply provided synonyms for context, referring, for example, to context as the environment or situation. M.G. Brown (1996) defines context as the elements of the user's environment that the user's computer knows about. Franklin and Flaschbart (1998) consider context to be the situation of the user. Ward, Jones, and Hopper (1997) view context as the state of the application's surroundings while Rodden and colleagues (1998) define it as the application's setting.

Pascoe (1998) defines context as the subset of physical and conceptual states of interest to a particular entity. Hull, Neaves, and Bedford-Roberts (1997) include the entire environment by defining context as aspects of the current situation (also introducing the term "situated computing"). Jameson (2001) extend the previous definitions by adding the user's behavior and current interactions with the pervasive system while Harter and colleagues (2001) and Van Laerhoven and Aidoo (2001) emphasize the importance of sensors embedded in the environment in order to sense the location and current movement of the user and add it to the properties of a context-aware system. Ljungstrand (2001) examines context from the perspective of the pervasive device (in his case, the mobile phone). It is worth mentioning that several attempts have been to model context-sensitive applications and systems (Jameson, 2001; Lei et al., 2002; Petrelli et al., 2001; Urnes, Malm, and Myhre, 2001; Yau et al., 2002). Still, these models take into account only subsets of the aforementioned attributes.

All of these definitions provide indicative examples of attributes that identify the properties of context. In this chapter, we will follow the definitions provided by Dix and colleagues (2000) and Abowd and Mynatt (2000), which incorporate most of the important properties mentioned above. Dix and colleagues (2000) distinguish among four different types of context: infrastructure, system, domain, and physical. Infrastructure context takes into consideration particular technical elements: the network bandwidth, the reliability of the system/service used, and the display resolution of the end device. System context takes into consideration the interrelated components of the PS *as a system:* other devices, pervasive artifacts, applications, and users. Domain context considers the semantics of the application domain taking into account elements such as the style of use and the identity of the user. Finally, the physical context considers the environmental conditions, namely, the current location of the user, the physical nature of the devices used, and other sensory information. Building on previous work (Abowd, 1999; Abowd et al., 1997), Abowd and Mynatt (2000) decompose context into the who, where, when, and what (the current activities) of entities and use this information to determine why a situation is occurring. According to the authors, a context-aware system should identify the location of a user, the time an activity takes place, the identity of the user performing the activity, and the user's current interactions with the system. This definition has been prevalent in similar works of other researchers investigating the incorporation of context in pervasive systems (Dey, 2001; Truong, Abowd, and Brotherton, 2001).

Taking into account the above analysis, we will treat context as defined by Dey (2001) "as any information that can be used to characterise the situation of an entity. An entity is a person, place, or object that is considered relevant to the interaction between a user and an application, including the user and applications themselves." This definition makes it easier for the designer of a pervasive system to define the context for a given application scenario. If a piece of information can be used to characterize the situation of a participant in an interaction, then that information is context. Moreover, that information should be responsible for changing the environment within which the system operates. We distinguish among three different types of environments (following Dey, 2001; Dix et al., 2000): computing or infrastructure environment, user environment, and physical environment.

Having identified the properties and attributes of a context-aware system, a system designer should specify the important features of a context-aware system. In effect, context-aware systems have become somewhat synonymous with other terms: adaptive (Brown, 1996), reactive (Cooperstock et al., 1995), responsive (Elrod et al., 1993), situated (Hull, Neaves, and Bedford-Roberts, 1997), context-sensitive (Rekimoto et al., 1998), and environment-directed (Fickas, Kortuem, and Segall, 1997). Nevertheless, the capabilities of a context-sensitive system are generally common in the literature. Context-sensitive systems should be able to detect, sense, interpret, and respond to aspects of a user's local environment based on peripheral and behavioral elements (Abowd, Mynatt, and Rodden, 2002; Dey, 2001; Hull, Neaves, and Bedford-Roberts, 1997; Pascoe, 1998; Pascoe, Ryan, and Morse, 1998; Ryan, et al., 1998). Moreover, at the procedural level, Saha and Mukherjee (2003) distinguish between *context management* and *context awareness*. Context awareness, or perception, is the initial action taken by a pervasive system; the system perceives contextual information from multiple and possibly disagreeing sensors, models it, and merges it into a form that is capable of being processed at a later stage. Once a pervasive computing system can perceive the current context, it must have the means of using its perceptions effectively. Thus, context management, or perception, retrieves and processes contextual information and presents it in an appropriate form to the end user (or adapts the behavior of the pervasive system accordingly). In any case, the information that defines context awareness must be accurate; otherwise it can confuse or intrude on the user experience.

The most generic definition for the features of a context-aware system has been provided by Dey (2001), and it will be used as the basis for this chapter: "a system is context-aware if it uses context to provide relevant information and/or services to the user, where relevancy depends on the user's task." This definition encapsulates two important elements: (a) it is independent of any application domain and (b) it particulates the objective of the context-aware system to the provision of information that is relevant (to the task). This chapter will follow the system specifications originally proposed by Dey (2001), which combine ideas from previous taxonomies and attempt and generalize them to satisfy all existing context-aware applications. According to Dey, there are three categories of features that a context-aware system should support:

- Presentation of relevant information and services to a user.
- Automatic execution of a service for a user when needed or requested.
- Tagging of context to information and storing it in order to support later retrieval.

The common denominators among all the different approaches to context awareness, refer to the capabilities of the pervasive system to perceive the relevant information of its environment (with location sensitivity and user identity capture being the minimum requirement), process it, and adapt to changes in the environment, taking into account both historical and current data. Another issue with context-aware PS is their capacity to deal with ambiguity. Dey and Mankoff (2005) discuss ways to mediate imperfectly sensed context. Although at present contextual information refers mainly to the user's current location, we expect that in the near future PS will be able to perceive multiple stimulants that may simultaneously contradict each other. Thus, we suggest that PS should accommodate an appropriate mechanism that will filter the different contextual information particles, process them, and adjust their behavior according to the information that best suits the current occasion. This might be accomplished by taking into account historical system behavior based on similar conditions or giving priority to the user's behavior.

Summary

The previous sections discussed several design challenges related to the infrastructure layer of PS. Table 2.3 aggregates these challenges in categories for each infrastructure dimension.

Table 2.3

Summary of Design Challenges for Pervasive Information Systems Infrastructure Components

Infrastructure dimension	Design challenge	Possible design solution
Pervasive networks	Connectivity	Network management centrally, through the pervasive middleware.
	Quality of service (QoS)	QoS management centrally, through the pervasive middleware, based on established methods or models (e.g., QADA [Matinlassi, Niemelä, and Dobrica, 2002]).
	Multiple networks management	Network management centrally, through the pervasive middleware.
	Security	Wireless encryption techniques and protocols (e.g., WEP). Auditing mechanisms preventing unauthorized access and use of any system component.
Wireless sensor networks	Uncertainty or latency of sensed information/node failure	Middleware solution that identifies proximity nodes and utilizes their sensed data. Usually, these software solutions use localized or adaptive fidelity algorithms to cope with data uncertainty.
	Information update and synchronization	Middleware solution that synchronizes and updates data among the participating nodes.
	Power management	• Alternative power sources (e.g., solar energy, ambient RFID scavenging, mechanical vibrations, and so on). • Energy sharing through the network. • Selection of the most cost-efficient wireless communication solution (e.g., wireless hierarchy [Pering, Ranghunathan, and Want, 2005]) • Selectively slow down or deactivate sensor capabilities (e.g., DVM [Pering, Burd, and Brodersen, 2000]).

Pervasive access devices	Wireless discovery	Employment of established communication and connection protocols such as Universal Plug and Play (UPnP) (Jeronimo and Weast, 2003) and Apple's Bonjour (Apple, 2006). These wireless discovery methods may be included in the pervasive middleware.
	User interface adaptation	User interface (UI) adaptation mechanisms that generate UIs based on an abstract definition of them and in combination with knowledge of the capabilities of the target display generate the UI components on the fly (e.g., PUC [Nichols, Myers, and Litwack, 2004], SUPPLE [Gajos and Weld, 2004], iCrafter [Ponnekanti et al. 2001]). These adaptation mechanisms may be incorporated in the pervasive middleware.
Pervasive middleware	Component heterogeneity	Centralized components management through meta-models or components abstractions (e.g., Gaia [Roman et al. 2002b] and Aura [Sousa and Garlan 2002]).
	Application interoperability	Software components should be designed to be independent of the context in which they are used, as this allows their use in different computing environments and applications. If a uniform description language is used for software specification, this description can be used for binding components dynamically. Distributed systems design principles may be employed (Colouris, Dollimore, and Kindberg, 2001).
Context awareness	Location aware computing	Selection of an appropriate mechanism to identify user location (e.g., RADAR [Bahl and Padmanabhan, 2000], Active Badge [Want et al. 1992], etc.).
	Context aware representation and coordination	Implementation of context toolkits or architectures that use a common representation format for contextual information, and coordinate/manage contextual information among the system components (e.g., MARS [Cabri, Leonardi, and Zambonelli, 2002], Context Shadow [Jonsson 2002], and Context Toolkit [Salber, Dey, and Abowd 1999]).
	Personal data (privacy) management	Design of the context toolkits/solutions according to established privacy-by-design PS principles (e.g., Langheinrich 2001, 2002).

THE SERVICES LAYER

Introduction

The previous sections provided a thorough discussion on the novel features of pervasive information systems irrespective of their application domain. However, these novel features should not delineate the scope of this chapter. Pervasive information systems are purposeful systems; they are developed, used, and administered by humans aiming to attain particular goals and objectives. As such, they may be applied in several contexts supporting multiple purposes. Yet, both academia and industry agree that the current technology limits the provision of truly pervasive services, especially in commercial conditions. A truly pervasive environment should not be distractive in terms of user interaction with the system. The examples of ambient displays that were discussed in the previous sections reveal that significant work remains before organizations will be able to deploy economically viable pervasive systems for commercial use. Nevertheless, the literature reveals a substantial number of research initiatives. The following paragraphs will briefly discuss some pioneering examples of pervasive information systems. Although this selection is far from exhaustive, it illustrates the main drivers behind this vision.

Pervasive Information Systems Initiatives

One of the most well-known initiatives is project Aura at Carnegie Mellon University (Hengartner and Steenkiste, 2004; Judd and Steenkiste, 2003; Sousa and Garlan, 2002). The people involved in the project characterize it as "distraction-free ubiquitous computing." Aura's goal is to provide each user with an invisible halo of computing and information services that persists regardless of location. Aura is a large umbrella project with many individual research thrusts, including task-driven computing, energy-aware adaptation, nomadic data access, and multimodal user interfaces.

Along the same line, the Oxygen project at the Massachusetts Institute of Technology (MIT) enables pervasive, human-centered computing through a combination of specific user and system technologies (Saif, 2006). Oxygen aims to combine speech and vision technologies to directly address human needs. Speech and vision technologies enable us to communicate with Oxygen as if we are interacting with another person, thus saving much time and effort. The project has developed two types of computational devices to enhance user interaction with the system services. The first type of devices, called Envir021s (E21s), may be embedded in environments such as homes, offices, and cars, and are capable to sense and affect them directly. The second type of devices, called Handy21s (H21s), empowers users to communicate and compute no matter where they are. H21s accept speech and visual input, and they can reconfigure themselves to support multiple communication protocols or to perform a wide variety of useful functions (e.g., to serve as cellular phones, beepers, radios, televisions, geographical positioning systems, cameras, or personal digital assistants) (Steele, Waterman, and Weinstein, 2002). Dynamic, self-configuring networks (called N21s) help pervasive devices to locate each other as well as the people, services, and resources they want to reach and serve. Finally, the project has developed specialized software that adapts to changes in the environment or in user requirements (02S) and helps them to do what they want at the moment they wish. The project has also developed two application scenarios to demonstrate the practical utility of the aforementioned technologies. *Business conference* supports conference visitors in managing and administering their business arrangements, while *Guardian Angel* provides emergency and notification services.

The Portolano project from the University of Washington, shifts away from technology-driven general-purpose devices to focus on the needs of consumers and develop easy-to-use, low-mainte-nance, portable, ubiquitous, and ultra-reliable task-specific devices (Esler et al., 1999). The project emphasizes invisible, intent-based computing, which infers users' intentions via their actions in the environment and their interactions with everyday objects. Similarly, the Cooltown project at Hewlett-Packard (HP) Labs develops systems that support users of wireless, handheld devices in interacting with their environment, regardless of where they may be (Caswell and Debaty, 2000; Kindberg et al., 2002). The project aims to develop new experiences for users through new interac-tion schemes and access devices. As empirical evidence, museum users are studied to measure the efficacy of several types of handheld devices in augmenting museum exhibits with various types of Web content in order to understand the influence of physical factors, such as the device's size and input modes and the interaction styles involved in viewing both physical exhibits and virtual resources.

Classifying Pervasive Information Systems

The aforementioned initiatives comprise large, integrated projects, each focusing on the practical utility and usability of technology-augmented environments, especially in terms of supporting everyday life. As umbrella projects, they try to validate their findings through the implementa-tion and testing of particular applications in different contexts. In this section we will provide a classification of pervasive systems based on their functionality, or, to be more precise, on the application context they support.

An initial classification of PS has been provided by Kostakos and O'Neill (2004), who distinguish between two types of PS, domestic and public. This distinction reflects the difference between the *provision* and *accessibility* of each information system. According to the authors, *domestic PS* refer to systems deployed in *tightly constrained domains* and are usually small in scale (such as the home environment or a car). Moreover, they are optimized to provide a particular functional-ity within the given requirements of their contextual environment. *Public PS* cover a much wider area that provides accessibility to social units. These systems may be provided by a public sector body (such as a municipality), and they are flexible enough to supply useful resources to a wide range of potential users.

This classification does not include wearable (or personal) systems. Moreover, it positions pervasive systems in the domestic environment under the same umbrella with pervasive systems that are deployed in commercial or interorganizational environments. Although both systems are deployed in a constrained environment, their primary objectives can be, with a few exceptions, totally opposite. *Corporate pervasive systems* focus on supporting and enhancing particular busi-ness processes of an organization, while *domestic pervasive systems* support mainly entertainment or the routine demands of household residents. Moreover, social activities in offices differ from those in the home. Office activities tend to be more formal, structured, task oriented, and focused on productivity. Home activities are mostly informal, not necessarily structured, and focused on convenience, safety, pleasure, and entertainment (Meyer and Rakotonirainy, 2003). Finally, users are different. Domestic pervasive systems users usually reside relaxed in their environment and may be passively supported by the system. Conversely, corporate pervasive systems users fall into two main categories: *intraorganizational users* who utilize the system to facilitate them in a particular work activity (e.g., in the case of an office pervasive system) and *extraorganizational users* who may use the system opportunistically to support them in a consumer- or entertainment-related activity (e.g., in the case of a shopper or a museum visitor). The following sections briefly discuss the four different types of pervasive information systems and present examples of each.

Personal Pervasive Information Systems

Personal systems are commonly referred to as *wearable systems* (Smailagic and Siewiorek, 2002). These systems rely on hardware such as heads-up displays and one-handed keyboards to provide the interface to the computer. This model is attractive because it provides a fully functional computing experience wherever the user may be. However, these interfaces can be overly intrusive and require a great deal of the user's attention, thus mitigating their widespread acceptance. Currently, these devices are typically somewhat bulky belt-worn devices, but they will shrink as technology progresses, thereby lending themselves to better industrial design and integration. Several researchers have already proposed design considerations for wearable systems, emphasizing mainly wearability, the interaction of the user with the wearable object (Fishkin, Partridge, and Chatterjee, 2002; Gemperle et al., 1998; Siewiorek, 2002; Smailagic and Siewiorek, 2002), and ergonomics (Baber et al., 1999; Siewiorek, 2002). Such properties refer primarily to smooth (and aesthetic) integration of the wearable device with the end user, efficient power management, and unobtrusive user interaction by employing an interface that is easy to use and easy to learn. Moreover, in contrast to desktop or mobile systems that attempt to pack as much capacity and performance as possible into an integrated package, wearable systems require a minimalistic design. The provision of a wide-range service portfolio in a wearable module may not only compromise ease of use by generating information overload but also can require substantial resources. To support these requirements, initial research efforts in the area focused on the development of wireless, comfortable (in terms of size and weight) hardware modules for users, an objective that is characterized as "kinesthetics" (Fishkin, Partridge, and Chatterjee, 2002).

Wearable systems started to evolve in the early 1970s. Since then, they have been widely accepted in multiple application domains and have evolved from simple presentation of text and graphics to team maintenance and collaboration with other field workers (Smailagic and Siewiorek, 2002). Table 2.4 presents just a few domains in which wearable systems have been applied over the past few years.

Domestic Pervasive Information Systems

The second type of PS demonstrates how interactive technologies may be embedded into the fabric of our everyday environment: the household. Research in this area was initiated by established appliance manufacturers, such as Philips, Siemens, and Hewlett-Packard, which recognized a market opportunity with respect to embedding additional interactive and computational capabilities into their products (e.g., Internet TV, smart refrigerators, etc.). To postulate how the home of the future will look and operate, visionary publications (e.g., Philips Design Visions of the Future) and integrated research projects (e.g., the Cooltown project by HP) were developed. At the same time, the research community embraced these visions by constructing "living laboratories" that allowed researchers to investigate how inhabitants react in and experience the new home environment. As such, new research programs were established jointly by academia and industry. MIT's School of Architecture and Planning project, Home of the Future, is one of the most well-known initiatives in the area (Intille, 2002).

Domestic PS support a number of services in the home environment. In general, there is a bias toward automation of tasks that otherwise require human supervision and action, such as controlling heat and lighting, cooking, monitoring the home inventory, and so on (Coen, 1998; Kidd et al., 1999; Mozer, 1998). Nevertheless, pervasive technologies may also support household residents in additional ways. We classify the services that domestic PS offer into three broad categories: automation, protection, and entertainment. Table 2.5 summarizes the functionality of each service category and provides a set of examples.

Table 2.4

Personal Pervasive Information Systems

Application domain	Functionality	Examples
Military	• Navigation	Collected from Mann (1997), and Zieniewicz et al. (2002):
	• Communication	• Soldier Integrated Protective Ensemble (SIPE)
	• Multimedia content broadcasting and reception (maps, mission reports)	• VulMan
	• Target management (locating, aiming, identifying)	• 21st Century Land Warrior
		• Land Warrior
Medical	• Patient monitoring	• Metronaut (Smailagic and Martin, 1997)
	• Events management/ notification	• Medical Jacket (Jafari et al., 2005)
		• LifeMinder (Suzuki and Doi, 2001)
		• iGlove (Philipose et al., 2004)
		• iBracelet (Smith et al., 2005)
		• Biomedical wearable healthcare system (Huang and Hsu, 2005)
Engineering	• Maintenance	• VuTech (Smailagic and Siewiorek, 1994)
	• Field worker collaboration	• Georgia Tech's wearable computer for quality assurance in a food-processing plant (Najjar, Thompson, and Ockerman, 1997)
	• Field engineer support	• OSCAR
	• Plant operation	• MoCCA (Smailagic et al., 1999)
	• Parts inspection and replacement	• Nomadic Radio (Sawhney and Schmandt, 2000)
	• Error notifications	
Office automation and support	• E-mail management	• W-Mail (Ueda, Tsukamoto, and Nishio, 2000)
	• Office documents management	• Meetings recorder (Kern et al., 2003)
	• Notifications/alerts	• Factory automation support technology (FAST) (Najjar, Thompson, and Ockerman, 1999)
	• Learning/training	• Aware-Mail (Miura et al., 2004)
Infotainment	• Language translation	• Touring Machine (Feiner et al., 1997)
	• Advice provision	• CMU's Synthetic Assistant (Marinelli and Stevens, 1998; Smailagic 1998)
	• Information provision	• Martial Arts Protector (Chi, Song, and Corbin, 2004)
	• Multimedia content reproduction	• Human Pacman (Cheok et al., 2004)
	• Interactive games support	• iBand (Kanis et al., 2005)
	• Virtual communities	• NetMan (Kortuem et al., 1999)
		• Pirates! (Bjork et al. 2001)
		• The SpyGame, Multi Monster Mania, The Guild (Bjork et al., 2002)
		• Smart playing cards (Romer and Domnitcheva 2002)

Table 2.5

Domestic Pervasive Information Systems

Service category	Functionality	Examples
Automation	• Adjustment of lights, Venetian blinds, heating, and/or air-conditioning based on environmental conditions or preferences	• MIT Home of the Future (Intille, 2002)
	• Real-time home inventory management (consumed products, lost items, compilation of shopping list)	• Neural Network House (Mozer, 1998)
	• Phones ringing only in the room where the addressee is located	• Casablanca (Hindus et al., 2001)
	• Interactive communication of family members even when they are in different rooms	• Family Intercom (Nagel et al., 2001)
		• Aware Home (Kidd et al., 1999)
		• Intelligent Room (Brooks, 1997)
Protection	• Fully integrated security and monitoring systems including emergency call-out alarms for burglars, fire, or injuries	• Stanford (2002b)
	• Monitoring of the condition of elders or amputees and alerting family members or other supervisory staff in emergency situations	• Mynatt, Essa, and Rogers (2000)
		• Millennium Homes (Lines and Hone, 2002)
		• The Information Furnace (Spinellis, 2003)
Entertainment	• Multimedia content broadcasting in different rooms (music, videos/movies)	• The KidsRoom (Bobick, 1999)
	• Interactive play spaces for children	• The Networked Home (Mani et al., 2004)
	• Adjusting the pictures in the frames in each room based on the preferences of the person currently in the room	• Coordinated displays (Crabtree, Hemmings, and Rodden, 2002a)

To support the aforementioned services, domestic PS incorporate several technological solutions that alter the usual interaction of residents with their environment. Rodden and Benford (2003) summarize these developments/approaches:

- *Interactive household objects* that incorporate computational and interactive properties in contemporary household objects. Examples include interactive picture frames (Mynatt, Essa, and Rogers, 2000), adding new communication means to notice boards (Hindus et al., 2001), and augmented cups (Beigl, Gellersen, and Schmidt, 2001).
- *Augmented furniture* (including *information appliances*), which implies the addition of interactive capabilities to various furniture in the home. Examples include the DiamondTouch (Dietz and Leigh, 2001) and the Drift (Gaver et al., 2004) interactive tables, the Smart Sofa, Bed and Pillow (Park et al., 2003), the Sense Lounger (supporting elderly citizens) (Hurst et al., 2005), and garden furniture (Graver and Martin, 2000).

Still, domestic PS should not be viewed solely in the context of technology. Designing a smart home implies much more than simple embedment of information technology. On the contrary, it is a process of developing both the environment and the infrastructure. Thus, various people may be involved in the design process. Domestic PS designers may need to intervene in the following layers that generically characterize how domestic environments change (Brand, 1994):

- *Site,* which refers to the geographical setting and location of domestic settings.
- *Structure,* which refers to the materials used to build the domestic setting.
- *Skin,* which refers to the exterior surfaces.
- *Services,* which incorporate the backbone infrastructure of the domestic place such as electrical and communications wiring, plumbing, and so on.
- *Space plan,* which refers to the overall layout and available space of each room and the setting in general.
- *Stuff,* which characterizes all of the furniture and appliances.

Domestic PS designers will seldom affect the first three layers (site, structure, and skin). Nevertheless, the remaining three layers (services, space plan, and stuff) will most certainly be affected with the integration of information technology. Crabtree, Hemmings, and Rodden (2002) characterize this interplay as an "ongoing configuration and reconfiguration of artefacts and media." Thus, the deployment of a pervasive PS involves the following activities (adapting Rodden et al., 2004):

- *Analysis.* The first activity aims to determine ways in which the technology might be appropriated, specifying the functionality of the domestic PS, identifying intervention requirements with the services, space plan, and stuff layers, and eliciting the feasibility of the proposed changes. This activity presupposes the collaboration of multiple professionals apart from the inhabitants and system designers. These can include architects, service providers, and decorators. Consequently, creating synergies with external parties is a major requirement in building smart homes.
- *Sketching.* The second activity aims to lay down a detailed design of the technology-augmented domestic setting. Similar to the previous activity, designers should collaborate with both inhabitants and the aforementioned professionals. This activity will guide the development and deployment of the pervasive system so that inhabitants (the actual users of the system) are

able to recognize the relevance of technology to their practical activities and circumstances (Rodden et al., 2004).

- *Placement and assembly.* The final activity involves the actual deployment of the technology-augmented domestic setting. Special care should be taken to maintain a sense of responsiveness to the current organization of the space plan and services layers and to situate the new technologies at functional sites within the environment. In addition, designers should preserve the personal and historic values of the technology-augmented objects or appliances since people in their homes are accustomed to being surrounded by items that have history and biographies. Finally, the pervasive system should be able to dynamically accommodate to inhabitants' needs and demands by enabling them to configure (and reconfigure) its functionality.

Corporate Pervasive Information Systems

The third type of pervasive information systems addresses the embedment of pervasive computing technologies in the organization. Mobile and wireless forms of connectivity, as with most information and communication technologies, play an important role in determining competitiveness, employment, and economic growth. In particular, mobile and wireless technologies have created new business opportunities, while at the same time affecting many existing organizational norms and practices by bridging the gap between the physical company reality and its information-technological representation (Borriello and Want, 2000).

In particular, office workers may have nomadic access to corporate information, regardless of time and space. They may use laptops or PDAs to perform their duties without feeling restricted by desktop computing facilities. Moreover, they may have enhanced capabilities for communication, coordination, collaboration, and knowledge exchange because of mobility and remote access to valuable information. This phenomenon led researchers to invent new terminology such as sales force automation, field force automation, mobile supply chain management, and mobile office support (Spriestersbach et al., 2001). Grudin (2002) discusses the potential of pervasive computing technologies to support group meetings while Davis (2002) presents application examples that may enhance the productivity of knowledge workers. Likewise, the pervasive computing literature presents several prototype systems aimed at supporting office workers through collaboration tools (e.g., digital notification flyers, plasma posters, etc.) (Churchill, Nelson, and Denoue, 2003; Stanford, 2002a).

Moreover, pervasive technologies in the form of mobile and wireless networks enable physical and computational resources to communicate automatically, eliminating the requirement for human mediation and intervention in performing tasks. For example, by attaching RFID tags to consumer products or pallets, a retailer or manufacturer can streamline core supply chain management processes, such as inventory management, reverse logistics, and product tracking (Wong et al. 2002). As examples of the potential of RFID technology, many industries and government agencies, including some of the largest U.S. retailers (such as Wal-Mart and Target), as well as the largest U.S. government agency (the Department of Defense), mandate the use of RFID tags at the pallet level by all of their suppliers (Borriello, 2005).

Finally, pervasive technologies enable the implementation of new business services, creating new communication channels with consumers and ultimately generating revenue for organizations. Fano and Gershman (2002) discuss the potential of pervasive computing technologies for the provision of new customer-related services. Mobile technologies may be used to sustain long-term relationships with customers, thus extending traditional customer-relationship management (CRM) schemes. Through the mobile phone, a personalized medium for every consumer, organizations can provide targeted promotions and advertisements. Likewise, advertisements can be projected to public displays in supermarkets, subway stations, and other public places, enabling a new form of advertisement called "serendipitous advertising" (Ranganathan and Campbell, 2002). According to the authors, this new form of advertising will enable new business models and business entities in the form of "pervasive service providers" that deploy a variety of sensors in public places to detect or track various contexts (e.g., people's location, the temperature, and the activities of people or groups of people, and sending promotional information to individuals through various means such as instant messaging, wall displays, etc.). Moreover, organizations can implement new tools to facilitate shopping for consumers. Several personal shopping assistants have already appeared in the literature; they provide value-added services to supermarket shoppers such as automatic checkout, personalized recommendations, in-store navigation, and targeted promotions, to name a few (Asthana, Cravatts, and Krzyzanowski, 1994; Kourouthanassis and Giaglis, 2004).[3]

Pervasive technologies allow rapid response to all service requests by first establishing the customer's context, identifying available service channels such as the customer's mobile device, nearby screens, or other access devices, and then delivering the highest fidelity service through the available channels. As Fano and Gershman (2002) highlight, corporate pervasive systems create new relationships between organizations and their customers based on three characteristics: *awareness*, *access*, and *responsiveness*. Corporate pervasive systems are aware of the customer because they can interpret contextual data and past consumption information to extrapolate current needs. They can access the customer through multiple channels and provide targeted and value-added services. As a result, they can respond to the specific needs of the customer and take advantage of the resources available at the customer's location.

Classifying the various application types of corporate pervasive information systems is difficult because they come in many "flavors." Nevertheless, an initial typology identifies three major classes of applications:

- *Business process applications* refer to all types of corporate applications aimed at augmenting, enabling, or strengthening existing organizational business processes through the use of pervasive computing technologies. Typical business processes that can benefit from the introduction of mobile applications are supply chain management and enterprise resource planning, providing the conditions for more efficient decision making and prompt reaction in the presence of unexpected problems in the supply chain or within the company.
- *Workforce applications* enable remote workers to utilize mobile and wireless applications to be more productive in their jobs. As such, they are not isolated from the business process systems described above, but, rather, they enable employees to take part in such business processes more efficiently. Typical workforce applications include:
  a. *Field force automation (FFA):* Field-workers (such as engineers, consultants, inspectors, and surveyors) spend the majority of their time on the move and away from corporate premises. Hence, the ability to always be connected to the organization to which they belong, either to receive instructions and support or to access and update critical company information, is of paramount importance. Wireless connectivity and mobile computing thus become powerful weapons supporting the job of field-workers in a seamless fashion. Moreover, over the past few years we have seen a rapid growth of workers who are independent of a formal organization, and, in many cases, do their jobs on a freelance and contract basis, establishing ongoing relationships with several different client firms (Segal and Sullivan, 1997). They represent the "temporary labor force" (Segal and Sul-

livan, 1995) for which the company has not allocated any resources with which to work. Pervasive technologies can enable this workforce to engage in their activities using their own resources and connecting to the corporate database on an ad hoc basis.

b. *Sales force automation (SFA):* Sales personnel need constant access to company data such as customer profiles, credit limits, and inventory information, which they can obtain through mobile or wireless connectivity. SFA systems consist of centralized databases that can be accessed remotely through laptop computers, tablet PCs or PDAs using special SFA software. SFA systems enable sales personnel to obtain constantly refreshed information regarding various facets of the job, such as contact information, inventory and shipping statistics (to avoid backorders), customer service information, and transportation logistics. Moreover, they enable salespeople to file regular reports electronically without having to travel to the central office in person (Parthasarathy and Sohi, 1997). The direct benefits of SFA systems are improved efficiency and productivity (Swenson and Parrella, 1992). Still, the adoption of such systems by sales personnel is affected by several factors. Recent studies have found that salespeople's perceptions concerning the level of managerial commitment, training adequacy, user involvement, user experience, and user expectations all have a major impact on the acceptance and use of SFA systems (Gohmann et al., 2005; Speier and Venkatesh, 2002).

c. *Pervasive office support (POS):* POS embraces all kinds of applications that are used by employees, managers, and executives to handle various corporate administration duties while on the move. We are increasingly becoming a globally connected society; thus, the ability to check e-mail, access the corporate intranet, and schedule tasks while away from the organization become critical to market success. At the same time, white-collar workers need no longer be tied to their desks; mobile and wireless applications allow them to carry their complete information and communications environment with them wherever they go.

- *Customer relationship management applications:* Pervasive CRM aims at increased profitability through improved customer loyalty. Pervasive computing technologies can allow organizations to remain close to their customers regardless of time or space limitations, either remotely (e.g., through a mobile phone) or while visiting the physical store.

Table 2.6 summarizes the functionality of each application category and provides a set of examples.

The design challenges of corporate PS are closely related to those presented in the previous section. Smooth and unobtrusive placement of the pervasive system components (sensors, access points, interaction devices, etc.) represents the major design challenge. At the same time, the PS user interfaces should be designed to enhance overall system usability. It should be noted that corporate PS users range from people who are very experienced with information technology to those who have never used an information system in the past. This refers to both intraorganizational users and extraorganizational users. For example, according to recent studies, the acceptance and use of sales force automation systems are significantly affected by issues related to enhanced usability and user experience (Gohmann, et al., 2005; Speier and Venkatesh, 2002). Similarly, personal shopping assistants (Cumby et al., 2005; Ellis and Lambright, 2002) address a target group that cannot be easily profiled (supermarket shoppers). Consequently, Wolfram, Scharr, and Kammerer (2004) suggest that the system's ease of use will determine the eventual acceptance of such PS. Finally, an important functional design consideration seems to be the issue of privacy.

Table 2.6

Corporate Pervasive Information Systems

Applications category	Functionality	Examples
Business process applications		
Supply chain management	• Warehouse/inventory management • Distribution (fleet) management • Logistics management • Procurement • Order fulfillment • Sales management • Anticounterfeiting	• Smart toolbox/smart tool inventory (Lampe, Strassner, and Fleisch, 2004) • RFID smart tags (Staake, Thiesse, and Fleisch, 2005) • Automated inventory management (McKelvin, Williams, and Berry, 2005) • Sainsbury's (Karkkainen 2003) • 3M Digital Materials Flow Management System (Fabbi et al., 2005) • WhereNet (Johnson, 2000) • Wal-Mart, Home Depot, and Gillette (Prater, Frazier, and Reyes, 2005)
Enterprise resource planning	• Alerts and notification • Access to corporate information • Remote monitoring	• Connexions (Watson and Lightfoot, 2003)
Workforce applications		
Sales force automation (SFA)	• Lead maintenance and discovery • Contact management • Review customer history and product specifications • Review pricing details and product availability	• Life insurance industry in Thailand (Larpsiri and Speece, 2004) • Pharma Corp. (Alt and Puschmann, 2005)
Field force automation	(Inherits the functionality of SFA applications) • Remote access to corporate information	• Connexions (Watson and Lightfoot, 2003)

(continued)

Table 2.6 *(continued)*

Applications category	Functionality	Examples
Pervasive office support	• E-mail access • Chatting/instant messaging • Virtual communities • Interactive bulletin boards • Sharing and exchanging of files and multimedia content	• Plasma Poster (Churchill et al., 2004) • Community Wall (Grasso, 2003) • Multimedia Fliers (Churchill, Nelson, and Denoue, 2003) • Notification Collage (Greenberg and Rounding, 2001) • Kimura (Voida et al., 2002) • Blueboard (Russell and Sue, 2003) • AvantGo (Stanford, 2002a) • WorkSPACE (Buscher, Kramp, and Krogh, 2003) • Caretta (Sugimoto, Hosoi, and Hashizume, 2004)
Customer relationship management applications		
Shopping assistants	• Personalized recommendations • In-store navigation • Automatic checkout • Product comparisons • Entertainment • Wireless payment	• MyGROCER (Kourouthanassis and Roussos, 2003) • SpeedPass (Ellis and Lambright, 2002) • Intelligent Shopping Assistant (Cumby et al., 2005) • SuperTag (Hawkes, 1994) • IntelliShopper (Menczer et al., 2002) • PDA Shopping Assistant (Newcomb, Pashley, and Stasko, 2003)
Pervasive advertising	• Frequently asked questions • Targeted promotions	Mostly conceptual papers such as: • Robins (2003)

We consider privacy to be a horizontal design challenge for PS, involving mainly corporate and public PS. Thus, we will provide an initial discussion in the forthcoming section, and extensively address this challenge in the social design challenges section.

Public Pervasive Information Systems

The final application type refers to the provision of interactive services to public environments. These can refer to services involving the public good (e.g., health services, educational services, etc.) or services that are provided by a public institution or body (e.g., e-government services, public transportation, etc.). In Table 2.7, we classify the potential functionality of public pervasive information systems into five broad service categories. Although these categories are not exhaustive, they provide a comprehensive overview of potential interactions with a public system.

An important design consideration for public PS is the issue of usability. In public pervasive information systems, the degree of temporality and circumstantiality is greater in comparison with the other system types. Public system users can range from inexperienced to disabled individuals. Even an experienced user may encounter difficulties in using an informational system in a hospital for a variety of reasons (the obvious one being current health condition). Especially in the case of public displays, Churchill and colleagues (2003) observe that constant encouragement and demonstration are required for people to interact with them, a statement also supported by Agamanolis (2003). As a result, clarity of presentation and ease of use are key design requirements. We argue that *immediate usability* will encourage individuals to use the public system by minimizing the degree of prior training required. Vogel and Balakrishnan (2004) suggest that interactions with a public system should be short in duration and explicit; they should encourage learning by exploration; and they should incorporate responsive display techniques. At the same time, information should be presented in a comprehensive manner, even if this involves a certain amount of abstraction (Skog, Ljungblad, and Holmquist, 2003) or ambiguity (Gaver, Beaver, and Benford, 2003). In any case, users will eventually discover the system's functionality by simply observing others using it (Brignull and Rogers, 2003).

The aforementioned considerations refer to functional design requirements for public pervasive systems. A critical—yet nonfunctional—design consideration is the issue of privacy. Although we will discuss this topic in more detail in a forthcoming section, it is worth mentioning that, especially in public places, our interaction with a system may be visible to several persons including total strangers or "familiar strangers" (Paulos and Goodman, 2004), individuals whom we repeatedly observe and yet with whom we do not directly interact. Arguably, it is very difficult to separate the "private" from the "public" in such places. Vogel and Balakrishnan (2004) identify four interaction zones that may be applied to public pervasive systems, ranging from up-close explicit personal interaction to ambient implicit awareness regarding other users' interactions with system components. In particular, they distinguish among personal interactions (direct system use), subtle interactions (observations by individuals who are in close proximity to the person actually using the system), implicit interactions (peripheral notification when a user passes by), and ambient interactions (generic awareness of an individual's activities while using the system). Although private information (such as the personal identification number [PIN] in banks' automated teller machines [ATMs]) may be visible to others only when they enter the first two interaction spaces, any interaction of a user with the system (especially if it involves multimodal means) can raise the attention of other parties in the nearby area.

Table 2.8 summarizes the key characteristics of all four types of pervasive information systems.

Table 2.7

Public Pervasive Information Systems Functionality

Service category	Functionality	Examples
Informational	• Provision of real-time, ad-hoc information through ambient displays in public spaces • Provision of informational services to public indoor environments (museums, exhibitions, etc.) • Provision of Internet access through hotspots	• Interactive displays in hospitals (Dearden and Walker, 2003; Xiao et al., 2001) • Interactive displays in external spaces (Churchill et al. 2004; Kray, Kortuem, and Kruger, 2005; Vogel and Balakrishnan, 2004) • Museum guides (Bellotti et al., 2001; Fleck et al., 2002; Hsi and Fait, 2005; Ing, 1999; Yamada, Hong, and Sugita, 1995) • Travel guides (Abowd et al., 1997; Broadbent and Marti, 1997; Cheverst et al., 2000; Davies et al., 2001; Long et al., 1996)
Transactional	• Provision of e-government services • Provision of support services to public transportation	• TramMatena (Kjeldskov et al., 2003) • TESS (Gransart, Ambellouis, and Rioult, 2004) • Visions (Davies, Stock, and Wehmeyer, 2002)
Educational	• Provision of support services to campuses, schools, and other educational institutions • Course calendars • Notifications/alerts • Lecture broadcasting • New learning experiences	• KidPad (Benford et al., 2000) • eFuzion (Peiper et al., 2005) • E-Chalk (Friedland et al., 2004) • Ambient Horn (Randell et al., 2004)/Ambient Wood (Rogers et al., 2004) • Technology Learning Center (Kornkven, 2003) • MIT.EDU (Sung et al., 2004)
Communication	• E-mail • Chatting/instant messaging • Virtual communities • Interactive bulletin boards • Sharing and exchanging of files and multimedia content	• Dynamo (Izadi et al., 2003) • IM Here (Huang, Russell, and Sue, 2004) • YeTi (Yamada et al., 2004) • InfoRadar (Rantanen et al., 2004)
Entertainment	• Interactive multi-user gaming • Music and video content broadcasting	• FishPong (Yoon et al., 2004) • WorldBeat (Borchers, 1997)

Table 2.8

Characteristics of Personal, Domestic, Corporate, and Public Pervasive Information Systems

	Personal	Domestic	Corporate	Public
Provision	Provided by a private company for personal use	Private ownership, for use by members of a household/family	Provided by a private company	Provided by a community, municipality, or other public sector property
Coverage	Extremely small in scale, worn on a part of the human body	Very small in scale, applicable, for example, in the home environment, the car, and so on	Small in scale, applicable to a specific domain environment (e.g., the office, the warehouse, the retail outlet)	Large in scale, applicable to public areas (such as squares and parks), social units (such as towns, or cities); alternatively, small in scale, applicable to a specific public environment such as a museum, an exhibition, or a library
Functionality	Optimized to support task-specific operations (e.g., remote control of equipment)	Optimized for specific purposes in the home environment (e.g., infotainment, control of household appliances, etc.)	Optimized to automate or streamline particular business processes; alternatively, targeted to provide customers with multichannel access to corporate information/products	Flexible, in order to provide useful, usable resources to a wide range of potential users, individuals, and groups

Source: Adapted from Kostakos and O'Neill (2004).

Summary

The previous sections presented the design challenges for the service layer of PS. Based on this analysis, we highlight the following:

Smooth embedment of pervasive components (artifacts) to the physical space seems to be of equal importance for all PS types. The key consideration in this design challenge is to design the PS architecture in such a way that does not superimpose information technology on users, and, consequently, preserves the physical space so that the actual users of the system will recognize the relevance of technology to their practical activities and circumstances.

Privacy is of paramount importance, especially for corporate and public PS. This design challenge stems mainly from the capability of PS to collect personal information, store it, and process it in order to provide personalized services.

Finally, the design of easy-to-use interfaces is likely to increase the system's usability, and, consequently, its acceptance, especially by users who are not familiar with information technology.

THE SOCIAL LAYER

Introduction

PS consist of a multitude of heterogeneous tools/artifacts designed to perform a specific function. These tools perform the tasks for which they have been designed very well from a usability point of view. Until recently, the main purpose of information technology has been to make people more efficient in carrying out certain tasks. This is due to the use of traditional information systems in organizational contexts. However, as information technology is now being used far outside its origin in the office environment and scientific computation centers, and no longer by a selected group of business professionals and scientists, the traditional use of IT is being reconsidered. When information technology becomes totally pervasive, it will eventually be transformed from explicit use in specific situations to more or less continuous presence as a part of a designed environment.

Still, humans sometimes respond socially to IT artifacts. IT artifacts may be intentionally designed to encourage social responses, but more often, they affect people in social ways unimagined by their creators. Researchers have found, for example, that individuals expect machines with female voices, in contrast to computers with male voices, to give better advice on love and worse advice on technology (Nass, Moon, and Green, 1997). Social interface theory is built on the results of various studies demonstrating that humans respond socially in their interactions with artificial machines (Dryer, 1999; Kiesler and Sproull, 1997; Reeves and Nass, 1996). Humans are inclined to treat everything as social and natural. Therefore, whenever possible, they automatically and subconsciously use what they know about their natural and social experiences to help them with their technological experiences. Carroll (1990) describes an experiment in which simulated intelligent help was given to users. Although the users praised the help system for assisting them in certain situations, in other situations they blamed the system for their problems and attributed social traits to the system such as "fussy" and "untrustworthy."

In the case of PS, many features would seem to encourage social responses. For example, speech-based user interfaces have been proposed as an alternative to standard keyboards, because speech is a natural form of communication, uses little physical space, and offers high mobility. PS will often fulfill certain social roles for people, acting as assistants, delegates, or guides. These systems might also appear to have a considerable level of intelligence and ability to attain knowledge about the relationships among persons, places, and events. In addition, pervasive devices themselves will take on a personal nature by virtue of their extreme physical proximity. Pervasive social interactions may be excessive; individuals are already faced with the problem of being bombarded by too much information, and a new load of social information may be unnecessarily burdensome. Designers have a new challenge: to create successful "personalities" for the intimate devices that will live in people's cars, meeting rooms, shirt pockets, and even in their households.

Nevertheless, the social implications differ fundamentally based on the category into which a particular pervasive system falls. Public and corporate PS, due to their nature (increased numbers of users interacting with the system, each having different IT skills and experience), are highly embedded in society and thus have to follow certain norms and guidelines in order to be more "socially acceptable." On the other hand, domestic PS have a narrower social impact because they are restricted to the home environment and address more personal needs and requirements. Figure 2.4 illustrates the distinction among the four types of pervasive systems.

The increased social integration of PS suggests that their aesthetics and the smooth embedment of pervasive artifacts into the physical environment are of paramount importance. Researchers investigating this aspect have proposed new research agendas dedicated to designing philosophies

Figure 2.4   **Social Impact of Pervasive Information Systems**

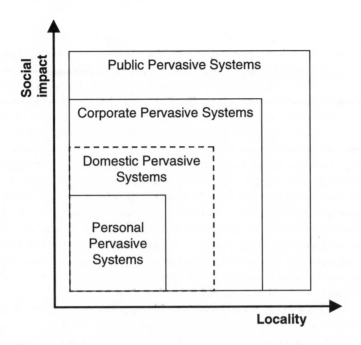

of a computer-augmented everyday life. In 1995 Weiser and Brown (1995) were the first to intro-duce the term "calm technology," explaining that technology should alternate between the center and the periphery of the user's consciousness in order to better convey informational context and to avoid sensory overload. Norman (1999) characterized this new design discipline as the "invis-ible computer," supporting users continuously during their everyday tasks. Hallnas and Redstrom (2001) introduced the term "slow technology," a design agenda for technology aimed at reflection and moments of mental rest rather than efficiency in performance, and also proposed specific design guidelines. Finally, the integration of pervasive technologies into the physical environ-ment raises *social concerns* mainly in the form of public pervasive systems where *privacy*, *trust*, and *conformity to rules and regulations* play an important role (Dryer, Eisbach, and Ark, 1999; Jessup and Robey, 2002). The following sections discuss some key social issues arising from the deployment of pervasive systems.

Security and Privacy in Pervasive Information Systems

User privacy has been a major concern in computer science since the late 1970s, when networks and distributed systems started to evolve, initially as a social issue (Agre, 2001; Hoffman, 1969) and then as a core organizational matter (Agre, 1999; Smith, 1993). With the embedment of computational material in everyday life, multiple surveys indicate that fear of privacy violations increases (Robbin, 2001). As Lahlou, Langheinrich, and Rocker (2005) observe, when the bound-aries between public and personal spaces merge, users tend to feel uncomfortable because they are no longer certain with whom they are sharing information. In fact, in the early 1990s, several visionary papers outlined the potential privacy risks driven by the widespread use of information technology in our lives (Baer, 1993; Dutton, 1992; Spector, 1993).

Privacy is about protection from intrusion and information gathering by others (Tavani and Moor, 2001). Therefore, privacy can be viewed as a term that embodies a duality of perspectives:

- The "claim," "entitlement," or "right" of any person to determine the degree of personal information that may be communicated to others (Schoeman, 1984; Walters, 2001).
- The ability to selectively maintain control over and make adjustments concerning (1) access to information about oneself, (2) the intimacies of personal identity, and (3) those possessing sensory information related to an individual (Altman, 1977; Bennett, 1992; Bennett and Grant, 1999; Gavison, 1980; Inness, 1992).

On the Internet, users interact with many remote computers. These computers have a variety of ways to collect information that may be used to characterize each individual. Usually, this information refers to the navigation path followed (commonly referred to as click-throughs), past transactions (at commercial Web sites), and the data that the individual submits to the system (such as demographics, behavioral information, etc.). In any case, users maintain a certain level of control over the information that they exchange with the remote system. Moreover, manipulation or processing of their personal information is prohibited by law unless the users themselves consent by intentionally agreeing to disclaimers. Although the aforementioned information may be used for direct marketing purposes, privacy breaches can lead to *identity theft* enabling others to conduct unauthorized financial transactions, alter or review medical histories, and so on.

The established portfolio of Internet privacy concerns and risks becomes blurred in PS environments. PS are capable of monitoring *what users do and how they do it*, and extrapolating *how they feel about doing it*. This is the result of the following properties of pervasive systems properties that augment privacy risks compared with online environments.

- *Diffusion.* Computerized artifacts may be embedded almost anywhere in the pervasive space, sensing and monitoring different types of information apart from those submitted by users through their interactions with the system. In effect, context awareness implies that the system may be in a continuous surveillance mode, capable of monitoring and processing personal information, such as the user's current location, activities, and even information related to the human body such as temperature, heartbeat, and respiration.
- *Storage and processing amplification.* Building on the aforementioned observation, personal information may be stored and processed in multiple places and communicated through nonsecure means (such as wireless networks). This amplification of memory and processing capabilities may lead to faster correlation and extrapolation of each individual's profile, not only affecting the individual but also creating social knowledge by constructing patterns, norms, and clusters of people, events, or places (Phillips, 2005).
- *Miniaturization and cloaking.* A pervasive environment may hide from users the number and type of sensing devices in operation. If a device is not explicitly visible or does not interact with the user, then it is highly probable that he or she will not be aware of its presence. Moreover, the need to smoothly integrate the participating pervasive devices into the physical environment, along with current miniaturization trends, may make even harder for users to detect them.
- *Visibility.* On the Internet, interactions occur through the desktop, a—more or less—personal access device. They are "black-box" and can pass completely unnoticed by outsiders. In PS, many interactions may occur in public places (public PS) or places with high concentrations of people (e.g., office environments). Consequently, not only the interactivity itself may be

visible to others, but also the user's *expressions and reactions* while using the system. This means that each individual's personal traits may be publicly visible, including body language, voice and speech tone, complexion, and so on.

To protect user privacy in online environments, several means have been established that can be classified in three broad categories:

- *Regulations and laws* enforced by governmental or other public bodies and to shape a generic framework that will govern the manipulation of personal information by (mainly commercial) parties.
- *Formation of social units,* comprising mainly nonprofit organizations to inform and advise the average consumer regarding privacy threats and/or violations. For example, the Privacy Rights Clearinghouse (www.privacyrights.org) acts as a forum that generates awareness on privacy-related subjects, responds to complaints from consumers, intercedes on their behalf, and, when appropriate, refers them to the proper organizations for further assistance.
- *Implementation of technical solutions* to secure online transactions, prevent repudiations, and protect personal identities.

A critical question to be answered is whether these means are adequate to protect user privacy in pervasive environments, especially taking into consideration the aforementioned risk factors. The Directive on Privacy and Electronic Communications (2002/58/EC) addresses mobility by preventing telecommunications companies from manipulating location-related information unless indicated by emergency or security conditions. This is a first attempt to address electronic transactions beyond the "desktop" paradigm. Still, this directive mainly addresses subscribers to mobile networks and not individuals who may use a public or commercial hotspot and who thus indirectly provide their location for the provision of location-based services (e.g., mobile advertising). Likewise, the directive does not address issues relating to the manipulation of sensory data or the extent to which a particular organization can deploy wireless sensor networks and what type of data they have the right to collect. Nevertheless, growing concerns and protests by consumer advocates will eventually force legislative bodies to revise their privacy protection laws. Recently, two protest campaigns were organized against the apparel manufacturer Benetton in Italy and the supermarket Tesco in the United Kingdom (Ohkubo, Suzuki, and Kinoshita, 2005). In particular, the Consumers Against Supermarket Privacy Invasion and Numbering (CASPIAN, www.nocards. org) criticized Benetton's and Tesco's plans to attach RFID tags to their products in 2003, which led to a boycott of Benetton's products.

The technical dimension of the problem is more straightforward. Researchers have already suggested for the online environment several technical solutions that enable individuals to manage their personal privacy and express their subjective expectations of privacy (Cavoukian, 1999; Davies, 1999; Goldman, 1999; Reidenberg, 1999). These are commonly referred to as "privacy-enabling technologies" or PETs. Burkert (1998) defines PETs as "technical and organizational concepts that aim at protecting personal identity." This definition clearly distinguishes among the components of PETs, which suggest *conceptual principles* that are supported by adequate *technical solutions.* These solutions mainly derive from established security schemes and involve encryption in the form of digital signatures, blind signatures, anonymizing agents, or pseudonym agents (Burkert, 1998; Cranor, 1999).

In the context of PS, many researchers have attempted to apply the suggestions of PETs in order to accommodate the new requirements for privacy protection. As such, most of these efforts emphasize avoiding the unnecessary disclosure of necessary information to a third party as well as masking the information transmitted so that it cannot be associated with an individual. Examples in the literature appear in the works of Beckwith (2003), Bellotti and Sellen (1993), Beresford and Stajano (2003), Jacobs and Abowd (2003), Jiang and Landay (2002), Langheinrich (2001), Palen and Dourish (2003), and Pottie (2004), among others. We classify these efforts into three broad categories:

- *Guidelines, principles, frameworks, or suggestions* that should be taken into consideration during the design process of a pervasive system. Langheinrich (2001) proposed six design principles for privacy-aware pervasive systems (clear notice, explicit consent, support for anonymity and pseudonimity, disclosure of information only to proximate entities, adequate security, and regulated access and recourse), which were later implemented in the Panther Access to Web Services (PAWS) system enabling users to negotiate their privacy preferences through trusted devices (Langheinrich, 2002). The most recent effort to develop privacy-related guidelines has been accomplished by the project Ambient Agoras, which belongs under the umbrella of the disappearing computer initiative. The project proposes nine privacy design guidelines that may be applied in pervasive computing environments,[4] and aims explicitly to incorporate privacy considerations early in the design process, making privacy a core design objective. These are *generic* design principles that may be applied to all types of pervasive systems. It should be noted that several authors have proposed specific guidelines pertaining to privacy protection in particular types of pervasive systems. For example, Gunther and Spiekermann (2005) and Pottie (2004) propose design considerations that may be applied to RFID-augmented pervasive retail systems, while Duri and colleagues (2002) have developed a framework for privacy-aware automotive telematics computing platforms.
- *Tools, protocols, and platforms* that embed privacy protection mechanisms. Hong and Landay (2004) developed Confab, a toolkit that facilitates the construction of privacy-sensitive pervasive applications. Kong and Hong (2003) proposed ANODR, a routing protocol addressing the problems of route anonymity and location privacy. Beresford and Stajano (2003) proposed the Mix Zones, an infrastructure that delays and reorders messages within a network to confuse an observer. Gruteser and Grunwald (2003) proposed a mechanism based on temporal and spatial cloaking where a trusted proxy manages location-related information based on the density of users in a region. Brodie and colleagues (2005) developed a policy management workbench entitled SPARCLE. Kaufman, Edlund, and Ford (2002) proposed the Social Contract Core and Agrawal and colleagues (2005) proposed XPref, both XML-based specifications that extend the Platform for Privacy Preferences (P3P) properties used on the Internet (Cranor et al., 2002).
- *Hardware solutions* to protect user privacy. For example, Juels, Rivest, and Szydlo (2003) implemented the Blocker Tag, a special RFID tag that may selectively prevent RF-readers from identifying its contents.

The protection of user privacy is directly related to user feelings of safety and trust with respect to using the system since their perception that their personal information may be publicly available may deter them from using and adopting pervasive environments. Nevertheless, to what extent should we follow these privacy protection guidelines? Is it possible that overprotecting a user may affect the quality of service provided by the pervasive system? We agree with Altman (1975) that privacy should be a dialectic and dynamic boundary regulation process. It should be a process of trade-offs among social entities: people, institutions, groups, and organizations. Privacy should be regulated and understood based on the expectations and experiences of all parties involved. Palen and Dourish (2003) specify three privacy management boundaries that may be applied to pervasive environments. These are:

- The *disclosure* boundary, which suggests that individuals should maintain selective disclosure of personal information.
- The *identity* boundary, which suggests that either parties involved in a communication or transaction should maintain their identities but reveal them only if required (e.g., for authentication purposes in a financial transaction).
- The *temporal* boundary, which suggests that any privacy management scheme depends on the time the transaction or communication occurs.

In the previous sections we argued that strict privacy protection rules and mechanisms should be applied in public pervasive systems where social borders are loose. Indeed, when a pervasive system applies to close social groups (such as families, coworkers, etc.), privacy concerns seem to be less important. System users already share close relationships and tend to know a great deal of personal information about each other. This does not imply that the aforementioned generic rules should not be incorporated into these systems. The first rule (control of disclosed information) should most definitely be supported to prevent unwanted social border crossings (e.g., reading personal information that was not intended for anyone else).

Designing Pervasive Information Systems for Everyday Life

Pervasive systems imply that information technology is increasingly used in everyday life. We can argue that these IT artifacts enter our *lifeworld*. As we take them for granted, they often become more than just tools to be used to accomplish given tasks. Contemporary information systems, in the form of personal computers or other stationary access devices, were designed to fit into an office environment and the activities taking place there. They were designed to be efficient tools in the hands of professionals. Thus, their interaction design practice is directed toward this setting. Obviously, everyday life is quite different from office work, and, therefore, other "places," interfaces, and appearances must be explored to find a broader repertoire of strategies for creating human-centered technology. Moreover, these systems are designed *for use*; this means that their design and evaluation are accomplished on the basis of some definition of their functionality and perceived usage. Thus, designers seek a solution that satisfies the basic criteria for usability such as efficiency in use, low error rate, and support for recovery from error, based on a general knowledge about what to do and what not to do to meet such criteria (Hackos and Redish, 1998; Nielsen, 1994). The objective is to achieve *maximum usability* with respect to a general, precise notion of use, and design is motivated by this ambition.

Although use is still a very important driver of design, the notion of the *user* is somewhat blurred (Grudin, 1993). Interactions are physically embedded, which means that they may refer to human–artifact, artifact–artifact, or even human–human interactions (Shafer, Brummitt, and Cadiz, 2001). This notion of "living with" rather than "simply using" information technology introduces significant novel elements to designers of PS. According to Hansmann and colleagues (2003), information access and management should be applicable without the need to spend significant time learning how to use the technology. In contrast to a desktop environment where the user is always *actively* involved with the system, pervasive systems should be capable of supporting *passive users* who may not even be aware that such systems exists. To this end, the traditional lever of usability that drives the design process of desktop systems should be reconsidered for the design of PS.

Moreover, PS revisit the sequence based on which a user interacts with the system. In traditional computing environments, the user is the trigger that initiates interaction with the system. Pervasive computing suggests that the system itself is capable of triggering interaction with the system. This can be accomplished through sensors that are deployed in the physical environment. For example, the SmartKG pervasive system is able to "sense" whether a child is isolated from the other children and automatically inform a kindergarten teacher (Chen et al., 2002); the Smart Doorplate system automatically navigates office workers to the closest exit if it "senses" that they are lost (Trumler et al., 2003); sensors have been deployed in a vineyard to constantly monitor the conditions in wine barrels to notify workers if any problems occur, and biological and habitat research to provide valuable information (Burrell, Brooke, and Beckwith, 2004).

Finally, pervasive system users should not be overwhelmed by information technology. In essence, any IT artifacts that are components of the pervasive system (e.g., sensors, actuators, etc.) should be naturally conceived as *an extension* of the physical environment. It should be noted that this smooth integration does not suggest that information technology be completely invisible to system users, as implied by many researchers (Norman, 1999; Satyanarayanan, 2001; Weiser, 1993, 2002). On the contrary, following Redstrom (2001), we believe that pervasive technology should be governed by *meaningful presence* promoting unobtrusiveness. Invisibility poses a dilemma. On the one hand, it is desirable to hide the infrastructure of computer technology from its users, because it can potentially make the PS easier to use and comprehend. A common view is that most users seem to have no interest in how a technology works as long as it does work. On the other hand, completely obliterating IT may cause frustrations in the form of *perceived system exclusion* (Kostakos and O'Neill, 2004). If we do not know how to access the system, we will not be able to use it. Moreover, in case of system failure or error, it will be difficult to identify the failed component, not to mention to proceed to corrective actions. In this chapter we propose that invisibility should be comprehended differently; instead of designing to hide pervasive technology *from the physical space,* we should focus on hiding the pervasive technology *from the user's consciousness* allowing him to interact with the system at an almost subconscious level. Thus, the challenge is to design systems in such a way that users perceive them as *part of the environment.* Universal design principles (Story, Mueller, and Mace, 1998) may be applied to create reminders allowing for system usage with minimal distraction.

Consequently, *aesthetics* receive increased attention during the design of a pervasive system, especially in terms of ensuring that the supporting pervasive system components are indeed smoothly embedded in the physical environment. Still, this does not mean that designers should simply give a new and more colorful shell (Djajadiningrat, Gaver, and Fres, 2000) to pervasive systems artifacts. Aesthetic "beauty" should be seen in terms of interaction of the system with the user and the environment in a way that does not disrupt the user's performance of a task.

The first goal of aesthetics is the enhancement of user experience. Preece, Rogers, and Sharp (2002) were the first to introduce the notion of a transition from traditional human–computer interaction to interaction design. According to them "the goals of designing interactive products to be fun, enjoyable, pleasurable, aesthetically pleasing and so on are concerned primarily with the user experience. By this we mean what the interaction with the system feels like to the users. . . . Hence, user experience goals differ from the more objective usability goals in that they are concerned with how users experience an interactive product from their perspective, rather than assessing how useful or productive a system is from its own perspective." Similar notions appear in the PS literature as "beauty in interaction" (Djajadiningrat et al., 2004), "beauty in use" (ibid.), "aesthetics of interaction" (ibid.), "aesthetics of use" (Dunne, 2006; Petersen et al., 2004), and "aesthetics of functionality" (Hallnas and Redstrom, 2001). All of these notions relate to a property additional to just static appearance of the design product; they are concerned with expressions of what we do with it.

This leads us to the notion of meaningful presence for PS artifacts. Meaningful presence concerns the existence of pervasive artifacts on the basis of an act of invitation and acceptance. In particular, an artifact can be the bearer of certain expressions as we encounter it or use it in our everyday or work lives. The focus here is on the internal structure of a design and its inner logic. As such, PS designers should explore how computational artifacts build their presence when they are embedded in the physical environment, their expression as design material, and the relation between spatial and temporal form elements in the combination of computational (IT) and traditional design materials (Hallnas and Redstrom, 2001, 2002). At the same time, this fusion of the physical with the virtual should take into consideration the architectural and structural qualities of the environment.

Hallnas and Redstrom (2001), building on previous work from Redstrom (2001), introduce the term *expressional interaction*, referring to artifacts designed to be the bearer of certain *expressions*, instead of simply the bearer of a certain *functionality*. Aesthetics represent the natural means to create positive or negative expressions pertaining to the interaction of a user with a pervasive information system. Indeed, pervasive information systems revisit the traditional interactions between man and machine (Thackara, 2001). The new paradigm suggests that a user may interact with multiple pervasive artifacts simultaneously (e.g., access devices, sensors that collect, process, and disseminate contextual information, etc.), and the user might not even be aware that these are present in the surrounding environment. This notion of "invisibility" is closely related to the appearance of pervasive artifacts. If users consider a pervasive artifact as part of the natural environment, then they will not express feelings of discomfort or disturbance about its physical presence.

To design with aesthetics in focus means to concentrate on appearance as constituting the essence of things—how a thing manifests itself in a world of expressions (Zaccai, 1995). Moreover, retaining this focus provides pervasive information systems designers with a clear advantage: instead of trying to *conceal* pervasive artifacts in the environment, they can *manipulate* the material forming their external appearance so that for users they constitute "just another everyday life object," such as a doorknob, a coffee cup, and so on. Norman (2002a) provides an extensive discussion on how we should treat the design of everyday objects. In his view, design products (regardless of whether they consist of commodity objects or sophisticated information systems) should be both useful and beautiful since attractive things work better (Norman, 2002b).

Thus, one of the more prevalent tendencies at this time is to design for emotions (Desmet and Dijkhuis, 2003; Monk, 2000; Nielsen, 2002; Overbeeke et al., 2002; Shusterman, 1992). Most of this work focuses primarily on the properties of form as perceived visually, with vague relationships to the functionality and instrumentality of systems. The objectives of this kind of design are pleasure and attraction, emphasizing the design of smart and seductive user interfaces. However, the "aesthetic design" of pervasive artifacts does not mean that designers should simply give them a new and more colorful shell (Djajadiningrat, Gaver, and Fres, 2000). Aesthetic "beauty" can also be seen in terms of interaction of the system with the user and the environment. Petersen and colleagues (2004) explicitly consider aesthetics as a core interaction element focusing on the experiential aspects of an information system. Indeed, pervasive information systems may create new experiences for their users, especially if these systems provide users with alternative means of conducting particular tasks (e.g., an interactive visit to the museum, accurate navigation of the user in an exhibition environment, automatic translation of a lecture in a seminar, etc.). Finally, pervasive information systems designers should embed aesthetic attributes in the early phases of the design process and not simply consider them as "an added bonus" (Fogarty, Forlizzi, and Hudson, 2001).

Designing Pervasive Information Systems for All

As mentioned in the previous section, the profile of pervasive systems users is—at best—uncertain. Taking into consideration the users of the different implementations of pervasive tour guides (Abowd et al. 1997; Bederson 1995; Bellotti et al. 2001; Davies et al., 2001), users can range from people who are vaguely familiar with information technology (mainly due to their interaction with commonplace IT artifacts such as mobile phones) to people who are technophobic, even if only in extreme cases. Moreover, these types of users are *opportunistic* in the sense that they will use the system for a particular time frame and for a particular reason (in this example, to augment their visiting experience). To this end, it is highly unlikely that these users will be subject to thorough training in the system's use. As a result, pervasive systems should be able to support all of the different user types by employing sufficient means of enhancing or facilitating their interaction with the pervasive system while at the same time hasting their learning curve.

Still, pervasive systems might also be used by people who are very experienced and competent in using information technology; at the same time, continuous or frequent use of the system can be considered "informal training," implying that inexperienced users will eventually develop the skills necessary to use even the most advanced features of the pervasive system. Finally, designers should incorporate into the system's design the ability to identify users' current skills and to adapt, providing advanced features as required.

It should be noted that in some cases a PS designer might need to incorporate particular elements that "attract" users to the system and increase their motivation. Studies in the wearable computing literature (Fickas, Kortuem, and Segall, 1997; Hull, Neaves, and Bedford-Roberts, 1997; Hull, Reid, and Geelhoed, 2002; Pascoe, 1998; Rekimoto, Ayatsuka, and Hayashi, 1998; Smailagic and Siewiorek, 2002; Starner, 1996) have revealed that, apart from the expected elements of a wearable computing system (appearance, ergonomics, and user model), user experience is affected (and sometimes enhanced) by the introduction of application probes (such as aesthetic elements or sounds/music) into the wearable system.

This unpredictability of users raises another problem for PS designers. Since the user is not known in advance, the requirements elicitation phase is characterized by increased uncertainty due to the fact that designers will not have the luxury of systematic requirements analysis; they must plan for very infrequent use of the PS (at least in terms of user sessions), implying that the design process should clearly identify the various—and sometimes opposite—needs and wants of the system users, and they cannot even assume that the intended users will want to use the PS at all, or that they can be required to do so.

Finally, in some extreme cases, PS designers may not be able to collect feedback from the actual system users due to their inability to provide tangible (and valuable) system requirements. Consider the smart kindergarten pervasive system discussed by Chen and colleagues (2002). The main users of the system are small children, who, by definition, cannot participate actively during the requirements analysis phase. This constraint forces PS designers to search for additional actors (in the aforementioned case, the children's teachers and external psychologists) to act as system requirements providers based on their experience with the domain in which the PS will be applied.

Environmental Challenges for Pervasive Information Systems

A final social issue, yet one rarely raised by researchers, in the design of PS is their environmental impact. Embedding computational devices in the environment may ultimately lead to pollution in terms of physical waste and energy consumption. Although the actual environmental implications of PS will be apparent in forthcoming years, some are evident today. The most overt example is the saturation of wireless frequencies and especially the band of 2.4 GHz within which multiple wireless networks operate (e.g., Bluetooth, RFID, IEEE 802.11b, IEEE 802.11g). Likewise, energy consumption (and consequent waste in the form of dead batteries or other chemical power sources) is a critical issue in PS design. Although mobile and wireless devices gradually become more energy efficient, their overall energy consumption increases due to their exponential growth in numbers and the integration of more sophisticated and energy-consuming peripherals. Jain and Wullert (2002) summarized the environmental challenges for pervasive information systems design, pointing out the following considerations:

- Minimize as much as possible physical materials and energy usage, while at the same time sharing—if possible—resources and power among the participating computing artifacts (Anderson and Kubiatowicz, 2002).
- Do not store redundant information, while at the same time installing only the software that is absolutely necessary for manipulating the stored information.
- Recycle waste materials/obsolete devices to extract new raw materials.

Summary

Social design challenges are horizontal for all PS types. Protection of privacy information seems to be the most important design challenge. In effect, PS designers need to assess whether the pervasive system that they design raises any privacy concerns. This analysis should be conducted during the early stages of the design process so that designers can incorporate sufficient privacy protection mechanism at the design level.

Moreover, we have observed that privacy concerns rise exponentially depending on the social impact of the PS. Specifically, those who design public and corporate PS may need to more thoroughly address the issue of privacy than those who design personal or domestic PS. This is attributed to the characteristics of the entity that provides the PS, and a lack of familiarity between expected users. Indeed, in close social groups (such as a family), privacy concerns seem to be less important. Conversely, in an organizational setting, privacy may be the determinant of user trust with respect to the pervasive system.

Moreover, this section identified that usability and aesthetics seem to affect the perceived usefulness of the PS. This is the result of the unpredictability of PS user profiles regarding IT expertise. According to PS scholars, providing natural and easy-to-use user interfaces will, most likely, increase the system's usefulness while at the same time minimizing user learning curves.

Finally, this section recognized the importance of aesthetics as a determinant of smooth placement of pervasive artifacts in the physical environment. According to this challenge, if users consider a pervasive artifact as part of the natural environment, they will not express feelings of discomfort or disturbance about its physical presence. Consequently, the aesthetic properties of pervasive artifacts should be addressed during the design of a PS.

We should acknowledge that this section also recognized the importance of protecting the environment from "waste materials" such as increased energy/radiation usage, redundant information, obsolete devices, and so on. While these are important design challenges, we believe that they should be addressed by regulatory bodies rather than system designers. Indeed, over the past few years, we have witnessed several attempts in both the European Union and the United States to register wireless hotspots as a first attempt to minimize bottlenecks in the frequencies of 2.4 and 5 GHz. Consequently, we expect that when the total number of implemented PS reaches a critical level, regulatory bodies will eventually intervene in order to protect the environment.

CONCLUSIONS

The previous sections classified the design capabilities and challenges for PS into three broad categories: infrastructure (technological), service, and social. Based on this analysis, we conclude that PS introduce new elements in multiple dimensions, spanning different IS domains, such as human–computer interaction and software engineering, which admonish us to examine them as a new class of information systems. In essence, PS revisit the way we interact with computers by introducing new input modalities and system capabilities.

So far, PS design has stemmed from practice. It is a trial-and-error process. Thus, the knowledge generated to date presents only fragments of the PS picture as a whole. Since PS is a technology-driven phenomenon, some efforts that attempt to guide designers in a systematic way also perceive PS design from a technical perspective. Others, view PS design from a purely social perspective and emphasize privacy management or environmental management issues. Indeed, most current PS implementations follow a vertical, ad hoc approach, implementing from scratch all of the required elements based on the unique characteristics of the application domain. Based on the above, we classify the current design areas for PS into three broad categories:

- *Engineering-oriented design* to provide solutions or toolkits for the various PS technical challenges. Design research in this area emphasizes the specification of efficient middleware solutions, context representation and management mechanisms, and sensor fusion.
- *Interaction-oriented design* to provide guidelines on how users may interact with a pervasive system.
- *Application-oriented design* to provide generic guidelines for the development of PS in specific application domains, such as office environments, public areas, and so on.
- *Social-oriented design* to generate guidelines for the development of socially accepted PS emphasizing environmental and privacy-related issues.

This chapter provides an aggregated approach to describe PS characteristics and prescribe alternative approaches that may assist designers during PS development. Moreover, it represents the only consolidated approach, to our knowledge, that investigates the problem of PS design. In any case, PS will be a fertile source of challenging research problems for many years to come. Solving these problems will require IS scholars to fuse multiple disparate research areas (e.g., human–computer interaction, distributed systems, operating systems, and software engineering, to name a few) and to revisit long-standing design assumptions in others. Still, while several research challenges remain in all areas of PS, most of the basic component technologies exist today. Hence, in the near future, we can expect several commercial implementations of PS that will be an indistinguishable part of our everyday lives.

NOTES

1. SUN JAVA 2 Micro and Enterprise Editions. http://java.sun.com.
2. R. Katz, Sahara Overview. http://sahara.cs.berkeley.edu.

3. See also J. Chu and G.P. Morrison, *Enhancing the customer shopping experience: 2002 IBM/NRF "Store of the Future" survey.*

4. S. Lahlou and F. Jegou, *European Disappearing Computer Privacy Design Guidelines Version 1.1.* Available at http://www.ambientagoras.org/downloads/D15%5B1%5D.4_-_Privacy_Design_Guidelines.pdf

REFERENCES

Abowd, G.D. 1999. Classroom 2000: An experiment with the instrumentalization of a living educational environment. *IBM Systems Journal,* 38, 4, 508–530.

Abowd, G.D. and Mynatt, E.D. 2000. Charting past, present, and future research in ubiquitous computing. *ACM Transactions on Computer-Human Interaction,* 7, 1, 29–58.

Abowd, G.D.; Mynatt, E.D.; and Rodden, T. 2002. The human experience. *IEEE Pervasive Computing,* 1, 1, 48–57.

Abowd, G.D.; Atkeson, C.G.; Hong, J.; Long, S.; Kooper, R.; and Pinkerton, M. 1997. Cyberguide: A mobile context-aware tour guide. *Wireless Networks,* 3, 5, 421–433.

Abraham, S.; Meylan, A.; and Nanda, S. 2005. 802.11n MAC design and system performance. In *Proceedings of the IEEE International Conference on Communications (ICC 2005).* Seoul, 2957–2961.

Agamanolis, S. 2003. Designing displays for human connectedness. In K. O'Hara, M. Perry, E.F. Churchill, and D.M. Russell, eds., *Public and Situated Displays. Social and Interactional Aspects of Shared Display Technologies.* Norwell, MA: Kluwer, 309–334.

Agrawal, R.; Kiernan, J.; Srikant, R.; and Xu, Y. 2005. XPref: A preference language for P3P. *Computer Networks,* 48, 5, 809–827.

Agre, P. 1999. The architecture of identity: Embedding privacy in market institutions. *Information, Communication, and Society,* 2, 1, 1–25.

———. 2001. Changing places: Contexts of awareness in computing. *Human-Computer Interaction,* 16, 2–4, 177–192.

Alt, R. and Puschmann, T. 2005. Developing customer process orientation: The case of Pharma Corp. *Business Process Management Journal,* 11, 4, 297–315.

Altman, I. 1975. *The Environment and Social Behavior: Privacy, Personal Space, Territory and Crowding.* Monterey, CA: Brooks/Cole.

———. 1977. Privacy regulation: Culturally universal or culturally specific? *Journal of Social Issues,* 33, 3, 66–84.

Anderson, D.P. and Kubiatowicz, J. 2002 The worldwide computer. *Scientific American* March, 40–47.

Arora, A.; Dutta, P.; Bapat, S.; Kulathumani, V.; Zhang, H.; Naik, V.; Mittal, V.; Cao, H.; Demirbas, M.; Gouda, M.; Choi, Y.; Herman, T.; Kulkarni, S.; Arumugam, U.; Nesterenko, M.; Vora, A.; and Miyashita, M. 2004. A line in the sand: A wireless sensor network for target detection, classification, and tracking. *Computer Networks,* 46, 5, 605–634.

Ashok, R.L. and Agrawal, D.P. 2003. Next-generation wearable networks. *IEEE Computer,* 36, 11, 31–39.

Asthana, R.; Cravatts, M.; and Krzyzanowski, P. 1994. An indoor wireless system for personalized shopping assistance. In *Proceedings of the IEEE Workshop on Mobile Computing Systems and Applications.* Santa Cruz, CA: IEEE Computer Society Press, 69–74.

Asunmaa, P.; Inkinen, S.; Nykanen, P.; Paivarinta, S.; Suormunen, T.; and Suoknuuti, M. 2002. Introduction to Mobile Internet Technical Architecture. *Wireless Personal Communications: An International Journal,* 22, 2, 253–259.

Baber, C.; Knight, J.; Haniff, D.; and Cooper, L. 1999. Ergonomics of wearable computers. *Mobile Networks and Applications,* 4, 1, 15–21.

Baer, W.S. 1993. Technology's challenges to the First Amendment. *Telecommunications Policy,* 17, 1, 3–13.

Bahl, P. and Padmanabhan, V. 2000. RADAR: An in-building RF-based user location and tracking system. In *Proceedings of the IEEE Infocom 2000.* Los Alamitos, CA: IEEE Computer Society Press, 775–784.

Banavar, G. and Bernstein, A. 2002. Software infrastructure and design challenges for ubiquitous computing applications. *Communications of the ACM,* 45, 12, 92–96.

Barfield, W. and Thomas, C., eds. 2001. *Fundamentals of Wearable Computers and Augmented Reality.* Mahwah, NJ: Lawrence Erlbaum.

Beckwith, R. 2003. Designing for ubiquity: The perception of privacy. *IEEE Pervasive Computing,* 2, 2, 40–46.

Bederson, B.B. 1995. Audio augmented reality: A prototype automated tour guide. In *Proceedings of the ACM Conference on Human Factors in Computing (CHI '95)*. New York: ACM Press, 210–211.

Beigl, M.; Gellersen, H.W.; and Schmidt, A. 2001. Mediacups: Experience with design and use of computer-augmented everyday artefacts. *Computer Networks,* 35, 4, 401–409.

Bellotti, F.; Berta, R.; De Gloria, A.; and Margarone, M. 2001. User testing a hypermedia tour guide. *IEEE Pervasive Computing,* 1, 2, 33–41.

Bellotti, V. and Sellen, A. 1993. Design for privacy in ubiquitous computing environments. In *Proceedings of the Third European Conference on Computer Supported Cooperative Work (ECSCW '93)*: New York: Springer, 77–92.

Benford, S.; Bederson, B. B.; Akesson, K.; Bayon, V.; Druin, A.; Hansson, P.; Hourcade, J.P.; Ingram, R.; Neale, H.; O'Malley, C.; Simsarian, K.; Stanton, D.; Sundblad, Y.; and Taxén, G. 2000. Designing story-telling technologies to encourage collaboration between young children. In *Proceedings of the Conference on Human Factors in Computing Systems*. New York: ACM Press, 556–564.

Bennett, C.J. 1992. *Regulating Privacy.* Ithaca, NY: Cornell University Press.

Bennett, C.J. and Grant, R., eds. 1999. *Visions of Privacy: Policy Choices for the Digital Age.* Toronto: University of Toronto Press.

Bennewitz, M.; Faber, F.; Joho, D.; Schreiber, M.; and Behnke, S. 2005. Towards a humanoid museum guide robot that interacts with multiple persons. In *Proceedings of the Fifth IEEE-RAS International Conference on Humanoid Robots*. IEEE Press, 418–423.

Beresford, A.R. and Stajano, F. 2003. Location privacy in pervasive computing. *IEEE Pervasive Computing,* 2, 1, 46–55.

Betts, B. 2006. Smart sensors. *IEEE Spectrum,* 43, 4, 50–53.

Bianchi, G.; Tinnirello, I.; and Scalia, L. 2005. Understanding 802.11e contention-based prioritization mechanisms and their coexistence with legacy 802.11 stations. *IEEE Network,* 19, 4, 28–34.

Bjork, S.; Falk, J.; Hansson, R.; and Ljungstrand, P. 2001. Pirates! Using the physical world as a game board. In *Proceedings of the Conference on Human-Computer Interaction*. Tokyo: ACM Press, 119–120.

Bjork, S.; Holopainen, J.; Ljungstrand, P.; and Akesson, K. 2002. Designing ubiquitous computing games—A report from a workshop exploring ubiquitous computing entertainment. *Personal and Ubiquitous Computing,* 6, 443–458.

Bobick, A.F. 1999. The KidsRoom: A perceptually-based interactive and immersive story environment. *Presence,* 8, 4, 369–393.

Bocquet, M.; Loyez, C.; and Benlarbi-Delai, A. 2005. Embedded technologies: Millimeter wave up-converted UWB based positioning system. In *Proceedings of the Conference on Smart Objects and Ambient Intelligence: Innovative Context-Aware Services: Usages and Technologies*. New York: ACM Press, 293–296.

Borriello, G. 2005. RFID: Tagging the world (Editorial). *Communications of the ACM,* 48, 9, 34–37.

Borriello, G. and Want, R. 2000. Embedded computation meets the World Wide Web. *Communications of the ACM,* 43, 5, 59–66.

Brand, S. 1994. *How Buildings Learn.* New York: Viking.

Brignull, H. and Rogers, Y. 2003. Enticing people to interact with large public displays in public spaces. In *Proceedings of the INTERACT Conference,* Amsterdam: IOS Press, 17–24.

Broadbent, J. and Marti, P. 1997. Location aware mobile interactive guides: Usability issues. In *Proceedings of the Fourth International Conference on Hypermedia and Interactivity in Museums (ICHIM97),* 162–172.

Brodie, C.; Karat, C.M.; Karat, J.; and Feng, J. 2005. Usable security and privacy: A case study of developing privacy management tools. In *Proceedings of the Symposium on Usable Privacy and Security (SOUPS)*. ACM International Conference Proceeding Series, vol. 93. New York: ACM Press, 35–43.

Brooks, R. 1997. The Intelligent Room Project. In *Proceedings of the Second International Cognitive Technology Conference*. Los Alamitos, CA: IEEE Computer Society Press, 271.

Brown, M.G. 1996. Supporting user mobility. In *Proceedings of the IFIP Conference on Mobile Communications (IFIP'96)*. Chapman & Hall, 69–77.

Brown, P.J. 1996. The stick-e document: A framework for creating context-aware applications. In *Proceedings of the IFIP Electronic Publishing '96*. Chapman & Hall, 259–272.

Brown, P.J.; Bovey, J.D.; and Chen, X. 1997. Context-aware applications: From the laboratory to the marketplace. *IEEE Personal Communications,* 4, 5, 58–64.

Burkert, H. 1998. Privacy-enhancing technologies: Typology, critique, vision. In P.E. Agre M. and Rotenberg, eds., *Technology and Privacy: The New Landscape*. Cambridge: MIT Press, 125–142.

Burrell, J.; Brooke, T.; and Beckwith, R. 2004. Vineyard computing: Sensor networks in agricultural production. *IEEE Pervasive Computing*, 3, 1, 38–45.

Buscher, M.; Kramp, G.; and Gall Krogh, P. 2003. In formation: Support for flexibility, mobility, collaboration, and coherence. *Personal and Ubiquitous Computing*, 7, 136–146.

Buttery, S. and Sago, A. 2003. Future applications of Bluetooth. *BT Technology Journal*, 21, 3, 48–55.

Cabri, G.; Leonardi, L.; and Zambonelli, F. 2002. Engineering mobile agent applications via context-dependent coordination. *IEEE Transactions on Software Engineering*, 28, 1039–1055.

Cardinali, R., and Lombardo, L.M.-G.P. 2006. UWB ranging accuracy in high- and low-data-rate applications. *IEEE Transactions on Microwave Theory and Techniques*, 54, 4, 1865–1875.

Carroll, J.M. 1990. *The Nurnberg Funnel: Designing Minimalist Instruction for Practical Computer Skill*. Cambridge: MIT Press.

Carter, S.; Churchill, E.F.; Denoue, L.; Helfman, J.; and Nelson, L. 2004. Digital graffiti: Public annotation of multimedia content. In *Proceedings of the Conference on Human Factors in Computing Systems*. New York: ACM Press, 1207–1210.

Caswell, D., and Debaty, P. 2000. Creating Web representations for places. In *Proceedings of the Second International Symposium on Handheld and Ubiquitous Computing*. Lecture Notes in Computer Science, vol. 1927. London: Springer-Verlag, 114–126.

Cavoukian, A. 1999. The promise of privacy-enhancing technologies: Applications in health information networks. In C.J. Bennett and R. Grant, eds., *Visions of Privacy: Policy Choices for a Digital Age*. Toronto: University of Toronto Press, 116–128.

Cayirci, E.; Govindan, R.; Znati, T.; and Srivastava, M. 2003. Wireless sensor networks (Editorial). *Computer Networks*, 43, 4, 417–419.

Chaczko, Z.; Ahmad, F.; and Mahadevan, V. 2005. Wireless sensors in network based collaborative environments. In *Proceedings of the Sixth International Conference on Information Technology Based Higher Education and Training (ITHET 2005)*. Los Alamitos, CA: IEEE Computer Society Press, 7–13.

Chan, H. and Perrig, A. 2003. Security and privacy in sensor networks. *IEEE Computer*, 36, 10, 103–105.

Chandrakasan, A. 1999. Design considerations for distributed microsensor systems. In *Proceedings of the IEEE Custom Integrated Circuits Conference*. Los Alamitos, CA: IEEE Computer Society Press, 279–286.

Chatzigiannakis, I.; Nikoletseas, S.; and Spirakis, P. 2002. Efficient communication: Smart dust protocols for local detection and propagation. In *Proceedings of the Second ACM International Workshop on Principles of Mobile Computing*. New York: ACM Press, 9–16.

Chen, A.; Muntz, R.R.; Yuen, S.; Locher, I.; Park, S.I.; and Srivastava, M.B. 2002. A support infrastructure for the smart kindergarten. *IEEE Pervasive Computing*, 1, 2, 49–57.

Cheok, A.D.; Goh, K.H.; Liu, W.; Farbiz, F.; Fong, S.W.; Teo, S.L.; Li, Y.; and Yang, X. 2004. Human Pacman: A mobile, wide-area entertainment system based on physical, social, and ubiquitous computing. *Personal and Ubiquitous Computing*, 8, 2, 71–81.

Cheverst, K.; Davies, N.; Mitchell, K.; Friday, A.; and Efstratiou, C. 2000. Developing a context-aware electronic tourist guide: Some issues and experiences. In *Proceedings of the ACM Human Factors in Computing (CHI'00)*. New York: ACM Press, 17–24.

Cheverst, K. et al. 2001. The role of a shared context in supporting cooperation between city visitors. *IEEE Computer Graphics and Applications*, 25, 4, 555–562.

Chi, E.H.; Song, J.; and Corbin, G. 2004. "Killer App" of wearable computing: Wireless force sensing body protectors for martial arts. *CHI Letters*, 6, 2, 277–285.

Chivers, H., and Clark, J.A. 2004. Smart dust, friend or foe? Replacing identity with configuration trust. *Computer Networks*, 46, 5, 723–740.

Choi, H.H.; Song, O.; and Cho, D.H. 2005. A seamless handoff scheme for UMTS-WLAN interworking. In *Proceedings of the IEEE Global Telecommunications Conference (GLOBECOM '04)*, vol. 3. Los Alamitos, CA: IEEE Computer Society Press, 1559–1664.

Churchill, E.F.; Nelson, L.; and Denoue, L. 2003. Multimedia Fliers: Information Sharing With Digital Community Bulletin Boards. In *Proceedings of the Communities and Technologies*. Amsterdam: Kluwer, 97–117.

Churchill, E.F.; Nelson, L.; Denoue, L.; Helfman, J.; and Murphy, P. 2004. Sharing Multimedia Content with Interactive Public Displays: A Case Study. In *Proceedings of the Conference on Designing Interactive Systems: Processes, Practices, Methods, and Techniques*. New York: ACM Press, 7–16.

Coen, M. 1998. Design principles for intelligent environments. In *Proceedings of the Fifteenth National Conference on Artificial Intelligence*. Menlo Park, CA: AAAI Press, 547–554.

Colouris, G.; Dollimore, J.; and Kindberg, T. 2001. *Distributed Systems Concepts and Design.* Boston, MA: Addison-Wesley.

Cooperstock, J.R.; Tanikoshi, K.; Beirne, G.; Narine, T.; and Buxton, W.A.S. 1995. Evolution of a reactive environment. In *Proceedings of the ACM Conference on Human Factors in Computing Systems (CHI '95).* Denver, CO: ACM Press, 170–177.

CORBA. 2004. CORBA Specification. www.omg.org.

Crabtree, A.; Hemmings, T.; and Rodden, T. 2002a. Coordinate displays in the home. In *Proceedings of the ACM Conference on Computer Supported Cooperative Work.* New York: ACM Press, Available at: http://www.mrl.nott.ac.uk/~axc/documents/workshops/CSCW02W3.pdf (accessed November 10, 2005).

Cranor, L.; Langheinrich, M.; Marchiori, M.; Presler-Marshall, M.; and Reagle, J. 2002. *The Platform for Privacy Preferences 1.0 (P3P1.0) Specification.* Available at: http://www.w3.org/TR/P3P/ (accessed October 10, 2005).

Cranor, L.F. 1999. Internet privacy. *Communications of the ACM,* 42, 2, 29–31.

Cumby, C.; Fano, A.; Ghani, R.; and Krema, M. 2005. Building intelligent shopping assistants using individual consumer models. In *Proceedings of the 10th International Conference on Intelligent User Interfaces.* New York: ACM Press, 323–325.

Davcevski, M., and Janevski, T. 2005. Analysis of IEEE 802.11e QoS in multimedia environment. In *Proceedings of the Seventh International Conference on Telecommunications in Modern Satellite, Cable and Broadcasting Services,* vol. 1. Los Alamitos, CA: IEEE Computer Society Press, 45–48.

Davies, D.; Stock, S.; and Wehmeyer, M. 2002. Enhancing independent task performance for individuals with mental retardation through use of a handheld self-directed visual and audio prompting system. *Education, Training, and Development for Disabled,* 37, 2, 209–219.

Davies, N.; Cheverst, K.; Mitchell, K.; and Efrat, A. 2001. Using and determining location in a context-sensitive tour guide: The GUIDE experience. *IEEE Computer,* 34, 8, 35–41.

Davies, S. 1999. Spanners in the works: How the privacy movement is adapting to the challenge of Big Brother. In C.J. Bennett and R. Grant, eds., *Visions of Privacy: Policy Choices for a Digital Age.* Toronto: University of Toronto Press, 224–261.

Davis, G.B. 2002. Anytime/anyplace computing and the future of knowledge work. *Communications of the ACM,* 45, 12, 67–73.

Dearden, A. and Walker, S. 2003. Designing for civil society. In *Proceedings of the Conference on Human-Computer Interaction.* New York: ACM Press, 157–158.

Deng, D.J., and Yen, H.C. 2005. Quality-of-service provisioning system for multimedia transmission in IEEE 802.11 Wireless LANs. *IEEE Journal on Selected Areas in Communications,* 23, 6, 1240–1252.

Desmet, P. and Dijkhuis, E. 2003. A Wheelchair can be fun: A case of emotion-driven design. In *Proceedings of the DPPI'03.* New York: ACM Press, 22–27.

Dey, A. and Mankoff, J. 2005. Designing mediation for context-aware applications. *Communications of the ACM,* 12, 1, 53–80.

Dey, A.K. 2001. Understanding and using context. *Personal and Ubiquitous Computing,* 5, 4–7.

Dey, A.K.; Abowd, G.D.; and Wood, A. 1998. CyberDesk: A framework for providing self-integrating context-aware services. *Knowledge Based Systems,* 11, 1, 3–13.

Dietz, P. and Leigh, D. 2001. DiamonTouch: A multi-user touch technology. In *Proceedings of the ACM UIST 2001.* New York: ACM Press, 209–216.

Dix, A.; Rodden, T.; Davies, N.; Trevor, J.; Friday, A.; and Palfreyman, K. 2000. Exploiting space and location as a design framework for interactive mobile systems. *ACM Transactions on Computer-Human Interaction,* 7, 3, 285–321.

Djajadiningrat, J.P.; Gaver, P.; and Fres, J.W. 2000. Interaction relabelling and extreme characters: Methods for exploring aesthetic interactions. In *Proceedings of the Designing Interactive Systems (DIS'00).* New York: ACM Press, 66–71.

Djajadiningrat, T.; Wensveen, S.; Frens, J.; and Overbeeke, K. 2004. Tangible products: Redressing the balance between appearance and action. *Personal and Ubiquitous Computing,* 8, 5, 294–309.

Dodgson, N.A. 2005. Autostereoscopic 3D displays. *IEEE Computer,* 38, 8, 31–36.

Dryer, D.C. 1999. Getting personal with computers: How to design personalities for agents. *Applied Artificial Intelligence,* 13, 3, 273–295.

Dryer, D.C.; Eisbach, C.; and Ark, W.S. 1999. At what cost pervasive? A social computing view of mobile computing systems. *IBM Systems Journal,* 38, 4, 652–676.

Dubberley, M.; Agogino, A.M.; and Horvath, A. 2004. Life-cycle assessment of an intelligent lighting system using a distributed wireless mote network. In *Proceedings of the IEEE International Symposium on Electronics and the Environment.*, Los Alamitos, CA: IEEE Computer Society Press, 122–127.

Dunlop, J.; Girma, D.; and Irvine, J. 1999. *Digital Mobile Communications and the TETRA System.* New York: Wiley.

Dunne, A. 2006. *Hertzian Tales: Electronic Products, Aesthetic Experience and Critical Design.* Cambridge: MIT Press.

Duri, S.; Gruteser, M.; Liu, X.; Moskowitz, P.; Perez, R.; Singh, M.; and Tang, J.M. 2002. A framework for security and privacy in automotive telematics. In *Proceedings of the International Conference on Mobile Computing and Networking.* New York: ACM Press, 25–32.

Dutton, D.H. 1992. The social impact of emerging telephone services. *Telecommunications Policy,* 16, 5, 377–387.

Eddon, G. and Eddon, H. 1998. *Inside Distributed Com.* Redmond, WA: Microsoft Press.

Ellis, S. and Lambright, S. 2002. Real time tech—Unilever sees intelligent product tags as the brains behind real-time supply chains. *Optimize,* 44.

Elrod, S.; Hall, G.; Costanza, R.; Dixon, M.; and Des Rivieres, J. 1993. Responsive office environments. *Communications of the ACM,* 36, 7, 84–85.

Esler, M.; Hightower, J.; Anderson, T.; and Borriello, G. 1999. Next century challenges: Data-centric networking for invisible computing: The Portolano Project at the University of Washington. In *Proceedings of the ACM SIGMOBILE Fifth International Conference on Mobile Computing and Networking.* Seattle, 256–262.

European Commission. 1999. The disappearing computer. Available at www.disappearing-computer.net.

Fabbi, J.L.; Watson, S.D.; Marks, K.E.; and Sylvis, Z. 2005. UNLV libraries and the digital identification frontier. *Library Hi Tech,* 23, 3, 313–322.

Fano, A. and Gershman, A. 2002. The future of business services in the age of ubiquitous computing. *Communications of the ACM,* 45, 12, 83–87.

Favalora, G.E. 2005. Volumetric 3D displays and application infrastructure. *IEEE Computer,* 38, 8, 37–44.

Feiner, S.; MacIntyre, B.; Hollerer, T.; and Webster, A. 1997. A touring machine: Prototyping 3D mobile augmented reality systems for exploring the urban environment. *Personal Technologies,* 1, 4, 208–217.

Feldman, A.; Tapia, E.M.; Sadi, S.; Maes, P.; and Schmandt, C. 2005. ReachMedia: On-the-move interaction with everyday objects. In *Proceedings of the Ninth IEEE International Symposium on Wearable Computers,* Los Alamitos, CA: IEEE Computer Society Press, 52–59.

Fickas, S.; Kortuem, G.; and Segall, Z. 1997. Software organization for dynamic and adaptable wearable systems. In *Proceedings of the First International Symposium on Wearable Computers (ISWC'97).* Los Alamitos, CA: IEEE Computer Society Press, 56–63.

Fishkin, K.P.; Partridge, K.; and Chatterjee, S. 2002. Wireless user interface components for personal area networks. *IEEE Pervasive Computing,* 1, 4, 49–55.

Fleck, M.; Frid, M.; Kindberg, T.; O'Brien-Strain, E.; Rajani, R.; and Spasojevic, M. 2002. From informing to remembering: Ubiquitous systems in interactive museums. *IEEE Pervasive Computing,* 1, 2, 13–21.

Flinn, J. 2001. Extending mobile computer battery life through energy-aware adaptation. PhD dissertation. Computer Science Department, Carnegie Mellon University, Pittsburgh.

Fogarty, J.; Forlizzi, J.; and Hudson, S.E. 2001. Aesthetic information collages: Generating decorative displays that contain information. In *Proceedings of the UIST'01.* New York: ACM Press, 141–150.

Franklin, D. and Flaschbart, J. 1998. All gadget and no representation makes Jack a dull environment. In *Proceedings of the AAAI 1998 Spring Symposium on Intelligent Environments (AAAI Technical Report SS-98–02).* Palo Alto, CA: AAAI Press, 155–160.

Friedland, G.; Knipping, L.; Rojas, R.; and Tapia, E. 2004. Teaching with an intelligent electronic chalkboard. In *Proceedings of the International Multimedia Conference.* New York: ACM Press, 16–23.

Gajos, K. and Weld, D. 2004. SUPPLE: Automatically generating user interfaces. In *Proceedings of the Intelligent User Interfaces (IUI) 2004.* New York: ACM Press, 93–100.

Gaver, W.; Beaver, J.; and Benford, S. 2003. Ambiguity as a resource for design. In *Proceedings of the Conference on Human Factors in Computing Systems.* New York:ACM Press, 233–240.

Gaver, W.W.; Bowers, J.; Boucher, A.; Gellerson, H.; Pennington, S.; Schmidt, A.; Steed, A.; Villars, N.; and Walker, B. 2004. The drift table: Designing for ludic engagement. In *Proceedings of the Conference on Human Factors in Computing Systems.* New York: ACM Press, 885–900.

Gavison, R. 1980. Privacy and the limits of law. *Yale Law Journal,* 89, 421–471.

Gemperle, F.; Kasabach, C.; Stivoric, J.; Bauer, M.; and Martin, R. 1998. Design for wearability. In *Proceed-*

ings of the Second International Symposium on Wearable Computers. Los Alamitos, CA: IEEE Computer Society Press, 116–122.

Gibbons, P.B.; Karp, B.; Ke, Y.; Nath, S.; and Srinivasan, S. 2003. IrisNet: An architecture for a Worldwide Sensor Web. *IEEE Pervasive Computing,* 2, 4, 22–33.

Gohmann, S.F.; Barker, R.M.; Faulds, D.J.; and Guan, J. 2005. Salesforce automation, perceived information accuracy and user satisfaction. *Journal of Business & Industrial Marketing,* 20, 1, 23–32.

Goldman, J. 1999. Privacy and individual empowerment in the interactive age. In C.J. Bennett and R. Grant, eds., *Visions of Privacy: Policy Choices for a Digital Age.* Toronto: University of Toronto Press, 97–115.

Gong, M.; Xu, Y.; and Yu, Y. 2004. An enhanced technology acceptance model for Web-based learning. *Journal of Information Systems Education,* 15, 4, 365–374.

Gracanin, D.; Eltoweissy, M.; Wadaa, A.; and DaSilva, L.A. 2005. A service-centric model for wireless sensor networks. *IEEE Journal on Selected Areas in Communications,* 23, 6, 1159–1166.

Gransart, C.; Ambellouis, S.; and Rioult, J. 2004. Providing information to the users of public transportation by combining Wi-Fi network and satellite communications. In *Proceedings of the First French-Speaking Conference on Mobility and Ubiquitous Computing.* ACM International Conference Proceedings Series, vol. 64. New York: ACM Press, 29–35.

Grasso, A. 2003. Supporting communities of practice with large screen displays. In K. O'Hara, M. Perry, E.F. Churchill, and D.M. Russell, eds., *Public and Situated Displays. Social and Interactional Aspects of Shared Display Technologies.* Dordrecht, The Netherlands: Kluwer, 261–282.

Graver, B. and Martin, H. 2000. Alternatives. In *Proceedings of the CHI 2000.* New York: ACM Press, 209–216.

Greenberg, S. and Rounding, M. 2001. The notification collage: Posting information to public and personal displays. *CHI Letters,* 3, 1, 515–521.

Grudin, J. 1993. Interface: An evolving concept. *Communications of the ACM,* 36, 4, 110–119.

Grudin, J. 2002. Group dynamics and ubiquitous computing. *Communications of the ACM,* 45, 12, 74–78.

Gruteser, M. and Grunwald, D. 2003. Anonymous usage of location-based services through spatial and temporal cloaking. In *Proceedings of the MobiSys.* New York: ACM Press, 31–42.

Gunther, O. and Spiekermann, S. 2005. RFID and the perception of control: The consumer's view. *Communications of the ACM,* 48, 9, 73–76.

Hackos, J. and Redish, J. 1998. *User and Task Analysis for Interface Design.* New York: Wiley.

Hallnas, L., and Redstrom, J. 2001. Slow technology—Designing for reflection. *Personal and Ubiquitous Computing,* 5, 201–212.

———. 2002. From use to presence: On the expressions and aesthetics of everyday computational things. *ACM Transactions on Computer-Human Interaction,* 9, 2, 106–124.

Hansmann, U.; Merk, L.; Nicklous, M.S.; and Stober, T. 2003. *Pervasive Computing: The Mobile World.* Berlin: Springer-Verlag.

Harter, A.; Hopper, A.; Steggles, P.; Ward, A.; and Webster, P. 2001. The anatomy of a context-aware application. *Wireless Networks,* 1, 1–16.

Hawkes, P. 1994. Supertag—Stock counting off its trolley. *Sensor Review,* 14, 3, 23–25.

Hengartner, U. and Steenkiste, P. 2004. Implementing access control to people location information. In *Proceedings of the Ninth ACM Symposium on Access Control Models and Technologies (SACMAT'04).* New York: ACM Press, 11–20.

Hermann, R.; Husemann, D.; Moser, M.; Nidd, M.; Rohner, C.; and Schade, A. 2001. DEAPspace—Transient ad hoc networking of pervasive devices. *Computer Networks,* 35, 4, 411–428.

Hill, J.; Szewczyk, R.; Woo, A.; Hollar, S.; Culler, D.; and Pister, K. 2000. System architecture directions for networked sensors. *Operating Systems Review,* 34, 5, 93–104.

Hindus, D.; Mainwaring, S.; Leduc, N.; Hagstrom, A.E.; and Bayley, O. 2001. Casaclanca: Designing social communication devices for the home. In J.A. Jacko, A. Sears, M. Beudoin Lafon, and R.J.K. Jacob, eds., *Proceedings of the Conference on Human Factors in Computing Systems.* New York: ACM Press, 325–332.

Hoffman, L.J. 1969. Computers and privacy: A survey. *ACM Computing Surveys,* 1, 2, 85–103.

Hong, J.I. and Landay, J.A. 2004. An architecture for privacy-sensitive ubiquitous computing. In *Proceedings of the MobiSys'04.* New York: ACM Press, 177–189.

Hoymann, C. 2005. Analysis and performance evaluation of the OFDM-based metropolitan area network IEEE 802.16. *Computer Networks,* 49, 3, 341–363.

Hsi, S. and Fait, H. 2005. RFID enhances visitors' museum experience at the exploratorium. *Communications of the ACM,* 48, 9, 60–65.

Hu, W.C.; Lee, C.W.; and Kou, W., eds. 2005. *Advances in Security and Payment Methods for Mobile Commerce.* Hershey, PA: Idea Group.

Huang, A.C.; Ling, B.C.; Ponnekanti, S.; and Fox, A. 1999. Pervasive computing: What is it good for? In *Proceedings of the Workshop on Mobile Data Management (MobiDE) in Conjunction with ACM MobiCom '99.* New York: ACM Press, 84–91.

Huang, E.M.; Russell, D.M.; and Sue, A.E. 2004. IM here: Public instant messaging on large, shared displays for workgroup interactions. In *Proceedings of the SIGCHI Conference on Human Factors in Computing Systems.* New York: ACM Press, 279–286.

Huang, H.P. and Hsu, L.P. 2005. Development of a wearable biomedical health-care system. In *Proceedings of the IEEE/RSJ International Conference on Intelligent Robots and Systems (IROS 2005).* Los Alamitos, CA: IEEE Computer Society Press, 1760–1765.

Hull, R.; Neaves, P.; and Bedford-Roberts, J. 1997. Towards situated computing. In *Proceedings of the First International Symposium on Wearable Computers (ISWC'97).* Los Alamitos, CA: IEEE Computer Society Press, 146–153.

Hull, R.; Reid, J.; and Geelhoed, E. 2002. Creating experiences with wearable computing. *IEEE Pervasive Computing,* 1, 4, 56–61.

Hum, A.P.J. 2001. Fabric area network—A new wireless communications infrastructure to enable ubiquitous networking and sensing on intelligent clothing. *Computer Networks,* 35, 4, 391–399.

Hurst, A.; Zimmerman, J.; Atkeson, C.; and Forlizzi, J. 2005. The sense lounger: Establishing a Ubicomp beachhead in elders' homes. In *Proceedings of the Conference on Human Factors in Computing Systems.* New York: ACM Press, 1467–1470.

Ing, D.S.L. 1999. Innovation in a technology museum. *IEEE Micro,* 19, 6, 44–52.

Inness, J.C. 1992. *Privacy, Intimacy and Isolation.* New York: Oxford University Press.

Intille, S.S. 2002. Designing a home of the future. *IEEE Pervasive Computing,* 1, 2, 76–82.

Irahhauten, Z.; Nikookar, H.; and Janssen, G.J.M. 2005. An overview of ultra wide band indoor channel measurements and modeling. *IEEE Microwave and Wireless Components Letters,* 14, 8, 386–388.

Izadi, S.; Brignull, H.; Rodden, T.; Rogers, Y.; and Underwood, M. 2003. Dynamo: A public interactive surface supporting the cooperative sharing and exchange of media. In *Proceedings of the Sixteenth Annual ACM Symposium on User Interface Software and Technology.* New York: ACM Press, 159–168.

Jacobs, A.R. and Abowd, G.D. 2003. A framework for comparing perspectives on privacy and pervasive technologies. *IEEE Pervasive Computing,* 2, 3, 78–84.

Jafari, R.; Dabiri, F.; Brisk, P.; and Sarrafzadeh, M. 2005. Adaptive and fault tolerant medical vest for life-critical medical monitoring. In *Proceedings of the ACM Symposium on Applied Computing.* New York: ACM Press, 272–279.

Jain, R. and Wullert II, J. 2002. Environmental design for pervasive computing systems. In *Proceedings of the MOBICOM2002.* New York: ACM Press, 263–270.

Jameson, A. 2001. Modelling both the context and the user. *Personal and Ubiquitous Computing,* 5, 29–33.

Jeronimo, M. and Weast, J. 2003. *UPnP* Design by Example: A Software Designer's Guide to Universal Plug and Play.* Intel Press.

Jessup, L.M. and Robey, D. 2002. The relevance of social issues in ubiquitous computing environments. *Communications of the ACM,* 45, 12, 88–91.

Jiang, X. and Landay, J.A. 2002. Modeling privacy control in context aware systems. *IEEE Pervasive Computing,* 1, 3, 59–63.

Johnson, J.R. 2000. RFID gets the green light. *Warehousing Management,* 7, 4, 28–29.

Jonsson, M. 2002. Context shadow: An infrastructure for context aware computing. In *Proceedings of the Workshop on Artificial Intelligence in Mobile Systems (AIMS) in conjunction with ECAI 2002.* Available at: http://dsv.su.se/FEEL/DSV/ContextShadow.pdf (accessed November 10, 2005).

Judd, G. and Steenkiste, P. 2003. Providing contextual information to pervasive computing applications. In *Proceedings of the IEEE International Conference on Pervasive Computing (PERCOM).* IEEE Press, 133.

Juels, A.; Rivest, R.L.; and Szydlo, M. 2003. The blocker tag: Selective blocking of RFID tags for consumer privacy. In V. Atluri, ed. *Proceedings of the Eighth ACM Conference on Computer and Communications Security.* New York: ACM Press, 103–111.

Kadous, M.W. and Sammut, C. 2005. MICA: Pervasive middleware for learning, sharing and talking. In *Proceedings of the Second IEEE Conference on Pervasive Computing and Communications*. Los Alamitos, CA: IEEE Computer Society Press, 176–180.

Kahn, J.M.; Katz, R.H.; and Pister, K.S.J. 1999. Mobile networking for "smart dust." In *Proceedings of the ACM/IEEE International Conference on Mobile Computing and Networking (MOBICOM 99)*. 271–278.

Kanis, M.; Winters, N.; Agamanolis, S.; Gavin, A.; and Cullinan, C. 2005. Toward wearable social networking with iBand. In *Proceedings of the Human Factors in Computing Systems*. New York: ACM Press, 1521–1524.

Karkkainen, M. 2003. Increasing efficiency in the supply chain for short life goods using RFID tagging. *International Journal of Retail & Distribution Management,* 31, 10, 529–536.

Katz, R.H. 1994. Adaptation and mobility in wireless information systems. *IEEE Personal Communications,* 1, 1, 6–17.

Kaufman, J.H.; Edlund, S.; and Ford, D.A. 2002. The social contract core. In *Proceedings of the WWW 2002*. New York: ACM Press, 210–220.

Kern, N.; Schiele, B.; Junker, H.; Lukowicz, P.; and Tröster, G. 2003. Wearable sensing to annotate meeting recordings. *Personal and Ubiquitous Computing,* 7, 5, 263–274.

Kidd, C.D.; Orr, R.; Abowd, G.D.; Atkeson, C.; Essa, I.; MacIntyre, B.; Mynatt, E.D.; Starner, T.; and Newstetter, W. 1999. The aware home: A living laboratory for ubiquitous computing research. In *Proceedings of the Second International Workshop on Cooperative Buildings*. Berlin: Springer-Verlag, 190–197.

Kiesler, S. and Sproull, L. 1997. "Social" human–computer interaction. In B. Friedman, ed., *Human Values and the Design of Computer Technology*. New York: CSLI Publications, 191–199.

Kindberg, T. and Barton, J. 2001. A Web-based nomadic computing system. *Computer Networks,* 35, 4, 443–456.

Kindberg, T.; Barton, J.; Morgan, J.; Becker, G.; Caswell, D.; Debaty, P.; Gopal, G.; Frid, M.; Krishnan, V.; Morris, H.; Schettino, J.; Serra, B.; and Spasojevic, M. 2002. People, places, things: Web presence for the real world. *Mobile Networks and Applications,* 7, 5, 365–376.

Kjeldskov, J.; Howard, S.; Murphy, J.; Carroll, J.; Vetere, F.; and Graham, C. 2003. Designing TramMatena context-aware mobile system supporting use of public transportation. In *Proceedings of the Conference on Designing for User Experiences*. New York: ACM Press, 1–4.

Kong, J. and Hong, X. 2003. ANODR: Anonymous on demand routing with untraceable routes for mobile ad-hoc networks. In *Proceedings of the Fourth ACM International Symposium on Mobile Ad-Hoc Networking & Computing*. New York: ACM Press, 291–302.

Kornkven, S. 2003. The Technology Learning Center (TLC): A comprehensive learning environment for students. In *Proceedings of the Thirty-first Annual ACM SIGUCCS Conference on User Services*. New York: ACM Press, 222–224.

Kortuem, G.; Bauer, M.; Heiber, T.; and Segall, Z. 1999. Netman: The design of a collaborative wearable computer system. *Mobile Networks and Applications,* 4, 1, 49–58.

Kostakos, V., and O'Neill, E. 2004. Designing pervasive systems for society. In *Proceedings of the Second International Conference on Pervasive Computing*. Berlin: Springer-Verlag. Available online at: http://www.cs.bath.ac.uk/pervasive/publications/pervasive04.pdf [2005, November 7].

Kourouthanassis, P.E. and Giaglis, G.M. 2004. Shopping in the 21st century: Embedding technology in the retail arena. In G.J. Doukidis and A.P. Vrechopoulos, eds., *Consumer Driven Electronic Transformation: Applying New Technologies to Enthuse Consumers and Transform the Supply Chain*. Berlin: Springer-Verlag, 227–239.

Kourouthanassis, P., and Roussos, G. 2002. Developing consumer-friendly pervasive retail systems. *IEEE Pervasive Computing,* 2, 2, 32–39.

———. 2003. Developing consumer-friendly pervasive retail systems. *IEEE Pervasive Computing,* 2, 2, 32–39.

Kray, C.; Kortuem, G.; and Krüger, A. 2005. Adaptive navigation support with public displays. In *Proceedings of the Tenth International Conference on Intelligent User Interfaces*. ACM Press: 326–328.

Kumagai, J. 2004. Life of birds: Wireless sensor network for bird study. *IEEE Spectrum,* 41, 4, 42–49.

Kwon, T.H., and Zmud, R. 1987. Unifying the fragmented models of information systems implementation. In R.J. Boland and R.A. Hirschheim, eds., *Critical Issues in Information Systems Research*. New York: John Wiley & Sons, Inc., 227–251.

Lahlou, S.; Langheinrich, M.; and Rocker, C. 2005. Privacy and trust issues with invisible computing. *Communications of the ACM,* 48, 3, 59–60.

Lal, A.; Duggirala, R.; and Li, H. 2005. Pervasive power: A radioisotope-powered piezoelectronic generator. *IEEE Pervasive Computing,* 4, 1, 53–61.

Lampe, M.; Strassner, M.; and Fleisch, E. 2004. A ubiquitous computing environment for aircraft maintenance. In *Proceedings of the ACM Symposium on Applied Computing.* New York: ACM Press, 1586–1592.

Langheinrich, M. 2001. Privacy by design—Principles of privacy-aware ubiquitous systems. In G. D. Abowd, Brumitt, B.; and Shafer, S.A.N., eds., *Proceedings of the Ubicomp 2001.* Berlin: Springer-Verlag, 273–291.

———. 2002. A privacy awareness system for ubiquitous computing environments. In the *Proceedings of the Fourth International Conference on Ubiquitous Computing.* London, UK: Springer, 237–245.

Larpsiri, R. and Speece, M. 2004. Technology integration—Perceptions of sales force automation in Thailand's life assurance industry. *Marketing Intelligence & Planning,* 22, 4, 392–406.

Lei, H.; Sow, D.M.; Davis II, J.S.; Banavar, G.; and Ebling, M.R. 2002. The design and applications of a context service. *Mobile Computing and Communications Review,* 6, 4, 45–55.

Lenzini, L. and Mingozzi, E. 2001. Performance evaluation of capacity request and allocation mechanisms for HiperLAN2 wireless LANs. *Computer Networks,* 37, 1, 5–15.

Lines, L. and Hone, K.S. 2002. Millenium homes: A user centered approach for system functionality. In S. Keates, P. Langdon, P.J. Clarkson, and P. Robinson, eds., *Proceedings of the First Cambridge Workshop on Universal Access and Assistive Technology (CWUATT).* Cambridge, UK: Springer-Verlag, 91–92.

Ljungstrand, P. 2001. Context awareness and mobile phones. *Personal and Ubiquitous Computing,* 5, 58–61.

Long, S.; Kooper, R.; Abowd, G.D.; and Atkeson, C.G. 1996. Rapid prototyping of mobile context-aware applications: The Cyberguide Case Study. In *Proceedings of the Second International Conference on Mobile Computing and Networking.* New York: ACM Press, 97–107.

Lubrin, E.; Lawrence, E.; and Navarro, K.F. 2005. Wireless remote healthcare monitoring with Motes. In *Proceedings of the International Conference on Mobile Business (ICMB 2005).* Sydney, Australia, 235–241.

Luff, P., and Heath, C. 1998. Mobility in collaboration. In *Proceedings of the CSCW'98.* Seattle, 305–314.

Lyytinen, K. and Yoo, Y. 2002. Issues and challenges in ubiquitous computing. *Communications of the ACM,* 45, 12, 63–65.

Mamei, M. and Zambonelli, F. 2005. Programming stigmergic coordination with the TOTA middleware. In *Proceedings of the Fourth International Joint Conference on Autonomous Agents and Multiagent Systems.* New York: ACM Press, 415–422.

Mani, A.; Sundaram, H.; Birchfield, D.; and Qian, G. 2004. The networked home as a user-centric multimedia system. In *Proceedings of the NRBC'04.* New York: ACM Press, 19–30.

Mann, S. 1997. An historical account of the "WearComp" and "WearCam" inventions developed for applications in "Personal Imaging." In *Proceedings of the First International Symposium on Wearable Computers.* Piscataway, NJ: IEEE Press, 66–73.

Marinelli, D. and Stevens, S.M. 1998. Synthetic interviews: The art of creating a "dyad" between humans and machine-based characters. In *Proceedings of the Fourth IEEE Workshop Interactive Voice Technology for Telecommunications Applications.* Los Alamitos, CA: IEEE Computer Society Press, 43–48.

Matinlassi, M.; Niemelä, E.; and Dobrica, L. 2002. *Quality-driven architecture design and quality analysis method—A revolutionary initiation approach to product line architecture.* Espoo, VTT Electronics, VTT Publications.

McKelvin, M.L.; Williams, M.L.; and Berry, N.M. 2005. Integrated radio frequency identification and wireless sensor network architecture for automated inventory management and tracking applications. In *Proceedings of the Richard Tapia Celebration of Diversity in Computing Conference.* New York: ACM Press, 44–47.

Menczer, F.; Street, W.N.; Vishwakarma, N.; Monge, A.E.; and Jakobsson, M. 2002. IntelliShopper: A proactive, personal, private shopping assistant. In *Proceedings of the International Conference on Autonomous Agents.* New York: ACM Press, 1001–1008.

Meyer, S., and Rakotonirainy, A. 2003. A survey of research on context-aware homes. In C. Johnson, P. Montague, and C. Steketee, eds., *Proceedings of the Conference in Research and Practice in Information Technology.* Darlinghurst: Australian Computer Society, Inc., 159–168.

Miura, N.; Miyamae, M.; Terada, T.; Tsukamoto, M.; and Nishio, S. 2004. Aware-mail: An event-driven mail system for wearable computing environments. In *Proceedings of the Twenty-fourth International Conference on Distributed Computing Systems*, 402–407.

Monk, A. 2000. User centered design: The home use challenge. In A. Sloane and F. Van Rijn, eds., *Home Informatics and Telematics: Information, Technology and Society*. Hingham, MA: Kluwer Academic, 181–190.

Mozer, M. 1998. The neural network house: An environment that adapts to its inhabitants. In *Proceedings of the AAAI Spring Symposium on Intelligent Environments*. Menlo Park, CA: AAAI Press, 110–114.

Mynatt, E.D.; Essa, I.; and Rogers, W. 2000. Increasing the opportunities for aging in place. In J. Scholtz and J. Thomas, eds. *Proceedings of the ACM Conference on Universal Usability*. New York: ACM Press, 65–71.

Nagel, K.; Kidd, C.D.; O'Conell, T.; Dey, A.K.; and Abowd, G.D. 2001. The family intercom: Developing a context-aware audio communication system. In G.D. Abowd, B. Brumitt, and S. Shafer, eds., *Proceedings of the Ubicomp 2001*. Springer-Verlag, 176–183.

Najjar, L.; Thompson, J.C.; and Ockerman, J.J. 1997. A wearable computer for quality assurance in a food-processing plant. In *Proceedings of the First International Symposium on Wearable Computers*. Los Alamitos, CA: IEEE Computer Society Press, 163–164.

———. 1999. Using a wearable computer for continuous learning and support. *Mobile Networks and Applications,* 4, 1, 69–74.

Nass, C.; Moon, Y.; and Green, N. 1997. Are machines gender neutral? Gender-stereotypic responses to computers with voices. *Journal of Applied Social Psychology,* 27, 864–876.

Newcomb, E.; Pashley, T.; and Stasko, J. 2003. Mobile computing in the retail arena. In *Proceedings of the Conference on Human Factors in Computing Systems*. New York: ACM Press, 337–344.

Ni, Q. 2005. Performance analysis and enhancements for IEEE 802.11e wireless networks. *IEEE Network,* 19, 4, 21–27.

Nichols, J.; Myers, B.A.; and Litwack, K. 2004. Improving automatic interface generation with smart templates. In *Proceedings of the International Conference on Intelligent User Interfaces*, ACM Press, 286–288.

Nielsen, C. 2002. Designing to support mobile work with mobile devices. PhD dissertation, University of Aarhus.

Nielsen, I. and Pullin, G. 2005. A simple secret for design. *Interactions,* 12, 4, 48–50.

Nielsen, J. 1994. *Usability Engineering*. Boston: Academic Press.

Norman, D.A. 1999. *The Invisible Computer: Why Good Products Can Fail, the Personal Computer Is So Complex, and Information Appliances Are the Solution*. Cambridge: MIT Press.

———. 2002a. *The Design of Everyday Things*. New York: Basic Books.

———. 2002b. Emotion and design: Attractive things work better. *Interactions,* 9, 4, 36–42.

O'Brien, J.; Rodden, T.; Rouncefield, M.; and Hughes, J. 1999. At home with the technology: An ethnographic study of a set-top-box trial. *ACM Transactions on Computer-Human Interaction,* 6, 3, 282–308.

Odlyzko, A. 1999. *The Visible Problems of the Invisible Computer: A Skeptical Look at Information Appliances*. First Monday, 4, 9, Available online at: http://www.firstmonday.org/issues/issue4_9/odlyzko/ (accessed December 8, 2005).

Ohkubo, M.; Suzuki, K.; and Kinoshita, S. 2005. RFID privacy issues and technical challenges. *Communications of the ACM,* 48, 9, 66–71.

Overbeeke, C.J.; Djajadiningrat, J.P.; Hummels, C.C.M.; and Wensveen, S.A.G. 2002. Beauty in usability: Forget about ease of use. In W.S. Green and P.W. Jordan, eds., *Pleasure With Products: Beyond Usability*. London: Taylor & Francis, 9–18.

Palen, L. and Dourish, P. 2003. Unpacking "privacy" for a networked world. *CHI Letters,* 5, 129–136.

Paradiso, J.A. and Starner, T. 2005. Energy scavenging for mobile and wireless electronics. *IEEE Pervasive Computing,* 4, 1, 18–27.

Park, S.H.; Won, S.H.; Lee, J.B.; and Kim, S.W. 2003. Smart home—Digitally engineered domestic life. *IEEE Personal and Ubiquitous Computing,* 7, 3–4, 189–196.

Parthasarathy, M. and Sohi, R.S. 1997. Salesforce automation and the adoption of technological innovations by salespeople: Theory and implications. *Journal of Business & Industrial Marketing,* 12, 3–4, 196–208.

Pascoe, J. 1998. Adding generic contextual capabilities to wearable computers. In *Proceedings of the Second IEEE International Symposium on Wearable Computers (ISWC'98)*. Los Alamitos, CA: IEEE Computer Society Press, 92–99.

Pascoe, J.; Ryan, N.S.; and Morse, D.R. 1998. Human–computer–giraffe interaction—HCI in the field. In *Proceedings of the Workshop on Human Computer Interaction with Mobile Devices*. Available online at:

http://www.dcs.gla.ac.uk/~johnson/papers/mobile/HCIMD1.html (accessed December 10, 2005).

Paulos, E. and Goodman, E. 2004. The familiar stranger: Anxiety, comfort, and play in public places. In *Proceedings of the SIGCHI conference on Human Factors in Computing Systems.* New York: ACM Press, 223–230.

Peiper, C.; Warden, D.; Chan, E.; Capitanu, B.; and Kamin, S. 2005. eFuzion: Development of a pervasive educational system. In *Proceedings of the Conference on Innovation and Technology in Computer Science Education.* New York: ACM Press, 237–240.

Pering, T.; Burd, T.; and Brodersen, R.W. 2000. Voltage scheduling in the lpARM microprocessor system. In *Proceedings of the International Symposium on Low Power Electronics and Design.* New York: ACM Press, 96–101.

Pering, T.; Ranghunathan, V.; and Want, R. 2005. Exploiting radio hierarchies for power-efficient wireless discovery and connect setup. In *Proceedings of the Eighteenth International Conference on VLSI Design.* Los Alamitos, CA: IEEE Press, 774–779.

Petersen, M.G.; Iversen, O.S.; Krogh, P.G.; and Ludvigsen, M. 2004. Aesthetic interaction: A pragmatist's aesthetics of interactive systems. In *Proceedings of the Designing Interactive Systems: Processes, Practices, Methods, and Techniques (DIS2004).* New York: ACM Press, 269–276.

Petrelli, D.; Not, E.; Zancanaro, M.; Strapparava, C.; and Stock, O. 2001. Modelling and adapting to context. *Personal and Ubiquitous Computing,* 5, 20–24.

Philipose, M.; Smith, J.R.; Jiang, B.; Mamishev, A.; Roy, S.; and Sundara-Rajan, K. 2005. Battery-free wireless identification and sensing. *IEEE Pervasive Computing,* 4, 1, 37–45.

Philipose, M.; Fishkin, K.; Patterson, D.; Perkowitz, M.; Hahnel, D.; Fox, D.; and Kautz, H. 2004. Inferring activities from interactions with objects. *IEEE Pervasive Computing,* 3, 4, 50–57.

Phillips, P. 2005. Texas 9-1-1: Emergency telecommunications and the genesis of surveillance infrastructure. *Telecommunications Policy,* 29, 11, 843–856.

Ponnekanti, S.R.; Lee, B.; Fox, A.; Hanrahan, P.; and Winograd, T. 2001. I-Crafter: A service framework for ubiquitous computing environments. In *Proceedings of the UBICOMP2001,* London: Springer-Verlag, 56–75.

Pottie, G.J. 2004. Privacy in the global E-village. *Communications of the ACM,* 47, 2, 21–23.

Prater, E.; Frazier, G.V.; and Reyes, P.M. 2005. Future impacts of RFID on e-supply chains in grocery retailing. *Supply Chain Management: An International Journal,* 10, 2, 134–142.

Preece, J.; Rogers, Y.; and Sharp, H. 2002. *Interaction Design: Beyond Human-Computer Interaction.* New York: Wiley.

Preece, J.; Rogers, Y.; Sharp, H.; and Benyon, D. 1994. *Human–Computer Interaction.* Essex, UK: Addison-Wesley.

Raatikainen, K.; Christensen, H.B.; and Nakajima, T. 2002. Application requirements for middleware for mobile and pervasive systems. *Mobile Computing and Communications Review,* 6, 4, 16–24.

Raj, H.; Schwan, K.; and Nathuji, R. 2005. M-ECho: A middleware for morphable data-streaming in pervasive systems. In *Proceedings of the M-ECho: A Middleware for Morphable Data-Streaming in Pervasive Systems.* Seattle, WA: USENIX Association, 13–18.

Randell, C.; Price, S.; Rogers, Y.; Harris, E.; and Fitzpatrick, G. 2004. The ambient horn: Designing a novel audio-based learning experience. *Personal and Ubiquitous Computing,* 8, 3–4, 177–183.

Ranganathan, A.; Al-Muhtadi, J.; Chetan, S.; Campbell, R.; and Mickunas, M.D. 2004. MiddleWhere: A middleware for location awareness in ubiquitous computing applications. In *Proceedings of the Fifth ACM/IFIP/USENIX International Conference on Middleware.* New York: Springer-Verlag, 397–416.

Ranganathan, A. and Campbell, R. 2002. Advertising in a pervasive computing environment. In *Proceedings of the WMC2002.* New York: ACM Press, 10–14.

Rantanen, M.; Oulasvirta, A.; Blom, J.; Tiitta, S.; and Mäntylä, M. 2004. InfoRadar: Group and public messaging in the mobile context. In *Proceedings of the Third Nordic Conference on Human-Computer Interaction.* New York: ACM Press, 131–140.

Rasheed, Y.; Edwards, J.; and Tai, C. 2002. Home interoperability framework for the digital home. *INTEL Technology Journal,* 6, 4, 5–16.

Ratsimor, O.; Chakraborty, D.; Joshi, A.; Finin, T.; and Yesha, Y. 2004. Service discovery in agent-based pervasive computing environments. *Mobile Networks and Applications,* 9, 6, 679–692.

Redstrom, J. 2001. Designing everyday computational things. PhD dissertation. Department of Informatics, Göteborg University, Sweden.

Reeves, B. and Nass, C. 1996. *The Media Equation.* New York: Cambridge University Press.

Reidenberg, J.R. 1999. The globalization of privacy solutions: The movement towards obligatory standards for fair information practices. In C.J. Bennett and R. Grant, eds., *Visions of Privacy: Policy Choices for a Digital Age.* Toronto: University of Toronto Press, 217–228.

Rekimoto, J.; Ayatsuka, Y.; and Hayashi, K. 1998. Augmentable reality: Situated communication through physical and digital spaces. In *Proceedings of the Second IEEE International Symposium on Wearable Computers (ISWC'98).* New York: IEEE Press, 68–75.

Robbin, A. 2001. The loss of personal privacy and its consequences for social research. *Journal of Government Information,* 28, 493–527.

Robins, F. 2003. The marketing of 3G. *Marketing Intelligence & Planning,* 21, 6, 370–378.

Robinson, J.W. and Randhawa, T.S. 2004. Saturation throughput analysis of IEEE 802.11e enhanced distributed coordination function. *IEEE Journal on Selected Areas in Communications,* 22, 5, 917–928.

Rodden, T. and Benford, S. 2003. The evolution of buildings and implications for the design of ubiquitous domestic environments. In *Proceedings of the CHI 2003: New Horizons.* New York: ACM Press, 9–16.

Rodden, T.; Cheverst, K.; Davies, N.; and Dix, A. 1998. Exploiting context in HCI design for mobile systems. In *Proceedings of the Workshop on Human Computer Interaction with Mobile Devices.* Glasgow: Available at: http://www.dcs.gla.ac.uk/~johnson/papers/mobile/HCIMD1.html (accessed November 8, 2005).

Rodden, T.; Crabtree, A.; Hemmings, T.; Koleva, B.; Humble, J.; Akesson, K.P.; and Hansson, P. 2004. Between the dazzle of a new building and its eventual corpse: Assembling the ubiquitous home. In *Proceedings of the Designing Interactive Systems: Processes, Practices, Methods, and Techniques.* New York: ACM Press, 71–80.

Rogers, Y.; Price, S.; Fitzpatrick, G.; Fleck, R.; Harris, E.; Smith, H.; Randell, C.; Muller, H.; O'Malley, C.; Stanton, D.; Thompson, M.; and Weal, M. 2004. Ambient wood: Designing new forms of digital augmentation for learning outdoors. In *Proceedings of the Interaction Design and Children Conference.* New York: ACM Press, 3–10.

———. 2002. A middleware infrastructure for active spaces. *IEEE Pervasive Computing,* 1, 4, 74–83.

Romer, K. and Domnitcheva, S. 2002. Smart playing cards: A ubiquitous computing game. *Personal and Ubiquitous Computing,* 6, 371–377.

Romer, K.; Kasten, O.; and Mattern, F. 2002. Middleware challenges for wireless sensor networks. *Mobile Computing and Communications Review,* 6, 4, 59–61.

Roundy, S.; Leland, E.S.; Baker, J.; Carleton, E.; Reilly, E.; Lai, E.; Otis, B.; Rabaey, J.M.; Wright, P.K.; and Sundararajan, V. 2005. Improving power output for vibration-based energy scavengers. *IEEE Pervasive Computing,* 4, 1, 28–35.

Roussos, G. 2003. Appliance design for pervasive computing. *IEEE Pervasive Computing,* 2, 4, 75–77.

Russell, D. and Sue, A. 2003. Large interactive public displays: Use patterns, support patterns, community patterns. In K. O'Hara, M. Perry, E.F. Churchill, and D.M. Russell, eds., *Public and Situated Displays. Social and Interactional Aspects of Shared Display Technologies.* Boston: Kluwer, 3–17.

Ryan, N.; Pascoe, J.; and Morse, D.R. 1998. Enhanced reality fieldwork: The context-aware archaeological assistant. In V. Gaffney, M. Van Leusen, and S. Exxon, eds., *Computer Applications and Quantitative Methods in Archaeology.* Oxford: Available at: http://www.cs.kent.ac.uk/pubs/1998/616/content.html (accessed October 22, 2006).

Saha, D. and Mukherjee, A. 2003. Pervasive computing: A paradigm for the 21st century. *IEEE Computer* (March), 25–31.

Saif, U. 2006. How the "What" Becomes the "How". In *Proceedings of the First International Symposium on Pervasive Computing and Applications.* IEEE Press, 4.

Salber, D.; Dey, A.K.; and Abowd, G.D. 1999. The context toolkit: Aiding the development of context-enabled applications. In *Proceedings of the ACM Conference on Human Factors in Computer Systems (CHI '99).* Pittsburgh, PA: ACM Press, 434–441.

Salkintzis, A.K.; Dimitriadis, G.; Skyrianoglou, D.; Passas, N.; and Pavlidou, N. 2005. Seamless continuity of real-time video across UMTS and WLAN networks: Challenges and performance evaluation. *IEEE Wireless Communications,* 12, 3, 8–18.

Satyanarayanan, M. 2001. Pervasive computing: Visions and challenges. *IEEE Personal Communications* (August), 10–17.

Sawhney, N. and Schmandt, C. 2000. Nomadic radio: Speech and audio interaction for contextual messaging in nomadic environments. *ACM Transactions on Computer-Human Interaction,* 7, 3, 353–383.

Schilit, B.N.; Adams, N.I.; and Want, R. 1994. Context-aware computing applications. In *Proceedings of the*

First International Workshop on Mobile Computing Systems and Applications. Santa Cruz, CA: IEEE, 85–90.

Schindler, E. 2004. The buzz in the background. *netWorker,* 8, 3, 24–29.

Schmidt, A. and Van Laerhoven, K. 2001. How to build smart appliances? *IEEE Personal Communications,* 8, 4, 66–71.

Schoeman, F.D., ed. 1984. *Philosophical Dimensions of Privacy: An Anthology.* Cambridge: Cambridge University Press.

Segal, L.M. and Sullivan, D.G. 1997. The growth of temporary services work. *Journal of Economics Perspectives,* 11, 2, 117–136.

Segal, L.M. and Sullivan, D.G. 1995. The temporary labor force. *Economics Perspectives,* 12, 2, 2–19.

Shafer, S.; Brummitt, B.; and Cadiz, J.J. 2001. Interaction issues in context-aware intelligent environments. *Human-Computer Interaction,* 16, 2–4, 363–378.

Shenck, N. and Paradiso, J. 2001. Energy scavenging with shoe-mounted piezoelectrics. *IEEE Micro,* 21, 3, 30–42.

Shi, Y.; Hou, Y.T.; Sherali, H.D.; and Midkiff, S.F. 2005. Cross-layer optimization for routing data traffic in UWB-based sensor networks. In *Proceedings of the Eleventh Annual International Conference on Mobile Computing and Networking (MobiCom '05).* New York: ACM Press, 299–312.

Shusterman, R. 1992. *Pragmatic Aesthetics: Living Beauty, Rethinking Art.* Oxford: Blackwell.

Siewiorek, D. 2002. New frontiers of application design. *Communications of the ACM,* 45, 12, 79–82.

Skog, T.; Ljungblad, S.; and Holmquist, L. 2003. Between aesthetics and utility: Designing ambient information visualizations. In *Proceedings of the IEEE Symposium on Information Visualization.* New York: IEEE Press, 233–240.

Slinger, C.; Cameron, C.; and Stanley, M. 2005. Computer-generated holography as a generic display technology. *IEEE Computer,* 38, 8, 46–53.

Smailagic, A. 1998. An evaluation of audiocentric CMU wearable computers. *ACM Journal on Special Topics in Mobile Networking,* 6, 2, 59–68.

Smailagic, A., and Martin, R. 1997. Metronaut: A wearable computer with sensing and global communication capabilities. In *Proceedings of the 1st IEEE International Symposium on Wearable Computers.* Los Alamitos, CA: IEEE Computer Society Press, 116–122.

Smailagic, A., and Siewiorek, D. 2002. Application design for wearable and context-aware computers. *IEEE Pervasive Computing,* 1, 4, 20–29.

Smailagic, A. and Siewiorek, D.C. 1994. The CMU mobile computers: A new generation of computer systems. In *Proceedings of the IEEE COMPCON 94.* Piscataway, NJ: IEEE Press, 467–473.

Smailagic, A.; Siewiorek, D.; Iannucci, B.; Dahbura, A.; and Bass, L. 1999. MoCCA: A mobile communication and computing architecture. In *Proceedings of the Third International Symposium on Wearable Computers.* Los Alamitos, CA: IEEE Computer Society Press, 64–71.

Smith, H.J. 1993. Privacy policies and practices: Inside the organizational maze. *Communications of the ACM,* 36, 12, 104–122.

Smith, J.R.; Fishkin, K.; Jiang, B.; Mamishev, A.; Philipose, M.; Rea, A.D.; Roy, R.; and Sundara-Rajan, K. 2005. RFID-based techniques for human-activity detection. *Communications of the ACM,* 48, 9, 39–44.

Soltan, P.; Lasher, M.; Dahlke, W.; Acantilado, N.; and McDonald, M. 1995. Laser-based 3-D volumetric display system (second generation). *Naval Engineers Journal,* 107, 3, 233–243.

Sousa, J.P. and Garlan, G. 2002. Aura: An architectural framework for user mobility in ubiquitous computing environments. In J. Bosch, M. Gentleman, C. Hofmeister, and J. Kuusela, eds., *Proceedings of the Third Working IEEE/IFIP Conference on Software Architecture.* Deventer, The Netherlands: Kluwer Academic, 29–43.

Spector, P.L. 1993. Wireless communications and personal freedom. *Telecommunications Policy,* 17, 6, 403–406.

Speier, C. and Venkatesh, V. 2002. The hidden minefields in the adoption of salesforce automation technologies. *Journal of Marketing,* 66, 98–111.

Spinellis, D. 2003. The information furnace: Consolidated home control. *Personal and Ubiquitous Computing,* 7, 1, 53–69.

Spriestersbach, A.; Vogler, H.; Lehmann, F.; and Ziegert, T. 2001. Integrating context information into enterprise applications for the mobile workforce—A case study. In *Proceedings of the WMC2001.* New York: ACM Press, 55–59.

Staake, T.; Thiesse, F.; and Fleisch, E. 2005. Extending the EPC network: The potential of RFID in anti-counterfeiting. In *Proceedings of the ACM Symposium on Applied Computing*. New York: ACM Press, 1607–1612.

Stanford, V. 2002a. Pervasive computing goes to work: Interfacing to the enterprise. *IEEE Pervasive Computing*, 1, 3, 6–12.

———. 2002b. Using pervasive computing to deliver elder care. *IEEE Pervasive Computing*, 2, 1, 10–13.

Starner, T. 1996. Human-powered wearable computing. *IBM Systems Journal*, 35, 3–4, 618–629.

Steele, K.; Waterman, J.; and Weinstein, E. 2002. HPCA-8 work-in-progress session: The oxygen H21 handheld. *ACM SIGARCH Computer Architecture News*, 30, 3, 3–4.

Story, M.F.; Mueller, J.L.; and Mace, R.L. 1998. *The Universal Design File: Designing for People of All Ages and Abilities*. Raleigh, NC: Center for Universal Design, North Carolina State University.

Streitz, N.A. 2003. Smart artefacts and the disappearing computer. In *Proceedings of the Smart Objects Conference 2003*, 1–2.

Streitz, N.A.; Rocker, C.; Prante, T.; Van Alphen, D.; Stenzel, R.; and Magerkurth, C. 2005. Designing smart artifacts for smart environments. *IEEE Computer*, 38, 3, 41–49.

Sugimoto, M.; Hosoi, K.; and Hashizume, H. 2004. Caretta: A system for supporting face-to-face collaboration by integrating personal and shared spaces. In *Proceedings of the Conference on Human Factors in Computing Systems*. New York: ACM Press, 41–48.

Sung, M.; Gips, J.; Eagle, N.; DeVaul, R.; and Pentland, A. 2004. MIT.EDU: System architecture for real-world distributed multi-user applications in classroom settings. In *Proceedings of the Second IEEE Workshop on Wireless and Mobile Technology for Education*. Jungli, Taiwan: Washington, DC: IEEE Press, 43–50.

Suzuki, T., and Doi, M. 2001. LifeMinder: An evidence-based wearable healthcare assistant. In *Proceedings of the Human Factors in Computing Systems*. aNew York: ACM Press, 127–128.

Swenson, M.J., and Parrella, A. 1992. Cellular telephones and the national sales force. *Journal of Personal Selling and Sales Management*, 12, 4, 67–74.

Szewczyk, R.; Osterweil, E.; Polastre, J.; Hamilton, M.; Mainwaring, A.; and Estrin, D. 2004. Habitat monitoring with sensor networks. *Communications of the ACM*, 47, 6, 34–40.

Takeuchi, Y.; Shimizu, Y.; and Sanada, Y. 2005. Experimental examination of antennas for a UWB positioning system. In *Proceedings of the IEEE International Conference on Ultra-Wideband (ICU 2005)*, 269–274.

Tavani, H.T., and Moor, J.H. 2001. Privacy protection, control of information and privacy-enhancing technologies. *Computers and Society*, 31, 1, 6–11.

Thackara, J. 2001. The design challenge of pervasive computing. *Interactions* (May–June), 46–52.

Trumler, W.; Bagci, F.; Petzold, J.; and Ungerer, T. 2003. Smart doorplate. *Personal and Ubiquitous Computing*, 7, 3–4, 221–226.

Truong, K.N.; Abowd, G.D.; and Brotherton, J.A. 2001. Who, what, when, where, how: design issues of capture & access applications. In G.D. Abowd, B. Brumitt, and S. Shafer, eds., *Proceedings of the Ubicomp 2001*. Berlin: Springer-Verlag, 209–224.

Ueda, H.; Tsukamoto, M.; and Nishio, S. 2000. W-mail: An electronic mail system for wearable computing environments. In *Proceedings of the Sixth Annual International Conference on Mobile Computing and Networking*. New York: ACM Press, 284–291.

Urnes, T.; Hatlen, A.; Malm, P.; and Myhre, O. 2001. Building distributed context-aware applications. *Personal and Ubiquitous Computing*, 5, 38–41.

Van Laerhoven, K., and Aidoo, K. 2001. Teaching context to applications. *Personal and Ubiquitous Computing*, 5, 46–49.

Vazquez, R.; Rodriguez-Del Bosque, A.; Ma Diaz, A.; and Ruiz, A.V. 2001. Service quality in supermarket retailing: Identifying critical service experiences. *Journal of Retailing and Consumer Services*, 8, 1–14.

Vogel, D. and Balakrishnan, R. 2004. Public ambient displays: Transitioning from implicit to explicit, public to personal, interaction with multiple users. In *Proceedings of the Seventeenth Annual ACM Symposium on User Interface Software and Technology*. New York: ACM Press, 137–146.

Voida, S.; Mynatt, E.D.; MacIntryre, B.; and Corso, M. 2002. Integrating virtual and physical context to support knowledge workers. *IEEE Pervasive Computing*, 1, 3, 73–79.

Walters, G.J. 2001. Privacy and security: An ethical analysis. *Computers and Society*, 31, 2, 8–23.

Want, R.; Hopper, A.; Falco, V.; and Gibbons, J. 1992. The active badge location system. *ACM Transactions on Information Systems*, 10, 1, 91–102.

Want, R.; Pering, T.; Borriello, G.; and Farkas, K.I. 2002. Disappearing hardware. *IEEE Pervasive Computing,* 1, 1, 36–47.

WAPForum. 2001. WAP Wireless application environment specification. Available at www.wapforum.org.

Ward, A.; Jones, A.; and Hopper, A. 1997. A new location technique for the active office. *IEEE Personal Communications,* 4, 5, 42–47.

Warneke, B.; Last, M.; Liebowitz, B.; and Pister, K.S.J. 2001. Smart dust: Communicating with a cubicmillimeter computer. *IEEE Computer,* 34, 1, 44–51.

Watson, I. and Lightfoot, D.J. 2003. Mobile working with connexions. *Facilities,* 21, 13–14, 347–352.

Weiser, M. 1993. Some computer science issues in ubiquitous computing. *Communications of the ACM,* 36, 7, 75–84.

———. 1994. Scheduling for reduced CPU energy. In *Proceedings of the First Symposium on Operating Systems Design and Implementation.* USENIX, 13–23.

———. 2002. The computer of the 21st century. *IEEE Pervasive Computing,* 1, 1, 19–25.

Weiser, M., and Brown, J.S. 1995. Designing calm etchnology. Available at www.ubiq.com/hypertext/weiser/calmtech/calmtech.htmWolfram, G.; Scharr, U.; and Kammerer, K. 2004. RFID: Can we realise its full potential? *ECR Journal,* 3, 2, 17–29.

Wong, C.Y.; McFarlane, D.; Zaharudin, A.; and Agarwal, V. 2002. The intelligent product driven supply chain. In *Proceedings of the IEEE International Conference on Systems, Man and Cybernetics.* IEEE Press, 4–9.

Wong, K.L.; Chou, L.C.; and Wang, C. 2005. Integrated wideband metal-plate antenna for WLAN/WMAN operation for laptops. In *Proceedings of the IEEE Antennas and Propagation Society International Symposium,* 235–238.

Xiao, Y.; Lasome, C.; Moss, J.; Mackenzie, C.; and Faraj, S. 2001. Cognitive properties of a whiteboard: A case study in a trauma centre. In *Proceedings of the Seventh European Conference on Computer Supported Cooperative Work.* Kluwer, 259–278.

Yamada, S.; Hong, J.; and Sugita, S. 1995. Development and evaluation of hypermedia for museum education: Validation of metrics. *ACM Transactions on Computer-Human Interaction,* 2, 4, 284–307.

Yamada, T.; Shingu, J.; Churchill, E.F.; Nelson, L.; Helfman, J.; and Murphy, P. 2004. Who cares? Reflecting who is reading what on distributed community bulletin boards. In *Proceedings of the Seventeenth Annual ACM Symposium on User Interface Software and Technology.* New York: ACM Press, 109–118.

Yao, Y. and Gehrke, J.E. 2002. The Cougar approach to in-network query processing in sensor networks. *Sigmod Record,* 31, 3, 9–18.

Yau, S.S.; Karim, F.; Wang, Y.; Wang, B.; and Gupta, S.K.S. 2002. Reconfigurable context-sensitive middleware for pervasive computing. *IEEE Pervasive Computing,* 1, 3, 33–40.

Ye, W.; Heidemann, J.; and Estrin, D. 2002. An energy-efficient MAC protocol for wireless sensor networks. In *Proceedings of the Twenty-first International Annual Joint Conference of the IEEE Computer and Communications Societies (INFOCOM 2002).* Washington, DC: IEEE Press, 1567–1576.

Yoon, J.; Oishi, J.; Nawyn, J.K.; Kobayashi, K.; and Gupta, N. 2004. FishPong: Encouraging human-to-human interaction in informal social environments. In *Proceedings of the ACM Conference on Computer Supported Cooperative Work.* New York: ACM Press, 374–377.

Zaccai, G. 1995. Art and technology: Aesthetics redefined. In R. Buchanan and V. Margolin, eds., *Discovering Design: Explorations in Design Studies.* Chicago: University of Chicago Press, 3–12.

Zeng, H.; Ellis, C.S.; and Lebeck, A.R. 2005. Experiences in managing energy with ECOSystem. *IEEE Pervasive Computing,* 4, 1, 62–68.

Zhai, H.; Chen, X.; and Fang, Y. 2005. How well can the IEEE 802.11 wireless LAN support quality of service? *IEEE Transactions on Wireless Communications,* 4, 6, 3084–3094.

Zieniewicz, M.J.; Johnson, D.C.; Wong, D.C.; and Flatt, J.D. 2002. The evolution of army wearable computers. *IEEE Pervasive Computing,* 1, 4, 30–40.

CHAPTER 3

REQUIREMENTS FOR MIDDLEWARE FOR PERVASIVE INFORMATION SYSTEMS

GREGORY BIEGEL AND VINNY CAHILL

Abstract: Pervasive information systems are predicated on cooperation between a very large number of distributed heterogeneous devices and services, including information processing and communication devices, sensors, and actuators. As a result, a crucial requirement of pervasive information systems is the need to make the operation of these underlying enabling technologies transparent to the end user, allowing the user's immersion in the pervasive computing environment without distraction. In order for computing infrastructure to truly fade into the background of users' consciousness, application components that act autonomously and proactively, based solely on the acquisition of data from the environment and their own knowledge, are necessary. The inherent heterogeneity and distribution of devices, services, and data associated with pervasive information systems has so far hampered the wide-scale development and deployment of the type of applications that will eventually lead to a reduction in the need for explicit user interaction.

Middleware, or software that provides applications and their developers with high-level interfaces to lower-level software, has the potential to address this problem by providing support to application developers, thereby enabling the widespread deployment and use of robust and useful pervasive information systems. A number of existing approaches to the provision of middleware for pervasive information systems have been proposed to address such challenges as low-level heterogeneous device interaction, ad hoc communication, capture, storage, and inference based on uncertain context data, as well as support for application developers. However, these approaches remain incomplete, with no single middleware solution providing an integrated approach to supporting all requirements.

This chapter provides a core set of requirements that must be addressed in providing middleware support for pervasive information systems, thus providing a basis for the implementation of effective middleware architectures. The set of requirements derives from the challenges inherent in building pervasive information systems and is provided in the context of current efforts toward the provision of middleware for pervasive information systems.

Keywords: Context Aware, Middleware, Pervasive Information Systems

INTRODUCTION

The development of middleware for pervasive information systems remains fragmented with a variety of approaches proposed that address individual technical challenges, but with no unified and commonly adopted approach having emerged. Essential to the development of effective middleware for pervasive information systems is a clear understanding of the set of requirements for such middleware. The requirements presented in this chapter are based on the major challenges inherent in building pervasive information systems and provide a basis both for the evaluation of existing middleware approaches and for the implementation of future solutions. Support for this set of requirements is considered integral to the widespread development and deployment of applications as envisaged in the pervasive computing environment.

PERVASIVE INFORMATION SYSTEMS AS ENVIRONMENTAL INTERACTION

A central tenet of pervasive information systems is that the computing infrastructure should fade into the background of the user's consciousness, and become part of the environment (Weiser, 1991). Current infrastructure clearly falls well short of this goal with a great deal of explicit input still required from a relatively small set of devices, while the addition of new sources of input remains overly complex. For infrastructure to truly fade into the background, middleware that hides the complexities inherent in basing application behavior on the acquisition of information from the environment is necessary. A number of factors contribute to the perceived importance of interaction with the environment in the emerging field of pervasive information systems. First and foremost, saturation of the environment with heterogeneous networked devices makes environmental parameters an important system input and enables applications to be aware of the context in which they operate. The importance of environmental awareness is truly realized when we consider mobility, and, consequently, the rapidly changing environment. Whereas stationary desktop computers of the preceding era operated in a constant physical environment, rarely if ever changing location, administrative domain, or proximity to other devices, the opposite is true of mobile devices. Ad hoc mobility causes rapid changes in execution environment and awareness of these changes can be used to enhance the flexibility, adaptiveness, and efficiency of existing applications, while making a host of new applications possible. Furthermore, although the value of environmental awareness is realized in mobile computing, the mechanisms by which it is achieved are due to recent progress in the miniaturization and fabrication of sensor components. Advances in manufacturing processes leading to low cost-to-performance ratios coupled with novel signal processing methods and high-speed, low-cost electronic circuits have provided cheap, compact sensors able to measure a range of environmental parameters. *Context* is the commonly accepted term used to describe the state of the environment in which an application operates, and, in order to be minimally intrusive, an application needs to be *context aware*, defined as the ability to sense and react to context. A widely accepted definition of *context* is given by Dey and Abowd (1999), as any information that can be used to characterize the situation of an entity, where an entity is a person, place, or object that is considered relevant to the interaction between a user and an application, including the user and the application themselves. *Context awareness* is in turn defined as the use of context to provide relevant information and/or services to the user, where relevancy depends on the user's task (ibid.). We view context awareness as the enabler behind pervasive information systems, and believe that pervasive middleware should mediate between application requirements for high-level context information, on the one hand, and multiple software entities and networked heterogeneous devices, on the other.

MIDDLEWARE FOR PERVASIVE INFORMATION SYSTEMS

Middleware is the general term used to describe software that exists between low-level hardware and software infrastructure and high-level applications, and its purpose is to address heterogeneity and distribution (Blair et al., 1998), offering to application developers higher-level interfaces that mask lower-level complexities. Middleware has a long history in distributed systems, where the broad aim has been to enable developers to program distributed systems much like stand-alone applications, without the need to deal with aspects such as location, communication protocols, and specific hardware (Schantz and Schmidt, 2002). Middleware provides substantial advantages to distributed application development, including shielding developers from low-level programming details, and significantly reducing the development lifecycle by offering reusable implementations of key components, eliminating the need to manually develop them for individual applications (Schantz and Schmidt, 2002). Traditional middleware for distributed systems (e.g., CORBA, Java RMI.NET) is, however, ill-suited to the development of pervasive information systems due to the challenges posed by the environment in which they must operate.

In light of this, several middleware solutions have been proposed in the past to ease the development of pervasive information systems, predominantly by abstracting away from the complexity of low-level, heterogeneous sensors. Most notable among these is the Context Toolkit (Salber, Dey, and Abowd, 1999), which separates context acquisition from the rest of the application through abstractions known as "context widgets." Other approaches, such as Gaia (Roman et al., 2002), provide middleware support for sensor fusion and intelligent inference in addition to sensor abstraction. A significant disadvantage of existing middleware approaches to support pervasive information systems is that although interaction with sensors at a low level is simplified, a tight coupling remains between low-level devices and high-level applications. In the type of mobile ad hoc networks that are envisaged underpinning pervasive information systems, the assumption that the identities and addresses of various data sources are known in advance does not hold, and, consequently, such applications require a highly decoupled communication method (Payton, Roman, and Julien, 2004).

In addition, current middleware approaches to supporting the development of pervasive information systems place a disproportionate focus on environmental sensing, neglecting actuation on the environment but rather focusing predominantly on the manipulation of user interfaces. The realization of technology that truly *fades* into the background dictates that a more autonomous style of interaction is required, with less emphasis on user interaction.

Despite the availability and maturity of enabling technologies, the development of pervasive information systems remains a highly application-specific process, with a lack of development support and no generally accepted programming model available. This chapter acknowledges the limitations of existing approaches and proposes a set of specific requirements and research challenges that must be addressed for middleware to successfully support the development of pervasive information systems in the future.

This chapter begins by introducing mobile computing as an important technology underlying pervasive information systems due to the fact that mobility causes frequent and interesting changes in application context, which may be used to proactively influence application behavior without the need for user interaction.

MOBILE COMPUTING

Although truly pervasive information systems could conceivably be realized to some degree through widespread deployment of fixed computing and networking technology, we take the view that this is highly unlikely, due to two major considerations. First, the cost of deploying fixed networking infrastructure throughout the environment is prohibitive, and second, it would be physically impossible to network mobile entities such as vehicles and aircraft in this way. Current trends indicate the increasingly widespread adoption of wireless networking between mobile devices, and we believe future advances in pervasive computing will be based predominantly on mobile computing. Furthermore, we believe that these advances will be based on ad hoc mobile networks, obviating the need for extensive deployment of gateway infrastructure.

Additionally, in a consideration biased toward context-aware computing as the enabling paradigm behind pervasive information systems, mobility causes frequent changes to the context in which an application executes. In marked contrast to stationary systems, mobile systems may experience rapid changes in location, administrative domain, bandwidth availability, temperature, speed, proximity to other devices, and a host of other environmental parameters. Related to this consideration is the fact that awareness of the dynamic execution context by an application on a mobile device allows the application to initiate specific activity, for instance, reallocation of resources. As a result, mobile computing environments exhibit a range of characteristics that challenge the developer of applications for such environments, as well as provide a source of input to applications that may be used to control behavior.

Characteristics of Mobile Computing

Mobile computing poses a set of fundamental technical challenges to software design stemming primarily from the use of wireless communication, the ability to change locations, and the need for portability of the device. There has been extensive research carried out in the field of mobile computing and the challenges posed therein have been understood for some time (Forman and Zahorjan, 1994). Although these constraints are becoming less noticeable, the portability of mobile devices will always induce additional constraints relative to stationary computing. These constraints are predominantly in the areas of bandwidth and latency, resource poverty, address and locality migration, and security.

Mobile Network Models

Wireless mobile networks may adopt one of two communication models (Crow et al., 1997), which are differentiated by the level of infrastructure deployed in the environment. As Haahr notes, the two models are not mutually exclusive and a given environment may contain both types (Haahr, 2005).

The Infrastructure Model

In the *infrastructure* network model, a set of stationary *access points* coordinate communication between mobile devices and provide gateway access to a fixed network. Access points have both fixed and wireless network interfaces, and to connect to the network a mobile device has to be within transmission range of an access point. This requirement imposes a severe restriction on the infrastructure model in terms of pervasive information systems, since it may only operate in close proximity (currently hundreds of meters at best) to fixed infrastructure.

The Ad Hoc Model

In the *ad hoc* network model, the network is composed only of a set of mobile nodes interconnected by wireless links, which may move randomly, leading to rapid and unpredictable changes to the network topology. Perkins and Royer (1999) define an ad hoc network as "the co-operative

Figure 3.1   **A Mobile, Ad Hoc Wireless Network with Three Nodes**

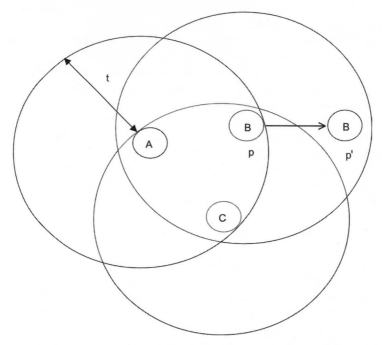

engagement of a collection of mobile nodes without the required intervention of any centralised access point or existing infrastructure." Ad hoc networks are becoming popular due to the ease with which they may be deployed as well as the flexibility they offer in contrast to the overhead of setting up traditional fixed networks. Such networks are particularly attractive in situations where fixed infrastructure is not deployed, or has been destroyed, and communication ability is required rapidly, for example, in a disaster area or war zone. The ad hoc network model is vital to the realization of pervasive computing where multitudes of mobile devices interact with each other in a dynamic and unpredictable manner in the absence of costly fixed infrastructure.

Each mobile node in a mobile ad hoc network (MANET) can combine the functionality of a router and a host, forming the network routing infrastructure in an ad hoc manner, or simply sharing a common broadcast region in a limited spatial area. The union of nodes forms an arbitrary graph in which nodes may move randomly. An example mobile ad hoc network consisting of three nodes, each with the same transmission range (*t*) is illustrated in Figure 3.1, where node B of the network is moving from position *p* to *p'*.

Fixed and infrastructure-based wireless networks use protocols that leverage their relatively static network topology and the fact that links between nodes in the network are reliable. Such assumptions do not hold in ad hoc networks and result in the following characteristics.

    1. Network partitions—as a result of rapid and unpredictable mobility, *partitions* can occur frequently in the network, whereby the network is split into a set of disconnected portions. For example, a mobile ad hoc network consisting of three nodes, each with transmission range *t*, is illustrated in Figure 3.1. It can be seen that if node B, at position *p* continues to move in the direction indicated by the arrow, then when it reaches position *p'* it will be out of range of the other nodes in the network and will be partitioned from them. Network

partitions can cause severe disruption to network routing if they are not merged rapidly, which in turn affects higher-level applications.

2. Routing—most routing protocols, designed for networks with infrequent topology changes, rely on the proactive exchange of topology information between nodes and the use of routing algorithms to inexpensively compute routes through the network. However, in a MANET, where the topology changes constantly and bandwidth, power, and transmission range are constrained, traditional routing protocols do not perform well, and both reactive (Perkins and Royer, 1999) and proactive (Perkins and Bhagwat, 1994) ad hoc routing protocols have been proposed.

It is clear that the ad hoc network model is of particular value in pervasive information systems, where application components may collaborate anywhere, potentially in the absence of any fixed network infrastructure. The characteristics of mobile, ad hoc networks may also be leveraged by the application developer to react to contextual events such as an impending network partition.

CHALLENGES IN BUILDING PERVASIVE INFORMATION SYSTEMS

While the incorporation of context data into applications to make them context aware is fundamental to the realization of pervasive information systems that support the disappearance of the computing function into the background, building mobile context-aware applications in an ad hoc environment remains a challenging undertaking. This is due to the fact that, at present, application developers are required to develop, from scratch, software to capture, represent, and process context data, in addition to developing the application itself. There is little middleware support and no commonly accepted programming model promoting scalability, extensibility, and reuse of application components, and, most important, ease of development.

Capture of Context Data

In addition to identifying the relevant sources of context data for a particular application, the application developer often has to write low-level code to interact with sensor hardware, often at the device protocol level (e.g., Ryan, Pascoe, and Morse, 1999). Such development is time-consuming, error-prone, and only accessible to fairly experienced programmers. While a number of approaches to developing context-aware applications define abstractions to assist in context capture (e.g., Castro and Muntz, 2000; Dey, Salber, and Abowd, 2001; Schmidt et al., 1999), most do not provide further support to the developer for the representation and processing of context data.

A usable abstraction for dealing with the capture of context data from low-level sensor hardware is an essential requirement of pervasive middleware, as is the incorporation of the abstraction into an overall programming model supporting the capture, representation, and processing of context data.

Uncertainty of Context Data

Measurements made of the real world by sensors based on physical transducers will always contain a degree of *uncertainty* and *incompleteness*, which together result in an inherent unreliability of context data based on such measurements. Uncertainty regarding the true value of what the sensor is measuring is inherent in data resulting from a physical measurement and stems from hardware limitations in the manufacturing of the sensor and the fact that the physical operation of the sensor is too complex to model.

Figure 3.2   **Inherent Uncertainty in an Ultrasonic Range Finder Reading**

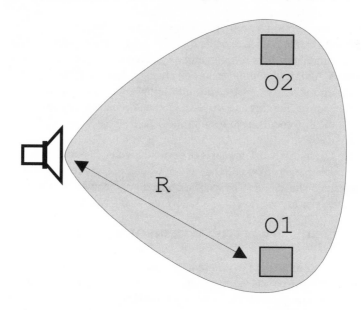

Hardware sensors typically produce a time-continuous *analogue* signal, with infinite precision. In order to use this analogue signal in a computer, it has to be converted into a digital signal, in a process known as *quantization*, whereby the state is constrained to a set of discrete values, rather than varying continuously. A *digital* signal is thus a discrete-time, discrete amplitude signal defined only at sampling times with finite precision. The process of analogue to digital conversion involves the systematic loss of data, since the conversion process only has a finite resolution. This quantization error is one source of uncertainty in sensor data, with others arising from measurement errors made by the sensor, or through the interpolation of measurements when the sensor is temporarily unavailable. In addition to the inherent uncertainty of sensor data, each type of sensor performs a narrow and specific sensing task and is unable to capture completely all aspects of a particular context.

A classic example of the uncertainty inherent in a sensor reading is given by Visser[1] for an ultrasonic range finding sensor, as illustrated in Figure 3.2. This type of sensor can detect the distance to an obstacle within its "cone" of vision, but is not able to determine the position of the obstacle. In the figure, the sensor would not be able to discriminate between the position of obstacle 01 and obstacle 02—the range value R will be the same for both obstacles. In addition to the inherent uncertainty of sensor data, each type of sensor performs a narrow and specific sensing task and is unable to capture completely all aspects of a particular context. For example, for the sensor illustrated in Figure 3.2, if one obstacle lies slightly closer to the sensor than the other, the sensor will only detect the nearest obstacle.

It is an important requirement of pervasive middleware to provide systematic support for dealing with the uncertainty of context data. While numerous approaches to managing uncertainty have been proposed for context-aware applications (e.g., Castro and Muntz, 2000; Chen, Schmidt, and Gellesen, 1999; Dey et al., 2002; Ranganathan, Al-Muhtadi, and Campbell, 2004; Wu, Siegel, and Ablay 2002 and Wu et al., 2002a), there remains no commonly accepted and generic approach that is part of an overall middleware, with most developers rather managing uncertainty in an ad hoc and application-specific manner that is not reusable between applications.

Representation of Context Data

In order to process, reason about, and react to context data, a systematic approach to the representation of context is an important requirement of middleware for pervasive information systems. Since context data is derived from a plethora of heterogeneous devices, each representing data in different formats and at different frequencies, an effective and reusable approach to storing these data is essential. The selected representation format should be efficient to process and reason about by the application. A variety of approaches to representing context data have been proposed (e.g., by Fersha, Vogl, and Beer, 2002; Henricksen, Indulska, and Rakotonirainy, 2002; Ranganathan and Campbell, 2003a; and Winograd, 2001), but no commonly accepted approach has emerged.

Developers of pervasive information systems need a systematic and powerful approach to the representation of context data in order to incorporate inference based on these data into applications.

Scalability

Scalability refers to the ability to incrementally increase the abilities of a system, while maintaining, or improving, performance. Context-aware applications in mobile ad hoc environments will form a part of an overall pervasive information systems infrastructure consisting of very large and dynamic distributed populations of entities, and thus scalability of communication is an important consideration to application developers.

Scalability is a significant challenge in the mobile ad hoc networks we envisage as being crucial to pervasive computing environments, due to the large increase in the network protocol control overhead experienced with an increase in the number of nodes in the network (Li et al., 2001). Within such an environment, the provisioning of quality of service (QoS) is a significant challenge, and a number of proposals have been made to address the characteristics of such networks (e.g., Lee et al., 2000; Xu et al., 2003).

It is essential that middleware to support context-aware applications in mobile environments provide appropriate abstractions and system support to ensure the scalability and ubiquitous adoption of applications.

Synchrony

Most existing distributed applications are based on *synchronous* operation, whereby an operation has to wait for a response before execution can continue. Synchronous operations in context-aware applications imply expensive polling behavior in order to determine when the requisite information is available (Bacon et al., 2000). Such blocking communication behavior, as illustrated in Figure 3.3, is not suited to pervasive environments where networks are likely to be slow and unreliable.

Support for asynchronous communication between application components in mobile ad hoc networks is an important component of middleware support for pervasive information systems for which limited support is currently available. Most current approaches to pervasive information system development utilize tightly coupled client–server architectures based exclusively on synchronous invocations using mechanisms such as HTTP (Dey, Salber, and Abowd, 2001) and CORBA (Ranganathan and Campbell, 2003b), and there remains poor middleware support for developing context-aware applications based on asynchronous communication.

Figure 3.3 **Synchronous vs. Asynchronous Communication**

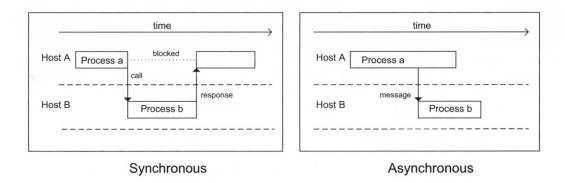

Synchronous   Asynchronous

Extensibility and Reusability

Extensibility may be defined as the ability to add new functionality to an application, while reusability may be defined as the ability of a piece of functionality to be used again, unmodified, in a different system than that for which it was originally written. It is likely that in the future multiple, unanticipated types and sources of context will become available, while new applications will emerge that use existing sources of context. The ability to seamlessly integrate new sources of context data into applications, while at the same time reusing existing functionality is essential to the realization of pervasive computing. Current approaches to context-aware application development with ad hoc integration of devices and application logic results in applications that are neither extensible nor reusable.

Support for extensibility and reusability is an essential requirement of pervasive middleware. Facilitating extensibility and reusability of application components enables the incremental evolution of applications, reducing development effort and reducing the need to develop from scratch.

SUPPORTING THE DEVELOPMENT OF PERVASIVE INFORMATION SYSTEMS

The previous section has discussed the major challenges posed to pervasive information systems development. In this section, we identify a set of requirements based upon these challenges, which we believe are necessary in providing generic middleware support to the developers of pervasive information systems.

Loosely Coupled Communication

The communication paradigm adopted by context-aware applications in mobile, ad hoc environments as envisaged in pervasive computing scenarios should be dynamic, supporting the frequent mobility and unpredictable interaction patterns characteristic of such networks. Applications operating in such environments cannot rely on traditional distributed computing communication paradigms where the sender of a message knows the identity of the intended recipient a priori. Traditional methods of communication based on point-to-point, request/reply semantics are infeasible because (1) the addresses of all interacting entities has to be known a priori; and (2) this paradigm only supports one-to-one communication semantics and does not scale well to the large numbers of entities envisioned in pervasive environments.

An anonymous, generative event-based communication paradigm is well suited to mobile ad hoc environments since it is not based on synchronous, connection-oriented communication between distributed components. This communication paradigm is anonymous since an entity producing an event need not know which entities (if any) have subscribed to the type of event and will thus receive it. The anonymity and many-to-many style of asynchronous event-based communication addresses the requirement for asynchronous communication between application components as well as both scalability and extensibility issues inherent in mobile environments.

Event-Based Communication

The event-based communication paradigm provides anonymous, loosely coupled, many-to-many communication between application components via asynchronous event notifications (Bacon et al., 2000). *Event notifications* represent a change in the state of the sending application component and are propagated from *producers* (sending application components) to *consumers*, according to subscriptions made by consumers (Meier and Cahill, 2002). Events typically have a name and a set of typed attributes, and *event filters* provide a mechanism to scope the delivery of events to consumers based on declared interest.

Event-based communication in an ad hoc wireless environment poses additional challenges since the event middleware cannot rely on the presence of access points to route messages, nor can it rely on intermediate components that may apply event filters or enforce nonfunctional attributes (Meier and Cahill, 2003). An event-based communication system designed specifically for operation in mobile, ad hoc network environments should form the basis of middleware support for pervasive information systems.

Sensor Abstraction

A number of enabling technologies have contributed to the rise of cheap, ubiquitous, and high-performance sensors. Among these technologies are microelectromechanical systems (MEMS), piezo materials, charge-coupled devices (CCD), and at a higher level, global positioning system (GPS) (Hoffmann-Wellenhof, Lichtenegger, and Collins, 1994) satellites for location sensing.

A sensor is defined as a device that responds to some form of physical stimuli (such as a change in temperature) by producing an electrical signal. As such, a sensor is essentially a transducer, a component that converts one type of energy to another. For example, a temperature sensor may convert a change in physical temperature to an analogue electric signal, such as a varying voltage. In addition to the traditional definition of a sensor as responding to *physical* stimuli, context-aware applications often depend on components that respond to digital stimuli from software rather than the physical environment, for example, a Web service that reports estimated travel time between two towns.

Hardware sensors usually produce numerical output using low-level, device-specific protocols. Integrating the output of sensors into applications typically requires significant low-level knowledge, and often results in tightly coupled applications and limited reusability. Crucial in easing the development of context-aware applications is the provision of software components that abstract away from physical device protocols and support the conversion of numerical protocols into a higher-level symbolic representation. Few application-level developers have experience in working with low-level hardware, and to ensure that the development process is accessible to as wide an audience as possible, it is essential that some way of abstracting away from individual devices is provided.

Sensor Fusion

Although expensive sensors may offer a higher degree of reliability than their more economical counterparts, by definition, pervasive computing implies the adoption of inexpensive sensors, while requiring resolution and accuracy commensurate with human perceptive ability (Wu et al., 2002b). A scheme that manages the unreliability of inexpensive sensors is consequently an essential requirement of a programming model for context-aware applications in pervasive environments. A proven approach to managing sensor uncertainty is the combination of readings from multiple sensors, or multiple readings from the same sensor. This technique is known as *sensor fusion*, and allows inferences to be made that might not be possible from a single reading from a single sensor. In general, there are two broad categories of sensor fusion.

Monomodal Sensor Fusion

The potential uncertainty present in a single reading produced by a single sensor may be reduced by fusing multiple readings from the same sensor at different points in time, using techniques such as the Kalman filter (Kalman, 1960). This provides a more accurate description of the measured parameter than a single reading and may be applied by using sensor readings to successively update the estimation of the parameter being measured.

The uncertainty of readings from an individual sensor may further be reduced by fusing the output of a set of redundant sensors measuring the same parameter at the same point in time, using numerical techniques such as sum and average. Monomodal sensor fusion reduces the uncertainty of sensor data and increases its accuracy.

Multimodal Sensor Fusion

The incompleteness of sensor data may be mitigated by fusing the output of several disparate sensors measuring different environmental parameters in a complementary approach known as *multimodal* sensor fusion.

While the majority of approaches to sensor fusion deal with fusing the output of multiple sensors of a similar type, fusing sensory output of different modalities is a substantially more difficult task. Pervasive information systems typically rely on a wide range and type of sensors in order to accurately derive their context, and thus, for example, may need to fuse the output of a passive infrared sensor, a pressure sensor, and a light sensor to determine the action currently taking place within an office. Monomodal techniques that exploit the similarity of their inputs, extracting features and merging these together, are not applicable. The difficulties inherent in fusing sensor readings of different modalities has caused most solutions to be highly application specific and not extensible beyond a specific set of sensors and a specific task. A number of approaches to fusing multimodal sensor data in context-aware applications have been proposed, including rule-based approaches (e.g., Schmidt et al., 1999), Dempster-Schafer Theory (e.g., Wu, Siegel, and Ablay 2002), and probabilistic networks (e.g., Ranganathan, Al-Muhtadi, and Campbell, 2004), but until now these have been tightly integrated with specific applications.

It is essential that middleware for pervasive information systems provide application developers with a systematic approach to managing the uncertainty inherent in a single sensor reading. While sensor fusion requires a degree of application specificity in order to support pervasive information system development, a reusable approach is necessary that is applicable across a range of applications and ensures accessibility to a range of developers.

Context Representation

Context data obtained from sensors needs to be represented and stored in a structure that eases its integration and use by applications. Chen and Kotz (2000) argue that although most existing applications use ad hoc data structures to represent context data, they typically fall into one of the following broad categories.

Key-Value Pairs

Context data may be represented as a set of key-value pairs, as in pioneering work by Schilit, Theimer, and Welch (1993), where the key represents an environmental variable of interest to the application, and the value its current value.

Tagged Encoding

This approach models context data as standard generalized mark-up language (SGML) documents containing tags and corresponding fields. One approach to the representation of context data using tagged encoding is the use of an application-specific schema, others include using resource description framework (RDF) as in (Ferscha, Vogl, and Beer, 2002).

Object-Oriented

Context data may be represented as a set of objects encapsulating variables and associated accessors and mutators. An object-oriented approach to context representation is adopted in the GUIDE project (Cheverst, Mitchell, and Davies, 1999), where a *position sensor* object represents location context data based on signals received from remote base stations. Another approach appears in (Harter et al., 1999) which model real-world objects in a sentient application. This approach supports the features associated with object orientation, namely, inheritance, encapsulation, and polymorphism.

Logic-Based

Following this approach, context data is expressed as a set of facts in the working memory of a rule-based system. By storing context data as facts directly within the rule-based system, context data is closely coupled with the rules that perform inference based on it. This approach is successfully adopted by López de Ipiña and Katsiri (2001) to store sensor data.

It is vital to provide developers of context-aware applications with a systematic and structured approach to the representation of context data within applications. The selected representation format should be integrated with the inference mechanism to allow the application to reason efficiently about context data.

Inference

Context-aware systems perform actions based on context data derived from sensor inputs. This requires the system to reason from observations made by sensors to conclusions in a process known as *inference*. While there is a wide range of possible approaches to providing inference capabilities to context-aware applications, rule-based systems and machine-learning approaches have emerged as the most effective approaches.

Rule-Based Systems

Rule-based systems provide one approach to inference that is widely adopted among context-aware systems (e.g., López de Ipiña and Katsiri, 2001; Ranganathan and Campbell, 2003a). In such systems, the reasoning process uses a set of *facts* and knowledge captured as *rules* applied to these facts to draw conclusions, given a set of observations. For example, from a very early age humans use the observation that someone is crying, combined with rules learned by experience, to infer that the person is unhappy. The certainty of an inference is based on the quality of both the observation and the underlying rules. Rule-based systems are programmed declaratively, that is, the programmer specifies a set of conditions and actions, leaving it to the system to work out how to fulfill them—the order in which the logic is specified is not important. Declarative programming provides a higher level of abstraction than procedural programming and is more flexible when inputs are incomplete or poorly specified, as in pervasive information systems.

Machine Learning

Machine learning refers to the use of a set of algorithms to infer a model from a set of data. In terms of inference in context-aware applications, machine-learning algorithms are of interest both in the classification of contexts from noisy sensor data and in the learning of appropriate behavior in different contexts, rather than relying on behavioral rules specified by developers. Although not yet widely employed as an inference mechanism in context-aware applications, some machine-learning algorithms have been adopted, including the Naive Bayes classifier (Bayes, 1958), reinforcement learning (Kaelbling, Littman, and Moore, 1996), and artificial neural networks (Callan, 2003; Mozer, 1998).

Machine learning has been proposed as a more flexible approach to inference in pervasive information systems, allowing applications to "learn" behaviors in different contexts, rather than following a rigid rule-set defined by an application developer.

Developers of context-aware applications should be provided with a structured means to reason about context data. None of the inference mechanisms described is readily accessible to average developers due to their relatively complex programming models, and higher-level support is necessary in order to offer this functionality to developers.

Actuator Abstraction

Actuators provide a useful abstraction for dealing with the actions taken by context-aware applications. An *actuator is* traditionally defined as a device that responds to an electrical signal by producing a mechanical action, such as motion, or acoustic or thermal energy. This fairly narrow definition constrains actuation to effecting a change in the physical environment and in its current form is not adequate for context-aware applications, since not all applications' actions effect a change in the physical environment. Many context-aware applications only perform actions that effect a change in software, for example, customizing a graphical user interface (GUI), and this needs to be taken into account when considering actuation.

Interaction with most hardware actuator devices is via low-level, device-specific protocols, while interaction with software actuator devices is via custom Application Program Set (APS). Programming interaction with actuator devices is a complex task, which is only available to experienced developers with experience in either the hardware or relevant Application Programming Interface

(API). It is thus essential that any approach to supporting the development of context-aware applications provides an appropriate abstraction for interacting with actuator devices. The major function of such an actuator abstraction is the conversion of high-level, symbolic commands, into low-level commands based on numerical, device-specific protocols.

Application Developer Support

Consolidating the set of other components required of middleware for pervasive information systems, developer support is required in the form of a programming environment that exposes the middleware to the application developer in a coherent and usable manner. Generic support has been offered to developers to some degree for a subset of the requirements discussed above, (e.g., Dey and Sohn, 2003; Ranganathan and Campbell, 2003b; and Schmidt et al., 1999), but often this support is inaccessible to all but the most experienced of developers or does not provide comprehensive support for all the requirements identified in the preceding sections. The majority of middleware developed thus far to support pervasive information systems has remained firmly in the research laboratory and is not readily available to the wider development community, hampering widespread adoption. This situation clearly needs to be addressed, making the development of pervasive information systems by industrial developers possible.

REQUIREMENTS

Based on the discussion of the challenges faced by the developers of pervasive information systems, the set of requirements derived as essential in the development of effective middleware for such applications is summarized below:

- *Requirement 1: Loosely coupled communication*—the middleware should support the development of application components that communicate using a loosely coupled, asynchronous communication mechanism that addresses ad hoc device mobility as well as application scalability and extensibility.
- *Requirement 2: Sensor abstraction*—the middleware should provide suitable high-level abstractions to facilitate the incorporation of sensor data from a range of sensing technologies, implemented both in hardware and software. These abstractions will facilitate the reuse of sensor components among applications, and ease the incorporation of novel sources of data into applications.
- *Requirement 3: Sensor fusion*—the middleware should provide a systematic and efficient approach to fusing the output of potentially multimodal sensors as a way of mitigating the uncertainty of individual sensor readings in a timely manner. The approach should be suitably generic, that is, applicable to a wide range of potential application scenarios, while at the same time supporting domain- and application-specific fusion functions.
- *Requirement 4: Context representation*—the middleware should provide an effective means to represent context information that may be used by applications. Given the potentially large volumes of context data, efficiency should be emphasized in the approach.
- *Requirement 5: Inference engine*—the middleware should provide a systematic and efficient approach to reasoning about context information, allowing applications to make effective decisions and influence their behavior in a context-aware manner.
- *Requirement 6: Actuator abstraction*—the middleware should provide suitable abstractions for applications to be able to interact with their environment via a range of actuator devices,

both hardware and software. As with sensor abstractions, these should emphasize reuse between applications and reduce the amount of development effort required to incorporate actuation into applications.

- *Requirement 7: Application developer support*—the most important requirement is that support offered by the middleware be exposed to the application developer in an intuitive and accessible programming model. To achieve the wide-scale development and deployment of applications required for truly pervasive information systems, their development has to be available to as wide a range of potential developers as possible.

Privacy Within Pervasive Information Systems

The need to protect the privacy of users of pervasive information systems is an overarching concern that needs to be addressed across all other identified requirements of middleware for pervasive information systems. Traditional concerns regarding privacy are vastly amplified in applications that are predicated on access to a wide range of sensitive data and involve ad hoc collaborations between entities. Context-aware computing connotes the storage of more data, with the associated increased risk of theft and misuse.

The explicit incorporation of location, activity, and identity data into applications raises serious privacy concerns (Langheinrich, 2002), which have been voiced since early applications emerged. If pervasive information systems are to be broadly embraced, privacy of sensitive data has to be assured, and middleware is required that will provide appropriate tools to manage privacy and security. Although approaches to managing privacy in context-aware applications have been proposed (Canny, 2002), there remains no common approach to managing these concerns as part of an overall programming model.

SUMMARY

This chapter has identified the major challenges that must be addressed by middleware support for pervasive information systems, and has derived a concrete set of requirements of such middleware that addresses these challenges. Where they exist, current approaches to addressing these requirements in middleware architectures have been discussed. While a number of promising approaches address individual requirements, there remains no unified approach in common use that fulfills the complete set of identified requirements of middleware for pervasive information systems.

Effective middleware support for pervasive information systems is likely to have a significant impact on the emergence of truly ubiquitous computing and on an end to traditional forms of interaction with applications. The ultimate goal is to make the operation of complex information systems as accessible in the future as the operation of complex mechanical systems, such as automobiles, is today.

NOTE

1. Visser, Design and organisation of autonomous systems. Available at http://www.science.uva.nl/~arnoud/education/DOAS/2007/.

REFERENCES

Bacon, J.; Moody, K.; Bates, J.; Hayton, R.; Ma, C.; McNeil, A; Seidel, O.; and Spiteri, M. 2000. Generic support for distributed applications. *IEEE Computer,* 33, 3, 68–76.

Bayes, T. 1958. An essay towards solving a problem in the doctrine of chances (Reprint of 1763). *Biometrika*, 45, 293–315.

Blair, G.S.; Coulson, G.; Robin, P.; and Papathomas, M. 1998. An architecture for next generation middleware. In *Proceedings of the IFIP International Conference on Distributed Systems Platforms and Open Distributed Processing (MIDDLEWARE 1998)*. London, 191–206.

Callan, R. 2003. *Artificial Intelligence*. Basingstoke, UK: Palgrave Macmillan.

Canny, J. 2002. Some techniques for privacy in Ubicomp and context-Aware applications. *Paper presented at the Workshop on Socially-Informed Design of Privacy-Enhancing Solutions in Ubiquitous Computing (UbiComp)*.

Castro, P. and Muntz, R. 2000. Managing context data for smart spaces. *IEEE Personal Communications*, 7, 5, 44–46.

Chen, G. and Kotz, D. 2000. A survey of context-aware mobile computing research. Dept. of Computer Science, Dartmouth College Technical Report TR2000–381 (November).

Chen, D.; Schmidt, A.; and Gellesen, H-W. 1999. An architecture for multi-sensor fusion in mobile environments. In *Proceedings of the International Conference on Information Fusion*. IEEE Press, 861–868.

Cheverst, K.; Mitchell, K.; and Davies, N. 1999. Design of an object model for a context sensitive tourist. *Computers and Graphics*, 23, 6, 883–891.

Crow, B.P; Widjaja, I.; Kim, J.G.; and Sakai, P.T. 1997. IEEE 802.11 wireless local area networks. *IEEE Communications Magazine*, 35, 9, 116–126.

Dey, A.K. and Abowd, G.D. 1999. Towards a better understanding of context and context-awareness. Technical Report GIT-GVU-99–22, Georgia Institute of Technology (June).

Dey, A.K. and Sohn, T. 2003. Supporting end user programming of context-aware applications. Paper presented at the *Conference on Human Factors in Computing Systems (CHI), Workshop on Perspectives in End User Development*.

Dey, A.K.; Mankoff, J.; Abowd, G.D.; and Carter, S. 2002. Distributed mediation of ambiguous context in aware environments. In *Proceedings of the Fifteenth Annual Symposium on User Interface Software and Technology (UIST 2002)*. New York: ACM Press, 121–130.

Dey, A.K.; Salber, D.; and Abowd, G.D. 2001. A conceptual framework and a toolkit for supporting the rapid prototyping of context-aware applications. *Human-Computer Interaction (HCI) Journal*, 16, 2–4, 97–166.

Ferscha, A.; Vogl, S.; and Beer, W. 2002. Ubiquitous context sensing in wireless environments. Paper presented at *the Fourth Austrian-Hungarian Workshop on Distributed and Parallel Systems (DAPSYS)*. Kluwer.

Forman, G.H. and Zahorjan, J. 1994. The challenges of mobile computing. *IEEE Computer*, 27, 6, 38–47.

Haahr, M. 2005. Supporting mobile computing in object-oriented middleware architectures. PhD thesis, Department of Computer Science, University of Dublin, Trinity College. Technical Report TCD-CS-2005–55 (July).

Harter, A.; Hopper, A.; Steggles, P.; Ward, A.; and Webster, P. 1999. The anatomy of a context-aware application. In *Proceedings of the Fifth Annual ACM/IEEE International Conference on Mobile Computing and Networking (MOBICOM '99)*. New York: ACM Press, 59–68.

Henricksen, K.; Indulska, J.; and Rakotonirainy, A. 2002. Modeling context information in pervasive computing systems. In *Proceedings of the First International Conference on Pervasive Computing*. Lecture Notes In Computer Science, vol. 2414. London: Springer-Verlag, 167–180.

Hoffmann-Wellenhof, B.; Lichtenegger, H.; and Collins, J. 1994. GPS: Theory and practice. 3d ed. New York: Springer-Verlag.

Kaelbling, L.P.; Littman, M.L.; and Moore, A.W. 1996. Reinforcement learning: A Survey. *Journal of Artificial Intelligence Research*, 4, 237–285.

Kalman, R.E. 1960. A new approach to linear filtering and prediction problems. Transactions of the ASME, *Journal of Basic Engineering*, 82, Series D, 35–45.

Langheinrich, M. 2002. Privacy invasions in ubiquitous computing. Paper presented at the *Workshop on Socially-Informed Design of Privacy-Enhancing Solutions in Ubiquitous Computing (UbiComp)*.

Lee, S.; Ahn, G.; Zhang, X.; and Campbell, A. 2000. INSIGNIA: An IP-based quality of service framework for mobile ad hoc networks. *Journal of Parallel and Distributed Computing*, 60, 4, 374–406.

Li, J.; Blake, C.; De Couto, D.S.J.; Lee, H.I.; and Morris, R. 2001. Capacity of ad hoc wireless networks. In *Proceedings of the Seventh ACM International Conference on Mobile Computing and Networking*, New York: ACM Press, 61–69.

López de Ipiña, D., and Katsiri, E. 2001. An ECA rule-matching service for simpler development of reactive applications. *IEEE Distributed Systems Online*, 2, 7.

Meier, R. and Cahill, V. 2002. STEAM: Event-based middleware for wireless ad hoc networks. In *Proceedings of the International Workshop on Distributed Computer Systems (ICDCS/DEBS'02)*, 639–644.

———. 2003. Exploiting proximity in event-based middleware for collaborative mobile applications. In *Proceedings of the Fourth IFIP International Conference on Distributed Applications and Interoperable Systems (DAIS '03)*. Lecture Notes in Computer Science. Berlin: Springer-Verlag, 285–296.

Mozer, M.C. 1998. The neural network house: An environment that adapts to its inhabitants. In *Proceedings of the American Association for Artificial Intelligence Spring Symposium on Intelligent Environments*. Menlo Park, CA: AAAI Press, 110–114.

Payton, J.; Roman, G.-C.; and Julien, C. 2004. Context sensitive data structures supporting software development in ad hoc mobile settings. In *Proceedings of the Third International Workshop on Software Engineering for Large-Scale Multi-Agent Systems (SELMAS'2004)*, 34–41.

Perkins, C.E. and Royer, E.M. 1999. Ad hoc on-demand distance vector routing. In *Proceedings of the Second IEEE Workshop on Mobile Computing Systems and Applications*. IEEE Press, 90–100.

Perkins, C. and Bhagwat, P. 1994. Highly-dynamic destination-sequenced distance-vector routing (DSDV) for mobile computers. In *Proceedings of the Conference on Communications Architectures, Protocols, and Applications*. New York: ACM Press, 234–244.

Ranganathan, A.; Al-Muhtadi, J.; and Campbell, R.H. 2004. Reasoning about uncertain contexts in pervasive computing environments. *IEEE Pervasive Computing*, 3, 2, 62–70.

Ranganathan, A. and Campbell, R.H. 2003a. An infrastructure for context-awareness based on first order logic. *Personal and Ubiquitous Computing*, 7, 6, 353–364.

Ranganathan, A. and Campbell, R.H. 2003b. A middleware for context-aware agents in ubiquitous computing environments. In *Proceedings of the ACM/IFIP/USENIX International Middleware Conference*. Springer, 143–161.

Roman, M.; Hess, C.K.; Cerqueira, R.; Ranganathan, A.; Campbell, R.H.; and Nahrstedt, K. 2002. Gaia: A middleware infrastructure to enable active spaces. *IEEE Pervasive Computing*, 1, 4, 74–83.

Ryan, N.S; Pascoe, J.; and Morse, D.R. 1999. FieldNote: A handheld information system for the field. In *Proceedings of the First International Workshop on TeleGeoProcessing* (May 6–7). Boston: Kluwer Academic Publishers, 156–163.

Salber, D.; Dey, A.K.; and Abowd, G.D. 1999. The context toolkit: Aiding the development of context-enabled applications. In *Proceedings of the SIGCHI Conference on Human Factors in Computing Systems*. New York: ACM Press, 434–441.

Schantz, R.E. and Schmidt, D.C. 2002. Research advances in middleware for distributed systems: State of the art. Paper presented at the IFIP World Computer Congress, Montreal, August, 1–36.

Schilit, B.; Theimer, M.; and Welch, B. 1993. Customizing mobile applications. In *Proceedings of USENIX Symposium on Mobile and Location-Independent Computing*, 129–138.

Schmidt, A.; Aidoo, K.A.; Takaluoma, A.; Tuomela, U.; Van Laerhoven, K.; and Van de Velde, W. 1999. Advanced interaction in context. In *Proceedings of the First International Symposium on Handheld and Ubiquitous Computing (HUC99)*. Lecture Notes in Computer Science; Vol. 1707. London: Springer-Verlag, 89–101.

Weiser, M. 1991. The computer for the 21st century. *Scientific American*, 265, 3, 94–104.

Winograd, T. 2001. Architectures for context. *Human-Computer Interaction (HCI) Journal*, 16, 2–3, 401–419.

Wu, H.; Siegel, M.; and Ablay, S. 2002. Sensor fusion for context understanding. In *Proceedings of the IEEE Instrumentation and Measurement Technology Conference (IMTC)*, Vol. 1. IEEE Press, 17–21.

Wu, H.; Siegel, M.; Stiefelhagen, R.; and Yang, J. 2002. Sensor fusion using Dempster-Shafer Theory. In *Proceedings of the IEEE Instrumentation and Measurement Technology Conference (IMTC)*.

Xu, K.; Tang, K.; Bagrodia, R.; Gerla, M.; and Bereschinsky, M. 2003. Adaptive bandwidth management and QoS provisioning in large scale ad hoc networks. In *Proceedings of the IEEE Military Communications Conference (MILCOM)*, Vol. 2. IEEE Press, 1018–1023.

CHAPTER 4

A SOFTWARE FACTORY FOR PERVASIVE SYSTEMS DEVELOPMENT

JAVIER MUÑOZ AND VICENTE PELECHANO

Abstract: *The rise in the number and complexity of pervasive systems is a fact. Pervasive systems developers need advanced development methods in order to build better systems in an easy way. Software factories and model-driven architecture (MDA) are two important trends in the software engineering field. This chapter applies the guidelines and strategies described by these proposals in order to build a methodological approach for the development of pervasive systems. Software factories are based on the definition of software families supported by frameworks. Individual system requirements are specified by means of domain-specific languages. Following this strategy, our approach defines a domain-specific language for pervasive systems (PervML). In order to support our modeling language, we introduce a software architecture for pervasive systems, which is implemented by a software framework using OSGi technology. The methodological approach presented in this chapter raises the abstraction level in the development of pervasive systems and provides highly reusable assets to reduce the effort in development projects.*

Keywords: *Automatic Code Generation, MDA, Pervasive Systems Development, Software Architecture, Software Factories*

INTRODUCTION

Computing-based systems growth is becoming an element of all environments of our daily life. Pervasive systems surround around us providing services to people in their homes, workers in offices, or drivers in car parks. We know that the requirements for current and future pervasive systems involve a great diversity of types of services (Want et al., 2002). Different services such as multimedia, communications, or automation services require hardware devices provided by various manufacturers. These devices reside in several networks running on different platforms. The development of such systems is a difficult task in that the devices must be interoperable in a heterogeneous environment in order to satisfy system requirements.

Recently, two compatible approaches have been proposed for developing software systems in a highly productive and cost-effective way. Software Factories (Greenfield et al., 2004) and Model-Driven Architecture (MDA) (OMG, 2003a) provide strategies for raising the abstraction level in the software development process and making the development of complex systems affordable. The application of the guidelines defined in these approaches to pervasive systems development can help to build better systems more easily than is the case using traditional application methods. Software Factories focus on producing reusable assets that reduce overall development time. On the other hand, MDA promotes the use of models of high-level abstraction, which provide developers with an intuitive method of describing the system. These models are transformed into final implementation following the MDA approach.

This chapter introduces a methodological approach to pervasive systems development following the software factories principles and MDA guidelines. Our approach contributes to the state of the art in pervasive systems development by providing a model-driven development method for the specification and implementation of pervasive systems. This method raises the abstraction level in the development of pervasive systems and provides highly reusable assets to reduce the effort on development projects. The structure of the chapter is as follows: the next section describes the MDA and the software factories approaches and introduces our strategy for pervasive systems development. Then, we present PervML, our modeling language for pervasive systems specification and introduce a case study. Next, we define a product line for pervasive systems following the software factories guidelines. The product line specifies the architecture of the pervasive systems we are going to develop. In order to support the architecture, an implementation framework using OSGi technology is provided. The next section describes the transformation steps required to generate code from PervML specifications. Then we describe some details of the implementation of the system developed in the case study. The final two sections introduce some related work and some conclusions.

A SOFTWARE FACTORY FOR PERVASIVE SYSTEMS

A software factory, as defined by Greenfield and colleagues (2004), is a software product line that configures extensible tools, processes, and content [. . .] to automate the development and maintenance of variants of an archetypical product by adapting, assembling, and configuring framework-based components. Therefore, software factories focus on the development of similar systems encouraging the reuse of architectures, components, and know-how.

In order to achieve these goals, software factories integrate several existing software development practices. The main activities promoted by software factories are:

- *Building families of similar software*. This activity involves the analysis and design of a common architecture for a set of systems and the development of a framework to support this architecture.
- *Assembling components*. The construction of a new system implies the use, assembly, and/or configuration of the components provided by the framework.
- *Developing domain-specific languages and tools*. Developers use this language in order to describe the specific requirements of a member of the systems family. Then, the specific source code is automatically generated.
- *Using constraint-based scheduling and active guidance*. All steps of the development project must be taken according to a well-defined process properly adapted to the domain of the systems that are going to be developed.

On the other hand, MDA, as described in the *IEEE Software* special issue on "Model Driven Development" (Mellor, Clark, and Futagami, 2003), is "a set of OMG [Object Management Group] standards that enables the specification of models and their transformation into other models and complete systems." Following this approach, system developers build high-level abstraction models (called platform independent models, PIM) and transform them obtaining models that directly represent the final software product (called platform specific model, PSM).

Thus, there is a natural integration of these two approaches. MDA techniques can be used to

Figure 4.1   **Our MDA-based Methodological Approach to Pervasive Systems Development**

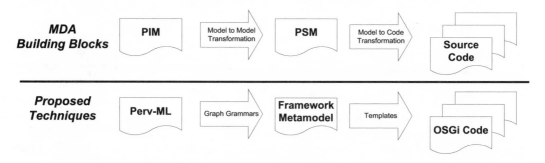

support the development of domain-specific languages in building high-level abstraction models. Then, these models can be transformed in order to obtain the specific source code of a system in the context of a family of systems.

In short, we are interested in *the strengths of both approaches:*

- *from the software factories* we borrow the focus on reuse by means of domain-specific development.
- *from MDA* we borrow the focus on constructing high-level abstraction models and providing automatic code generation.

This mixed approach can contribute to the improved development of pervasive systems. Software factories focus on domain-specific development, and we are dealing with a specific domain: pervasive systems. On the other hand, MDA promotes the use of platform independent models in order to separate the system description and its implementation using a specific technology. This characteristic can provide many benefits to pervasive systems development since this is a field where new implementation technologies emerge continuously.

Following the combined strategy, which is shown in Figure 4.1, our proposed methodological approach to pervasive systems development is based on:

- the *construction of a domain-specific language (DSL),* based on unified modeling language (UML) (OMG, 2004), for the description of pervasive systems. This language is called Perv-ML and is introduced in a further section.
- the *construction of a software framework* that provides implementation constructs similar to those defined by the domain-specific language. This framework facilitates transformation of the system specifications using the DSL into the final implementation code. Moreover, it should support a common architecture for the development of all of the systems we want to build.
- the *definition of mappings or rules for the transformation* of models, which are built using the domain-specific language, to code that instantiates the defined framework.

Pervasive Systems as Integrator Systems

Following the software factories strategy, this work requires a clear analysis and definition of the characteristics of the software systems that we want to develop. As was outlined in the introduction, requirements for current and future pervasive systems involve a great diversity of types of

Figure 4.2 **The Plan for a Smart Meeting Room**

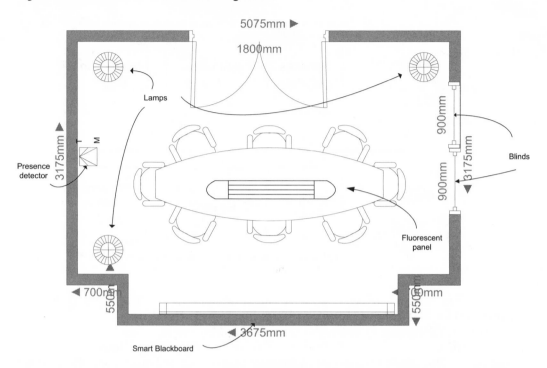

services. Different services such as multimedia, communications, or automation services need hardware devices that are provided by different manufacturers and external software systems. These elements reside in several networks that run on different technological platforms, but they can not satisfy isolated all-system requirements. The elements that constitute the system must work together to achieve system goals. Therefore, we can distinguish two sources of service providers: *commercial off-the-shelf (COTS) elements*[1] and the *software system* that is in charge of integrating all the elements of the system.

From this point of view, the development of a pervasive system consists of:

- *The selection of suitable COTS devices or external software systems.* These elements should provide the services that users require either in isolation from or interaction with other elements.
- *The development of a software system that integrates the external elements in order to provide the services that users require.* The development of that software can imply the use of different technologies where some gateway technology is required.

In order to illustrate our approach, we introduce a pervasive system for a meeting room. In such a system, which is depicted in Figure 4.2, users require services such as *lighting management by presence*, *window blind management,* or *shared drawings.* Users do not care which devices constitute the system; they just need a particular functionality. Therefore, system architects deal with selecting the most suitable devices (e.g., lamps or a smart blackboard in our case study) for providing that functionality.

After introducing the overall strategy, the following sections examine in depth all of the building blocks of the software factory for pervasive systems development.

Figure 4.3 **The Six Models of PervML**

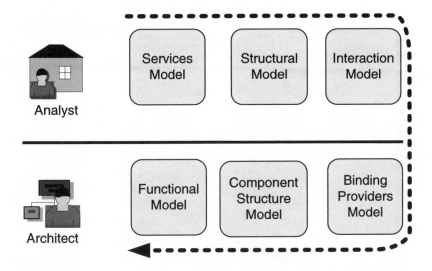

3. PERVASIVE MODELING LANGUAGE (PERVML): A DOMAIN-SPECIFIC LANGUAGE FOR PERVASIVE SYSTEMS

As introduced above, our methodological approach proposes the construction of a DSL for pervasive systems. The use of domain specific languages has several advantages and disadvantages. The main advantage is that it provides conceptual primitives that are suitable to specifying the requirements of a given kind of system. Therefore, it is easier to describe a system using a DSL than using a general purpose language. On the other hand, system developers must invest time in learning this new language. Moreover, DSLs lack well-known tools. It is hoped that new technologies such as *DSL Tools* by Microsoft and the *EMF* and *GEF* plug-ins for Eclipse will help to develop tools to support DSLs. We believe that the benefits of using DSLs are greater than the drawbacks.

Pervasive modeling language is a DSL designed to provide system developers with a set of constructs that allow a precise description of the pervasive system. The abstract syntax of PervML is defined by a meta object facility (MOF) compliant metamodel (which is different from the unified modeling language [UML] metamodel), but we use the UML notation as a concrete syntax, since it provides a well-known representation of many concepts used by PervML.

PervML promotes a separation of roles whereby developers can be categorized as analysts and architects. Figure 4.3 shows the language organization. The dashed arrow of Figure 4.3 defines the construction order of the conceptual models that our approach proposes. In short, pervasive systems analysts capture system requirements and describe the pervasive system at a high level of abstraction using the service metaphor as the main conceptual primitive. Analysts build three graphical models that constitute what we call the "analyst view." On the other hand, pervasive system architects specify COTS devices and/or the existing software systems that are in charge of realizing the services of the systems. Pervasive system architects build three other models that constitute what we call the "architect view." Next we give a more detailed description of the language.

Figure 4.4   **Meeting Room Services Model**

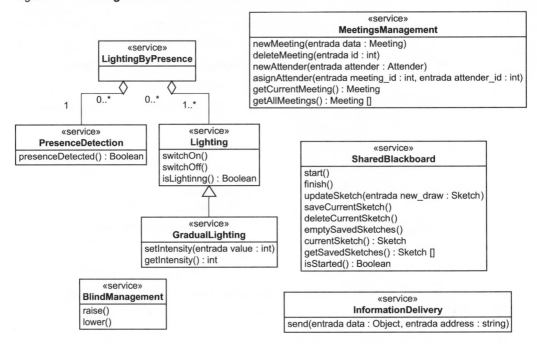

The Analyst View

The analyst describes a pervasive system by specifying a set of functional elements that provide a specific set of services required by the user. Those functional elements are what we call "service instances." For example, if the meeting room described above has two window blinds and a user wants to control them independently, the pervasive system must provide two elements (instances) that provide the blind management service. Following this approach we propose a step previous to the building of the pervasive system conceptual structure. In this step, we introduce the "services model" where the analyst defines services and their relationships. PervML uses and extends the UML class diagram for representing a description of the services, and protocol state machines for modeling the behavior (OMG, 2004). Figure 4.4 shows the service model of our meeting room.

The analyst defines the pervasive system component structure in the *structural model*. This model specifies the service instances of the system, which are represented by a component, using the UML component diagram. PervML provides components as abstractions of the low-level elements that implement the services. Every system component provides one of the services described in the services model. In Figure 4.5 we can see that the *LightingManagement* component has dependence relationships with the *MainLighting* and the *Presence* components due to the aggregation relationship defined in the services model. PervML represents the structural model as a UML component diagram.

System services should cooperate in order to satisfy all of the system requirements. The analyst describes services cooperation in the *interaction model*. An interaction is a communication between services for providing a specific functionality, so the analyst must describe as many interactions as the combined functionality the system provides. Every interaction is described by a subset of a UML sequence diagram (for instance, fragments and some interaction operators are not allowed);

Figure 4.5 **Components That Provide the Services**

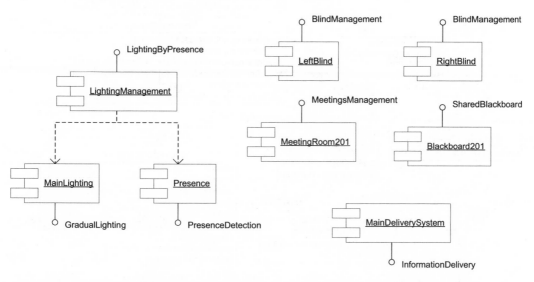

Figure 4.6 **An Interaction That Lowers Blinds and Sets Lighting to 20 Percent of Its Maximum Intensity**

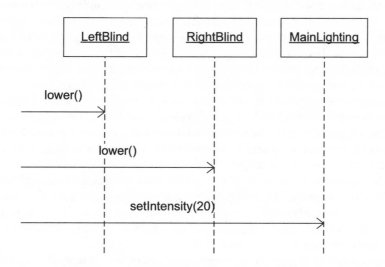

therefore, the interaction model is composed of several sequence diagrams. Figure 4.6 shows an interaction for regulating the light when the blackboard service is being used. The system lowers both blinds and sets the lighting service at a 20 percent of its maximum power. This interaction takes place when somebody starts using the blackboard.

Figure 4.7   **Some Elements of a Binding Providers Model**

«actuator» **Lamp**
switch() : void currentState() : Boolean

«actuator» **FluorescentPanel**
onAll() offAll() onOne(entrada tube_id : int) offOne(entrada tube_id : int) getTubesNumber() : int

«software_service» **EmailService**
send(entrada message : Text, entrada attachments : List, entrada e-mail : string)

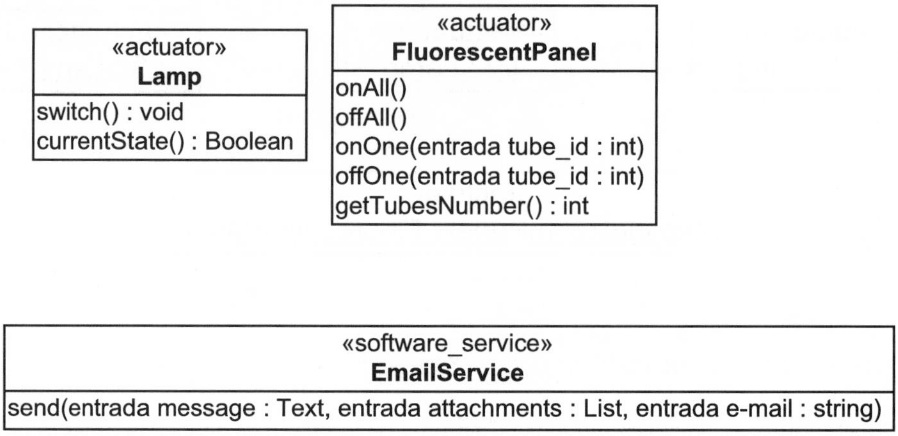

The Architect View

A detailed specification of the lower-level artifacts that realize system services should be built, in order to have a complete and operative pervasive system description. We use the term *binding provider* to refer to artifacts that the pervasive system manages to interact with its physical or logical environment. A *device*, a *sensor*, an *actuator* or *an external software system* can be binding providers. The architect describes every binding provider type, which is introduced to implement system services, in the binding providers model. A type of binding provider represents a set of devices or software systems that provide a similar functionality without detailing manufacturer-specific information. The *binding provider model* is depicted using a stereotyped UML class diagram. Figure 4.7 shows some binding providers for our meeting room. The usage of *Lamp* and *FluorescentPanel* actuators is different, although both can be used to light a room.

The system architect uses the *component structure specification* to specify the binding providers that realize a component of the structural model. For instance, a component that provides a lighting management service can be realized by three lamps and a fluorescent panel. Figure 4.8 shows the component structure specification for the *MainLighting* component, which was included in the structural model of our meeting room (see Figure 4.8).

Finally, the architect must specify how every component operation is realized. In the *component functional specification,* the architect defines the sequence of actions that the component realizes when an operation is invoked. The architect specifies actions using the UML action semantic language (ASL). ASL does not have an official concrete syntax, but many proposed syntaxes are available, for example, the one provided by Kennedy Carter (Wilkie et al., 2001).

Using the PervML approach, the system can be completely described in a technology- and manufacturer-independent way. When a new technology emerges, the system description does not need to be modified. Moreover, if the system architect decides to change a component specification, the analyst view remains unmodified. We isolated these changes by means of a stratification policy that was achieved by introducing several abstraction levels.

Figure 4.8 **Structure Specification of the MainLighting Component**

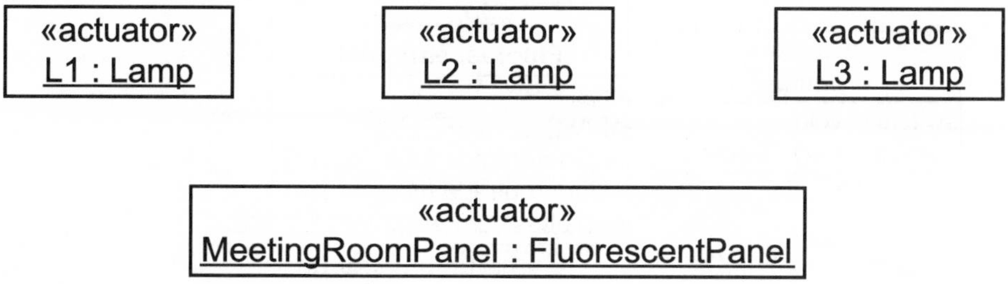

«actuator»	«actuator»	«actuator»
L1 : Lamp	L2 : Lamp	L3 : Lamp

«actuator»
MeetingRoomPanel : FluorescentPanel

A PRODUCT LINE FOR PERVASIVE SYSTEMS

Following the software factories guidelines, a product line should be defined in order to facilitate the development of pervasive systems. The product line definition is constructed, in short, by means of the following steps (Greenfield et al., 2004):

1. *Product line analysis.* Its purpose is to decide what kind of systems the product line will develop. In order to achieve that goal, the scope of the systems to be developed should be specified.
2. *Product line design.* Its purpose is to decide how the product line will develop the software products. In order to achieve that goal, the architecture for the systems to be developed should be specified.
3. *Product line implementation.* Its purpose is to provide the implementation assets that are required by the product line architecture. In our case, we implement a software framework for supporting the specified architecture.

The following subsections give an overview of each step.

Product-Line Analysis

As described above, the purpose of this step is to decide what kind of systems the product line will develop. In the section entitled "Pervasive Systems as Integrator Systems" we introduced our point of view concerning pervasive systems development. In short, we aim to develop systems that are built using several COTS devices or external software applications that are integrated by a software system in order to provide a set of services to users of the pervasive system.

In order to provide a software architecture that correctly fits the requirements of such systems, we should clearly determine the scope of our applications and identify some basic nonfunctional requirements that must be satisfied by the assets (the software architecture and the implementation framework) that are produced to support the product line. These are the required characteristics:

- *Support for the conceptual primitives that are provided by the modeling language.* As introduced in the previous sections, a key goal of our framework is to raise the abstraction level of the implementation technology in order to facilitate code generation from our DSL. Therefore, it is very important issue to support the PervML conceptual primitives.

Figure 4.9 **Overview of the Proposed Architecture**

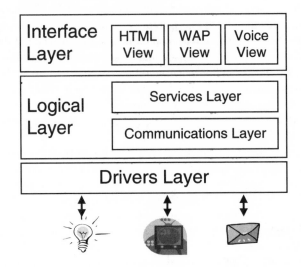

- *Integration with external software systems.* Services provided by pervasive systems can be implemented by physical devices and also by existing software systems (multimedia servers, contacts management software, etc.). Therefore, integration with external software systems should be supported by our framework.
- *Isolation of the manufacturer-dependent components.* As outlined above, a pervasive system is built from several COTS elements. However, on the other hand, our framework should support the DSL for pervasive systems. Therefore, in order to integrate these two requirements, the framework should clearly isolate the manufacturer-dependent parts from those that can be generated automatically.
- *Support for multiple user interfaces.* Pervasive systems emphasize new modes of human–computer interaction. Different kind of devices and platforms can be used. Therefore, our systems should be prepared to support several kinds of user interfaces.

Product-Line Design: Definition of a Software Architecture

Our proposed architecture for pervasive systems was designed to support the requirements introduced in the product-line analysis. We applied layers and model-view-controller architectural patterns (Buschmann et al., 1996) to provide a multitiered architecture for pervasive systems (see Figure 4.9).

The *drivers layer* is the lowest layer in the architecture. It is in charge of managing access to the devices and the external software services. In order to achieve these goals, drivers should be manually developed for dealing with manufacturer-dependent issues. Following this strategy, the drivers adapt the specific mechanisms for using the binding providers (the drivers or APS should be supplied by the manufacturers), so a common interface is provided for every kind of binding provider. This means that, for instance, all the lamp devices must be adapted to a generic interface with common operations like *switchOn* and *switchOff*.

The *communications layer* provides a representation of the binding providers that can be used by the services layer, thus providing a bridge between these two layers. There is a one-to-one relationship between the elements in the communication layer and the elements in the drivers layer. Concretely, this layer holds the manufacturer-independent part of the binding providers whereas the drivers layer holds the manufacturer-dependent issues. For instance, if there is a driver in the drivers layer for accessing a presence sensor that is located in a particular technology control network (e.g., EIB or LonWorks in home-automation systems), there will also be a presence sensor element in the communications layer. The driver would be in charge of dealing with specific issues of the control technology, whereas their representation in the communication layer would be in charge of logging the operations calls, updating an icon image representing the state of the device, and so on.

The *services layer* provides functionality as required by users of the system. The components that implement the services make use either of the elements in the communications layer or other services in the same layer. Note that one component can make use of many binding providers for implementing a service. On the other hand, one binding provider can be used by many components. For instance, a lighting service could be provided by several lamps and one of these lamps could be used as part of an alarm service. Moreover, interactions between services that are triggered by some condition can also occur.

Finally, the *interface layer* manages access to the system by any kind of client (human users or other software applications). In a pervasive context, several interfaces may be provided to access the same system. Therefore, we apply the model-view-controller pattern in this layer. Following this strategy, the components of the services layer can be seen as the model whereas specific controller and viewers for every supported interface should be implemented.

Other architectures for pervasive systems have been proposed. For example, *one.world*, proposed by (Grimm et al., 2004), is based on tuples, as the data model; environments, as the structuring mechanism for building pervasive applications; and events, as the communication mechanism. Moreover, it provides many low-level services (such as a query engine, checkpointing, and migration) to support the construction of applications. MediaBroker (Modahl et al., 2004) is a distributed framework. The main components of MediaBroker are clients (which produce or consume some kind of data), transports (which distribute the data), and transformation engines (which convert the data). This architecture was implemented using C programming language. Kirby and colleagues (2003) propose an active architecture that focuses mainly on supporting context awareness. They describe a global event service that uses P2P architecture to broadcast the context data. Pervasive applications should activate their functionality as a response to these events.

Product-Line Implementation: Building an Implementation Framework

In order to provide support to the architecture introduced in the preceding section, we developed an implementation framework. As described above, there are many implementation technologies for the development of pervasive systems. Using only a low-level technology for control (LonWorks, EIB, UPnP), data (Ethernet, Bluetooth, WiFi), or multimedia (IEEE1394, HAVi) networks is not possible because of the diversity of services required. For that reason, we selected OSGi, a middleware platform that has bridges to many of these networks and provides high-level constructs for building pervasive systems. This middleware helps to fill the abstraction gap between the domain-specific language and the target implementation technology.

The Open Service Gateway Initiative (OSGi) (Marples and Kriens, 2003) is an association of companies that includes Sun Microsystems, IBM, Oracle, and Nokia, created with the aim of developing an open standard for service gateways. A service gateway is the platform in which the

Figure 4.10   **Design Classes for the System Logic Layer of the Framework**

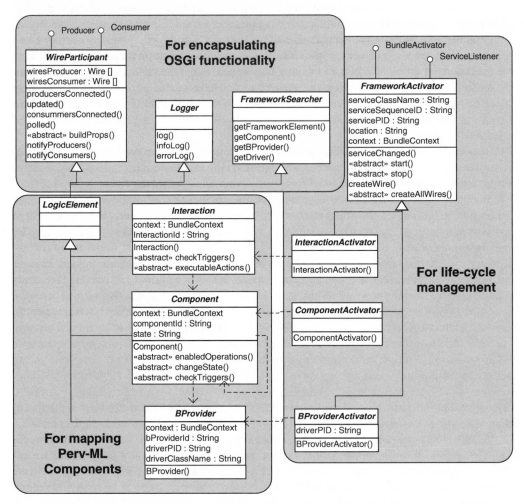

software for providing home services resides. It manages home devices and communicates with external networks. The standard defines Java APS for libraries that the OSGi platform provides and several standard services such as logging, HTTP server, device management, and so on. Our framework is built on top of this middleware using their runtime environment and services.

This section briefly describes the implementation framework for pervasive systems that was developed to support the proposed architecture. We did not implement the drivers layer because its software components should be manually developed in order to deal with manufacturer dependencies.

The Logic Layer

Figure 4.10 shows the design diagram that represents the framework classes of the system logic layer. Classes in this layer can be classified in three functional groups:

- *Classes for mapping PervML conceptual primitives.* This functional group is composed of the *Component, BProvider,* and *Interaction* classes. The goal of this group is to support PervML execution strategy. In order to achieve this goal, these classes define abstract methods that implement the steps in the PervML execution strategy. For instance, when an operation of a component class is executed: (1) the specific actions of the operation are performed (invoking operations of *BProvider* classes or other *Components*), (2) the class should change its current state and (3) check whether any triggering condition is satisfied. The implementation of these steps depends on the PervML specification, so the automatically generated code must extend and fulfill the classes that comprise this group in order to implement the behavior of the pervasive system.
- *Classes for encapsulating OSGi-related functionality.* This functional group is composed of the *Logger, FrameworkSearcher,* and *WireParticipant* classes. The goal of this group is to isolate some OSGi-related functionality that was inherited by the classes of the previous functional group. Classes in this group provide facilities for logging events (*Logger*), for searching services in the OSGi framework (*FrameworkSearcher*), and for participating in the event notification mechanism supplied by OSGi (*WireParticipant*).
- *Classes for dealing with the system of life-cycle management.* This functional group is composed of the *ComponentActivator, BproviderActivator,* and *InteractionActivator* classes. The goal of this group is to support the construction of the classes (activators) that are in charge of registering and unregistering the services in the OSGi framework. In our case, the mechanisms for notifying and receiving notification of changes in the OSGi services (wires, in OSGi terminology) are also created. Most of the functionality supplied by the activators is shared by the three elements, so an abstract class (*FrameworkActivator*) was implemented.

The Interface Layer

To provide support to interfaces for multiple devices, the *abstract factory* design pattern was applied. Moreover, abstract classes were included to facilitate the fulfillment of two critical user tasks:

- *Selecting the services of the system.* The *ServiceListing* class provides mechanisms for accessing the system services. Users can index the services by the kind of service, by their location or by their last usage. In order to achieve that goal, the abstract class provides several methods that return service lists. The screenshot on the left side of Figure 4.10 shows an instance of this class. Concretely, the figure shows an automatically generated Web interface for accessing all of the services available in the meeting room of our example.
- *Managing an instance of a kind of service.* The *ServiceUI* class supports the creation of interfaces for the management of instances of a kind of service. The *showServiceData* method creates the interface part that shows general information about the service, such as its location or its last usage. The *showServiceState* method creates the interface part that shows specific information about that kind of service, for instance, when a lighting service is switched on or off. The *showServiceOperations* method should create the interface part that shows the mechanism for using the functionality provided by that kind of service, for instance, creating the buttons for switching the state of a lighting service. Finally, the *manageOperation* method is in charge of obtaining the data from the user interface in order to execute the operation invoked by the user. The screenshot on the right side of Figure 4.10 shows a Web interface for managing a lighting service that has been generated by an instance of the *ServiceUI* class.

GRAPH GRAMMARS + TEMPLATES: THE TRANSFORMATION ENGINES

The last step in constructing the method is the definition and implementation of the rules for the transformation of the models (specified using PervML) into code. The generated code instantiates our framework for pervasive systems. Following the MDA proposal, this task is divided into two stages: first, the high-level abstraction model (PIM) should be transformed into a model (PSM) that is expressed using concepts of the final technology (in our case, using the primitives of our framework for pervasive systems). Then, the PSM is serialized to source code that can be compiled to produce the final software product. Note that the first stage is a model-to-model transformation, but the second one is a model-to-code transformation, so we need different techniques for every stage.

From PervML to the Framework Specification

As we introduced above, this step implies a transformation of the models expressed using the concepts of PervML into models expressed using the concepts of the implementation framework. In an MDA context, the structure of modeling languages is specified by metamodels that are built using the MOF language. Therefore, we developed the PervML and the framework metamodels. Figure 4.11 shows the framework metamodel. Following this approach, transformation from the PervML metamodel elements to the framework metamodel elements must be defined in order to convert PervML models into framework models. Note that the framework provides constructs (abstract classes) similar to those defined by PervML; therefore, the complexity of the model-to-model transformation was reduced.

Today, there are no standards for the definition of model-to-model transformations (Czarnecki and Helsen, 2003). In this direction, the OMG published a *Request For Proposal* (OMG, 2003b) in order to achieve a language for defining transformation between metamodels built using MOF. Therefore, in the meantime, we use graph grammars (Ehrig et al., 1999) as the model-to-model transformation engine. Many works (e.g., Csertan et al., 2002; Heckel, Küster, and Taentzer, 2002; Sendall, 2003) propose graph grammars as a suitable technique for model transformation. From a mathematical point of view, a model can be seen as a graph where model elements are labeled nodes and the relationships between model elements are edges. In this way, we apply all of the existing knowledge for defining graph transformations in order to achieve model transformations in the MDA context.

Figure 4.12 shows a rule for model transformation from PervML models to models expressed using the concepts of our framework. Every rule consists of a left-hand side that defines a pattern to be matched in the source graph and a right-hand side that defines the replacement for the matched subgraph. The example rule converts a PervML component into a framework component and sets the properties of the framework element using the values of the matched elements. Moreover, it removes the link between the component and the location elements. We are currently working with the AGG[2] graph grammars engine to implement our model-to-model transformation tool.

From the Framework Specification to OSGi Code

As a result of the model-to-model transformation introduced above, we obtain a graph-like representation of the pervasive systems. Figure 4.13 shows an excerpt of a framework specification

Figure 4.11 **Metamodel of Our Framework for Pervasive Systems**

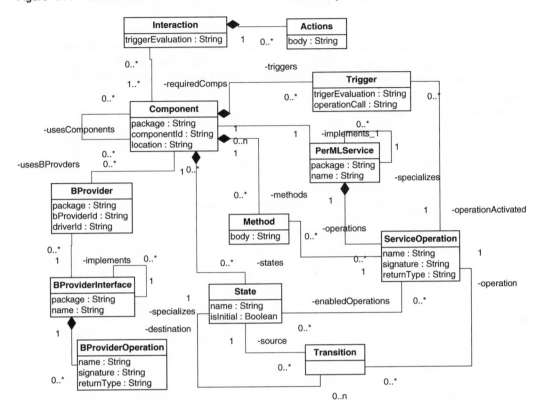

represented as a UML object diagram. To automatically obtain the source code of the final application, we need to transform that representation into Java files (since our aim is to produce OSGi code) and other textual resources (manifest files, build files, etc.).

Several techniques can be used to perform this task. Templates are a flexible and powerful solution that has previously been applied in this field (Rausch, 2001; Sturm, Voss, and Boger, 2002). Using a templates engine, we can independently specify the main structure and the syntax issues of the files that we want to generate.

In order to put our software factory into practice, we used the FreeMarker[3] template engine. FreeMarker is a free software engine that works on Java data structures, and provides a powerful syntax for specifying templates. We specified a set of templates for the main metamodel elements. These templates navigate through the metamodel structure (which was implemented as a library of Java classes) in order to obtain the data required to fill the gaps. Then, a simple Java program is in charge of (1) loading the metamodel data and (2) applying the templates for automatic code generation. Figure 4.14 shows a detailed view of the method strategy, which emphasizes the steps described in this section.

Figure 4.15 shows an excerpt of a FreeMarker template for generating a *Component* element of the framework. This template receives a *Component* metamodel element in the *comp* variable. Using a dot notation we extract data from the element properties and navigate to their related elements. For instance, the first line of the template builds the name of the package using three different variables: the base package of the component, the name of the service that the compo-

Figure 4.12 **A Transformation Rule**

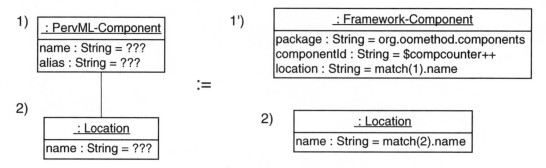

Figure 4.13 **A Partial Framework Specification**

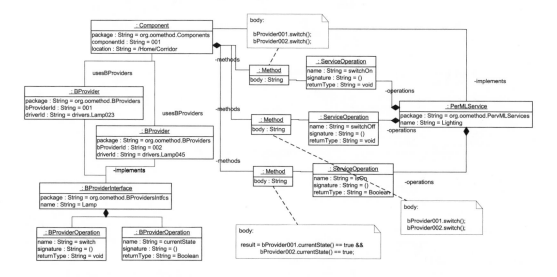

nent implements, and the component identifier. We make use of the <#list> and <#if> directives for iterating through collections and for conditionally generating some parts of the file. Note that some parts of the template have been omitted due to space constraints.

Templates like this one were developed for the *Interaction* and *BProvider* elements. Moreover, templates for generating their corresponding activators were also developed, using the data of the main elements (the *ComponentActivator* using the *Component* data, etc.). Figure 4.16 shows the generated code that was obtained from the application of the template to the component presented in Figure 4.13. We can see how the holes in the template have been fulfilled with the model data.

Finally, the automatically generated code is compiled and packaged into bundles (JAR files with specific manifest headers), which are loaded into the OSGi environment. Figure 4.17 shows two screenshots of the automatically generated Web interface for the system described in the example. Note that the framework and the manually implemented drivers for accessing the external elements must be previously loaded in order to obtain the complete pervasive system.

Figure 4.14   **A Detailed View of the Transformation Strategy**

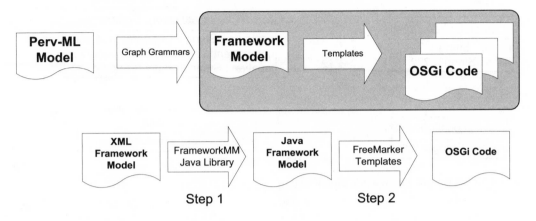

Figure 4.15   **An Excerpt of a FreeMarker Template**

```
Search  View  Tools  Options  Language  Help

<#assign packageName = "${comp.package}.${comp.implements.name}${comp.componentId}">
package ${packageName};

//Imports here
public class Component  extends org.oomethod.framework.Component
        implements ${implements.name} {
  //Defining variables for the binding providers
  <#list comp.usesBProviders as bProv>
  public static String bProvider${bProv.bProviderId}PID =
        "${bProv.implements.name}${bProv.bProviderId}";
  </#list>

  //For all the methods of the component
  <#list comp.method as meth>
  public ${meth.ServiceOperation.returnType}
  ${meth.ServiceOperation.name}  ${meth.ServiceOperation.signature} {
          //Searching the BindingProviders
          <#list comp.usesBProviders as bProv>
          ${bProv.BProviderInterface.name} bProvider${bProv.bProviderId};
          bProvider${bProv.bProviderId} = (${bProv.BProviderInterface.name})
          this.getBProvider(${bProv.BProviderInterface.name}.class.getName(),
                           bProvider${bProv.bProviderId}PID);
          </#list>
          //Defining the result variable, if needed
          <#if meth.ServiceOperation.returnType != "void">
          ${meth.ServiceOperation.retrunType} result;
          </#if>
          //Body of the method
          ${meth.body}
          //Updating the state of the component and loggint the action
          this.changeState("${meth.ServiceOperation.name}");
          this.log("Operation '${meth.ServiceOperation.name}'invoked on Component ${packageName}");
          //Returning the result of the operation, if needed
          <#if meth.ServiceOperation.returnType != "void">
          return result;
          <#else> //Or notifying of changes in the component
          this.notifyConsumers();
          </#if>
  }
  </#list>
  //constructor, checkTriggers, changeState, enabledOperations and buildProps definition here.
}
```

Figure 4.16 **Code Automatically Generated**

```
Search  View  Tools  Options  Language  Help

package org.oomethod.Components.Lighting001;
//Imports here

public class Component  extends org.oomethod.framework.Component
                       implements Lighting {
  //Defining variables for the binding providers
  public static String bProvider001PID = "Lamp001";
  public static String bProvider002PID = "Lamp002";

  //For all the methods of the component
  public void switchOn () {
    //Searching the BindingProviders
    Lamp bProvider001;
    bProvider001 = (Lamp) this.getBProvider(Lamp.class.getName(),
                   bProvider001PID);
    Lamp bProvider002;
    bProvider002 = (Lamp) this.getBProvider(Lamp.class.getName(),
                   bProvider002PID);

    //Body of the method
    bProvider001.switch();
    bProvider002.switch();

    //Updating the state of the component and logging the action
    this.changeState("switchOn");
    this.log("Operation 'switchOn' invoked on Component org.oomethod.Components.Lighting001");
    //Or notifying changes in the component
    this.notifyConsumers();

  }
  //The switchOff and isOn operations has been omitted due to space restrictions.
  //constructor, checkTriggers, changeState, enabledOperations and buildProps definition here.
}
```

IMPLEMENTATION DETAILS

In this section, we provide some details about the implemented pervasive system. The central server of the system is a Pentium IV barebone, with 512Mb RAM and connectivity by ethernet, 802g and serial port. The barebone runs Windows XP Professional Edition. We selected the Prosyst Embedded Server 5.2 as the OSGi implementation.

To support the control devices (lights, switches, and presence detector), an EIB network was deployed. The pervasive system accesses this network by means of the EIB bundle provided by Prosyst. The barebone is physically connected to the network by the serial port.

Figure 4.18 shows the overall network structure of our pervasive system. Next we summarize the devices selected for implementing the system services.

- The lighting lamps were implemented using common bulbs. These bulbs are controlled by the output ports, which are embedded in a Lingg & Junke eibDUO programmer.
- The blinds were also implemented using common blinds with an engine attached. The engines are controlled by a Moeller four-way blind actuator.
- The presence detector was implemented using a Jung 180 degree movement sensor.
- The blackboard was implemented using a common projector attached to a Pentium III. This computer runs Windows XP Home with a Windows Media Player in full screen mode. The projector computer hosts a program that provides Web services for controlling the Media Player. We developed an OSGi driver for accessing these Web services from the pervasive system.

121

Figure 4.17 Screenshots of Two Automatically Generated Web Interfaces

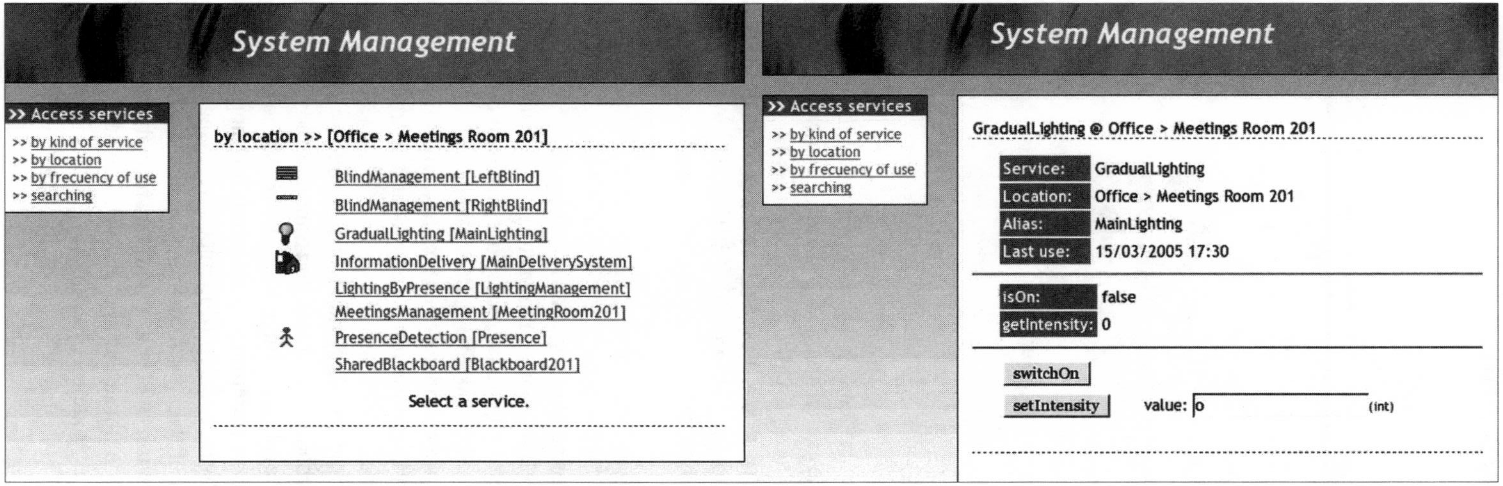

Figure 4.18 **Network Structure of the Final Pervasive System**

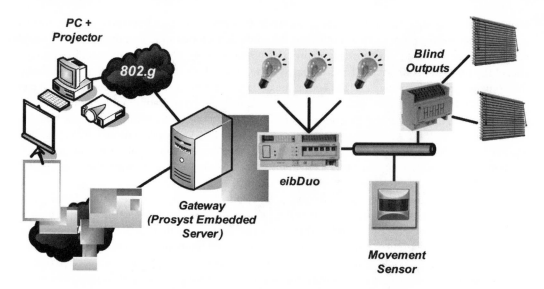

- The meetings management service was implemented using the OlivaNova Model Execution System.[4] This tool produces fully functional information systems from UML-like specifications. The generated system provides a Web services facade. As with the projector, we developed an OSGi driver to access these Web services from the pervasive system.
- E-mail service was implemented by an OSGi driver that connects to a predefined SMTP server by means of a Telnet connection and delegates mail delivery to this server.

RELATED WORK

Currently, most pervasive systems are developed ad hoc using very novel technologies. Sometimes the implementation technologies are just research prototypes. It is also common to use self-developed devices. We follow a different approach, since our aim is to build pervasive systems using current commercial technologies (such as EIB, UPnP, OSGi, Jini, X-10, etc.) that can be applied to such systems. Moreover, we use a model-driven strategy. Therefore, our work should be compared to other proposals for pervasive systems development that are based on the specification of system models and their implementation.

Modeling methods for real-time and embedded systems can be applied to pervasive systems development (Powel, 2000; Machado, Fernandes, and Santos, 2000; Peleg and Dori, 1999). These techniques usually provide the developer with low-level abstraction constructs (e.g., input/output ports) that directly describe hardware entities. Following this approach, system description is strongly dependent on the hardware system. Moreover, any change in the system requirements usually affects a broad segment of the system model. Another weak point associated with these approaches is the lack of well-defined and automated transformations from models to implementation. Finally, most of these techniques assume that developers can program system devices, but we think pervasive systems that are intended to be widely introduced should use black-box commercial devices.

CONCLUSIONS

This chapter presents a methodological approach to the development of pervasive systems from a software engineering point of view. Following the software factories strategy, our approach is based on the construction of a framework for a family of similar systems and a domain-specific language (PervML) for the specification of individual systems. We follow the MDA standard for defining the domain-specific language and the automatic code generation step. This merged approach can help to build better pervasive systems more easily than by applying traditional methods.

We have experimented in the development of information systems with many of the benefits provided by a model-driven approach. Our research group has developed a model-driven method (called OO-Method [Pastor et al., 2001]) with full code generation capabilities that has been implemented in the OlivaNova Model Execution System. Our aim is to apply these successful ideas to pervasive systems development.

We are currently using the home environment as a test-bed for our ideas and results. In this area, we have developed several pilot projects to test the expressivity of PervML and the implementation framework. These projects have produced fully functional systems that accurately implement the PervML specifications. Our experiments have revealed several future lines of research. For instance, our approach manages context information as any other information provided by a service (e.g., a presence-detection service or temperature-measurement service provide context information). A possible extension of PervML could manage context information explicitly as a first-class citizen. This extension could also influence the implementation framework. On the other hand, we currently generate default interfaces for several kinds of devices and/or platforms (Web for desktop browsers, Web for PDAs, WAP, and native PDA on Windows CE devices). We know that a system developer could require the adaptation of these interfaces in order to satisfy user requirements. We plan to extend PervML to support the detailed specification of user interfaces for multiple devices. Finally, we want to work with other implementation platforms. Today's systems are highly dependent on OSGi for providing functionality such as dynamic service discovery or hot update of software pieces. However, we aim to use other middleware or even to develop our own to implement all of the features required for pervasive systems. This line of research involves the definition of new mappings and transformations from PervML into the target technology, which will require a great effort. Fortunately, our approach facilitates the migration of all previously developed systems. The only requirement is to regenerate these systems using the new transformation engine.

In summary, this chapter has provided a broad overview of the development of pervasive systems from a software engineering point of view. A methodological approach to the construction of large and complex pervasive systems is needed. We think that current exciting trends in software engineering (MDA and software factories) can help in achieving that goal, and our method is a novel application of those proposals to pervasive systems development.

ACKNOWLEDGMENTS

This work was supported by MEC under the project DESTINO TIN2004-03534 and co-financed by FEDER.

NOTES

1. We extend the definition of COTS to include hardware devices.
2. http://tfs.cs.tu-berlin.de/agg/.
3. http://freemarker.sf.net.
4. http://www.care-t.com/.

REFERENCES

Buschmann, F.; Meunier, R.; Rohnert, H.; Sommerland, P.; and Stal, M. 1996. *Pattern-Oriented Software Architecture. Vol. 1: A System of Patterns*. New York: Wiley.

Csertan, G.; Huszerl, G.; Majzik, I.; Pap, Z.; Pataricza, A.; and Varro, D. 2002. VIATRA—Visual automated transformations for formal verification and validation of UML models. In *Proceedings of the Seventeenth IEEE International Conference on Automated Software Engineering (ASE'02)*. Edinburgh: IEEE CS Press, 267–270.

Czarnecki, K. and Helsen, S. 2003. Classification of model transformation approaches. In *Proceedings of the Second OOPSLA Workshop on Generative Techniques in the Context of the Model Driven Architecture*. Anaheim, CA. Available at www.softmetaware.com/oopsla2003/mda-workshop.html.

Ehrig, H.; Engels, G.; Kreowski, H.-J.; Montanari, U.; and Rozenberg, G. 1999. *Handbook of Graph Grammars and Computing by Graph Transformation. Volume 2: Applications, Languages and Tools*. Singapore: World Scientific.

Greenfield, J.; Short, K.; Cook, S.; and Kent, S. 2004. *Software Factories: Assembling Applications with Patterns, Models, Frameworks, and Tools*. New York: Wiley.

Grimm, R.; Davis, J.; Lemar, E.; MacBeth, A.; Swanson, S.; Anderson, T.; Bershad, B.; Borriello, G.; Gribble, S.; and Wetherall, D. 2004. System support for pervasive applications. *ACM Transactions on Computer Systems*, 22, 4, 421–486.

Heckel, R.; Küster, J.; and Taentzer, G. Towards automatic translation of UML models into semantic domains. In *Proceedings of the APPLIGRAPH Workshop on Applied Graph Transformation (AGT 2002)*. Grenoble, 11–22.

Kirby, G.; Dearle, A.; Morrison, R.; Dunlop, M.; Connor, R.; and Nixon, P. 2003. Active architecture for pervasive contextual services. In *Proceedings of the International Workshop on Middleware for Pervasive and Ad-hoc Computing (MPAC 2003)*. Rio de Janeiro, 21–28.

Machado, R.J.; Fernandes, J.M.; and Santos, H.D. 2000. A methodology for complex embedded systems design: Petri nets within a UML approach. In *Proceedings of the Second IFIP International Workshop on Distributed and Parallel Embedded Systems—DIPES'00*. IFIP Conference Proceedings; Vol. 189. Kluwer: Deventer, Netherlands, 1–10.

Marples, D. and Kriens, P. 2003. The Open Services Gateway Initiative: An introductory overview. *IEEE Communications Magazine*, 39, 12, 110–114.

Mellor, S.J.; Clark, A.N.; and Futagami, T. 2003. Guest editors' introduction: Model-driven development. *IEEE Software*, 20, 5, 14–18.

Modahl, M.; Bagrak, I.; Wolenetz, M.; Hutto, P.; and Ramachandran, U. 2004. MediaBroker: An architecture for pervasive computing. In *Proceedings of the Second IEEE International Conference on Pervasive Computing and Communications (PerCom'04)*, 253–262.

Object Management Group (OMG). 2003a. *Model Driven Architecture Guide*, 1.0. Needham, MA: Object Management Group. Available at www.omg.org/cgi-bin/doc?omg/03-06-01.

———. 2003b. *OMG/RFP/QVT MOF 2.0 Query/Views/Transformations RFP*. Needham, MA: Object Management Group. Available at www.omg.org/docs/ad/02-04-10.pdf.

———. 2004. *UML 2.0 Superstructure Specification*. Needham, MA: Object Management Group. Available at www.omg.org/cgi-bin/doc?ptc/2004-10-02.

Pastor, O.; Gómez, J.; Insfrán, E.; and Pelechano, V. 2001. The OO-Method approach for information systems modeling: From object-oriented conceptual modeling to automated programming. *Information Systems*, 26, 7, 507–534.

Peleg, M. and Dori, D. 1999. Extending the object-process methodology to handle real-time systems. *Journal of Object-Oriented Programming*, 11, 8, 53–58.

Powel, B. 2000. *Real-time UML: Developing Efficient Objects for Embedded Systems*. 2d ed. Essex: Addison-Wesley Longman.

Rausch, A. 2001. A proposal for a code generator based on XML and code templates. In *Proceedings of the Workshop on Generative Techniques for Product Lines*. Toronto. Available at users.encs.concordia.ca/~gregb/icse-workshop/.

Sendall, S. 2003. Combining generative and graph transformation techniques for model transformation: An effective alliance? In *Proceedings of the Second OOPSLA Workshop on Generative Techniques in the Context of Model Driven Architecture*. Anaheim, CA. Available at www.softmetaware.com/oopsla2003/mda-workshop.html.

Sturm, T.; Voss, J. von; and Boger, M. 2002. Generating code from UML with velocity templates. In *Proceedings of the Fifth International Conference on the Unified Modeling Language*. Dresden: Springer-Verlag, 150–161.

Want, R.; Pering, T.; Borriello, G.; and Farkas, K.I. 2002. Disappearing hardware. *Pervasive Computing*, 1, 1, 36–47.

Wilkie, I.; King, A.; Clarke, M.; Weaver, C.; and Rastrick, C. 2001. *The UML Action Specification Language (ASL) Reference Guide*. Available at http://www.kc.com/download/index.php. Kennedy Carter Ltd.

PART II

APPLICATIONS OF PERVASIVE INFORMATION SYSTEMS

DOMESTIC PERVASIVE INFORMATION SYSTEMS

End-user Programming of Digital Homes

VICTOR CALLAGHAN, JEANNETTE CHIN, VICTOR ZAMUDIO,
GRAHAM CLARKE, ANUROOP SHAHI, AND MICHAEL GARDNER

Abstract: *This chapter presents the background to the development of the digital home of the future and the ways in which it might be controlled by the end user. We describe the technical background to the development of the digital home out of the ubiquitous availability of networks and devices. We then describe two different approaches to user control that are already under development—task-based computing (TBC) and Pervasive Interactive Programming (PiP). We discuss theoretical work on combining, formalizing, and visualizing these processes. In addition, we report on a user evaluation that demonstrates that nonexpert users find these methods simple, enjoyable, and useful. Although this chapter confines itself to end-user programming of the digital home, we argue that the underlying mechanisms and concerns apply to all levels of pervasive computing.*

Keywords: *Digital Home, End-User Programming, Intelligent Buildings, Smart Home, Task Computing*

INTRODUCTION

In "Towards a New Architecture," a ground-breaking text of the Modern Movement in architecture in the 1920s, Le Corbusier (1970) famously remarked that, "A house is a machine for living in." More recently Craig Mundie, one of three chief technology officers at Microsoft, the world's largest software company was quoted in the *Economist* as saying "We view the digital home as critically important" and "the home is much more exciting than the workplace." Microsoft is not alone as, for example, Intel, the world's largest semiconductor maker, was reported in the same article as reorganizing itself into new business divisions including one called the "digital home" (*Economist*, 2005). The importance of the home market is further reinforced by market research conducted by the Diffusion Group, which reported that in 2005, more than half of U.S. households were interested in some sort of home control system (DTI, 2005). Modern buildings bear strong physical similarities to machines in that they contain a myriad of sensors, effectors, computer-based devices, and networks. By facilitating programmed coordination and interaction between distributed computer-enabled networked appliances, sensors, and actuators, the so-called smart home is created in which the home senses people's actions and responds in programmable ways. Thus, an essential aspect of a smart or digital home is "programming." We will describe the technical background to the development of smart homes and then look at different ways in which such systems might be programmed. We will argue that personal choice and control is of the essence when it comes to choosing a programming approach. We will describe a number of potential scenarios of a digital home of the future to illustrate the approach we have adopted. We will then examine in detail two existing approaches—task-based computing (TBC) and Pervasive Interactive Programming (PiP)—and discuss the implications of these approaches for the underlying methods required to enable this vision for enabling nontechnical people to program the functionality of their own digital homes. PiP has been evaluated by a number of users and the results of these finding will be reported.

BACKGROUND TO THE DEVELOPMENT OF THE DIGITAL HOME

In terms of domestic homes, the roots of building automation can be traced to a small Scottish company, PICO, that, in 1975, started the X10 project, which in 1978 resulted in Radio Shack's introduction of X10 home-automation technology to the American market. The X10 standard enables a computer, with suitable software, to control electrical power outlets by propagating signals along the power line. However, X10 has its limitations, such as speed (it takes about 600 milliseconds to send a single command), collisions (simultaneous signaling causes the system to fail), signal strength (poor or noisy wiring environments cause failure), and limited addressing range (256 addressable modules, based on 16 house codes [A–P] and 16 unit codes). As a consequence, there are numerous newer standards (e.g., LonTalk, BatiBus, CEbus, EIB, EHS, HBS, etc.) that seek to overcome these constraints and to expand the applications beyond simple actuator and sensor input/output into areas such as media streaming and interaction with internal functions of appliances (Wacks, 1998). The arrival of the Internet in the early 1990s and broadband networking for the home at the turn of the millennium have also impacted the functions and performance of home networks. This improved functionality has meant that the home computer is no longer just a gateway for the home, but can now be a contender for the home control network. Only time will tell which of the many standards will eventually dominate the domestic market but, for the time being, the simple and low-cost nature of X10 means it has remained one of the most enduring standards (Adair, 2005). Home automation standards are essentially descriptions of network transport mechanisms and communication protocols.

PROGRAMMING THE HOME OF THE FUTURE

The main focus of this chapter is how the digital home of the future can be programmed and managed by ordinary nonexpert home occupants. An alternative approach involves the use of autonomous intelligent agents that monitor occupants' habitual behavior, learning their needs, and creating rules (self-programming) so they can preemptively set the environment to what they anticipate the user would like (Callaghan et al., 2005). While autonomous agents may appeal to many people, their acceptance is not universal. Some lay people distrust autonomous agents and prefer to exercise direct control over what is being learned, when it is being learned, and to whom (or what) any information is being communicated. These concerns are particularly acute when such technology is in the private space of our homes. Often, end users are given very little, if any, choice in setting up such systems, but rather, they are required to "surrender their rights" and "put up with" whatever is provided (Chin et al., 2004). Moreover, there are other good arguments in support of a more personal involvement, such as enabling people's creative abilities by providing them with the means to become "designers" of their own "pervasive computing spaces," while at the same time shielding them from unnecessary technical details. In this approach, if people are given the means to configure their own "electronic spaces" then personal expression will be able to extend beyond the current do-it-yourself (DIY) approach of "paint and wallpaper" into information and control spaces. To achieve this vision it is necessary to solve the formidable challenge of enabling nontechnical people to program coordinating sets of pervasive computing-based home appliances. Current end-user programming systems for the home are built around extensions of the principles of conventional computer languages involving a sequence of logical instructions. In an attempt to make the process simpler for nontechnical users, some applications, such as ActiveHome Pro (Asaravala, 2004), employ a graphical interface front-end approach that represents text-based program constructs (i.e., instructions) with graphical objects for the user to manipulate into program flows or sequences of actions. The disadvantages of this approach are that it requires users to mentally manipulate programming abstractions; it is restricted to sequential actions (macros); and it is limited to single monolithic processor control rather than the distributed computation afforded by pervasive computing. The remainder of this chapter will present new research aimed at enabling nontechnical home users to control and program distributed pervasive home networked devices in as unconstrained a way as possible.

An Illustrative Scenario

The following scenario is offered to crystallize some of the ideas discussed in this chapter. We will refer back to this scenario later in the chapter when discussing different techniques.

1. *Background*—Tessa is a visiting researcher at the University of Essex. She arrives at the University and moves into her new temporary accommodation, an intelligent apartment. Like all environments in the future, the "radio-sphere" is awash with services that are available for her use. Many of these services are local, such as lighting and heating, while others are remote, such as video, music, news, and e-mail. Monolithic appliances and computer applications have given way to more atomic networked functions, such as switches, video displays, codecs, editors, mp3 files, and so on. Tessa interacts with the environment via her personal "wireless assistant" (WA), which also holds descriptions of her preferred world.

2. *Virtual appliances and applications*—The concept of appliances and applications has lingered on as people still need to utilize functions akin to televisions, telephones, word processors, and the like. Consequently, all environments have their networked devices/applications preformed into familiar default configurations (called Meta-Application-appliances [MAps]). Each MAp describes a familiar everyday appliance. Thus, both physical and information spaces function as normally. It is possible for users to purchase new MAps, and for more creative individuals to devise their own.

3. *Mobility*—On entering her apartment, Tessa's WA starts to flash in an unobtrusive manner indicating she is within a "smart space." Her WA contains her ontology-based descriptions of her preferred MAp. It discovers what is available in the environment, and then requests that matches as near as possible be constructed. If devices move out of the room or fail, the system will similarly try to find suitable replacements. Of course, this is not always possible but her WA will indicate what is missing, so she has the option to borrow, buy, or replace any missing devices. One such MAp is her "communication center" (CC). On moving to other rooms and environments the WA attempts to maintain Tessa's preferred configuration for her CC MAp.

4. *Programming*—The original CC MAp consists of a telephone service, audio transducer, and dialer. Tessa has modified the MAp to add in a light and then programs rules using an end-user programming tool that is resident in her WA to be associated with this new device. For example she reprograms the CC MAp configuration and rules to: "on receipt of a call, pause other incoming media streams, divert the call to the audio/video-transducer in use at the time, and raise the light if it is dark." While Tessa generally only modifies existing MAps, numerous hobby clubs and small industries generate novel and sometimes highly complex MAps, which they then trade.

5. *Interaction*—Tessa selects the "News" menu, which causes the smart space to invoke an interactive display MAp, connecting it to her preferred RSS news feeds. As she reads her news feed, a video-conference request arrives, and the CC acts as a sophisticated "soft appliance," activating previously programmed rules that cause the news feed to be suspended, lights to be raised, and the video conference to be patched through to the current audio and video system. As with a normal appliance, Tessa can manually override any of the settings on this "soft appliance."

From this scenario it can be inferred that, in order to realize this particular vision, a number of issues need to be resolved. These include the question of how communities of devices are formed and managed, how the capabilities of devices and communities are described, how lay users can program these communities, how the system deals with mobility of the devices and users, how the user interacts with the programmed systems, and how the end user can maintain and debug the system. We hope to answer these questions in the process of describing this approach further.

Decomposition, Deconstruction, Disintegration, and Disaggregation

While traditional stand-alone home appliances provide useful functionality to users, when you add a network connection a number of significant possibilities arise. For instance, manufacturers can provide access to individual subfunctions within an appliance or application allowing, for example, the mute function on a television to be accessed by other networked appliances. More significantly *soft appliances* and *applications* can be created by establishing logical connections between subfunctions. This can serve to create replicas of traditional appliances and applications, or to invent altogether new appliances or applications (Chin 2006). In essence, this paradigm involves the *deconstruction* (alternatively described as decomposition, disaggregation, or disintegration) of traditional appliances and applications into their atomic functionalities (physically or logically), allowing the user to reconstruct appliances and applications by reconnecting the basic atomic functionalities in various ways. Some current examples of this approach include SUN's Epsilon Project (Epsilon, 2005), which explores how appliances are decomposed into small independent devices each having a virtual world proxy that can be "connected" to other proxies to create meta systems (offering conventional appliance functions, or novel ones created by user-chosen combinations). A particularly interesting aspect of the Epsilon work is that it explores the notion of ultra-thin clients where the physical manifestation of the appliance becomes nearly stateless with most state and process residing in proxies whose location is almost irrelevant. This work at SUN is wide ranging and includes studies on supporting middleware (Horan, 2005). As part of their Easy Living project, Microsoft is also exploring the notion of deconstruction ("disaggregation," in their terminology) to personal computers (PCs) and services, demonstrating how a disconnected pool of screens, keyboards, and applications can be dynamically reconnected to create a virtual PC for a user in differing contexts (Easy Living, 2005). In terms of decomposed applications, Apple's

Unix Mac OS X (aka "Tiger") provides an "AppleEvent subsystem" that allows developers to get at the internal interface descriptions of applications (i.e., application subfunctions) and combine them in differing ways (Jobs 2004).

Communities and Tasks

The key to creating soft-appliances and applications from deconstructed functions is to connect them into coordinating communities or collectives that synergistically form new functions. Clearly, the richer the pool of (sub-) functions or services, the greater the possible permutations for new utilities. How such communities or collectives are created is one of the central issues that we address in this chapter.

A useful way to view people and their activities, which is consistent with the deconstructed worldview we are developing, is to see their activity as being task based. For example, rather than describing user requirements in terms of the physical model of the world—"I will switch on the TV in the corner of the living room, and turn to channel 3"—one might abstract to the higher-level task "I want to watch the news now (where I am)." Later in this chapter we will show how such a task-based approach can be implemented to provide a user-friendly means of interacting with home-based pervasive information systems.

Making Sense of the World: Ontology and Epistemology

In order for the tools we provide users to make sense of their world, it is necessary to develop a description of the properties and capabilities of devices and applications that can be shared. An ontology formally describes devices and applications, and provides axioms that constrain the form and interpretation of these terms. An ontology can therefore help with mobility and failure by searching for nearest matches to missing devices or community functions, or by alerting the user to other possibilities given the particular context. For user-generated communities of coordinating computer-based devices, community-related information can be described and reasoned about using an ontology. Ontologies also provide a convenient means for storing rules that embody the autonomous functionality of a community. Since we are concerned with user-defined communities that are both personal and subjective descriptions based upon the limited knowledge of the user, their representation within an ontology is referred to here as an epistemology. As the techniques described in this chapter are user-centric, epistemologies are intrinsic to many of the approaches we describe and are discussed in greater detail in a later section.

TASK-BASED COMPUTING

Task-based computing was pioneered by Wang and Garlan (2000) of Carnegie Mellon University and by Fujitsu (Masuoka, Parsia, and Labrou, 2003). It seeks to provide a programming environment that allows users to interact with computing spaces in terms of high-level tasks. It can be viewed as a method to allow users to discover, combine, and execute coordinated contextual actions (tasks); this differs from more common usages such as capturing system requirements and specifying users interfaces (O'Neill and Johnson, 2004). Thus, in our interpretation, tasks are high-level collectives composed of numerous lower-level actions, for example, the task "play my MP3 files" could be decomposed into a series of smaller steps that need to be combined to carry out this task. In the Fujitsu work, a graphical user interface tool referred to as STEER (semantic task execution editor) is used to do this. The basic unit of task composition is

Figure 5.1   **Task Definition for Grouping Tasks Available in the IIE Room**

```
<taskgrouplabel="IIE Room">
    <taskgrouplabel = "Control Space">
        <taskgroup label = "Lighting">
            <task label="Switch On" target="http://essex.ac.uk.idorm#LightOn"
            oncomplete="Let there be light"/></taskgroup>
    </taskgroup>

    <taskgroup label = "Personal Space">
        <task label="News" target="http://essex.ac.uk/idorm#NEWS"/></taskgroup>

    <taskgroup label = "NoticeBoard">
        <task label="Add Note" target="http://essex.ac.uk/idorm#ADDNOTE"
        oncomplete="Enter NOTE on Board"/> </taskgroup>
</taskgroup>
```

a pair of service inputs and outputs, which, when associated, can be executed on command by the user. Using STEER makes it possible to create more complex compositions. This approach bears similarities to scripting mechanisms (e.g., AppleScript) that enable the user to combine the functionality of multiple applications. For example, Apple's "drag and drop" automator tool allows developers to create lists of actions (workflows) in new and unexpected ways (Jobs, 2004). In general terms, task-based computing provides a simple and quick way for users to interact with and control such environments since they need simply to select the required actions from a menu of available high-level tasks with minimal configuration and interaction.

Task Discovery

Pervasive computing environments, such as smart spaces, contain a range of services that are resources provided to network clients by one or more servers, such as room lighting, for example. In this implementation, a service keeps no record of its own or its client's state and does not have to provide a unique identifier. However, tasks are normally constructed from a set of services and keep state on themselves and clients. Before interacting with services, some form of service discovery is necessary, and it should be seamless and intuitive.

With a user-oriented task layer, pervasive computing environments are able to discover and present combinations of services to users as high-level tasks that may be organized according to contextual information. Figure 5.1 shows a task definition describing tasks available within the iDorm. Tasks are grouped according to context-based namespaces, such as "IIE Room/Control Space/Lighting/Switch On." This namespace indicates that "Switch On" is an atomic task for controlling lighting in the IIE Room. For this simple case, the low-level service (switch on) directly equates to a task (i.e., one source, one sink). In such simple cases, services will belong to well-defined types, allowing task definitions to be generated by pairing sources and sinks, inferring the type of task by making use of a service's low-level interface description, as provided by conventional service-discovery protocols. Where multiple services are combined to form tasks, they can be organized automatically using available contextual information, without requiring any human intervention or being organized manually by the user. In this work, tasks are provided to

Figure 5.2   **Task Menu on Smart Phone**

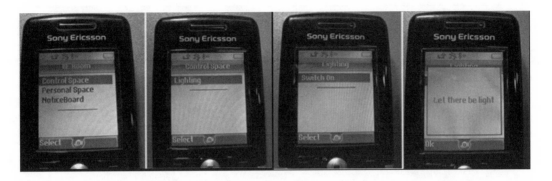

the user via a smart phone device using Bluetooth. Figure 5.2 depicts the results of transferring the tasks described in Figure 5.1 to such a phone, which a user may then use to discover and interact with the pervasive information systems environment.

The automated approach is crucially dependent on the ability of designers to prespecify all combinations of device types and users, and developers to adhere rigidly to type constraints. Thus, for more complex collectives involving numerous sources, sinks, conditional relationships, and/or user-created communities, automated task formation is infeasible. In such cases a method for translating composite sets of services into tasks is required. Pervasive Interactive Programming is one such tool, which will be described later in this chapter.

Task Interaction

Task-based computing shields users from knowing the esoteric details associated with a service's interface definition. This is provided by linking a task definition to a service's interface definition (Figure 5.1). Figure 5.3 depicts an architecture describing a task-based computing environment where a mobile device, such as a smart phone, is present within a space, and interacts with a lighting service provided by the space.

The architecture is divided into a number of components:

- *Mobile device mediator* (MDM): Provides mechanisms for discovering and interacting with any services that are available. Interacts with the task model to obtain a task definition (Figure 5.1), which is then translated and adapted to a form interpretable by the device. When a user invokes a task, such as "Lighting On," the MDM forwards the request to the event heap.
- *Task model* (TM): Stores all task definitions and their mapping to task descriptions. Organizes tasks according to user-defined notions of space. For example, one may wish to split a room into many subspaces or tag objects using radio frequency identification, consider a whole floor using Wi-Fi, or just a room by using Bluetooth. This will associate tasks with physical spaces within a building.
- *Tasks*: Abstracts environmental and application services into processes as defined by the OWL-S. Tasks are embedded with semantics to allow for automated and seamless service composition, invocation, and configuration. Tasks may correspond to either atomic or composite processes. For example, in Figure 5.1, the task "Lighting/Switch On" is mapped to

Figure 5.3   **Task Interaction in a Pervasive Computing Environment**

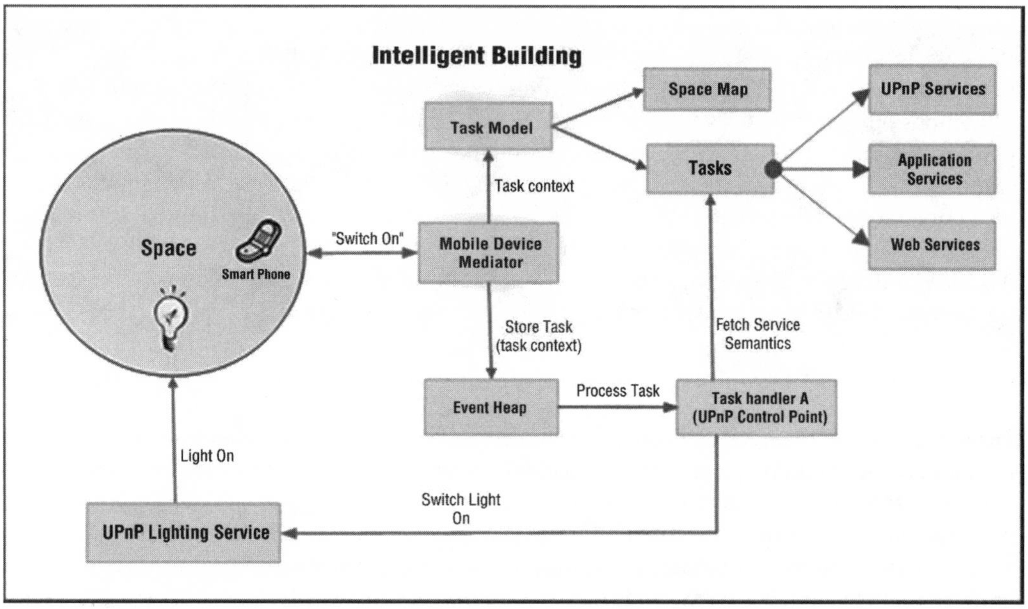

an atomic service identified by http://essex.ac.uk/idorm#LightOn, which, in turn, links to a semantic description that wraps an operation from a Universal Plug and Play (UPnP)-based lighting service.
* *Event heap and handlers*: All task invocations received from the MDM are forwarded to the event heap, which then notifies any relevant task handlers registered for a particular task type. The "task invocator" handler processes events by using the task to invoke a relevant service, for example, a UPnP-based lighting service.

Prior to their use, simple tasks are generated from automated parsing, but more complex collectives need to be explicitly programmed.

PERVASIVE INTERACTIVE PROGRAMMING

In this section we describe an end-user tool that takes the notion of task-based computing forward by enabling the creation of nonterminating tasks or meta-appliances (and meta-applications) from locally available appliances (and application) services. These nonterminating tasks can be programmed by the user.

Overview

Pervasive Interactive Programming (UK Patent No: GB 0523246.7) is based on the idea of putting the end-user at the center of control of a pervasive information system environment by providing a simple means that requires no technical skills. This approach allows the user to define communities of pervasive devices and to program them by using this community to produce the required behavior. Such coordination creates behaviors above and beyond those available from an individual application or appliance giving rise to a possible alternative name for the process, meta application-appliance program (MAp). PiP has its roots in Programming by Example (PBE), a programming paradigm pioneered by Canfield-Smith in the mid-1970s whereby functionalities are not described abstractly but rather demonstrated in concrete examples (Canfield-Smith, Cypher, and Tesler, 2000; Lieberman 2001); Tangible Computing, a way of bringing a physical metaphor to software abstractions pioneered by Ishii (Ishii et al., 2004); Palpable Computing (Andersen et al., 2005), an approach to promote user control and choice through increased visibility of pervasive computing technology, and Learning from the User (LFU), an embedded-agent learning paradigm that Essex University has been developing for many years (Callaghan et al., 2005). In addition, PiP utilizes ontologies mainly drawn from research work on the semantic Web (Berners-Lee, Hendler, and Lassila, 2001). PiP differs from PBE in that, first, it aims at real rather than graphical objects; second, it is directed at distributed computing rather than a single processor; and third, it spawns distributed nonterminating sequence-independent tasks rather than creating macros or other procedural structures. PiP shares the same motivation as many of the approaches mentioned above but aims to take this vision forward by enabling nontechnical people to become designers and programmers of their own unique environments. In addition, the motivation for PiP was driven by experience with autonomous agent-based systems where concerns about privacy and trust were voiced (Basu and Callaghan, 2005; Chen, Finin, and Joshil, 2004; Lyons 2005). In the PiP approach, the system is explicitly put into a learning mode and taught how to behave by the end user's demonstration of the activity required. For example, as discussed in the scenario provided earlier, the television- or sitting-room light could be made to react to an incoming call on the telephone, thus the telephone, TV, and light could coordinate their actions to form a new meta-utility (soft appliance). In this approach functional subunits of appliances can be shared while devices interoperate seamlessly together. For example, the audio amplifier in a TV could be made use of by the HiFi system, or vice versa. Consequently, MAps could be created by establishing logical connections between the subfunctions of appliances, creating replicas of traditional appliances, or inventing altogether new appliances. Of course, there are also stand-alone appliances that provide all of these functions in an "off the shelf" box. Additionally, the vision for PiP includes the notion of prefabricated interconnection MAps, which are descriptions of previously made communities, such as a TV.

PiP Architecture

Pervasive Interactive Programming supports the setting up of communities. Users first select and define a community that they wish to program, and then carry out a set of coordinated actions that are taught to the system. The members of the community that are going to be the actuators and those that are going to be the environment for such actuation need to be chosen. A user action in the teaching mode causes an appliance to generate an associated event, and this event is then used to generate appropriate rules based on a "snapshot" of the environment (community) state at the time. A device can be involved in more than one community. The user interface with PiP is via a PiP editor, shown in Figure 5.4. This editor provides a means for:

1. displaying discovered devices,
2. setting up/amending communities; and
3. managing the user's demonstration sessions (teaching).

Tasks (e.g., MAps) can be taught by interacting either with on-screen representations of the devices or with the real devices themselves. Once created, tasks can be played back on demand,

Figure 5.4   **The MaP Editor with Example of Community Setup**

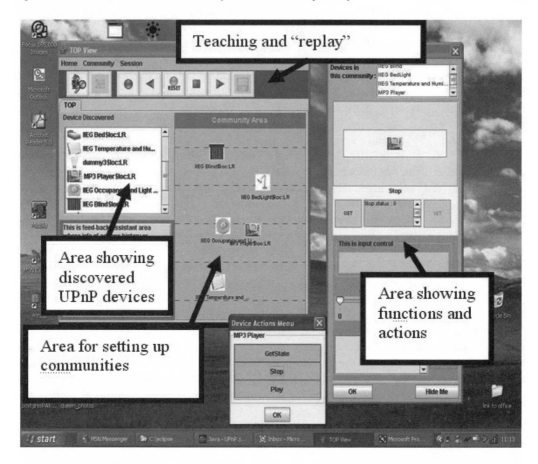

either from the user-generated event, as in a task computing meta-application, or in response to an environmentally originated event.

The PiP architecture, shown in Figure 5.5, comprises the following modules:

1. PiP engine—this module is responsible for discovering and subscribing to community events. This module contains a Rule Manager that is responsible for gathering, generating, and *executing* rules, together with an Event Handler that manages PiP events.
2. Data Modeling Manager—this module is responsible for maintaining and providing consistent data.
3. Community Manager—this module manages (sets up and maintains) the communities of coordinating devices.
4. PiPeditor—this is the interface the user uses to program and interact with the system.
5. Rule Manager—this module is responsible for compiling and executing rules.
6. Ontology Manager—this module manages the translation of ontology.

To facilitate the information to be used within and beyond the community, data need to be standardized so that they can be understood by all other parties in the network. For this aspect of the

Figure 5.5   **The Pervasive Interactive Programming (PiP) Architecture**

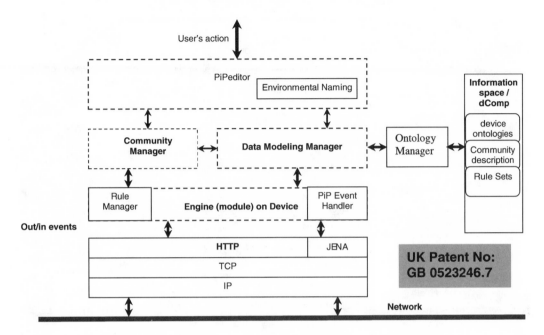

work, the semantics in PiP (described in the following section) support information interoperability between applications, providing a common machine "understanding" knowledge framework.

Semantics of Home Devices and dComp Ontology

To enable computers and users to utilize devices it is necessary to provide descriptions of their capabilities; an ontology provides such a description. PiP leverages ontology semantics as the core vocabulary for its information space, generating ontology-based rule sets when a user demonstrates his/her desired tasks to the system.

The SOUPA ontology from Ubicomp (Chen, Finin, and Joshil, 2004) is aimed at pervasive computing but lacks support for crucial PiP mechanisms such as community, decomposed functions, and coordinating actions, which are essential to produce higher-level meta functionality. In addition, the current SOUPA standard has only limited support for the UPnP standard (which our research testbed, the iDorm2 described later in this chapter, depends on). OWL-S, previously called DAML-S (OWL, 2005) is based around the notion of services. It primarily targets the World Wide Web, enabling agents to evoke services, and thus facilitating the automation of Web tasks. It provides a useful abstraction called "composite processes," which is still under development and, at the time of writing, does not give a precise specification of what it means to perform a process. Thus, we have developed our own ontology, dComp (deconstructionist and community programming), which provides a better match with domestic environments and has a well-defined specification of communities (akin to composite processes on OWL-S). dComp (see Table 5.1) is based around the OWL language, which is widely used (especially for the semantic Web). Numerous supporting tools such as the Jena (McBride, 2002), RACER (Haarslev and Moller, 2001), and

Table 5.1

dComp Ontology (v.1.1)

DCOMPDevice Class	DCOMPHardware Class	DCOMPService Class	Rule Class	Policy Class
DCOMPDevice	Hardware	DCOMPService	Rule	Policy
MobileDevice	CPU	LightsNFittingsService	FixedRule	Mode
StaticDevice	Memory	LightService	PersistentRule	
NomadicDevice	DisplayOutput	SwitchService	NonPersistentRule	_Time Class_
Light	DisplayScreenProperty	TelephoneService	Preceding	
Switch	AudioOutput	AlarmService	Device	_DCOMPperson Class_
Telephone	AudioOutputProperty	TemperatureService		
Alarm	Tuner	EntertainmentService	_Preference Class_	_Action Class_
Blind	Amplifier	AudioService	Preference	Action
Heater		VideoService	SituationalCondition	PermittedAction
FileRepository	_DCOMPCommunity Class_	FollowMeService	CommunityPreference	ForbiddenAction
DisplayDevice	SoloCommunity	SetTopBoxService		Recipient
AudioDevice	NotJointCommunity	StateVariable		TargetAction
SetTopBox	PersistentCommunity	TOPService		
Characteristic	TransitoryCommunity			
DeviceInfo	CommunityDevice			

Figure 5.6   **A Partial TV Community Definition**

```
<com:TransitoryCommunity rdf:ID="JCTV">
 <com:communityID>Tran-JCTV</com:communityID>
 <com:communityName>JC TV</com:communityName>
 <com:communityDescription>The first JC testing
TV</com:communityDescription>
 <com:timeStamp rdf:datatype="&xsd;dateTime">2004-09-
06T19:43:08+01:00</com:timeStamp>
 <com:hasOwner>
  <person:Person>
   <person:firstName
rdf:datatype="&xsd;String">Jeannette</person:firstName>
    <person:nickname rdf:datatype="&xsd;String">JC</person:nickname>
    <person:gender rdf:resource="#Female"/>
   </person:Person>
  </com:hasOwner>
 <com:hasCommunityDevice>
  <com:CommunityDevice>
   <device:deviceUUID>UUID:PHLCRT17</device:deviceUUID>
  </com:CommunityDevice>
  <com:CommunityDevice>
   <device:deviceUUID>UUID:PHLAudioMMS223</device:deviceUUID>
  </com:CommunityDevice>
  <com:CommunityDevice>
   <device:deviceUUID>UUID:NetGem442</device:deviceUUID>
  </com:CommunityDevice>
 </com:hasCommunityDevice>
 </com:TransitoryCommunity>
```

F-OWL (Zou, Chen, and Finin, 2004) inference engines are also widely available. The full dComp specification is available online (dComp, 2005).

In the current implementation we have defined a few classes supporting the notion of community and rules (Chin 2006). Wherever possible we have sought to adopt suitable ontology for our other needs. For example our Person, Policy, and Time ontologies are adopted from Ubicomp SOUPA ontology. In dComp, preferences are referred to as "situated preferences," which is akin to Vastenburg's (2004) "situated profile" concept, which uses situation as a framework for user profile so that the values of the profile are relative to situations. By way of illustrating a virtual appliance definition, Figure 5.6 shows the partial description of a TV community. In it, the community has a label "JC TV" with a description of "The first JC testing TV"; it was created on 2004-09-06 at 19:43 and has an owner "Jeannette"; it was composed from three other devices on the network. These devices are identified by their unique id numbers: UUID:PHLCRT17, UUID: PHLAudioMMS223, and UUID:NetGem442.

AGENT SERVICES

At the outset of this chapter we described how automated services, such as agents, were deliberately made to be subservient to the end-user programming interface, allowing the user to choose the level of autonomy given to various parts of the system. Invariably, some aspects of any system will need to be automated that users are incapable of carrying out or that they do not want to be involved in at the given level of complexity or abstraction. For example, searching the available network services and functions and mapping these to higher-level task-based user requirements would be a complex and tedious process that is better left to automated assistance. This difficulty is compounded by the highly dynamic nature of users and devices; with both users and devices joining and leaving networks and the variability of devices, it is not possible to prespecify every device or combination of devices. In the following we provide a formalism that describes how continuity of function might be supported when people and devices change in ways illustrated in the Home of the Future scenario earlier in this chapter.

In general terms we could describe this problem as follows: an *allocation* is a duple *(d, T)* where *d* is a device and *T* is a nonempty set of *k* tasks, that is, $T = \{t_1, t_2, t_3, ..., t_k\}$, with $k \geq 1$. If $k = 1$, we have a simple device that is able to handle only one kind of task. This is the case of a speaker, or a microphone. If $k > 1$, then *d* is a complex device, which is comprised of other subdevices, that is, *d* can handle more than one task. This could be the case of a TV, comprised of a device that can handle two different kinds of signals: audio and video.

When the user configures a new appliance, he defines a new *community*. A *community,* denoted by *C*, is a finite nonempty collection of *n* allocations, that is,

$$C = \{(d_1, T_1), (d_2, T_2), (d_3, T_3), ..., (d_n, T_n)\}, \text{ with } n \geq 1.$$

If the user goes to a new environment, the agent should attempt to create an *equivalent community* C_{eq}. In order to create this equivalent community, for each allocation $(d, T) \geq C$, the agent should find an equivalent allocation (d_{eq}, T_{eq}) in the new environment. As we mentioned before, we have two cases: $k = 1$ and $k > 1$.

1. If $k = 1$, then *d* is a simple device and $T = \{t_1\}$. The agent should find a new allocation $(d_{eq}, \{t_1\})$ such that the device d_{eq} is able to perform the only task. t_1.

2. If $k > 1$ then *d* is a complex device, and $T = \{t_1, t_2, t_3, ..., t_k\}$. The agent should find, in the worst case, *k* allocations $(d^1_{eq}, \{t_1\}), (d^2_{eq}, \{t_2\}), (d^3_{eq}, \{t_3\}), ..., (d^k_{eq}, \{t_k\})$, where every device d^i_{eq} is able to perform the task t_i, with $1 \leq i \leq k$.

We could extend this framework in order to include time. A *temporal allocation* is a tuple (d, T, t_i, t_f) where *d* is a simple device, *T* is a (simple) task, t_i is the initial time, and t_f is the final time. In other words, the device *d* will be performing task *T* during $t_f - t_i$ units of time, beginning at instant t_i. So, a *temporal community,* denoted by C_t is a nonempty set of temporal allocations:

$$C_t = \bigcup_{j=1}^{k} \left\{ \left(d_j, T_j, t_{ji}, t_{jf} \right) \right\}$$

From this approach other issues arise, such as scheduling and time-dependent sequences of tasks (Zamudio, Callaghan, and Chin, 2005). A temporal community representation in agent service is shown in Figure 5.7.

Figure 5.7   **Representation of a Temporal Community**

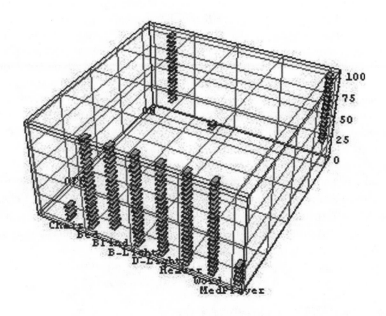

Figure 5.8   **The iDorm2**

EVALUATION

Research Platform

For our experimental work we have built a pervasive computing testbed called the iDorm2, which takes the form of a two-bedroom apartment (see Figure 5.8). It is a full-size domestic apartment containing the usual rooms for activities such as sleep, work, eating, washing, and entertaining. It comprises numerous networked artifacts such as telephones, MP3 players, lights, beds, and chairs.

Connectivity and a common interface to the iDorm2 devices are implemented via IP networking and UPnP. UPnP is a distributed middleware that employs event-based communication, supporting automatic discovery and configuration. Our experimental PiP architecture aims to be independent

Figure 5.9   **Some Participants Evaluating MaP**

of any particular middleware, although the current version utilizes UPnP as its underlying network communication infrastructure. The PiP user interface can be accessed via a variety of means ranging from mobile devices such as tablet PCs to an LG iFridge.

Procedures and Apparatus

The work described in this chapter was evaluated based on a trial involving eighteen participants drawn from a diverse set of backgrounds (e.g., housewives, students, secretaries, teachers, etc). There were ten females and eight males ranging in age from twenty-two to sixty-five. The participants also formed a multicultural group including Asians, Europeans, Latin Americans, and Australians. All participants had some computing experience (i.e., they knew how to use a mouse).

Table 5.2

The Evaluation Ratings

| | N | Mean | Standard deviation | Standard error | 95% confidence interval for mean | |
					Lower bound	Upper bound
Conceptual	113	4.3186	0.53894	0.05070	4.2181	4.4190
User control	191	4.1990	0.59134	0.04279	4.1146	4.2834
Cognitive load	155	4.2710	0.57332	0.04605	4.1800	4.3619
Information presentation	112	4.4107	0.54613	0.05160	4.3085	4.5130
Affective experience	240	4.6083	0.50596	0.03266	4.5440	4.6727
Future potential	83	4.1687	0.76221	0.08366	4.0022	4.3351
Total	894	4.3602	0.59489	0.01990	4.3211	4.3992

While 20 percent of the participants had a very good knowledge of programming, 60 percent had none at all. For the evaluation sessions they were given five sets of devices (drawn from a set of lights, a telephone, a smart sofa, and an MP3 player). During the evaluation, no specific tasks were set for the participants but they were encouraged to use their imagination to create their own desired environment based on the devices available. The evaluation was preceded by a twenty-minute training session.

The evaluation methodology was developed with the assistance of Chimera (a sociotechnical research unit based in the BT Research Park at Martlesham Heath in Suffolk, UK) to assess the participants' subjective views on the usability of the system (DiDuca and Van Helvert, 2005). It consisted of both observations and a questionnaire measuring attitudes over six usability dimensions, which are shown in Table 5.2 (a higher rating score on the dimensions shows greater usability). Each of these dimensions consisted of a series of from two to four statements and each statement offered a range of ratings (from 1 to 5). A higher rating score on the dimensions demonstrates greater usability of PiP.

Results

Because of space limitations, it is not possible to present all of the evaluation data or results; therefore, only highlights will be given to convey the general findings. It is clear that all of the dimensions rated well (scoring above 4), indicating that the users were generally well satisfied with the system. At the outset of the work, one of our contentions was that people would enjoy the experience of programming and find it relatively easy. Both of these assertions were supported by the evaluation: in terms of enjoying the experience, the mean of the affective dimension was 4.6 (the highest rating), indicating that people greatly enjoyed the experience of PiP programming, while the cognitive load dimensions had an overall average of 4.3, indicating that people found the process relatively simple. In fact, 88.9 percent of the participants reported that they used the controls with ease and 83 percent were able to use the system to create their desired environments with little or no assistance (see Figure 5.10).

Although not shown in the data presented here, we found no significant variation across cultures but found some minor variation on cognitive loading for age groups, with younger participants

Figure 5.10 **Ratings on Six Dimensions**

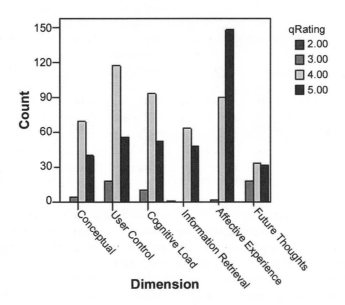

finding the system slightly easier to use. In general the "Information Presentation" dimension (how well information was presented to the user) scored the lowest but still higher than 4, indicating that overall people found it usable. Given that this is an early prototype, we were not surprised to find that the interface could be improved. None of the participants found the principles difficult to understand. A remark from one participant, "I thought the basic principles themselves were very simple and straightforward. I felt I could easily grasp the basic principles," was typical of many users. This comment was from someone in the group with no programming skills at all (a key target of our work). Overall 83.4 percent of the participants found the system intuitive to use and 94.4 percent stated that they felt it rewarding to use the system. Thus, these initial results support the original thesis of the work that it is possible to produce a system that empowers nonspecialists to be capable of and to enjoy programming-coordinated actions of distributed embedded computer systems that form a crucial aspect of the digital home.

DISCUSSION

Summary

In this chapter we have described how domestic pervasive systems of the future might be composed of potentially hundreds of coordinating deconstructed services and functions. Most of these will function in the same way as current appliances and applications, although their physical appearance might differ significantly from current products. We have described two complementary approaches to supporting nontechnical users of future digital homes; task-based computing and Pervasive Interactive Programming. Both approaches are based on the notion of constructing atomic computational elements into higher-level tasks. In PiP, tasks are wrapped within the "appliance" metaphor, which is a well-established idea in home environments, and are created by the user using real devices (or graphical emulations of them) to demonstrate what is required. The complexity and variety of tasks that can be programmed are limited only by the user's actions, which provide both its distinctive edge and principal research challenge. In TBC, tasks are created by the system, which associates service providers and consumers that the system has found within the local environment, on the basis of preprogrammed services. PiP is able to extend the capabilities of TBC by providing a mechanism for users to create tasks that go beyond the limits of anticipated or preprogrammed use.

We have described an ontology, dComp, that allows meta appliances and applications to be defined and configured. These descriptions can be supplied either with systems of possible behaviors so that the devices offer a default functionality akin to current appliances and applications or, for the more creative end user, with systems that will enable them to create their own novel meta-appliances and applications, thereby allowing them to decorate their domestic environments in new ways, something we have dubbed *DIY in the pervasive computing age*.

We have provided a formalism that describes the task translation and allocation problem needed to support MAps and movement of people and devices. Finally, although this work is aimed at the future digital home rather than those existing now, we have built and evaluated a prototype "proof of concept" system. While we have been able to undertake only a comparatively small-scale evaluation with eighteen users, the initial findings are most encouraging as they support our original hypothesis that it is possible to produce an end-user programming system that empowers nonspecialists to be capable of and to enjoy programming the coordinated actions of distributed embedded computer systems in a digital home.

Future Directions

Our longer-term work will involve the refinement of techniques elaborated in this chapter. While we have directed our work at a domestic setting, we believe that these methodologies are generic in nature and can be applied to other environments, something we will pursue in the future. Another area we are especially interested in exploring is the synergy in the interoperation of an *ontology engine* in support of user-based programming. How might this work and what would be gained? Taking a PiP user as an example, an ontology engine might be used to prompt the user with a set of possible communities that the ontology recognizes and that could be achieved with the currently available devices. This would help a novice user to setup an acceptable world with a minimum level of intervention on their part. The options offered might be graded, either all possibilities or options related to high-level functions described by the user, perhaps, with the high-level requirement itself captured as an ontology. This process might be implemented as a "virtual helper" suggesting the range of possible virtual devices that could be built from the currently available devices. As all technology has to have commercial potential, an opening for this might be that the ontology engine could suggest devices the user might consider buying. The ontology descriptions themselves (MAps) would also have a commercial value and open up the possibility for new forms of trading in virtual commodities. More speculatively, if the system included an agent-based learning mechanism, over and above any end-user programming, there might be patterns of use and behavior of the kinds of (implicit) communities formed and their use, which could be captured by an agent from the (implicit) rules created, in turn potentially being used to improve the advice offered by the helper system. In terms of the underlying science, such an approach could unify implicit autonomous agent learning mechanisms with explicit end-user programming. In terms of the levels of abstraction involved, one might characterize this as an epistemological level in that it seems to capture tacit knowledge from the user's behavior rather than to rely on what the user knows and wants consciously and explicitly. There would be a degree of recursion in this process as epistemological level processes could result in ontological instantiations, which in turn could feed the epistemological level modeling and potentially leading the user to possibilities nobody had considered. The point is that through PiP, the user's beliefs and desires are captured at an epistemological level, which, via an ontology, could add a more personal aspect to the prompts and suggestions offered to the user. Of course, using PiP, the user could still invent new virtual devices that could then become part of an expanded (personal) ontology, regardless of how well or badly they were formed. In some senses both the ontology and the epistemology described here are dynamic bodies of knowledge and belief that evolve as the pervasive system and the users evolve. The basic ontology of devices would probably be manufacturer based and refer to physical device descriptions and capabilities, whereas the virtual devices constructed by the user would be the equivalent of an epistemological level (i.e., what users want and know how to construct for their own purposes). Clearly, there is an equivalence between the epistemological level and the personal ontology creating the potential to encapsulate personal and subjective views that are especially in keeping with the domestic pervasive information systems in the private spaces of our homes.

ACKNOWLEDGMENTS

We wish to express our gratitude to those who, in various ways, have supported this work: The DTI (Next Wave Technologies and Markets Programme), Chimera (Institute for Sociotechnical Research), Essex University (our home university), and especially our colleagues Martin Colley, Hani Hagras, Martin Hicks, Greg Willat, and Malcolm Lear.

REFERENCES

Adair, M. 2005. *X10 Projects for Creating a Smart Home*. Indianapolis, IN: Indy-Tech Publishing.
Andersen, P.; Bardram, J.; Christensen, H.; Corry, A.; Greenwood, D.; Hansen, K.; and Schmid, R. 2005. Open architecture for palpable computing some thoughts on object technology, palpable computing, and architectures for ambient computing. Discussion document on palpable computing architecture. Available at www.ist-palcom.org (accessed October 15, 2005).
Asaravala, A. 2004. Give your home a brain for Xmas. *Wired*. Available at www.wired.com.
Basu, J. and Callaghan, V. 2005. Towards a trust based approach to security and user confidence in pervasive computing systems. Presented at *IE05*, Essex, June 28–29.
Berners-Lee, T; Hendler, J; and Lassila, O. 2001. The semantic Web. *Scientific American,* Vol. 284, 5, pp. 34–43.
Callaghan, V.; Colley, M.; Hagras, H.; Chin, J.; Doctor, F.; and Clarke, G. 2005. Programming iSpaces: A tale of two paradigms. In A. Steventon and S. Wright, eds., *Intelligent Spaces, The Application of Pervasive ICT*. Part of the series *Computer Communications and Networks*. Springer.
Canfield-Smith, D.; Cypher, A.; and Tesler L. 2000. Programming by example: Novice programming comes of age. *Communications of the ACM,* 43, 3, 75–81.
Chen, H.; Finin, T; and Joshil, A. 2004. SOUPA: Standard ontology for ubiquitous and pervasive applications. Presented at *International Conference on Mobile and Ubiquitous Systems: Networking & Services (MobiQuitous 2004)*, Boston, August 22–26.
Chin, J.; Callaghan, V.; Colley, M.; Hagras, H.; Clarke, G. 2005. Virtual appliances for pervasive computing: A deconstructionist, ontology-based, Programming-by-Example approach. Presented at *Intelligent Environments 2005 (IE05)*.
Chin J.; Callaghan,V.; and Clarke G. 2006. An end user tool for customising personal spaces in ubiquitous environments. Presented at *3rd International Conference on Ubiquitous Intelligence and Computing (UIC-06)*, Wuhan and Three Gorges, China, September 3–6, 2006.

dComp. 2005. *Deconstruction and Community Based Ontology for Pervasive Computing.* Available at http://iieg.essex.ac.uk/dcomp/ont/dev/2004/05/ (accessed October 15, 2005).

DiDuca, D. and Van Helvert, J. 2005. User experience of intelligent buildings: A user-centered research framework. Presented at *Intelligent Environments 2005.* Essex, June 28–29.

Department of Trade and Industry (DTI). 2005. *Next Wave Markets.* UK Department of Trade and Industry Web pages Available at www.nextwave.org.uk/docs/markets.htm (accessed October 15, 2005).

Easy Living. 2005. Microsoft's Easy Living Project. Available at http://research.microsoft.com/easyliving/ (accessed October 15, 2005).

Economist. 2005. The digital home: Science fiction? *Economist,* September 15.

Epsilon. 2005. SUN's Epsilon Project. Available at http://research.sun.com/projects/epsilon/ (accessed October 15, 2005).

Haarslev, V. and Moller, R. 2001. Description of the RACER system and its application. Presented at the *International Workshop on Description Logics (DL-2001).*

Horan, B. 2005. The use of capability descriptions in a wireless transducer network, SUN Microsystems Research Labs, Report no. TR-2005–131, February 1. Available at http://research.sun.com/techrep/2005/abstract-131.html (accessed October 15, 2005).

Ishii, H.; Ratti, C.; Piper, B.; Wang, Y.; Biderman, A.; and Ben-Joseph, E. 2004. Bringing clay and sand into digital design—continuous tangible user interfaces. *BT Technology Journal,* 22, 4 (October), 287–299.

Jobs, S. 2004. Tiger (Mac OS X). Presented at Apple Worldwide Developer Conference WWDC 2004. San Francisco, June 27–July 3. Available at http://developer.apple.com/macosx/automator.html (accessed October 15, 2005).

Le Corbusier. 1970. *Towards a New Architecture.* London: Architectural Press.

Lieberman, H. 2001. *Your Wish Is My Command.* San Francisco: Morgan Kaufmann Press.

Lyons, M. 2005. Privacy, freedom and control in intelligent environments. Keynote talk. Presented at *Intelligent Environments 2005 (IE05).* Essex, June 28–29. Available at www.iee.org/OnComms/PN/controlauto/Michael%20Lyons%20Presentation.pdf (accessed October 15, 2005).

Masuoka, R.; Parsia, B.; and Labrou, Y. 2003. Task computing—The semantic Web meets pervasive computing. Presented at *Second International Semantic Web Conference (ISWC2003).* Sanibel Island, FL, October 20–23.

McBride, B. 2002. Jena: A semantic Web toolkit. *IEEE Internet Computing* 9(6) (November/December): 55–59.

O'Neill, E. and Johnson, P. 2004. Participatory task modelling: Users and developers modelling users' tasks and domains. Presented at *Third International Workshop on Task Models and Diagrams for User Interface Design (TAMODIA 04).* Prague, November 15–16.

Smith, D.C. 1977. *Pygmalion: A Computer Program to Model and Stimulate Creative Thought.* Basel and Stuttgart: Birkhauser Verlag.

OWL-S. 2005. *Ontology Web Language for Services.* Available at www.w3.0rg/Submission/2004/SUBM-OWL-S-20041122/ (accessed October 15, 2005).

Vastenburg, M. 2004. SitMod: A tool for modelling and communicating situations. Presented at *Second International Conference, Pervasive 04.* Vienna, April 21–23.

Wacks, K. 1998. Home automation and utility customer services. (April). Arlington, MA: Cutter Information Corporation.

Wang, Z. and Garlan, D. 2000. Task-driven computing. Technical Report CMU-CS-00–154, School of Computer Science, Carnegie Mellon University.

Zamudio, V.; Callaghan, V.; and Chin, J. 2005. A multi-dimensional model for task representation and allocation in intelligent environments. Presented at the *Second International Symposium on Ubiquitous Intelligence and Smart Worlds (UISW2005).* Nagasaki, December 6–7.

Zou, Y.; Chen, H.; and Finin, T. 2004. F-OWL: An inference engine for semantic Web. Presented at the *Third NASA-Goddard/IEEE Workshop Formal Approaches to Agent-Based Systems,* Greenbelt, MD, April 26.

CHAPTER 6

CORPORATE PERVASIVE INFORMATION SYSTEMS

ANATOLE GERSHMAN AND ANDREW FANO

Abstract: The trend toward ubiquitous computing does not represent simply a change in the way people access and use information. In the end it will have a profound effect on the way people access and use services, enabling new classes of services that make sense only by virtue of being embedded in the environment. Ultimately, these technologies will lead us to a world of ubiquitous commerce. The prospect of ubiquitous computing, therefore, poses a fundamental question to businesses: What will it mean to conduct commerce in a world where our physical environments are teeming with a variety of technologies capable of providing new classes of services? In this chapter we explore this question in the context of a number of examples.

Keywords: Ubiquitous Computing, Pervasive Computing, Telematics, Mesh Networks, RFID, Sensors, Wireless Sensors

INTRODUCTION

Ubiquitous or pervasive computing enables real-time connection between external reality and corporate information systems (Estrin, 2002). This rapidly emerging capability challenges us to rethink all business functions of the enterprise: from customer relationship management and supply chain through public relations and corporate strategy. It will enable enterprises to be continuously aware of their customers' needs, of the state of their products and assets, and of the needs of their employees. It will close the gap between opportunity and action creating an important competitive advantage for those who harness this technology ahead of their competitors.

Ultimately, ubiquitous computing technologies challenge some of the fundamental assumptions about how businesses use technology. Traditionally, technology has been used to reduce variance to achieve economies of scale. Factories, for example, are designed to create as much regularity in a process as possible, enabling the process to be repeated efficiently. Factories, however, are environments over which businesses have complete control and to which they dedicate an enormous amount of capital. In a world of ubiquitous computing the opposite is true. One characterization of the opportunities offered by ubiquitous computing is to consider how services will be deployed in varying environments over which a particular service provider has limited control. For example, how should media services be delivered into a particular constellation of devices in different people's homes in a manner that creates unique and compelling experiences? What kind of services should support a salesperson's talking to a particular customer in a remote setting? How does an enterprise maintain expertise and capabilities when teams are distributed or being moved offshore? How does a business's ability to maintain awareness of the location of their products affect their business model?

At Accenture Technology Labs we have developed a variety of prototypes that explore these questions through a variety of technologies. A range of ubiquitous devices from radio frequency identification device tags to satellite-connected sensor packages enable enterprises to track their products and components through the supply chain, manufacturing processes, and the distribution network (Römer et al., 2003). While tagging and tracking provide only the most basic information about object identity and location, they can be used in a wide variety of applications, including supply-chain optimization, inventory control, manufacturing quality assurance, and safety compliance.

Beyond the basic information such as the identity and location of an object, ubiquitous sensors can detect and communicate the state of the object (e.g., its temperature, acceleration, illumination, etc.) and even some information about the environment surrounding the object (e.g., the presence of certain chemicals, air humidity, levels of radiation, etc.). The growing pervasiveness of camera phones—perhaps the newest ubiquitous sensor—represents the newfound ability of people to show (rather than verbally describe) their context. Camera phone sales are expected to reach $642.8 million worldwide by 2008 (Chute, 2004). While today they are used mostly for social purposes, we are already seeing their application for business purposes. Boston-based Strategy Analytics estimates that 700,000 people will use camera phones for business purposes in 2005 with the number topping 2 million by 2009 (Raskind, 2005).

More generally, we believe that three technology trends will be driving business innovation in the next five to ten years. These trends are:

1. The rise of intelligent sensor networks
2. The rise of scalable intelligence
3. The rise of experience technologies

Together, these trends create what we call Reality Online—the ability to connect physical world objects in real time with their virtual doubles in our information systems. In the first part of this chapter we examine these trends in greater detail; in the second part, we focus on the business implications of these trends.

INTELLIGENT SENSOR NETWORKS

Until recently, computers and therefore our information systems were mostly deaf and blind. All information about the physical, social, or commercial world had to be manually entered into these systems. In the past several years, however, this situation began to change. First, enterprise systems are routinely capturing data reflecting many of the central processes of the business. Secondly, many kinds of physical sensors have become available and are being integrated with business applications. One of the most talked about devices is a very small, flat electronic tag called an RFID (radio frequency identification device) that can be affixed to any physical object. The tag contains identifying information about the object and can be read at a short distance by a special tag reader. Identification tags automatically connect individual physical objects or people with the information in our systems. These sensing capabilities can be used in many business applications from tracking products through a distribution chain, to safety, security, and training (Lampe and Strassner, 2003). For example, when a worker approaches a particular piece of equipment he is not qualified to service, the system can simultaneously alert both the worker and his supervisors. The system can also automatically check to determine whether the worker has all the necessary safety tools.

Identification is only the first element that can be sensed about an object's context. Location is another critical component of an object's context that is becoming available. We now have sensors that can determine the geographic position of an object with great precision. The most common such sensor is the global positioning system (GPS) receiver that works mostly outdoors as it relies on satellite signals. Cellular phone-based systems are also entering the market. Indoors, precise local positioning is becoming possible based on the Ultra Wideband (UWB) technology. Another promising system under development is based on the signal from digital TV broadcasting, which is strong enough to penetrate most buildings. The combination of an object ID and its location enables another layer of business applications. For example, companies that operate fleets of trucks or rail cars or companies such as utilities that have a lot of geographically dispersed equipment will be able to tell exactly where their assets are at all times. Such companies will be able to optimize the use of this equipment and reduce the inventory they keep.

As valuable as the identity and the location of an object are, information about the state of an object is even more valuable. A truck owner may want to know how much gas the truck is using and how fast it is moving. A rail car owner might want to know how much the car weighs (i.e., whether the content has been unloaded). This is especially valuable for chemical commodities manufacturers as they own the content until it has been unloaded by their customer and the price of the commodity is determined at that moment. Temperature is an important factor for many goods, such as perishable food or sensitive chemicals. If a shipment of frozen food becomes partially defrosted during transport, it is not acceptable even if it appears frozen upon arrival. Some chemicals solidify when exposed to cold. Should this happen to a rail tanker, it becomes unusable and must be buried at great expense to its owners.

Today, inexpensive accelerometers can help solve the problem of improper handling, thus greatly reducing the associated cost. For example, to avoid unpleasant surprises to their customers, some retailers un-box and test expensive and fragile items such as plasma TVs every time they have been shipped from one place to another. Accelerometers placed in the package could indicate whether the item has been dropped or shaken during transit and help to avoid needless testing. Similarly, rail car owners would be able to pinpoint exactly when and where their cars were bumped and be able to precisely document violations of their service level agreements with the railroad. Figure 6.1 shows a rail car sensor package that includes a solar panel, GPS receiver, weight, temperature, and acceleration sensors, and a satellite communication link.

Finally, truly "smart" objects will detect and report not only their identity, location, and state but also their surrounding context. For example, a container with explosive chemical A would notice that another container in its immediate vicinity holds chemical B, which could be dangerous if combined. A smart valve in a nuclear power plant would notice that a maintenance worker lacks the proper equipment or that some steps in a critical maintenance procedure have been skipped. A smart store display would recognize a specific customer and offer a personalized message. Smart objects combined with the ability to communicate will help determine what kind of services are needed at a given time as well as what services can be provided.

The ability to detect context and provide services based on context is a highly competitive and controversial issue. For example, a GPS-equipped mobile phone may be able to detect your location. But who "owns" the knowledge of your location—your carrier? You? the handset manufacturer? Some of these questions will become particularly acute as the information proves increasingly valuable. In other circumstances, however, the information may prove useful, but it may be derivable in a multitude of ways. Today, location awareness is still a new and hardly universal capability for mobile devices. Serving as a location provider appears to be a valuable service. However, how long is it likely that there will be only one way to determine one's location? Consider the growing trend of

Figure 6.1   **Rail Car Sensor Package**

mobile devices equipped with short-range wireless capabilities that are exchanging information with each other and their environment. Many of these devices can, in practice, share location information. Therefore in the long term the problem is not likely to be getting access to your location, but rather, disambiguating which of several reported locations is most accurate and relevant. Finally, these devices may do more than provide information. They may serve as a resource to remote services. For example, in earlier work at our lab we showed how a mobile service, such as a product comparison service, could be switched to a nearby screen where it could be displayed better. Similar approaches have been explored at Lancaster University using Bluetooth (Cheverst et al., 2005). Ultimately, the real value will come when applications use location information to provide a useful service.

How will smart objects communicate information they gather to the central data management facility, which is in a better position to aggregate this information and optimize the system's behavior? Direct connections such as satellite links are not always readily available and they require too much power. However, solutions based on self-organizing low-power networks are beginning to emerge from research laboratories. In these networks, every node searches for its neighbors and collectively they form a dynamic network that transmits information from neighbor to neighbor until it reaches a base station. The nodes of such networks are becoming smaller and cheaper all the time. Some researchers, such as Kris Pister at University of California, Berkeley, believe that by 2010 single-chip low-power (10nJ/bit) short-range (1–100m) radios will cost about $0.10. (Pister, 2005). The ultimate goal of researchers working on this problem is to shrink them to the size of "smart dust" less than 1mm in size.

While many objects are destined to become smarter, inevitably they will constitute only a small minority of all objects. People will not necessarily carry smart tags and be easily identified. In many situations we will have to rely on external sensors such as surveillance cameras, microphones, chemical and radiation sensors to identify and track objects and people in an environment. Unfortunately, most such sensors have only a very fragmented and often distorted view of reality. For example, surveillance cameras do not see terrorists directly—they see only pixels and blobs. Pictures have to be analyzed, individuals have to be identified, suspicious behavior recognized. This is a difficult task that has to be automated if we want to apply it at scale. To produce reliable results intelligent sensor systems will have to combine multiple redundant sources of information while evaluating each source for its reliability and logically reconciling heterogeneous data. This problem, like the problem of resolving location, is often called *sensor fusion* and is becoming increasingly central to business information systems as sensors become more pervasive.

SCALABLE INTELLIGENCE

To achieve useful business results, our ability to collect real time data must be complemented by our ability to act intelligently in response to the information contained in these data. This means three things:

1. An ability to predict the future
2. An ability to optimize responses
3. An ability to learn from experience

In practice, our ability to act intelligently depends on our ability to predict the future and act accordingly. Today's business systems are reasonably good at producing monthly and quarterly forecasts at a fairly coarse level of granularity. For example, we can forecast monthly sales for categories of products such as milk or produce for a store or a region. We can forecast, on average, how many buses in a transportation fleet of a city will need repairs in the coming month. Based on these forecasts, we can optimize procurement and work schedules. What is changing dramatically is the accuracy, granularity, and timeliness of our predictions. Technology now enables us to predict with a high level of accuracy what Mrs. Jones will be likely to buy in aisle 3 this Tuesday afternoon. We can predict whether bus 4038 will need repairs today or tomorrow, and even when its engine and other components operate within nominally normal ranges.

Yet two questions remain: How can we achieve such accurate predictions and what are the consequences? We can do that because we are now in a position to collect a lot of data about Mrs. Jones's shopping habits and bus 4038's operating parameters. Based on these data and using the latest artificial intelligence and statistical techniques, we can build detailed models of Mrs. Jones's grocery consumption and shopping behavior and bus 4038's functioning. These are not generic models of a consumer or a bus. These are models of individual people and objects such as Mrs. Jones and bus 4038. Using these models and the specific contextual conditions such as weather, product promotions, and so forth, we can predict specific behaviors and detect any abnormalities as deviations from our predictions. For example, if the ball bearings in a bus start running at a higher temperature than what has been customary for that specific bus in otherwise similar circumstances, it may signal trouble ahead even when the temperature is still well within the absolute norm.

The advances in granularity and timeliness of predictions have the potential to lift the "fog of war" for businesses and to enable qualitative changes in their responses to business reality. The following simple example illustrates this idea. If we learn that a building is on fire, we call the fire department. If we learn that an arsonist is about to set the building on fire, we call the police. If we learn that a building is vulnerable to fire, we call for an inspection and improvements. If all we know about Mrs. Jones is a broad demographic category such as age, sex, and zip code, then our range of actions with respect to Mrs. Jones is limited to promotions through circulars and broad advertising. However, if we know how often Mrs. Jones buys a specific brand of yogurt; how loyal she is to that brand; how price sensitive she is with respect to this product; and when she last purchased this yogurt, we can act much more selectively, and at the right moment. For instance, we can offer Mrs. Jones a discount when she is physically located in front of the yogurt case, but only if, according to our model, she is ready to buy yogurt and is price sensitive. If she is not, the discount will not be offered.

Our model of Mrs. Jones specifies her likely behavior with respect to hundreds of products under different circumstances. Businesses have millions of customers such as Mrs. Jones each representing a different model. Clearly, for these individual models to be economically valuable, a business must be able to act in response to the individual differences represented in these models. The information about Mrs. Jones has likely been available for many years. The analytical approaches to deriving her individual model have as well. What is new, however, is the ability to actually take advantage of such a model by "acting" on Mrs. Jones individually as she shops, for example, through a shopping-cart mounted personal computer (PC) that selects promotions tailored to her based on her individual model. Figure 6.2 shows a shopping cart with a barcode scanner and a touch-sensitive display device manufactured by Symbol Technologies, Inc.

Predictions and intelligent action require intelligence, and anyone who thinks about intelligence is struck by the difference between the capabilities of computers today and the capabilities of our brains. Many tasks such as face recognition and common-sense reasoning seem so effortless to us and yet are still painfully difficult for computers. While we still do not know how our brains achieve this, a new generation of sensors is enabling neuroscientists to peer deeper into the brains of animals and people and begin to uncover the brain's architecture and processes. Some scientists even believe that advances in neuroscience within the next five to ten years will lead to a new generation of much more powerful algorithms for pattern recognition and reasoning (Hawkins and Blakeslee, 2004). In fact, Jeff Hawkins, a prominent engineer and entrepreneur, of Palm and Handspring fame, just announced the formation of a company called Numenta dedicated to developing a new type of computer memory system modeled after the human brain. If successful, this will provide a qualitative boost to our ability to implement scalable intelligence.

EXPERIENCE TECHNOLOGIES

While technology automates certain human decisions, in many instances, new human challenges are created. The abundance of information coming from emerging sensor networks and the analytical treatment of this data will introduce many new decision points where previously there were none (e.g., what promotions should be offered to Mrs. Jones right now?). Some of them will be handled automatically but many will not, greatly increasing the scope and complexity of human involvement. NASA space flight control is a good example of such complexity that requires coordination and collaboration among hundreds of human experts who receive and exchange prodigious amounts of real-time information. We believe that technology will enable businesses to exercise similarly detailed real-time control over their operations at a small fraction of the cost. In a business setting, experience technologies will enable three types of capabilities:

Figure 6.2 **Smart Shopping Cart**

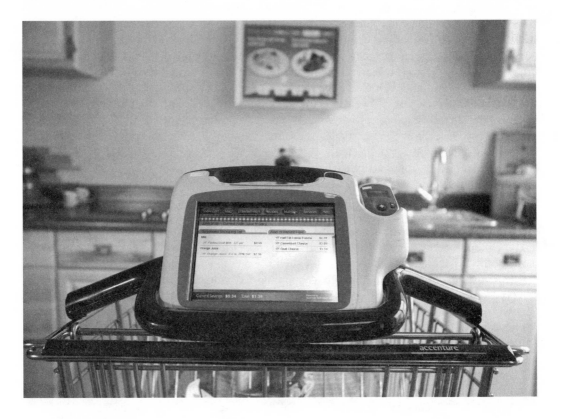

1. Visualization
2. Interaction
3. Collaboration

First, decision makers will need to have a way to absorb very large amounts of constantly changing information. Rapidly developing information visualization techniques are used to address this
problem. The falling prices of displays provide millions of pixels that can be used economically
for information visualization. A varied assortment of displays will be used to address different
needs of decision makers. Those in fixed control centers can use large information walls while
those in the field will make increasing use of pocket-size screens. In our own laboratory, we built
a 10′ x 4′ 6-mega-pixel information wall at a fraction of the cost of only a few years ago. The
wall is depicted in Figure 6.3. Inexpensive flexible screens currently being developed in research
laboratories will create a revolution in pocket displays. Another alternative could be a laser-based
projection technology similar to the one used today to project a virtual keyboard on almost any
surface. Kris Pister, whom we quoted earlier, believes that:

> In 2010 scanning 3-color laser projection systems will be no larger than a grain of rice,
> and cost under a dollar. They will be in augmented reality displays that appear to others as
> regular glasses. They will be in laser pointers, turning any wall into an electronic whiteboard.

Figure 6.3   **Accenture Technology Labs Interactive Information Wall**

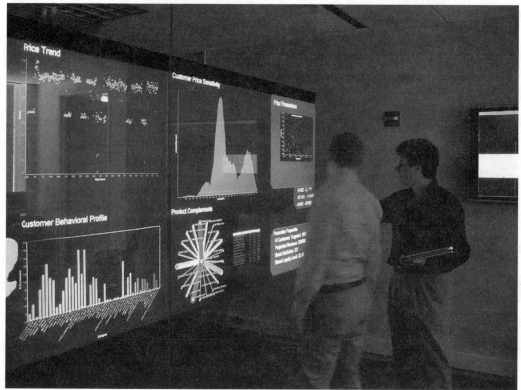

They will be in large arrays on walls, forming a truly staggering 3D display with brightness, contrast, and viewing angle unparalleled by any technology available or predicted today (Pister, 2005).

Display technologies will continue to evolve rapidly until they match human capabilities for visual perception. We will be surrounded by pixels and these pixels will drive the demand for content, bandwidth and processing power.

To be truly useful, visualizations of complex information must be coupled with our ability to interact with them. We are all familiar with a PC style of interaction, which involves one person using windows, menus, and mice with buttons. Interaction with large video walls will inspire entirely different styles and technologies, enabling simultaneous use by multiple people. Hand gestures such as pointing, waiving, sweeping, and so on, possibly accompanied by voice commands, will become the primary means of interaction. Pocket-size screens will also require different modes of interaction. Apple's iPod is a good example of ingenious interface design for one hand operation.

The value of large displays does not lie primarily in taking existing applications and projecting them on large surfaces. The nature of computer applications evolved dramatically when disk space, memory, and processing stopped being precious. Today we are happy to dedicate our CPUs and memory to running virtual aquariums in the form of screen savers when we are not there. Yet only a dozen years ago we optimized our programs by representing years with two digits to save a few bytes. Pixels, however, have yet to benefit from the kind of exponential growth seen in processing and storage. However, this is beginning to change as we find displays appearing on new surfaces and devices, from mobile devices to home appliances to office environments.

As pixels become less precious, we are starting to rethink what applications are like in these environments. Empty regions are acceptable, and arguably even desirable. Content, far from changing with every application, may begin to play a permanent role in an environment much the way furniture or other tools persist in a room. Applications, in sum, become part of the environment. One area where these principles may find early application is in control-room environments. Large information walls in control centers provide a natural venue for intense collaboration among several individuals sharing considerable amounts of data. Imagine several experts in a control center overseeing operations of a car manufacturing company. The information wall shows the entire supply and manufacturing chain, highlighting actual or predicted deviations from the norm. The experts who represent different competencies can use this common view as well as their own tools to change the time scale and the granularity of the presentation; to drill down into details; to access individual plants and assembly lines, and even to get a real-time camera view of specific production stations. Using these tools, the experts can quickly diagnose the problem and confer with local technicians about the best way to solve it. At the same time, other experts in the control room can plan workarounds using the same information and simulation tools.

Interaction with information will not be limited to displays. People will interact and exchange information with all kinds of smart objects from kitchen appliances and home furnaces to industrial robots. Today, researchers are busy developing new metaphors for such interactions. Even the proverbial VCR with its blinking 12:00 is giving way to personal video recorders such as TiVOs, which at first blush appear to have similar functionality, but in practice transform the experience of watching television. Other basic interaction paradigms are also being redesigned, such as the good old pen and paper. Today, you can buy a pen that not only captures your writing and sends it wirelessly to your computer: Using such a pen, a grandma can write a note to her granddaughter who will receive it as a text message on her cell phone. It also knows which form you are writing on and which field in that form you are filling out. It does this with the help of a special, almost invisible pattern printed on the paper. In a business setting, this paper form becomes an electronic form in real time. The result is that writing on a paper can culminate in an action. For example, a doctor may be paged if a patient's blood pressure is recorded above a threshold on their paper chart. Paper becomes a unique and disposable user interface we can start to attach to the world around us, and is appropriate in environments where screens or other mobile devices are inconvenient.

The three technology trends we have discussed so far in this chapter give businesses the abilities to:

1. *Sense* reality
2. *Think* through its implications, and
3. *Act* upon it

We will now discuss how these capabilities will change the way businesses conduct their most fundamental functions.

CUSTOMER RELATIONSHIPS

Today, most businesses have very narrow channels for interaction with their customers. Mass advertising is still the most common method of reaching them with promotional messages. Call centers are set up to handle customer-initiated interactions. Business–customer communications

Figure 6.4   **Online Medicine Cabinet and Online Wardrobe**

are at best sporadic and poorly targeted. Most businesses do not know exactly which of their products an individual consumer owns or even how valuable this customer is to their business. The technologies that we are discussing in this chapter will completely change this relationship. Companies will be able to track their products as they are being used by customers. They will be able to sense their customers' needs and communicate with them in the setting where their products are purchased—such as the previously mentioned smart shopping cart or in other cases where products are used. The ability to deliver services in these particular contexts alters the nature of these services. At Accenture Technology Labs we have developed a series of prototypes to illustrate these changes.

For example, at a time when a number of online health portals were being announced, allowing people to browse health information on the Web, we developed the Online Medicine Cabinet, enabling people to access health services in the bathroom—where people actually address their health care concerns (Wan, 1999). The online medicine cabinet provides a direct connection between health care providers and patients. The cabinet not only senses the inventory of medicines that are placed inside but also recognizes individual family members as they take their medicines out. It can collect many types of health-related data such as weight, blood pressure, and cardiovascular activity. Health care providers can use this channel for chronic disease management or even simply for wellness management.

The Online Wardrobe reads RFID tags built into clothing and maintains an inventory of one's possessions (Wan, 2000). It notices when various items go in and out. A clothing store that has a service contract with the wardrobe owner can use this information to suggest garments that might complement what the owner already has or offer fashion advice. The Online Medicine Cabinet and the Online Wardrobe are shown in Figure 6.4.

The above examples demonstrate a dramatically new way for businesses to interact with their customers. Instead of wondering how to reach their customers, businesses have to worry about when and what to say to their customers. This is the first challenge of Reality Online:

> Technology will enable continuous connection and interaction between businesses and their customers. Few businesses today have the capacity or business processes in place to pay that kind of detailed attention to their customers; even fewer can use the capability wisely and at scale.

SUPPLY, PRODUCTION, AND DISTRIBUTION

As discussed in the previous section, Reality Online technologies enable much closer connection between enterprises and their customers. This connection will enable detailed modeling of customer behavior and lead not only to a much more precise prediction of demand but also to active management of demand through precise, individually targeted promotions and price adjustments. This in turn will drive deep changes in the whole production chain and greatly reduce the "fog of uncertainty" on the demand side.

Similarly, Reality Online technologies will enable businesses to obtain much more frequent and detailed data about their operations, supplies, and the state of their machinery. The business process data from enterprise resource management and customer relationship management systems are already doubling every six months (Wesset, Morris, and Blumstein, 2003). Even more important, businesses will be able to model and predict equipment failures and process disruption. To illustrate the business implications of these new capabilities, let us return to our example of a municipal bus system where all bus engines are continuously monitored with the help of wireless sensors. This monitoring enables us to create individual bus models and accurately predict imminent engine failures. It is important to note that these predictions could not be made on the basis of periodic checks if the engine's operating parameters were within nominal limits. An engine failure in a bus during rush hour could be very costly and disruptive. Consequently, to achieve high reliability, the bus company in our example overmaintained its buses. With individualized predictive monitoring, a much more efficient business process could be established in which the buses would be maintained on an as-needed basis while achieving an even higher level of service reliability. Some analysts estimate that manufacturers could save 51 percent in maintenance labor costs alone by using a new class of predictive monitoring techniques (Radjou, 2003). Moreover, in industries such as utilities or rail, predictive monitoring solutions can lower the need for preventative maintenance and inspection by 60 percent (Maoz, 2004).

The ability to sense in real time also changes the nature of the services that are possible. For example, an insurance company that can detect, in real time, when an unsafe condition arises on a customer's factory floor can use that information to do something far more interesting than raise their rates a bit more quickly than before. They can begin providing risk mitigation or "compliance services." That is, why not provide a service that warns the company as the risk arises and helps bring it back into compliance as quickly as possible? This reduces risk and is a new kind of service offering.

Another example is package delivery. Reality Online technologies are increasingly enabling package delivery companies to monitor and analyze all factors that affect their performance. Detailed models of individual nodes and segments in their delivery networks combined with real-time data such as weather reports and traffic information can produce accurate predictions of likely delays and damage to the packages. Companies can react in real time by reallocating their resources, purchasing additional insurance, or changing the options available to their customers in particular locations. Technology can also be used to provide new services to customers and create additional revenues. For example, a package could be addressed to a person, not a physical address. The delivery company could be in contact with the customer, redirecting the delivery in real time as the customer moves from one location to another.

As the amounts and diversity of information about supply, manufacture, and distribution continue to increase exponentially, enterprise management will face the second challenge:

> Technology will enable continuous real-time predictive monitoring of enterprise functions. But are businesses truly ready to take advantage of this information and change their business processes to optimize their responses in real time?

One increasingly important area in which businesses will be challenged to take advantage of real-time supply-chain information is security. Supply-chain security is becoming a growing global concern; however, supply chain visibility is typically provided in the context of solutions deployed by private companies. The challenge lies in aligning public security interests with private business benefits. At our lab we are exploring ways to do just that. For example, in the case of cargo security, it is simply not economically viable to instrument every shipping container with sensors that would detect potential threats such as radiation; moreover, there are no mandates to do so. However, we are testing approaches that use a small subset of instrumented containers to monitor a neighborhood of containers. So while it may not be feasible to instrument every container, this approach allows us to refocus the question on identifying a business case for instrumenting a particular subset of containers, such as those that would benefit from "green lane," or expedited, treatment at ports. This is just one example of the growing confluence of business and government interests.

WORK AND WORKFORCE

Two key workforce-related factors are affecting enterprises. First, inexpensive communications combined with collaboration tools and other emerging technologies are increasingly enabling the transfer of ever more complex work to be transferred to labor forces throughout the world. Second, businesses face the prospect of an aging workforce, which can pose a threat in terms of the loss of critical expertise.

With respect to the mobility of work, most noticeably, call center-based customer service can be provided from anywhere in the world; radiologists in India are beginning to interpret x-rays for U.S. doctors. The ability to use remote labor effectively, however, poses its own set of challenges to an enterprise. At Accenture Technology Labs we created and deployed a series of tools that help to capture and transfer several classes of knowledge and skills. Consider a situation where application maintenance experts need to train new employees at a distant location. We begin with a detailed knowledge-transfer plan personalized for each learner. The software automatically generates a personalized Web portal for each learner to track his or her progress. We use virtual presence tools such as application sharing and desktop video-conferencing to enable learners to virtually "look over the shoulder" of their mentors as they conduct their work activities. This synchronous learning is augmented with asynchronous learning where the learners watch the expert through captured voice-annotated screenshots. This captured expertise is used as a reference for learner's exercises. As the training progresses, roles are switched and the expert begins to virtually look over the learner's shoulder both synchronously and asynchronously. Meanwhile, mentors and their students develop a sense of comradeship and shared culture by sharing personal stories and experiences through a media-rich communication interface. Our tools first addressed the tasks performed on a computer. We are now in the process of extending this approach to more physical tasks performed outside of an office environment.

Knowledge capture is also critical in coping with an aging workforce. In the United States, more than 25 percent of the working age population will reach retirement age by 2010, resulting in a potential worker shortage of 10 million people. In the United Kingdom, by 2006, forty-five- to fifty-nine-year-olds will become the largest single group in the workforce. Several large companies told us that up to 50 percent of their workers will reach retirement age in the next five to ten years. This loss of expertise combined with competitors' ability to use technology to bring inexpensive expertise from far away places will put a squeeze on companies that fail to master and take advantage of the Reality Online technologies.

As more and more types of work become mobile and as an experienced but aging workforce begins to leave the workplace, enterprises will face the third challenge:

> How to use the Reality Online technologies to efficiently allocate work and train workers on a global basis without sacrificing corporate culture and the cohesion, knowledge, and skills of the workforce?

The ability of these technologies to move labor flexibly also allows individual jobs to be addressed more flexibly at home. This allows retired workers to contribute by working part time in a flexible way, from their homes—and in a manner that is consistent with limitations imposed by their benefits.

RELATIONSHIPS WITH STAKEHOLDERS

In recent years, the Internet has become an enormous source of information and a medium of social exchange. Researchers at the School of Information Management at the University of California, Berkeley estimate that in 2002 about 800MB of stored information was produced for every one of the world's 6.3 billion people (Lyman and Varian, 2003). Since 1999, the amount of stored information has been growing at 30 percent per year. In 2002, the World Wide Web already contained about 170 terabytes of information on its surface—seventeen times the size of the Library of Congress print collections. Even more impressive are the estimated numbers for e-mail and instant messaging: 400,000 terabytes and 274 terabytes, respectively (Lyman and Varian, 2003). Weblogs or blogs is the most recent phenomenon in online communication. In 2004, it is estimated that more than 10 million blogs were created worldwide—a 105 percent increase over the previous year (Perseus/WebSurveyor Inc., 2005), while blog readership in the United States alone jumped 58 percent to 6 million readers (Pew Internet Project, 2005).

This flood of information and communication puts businesses into a virtual glass box. Every piece of information related to the company business is minutely examined, not only by industry analysts but also by every conceivable interest group or individual. Products, expansion plans, executive changes, employee morale, pollution, social contributions, and political connections are discussed in countless bulletin boards and blogs. Some information in these sources is accurate and some may be malicious inventions that are extremely harmful to a company's reputation. For example, a simple rumor claiming that a household cleaner is poisonous to pets can spread through the Internet with amazing speed, causing grave damage to a brand. One thing is clear—companies cannot afford to ignore this phenomenon. They can use the Internet to continually assess their standing with all stakeholders and to detect early potential threats and opportunities.

To achieve this capability, companies will need to harness technologies for information extraction from unstructured text sources. One of the early examples of such capabilities is a system for sentiment monitoring developed at Accenture Technology Labs. The system sifts through blogs, bulletin boards, and Web sites to assess how a company product or initiative is perceived by the authors. It compiles a report on the "buzz" around products and their features. One automobile company is using this insight to identify and prioritize features and enhancements for future models (Accenture Technology Labs, 2001). We expect that further research and development work in this area will lead to our ability to detect many more types of business-relevant events. These could include a range of events: changes in a competitor's marketing tactics; changes in price or popularity of complementary or competitive products; signs that an important supplier may be in trouble; changes in regulatory environment; and advocacy and pressure groups' activities. This brings us to the fourth and final business challenge discussed in this chapter:

> Are businesses ready to manage their image in a "glass house" of information transparency? Are they ready to systematically scan external information for business insights and integrate these insights into their business processes?

The information that is of value lies not just in what the public says about a company or its products, but in what companies say about themselves as well. The attributes that are formally represented in databases tend to be impoverished compared to what humans can glean from a rich description. An online catalog, for example, is designed to convey how trendy or conservative a featured blouse is. We have developed approaches that allow us to extract these soft attributes from marketing descriptions of products. This capability enables companies to compare the positioning of products, brands, and retailers and how it changes over time. Marketing messages can be tailored to achieve intended positioning. Similar capabilities allow us to map product offerings from different suppliers, helping to reduce the complexity of procurement decisions, while also enabling more suppliers to be efficiently considered in a procurement process.

CONCLUSIONS

Reality Online technologies enable businesses to *sense* reality, *think* through its implications, and *act* upon it in real time. We argue that these capabilities will create disruptive changes in all of the major business functions of an enterprise: its relationship with its customers, its supply, manufacturing, and distribution chains, its workforce and its relationship with all its stakeholders. With the "think, sense, and act" capabilities we are now entering the era of an intelligent enterprise whose challenges and opportunities we are only beginning to discover.

REFERENCES

Accenture Technology Labs. 2001. *Sentiment Monitoring Services Case Study*. Available at: www.accenture. com/Global/Services/Accenture_Technology_Labs/R_and_I/SentimentServices.htm (accessed March 20, 2007).

Cheverst, K.; Dix, A.; Fitton, D.; Kray, C.; Rouncefield, M.; Saslis-Lagoudakis, G.; and Sheridan, J. 2005. Exploring mobile phone interaction with situated displays. In *Proceedings of the First International Workshop on Pervasive Mobile Interaction Devices (PERMID)*, LMU Munich, 43–47.

Chute, C. and Slawsby, A. 2004. *Worldwide Still Camera and Camera Phone 2004–2008 Forecast*. IDC document no. 31772 (August). IDC: Framingham, MA.

Estrin, D.; Culler, D.; Pister, K.; and Sukjatme, G. 2002. Connecting the physical world with pervasive networks. *IEEE Pervasive Computing*, 1, 1 (January), 59–69.

Hawkins, J. and Blakeslee, S. 2004. *On Intelligence.* New York: Times Books.

Lampe, M. and Strassner, M. 2003. The potential of RFID for moveable asset management. Paper presented at the *Workshop on Ubiquitous Commerce at Ubicomp 2003.* Seattle, WA, October.

Lyman, P. and Varian, H.R. 2003. *How Much Information? 2003.* University of California at Berkeley, School of Information Management and Systems. Available at www.sims.berkeley.edu/research/projects/how-much-info-2003/execsum (accessed on March 20, 2007).

Maoz, M. 2004. *Intelligent Machines and the Enterprise Service Opportunity.* ID number T-23-0973 (July 7). Gartner Inc.: Stamford, CT.

Pew Internet Project (PIP). 2005. Data memo by PIP Director Lee Rainie (January). Available at www.pewinternet.org/pdfs/PIP_blogging_data.pdf (accessed March 20, 2007).

Perseus/WebSurveyor Inc. 2005. *The Blogging Geyser.* Blog studies, Perseus/WebSurveyor Inc. (April 5). Available at www.perseus.com/blogsurvey/geyser.html.

Pister, K. 2005. Smart dust. robotics.eecs.berkeley.edu/~PSter/SmartDust/in2010 (accessed September 2005).

Raskind, C. 2005. *Wireless Enterprise User-Level Market Forecast (2004–2009).* Research report, Strategy Analytics Inc., February 18.

Radjou, N. 2003. *Predicting When Machines Are About to Fail.* Brief No. 3, Continuous Asset Management Series, Forrester Research Inc. November 17.

Römer, K.; Schoch, T.; Mattern, F.; and Dübendorfer, T. 2003. Smart identification frameworks for ubiquitous computing applications. In *Proceedings of the First IEEE international Conference on Pervasive Computing and Communications* (PERCOM). Los Alamitos, CA: IEEE Computer Society Press, 253–262.

Wan, D. 1999. Magic medicine cabinet: A situated portal for healthcare. In *Proceedings of International Symposium on Handheld and Ubiquitous Computing.* Lecture Notes in Computer Science, vol. 1707. London: Springer–Verlag, 352–355.

Wan, D. 2000. Magic wardrobe: Situated shopping from your own bedroom. *Personal and Ubiquitous Computing,* 4, 4, 234–237.

Wesset, D.; Morris, H.D.; and Blumstein, R. 2003. *Worldwide Business Analytics Software Forecast and Analysis, 2003–2007.* IDC document no. 30076 (September). Framingham, MA.

CHAPTER 7

WEARABLE COMPUTING APPLICATIONS AND CHALLENGES

CLIFF RANDELL

Abstract: *The many opportunities offered by wearable computing have triggered the imaginations of designers and researchers in a wide variety of fields. The inevitability of computers and interfaces that are small enough to be worn on the human body has inspired the creation of devices and applications that can assist with specialized professional and personal activities, as well as aid and augment everyday life in the modern world. In reality, limitations imposed by factors such as battery life, processor power, display brightness, network coverage and form have conspired to delay the widespread introduction of wearable computers. Nevertheless, over the past ten years there have been many successful implementations, and, as the relentless miniaturization of computing devices continues, an increasing number of viable applications are emerging. In this chapter, a generic wearable computer architecture is outlined and its application to commercial and research designs presented. Applications are reviewed from early aircraft maintenance and military designs; designs for personal assistance, communication, and health monitoring; and prototype implementations for real-world gaming and smart fashion textiles. The challenges presented by these applications, including technical limitations, user interface and system design, and social issues are identified and discussed.*

Keywords: *Wearable Computing, Augmented Reality, Agents, Industry, Military, Medical, Health, Fashion, Games*

INTRODUCTION

The concept of wearable computing (wearables) emerged in the mid-1990s at a time when carrying an "always-on" computer combined with a head-mounted display (HMD) and control interface first became a practical possibility. In July 1996 a workshop, "Wearables in 2005," was sponsored by the U.S. Defense Advanced Research Projects Agency. This was attended by industrial, university, and military visionaries to work on the common theme of delivering computing to the individual. They defined wearable computing as "data gathering and disseminating devices which enable the user to operate more efficiently. These devices are carried or worn by the user during normal execution of his/her tasks" (DARPA, 1996). One of the first advocates and adopters of this form of computer usage, Steve Mann, further defined wearable computing and arrived at three fundamental properties. First, a wearable computer is worn, not carried, in such a way that it can be regarded as part of the user; second, it is user controllable, not necessarily involving conscious thought or effort; and third, it operates in real time—it is always active (though it may have a sleep mode) and able to interact with the user at any time (Mann, 1997).

Figure 7.1 **Wearable Computing Architectures**

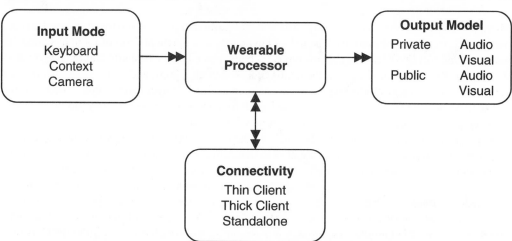

Using these definitions it was possible to retrospectively recognize early applications of wearable computing. These included the shoe-mounted roulette wheel prediction system by Thorp and Shannon, first implemented in 1961, later successfully developed and used by the Eudaemons, and by 1983 commercialized by Keith Taft and others (Bass, 1985; Thorp, 1998). These wearable computers were built into shoes with toe-operated switches enabling the wearer to analyze the characteristics of a roulette wheel and the types of balls in use. With this analysis complete it was possible, using the same design, preferably housed in a companion's shoe, to input the ball's position while in play and predict the quadrant of the wheel in which it would land. This was indicated to the player using solenoids in the shoes or elsewhere on the body with just enough time for a bet to be placed with a 44 percent chance of success.

As the development of the wearable computer was originally inspired by the availability of battery-powered head-mounted displays, it has been closely linked to this technology, either supporting augmented reality or providing personalized information directly to the user's eye(s). An overview of the challenges presented by these displays was summarized by Duchamp. These were the hassle of the headgear, low resolution, eye fatigue, and the requirement for dim lighting conditions (Duchamp, Steven, and Gerald, 1991). Battery life, processor power and size, sensor availability and form, and availability of suitable wireless communications also added to the challenge of building viable wearable computers. Fashion also played its part and HMDs needed to be become acceptable as everyday wear without arousing social antipathy.

Initially, the use of wearables aroused specific interest in four categories—industrial manufacturing, maintenance, and distribution; the military and emergency services; medicine and health; and academia. This resulted in a number of research programs that are outlined in below in the section on wearable applications. First, a broad outline of wearable architectures is given with discussions on the various input modes, output modes, and software architectures. In this chapter we explore the experience gained over the past ten years in each of these fields, and then identify challenges that are currently being addressed.

WEARABLE ARCHITECTURES

The wearable computer has developed into many different forms with a variety of input modes, output modes, and connection strategies. These are illustrated in Figure 7.1.

Input Modes

Three primary input modes have emerged as being of particular interest and these are used on their own or in different combinations. The use of keyboards as a practical form of input has persisted with hard and soft QWERTY keyboards typically being placed on the forearm; chording keyboards, such as the Twiddler, being used in the hand (Clarkson et al., 2005); and application-specific soft keys being tailored into clothes for applications such as music players and mobile phone control. While these do not provide continuous sensed input for an always-on device, they provide a practical way of controlling the wearable computer and for entering text.

For continuous input to an "always-on" wearable, context sensing devices have generated considerable interest. These devices are able to determine *where* the user is located and *what* the user is doing, as well as to monitor physical well-being, or the *how* of the user. The use of global positioning systems (GPS) and indoor positioning systems can bring situated, or location-based, information to the user and enable interaction with the environment; movement sensing devices such as microelectromechanical systems (MEMS) accelerometers and gyroscopes, along with magnetic sensors can be used to recognize movement patterns, including gestures (Hull, Neaves, and Bedford-Roberts, 1997; Rekimoto, 2001). Physical well-being and stress patterns are identified using heart-rate monitors, ECG, and ESR sensors (Crowe et al., 2004; Picard and Healey, 1997). Together they can gather a complete representation of the user's context and appropriately control the wearable application as well as collect useful data for analysis.

The use of wearable cameras can serve many purposes, for example, analysis of the surrounding environment to identify points of interest such as hazards; image gathering; and assisting with augmented, or mediated, reality (Mann, 1994). Images can be shared for online discussion, saved for future reference, or used to enable wearers of enclosed head-mounted displays to view their surroundings augmented with useful information.

Other input techniques include speech recognition and haptic interfaces. While these can perform acceptably in the laboratory, limitations in their performance restrict their viability as primary interfaces (Bonanni et al., 2006; Bürgy and Garret, 2002).

Output Modes

The output from a wearable can be private to the wearer or shared; audio or visual. The private audio mode has been widely adopted in other areas of mobile computing for mobile phones and music players whereas the private visual output, for example, from a head-mounted display raises questions of practicality and social acceptability (Bass, Mann et al., 1997). Nevertheless, the private visual display, which can provide an effective augmented reality experience, is one of the long-term goals of wearable computing.

A display capable of being shared, as in a wristwatch or body-mounted display, is more socially acceptable than a private display and can be designed for ease of use while carrying out different tasks. Indeed, wearable displays have been designed as part of fashion costumes specifically to enhance the presence of the user (Enlighted). Public audio outputs can also be used for performance by artists and musicians who use bodily movements to generate sound and music (Paradiso, 1997).

Further output modes include interaction with other users and servers creating group interactions or simply the recording and storage of data. Haptic outputs, for example, from Tactors, can also be employed, particularly for users with special needs; however, research in this field is limited (Toney, Dunne, and Thomas, 2003).

Connectivity

The earliest wearable applications were stand-alone, or had limited connectivity and were used as thick clients. This had a major impact on power requirements and all but the simplest applications suffered from power consumption issues. Either the user had to carry heavy and bulky batteries, or application usage time had to be kept short. Battery technology has improved, however, particularly with the development of flexible lithium polymer storage, and processor power consumption has also decreased. Both stand-alone and thick client wearable computers have thus become viable propositions.

The ready availability of high-speed wireless data connections has made it possible to realistically develop thin client applications where computationally expensive programs can be run on a server. Servers can also be used to support multiple wearable users with the main issue here being the range and quality of service of the wireless links (Vanegas et al., 1998).

Processing

The processing requirements of a wearable can benefit from a distributed approach. This is particularly important where power consumption is critical, as processors can sleep when they are not required. Processes can be categorized as sensor interface, main application, communications, and output drivers. A useful approach incorporates the sensor analysis programs into the sensors themselves using microcontrollers or field programmable gate arrays. This enables the remaining processor(s) to be put to sleep and only woken up when the sensors detect that something interesting is happening (Muller and Randell, 2000). A similar approach can be adopted with output and communications processes. An alternative strategy is to continuously scan the sensor devices for interesting matches—indeed, for augmented reality this is a necessity. This approach is particularly power hungry.

The different combinations of these modes of operation have principally been explored for industrial, military, medical, and personal applications. These are described in greater depth in the next section.

WEARABLE APPLICATIONS

Applications for wearable computing, by definition, can be proposed for almost all human activities. In reality, four application areas have emerged as being worthy of substantial research funding—industry assembly and maintenance using augmented reality techniques, and also warehouse distribution systems; military command and control systems both for battlefield and training purposes, and for the emergency services; medical and health systems for clinical use and for personal wellness monitoring; and personal information systems. In this section representative research in each of these fields is identified and described. In addition, the emerging field of computer technology integrated into fashion textiles is creating widespread interest. This section gives an overview of each of these application domains.

Industry

The quick and accurate availability of complex information to the worker in the field, or in a nonoffice workplace, has been an objective of many organizations since the establishment of computerized records in the 1950s. While this can be provided using handheld devices, many workers use one or both hands while carrying out their tasks, and also need to simultaneously maintain eye contact with their work. The wearable computer with a hands-free interface, for example, context sensing, and a head-mounted display can provide a solution for these workers. A high-speed connection to the organization's servers provides ready access to relevant data, and also enables the employer to monitor workforce progress.

The first organization to recognize this and to commit resources to researching the possibilities, was the Boeing Company. In the 1990s Boeing employed several hundred staff to assemble wiring harnesses for aircraft. These wire bundles were constructed using pegs in a number of 3′ x 8′ easel-like formboards with paper printouts glued to their surfaces, and a separate set of printouts for reference. It was proposed that a worker with a head-mounted augmented reality display could be guided through the assembly task with no need for reference to paper printouts (Caudell and Mizell, 1992). This project ran for a number of years testing many different HMD designs and tracking systems. It demonstrated that such a system was practical and it identified limitations that would need to be addressed as technology improved. Worker issues such as safety, comfort, and social compatibility needed special consideration. Several systems have been sold to companies in the wire bundle manufacturing business by TriSen, Inc., Boeing's partner in the project.

The maintenance of complex machinery also provides a potential application field for wearable computers. Maintenance manuals are often large, unwieldy documents that can deteriorate rapidly with frequent use in workshop environments. The possibility of using a head-mounted display to overlay technical drawing and maintenance procedures onto the actual equipment being maintained offers an attractive alternative. A wearable computer can also be used to efficiently update the maintenance records for the equipment while the procedures are being carried out. In addition, the availability of video clips illustrating procedures that are viewed while carrying out maintenance can assist with training. A series of prototypes were developed at Carnegie Mellon University to assess the issues associated with maintenance of airplanes, trains, and tractors (Bass, Kasabach, et al., 1997). These were principally the VuMan 3 and Navigator 2, both designed to help with performing inspections by recording the identification of imperfect aircraft skin panels as part of a job order process. By using checklists and forms on a wearable, a 50 percent reduction was observed in the time to record inspection information, with the data entry to the logistics computer being reduced from over three hours to two minutes. The C-130 system introduced a different emphasis by enabling the wearable to be used as a collaborative device to support user training. This project identified design issues that differentiated wearable and desktop computing, notably the user interface, and the opportunity for a focused design to provide a powerful yet simple tool for a limited function.

Warehousing and inventory control provides one of the most successful implementation areas of wearable computing. This, like many industrial applications, requires that the wearable is comfortable enough to wear for long periods—it should be lightweight, not generate heat, must not get in the way, and have minimal cabling. Vocollect's Talkman wearable voice computing terminal and integrated software suite provides a solution that has been adopted by office equipment supplier Corporate Express, Inc.[1] Following pilot studies it has implemented this system in twenty-two distribution centers. The studies showed that, compared with paper-based picking, the speech-based, wearable data collection system boosted productivity by 50–60 percent, increased picking accuracy to 99.99 percent, reduced worker training time, and would deliver payback in less than a year.

Many of the workplace challenges listed above are being addressed by the wearIT@work project in which thirty-six partners are aiming to prove the applicability of computer systems integrated into clothes in various industrial environments with funding of €14.6 million from the European

Commission. WearIT@work is the largest project worldwide in wearable computing and is being coordinated by the TZI—Mobile Research Center of the University of Bremen. The project centers around four application areas—emergency rescue, in particular, firefighters; health care procedures based on real hospital situations; mobile maintenance for the aeronautic industry; and information access and progress monitoring for workers and supervisors of a car production line. As well as the previously identified challenges, this project is addressing the need for especially accurate context sensing of both personal activity and environmental conditions. This sensing is intended to enable the delivery of a variety of services exactly tailored to the user's needs in a given situation (Boronowsky, Herzog, Knackfuss, and Lawo, 2006).

The previous examples of wearable applications illustrate how a wearable computer can assist effectively with indoor tasks. However, one of the main features of wearables is that they may be able to operate *anywhere*. For this to be realistic, the computer and its interfaces have to be especially rugged. To assist technicians working in the field, Bell Canada selected Xybernaut's Mobile Assistant to provide communications with the support infrastructure, gain access to data and schematics, and log progress as technicians climb utility poles and descend into manholes.[2] Time savings of fifty minutes per day per technician were recorded during a pilot study using this wearable.

Military and Emergency Services

The potential value of a wearable computer to an infantryman was quickly recognized by military organizations and law enforcement agencies. As well as providing command/control communication and navigation functions, a wearable can provide access to tactical information, assisting in distinguishing between friendly and hostile forces and potentially offering strategies for dealing with dangerous scenarios. Naturally, much of this research has been classified as confidential; however, examples of collaboration with nonmilitary researchers can be found in the United States, Australia, the United Kingdom, and Singapore. The U.S. Army in particular has funded the Land Warrior program, which initially provided positioning and targeting information, battlefield communications, and thermal sight imaging from the soldier's weapon. The objective was to merge the soldier and the technology into a cohesive, combat-effective system (Tappert et al., 2001). While the wearable computer has not yet fully met this objective, the Stryker experimental battalion has been using tethered wearables with head-mounted displays in the field. By tethering a wearable to a vehicle it is possible to effectively address communication and battery life challenges. Following the Iraq war a budget of $59 million was established to fund this battalion with Land Warrior technology provided by General Dynamics C4 Systems. This technology development effort is intended to create new capabilities for deployment to enhance the Ground Soldier suite of technologies and is interoperable with the joint Future Combat Systems network of military systems (one large system made up of eighteen individual systems plus the network and Soldier). A soldier linked to these platforms and sensors has access to data that can provide a much more accurate picture of what is going on around him.[3]

The Quantum3D Expedition uses augmented reality to provide a wearable computing training resource for the military (Quantum3D).[4] Using accurate simulations of fabricated situations, including visuals, surround sound, and voice command, the Expedition wearable computer design provides immersive training for the armed services and emergency response workers. As well as being able to reconstruct hazardous situations, it is particularly suited to rehearsal of future missions. Squad-level interaction based on a distributed network of individual soldiers all equipped with the Expedition training system is envisaged. With the ability to work within a correlated virtual world, squads will be able to plan missions via the wearable interface, rehearse their course of action prior to the actual training exercise, conduct virtual training exercises while engaging intelligent computer-generated forces, and review the action afterward with unit scoring and performance assessments.

Technology and applications developed for the military sector have common requirements to those needed for the emergency services, especially the ability to work reliably in adverse environments without inhibiting the user's normal way of working. Detailed studies of applications for firefighters and the police force have been carried out by the University of Birmingham, U.K., using scenario-based design methods enabling them to focus on user requirements rather than technical issues (Baber, Haniff, and Wooley, 1999). In their latest work, a wearable computer is employed to assist with crime scene investigation by aiding the investigating officer to use technology to record evidence in an accurate and reliable manner (Baber et al., 2005).

The health and well-being of service personnel also require special attention. The sensate liner developed at the Georgia Institute of Technology was designed specifically to monitor the vital signs of combat casualties, as well as automatically detect and characterize a wound in real time using bullet entry detection (Lind et al., 1997). Further health monitoring applications are presented in the following section.

Medical and Health

The applications described previously have used position-sensing technology to assist in a variety of tasks. The knowledge of *where* the user is located clearly provides the basis for many wearable designs. Wearables can also be designed to monitor well-being and activity—the *how* and *what* of the user. This form of context sensing has been put to use in wearable computers for medical and health applications and has met with more success than in any other field. Body-invasive devices, such as heart pacemakers, have become commonplace. However, as these devices are generally not user controllable they do not fall into our definition of wearable computers. Wearables have the potential to monitor health to assist with improving performance, for example, in sports; to prevent and detect illness through diagnosis; and even to provide treatment, although this usually involves some invasive procedure. Examples of treatment by a wearable are a brain implant to facilitate communication with speech-incapable patients (Siuru, 1999) and insulin pump therapy for diabetics (Doyle et al., 2004).

Health monitoring applications were initially explored for military purposes with the objective of remotely determining the physical status of troops in the field. The Personnel Status Monitor was designed to detect when a soldier is either injured or fatigued using a wide range of sensors, processing boards, and a wristwatch display (Satava, 1997). A simpler low-cost, lightweight, non-invasive, and adaptable system employed a single neck-mounted acoustic sensor to listen to the sounds of blood flow, respiration, and the voice, while minimizing ambient sound (Siuru, 1997). The sensor can collect information related to the function of the heart, lungs, and digestive tract or it can detect changes in voice or sleep patterns, other activities, and mobility. Extensive testing with soldiers and firefighters has demonstrated the effectiveness of this design in helping to understand the interrelations between physiology, the task at hand, and the surrounding environment.

More recently, health-monitoring wearables have become commercially available in the form of the Bodymedia product range.[5] This is based around an armband design with sensors for detecting movement, heat flux, skin temperature, near-body temperature, and galvanic skin response. Data can either be viewed in real time via a wireless link or downloaded for analysis using the Internet.

Providing assistance for people with special needs has also become an important role for wearables. Many systems have been explored to provide the visually impaired with guidance. Early examples of this were developed at the University of California, Santa Barbara (UCSB), using GPS (Loomis, 1985). Evolving from a bulky backpack design, the current system weighs only a few pounds and is worn in a pack slung over the shoulder. Using an electronic compass in conjunction with GPS and a spatial database of the UCSB campus with Geographic Information System functionality and a spatialized audio interface. Using this apparatus the visually impaired can achieve improved access to the environment as well as having greater independence of movement.

The PARREHA project led by Oxford Computer Consultants (Greenlaw et al., 2002) is directed at sufferers of Parkinson's disease. This disease causes inability to direct or control movement such as walking in a normal manner. The project assists sufferers to walk normally by placing virtual visual cues as part of an augmented reality display. This wearable design takes advantage of a little understood effect called "kinesia paradoxa" by using the user's head-mounted display to show brightly colored stripes that scroll toward the viewer as if they are walking down a tunnel.

The continuing challenge in the field of medical wearables is the achievement of interfaces that can be worn and will operate reliably without the conscious involvement of the user. Perhaps more than in any other wearable computing field it is important that the wearable augments and assists daily life and does not interfere with normal functions, especially for users who may have special needs.

Personal Assistance and Gaming

The concept of an "agent," an intelligent or semi-intelligent self-controlling process, can work powerfully on a desktop computer, especially in conjunction with the Internet. A user's agent can gather information and perform tasks with minimal input from the user, and is useful for tasks such as searching and communicating with other agents. An agent will often have knowledge of the user's identity, preferences, and interests. When the user's context—where the user is, what the user is doing, how the user is feeling—is added to the agent's knowledge base, the agent has the potential to become an indispensable tool. The wearable computer provides the essential components for this tool: computational ability, wireless communications, and context awareness. As with previous applications, the user interface becomes the major challenge and is critical to the success of agent-based applications as their regular use promotes the agent's learning, and hence the quality of performance.

The Wearable Computing Project at the Massachusetts Institute of Technology (MIT) Media Lab foresaw many of these agent-based applications that are being used to help "smooth" the user's daily interactions (Starner et al., 1997). The Remembrance Agent in particular was designed to provide timely information by searching for data associated with current location and activity; assisting with personal organization such as prompting the user when current, or future, activities might interfere with each other; and building an expert database of knowledge personalized to the user (Rhodes, 2003; Rhodes and Starner, 1996). Systems using physical context other than location have also been developed. The DyPERS system presents information about museum exhibits, but, instead of location, uses machine vision to detect which painting a wearer of the system is currently viewing (Schiele et al., 1999). Camera-based applications were also explored where an environment could be augmented with personalized digital information, for instance, using a wearable, a virtual museum exhibition could be overlaid with virtual information tailored to the user's interests (Mann, 1994). A team at Columbia University carried out related work under the title "Knowledge-Based Augmented Reality" (Feiner, MacIntyre, and Seligmann, 1993). In this project they explored overlaying graphical information onto complex objects in a way similar to the industrial maintenance applications described previously. The challenge identified here was how to design suitable content for the envisaged tasks in order to most effectively communicate with the user.

The challenges associated with mobile games are, as with desktop games, greater than with conventional mobile computer applications. Fast playability, realistic graphics, and intuitive user interfaces all require significant development for games to be practical on a wearable. Nevertheless, a team at the University of South Australia (UniSA) has developed a wearable version of the popular game Quake. Using a six-degrees-of-freedom GPS/compass tracking system and a 3D model of the university campus, they are able to overlay ARQuake monsters onto their normal vision using a head-mounted display. The player is able to "shoot" the monsters using a single-button handheld device. Though the research originally addressed issues of tracking and rendering, it also explored user interaction (Thomas et al., 2000). Similarly, a team from the Mixed Reality Lab at the National University, Singapore, has created an outdoor version of Pacman with real players represented by "pacmen" and "ghosts" in the virtual world. Again, using head-mounted displays, but in this case to view both the real and the digital worlds, this game explored immersion and interaction with the real world. As it is a multiplayer game, social interaction while playing was observed, and tangible artifacts, or "ingredients," were introduced, enabling the players also to interact with real objects with digital properties (Cheok et al., 2003). Research using games gives valuable insights into how the social challenges of wearable computing can be addressed, and has the potential to engage users at an early age.

Research on the use of wearables without head-mounted displays, such as that discussed in the previous section, has also produced a number of relevant applications. The University of Bristol's Cyberjacket, originally developed to deliver location-based multimedia messages, was used to prototype a tourist guide application in which content is related to the user's activity—with audio delivered when the user is active, and images when the user is stationary (Randell and Muller, 2002). The same platform was employed to investigate the future needs of the everyday shopper. Using a wearable with sensors to determine proximity to retail outlets, and further, to control a background data exchange, the user's agent was able to browse the stock of nearby shops without entering the premises (Randell and Muller, 2000).

While many forms of personal information devices are now available to the consumer, including mobile phones, personal digital assistants (PDAs), and portable game consoles, the wearable still provides the most advanced platform for personal applications. The wearable can go beyond supporting the provision of digital information and multimedia to actually supporting the wearer in the full production of images and video, not only text but also audio, in real time.

Fashionwear and Textiles

The connection between wearable computing and fashion was inevitable, and CyberFashion shows have taken place regularly since the 1990s. While many of the exhibits are conceptual or do not have the traditional qualities of fashion garments, technology is advancing to the point where sensors, computers, and displays can be integrated into garments in practical and aesthetically pleasing ways. One of the first products to reach the marketplace was the Philips/Levi Strauss ICD+ jacket incorporating an MP3 player and a mobile phone into a jacket, and this has led other manufacturers to incorporate device controls and interfaces into jackets. Full integration of a wearable with a fashion garment with expressive and aesthetic potential is in its early stages. Elise Co explored computational fashion in her MIT thesis with creations featuring bio- and movement sensors controlling displays in the garments structure. She concluded that "concept and quality

Table 7.1

Summary of Principal Wearable Computing Challenges

Technical issues	User interaction
Head-mounted displays	Wearable keyboards
Textile integration	Speech recognition
Wearable graphics processors	Gesture recognition
Power harvesting	Evaluation methods
System integration, privacy, and security	Social issues
Efficient server/client architectures	Cultural acceptability
Maintenance of privacy	Workplace adoption
Lightweight security	

of design in every aspect are the most crucial elements for meaningful research and creation" (Co, 2000). Subsequently Tom Martin at Virginia Tech has been researching the practicalities of integrating arrays of sensors into textiles as a basis for developing a design framework for "e-textiles" (Martin et al., 2003). The development of a comprehensive design tool for wearable designers was addressed by Jane McCann at the University of Wales, emphasizing the need for an informed multidisciplinary approach that incorporates an understanding of end-user needs, technology, garment manufacture, distribution and end-of-life recycling (McCann, Hurford, and Martin, 2005). Engagement with the textile and fashion industries is thus essential to progress in the development of technical textiles to produce clothing that successfully combines functionality with aesthetic appeal.

CHALLENGES

The wearable computer has achieved limited success with warehouse distribution systems and with health monitoring devices. To gain wider usage, technical, user interaction, system, and social issues still need to be addressed. These are summarized in Table 7.1.

Technical Issues

One of the goals of wearable computer design is to integrate the wearable system as fully as possible with the user's everyday or workday clothing so as to minimize the impact on normal activity as well as enhance the user's performance. Considerable progress has been made in reducing the size of head-mounted displays to enable them to be incorporated into what appear to be normal glasses,[6] and to improve their resolution and brightness by using lasers as part of a Virtual Retinal Display (Kasai et al., 2000; Kollin, 1993). Nevertheless, considerable progress still needs to be made for them to be competitive with a standard desktop display in indoor conditions, let alone outdoors.

The relentless miniaturization of processors and sensors has resulted in single-board computers and MEMS devices that can easily be integrated into overgarments. The challenge here is to fully integrate the devices with the textiles used to create the garments, or alternatively to develop textiles that can provide equivalent functionality. The other remaining semiconductor challenge is to produce low-power graphics processors that are capable of supporting augmented reality applications and can be comfortably placed on the body.

The rapid development of 3G mobile phone networks provides the necessary bandwidth for thick client applications for the personal wearable, and the 802.11 WiFi technology is also establishing itself as a suitable communication medium for thin clients, particularly in the workplace. Reliable on-body communication and power distribution continue to provide challenges with Bluetooth personal area networks becoming better understood and more widely used, and new battery technologies, such as flexible lithium polymer, making individually powered modules with long lives a practical proposition. Power harvesting from body movement continues to be an intriguing area of research, though the fundamental analysis by Thad Starner that advocated power generation through walking still appears to hold the most promise (Buren, Lukowicz, and Troster, 2003; Starner, 1996).

User Interaction

Alternatives to the QWERTY keyboard and mouse interface have been the subject of much research and are of particular relevance to wearable computing. Solutions range from chording keyboards, to speech recognition, to context sensing and gesture recognition. The two main challenges here are to make the interaction both intuitive and reliable. For the longtime user of a QWERTY keyboard, a chording keyboard can be a challenge—albeit not insurmountable. For others the use of a reduced keyboard with text prediction, such as on a mobile phone, appears to offer a viable alternative. Speech recognition becomes problematic in noisy environments, and context sensing does not yet provide a ready control input for a wearable. Gesture recognition, while seemingly intuitive, does not provide sufficient reliability. A significant challenge is to develop evaluation methods that can reliably compare different input methods, taking into account factors such as availability of one or two (or no) hands, the level of user attention required, error handling, and internationalization (MacKenzie and Soukoreff, 2002).

System Integration, Privacy, and Security

Any widespread development of wearables will bring with it a number of systems issues ranging from architecture to security. The issues of thick and thin clients have already been raised, but concerns and issues regarding user privacy will also need to be considered for each application, whether in the workplace or for personal use. Likewise the benefits of sharing personal and contextual information have to be weighed against the potential for malicious abuse and the need for security. The notion that your identity is represented by your various electronic representations, from credit card numbers to home pages or blogs on the Web, becomes more applicable when it is augmented with personal contextual data such as location, activity, or medical status. Thus, the need for lightweight, but highly effective, protection software is extremely relevant with respect to protecting the wearable from attack (Smart and Muller, 2000).

Social Issues

The widespread adoption of the mobile phone has made the use of personal technology socially acceptable and has become part of users' self-identity. The ways and circumstances in which this technology is used varies between cultures, and, in the case of use while driving a motor vehicle, is regulated according to legislation. The gradual increase of Bluetooth headset use has also demonstrated the acceptance of wearable technology in some cultures. The use of head-mounted displays in social circumstances can be acceptable, and regular users have adopted socially acceptable patterns of usage. When it is mutually agreed that a piece of information is needed as part of a social interaction, it is acceptable for the wearable user to use a display. However, switching one's focus during a personal interaction to view a display could be perceived as impolite, as would also be the case using a desktop display. A set of culturally acceptable usage situations must either be developed or evolve.

The use of specialized workwear is commonplace and should present no social problems in the modern workplace. Early introductions of wearables into a work environment were met with some unfavorable comparisons with fictional popular culture villains (Caudell and Mizell, 1992), but the use of wearables in futuristic movies has lessened this effect. Indeed, a warehouse management report includes the assertion that the wearables produced a "positive impact on team morale. Everyone likes the wearables because they are comfortable to wear and easy to use" (Symbol). In this case there appears to be a strong group identity associated with the wearable technology, which supports its use. Nevertheless, the introduction of new technology can produce concern from the workforce, and a recent communication from the U.K. GMB Union included the statement "we will not stand idly by to see our members reduced to automatons. The use of this (wearable) technology needs to be redesigned to be an aide to the worker rather than making the worker its slave" (GMB, 2005). Clearly, the introduction of wearables into the workplace can also be a serious industrial relations challenge requiring careful consideration of job descriptions and work relationships to ensure that the worker is empowered by the technology.

CONCLUSION

As with the desktop computer, there are many diverse applications for wearable computers. In this chapter, applications for industrial manufacturing and distribution, military use, medical and health, personal use, and emerging future designs have all been described. Prototypes of these applications have all been constructed and some of these have become commercially available. Nevertheless, many outstanding challenges must be addressed; this chapter has identified technical, user interaction, system, and social issues. These are being addressed, for example, as part of current research in the workplace, in the textile industry, and in mobile gaming applications. Wearable computing continues to provide a platform on which future mobile and personal applications can be developed, and, in doing so, contributes to the wider impact of pervasive computing. Early research on location-based applications and health monitoring using wearables has already influenced the design of mobile devices. Thus, the valuable lessons that have been learned can be applied in a wider context. The study of wearable applications also provides inspiration to future pervasive application designers, and will continue to explore the boundaries of technology.

NOTES

1. Product literature, Vocollect Inc. Available at www.vocollect.com (accessed February 9, 2006).
2. Product literature, Xybernaut Corp. Available at www.xybernaut.com (accessed February 9, 2006).
3. General Dynamics C4 systems product literature. Available at www.gdds.com (accessed February 9, 2006).
4. Product literature, Quantum3D Inc. Available at www.quantum3d.com (accessed February 9, 2006).
5. Product literature, Bodymedia Inc. Available at www.bodymedia.com (accessed February 9, 2006).
6. MicroOptical Corp. product literature. Available at www.microopticalcorp.com (accessed February 9, 2006).

REFERENCES

Baber, C.; Haniff, D.J.; and Wooley, S.I. 1999. Contrasting paradigms for the development of wearable computers. *IBM Systems Journal,* 38, 4, 551–565.

Baber, C.; Smith, P.; Cross, J.; Zasikowski, D.; and Hunter, J. 2005. Wearable technology for crime scene investigation. In *Proceedings of the Ninth International Symposium on Wearable Computers.* Los Alamitos, CA: IEEE Computer Society Press, 138–143.

Bass, L.; Mann, S.; Siewiorek, D.; and Thompson, C. 1997. Issues in wearable computing. *A CHI 97 Workshop. SIGCHI Bulletin* 29, 4, 34–39.

Bass, L.; Kasabach, C.; Martin, R.; Siewiorek, D.; Smailagic, A.; and Stivoric, J. 1997. The design of a wearable computer. In *Proceedings of CHI97.* New York: ACM Press, 139–146.

Bass, T.A. 1985. *The Eudaemonic Pie.* Boston: Houghton Mifflin.

Bonanni, L.; Lieberman. J.; Vaucelle, C.; and Zuckermann, O. 2006. TapTap: A haptic wearable for asynchronous distributed touch therapy. In *Proceedings of the SIGCHI conference on human factors in computing systems: CHI '06 extended abstracts on human factors in computing systems.* New York: ACM Press, 580–585.

Boronowsky, M.; Herzog, O.; Knackfuss, P.; and Lawo, M. 2006. wearIT@work—Empowering the Mobile Worker by Wearable Computing—the First Demonstrators. *In Proceedings of Information Societies Technologies—Africa* Pretoria, South Africa. IMC International Information Management Corporation ISBN: 1-905824-01-7.

Buren, T. von; Lukowicz, P.; and Troster, G. 2003. Kinetic energy powered computing—An experimental feasibility study. In *Proceedings of the Seventh International Symposium on Wearable Computers.* Los Alamitos, CA: IEEE Computer Society Press, 22–24.

Bürgy, C. and Garrett, J.H. Jr. 2002. Wearable computers: An interface between humans and smart infrastructure systems. In the CD, *Proceedings of Bauen mit Computern.* Bonn, Germany: VDI Verlag GmbH.

Caudell, T.P. and Mizell, D.W. 1992. Augmented reality: An application of heads-up display technology to manual manufacturing processes. In *Proceedings of the Twenty-fifth Hawaii International Conference on Systems Sciences,* vol. 2. Los Alamitos, CA: IEEE Computer Society Press, 659–669.

Cheok, A.D.; Fong, S.W.; Goh, K.H.; Yang, X.; Liu, W.; and Farbiz, F. 2003. Human Pacman: A mobile entertainment system with ubiquitous computing and tangible interaction over a wide outdoor area. In *Fifth International Symposium on Human Computer Interaction with Mobile Devices and Services,* 209–223.

Clarkson, E.; Clawson, J.; Lyons, K.; and Starner, T. 2005. An empirical study of typing rates on mini-QWERTY keyboards. In *Proceedings of the 2005 Conference on Human Factors in Computing Systems.* Portland, OR. ACM Press, 1288–1291.

Co, E.D. 2000. Computation and technology as expressive elements of fashion. Master's thesis, Program in Media Arts and Sciences, School of Architecture and Planning, Massachusetts Institute of Technology, June.

Crowe, J.; Hayes-Gill, B.; Sumner, M.; Barratt, C.; Palethorpe, B.; Greenhalgh, C.; Storz, O.; Friday, A.; Humble, J.; Setchell, C.; Randell, C.; and Muller, H. 2004. Modular sensor architecture for unobtrusive routine clinical diagnosis. In *Proceedings of the International Workshop on Smart Appliances and Wearable Computing.* Tokyo, Japan. IEEE Computer Society Press, 451–454.

DARPA. 2006. *Proceedings of the Wearables in 2005 Workshop,* 1996. Available at www.darpa.mil/MTO/Displays/Wear2005 (accessed February 9, 2006).

Doyle (Boland), E.A.; Weinzimer, S.A.; Steffen, A.T.; Ahern, J.H.; Vincent, M.; and Tamborlane, W.V. 2004. A randomized, prospective trial comparing the efficacy of continuous subcutaneous insulin infusion with multiple daily injection using insulin glargine. *Diabetes Care,* 27, 1554–1558.

Duchamp, D.; Steven, K.F.; and Gerald, Q.M. Jr. 1991. Software technology for wireless mobile computing. *IEEE Network Magazine,* 12, 18, 218.

Enlighted Designs, Inc. www.enlighted.com (accessed February 9, 2006).

Feiner, S.; MacIntyre, B.; and Seligmann, D. 1993. Knowledge-based augmented reality. *Communications of the ACM,* 36, 7, 53–62.

GMB. 2005. GMB congress demands end to electronic tagging of workers "battery farm" workplaces. Press release, June 6. Available at http://www.gmb.org.uk/Templates/PressItems.asp?NodeID=91861.

Greenlaw, R.; Wessel, I.D.; Katevas, N.; Andritsos, F.; Memos, D.; Prentza, A.; and Delprato, U. 2002. PAR-REHA—Assistive technology for Parkinson's rehabilitation. Presented at the *First Cambridge Workshop on Universal Access and Assistive Technology.* 25–27 March 2002, Cambridge, UK.

Hull, R.; Neaves, P.; and Bedford-Roberts, J. 1997. Towards situated computing. *First International Symposium on Wearable Computers.* Los Alamitos, CA: IEEE Computer Society Press, 146–153.

Kasai, I.; Tanijiri, Y.; Endo, T.; and Ueda, H. 2000. A forgettable near Eye Display. *Fourth International Symposium on Wearable Computers,* October, Atlanta, Georgia. IEEE Computer Society Press, 115–118.

Kollin, J. 1993. A retinal display for virtual-environment applications. Society for Information Display, 1993 International Symposium, *Digest of Technical Papers,* 24, 827.

Lind, E.J.; Jayaraman, S.; Park, S.; Rajamanickam, R.; Eisler, R.; Burghart, G.; and McKee, T. 1997. A sensate liner for personnel monitoring applications. In *Proceedings of the First International Symposium on Wearable Computers.* Los Alamitos, CA: IEEE Computer Society Press, 98–105.

Loomis, J.M. 1985. Digital map and navigation system for the visually impaired. Unpublished paper, Department of Psychology, University of California, Santa Barbara.

MacKenzie, I.S. and Soukoreff, R.W. 2002. Text entry for mobile computing: Models and methods, theory and practice. *Human-Computer Interaction,* 17, 147–198.

Mann, S. 1994. Mediated reality. Technical Report 260. MIT Media Lab, Perceptual Computing Group.

———. 1997. An historical account of the "WearComp" and "WearCam" inventions developed for applications in "Personal Imaging." In *Proceedings of the First International Symposium on Wearable Computers.* Los Alamitos, CA: IEEE Computer Society Press, 66–73.

Martin, T.; Jones, M.; Edmison, J.; and Shenoy, R. 2003. Towards a design framework for wearable electronic textiles. In *Proceedings of the Seventh International Symposium on Wearable Computers.* Los Alamitos, CA: IEEE Computer Society Press, 190–199.

McCann, J.; Hurford, R.; and Martin, A. 2005. A design process for the development of innovative smart clothing that addresses end-user needs from technical, functional, aesthetic and cultural viewpoints. In *Proceedings of the Ninth International Symposium on Wearable Computers.* Los Alamitos, CA: IEEE Computer Society Press, 70–77.

Muller, H. and Randell, C. 2000. An event-driven sensor architecture for low power wearables. *ICSE 2000, Workshop on Software Engineering for Wearable and Pervasive Computing.* New York: ACM Press, 39–41.

Paradiso, J. 1997. New ways to play: Electronic music interfaces. *IEEE Spectrum,* 34, 12 (December), 18–30.

Picard, R. and Healey, J. 1997. Affective wearables. In *Proceedings of the First International Symposium on Wearable Computers.* Los Alamitos, CA: IEEE Computer Society Press, 90–97.

Randell, C. and Muller, H. 2000. The shopping jacket: Wearable computing for the consumer. *Personal Technologies,* 4, 4, 241–244.

———. 2002. The well mannered wearable computer. *Personal and Ubiquitous Computing,* 6, 1 31–36.

Rekimoto, J. 2001. GestureWrist and GesturePad: Unobtrusive wearable interaction devices. In *Proceedings of the Fifth International Symposium on Wearable Computers.* Los Alamitos, CA: IEEE Computer Society Press, 21–27.

Rhodes, B. 2003. Using physical context for just-in-time information retrieval. *IEEE Transactions on Computers,* 52, 8 (August), 1011–1014.

Rhodes, B. and Starner, T. 1996. Remembrance agent: A continuously running automated information retrieval system. In *Proceedings of the First International Conference on the Practical Application of Intelligent Agents and Multi Agent Technology (PAAM '96),* London, UK, The Practical Application Company, 487–495.

Satava, R.M. 1997. Virtual reality and telepresence for military medicine. *ANNALS Academy of Medicine, Singapore,* 26, 1, 118–120.

Schiele, B.; Oliver, N.; Jebara, T.; and Pentland, A. 1999. An interactive computer vision system, DyPERS: Dynamic personal enhanced reality system. In *Proceedings of the First International Conference on Vision Systems,* Gran Canaria, Spain. Springer-Verlag, 51–65.

Siuru, B. 1997. Applying acoustic monitoring to medical diagnostics, *Sensors* (March), 51–52.

———. 1999. A brain/computer interface (neurotrophic electrode invented by Roy E. Bakay and Phillip R. Kennedy). *Electronics Now,* 70, 3 (March): 55–56.

Smart, N. and Muller, H. 2000. A wearable public key infrastructure (WPKI). In *Proceedings of the Fourth International Symposium on Wearable Computers.* Los Alamitos, CA: IEEE Computer Society Press, 127–133.

Starner, T. 1996. Human-powered wearable computing. *IBM Systems Journal,* 35, 3/4, 618.

Starner, T.; Mann, S.; Rhodes, B.; Levine, J.; Healey, J.; Kirsch, D.; Picard, R.; and Pentland, A. 1997.

Augmented reality through wearable computing. *Presence: Teleoperators and Virtual Environments,* 6, 4, 384–398.

Symbol. *Peacocks Case Study.* Available at www.symbol.com (accessed February 9, 2006).

Tappert, C.C.; Ruocco, A.S.; Langdorf, K.A.; Mabry, F.J.; Heineman, K.J.; Brick, T.A.; Cross, D.M.; and Kaste, R.C. 2001. Military Applications of Wearable Computers and Augmented Reality, In Barfield and Caudell (eds.) *Fundamentals of Wearable Computers and Augmented Reality.* New Jersey: Lawrence Erlbaum Associates, 625–662.

Thomas, B.; Close, B.; Donoghue, J.; Squires, J.; De Bondi, P.; Morris, M.; and Piekarski, W. 2000. ARQuake: An outdoor/indoor augmented reality first person application. In *Proceedings of the Fourth International Symposium on Wearable Computers.* Los Alamitos, CA: IEEE Computer Society Press, 139–146.

Thorp, E.O. 1998. The invention of the first wearable computer. In *Proceedings of the Second International Symposium on Wearable Computers.* Los Alamitos, CA: IEEE Press, 4–8.

Toney, A.; Dunne, L.; Thomas, B.H.; and Ashdown, S.P. 2003. A shoulder pad insert vibrotactile display. In *Proceedings of the Seventh International Symposium on Wearable Computers.* Los Alamitos, CA: IEEE Computer Society Press, 35–44.

Vanegas, R.; Zinky, J.A.; Loyall, J.P.; Karr, D.A.; Schantz, R.E.; and Bakken, D.E. 1998. QuO's runtime support for quality of service in distributed objects. In *Proceedings of the IFIP International Conference on Distributed Systems Platforms and Open Distributed Processing (Middleware'98),* The Lake District, UK. Springer-Verlag, 207–223.

CHAPTER 8

PERVASIVE ELECTRONIC SERVICES IN HEALTH CARE

ILIAS MAGLOGIANNIS AND STATHES HADJIEFTHYMIADES

Abstract: This chapter presents the state of the art in pervasive health care applications and the corresponding enabling technologies. In addition, it discusses pervasive health care applications in controlled environments, such as a health care unit or a hospital, and provides examples of pervasive applications in sites where immediate health support is not possible (i.e., the patient's home or an urban area). Furthermore, the chapter proposes a pervasive health care application that collects emergency biomedical data and correlates them with the patient's location and his electronic health record. Pilot results from a demonstrator are also provided along with a discussion concerning the remaining challenges of the near future in pervasive health care.

Keywords: 802.11, Biosignals, Bluetooth, Location-Based Services, On-body and Off-body Networks, Patient Monitoring, Pervasive Health Care Systems, WPANs

INTRODUCTION

During recent years computer-based patient record systems have been expanding in order to support more clinical activities. For this reason health care institutions are asking physicians and nurses to interact more often with computer systems during their everyday work. Existing systems suffer from a number of shortcomings including lack of mobility, bulky obtrusive hardware, and a lack of flexible functionality. Rapid development in wireless communications and the introduction of portable devices capable of reproducing multimedia, such as personal digital assistants (PDAs), have initiated new techniques in computer-based health systems by providing mobile access to a patient's medical data.

In this era of mobile computing, the trend in medical informatics is toward achieving two goals: the availability of software applications and medical information anywhere and anytime and the invisibility of computing; computing modules are hidden in multimedia information appliances, which are used in everyday life (Abowd, 1999). These two goals require the introduction of pervasive computing concepts in e-health applications. Applications and interfaces that will be able to automatically analyze data provided by medical devices and sensors, exchange knowledge, and make decisions in a given context are strongly desirable. Natural user interactions with such applications are based on autonomy, avoiding the need for the user to control every action, and adaptivity, so that they are contextualized and personalized, delivering to the medical personnel the right information and decision at the right moment (Birnbaum, 1997). All of the above pervasive computing features add value in modern pervasive e-health care systems.

Figure 8.1   **A Typical Pervasive Health Care System Architecture**

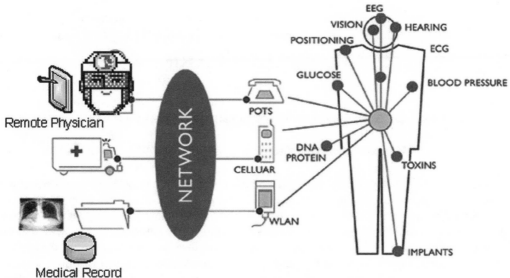

Pervasive health care systems refer mostly to patient telemonitoring, which is an important part of telemedicine. Telemonitoring involves the sensing of a patient's physiological and physical parameters and transmitting them to a remote location, typically a medical center, where expert medical knowledge resides (Hall et al., 2003; Stanford, 2002). A typical telemonitoring system has the ability to record physiological parameters and provide information to the doctor in real time through a wireless connection, while it requires sensors to measure parameters such as arterial blood pressure, heart rate, electrocardiogram, skin temperature and respiration, glucose, or patient position and activity (Barro et al., 1999; Dan and Luprano, 2003; Kara, 2001). Filtered signals and medical data are either stored locally on a wearable monitoring device for later transmission or directly transmitted, for example, over the public telephone network, to a medical center. Such an architecture is depicted in Figure 8.1.

The development of pervasive health care systems is a very promising area for commercial organizations active in the health monitoring domain. The pervasive infrastructure under consideration creates numerous business opportunities for players such as emergency medical assistance companies, telecommunication operators, insurance companies, and so on. The pervasive paradigm creates added value for all of these actors in the business chain. Currently, the cost effective provision of quality health care is a very important issue throughout the world because health care faces a significant funding crisis due to the increasing population of older people and the reappearance of formerly controlled diseases. Pervasive health care systems are capable of attacking all of these challenges in an efficient, ubiquitous, and cost-effective way. Pervasive hardware and software are gradually becoming affordable; they can be installed and operated at numerous sites (frequently visited by patients) and interfaced to a wide variety of medical information systems (e.g., patient databases, medical archives), and thus involve numerous actors. Pervasive e-health systems present a truly scalable architecture covering a wide spectrum of business roles and models (Lakshmi Narasimhan, Irfan, and Yefremov, 2004).

This chapter presents the use of such pervasive systems in the medical sector, and includes a discussion of the technologies that enable the use of pervasive health care computing. Pervasive health care applications in controlled environments, such as a health care unit or a hospital are presented. Examples are provided of pervasive applications at sites where immediate health support is not possible (i.e., the patient's home or an urban area). After a description of a pervasive health care application proposed by the authors, the final section presents the challenges of the near future and some conclusions.

ENABLING TECHNOLOGIES IN PERVASIVE HEALTH CARE

Applications that conform to the pervasive computing paradigm are continuously running and al·vays available. Pervasive applications are characterized by their functional adaptation to their current environment. This environment may refer to physical location, orientation, or a user profile. In a mobile and wireless environment, changes of location and orientation are frequent. Sensing the user's identity and location in e-health applications is quite important for adapting the services provided to the physician or patient in an intelligent manner. Mobile applications require dynamic formation of wireless ad hoc networks and on-the-fly system configuration. The development and standardization of the IEEE 802.x family of protocols, along with currently available 2.5G and 3G networks, offer sufficient networking technology for the development of "intelligent medical environments" that provide pervasive e-health services.

Networking Technologies

Regarding networking, there are two main enabling technologies according to their topology: *on-body* (wearable) and *off-body* networks. Recent technological advances have made possible a new generation of small, powerful, mobile computing devices. A wearable computer must be small and light enough to fit inside clothing. Occasionally, it is attached to a belt or other accessory, or is worn directly like a watch or glasses. An important factor in wearable computing systems is how the various independent devices interconnect and share data. An off-body network connects to other systems that the user does not wear or carry and it is based on a wireless local area network (WLAN) infrastructure, while an on-body or wireless personal area network (WPAN) connects the devices themselves—the computers, peripherals, sensors, and other subsystems—and runs in ad hoc mode. Tables 8.1 and 8.2 present the characteristics of wireless connectivity and the mobile networking technologies, respectively, related to off-body and on-body networks.

WPANs are defined within the IEEE 802.15 standard. The most relevant protocols for pervasive e-health systems are Bluetooth and ZigBee (IEEE 802.15.4 standard). Bluetooth technology, originally proposed by Ericsson in 1994 as an alternative to the cables that linked mobile phone accessories, is a wireless technology that enables any electrical device to communicate in the 2.5-GHz ISM (license free) frequency band. It allows devices such as mobile phones, headsets, PDAs, and portable computers to communicate and send data to each other without the need for wires or cables to link the devices together. It has been designed specifically as low-cost, small-size, and low-power radio technology, which is particularly suited to the short range of a personal area network (PAN). The main features of Bluetooth are: (a) real-time data transfer is usually possible in the range of 10–15 m,

Table 8.1

Wireless Connectivity

Technology	Data rate	Range	Frequency
IEEE 802.11a	54 Mbps	150m	5 GHz
IEEE 802.11b	11 Mbps	150m	2.4 GHz ISM
Bluetooth (IEEE 802.15.1)	721 Kbps	10m–150m	2.4 GHz ISM
HiperLAN2	54 Mbps	150m	5 GHz
HomeRF (Shared Wireless Access Protocol, SWAP)	1.6 Mbps (10 Mbps for Ver.2)	50m	2.4GHz ISM
DECT	32 kbps	100m	1,880–1,900 MHz
PWT	32 kbps	100m	1,920–1,930 MHz
IEEE 802.15.3 (high data rate wireless personal area network)	11–55 Mbps	1m–50m	2.4GHz ISM
IEEE 802.16 (Local and Metropolitan Area Networks)	120 Mbps	City limits	2–66 GHz
IEEE 802.15.4 (low data rate wireless personal area network), Zigbee	250 kbps, 20 kbps, 40 kbps	100m–300m	2.4 GHz ISM, 868 MHz, 915MHz ISM
IrDA	4Mbps (IrDA-1.1)	2m	IR (0.90 micrometer)

Table 8.2

Mobile Networks

Technology	Data rate	Frequency
GSM	GPRS (115 Kbps), EDGE (384 Kbps), HSCSD (57.6 Kbps)	900 MHz, 1,800 MHz, 1,900 MHz
IMT-2000	Picocell (2 Mbps), Microcell (512 Kbps), Macrocell (384 kbps)	WRC 2000 (806–960 MHz, 1,710–1,885 MHz, 2,500–2,690 MHz), WARC-92 (1,885–2,025 MHz, 2,110–2,200 MHz)
Metricom Ricochet	100 kbps	900 MHz ISM

(b) it supports point-to-point wireless connections without cables as well as point-to-multipoint connections to enable ad hoc local wireless networks, (c) data speed of 400 kb/s symmetrically or 700–150 kb/s of data asymmetrically. On the other hand, ZigBee (IEEE 802.15.4 standard) has been developed as a low data rate solution with multimonth to multiyear battery life and very low complexity. It is intended to operate in an unlicensed international frequency band. The maximum data rates for each band are 250, 40, and 20 kbps, respectively. The 2.4 GHz band operates worldwide while the sub-1-GHz band operates in North America, Europe, and Australia.

Pervasive health care systems have high demand requirements regarding energy, size, cost, mobility, connectivity, and coverage. Varying size and cost constraints result in varying limits on available energy, as well as on computing, storage and communication resources. Low power requirements are also necessary because of from safety considerations since such systems run near or inside the body.

Mobility is another major issue for pervasive e-health applications because of the nature of users and applications and the ease of connectivity to other available wireless networks. Off-body and personal area networks must not have line-of-sight requirements.

Various communication modalities can be used in different ways to construct an actual communication network. Two common forms are infrastructure-based networks and ad hoc networks. Mobile ad hoc networks represent complex systems that consist of wireless mobile nodes, which can freely and dynamically self-organize into arbitrary and temporary, "ad hoc" network topologies, allowing devices to seamlessly interwork in areas with no preexisting communication infrastructure or centralized administration. The effective range of the sensors attached to a sensor node defines the coverage area of a sensor node. With sparse coverage, only parts of the area of interest are covered by the sensor nodes. With dense coverage, the area of interest is completely (or almost completely) covered by sensors. The degree of coverage also influences information-processing algorithms. High coverage is a key to robust systems and may be exploited to extend the network lifetime by switching redundant nodes to power-saving sleep mode.

Positioning Technologies

Pervasive health services often require specific infrastructure for estimating the user's location. Several techniques that provide such estimation are currently available. The most prominent are: satellite-based (e.g., global positioning systems [GPS]) or terrestrial infrastructure-based (e.g., cell-ID, Time of Arrival [TOA]). Satellite-based positioning does not operate properly in deep canyons and indoors where cellular coverage may be denser. Terrestrial-based positioning may be more imprecise with sparse deployment of base stations in rural environments, where satellite visibility is better. Position fixing in indoor environments may also exploit other technologies such as WLAN. A WLAN positioning system requires ceiling mounted WLAN access points (e.g., 802.11) to be installed on the building structure, and portable or PDA devices (clients) equipped with WLAN network cards. In general, the location information can be physical or symbolic. Physical location information can be represented using a mathematical magnitude; for example, an emergency room is positioned at 47039'17"N by 122018'23"W, at a 20.5-meter elevation. Symbolic information presents abstract ideas about the position of the item under consideration (e.g., in the office, next to the parking sign). Finally, the information returned by an indoor positioning system can be absolute or relative. Absolute information is depicted on a shared grid or on a geographic coordinates system for all of the located systems. This information for a located object is the same and unique for all observers using the same grid or coordinates systems. In contrast, relative position information represents the position of a located object in reference to the observer and thus it is not unique and the same for all possible observers. In general, two types of positioning architectures exist. The first is a centralized scheme, where a server calculates the position of a client, based, for example, on triangulation or scene analysis. An example of centralized architecture is Ekahau's Positioning Engine (EPE),[1] which provides absolute positioning information to external applications, and works for a number of wireless environments, such as 802.11 and Bluetooth. EPE provides absolute position with 1 m of accuracy. The distributed scheme relies on specialized software that runs on clients (portables, PDAs). Each client uses its own radio frequency measurements in order to calculate its position. Examples of such architecture are the MS RADAR (Bahl and Padmanabhan, 2000) and the Nibble (Castro et al., 2001) systems. MS RADAR was developed by Microsoft Research in order to provide location positioning inside a building. It uses both scene analysis and triangulation through the received signal's attenuation. Developed for 802.11 networks, it provides positioning accuracy of 3–4 m, but with limited precision of 50 percent. It provides absolute location in a grid that covers the active area. Nibble, the location positioning components of the MUSE project developed by UCLA, uses the scene analysis technique to estimate the location of the user and provides symbolic and absolute positioning information. The accuracy of the system can reach up to 3 m. Other proprietary radio- or infrared-based positioning schemes also exist for indoor environments. Examples of such systems are the Active Badge and Active Bat systems. An extensive survey of similar platforms can be found in (Hightower and Borriello, 2001).

PERVASIVE HEALTH CARE APPLICATIONS IN CONTROLLED ENVIRONMENTS

The use of pervasive systems in controlled environments such as hospitals may be divided into two broad categories. The first one relates to applications, enabling the mobile ubiquitous delivery of medical data and implementations of mobile electronic health records, accessible by PDAs or tablet personal computers in a hospital equipped with WLAN infrastructure (Finch, 1999). Several research groups (Hall et al., 2003; Maglogiannis, Apostolopoulos, and Tsoukias, 2004) have experimented on the use of low-cost, high-portability handheld computers that are integrated through a wireless local computer network within the IEEE 802.11 or Bluetooth standards. Regarding medical data exchange, DICOM (www.dicom.org) and HL7 (www.hl7.0rg) standards are used in data coding and transmission via mobile client/server applications capable of managing health information.

On the other hand, pervasive systems are used to monitor and diagnose patients. A wide range of medical monitors and sensors enable the mobile monitoring of a patient, who is then able to walk freely without being restricted to a bed. Pervasive systems in a hospital environment are based mainly on Bluetooth communication technology. For example, Khoor and colleagues (2001) have used the Bluetooth system for short-distance (10 m–20 m) data transmission of digitized electrocardiograms (ECGs) together with relevant clinical data. Hall and colleagues (2003) have demonstrated a Bluetooth-based platform for delivering critical health record information in emergency situations, while J. Andreasson and colleagues (2002) have developed a remote system for patient monitoring using Bluetooth-enabled sensors. The above examples show that the merging of mobile communications and the introduction of handhelds along with their associated technology can have a potentially significant impact on emergency medicine. Moreover, many market projections indicate that mobile computers are both an emerging and enabling technology in health care (Finch, 1999). Table 8.3 presents the vital signals that can be monitored by pervasive systems and the corresponding dependent variables.

Each biosignal provides different and complementary information on a patient's status and for each specific person the anticipated range of signal parameters is different. For example, heart rate can vary between 30 and 250 beats/min for normal people under different circumstances; likewise, breathing rate can be between 5 and 50 breaths/min. Electroencephalogram (EEG) and electrocardiogram ECG are considerably more complex

Table 8.3

Physiological Signals and Dependent Variables

Signal	Dependent variables
Electrocardiogram	Heart rate, ventricular beat, ST/PR/ST segment, QT time, and so on
Noninvasive blood pressure	Systolic, diastolic, mean, pulse rate
Respiration	Breath rate, expired CO_2
Pulse oximetry	Pulse rate, pulse volume, oxygen saturation

Table 8.4

Biosignal Characteristics

Biomedical measurements	Voltage range (V)	Number of sensors K	Bandwidth (Hz)	Sample rate (Hz)	Resolution (b/sample)	Information rate (b/s)
ECG	0.5–4 m	5–9	0.01–250	1,250	12	15,000
Heart sound	Extremely small	2–4	5–2,000	10,000	12	120,000
Heart rate	0.5–4 m	2	0.4–5	25	24	600
EEG	2–200 μ	20	0.5–70	350	12	4,200
EMG	0.1–5 m	2+	0–10,000	50,000	12	600,000
Respiratory rate	Small	1	0.1–10	50	16	800
Body temperature	0–100 m	1+	0–1	5	16	80

biosignals with spectra up to 10 KHz (Gouaux et al., 2003). Voltage levels for the collected biosignals can vary from microvolts (EEG) to millivolts (ECG). Biosignal characteristics are summed up in Table 8.4. The ST/PR/ST segments and QT time metrics included in Table 8.3 are explained in Figure 8.2.

PERVASIVE HEALTH CARE IN NONHOSPITAL SETTINGS: HOME CARE APPLICATIONS

Facilities for medical practice in nonhospital settings are limited by the availability of medical devices suitable for producing biosignals and other medical data. Several active research and commercial projects are developing sensors and devices that do not require local intervention to enable contact with a clinician who is remote from the care environment (Mihailidis, Carmichael, and Boger, 2004). These new systems provide automated connection with remote access and seamless transmission of biological and other data upon request. Pervasive systems in nonhospital systems aim at better managing chronic care patients, controlling health delivery costs, increasing quality of life and quality of health services, and providing distinct possibilities for predicting, and, thus, avoiding, serious complications (Perry et al., 2004).

The patient will require mainly monitoring of his vital signals (i.e., ECG, blood pressure, heart rate, breath rate, oxygen saturation, and perspiration). Patients recently discharged from a hospital after some form of intervention, for instance, after a cardiac incident, cardiac surgery, or a diabetic comma, are less secure and require enhanced care. The most common forms of special home monitoring are ECG arrhythmia monitoring, post-surgical monitoring, respiratory and blood oxygen levels monitoring, and sleep apnea monitoring. In the case

Figure 8.2 **A Typical ECG and the Corresponding Segments that May Be Used as Variables for the Assessment of a Patient Condition**

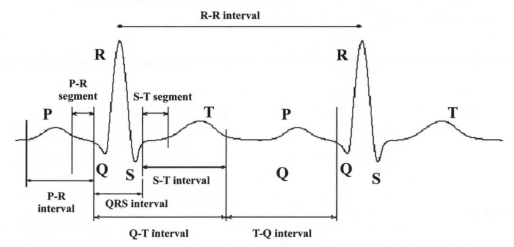

of diabetics, the monitoring of blood sugar levels permits patients to avoid repeated blood sampling, which is undesirable and invasive. One possible solution is the development of implantable wireless sensor devices that would be able to give this information quickly and continuously. Current conditions under which home monitoring might be provided include: hypertension, diabetes (monitoring glucose), obesity (monitoring weight), congestive heart failure (monitoring weight), asthma and chronic obstructive pulmonary disease (monitoring spirometry/peak flow), and, in the near future, conditions utilizing oximetry monitoring. Other home monitoring conditions might include pre-eclampsia, anorexia, low birth-weight infants, growth abnormalities, and arrhythmias. Most chronic health conditions in children and adults could be managed and/or enhanced by home monitoring.

Two monitoring modes are foreseen for most applications: the batch mode and the emergency mode. Batch mode refers to the everyday monitoring process, where vital signs are acquired and transmitted periodically to a health-monitoring center. The received data are monitored by the doctor on duty, then stored in the patient's electronic health record and maintained by the health care center. The emergency mode occurs when a patient does not feel well and, thus, decides to initiate an out-of-schedule session, or when the monitoring device detects a problem and automatically initiates the transfer of data to the corresponding center. Emergency episode detection and the corresponding alarm process are important for the patient's protection. An alarm represents a change in status of a physiological condition or a sensor reading that is outside of agreed limits.

A PERVASIVE SYSTEM FOR PATIENT TELEMONITORING

The typical requirements or prerequisites for a proposed patient telemonitoring pervasive system are summarized below:

- The patient wears (or carries) a personal device capable of monitoring his vital signals (i.e., ECG, EEG, blood pressure, heart rate, breath rate, oxygen saturation and perspiration, glucose, etc.), processing them, and transmitting alarm signals (along with recent vital signs) whenever predefined thresholds are exceeded and an emergency situation is imminent. Personal devices can be PDAs, mobile phones, or more complex devices such as wearable computers.

- The patient's attending doctor carries a portable device capable of receiving the alarm signals and the patient's full range of biosignals. Such a device is also capable of retrieving, upon request, data from the patient's medical record relevant to the vital signals that initiated the alarm.

- Communication flow is controlled by a patient central monitoring unit (CMU), possibly located within a hospital, which acts as a network operation center and a communications hub. Such a unit has full access to the patient's medical record. It is capable of receiving vital signals and intelligently relaying such information to the attending doctor. Moreover, the CMU can correlate the present location of both the doctor and the patient and provide specific guidance to the doctor on how to reach the patient.

The proposed system, from a technological point of view, involves the seamless use of heterogeneous network infrastructures (e.g., WLAN, PAN, global system for mobile communications/universal mobile telecommunications system [GSM/UMTS]) and exploitation of the position-fixing technologies that such networks offer. The positioning infrastructure may deliver location information continuously[2] (e.g., a PCMCIA GPS receiver mounted on the device) or on demand (e.g., the GSM/UMTS terrestrial position fixing). Irrespective of the frequency in the delivery of such information, the portable device relays (or requests) such information only when an emergency incident occurs. Such design orientation is adopted for energy efficiency reasons. The patient's device, apart from the monitoring/alerting facility, needs to report its present position (in a format such as WGS84—World Geodetic System[3]) to the interested parties (e.g., the CMU). Therefore, the device has multiple network interfaces and dynamically adjusts/regulates the transmitted information to the underlying infrastructure.

The proposed platform also requires a set of sensors that are attached on the patient's body, and a microcomputing unit (e.g., a PDA) responsible for processing and analyzing the data provided by the sensors, reaching meaningful conclusions, and, if deemed necessary, providing alarm signals. The sensors together with the intelligent unit form a wireless personal area network that monitors the patient's health status, gives advice to the patient, and in the case of an emergency, notifies, in time, the patient's doctor through the corresponding CMU (Figure 8.3).

The patient's portable equipment stores the biosignals for a period of time T. T is a function of the storage capacity (S) of the portable device and the sampling rate (F) for the collection of biosignals. Optionally, the portable device may also store the whole medical record of the patient along with the security credentials of the doctors who are allowed to access such sensitive information.

$$\text{Biosignal history} = T = f(S, F)$$

The CMU is linked to a location-based services (LBS) middleware and provisioning platform (e.g., the Canvas Location Enabling Server from Telenity). Within this LBS platform a minimalist crisis management system is operated. The type of LBS supported through the system is client-pull; the specific functionality of the LBS is invoked by the client only when some alarming situation arises. The CMU server can handle multiple open bearer services,

Figure 8.3 **Overall Architecture of the Proposed Pervasive System**

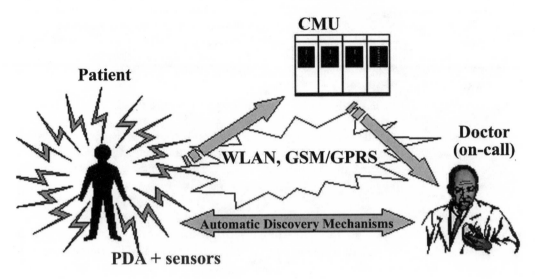

that is, it can receive distress signals through a WAP (wireless application protocol) or HTTP (hypertext transfer protocol) request conveyed through a GSM/GPRS or WLAN wireless/mobile interface (e.g., in the context of a 4G network). The LBS middleware determines which networking environment the distress signals come from. The doctor's device is very similar to the patient's device. However, in this device, the software requirement for the retrieval of information from sensors does not apply.

In case of an emergency, the transmitted messages contain (1) an overall estimation of the patient's status (e.g., serious, very serious), (2) the justification for the estimation, and (3) the most recent biosignal readings that where acquired by the microsensors. The CMU is able to handle multiple calls simultaneously. If a patient's intelligent device requests immediate support from the medical center or the attending doctor, then it is imperative that the latter have quick and efficient access to the information regarding the patient. Therefore, this information needs to be available to the system prior to the development of a crisis situation.

A patient's medical history is usually, and almost always in the case of patients who suffer from chronic diseases, quite long. It includes information such as initial and later diagnoses, current and prior medications, patient's sensitivities, the family's medical history (summarized), high risk factors that are related to the patient, operations, and so on. It is obvious that storing and retrieving the medical history in an unstructured text format is not ideal for handling emergency situations. In such cases, it is necessary for the doctor to have quick and efficient access to the parts of the history that he deems necessary for assessing the situation and deciding on measures to resolve it and to support the patient, especially when he is located in environments with low-speed network connections. The full medical record information is transmitted to the doctor's device only when he enters an area with a high-speed connection (i.e., the WLAN of the hospital). After assessing the patient's status, the doctor needs to be able to inform the CMU about what actions to take in order to deal with the current situation.

Figure 8.4 **Patient Tele-monitoring Application GUI**

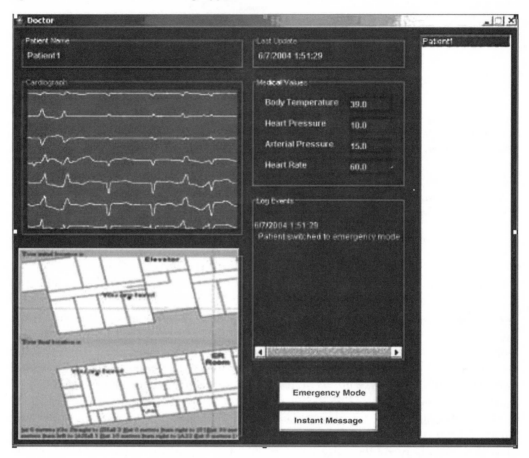

Part of the medical record along with the biosignal readings contained in the emergency notification signal will be relayed to the doctor. The selection procedure regarding which part of the medical record is to be transmitted in the emergency situation may be executed in two ways. The simple approach is preselection by the doctor attending the chronic or post-surgical patient. For instance, for a patient with chronic cardiovascular problems the physician selects recent incidents from his medical record that are related to the specific health problems. In a more sophisticated approach, the patient's device should be able to define, according to the biosignals that invoked the alarm situation, the type of incident (cardiovascular, stroke, diabetic, etc.) that has occurred. Then the patient device relays this information to the CMU, which extracts from the complete electronic health record only the medical history related to this type of incident. Such information is reproduced on the display of the doctor's personal computer (Figure 8.4).

A demonstration system was developed to assess feasibility in both controlled (hospital or health care unit with WLAN infrastructure) and open environments (an urban area with GSM/GPRS coverage). The terminal devices were Compaq iPAQ PDAs with IrDA, WLAN (802.11b), and Bluetooth capabilities. Additionally, some trials, focused mainly on positioning

Table 8.5

System Evaluation Results

Question	Responses average value	Responses standard deviation
Accuracy of results: GPS positioning	4.27	0.59
Accuracy of results: WLAN positioning	3.87	0.75
Correctness of information provided by routing services	3.27	1.12
Medical data display	4.14	0.71
Appropriate service execution time	3.37	0.69
Acceptable level of failed requests	4.67	0.59
Comprehensible and easy to read results	2.81	1.08

Note: Responses ranged from 1 (fully disagree) to 5 (fully agree).

issues, were performed using laptop PCs. GSM/GPRS connectivity was provided to the PDA by an Ericsson GSM handset, through the use of Bluetooth or IrDA interfaces.

Our experiments focused mainly on the transmission of medical images such as digital x-rays, CTs, MRIs, and ultrasounds (US) stored in electronic patient health records. Specifically, for the CT/MRI/US case, image specifications (in accordance with the ACR-199 specs) were 512 pixels × 512 pixels × 8 bits/pixel (256 KB). Over the IEEE 802.11 infrastructure, the transmission of such images lasts, on average, 2,900 msec (throughput ~ 88 KB/sec). For the transmission of digital x-rays (2,048 pixels × 2,048 pixels × 12 bits/pixel), through the same networking configuration, the observed throughput reached 105 KB/sec.

The transmission of the CT/MRI/US was also studied in the GSM/GPRS scenario. In the GSM (circuit switched data, CSD) case and for low signal quality conditions, throughput reached 2.5 KB/sec. In this scenario, the transmission of the CT image required, on average, 2 minutes. Slightly lower throughput was observed in the GPRS scenario with low signal quality conditions. In the GPRS scenario with high quality conditions, the observed throughput reached 3.7 KB/sec.

In terms of the positioning infrastructure used, during the GPS-based experiments, position fluctuations of 5–10m were observed. Such fluctuations were observed with commercially available GPS systems (e.g., Navitech, Garmin), pluggable to the PDA (or laptop) PCMCIA port. Given the overall objectives of this system, such fluctuation and location estimation accuracy is quite acceptable. Time-to-fix ranged from a few seconds to 2 minutes.

The demonstration system has been evaluated by a small number of physicians (fifteen) in a hospital environment. After using the system, users were asked to complete a questionnaire for the quantitative assessment of proposed implementation. The responses ranged from 1 (fully disagree) to 5 (fully agree). Table 8.5 presents the most important findings of the questionnaire analysis process.

CONCLUSIONS AND FUTURE CHALLENGES

The technological advances of the past few years in mobile communications, location- and context-aware computing have facilitated the introduction of pervasive health care applications.

These applications can assist medical personnel and people with health-related problems in two different ways:

- The remote monitoring of patients with chronic diseases (involving diagnosis and monitoring using biosensors and patients' history record) and the immediate notification of a doctor or a medical center in the case of an emergency.
- Coverage of the continuous needs of hospital units, involving the monitoring of the inpatient's status and mobile access to medical data.

In this chapter we discuss a novel pervasive health care application that relies on integrated state-of-the-art technologies such as wireless sensor networks, location-based services, and interworking heterogeneous wireless/mobile networks. Such technologies, glued together through a minimalist crisis-management system, effectively support demanding clinical operations such as the continuous monitoring of chronic diseases.

In the future, 4G network architectures will entail significant benefits for seamless operation of the proposed system. 4G will create an integrated system of existing wireless technologies such as UMTS, GSM, WLAN, Bluetooth, ZigBee, and other newly developed technologies. 4G advances will provide both mobile patients and citizens the choices that will fit their lifestyle and make it easier for them to get the medical attention and advice they need interactively, when and where this is required and in the way that they want it regardless of any geographical barriers or mobility constraints.

However, the use of such pervasive health care raises several challenges. Personal data security and location privacy are highly important aspects of such systems. Similar issues are currently being considered in the context of standardization bodies such as the Internet Engineering Task Force (IETF) (Working Group on Geographic Location/Privacy) (Cuellar et al., 2004). Furthermore, pervasive health care systems are very critical systems, as they deal with a person's health, and, therefore, call for high standards regarding reliability, scalability, privacy-enhancement, interoperability, and configurability, among other things. On the other hand, since health care systems are intended for use by those with low or medium computer literacy, usability issues come to the foreground.

Regardless the remaining challenges, it is anticipated that pervasive health care systems will be expanded in the near future through use of the most recent technological advances in a more active and direct way that offers more comprehensive and higher quality health services to citizens.

NOTES

1. Ekahau LBS. Available at www.ekahau.com (accessed September 26, 2005).
2. Or periodically with increased frequency.
3. The interested parties will convert the received location information according to their global information systems and spatial database models.

REFERENCES

Abowd G. 1999. Software engineering issues for ubiquitous computing. In *21st International Conference on Software Engineering.* Los Alamitos, CA: IEEE Computer Society Press, 75–84.

Andreasson, J.; Ekstrom, M.; Fard, A.; Castano, J.G.; and Johnson, T. 2002. Remote system for patient monitoring using Bluetooth/spl trade. *IEEE Sensors,* 1, June, 304–307.

Ashok, R. and Agrawal, D. 2003. Next-generation wearable networks. *IEEE Computer,* November, 31–39.

Bahl, P. and Padmanabhan, V.N. 2000. RADAR: An in-building RF-based user location and tracking system. In *Proceedings of IEEE Infocom 2000,* 775–784.

Barro, S.; Presedo, J.; Castro, D.; Fernandez-Delgado, M.; Fraga, S.; Lama, M.; and Vila, J. 1999. Intelligent telemonitoring of critical-care patients. *IEEE Engineering in Medicine and Biology,* July/August, 80–88.

Birnbaum, J. 1997. Pervasive information systems. *Communications of the ACM,* 40, 2, 40–41.

Castro, P.; Chiu, P.; Kremenek, T.; and Muntz R. 2001. A probabilistic room location service for wireless networked environments. In *Proceedings of the Third International Conference on Ubiquitous Computing.* Lecture Notes in Computer Science, vol. 2201. London: Springer, 18–34.

Cuellar, J.; Morris, J.; Mulligan, D.; Peterson, J.; Polk, J. 2004. Geopriv requirements. *IETF Network Working Group RFC 3693* (February).

Dan, J. and Luprano, J. 2003. Homecare: A telemedical application. *Medical Device Technology* (December), 25–28.

Finch, C. 1999. Mobile computing in healthcare. *Health Management Technology,* 20, 3 (April), 63–64.

Gouaux F.; Simon-Chautemps, L.; Adami, S.; Arzi, M.; Assanelli, D.; Fayn, J.; Forlini, M.C.; Malossi, C.; Martinez, A.; Placide, J.; Ziliani, G.L; and Rubel, P. 2003. Smart devices for the early detection and interpretation of cardiological syndromes. In *Proceedings of the Fourth International IEEE EMBS Special Topic Conference on Information Technology Applications in Biomedicine.* Los Alamitos, CA: IEEE Computer Society Press, 291–294.

Hall, E.S.; Vawdrey, D.K.; Knutson, C.D.; and Archibald, J.K. 2003. Enabling remote access to personal electronic medical records. *IEEE Engineering in Medicine and Biology Magazine,* May/June, 133–139.

Hightower, J. and Borriello, G. 2001. Location systems for ubiquitous computing. *IEEE Computer,* August, 57–66.

Kara, A. 2001. Protecting privacy in remote-patient monitoring. *Computing Practices,* May, 24–27.

Khoor, S.; Nieberl, K.; Fugedi, K.; and Kail, E. 2001. Telemedicine ECG-telemetry with Bluetooth technology. *Computers in Cardiology 2001,* 585–588.

Lakshmi Narasimhan, V.; Irfan, M.; and Yefremov, M. 2004. MedNet: A pervasive patient information network with decision support. *Proceedings of the Sixth International Workshop on Enterprise Networking and Computing in the Healthcare Industry.* Los Alamitos, CA: IEEE Computer Society Press, 96–101.

Maglogiannis, I.; Apostolopoulos, N.; and Tsoukias, P. 2004. Designing and implementing an electronic health record for personal digital assistants (PDAs). *International Journal for Quality of Life Research,* 2, 1, 63–67.

Mihailidis A.; Carmichael B.; and Boger J. 2004. The use of computer vision in an intelligent environment to support aging-in-place, safety, and independence in the home. *IEEE Transactions on Information Technology in Biomedicine,* 8, 3, 238–247.

Perry, M.; Dowdall, A.; Lines, L.; Hone, K. 2004. Multimodal and ubiquitous computing systems: supporting independent-living older users. *IEEE Transactions on Information Technology in Biomedicine,* 8, 3, 258–270.

Stanford, V. 2002. Pervasive health care applications face tough security challenges. *IEEE Pervasive Computing,* April/June, 6–12.

PART III

PROPERTIES OF PERVASIVE INFORMATION SYSTEMS AND THEIR EVALUATION

AESTHETIC CONCERNS IN PERVASIVE INFORMATION SYSTEMS

JOHAN REDSTRÖM

Abstract: Aesthetics is a subject receiving increasing attention in the design of pervasive information systems. One reason is the realization that existing approaches centered on usability and utility do not seem to cover aspects of use essential to the realm of the everyday. Another reason aesthetics enters the picture is that by leaving the established domain of personal computing, pervasive information technology comes in close contact with other design traditions engaged in the design of everyday things, and thus also a very different set of perspectives, values, and approaches. As we position pervasive information systems in relation to design traditions such as architecture and industrial design, it becomes apparent that we often lack even a rudimentary understanding of the expressiveness and aesthetics of the technology with which we are working.

This chapter presents the critical issues that need to be addressed during the design of aesthetically compliant pervasive information systems. Initially, the chapter discusses the rationale leading to the emergence of aesthetics as a core research topic for the design of pervasive systems. By adopting a holistic investigation viewpoint, the chapter discusses the most important developments in this field by focusing on the prospects of incorporating aesthetics on interaction design, extending the traditional information systems' design objectives, which were orchestrated around the system's utility and productivity.

Keywords: Aesthetics, Design Methodology, Design Theory, Pervasive Information Systems

INTRODUCTION

While the expressiveness and aesthetics of information technology have been explored in art for quite some time now, it is more recently that these issues have entered the discourse of human–computer interaction and interaction design. A central reason for this increasing interest in aesthetic concerns seems to be the introduction of ideas such as pervasive information systems, ubiquitous computing, and ambient intelligence.

A central reason that the notion of pervasive computing urges us to consider aesthetics is that, as a rather radical alternative to personal computing, it puts a certain focus on how we design things—"how" meaning the concrete form that we give the things we design. By revisiting questions such as whether to use screen, keyboard, mouse, and so on, we open up to alternative (re)solutions of the same functional requirements. An illustrative example of this is the notion of tangible user interfaces (TUIs). The difference between such interfaces and the (by now traditional) graphical user interfaces (GUIs) is not only a matter of what they do, but how they do it. While we can try to capture the difference between a given TUI and a GUI in terms of functions, what really sets them apart is how they appear in use, the expressions that define them.

Much of interaction design has been concerned with optimising this single path for speed and effectivity. Yet, it is exactly this repetition of a single, predictable path, time and time again, which, in the end, becomes a clear "aesthetics killer." Therefore, we have become interested in products that offer myriad ways of interacting with them. Interaction in which there is room for a variety of orders and combinations of actions. Freedom of interaction also implies that the user can express herself in the interaction. (Djajadiningrat et al., 2004, 297)

Another reason aesthetics becomes important, is, of course, because pervasive technology is designed to be present in a world not designed around technology—a world where the machine is not at the center. Some time ago, the shift in computer design toward the office domain implied many changes concerning what was considered important and, as a result, we now typically interact with our computers in ways inspired by and valued by the office and work context. The idea of pervasive information systems pushes computers even further into the realm of the everyday, a world dominated by other kinds of design traditions and values. To say that technology is becoming a fashion is not only to say that technology now needs to "look good"; it is also to say that technology is now being appropriated on the basis of cultural heritage, social structures, use patterns, personal identities, and so on, much the way we relate to other kinds of everyday things (cf. Aarts and Marzano, 2003). This is potentially a shift more fundamental than the one toward office work as a basis for designing computational things.

Given the rather immature state of aesthetics in our field, a reasonable starting point for an inquiry into such issues would be to try to better understand what the role and relevance of an aesthetic perspective could be like—and indeed, how one could go about developing one. To do so, we would probably have to say something about what an aesthetic perspective in general might be like, and whether it differs from the understanding we currently have as we develop new technology on the basis of practical functionality. The aim of this chapter is to examine a few such basic issues. Thus, some of what follows might appear rather elementary to many, perhaps trivial to some. Yet, there is a need to revisit these basic questions, as there are fundamental differences between typical technological and aesthetic perspectives that are likely to cause some confusion as we try to combine them. But let us start with the calls for aesthetics emerging in interaction design.

THE CALL FOR AN AESTHETICS OF PERVASIVE COMPUTING

A common feature of arguments for taking aesthetic issues more seriously in the development of pervasive computing applications is that the shift toward everyday life implies certain differences compared with the professional work setting in which personal computing evolved. Such differences include that there is a different set of values being sought, for example, engagement rather than efficiency, exploration rather than error-free performance, and so on. To optimize practical functionality with respect to utilitarian perspectives is not enough, or not even good at all (cf. Gaver and Martin 2000, Gaver et al 2004). Thus, aesthetics, and especially modern aesthetics with its rich framework for critique, may be used not only to expand the scope of technology development but also to critically examine it from within, that is, through design (cf. Dunne, 1999; Dunne and Raby, 2001).

Another set of arguments builds on the need to acknowledge what is, so to speak, already there for us—for example, that computational things need to be designed in ways that relate to existing environments (cf. Fogarty, Forlizzi, and Hudson, 2001; Hallnäs and Redström, 2001). Further, some arguments state the need for technology development to learn from more established areas of design such as industrial design and architecture, especially as it is combined with such traditions (cf. Ehn, 2002; Hallnäs, Melin, and Redström, 2002; McCullough 2004). Then there is the issue of foundations, and the need for aesthetics as a complement or alternative to existing approaches (cf. Bertelsen and Pold, 2004; Hallnäs and Redström, 2002a). Thus, there is not one, but a set of related issues and questions raised.

Complementary and Alternative Approaches

Embedded in the arguments of why an aesthetics of computational things is needed, there are ideas of what such a perspective might imply with respect to design. Roughly speaking, one can differentiate between two different development strategies. The first strategy argues for the need to complement existing design methods centered on usability and practical functionality, to broaden the set of issues dealt with in design in order to accommodate the needs and desires of everyday life (as opposed to, say, professional work). Thus, aesthetics is positioned as an extension of the current perspective. The second perspective argues that there is a need to more or less replace the existing usability-oriented design approach with a "new" one based on aesthetics—in other words, established methods based on practical functionality cannot provide a proper foundation for an expanding interest in aesthetics. For the purpose of this discussion, we refer to these approaches as either "complementary" or "alternative."

It is central to realize that the question of how to treat aesthetics differs from the question of whether one needs to consider both functional and aesthetic issues in a given design process. We must not confuse the question of whether aesthetics and functional concerns are both relevant with the question of how we aim to deal with the two, where we look for their respective foundations, and so on. Thus, the present discussion of a complementary versus an alternative approach is primarily a discussion of how to position emerging aesthetic concerns in relation to established usability-oriented approaches, and not whether or not they are both needed. As such, both strategies are "complementary" in some sense but, as we will see, there are reasons for distinguishing between the two, since they depend on different arguments and thus carry different sets of implications for how we might think about aesthetics. It is, however, important to remember that this seemingly divisive approach is a method this author uses to expose certain issues in the development of an aesthetics of interaction design, and thus is not necessarily a literal account of the intentions behind the work cited.

Complementary Approaches

The basic argument of the complementary approach is that the issues dealt with in a design process centered on practical functionality need to be expanded to include aesthetic aspects. The approach is one of adding aspects taken into consideration rather than a shift in basic understanding. It may, for instance, look like the following:

> A pleasure-based approach to fitting the product to the person would, however, require a far richer picture of the person for whom the product is to be designed. . . . Pleasure-based approaches still include looking at usability issues, so the cognitive and physical issues, including anthropometrics, are still important. However, because such approaches also take into account fitting the product to the person's lifestyle, there are many more issues that need to be considered. (Jordan, 2000, 60)

Another example of how to build on current practice is this suggestion of how to extend usability engineering to include a broader set of aspects of use:

Traditional usability engineering methods are not adequate for analyzing and evaluating hedonic quality and its complex interplay with usability and utility. The techniques we have suggested might significantly broaden usability engineering practices by shifting the focus to a more holistic perspective on human needs and desires. In the future, we might see usability engineering evolving toward more complete user experience design—one that encompasses the joy of use. (Hassenzahl, Beu, and Burmester, 2001, 7f)

While aesthetics is perhaps just one part of the new aspects intended here, clearly, it is a question of adding dimensions to existing methodologies. Norman presents a somewhat similar perspective:

We scientists now understand how important emotion is to everyday life, how valuable. Sure, utility and usability are important, but without fun and pleasure, joy and excitement, and yes, anxiety and anger, fear and rage, our lives would be incomplete. . . . The surprise is that we now have evidence that aesthetically pleasing objects enable you to work better. (Norman, 2004, 8–10)

Yet another example is Preece, Rogers, and Sharp's notion of a transition from human–computer interaction to interaction design:

The realization that new technologies are offering increasing opportunities for supporting people in their everyday lives has led researchers and practitioners to consider further goals. . . . The goals of designing interactive products to be fun, enjoyable, pleasurable, aesthetically pleasing and so on are concerned primarily with the user experience. By this we mean what the interaction with the system feels like to the users. . . . Hence, user experience goals differ from the more objective usability goals in that they are concerned with how users experience an interactive product from their perspective, rather than assessing how useful or productive a system is from its own perspective. (Preece, Rogers, and Sharp, 2002, 18f.)

The passage cited from Preece and colleagues entails an important distinction, namely, that there is a difference between the objective evaluation criteria of a system-centric perspective and the subjective judgments that characterize aesthetic statements. This leads us to a discussion of the "alternative" approach.

Alternative Approaches

The alternative approach is a more radical call for an aesthetics of pervasive computing. It not only states that present design methods centered on practical functionality are not enough, but that they are not suitable as a foundation at all. Here, the call for an aesthetic perspective is also a call for an alternative foundation for interaction design. Bertelsen and Pold argue:

The basic problem is that in order to understand the dynamics of use as not only contingency, it is necessary to introduce a cultural unit of analysis. We need to take into account the broader cultural context in order to understand and design IT-based artefacts today, and we need to introduce perspectives on the use situation taking experience rather than cognition as the basic unit of analysis. In other words we feel that there is a need for a redefinition of

HCI as an aesthetic discipline. . . . We propose that aesthetics could be a new foundational concept for HCI: taking aesthetic theories of representation, experience, and sense perception as basic categories. (Bertelsen and Pold, 2004, 24)

There is also a question of what set of values and objectives we build upon. Arguing that there is a need to reconsider the ambition to create a tight fit between user and product, Dunne states that:

> In the Human Factors world, objects, it seems, must be understood rather than interpreted. This raises the question: are conventional notions of user-friendliness compatible with aesthetic experience? Perhaps with aesthetics, a different path must be taken: an aesthetic approach might subsume and subvert the idea of user-friendliness and provide an alternative model of interactivity. (Dunne, 1999, 32)

> If user-friendliness characterises the relationship between the user and the optimal object, user-unfriendliness then, a form of gentle provocation, could characterise the post-optimal object. The emphasis shifts from optimising the fit between people and electronic objects through transparent communication, to providing aesthetic experience through the electronic objects themselves. (Ibid., 38)

Hallnäs and Redström have argued that aesthetics is the proper foundation for technology design as it turns from its current focus on efficient use toward a concern for meaningful presence:

> When computer systems change from being tools for specific use to everyday things present in our lives, we have to change focus from design for efficient use to design for meaningful presence. (Hallnäs and Redström, 2002a, 108)

> When we let things into our lifeworld and they receive a place in our life, they become meaningful to us. We can say that this act of acceptance is in a certain sense a matter of relating expression to meaning, or of giving meaning to expressions. . . . [T]he result is that a thing becomes the bearer of meaningfulness through its expressiveness. It is this expressiveness and meaningfulness that is basic to design for presence. (Ibid., 113)

> It follows that good design from an aesthetical point of view basically is a logical question, not primarily a question of psychology, ethnography, sociology, etc. It is a basic axiom here that it is through the force of its inner logic, its consistent appearance, that a thing receives depth in its expression and thus its strength to act as a placeholder for meaning. Behind each expressive thing present in our lives there is an expressional with a strong form. (Ibid., 116)

To summarize, we might say that aesthetics seems to mean several different things here, but that the call for aesthetics to a significant extent is made in relation/opposition to the typical focus on practical functionality. And so one thing we need to clarify in order to develop an aesthetics of pervasive computing is what this relation could be like, for example, whether the complementary or the alternative approach is more appropriate.

A central question here is how we think of aesthetics in relation to the empirical studies of use and users that is often argued to be the base of usability-oriented design, that is, if there could be such an empirical foundation for aesthetic decisions. Yet another issue is what notions such as "aesthetics of interaction" or "beauty in use" are about, what it is that we refer to. These are all rather complex issues that we perhaps cannot expect to be ready to answer at this point. What we can do, however, is to see how our situation relates to the established discourse on aesthetics. And, fortunately, most of these issues have been debated for a very long time.

HISTORICAL PERSPECTIVES

Though descriptions of aesthetics in dictionaries tend to center on the notion of beauty, our everyday use of "aesthetics" includes aspects from a series of transformations of the meaning of the term. Historically, our word "aesthetics" stems from "aisthesis," which was used by Aristotle and the philosophers of his time to describe perception. However, divisions between perception, cognition, consciousness, and so on, were not the same then as they are in contemporary thinking, and so their use of the term "aesthesis" is perhaps better understood as referring to a kind of "lived experience" (as opposed to reasoning and thinking) since it seems to include more than just sensory perception as we understand it today (Aristotle, *De Anima*).

The idea that aesthetics has to do with (the study of) the appreciation and creation of beauty, especially in art, was developed during the transition from "classical" ideals of beauty centered on normative rules, to "romantic" fascination with the individual genius and his/her ability to transcend given expectations and norms in the eighteenth century. These ideas are closely related to the shift in political and economic power that occurred at the time; the shift in influence from church and aristocracy to the rising bourgeois culture. Though rather different from each other, these two basic views are still with us: more or less normative rules and guidelines still matter (as, for instance, when we use notions such as the golden section to compose a "good" picture), as does the notion of beauty centered on the individual's experience (as when we say that beauty is in the eyes of the beholder).

However, we also have an understanding of aesthetics that is not so much about beauty, but about the ways in which we experience things in a more general sense. For instance, in contemporary art we might expect to find things that challenge us, make us reflect and rethink, things that question given norms, and so on, but that are not necessarily "beautiful." Though our notion of aesthetics centers on beauty, we do acknowledge that to try to understand such work in terms of beauty would be to miss the point entirely. Instead, this often seems to be concerned with questions of representation, mediation, interpretation, appropriation, and the like.

This wider notion of aesthetics as concerned with how we come to experience and understand the world in a rather profound sense is known as modern aesthetics, and can be said to originate with the work of Kant:

> Tradition had placed the aesthetic beyond words and Kant's ingenious move was to take its property of being resistant to conceptualization and make it the arena in which the interaction between consciousness and reality is worked out. For the first time, what exists beyond description is not placed beyond understanding or in opposition to everyday experience but argued to be the dynamic state of conceptual reappraisal that is constitutive of our attempts to deal with any new situation. (Cazeaux, 2000, xvi)

Of course, aesthetics as well as most other things have developed significantly since the eighteenth century, so why is this still relevant? Consider what Kant refers to as the "antinomy of taste," one of the issues he set out to resolve (Kant, 1790, 338f):

1. Thesis: A judgment of taste is not based on concepts; for otherwise one could dispute about it (decide by means of proofs).
2. Antithesis: A judgment of taste is based on concepts; for otherwise, regardless of the variation among [such judgments], one could not even so much as quarrel about them (lay claim to other people's necessary assent to one's judgment).

This is a rather precise description of a fundamental problem in aesthetics, namely, that although judgments of taste are expressed as if they were objective statements, they cannot be determined on the basis of proof. A statement like "this chair is comfortable" appears to be objective, that is, it appears to be stating something about the chair, yet it is inherently subjective and there is no way we can arrive at the conclusion that the chair is indeed comfortable either by empirical study or deductive proof. Still, somehow we are able to talk about the chair as being comfortable, although we might disagree about it.

PROSPECTS FOR AN AESTHETICS OF INTERACTION DESIGN

These historical perspectives have some interesting implications for how we might think about developing an aesthetics of pervasive computing. Let us begin with some implications of Kant's first thesis, and the question of whether aesthetics in interaction design is best seen as an extension of existing concerns for practical functionality or if it indeed is something else (again remembering that this is not a question of whether we need to consider both practical functionality and aesthetics in design, but whether or not the latter could be seen as an extension of the former). If we take into account the development of modern aesthetics by Kant and others, the answer to this question must be that it is by necessity something else, as it deals with judgments of taste and not properties of things that can be evaluated with respect to external criteria.

Though the two statements "this device is waterproof" and "this device is attractive" might appear to be similar, and thus possible to treat in similar ways, they are fundamentally different from each other. Whereas we can evaluate the "waterproofness" of a device (given a set of parameters and some mode of investigation, of course), we cannot, by means of any empirical investigation, determine whether a device is attractive or not. Of course, we can come up with operational criteria; for example, that attractiveness in this case means that 67 percent of the people in a study state that it is attractive when asked about their opinion, but that is a completely different thing from saying that the thing is attractive.

> By a principle of taste would be meant a principle under which, as condition, we could subsume the concept of an object and then infer that the object is beautiful. That, however, is absolutely impossible. For I must feel the pleasure directly in my presentation of the object, and I cannot be talked into that pleasure by means of any bases of proof. (Kant, 1790, 285)

This has consequences not only for how we think about evaluations. Though we might try to relate aesthetic design decisions to studies of users the way we relate decisions to measures of functional performance, there is an important difference between the two. From the discussion above, it follows that we cannot deduce aesthetic design decisions from any empirical material. In other words, aesthetic decisions will be made on grounds other than the empirical basis that human factors aim to build on. Thus, there does not seem to be a case for the complementary approach, that is, that we can build on the tradition of user studies and evaluations also when it comes to aesthetics. Rather, we need to think of the realm of aesthetics as something distinct from functional concerns and thus look for its foundation elsewhere.

This distinction is sometimes confused in user-centered design, and so let us consider another domain instead: how would one study what characterizes, say, a certain symphony by Beethoven? And how do we compare it with a symphony by Berlioz? Of course, we would learn something by asking people what they think of these works, or by studying people performing or experiencing these pieces—but that something would not help us understand the musical works as such. Rather, one would have to read the scores, perform them, listen and analyze how they were made, their use of form, material, compositional techniques, and so on. And so, why is it that we think we learn what a computational thing is by studying its use? Answering this question reveal the bias of our perspective.

Without a strong foundation in empirical studies, it may seem as if we do not have any real possibility for a systematic treatment of aesthetics in technology development. This, however, is not the case as we turn to the second thesis in Kant's analysis; that we indeed are able to talk about these matters. Whereas we cannot decide whether the chair I am sitting on now is comfortable or not by means of proof, we can certainly talk about it, discuss it, and through critical examination of the object find out more about it. Here, it is the inner logic of the thing that becomes the focus of our analysis.

Though certainly subjective and definitely embedded in various social and cultural contexts, critical examination of the expressions of a thing can be cultivated to the extent that it becomes systematic and reaches beyond statements about whether we like a given thing or not. Typical examples exist in the analysis of art and the field of art criticism, but we can find it elsewhere as well. Consider for instance more elaborate car enthusiast publications and magazines: the way the driving experience is described by relating technical terms such as power, torque, engine type, drivetrain, and so on to expressions of the car in use such as character, temperament, liveliness, power, balance, and the like. Often, we never get to drive the actual car ourselves, yet such descriptions seem to give (some of) us a rather precise idea of what it could be like and there are clearly certain principles according to which these reviews are made. Another relevant example is the growing area of review and critique of computer games. One would perhaps not argue that this criticism is scientific, but then again, neither is design. Still, it can be highly systematic and informative, and thus a basis for richer experience and deeper understanding. It is such a critical discourse that we need to develop and cultivate in pervasive computing to be able to deal with aesthetics.

DEVELOPING INTERACTION AESTHETICS

Though brief, it is hoped that the overview presented above illustrates that we find ourselves in a very rich context as we start developing frameworks for how to treat aesthetics in interaction design. The notion of an aesthetics of interaction puts us in an intriguing position with respect to the relation between the thing experienced and the person experiencing it. For instance, Kant describes the appreciation of beauty as a kind of "disinterested contemplation" (*interesseloses Anschauen*) (Kant, 1790), which does not really seem to characterize the rather active relation we have to the things we use and live with (cf. also, e.g., Gadamer, 1977). It seems reasonable to ask: When we shift from an interest in the expressions of things to the expressions of things in use, what is it that we refer to? This is perhaps the central question one has to address when developing frameworks for aesthetics in interaction design.

Let us compare the design of a typewriter keyboard and the keyboard of the piano. The design logic of the qwerty-keyboard centers on the way the keys have been arranged to enable us to type at maximum speed with respect to basic technical limitations of the mechanical device, that is, without jamming the keys. The design of the piano keyboard, on the other hand, has evolved to allow maximum expressiveness in terms of dynamics and how we control timbre through the way we press the keys (though of course which keys we press and when has some significance when performing music). Clearly, we can talk about the differences in design aesthetics between the typewriter and piano considered as physical objects, but we can also talk about design aesthetics in terms of expressions (and expressiveness) in use. As both keyboards are in many ways solutions to interaction design problems (i.e., how to enable quick but not too quick typing; how to enable control of dynamics and timbre), they also carry with them an explicit idea of what using them, and how to use them, could (or even should) be like.

We might say that what has been designed is not only an object but also a series of acts of using it (Hallnäs and Redström, 2006). These two layers are quite visible as we turn to the expressions of using these things—just picture someone using a typewriter in comparison with someone playing a piano. It is certainly not only the expressions of the things used that are different in these two pictures. Though related, the expressions of the thing as such and of the acts of using it are quite different—now picture someone typing on a typewriter the way a musician performs on an instrument, or playing the piano the way we type on a keyboard. The aesthetic potential of such combinations and recombinations of things and the acts of using them has been explored in art for some time now; in relation to our discussion of keyboards and the art of using them, the use of machinelike performance in electronic music can serve as an illustration, for example, Kraftwerk's *The Man Machine* (Capitol album of 1978).

We may now return to the question of what it is that we refer to when we say that we shift from a focus on the expressions of things to the expressions of things in use. As we design things meant to be used (by someone), we also design ways of using them, and it is toward the expressions of these ways, or acts, of use that we now turn. But it is not a shift from what a thing is to what it does as we use it, nor is it a shift from what the object is to what its user experiences; rather, it is a shift toward the user as performer, where the object becomes an instrument.

Emerging Frameworks for Aesthetics in Interaction Design

Though the area of aesthetics in pervasive computing is still far from presenting a more coherent framework such as the one we now have for handling usability issues, several attempts are being made to develop notions such as "beauty in interaction" (Djajadinigrat et al., 2004), "beauty in use" (ibid.), "aesthetics of interaction" (ibid.), "aesthetics of use" (Dunne, 1999; Graves Petersen et al., 2004), and "aesthetics of functionality" (Hallnäs and Redström, 2001). Four different approaches will be introduced to give the reader an idea of what issues are being addressed and how.

Based on an industrial design tradition, Djajadiningrat and colleagues (2004) have developed notions of "formgiving" with respect to issues in interaction design:

> To us, good interactive products respect all of man's skills: his cognitive, perceptual-motor and emotional skills. Current interaction design emphasises our cognitive abilities, our abilities to read, interpret and remember. We are interested in exploring the other two. (Djajadiningrat et al., 2004, 297)

As such, their approach centers on three aspects of interaction (ibid., 297):

- interaction patterns: the timing and rhythm linking user actions and product reactions
- richness of motor actions: to make use of a broader band of perceptual-motor skills
- freedom of interaction: the ability to choose how to interact

In the work of Dunne (1999), central elements concern instead the potential of the aesthetic to criticize and question, for example, by exposing certain values and structures in design. Introducing notions such as "para-functionality" and the "post-optimal" object, the approach of Dunne (1999, 109) aims at:

- going beyond optimisation to explore critical and aesthetic roles for electronic products
- using estrangement to open the space between people and electronic products to discussion and criticism
- designing alternative functions to draw attention to legal, cultural and social norms
- exploiting the unique narrative possibilities offered by electronic products
- developing forms of engagement that avoid being didactic and utopian

Bertelsen and Pold base their perspective on the practice of art criticism, especially in the field of new media. As a basis for evaluation of interfaces, they suggest considering the following issues (Bertelsen and Pold, 2004, 26):

- stylistic references in the interface
- use of standards and conformance to tradition
- materiality and remediation: immediacy and hypermediacy
- genres in the interface
- the interface as a hybrid between the functional (control interface) and the cultural interface
- representational techniques, e.g., realistic and naturalistic representations vs. symbolic and allegorical representations
- challenges to users' expectations
- developmental potentials, e.g., of unanticipated use

Yet another set of issues are the focus of work by Hallnäs and Redström (2001, 2002a, 2002b, 2006). Here, the focus is on the internal structure of a design, its inner logic, and so issues such as the following have been explored:

- how computational things build their presence
- the expressions of computational technology as design material
- the relation between spatial and temporal form elements in combinations of computational and traditional design materials
- interaction design as act design
- the expression-structure of acts

Clearly, these four examples of what an "aesthetics of interaction" could be like, point toward related but quite distinct directions. As such, the approaches presented also illustrate the complexity of the issues at hand and the need for us to leave more "classical" ideas such as set rules and guidelines behind (cf. Bertelsen and Pold, 2004). However, if we try to find recurring themes that could indicate general issues that are relevant to address in the development of new pervasive information systems, the central idea seems to be that we need to create a richer relation to our computational things, for example, through the exploration of:

- engagement rather than efficiency in use,
- temporal structures, for example, interaction patterns and expressions of use that evolve over time,
- alternative forms of use that even challenge expectations on use and user,
- relations to context, for example, cultural references, user identity, traditions, other design domains,
- alternative interface and material combinations.

Another common feature is, therefore, that, to a rather limited extent, they address issues related, for example, to the use of graphic design aesthetics in interface design or how to express basic functionality through physical form as is done in industrial design, but that instead they focus on what new areas for expression are opened up by pervasive technologies. This should not be understood as an exclusion of such already established issues and areas, as they are often relevant also within this area, but rather as the idea that is not where we will primarily find the new challenges posed to design by this technology.

Further, these accounts not only tell us that there are many different values and ideas promoted here, they also tell us something about where we can look for relevant work done in other fields, as they all relate to ideas developed elsewhere that can be of use in interaction design. As such, they point to the potentially very rich perspective that a more developed account of aesthetics could provide in interaction design.

CONCLUSION

In many ways, the technological and aesthetic perspectives seem to be in opposition. The technical object is typically characterized by its practical function. Kroes writes that "an essential aspect of any technical object is its function; think away from a technical object its function and what is left is just some kind of physical object. It is by virtue of its practical function that an object is a technical object." (Kroes, 2001, 1). The aesthetic object, on the other hand, can be something without "purpose" at all: a "purposeful purposelessness or a purposeless play," as Cage says about music (Cage, 1961, 12).

To further complicate things, this is not only a question of the object as such, but also our way of experiencing it, our basic perspective and understanding. For instance, Heidegger used the notion of a technological perspective to describe a way of looking at the world as being the means for one's ends, like a "standing reserve" (*Bestand*) (Heidegger, 1977). Aesthetic experience, on the other hand, was considered by Kant to be a kind of "disinterested contemplation" (Kant, 1790). Of course, things are not necessarily this polarized, and certainly these views have been contested many times since they were first presented. Nevertheless, they indicate that our present interest in the aesthetics of technology, from a designer's point of view, is a melting pot where sometimes seemingly contradictory perspectives and traditions come in contact with each other. It is no surprise that we sometimes become confused.

This cross-fertilization could, however, offer us an interesting and potentially highly creative future in terms of new methods of technology development and aesthetics in design (cf. Borgmann, 1995; Ehn, 2002; Zaccai 1999). The fact that aesthetic approaches differ significantly from the usability-oriented approaches currently in focus, need not be understood in terms of competition, that is, that we need to choose one and leave the other. Aesthetics provide us with an alternative foundation for technology development that builds on a different tradition, a different set of concepts, objectives, and methods, compared with those that now dominate the way we think and work.

As such, it gives us a complementary perspective that we can use to deepen our understanding of this new technology of ours. And a greater variety of perspectives on information technology is very much needed.

REFERENCES

Aarts, E. and Marzano, S., eds. 2003. *The New Everyday: Views on Ambient Intelligence.* Rotterdam: 010 Publishers.

Aristotle. 1986. *De Anima* [On the Soul], trans. H. Lawson-Tancred. London: Penguin Books.

Bertelsen, O.W. and Pold, S. 2004. Criticism as an approach to interface aesthetics. In *Proceedings of the Third Nordic Conference on Human–Computer Interaction.* New York: ACM Press, 23–32.

Borgmann, A. 1995. The depth of design. In R. Buchanan and V. Margolin, eds., *Discovering Design.* Chicago: University of Chicago Press, 13–22.

Cage, J. 1961. *Silence.* Middletown, CT: Wesleyan University Press.

Cazeaux, C., ed. 2000. *The Continental Aesthetics Reader.* London: Routledge.

Djajadiningrat, T.; Wensveen, S.; Frens, J.; and Overbeeke, K. 2004. Tangible products: Redressing the balance between appearance and action. *Personal and Ubiquitous Computing,* 8, 5, 294–309.

Dunne, A. 1999. *Hertzian Tales: Electronic Products, Aesthetic Experience and Critical Design.* London: RCA CRD Research Publications.

Dunne, A. and Raby, F. 2001. *Design Noir: The Secret Life of Electronic Objects.* Basel: August/Birkhäuser.

Ehn, P. 2002. Neither Bauhäusler nor nerd: Educating the interaction designer. In *Proceedings of the Conference on Designing Interactive Systems: Processes, Practices, Methods, and Techniques.* New York: ACM Press, 19–23.

Fogarty, J.; Forlizzi, J.; and Hudson, S.E. 2001. Aesthetic information collages: Generating decorative displays that contain information. In *Proceedings of the Fourteenth Annual ACM Symposium on User Interface Software and Technology.* New York: ACM Press, 141–150.

Gadamer, H.-G. 1977. Aesthetics and hermeneutics. In D.E. Linge, trans. and ed., *Philosophical Hermeneutics.* Berkeley: University of California Press, 95–104.

Gaver, B. and Martin, H. 2002. Alternatives: Exploring information appliances through conceptual design proposals. In *Proceedings of the SIGCHI Conference on Human Factors in Computing Systems.* New York: ACM Press, 209–216.

Gaver, W.W., et al. 2004. The drift table: Designing for ludic engagement. In *CHI '04 Extended Abstracts on Human Factors in Computing Systems.* New York: ACM Press, 885–900.

Graves Petersen, M.; Sejer Iversen, O.; Gall Krogh, P.; and Ludvigsen, M. 2004. Aesthetic interaction: A pragmatist's aesthetics of interactive systems. In *Proceedings of the 2004 Conference on Designing Interactive Systems: Processes, Practices, Methods, and Techniques.* New York: ACM Press, 269–276.

Hallnäs, L. and Redström, J. 2001. Slow technology: Designing for reflection. *Journal of Personal and Ubiquitous Computing,* 5, 3, 201–212.

———. 2002a. From use to presence: On the expressions and aesthetics of everyday computational things. *ACM Transactions on Computer-Human Interaction* (ToCHI), 9, 2, 106–124.

———. 2002b. Abstract information appliances: Methodological exercises in conceptual design of computational things. In *Proceedings of the Conference on Designing Interactive Systems: Processes, Practices, Methods, and Techniques.* New York: ACM Press, 105–116.

———. 2006. *Interaction Design: Foundations, Experiments.* Borås: Interactive Institute and the Textile Research Centre, Swedish School of Textiles, University College of Borås.

Hallnäs, L.; Melin, L.; and Redström, J. 2002. Textile displays: Using textiles to investigate computational technology as design material. In *Proceedings of the Second Nordic Conference on Human-Computer Interaction* (NordiCHI 2002). New York: ACM Press, 157–166.

Hassenzahl, M.; Beu, A.; and Burmester, M. 2001. Engineering joy. *IEEE Software,* January/February, 2–8.

Heidegger, M. 1977. *The Question Concerning Technology.* New York: Harper and Row.

Jordan, P.W. 2000. *Designing Pleasurable Products: An Introduction to the New Human Factors.* London: Taylor and Francis.

Kant, I. 1987. *Critik der Urtheilskraft.* Berlin: Lagarde und Friedrich, 1790. Citations taken from: *Critique of Judgment,* trans. W.S. Pluhar. Indianapolis, IN: Hackett.

Kroes, P. 2001. Technical functions as dispositions: A critical assessment. *Techné* (*Electronic Journal of the Society for Philosophy and Technology*), 5, 3, 1–16.

McCullough, M. 2004. *Digital Ground; Architecture, Pervasive Computing, and Environmental Knowing.* Cambridge: MIT Press.

Norman, D.A. 2004. *Emotional Design: Why We Love (or Hate) Everyday Things.* New York: Basic Books.

Preece, J.; Rogers, Y.; and Sharp. H. 2002. *Interaction Design: Beyond Human-Computer Interaction.* New York: Wiley.

Zaccai, G. 1999. Art and technology: Aesthetics redefined. In R. Buchanan and V. Margolin, eds., *Discovering Design.* Chicago: University of Chicago Press, 3–12.

CHAPTER 10

A FRAMEWORK FOR THE EVALUATION OF PERVASIVE INFORMATION SYSTEMS

Jean Scholtz, Mary Theofanos, and Sunny Consolvo

Abstract: As pervasive information systems weave their way into society, it is critical that these new systems are accepted and utilized. However, it is difficult to determine what makes for a good design and a successful interaction because evaluation methodologies and metrics are in their infancy for these types of systems. The complexity and diversity of these systems has made it difficult to establish common evaluation techniques and practices. However, the necessity for such a framework is overwhelmingly apparent. A framework will make it easier for researchers to learn from each other's results, create effective discount evaluation techniques and design guidelines for pervasive computing, provide a mechanism for researchers to share what they have learned about the appropriateness of different evaluation techniques, and provide structure so that key areas of evaluation are not overlooked.

In this chapter, we present a framework of areas of evaluation for pervasive information systems. The framework includes nine evaluation areas that include elements of usability, interaction, and values (such as privacy and trust). We present sample metrics and measures and examples for each area from the literature. We review a number of methodologies that have been used in evaluation and provide a case study of an evaluation using a number of the evaluation areas in the framework. We conclude with a discussion of future needs to enable researchers to share evaluation results.

Keywords: Evaluation, Measures, Methodologies, Metrics, Pervasive Computing

INTRODUCTION

Computing systems can achieve Weiser's (1991) vision of being pervasive only if they are seamlessly integrated into people's everyday lives. Such systems must go beyond the typical usability achieved by current desktop computer systems and consider the human experience in a larger context. In order to achieve this, we need to understand how to design and evaluate such systems. However, a challenge faced by the pervasive research community is that few guidelines exist that have been shown to be effective for evaluating pervasive or ubiquitous computing systems in the larger context. As they were for desktop systems, these guidelines must be developed using an iterative user-centered design process of designing, implementing, and evaluating the various classes of pervasive applications. However, the nature of pervasive systems presents many challenges that make the iterative design and development process time consuming and expensive. Additionally, such areas as security, privacy, enjoyment, and utility, while important to traditional desktop systems, are critical to effective pervasive information systems and therefore must be included in the systems' evaluations. We discuss the limitations of current efforts in the background section of this chapter.

We believe that the way to improve the sharing of results in the field is to create a user evaluation framework specifically for pervasive computing systems. Frameworks create structure, which ensures that key areas are not overlooked in evaluations. As evaluation efforts are expensive, frameworks also help developers identify areas of prime importance for their specific products. Selection and interpretation of evaluation areas will be covered in a later section of this chapter. Frameworks also establish terms that are used to describe results. By using the same terminology when publishing results, researchers should be able to learn from the results of others. Result sharing should lead to the establishment of design guidelines and sets of evaluation techniques that can be used to investigate different evaluation areas. It should also lead to the development of pervasive computing specific discount evaluation techniques to enable quicker and less costly evaluations. As this chapter represents early work, we have not been concerned with precise definitions of terminology. However, as work progresses, terms will be defined more precisely. Such was the case for the metrics of effectiveness, efficiency, and user satisfaction as defined by ISO 92411–11 (1998).[1]

In this chapter, we present the background used as the basis for our framework and we describe our framework of areas to consider for evaluation in pervasive computing applications. Another section of the chapter discusses different evaluation methodologies that have been used to assess pervasive computing evaluations. One of the authors conducted a case study using the framework to select evaluation areas and metrics for evaluation. This study is presented in the chapter as an example for the community. The final section discusses future work and the contributions that the community can make to the framework.

PERVASIVE COMPUTING'S NEED FOR NEW EVALUATIONS

One of the first things researchers may ask is why the design guidelines, metrics, and evaluation methodologies from desktop computing cannot be used "as is" for pervasive computing. While a number of evaluation methods, metrics, and design guidelines can be borrowed for pervasive computing, there are considerable differences with desktop computing that suggest different evaluation methodologies as well as metrics. Petersen, Madsen, and Kjaer (2002) note: "we see an increased complexity of especially domestic technology . . . our use continuously develops over time, new possibilities emerge, and others fade away. Unfortunately, present usability engineering methodologies provide little support in understanding how use develops right from the first meeting with the whole product until we later discover small facets of this technology and more importantly how this development in use may be supported by the design of the technology."

Today, pervasive computing applications are diverse in nature, ranging from small applications that help commuters to track train and bus schedules (Lunde and Larsen, 2001) to smart laboratories (Arnstein et al., 2002), smart museums (Fleck et al., 2002), and instrumented classrooms (Abowd, 1999). Moran and Dourish (2001) note that what is common to the various pervasive computing efforts is that "they move the site and style of interaction beyond the desktop and into the larger real world where we live and act" and that "the design challenge, then, is to make computation useful in the various situations that can be encountered in the real world—the ever changing context of use." Along this line is the concept that the application is secondary to other tasks the user is performing. Though this goal is shared by desktop computing, the differences between the computing environments mean different and often more serious implications for pervasive computing. This design challenge and the implications for pervasive computing motivate our user evaluation framework.

The pervasive computing environment may contain many devices with which the user interacts. Speech, gestures, and even physical interactions with devices can be used as interaction modalities. In some cases, the user may not need to consciously do anything. Likewise, the feedback to users is not limited to one particular display, or in fact to any display. Behavior by the user may cause actions in the physical world. For example, lying down in an intelligent room may cause the drapes to close, the lights to dim, and the music to be turned off (Brooks, 1997). Both input and output in a pervasive computing environment may be distributed.

Additionally, as pervasive computing occurs everywhere, there may be a number of users interacting with a system simultaneously (Fleck et al., 2002). This necessitates the question of how the interactions of one user might affect another user and whether/how pervasive computing impacts the normal social situation. As with desktop computing, there is the need to consider both direct and indirect stakeholders (Friedman, Kahn, and Borning, 2001). "*Direct stakeholders* refer to parties—individuals or organizations—who interact directly with [the system] or its output. *Indirect stakeholders* refer to all other parties who are affected by the use of the system. Often, indirect stakeholders are ignored in the design process." For pervasive computing applications to become adopted by the general public, it is crucial for evaluators to consider *all* stakeholders, not just direct stakeholders.

A number of pervasive computing applications are "context-aware." That is, the behavior of the application changes based on what the user is doing. Dey and Mankoff (2005) define context as "any information that characterizes a situation related to the interaction between humans, applications, and the surrounding environment." In practice, different types of sensory input are used to infer context. User location is a popular contextual attribute used in a number of context-aware applications such as mobile tour guides (Abowd et al., 1997; Feiner et al., 1997).

Evaluation of pervasive computing applications is currently a labor-intensive chore. First, evaluations are often carried out on a prototype of the application. This means that a robust prototype has to be developed and deployed, and though it does not have to be product-quality, it has to be reasonably safe (e.g., no sharp edges) and usable. Examples of different types of prototypes can be found in Smith and colleagues (2005) and Philipose and colleagues (2004), where a radio frequency identification device (RFID) glove was used in a prototyping environment, although this was known not to be appropriate for an extended evaluation. An RFID bracelet has since been developed for more extensive testing and, it is hoped, for use. Considerable development work has to be done to accomplish this, which has a tendency to decrease the willingness of the research team to make significant changes uncovered by evaluations. In some cases, Wizard of Oz (Dahlback, Jonsson, and Ahrenberg, 1993; Kelley, 1984) techniques, which allow a user to interact with an interface or system before it is really working, may be used. Wizard of Oz techniques allow the system to appear functional to a user because a person performs some or all of the responsibilities that will ultimately be performed by the computer. In other words, a person is pushing and pulling switches and levers. Even in this case, the "reasonably safe and usable" requirements apply. Pervasive computing applications often involve customized infrastructure, environments, and/or devices. This means it is difficult to conduct evaluations with large numbers of users (e.g., it may be too time consuming or cost prohibitive to produce more than a few prototypes of a device) and/or with several groups of users (e.g., though a study may be conducted with several inhabitants of an office in an instrumented space, it may be difficult to duplicate the study at other offices). Reasons such as these emphasize the importance of performing formative evaluations *before* any (or at least before significant) development occurs. Second, evaluations of pervasive computing applications are extremely diverse. Researchers conduct evaluations specific to their application and report results using their own terms to describe what they evaluated, making it difficult for other researchers in the community to use the lessons learned, or even to be able to apply the same evaluation techniques.

Our premise is that the identification of a set of areas for evaluation, along with measurable indicators and possible metrics for pervasive computing applications, would advance the field. Though researchers would select the measures appropriate for their particular application, having a standard framework from which to work and a standard set of terms to use should enable researchers to learn from each other's results. It should also enable others who are interested in evaluating the same metrics on their own applications to learn about the evaluation techniques they might use to conduct their studies. As we build up knowledge of the properties needed to ensure the success of pervasive computing systems, we will be able to develop design guidelines and lower-cost evaluation methodologies, as in the world of desktop computing. Work by Mankoff and colleagues (2003) has identified heuristics for ambient displays. While this work touches only a small portion of pervasive computing, we are encouraged and confident that many other aspects of pervasive computing can benefit from similar work.

RELATED WORK

Attempts have been made to start creating structure for designing and evaluating pervasive computing systems, but none of these is complete. Some focus on subsets of pervasive computing, such as sensing systems. Others focus solely on areas such as values. Our proposed framework encompasses the field of pervasive computing and is meant as a tool for evaluators. It follows the same spirit as the following work, but tries to create a structure for the entire field of pervasive computing. All of the works discussed here address important design and evaluation issues for different areas of computing research. Where appropriate, their suggestions have been incorporated into our framework.

Jameson (2003) proposes five usability challenges for adaptive interfaces: (1) predictability and transparency, (2) controllability, (3) unobtrusiveness, (4) privacy, and (5) breadth of experience. Jameson's work focuses solely on *adaptive interfaces* (i.e., systems that learn from the user's behavior and react accordingly) and *usability*[2] (e.g., though *privacy* is represented in his challenges, *trust* is not). Our framework encompasses the field of pervasive computing and addresses evaluation areas including, but not limited to, usability.

Bellotti and colleagues (2002) suggest five interaction challenges for designers and researchers of sensing systems: (1) address—"directing communication to a system," (2) attention—"establishing that the system is attending," (3) action—"defining what is to be done with the system," (4) alignment—"monitoring system response," and (5) accident—"avoiding or recovering from errors or misunderstandings." Bellotti focuses on challenges for the system designer and on communicative aspects of interaction in sensing systems (specifically, interactions that are not based on a graphical user interface [GUI]). Our framework is targeted at the evaluator, does not assume a particular style of interaction, and is not limited to interactions. It also encompasses the field of pervasive computing in general, not just sensing systems (e.g., text messaging is arguably pervasive computing, but does not involve sensing).

Friedman and Kahn (2003) suggest twelve key human values with ethical import: (1) human welfare, (2) ownership and property, (3) freedom from bias, (4) privacy, (5) universal usability, (6) trust, (7) autonomy, (8) informed consent, (9) accountability, (10) identity, (11) calmness, and (12) environmental sustainability. Friedman and Kahn's values are for the entire field of human–computer interaction (i.e., including Web sites and other desktop computing) and focus on design considerations. Usability issues such as *interaction* are not represented.

Though much about evaluating pervasive computing can be learned from desktop computing research, there are key differences that necessitate a framework specifically for pervasive computing.

A PROPOSED FRAMEWORK FOR USER EVALUATIONS OF PERVASIVE COMPUTING

We have developed a set of areas for evaluation, along with relevant categories and sample metrics. We call these "evaluation areas" (EAs) (Scholtz and Consolvo, 2004). They have been assembled from personal experience in evaluation efforts and a literature review (see the preceding section on related work.)

For each EA, we offer a definition, brief discussion, sample metrics and measures, and examples from desktop or pervasive computing as appropriate. We distinguish between metrics and measures. Measures are data or observables that are combined to produce the metrics. The metrics should be constant, regardless of the type of pervasive computing application or system that is being evaluated. The measures, however, will differ and are dependent on the application and what can be meaningfully collected.

EA 1: Attention

Attention is defined as "increased awareness directed at a particular event or action to select it for increased processing" (Proctor and Vu, 2003). Although the idea of *attention* has been explored in depth in the area of desktop computing, it is likely to be more of an issue for pervasive computing, as users are handling other physical or mental tasks in parallel, while interacting with pervasive computing devices.

Metrics	Measures
Focus	The number of times a user must change focus to use the technology
	The amount of effort (number of actions, displays to be checked) that users have to put forth to accomplish or check on the progress of an interaction
Overhead	The percentage of time a user spends switching between foci
	The time the user spends focusing on the technology

Metrics for *Attention* include focus and overhead. *Focus* refers to where the user is directing his/her attention. *Overhead* refers to any "wasted time" introduced by the technology. As part of the evaluation of Labscape, Consolvo, Arnstein, and Franza (2002) used lag sequential analysis to look at focus. Their premise was that the more interleaved Labscape and "regular work" were, the more likely it was that Labscape was being smoothly integrated into the environment, and therefore, the more the target users (i.e., biologists) were able to focus on their work (i.e., the biology) and not the new technology.

EA 2: Adoption

Adoption informs us about the acceptance of the technology and the incorporation into users' workplaces and homes. Metrics for adoption are rate, value, cost, and availability. This EA can be meaningfully measured only after the pervasive computing application is released to the general public (or at least the target population).

Metrics	Measures
Rate	New users/unit of time
	Why are users adopting/not adopting the technology? (e.g., is it a personal choice, employer mandate, etc.?)
	Usage patterns for users once they have purchased the product
Value	*Note:* When investigating value, it is important to consider all stakeholders.
	Change(s) in productivity
	Perceived cost/benefit
	User willingness to stop using the technology (e.g., how would their lives be impacted if it was taken from them?)
Availability	Number of actual users from each target user group
	Where are users getting the technology?
	If certain target user groups are not using it, why? (e.g., is the design appropriate for them?)
	Post-deployment, have new groups of users/usage scenarios emerged?
Flexibility	The number of tasks users can accomplish that were not originally envisioned for use
	The users' ability to incorporate new features and improvements easily.

Petersen, Madsen, and Kjaer (2002) conducted long-term interviews with and observations on several families who ordered new technology. The families were visited when the new technology was installed (the technology was an integrated television and video recorder), one month after the installation, two and a half months later, and six months later. One month after the installation, the researchers found that there were many functions that the user would like to do but could not manage. At the next visit, the user had managed to use the new technology as originally envisioned. Six months later, the user had managed all of the functionality, but found that the surround sound feature that she was looking forward to using for a "cinema experiment" was not really something she enjoyed. She used this feature for listening to music but no longer used it for watching movies. This result points to the need to design for evolution or flexibility.

The technology acceptance model (TAM) (Davis, Bagozzi, and Warshaw, 1989; Venkatesh and Davis, 2000) could also be used to collect user perceptions of software utility and ease of use. Future work for the framework should analyze adoption metrics and TAM surveys to determine any relationships with EAs that can be evaluated during formative studies.

EA 3: Trust

Pervasive computing applications and devices are present in places such as homes, offices, cars, schools, hospitals, elder-care facilities, and on the user him/herself. Parking garages and roadways know where and who we are as we come and go. Grocery stores know what we buy. Online bookstores know what we read. Information may be gathered both with and without direct participation or consent. Employees have to swipe badges to come and go within government and many industrial office facilities. Highway tollbooths read pass information and bill our accounts as we drive through the tollbooth. What are the policies on the information that is collected? Who has access to it? For what purposes is the information being used? Lahlou, Langheinrich, and Rocker (2005) note: "the design of adequate solutions [to privacy protection] will only succeed if privacy-related problems are methodically approached from the initial stages of development." We contend that this area is extremely important for evaluation.

Metrics	Measures
Privacy	The type and amount of information that the user has to provide to, or that can be collected by, the device (or system) to make it useful
	The availability of this information to others (both users and nonusers) of the application
Awareness	Ease of coordination with others in multiple user applications
	The number of collisions users have with others in multiple user applications
	User understanding of the types of data that are being recorded and their current and possible uses
Control	The ability of users to manage the use of their data
	The ability of users to stop the collection of their data, yet still use the technology in some meaningful way

Salvador, Barile, and Sherry (2004) presented design principles based on ethnographic and experimental research on retail transactions. The three design principles are accountability, real-time inspectability, and recourse. Accountability involves users' understanding of the actions. Accountability and inspectability could be added measures of awareness. Real-time inspectability allows users to monitor progress at various steps.

EA 4: Conceptual Models

A conceptual model (Gentner and Stevens, 1983) provides the basis for understanding an interactive device or program. It names and describes the various components and explains what they do and how they work together to accomplish tasks. Understanding the conceptual model makes it possible to anticipate the behavior of the application, to infer "correct" ways of doing things, and to diagnose problems when something goes wrong.

Different kinds of models exist to meet different needs. Though designers and developers may have different conceptual models for the same application, for the purposes of this chapter, we are interested in the *user's conceptual model*. For example, analogies or metaphors, such as the desktop metaphor, provide affordances which support the user's conceptual model. The distributed nature of pervasive computing makes it challenging for users to build unified models of behaviors and interactions. For example, how does a user know when he/she is in a "smart room?" When he/she is in a smart room, will the user know how to interact with the room? How will users distinguish improper interactions from technology problems?

Metrics	Measures
Predictability of application/system behavior	Degree of match between user's model and actual behavior of the application/system
Awareness of application/system capabilities	Degree of match between user's model and actual functionality of the application/system
Vocabulary awareness	Degree of match between user's model and the syntax of multimodal interactions

Lee and Kiesler (2005) did a study of how people formed a conceptual model of a robot's factual knowledge. They found that people formed a model based on their own knowledge, guided by characteristics they attributed to the robot based on the robot's language and origin. In terms of our framework, the researchers were measuring people's predictions of application behavior.

EA 5: Interaction

Usability evaluations in desktop computing apply measures of effectiveness, efficiency, and user satisfaction. While these measures are also applicable to interactions in pervasive computing, evaluations must take into consideration differences between desktop and pervasive computing. Shafer, Brummitt, and Cadiz (2001) suggest these differences:

- Interactions in pervasive computing can be physically embedded,
- the set of input and output devices are dynamic rather than static as in desktop systems,
- as multiple devices are used, there is no single focal point, and
- there can be multiple simultaneous users.

Additional measures are needed to evaluate these aspects of pervasive computing. Guidelines have been developed for the design of graphical user interactions based on mouse and keyboard input and a single display as output. The pervasive computing community needs studies and evaluations for distributed, multimodal interactions in a pervasive computing environment.

Metrics	Measures
Effectiveness	Percentage of task completion
Efficiency	Time to complete a task
Satisfaction	User rating of performing the task
Distraction	Time taken away from primary task to attend to technology
	Degradation in effectiveness or efficiency due to technology use
	Decrease in user satisfaction
Interaction transparency	Comparison of effectiveness using different sets of devices/input modalities
	Reduction in time/effort to accomplish interactions using new modalties
Scalability	The effectiveness of the interactions when large numbers of people are using the system
Collaborative interaction	The number and type of conflicts between users
	The percentage of conflicts that the system is able to resolve
	Users' ability to resolve conflicts
	Users' satisfaction with the conflicts and resolution

Other possible measures for collaborative interaction could be the benefits that are obtained from others working in the same spaces at the same time. Currently, these measures are much more difficult to obtain. We hope that evaluators will share with the community methodologies and measures for positive collaborative interactions.

While scalability in this EA refers to interactions involving a large number of people, there is also the aspect of scalability referring to a large number of devices. Russell, Streitz, and Winograd (2005) discuss building smart environments consisting of multiple display and interaction devices. Each device must be designed for the interactions appropriate to it, based on physical characteristics. However, there should be some common theme running through the interactions so that users will be easily able to move to other devices.

A study of Rememberer, a tool for recording museum experiences, was designed not to distract from the user's interaction with museum exhibits (by either physical or social interference) (Fleck et al., 2002, 2002a). The application was designed to encourage virtual interactions after the museum experience, allowing visitors to focus on the physical experience while at the museum. In the study, the researchers measured interference with any of the museum exhibits and use of the device while users were in the museum and whether the presence of a camera helped to increase use. The researchers found that users used the device in 80 percent of the visits, and that the device was used more often when it included a camera.

EA 6: Invisibility

"Smart" pervasive computing applications (i.e., context-aware applications) make inferences about the user's activities, goals, emotional state, and social situation, and attempt to act on behalf of the user. If the system has sensed and interpreted the context correctly, this initiative can result in time savings and a reduction in user workload. However, if the system has misjudged the situation, the user may have to intervene. This may result in a loss of time, embarrassment to the user, and even a potentially dangerous situation.

Smart systems may also allow users to customize how the system responds based on personal preferences. Users may be asked to explicitly input this information or the system may learn preferences based on a series of interactions.

Metric	Measures
Intelligibility	User's understanding of the system explanation
Control	Effectiveness of interactions provided for user control of system initiative
Accuracy	Match between the system's contextual model and the actual situation
	Appropriateness of action
	Match between the system action and the action the user would have requested
Customization	Time to explicitly enter personalization information
	Time for the system to learn and adapt to the user's preferences

One issue concerning context-aware applications involves dealing with ambiguity. Dey and Mankoff (2005) discuss ways to mediate imperfectly sensed context. They present a case study that looks at providing appropriate defaults and at postponing mediation of ambiguous context to an appropriate time. This study suggests that we might want to consider another measure of accuracy—the number of ambiguous situations that need mediation by the user.

EA 7: Impact and Side Effects

Applications that are designed for use outside of the office environment need to be assessed for their impact. For example, applications for use in the classroom should be evaluated to determine whether students and teachers/professors benefit. This could be assessed using grades or scores on achievement tests. Applications designed for use in social settings need to be evaluated to determine whether the insertion of technology changes people's behaviors and if it does, whether the change is positive. Side effects must also be evaluated. For example, if tourist facilities provide handheld devices for tourists to use in exploring an area, what will be the effect on the number of tour guides needed? Will the tourist facility need to hire technologists to maintain and upgrade these devices? What about elderly tourists who may not feel comfortable using these devices? What happens when devices are damaged, lost, or stolen? What happens if a hacker compromises the system?

Metrics	Measures
Behavior changes	Type, frequency, and duration
	User's willingness to modify behavior or tasks to use application
	Adapting dress to accommodate wearable devices
Social acceptance	Requirements placed on users outside of social norms
	Ratings of system components based on aesthetics
Environment change	Type, frequency, and duration
	User's willingness to modify his/her environment to use application

Theofanos and Scholtz (2005) discussed an application on a personal digital assistant (PDA) for taking customers' orders in restaurants. The waitstaff first used a tether to make sure that the device was not dropped. However, this did not look appropriate for use in an upscale restaurant, so the waitstaff abandoned the tether and simply used black aprons with pockets for the PDA. Waitstaff needed additional training to use the device. Although a game was provided on the device to help them learn quickly, the restaurant managers needed to make sure that new staff were willing and able to learn the device. Waitstaff were rewarded, however, with larger tips as service with the new device was faster and customers were appreciative. More drinks were sold as the staff did not have to leave the floor to enter orders. Fewer transcription errors were made, resulting in fewer complimentary meals being given. More desserts were ordered as the overall service was faster and customers had more time. All of this resulted in more profit for the restaurant. However, the waitstaff was able to handle more tables and, as a result, fewer personnel were needed. A positive result (cost reduction) for the restaurant was not a positive result when viewed from the perspective of the waitstaff. Thus, an application designed to replace a centralized ordering system with a distributed ordering system had numerous side effects on both direct and indirect stakeholders.

EA 8: Appeal

Applications beyond the desktop need more than functionality. They also need appeal. Does everyone else have one? Do I need one to be fashionable? An excellent current example of this is Apple's iPod[3] with its easy-to-recognize white earphone cord.

Metrics	Measures
Fun	Enjoyment level while using application
	Anticipation level prior to using application
	Sense of loss when unable to use application
Aesthetics	Ratings on look and feel of application/device
Status	Pride in owning the application
	Peer pressure to own and use the application

Eagle and Pentland (2005) designed a mobile information device profile that can be used for social encounters. The application uses the proximity to other mobile devices and detects proximity patterns. Coupled with an anonymous text message to users with related profiles who are in the same general area, this application serves as an introduction service. While privacy is certainly an area that must be evaluated for this application, the application has been well received by corporate workers as well as college students. This and other social applications might determine the need for a metric of "connectedness." This could be a measure of how well I stay in touch with those I already know or how effective the application is at finding others I would like to meet.

EA 9: Application Robustness

Although our framework deals primarily with user-centered metrics, performance measures contribute to the user's ability to use a system as well as his/her perception of the system. Our measures of application robustness look at performance, but from the eyes of the users.

Metrics	Measures
Robustness	Percentage of transient faults that the user is aware of
Performance speed	Measure of time from user interaction to feedback for user
	User's rating of speed (does the user feel he/she is driving the application or the application is forcing him/her to respond)
	User's ability to control the speed of the application
Volatility	Number of interruptions based on dynamically changing sets of users, hardware, and software

A recent article on the design of large displays for use in pervasive computing environments proposed four design guidelines based on lessons learned. This included robustness, heterogeneity, dynamism, and interaction techniques (Russell, Streitz, and Winograd, 2005). A number of different devices are integrated into these large spaces, and they must interoperate, despite differences in hardware and software operating systems. Moreover, user interfaces have to be designed to work easily on any size display and with any type of input/output modality.

SELECTION AND INTERPRETATION OF EA METRICS

All EAs are not applicable to all pervasive computing applications. Evaluators and other team members must decide which measures are most critical for the type and stage of system or application being evaluated. These decisions must consider the environments in which the application will be used and the needs of all anticipated categories of users.

How should evaluators prioritize the various EAs for pervasive computing? While it is too early to say definitely, we can make some predictions:

- Any applications that are designed to be "walk-up and use" will have to score well in metrics related to interaction and conceptual models.
- Applications that are developed to be used in a social setting, in addition to scoring well for interaction metrics and conceptual models, will need good impact scores.
- Applications that deal with personal information of users will certainly need high trust scores.
- If the pervasive computing application is targeting users involved in a time- or life-critical situation, interaction and attention will be of utmost importance.
- Wearable devices should score high on measures of appeal.
- Context-aware applications could score low on measures of predictability and conceptual models, but should score high on efficiency and effectiveness.

We may be able to predict adoption from looking at evaluation areas such as trust, impact and side effects, and appeal. While users often adapt to less-than-ideal interactions in an application, they do so only if there is a compelling attraction about the application. However, if users have issues with trust or have to drastically modify their behavior, they are less likely to use an application.

EVALUATION METHODOLOGIES

The Problem

Evaluation methodologies for pervasive computing applications must look beyond tasks done by one user at a desktop computer and focus on collecting data on the overall user experience. Pervasive computing applications require that evaluation methodologies examine the broader context of the environment. Thus, methodologies for evaluating pervasive computing applications must address the challenge of evaluating applications under realistic conditions (e.g., in situ), especially if data on values, emotion, privacy, trust, and other social aspects of pervasive computing applications are desired. This section will examine how various evaluation methodologies have been adapted to evaluate pervasive computing applications.

Categories of Evaluation Methodologies

Self-Reporting

One of the challenges in designing peripheral displays is the trade-off between awareness and distraction. For example, how do you notify the user of an e-mail's arrival without the peripheral display distracting the user from the primary task? Hsieh and Mankoff (2003) used laboratory and field studies to compare two peripheral displays for e-mail notification. Both studies used self-reporting of a set of questions to measure awareness, including how much attention users paid to a display, and knowledge questions to determine how much information the user retained. Distraction, primary task speed and accuracy, and usability were assessed. While the studies showed that the information gathered in each method was similar, the field study provided more insight into the complex relationship between awareness and distraction. The authors conclude that even a short field study is better than a lab study using this technique.

Ethnographic Techniques

Digital Ethnography. The traditional ethnography process involves immersion in the culture under study and generally requires a multidisciplinary team dispersed in numerous countries over short periods of time. Traditional ethnography is divided into three categories: self-reporting, passive observation, and participant observation. But with the Internet and wireless communication devices, traditional ethnography can now be extended through remote sensing devices and other creative techniques. Masten and Plowman (2003) have called this convergence of traditional methods with digital technology "Digital Ethno."

A Digital Ethno case study illustrates the use of remote sensing devices and digital technology to understand users' lives. Researchers were interested in participants' thoughts and attitudes toward Valentine's Day. The research replaced the face-to-face interactions of traditional ethnography with a variety of techniques including e-mail, cell phones, digital cameras, chatrooms, online questionnaires, and digitized audio diaries.

Traditional forms of ethnography can be time-intensive and cost-prohibitive. Digital Ethno enables an expansion of ethnographic studies at reduced costs. Advantages of the approach include the ability to: observe multiple participants simultaneously, automate data collection, and build digital user databases. Finally, gathering information from users in their natural environments encourages subjects to become active participants in the effort instead of passive data sources.

Mobile Probes. Another digital ethnography tool, mobile probes (Hulkko et al., 2004), addresses the need to study subjects in mobile contexts. In many instances, probes document behavior retrospectively rather than in real time. Although this information is useful, the context and action are lost. There is a need for more contextual interactive probing tools.

According to Hulkko and colleagues (2004), probing typically consists of a theme diary and a disposable camera; however, this technique is more difficult in mobile situations. Therefore, the technique was modified to include a mobile phone with a camera accessory and text-messaging services. The mobile probe data complemented the interviews and explained the social behaviors of the potential users.

Context-Aware Experience Sampling. The experience sampling method (ESM) is a technique that originated in the field of psychology in which users are prompted at random times, on a time schedule, or when events of interest occur to answer questions relevant to their current activities. Not only is ESM less susceptible than other self-report methods to subject recall errors, it can also produce a statistical model of behavior with enough subjects and samples (Intille et al., 2003).

A research group at the Massachusetts Institute of Technology has developed context-aware experience sampling software for PocketPC devices (Intille et al., 2003). This tool extends the benefits of ESM by using context sensors to enable researchers to gather information from a subject based on automatically triggering questions when a predefined behavior or activity occurs, instead of relying on the subject to recognize when the behavior or activity is happening and then manually trigger the questions him- or herself. The group is currently incorporating new attributes, including the ability to trigger questions based on heart-rate and particular activities. The University of Washington and Intel Research have developed context-aware experience sampling software for mobile phones (Froehlich et al., 2007). The tool, called My Experience, combines active context-triggered user experience sampling to collect subjective user feedback, and passive logging of device usage, user context, and environmental sensor readings to collect objective data. In addition to triggering questions based on various types of sensor readings to target moments of interest, My Experience supports logging of more than 140 event types, including device usage such as communication, application usage, and media capture; user context such as calendar appointments; and environmental sensing such as Bluetooth and Global Positioning System (GPS) readings.

The Image-Based Experience Sampling tool (Intille et al., 2003a) uses scene-based sensing. One drawback of ESM is that it is not always convenient for a subject to answer the questions when the trigger is activated. Using this tool, an audio-video image is recorded of the activity when the trigger occurs, instead of interrupting the subject to answer questions. These images are later used by researchers when interviewing the subject about the activity to jog the subject's memory. This tool is currently only available as a laboratory prototype. These tools have the potential to enable low-cost studies of people in natural environments.

Experience Clips. Traditional evaluation techniques do not permit accurately capturing feelings, emotions, and subjective information about users. Isomursu, Kuutii, and Vainamo (2004) developed a new technique, Experience Clips, to provide users with freedom to explore the system, and supporting mobile usage situations without altering the environment to change the user experience. The experience clip method captured a much wider range of usage situations and emotional responses than when a researcher was present, and it can be used to successfully capture data on emotions, feelings, and experiences in mobile situations.

Voice Mail Diary. The voice mail diary technique developed by Palen and Salzman (2002), an adaptation of the traditional paper diary study, is also designed to address user experiences in a natural environment. Instead of making notes on paper, participants use mobile phones to call into a dedicated voice mail line to record events. The voice mail diary approach offers several advantages over the traditional paper study for both the participant and the investigator. It is easier and faster for the participant to provide a report via voice mail than on paper, particularly in a mobile environment. From the researcher's perspective the reports provided are a richer description than paper notes and the researcher gets immediate access to reports, while the study is in progress. As in paper diary studies, frequent researcher involvement is a key to success, but now that can be accomplished remotely by updating greeting messages and providing regular acknowledgments of entries. Finally, the study can be structured or unstructured. In unstructured studies, open-ended, stream-of-consciousness reporting led to rich detailed accounts. Structured studies streamlined the process by supplying the participants with issues where they selected numbered options on the voice-mail system. Palen and Salzman advocate the voice mail diary technique for natural mobile environments based on its minimal intrusiveness. Examples of the use of voice mail diaries as a supplement to other information for longer-term studies can be found in Consolvo and colleagues (2005).

Testing in a Natural Setting

Quasi-naturalistic. Observing the user in context is critical when designing systems that are focused on mobile computing technologies accessible through pervasive wireless network connections. Jones and colleagues (2000) developed a working prototype to evaluate mobile information access and retrieval and tested it in a library setting. The study was "quasi-naturalistic" in that users were free to roam the library and experiment with the device beyond the scope of the tasks provided. This is a modified version of "usability testing" that allowed the developers to learn about the effectiveness and usefulness of a prototype in a natural setting.

Remote Testing. Remote Testing of mobile devices like PDAs and wireless application protocol-enabled cell phones is also designed to gather data in a realistic environment. Waterson, Landay, and Matthews (2002) performed two comparative studies (a traditional usability lab study and a test that remotely collected clickstream data in which audio/video was not recorded) of a mobile device. They note that clickstream data can be easily collected but lacks the qualitative information that traditional usability testing provides. However, it is difficult to resolve technology problems with remote prototypes.

Automatic Video Analysis. Direct observation can be a critical component of data gathering, providing researchers with detailed information on a subject's behaviors. Pervasive technology provides for the continuous capture of audio and video records, but the challenge is to transcribe this information into something useful. Hauptmann and colleagues (2004) have developed a technology that records and automatically analyzes video of the activities of nursing home patients as part of the CareMedia project.

During the study, four cameras and microphones were mounted in a Pittsburgh nursing home. The automated system was able to track people, identify and label individuals, and identify what the individual was doing. The system was quite effective in tracking individuals and automatically identifying their behaviors. The study was an evaluation of a specific type of technology, rather than a user evaluation of the technology. However, this type of technology could have far-reaching consequences for evaluating other types of pervasive systems where ethnographic observation is too invasive, expensive, or time intensive.

A CASE STUDY

To demonstrate how the evaluation framework can be applied to the evaluation of pervasive computing applications, we describe one of our recent projects in which we employed the framework.

Case Study: Installing Sensors in the Home

In one recent project, we investigated problems that end users may encounter when attempting to install sensors for a pervasive computing application in their homes (Beckmann and Consolvo, 2005). To conduct our investigation, we created an installation kit of high- and low-fidelity sensor mock-ups that were built in consultation with sensor hardware engineers to be as realistic as possible. The application concept that provided context for the investigation was the *Home Energy Tutor*—a pervasive computing application that a homeowner would receive on loan for one month from a sponsoring organization (such as the electric company) and deploy in his/her home to track household energy use and learn about ways to reduce it. The installation kit contained a sample of the types of sensors that would likely be used for such an application.

Fifteen nontechnical Seattle-area homeowners who were interested in conserving energy par-

Figure 10.1 **Home Energy Tutor Installation Kit**

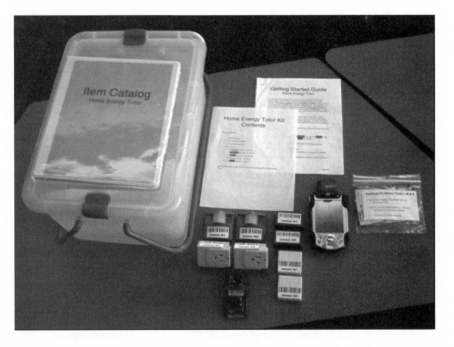

The kit contained a list of contents, printed instructions, an Item Catalog of various home appliances and rooms, the handheld scanner that was used to associate a sensor with an item from the catalog, a bag of removable adhesives, and ten mock sensors (two of each type: current, motion, vibration, image, and sound).

Figure 10.2 **Association in the Home Energy Tutor**

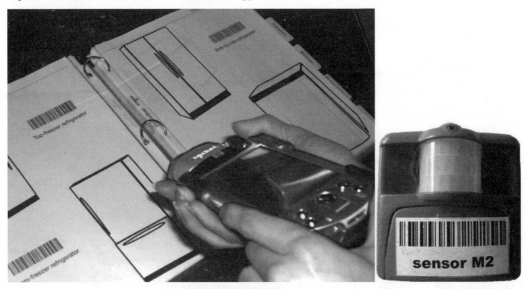

On the left, a user scans the barcode for the type of appliance to which she will attach a sensor; to complete the association, she also scans the barcode of the sensor (shown at right) that she will attach to the appliance. Screens on the handheld device guide the user through the installation process.

Figure 10.3 **An Example of a Correct Installation: Toaster**

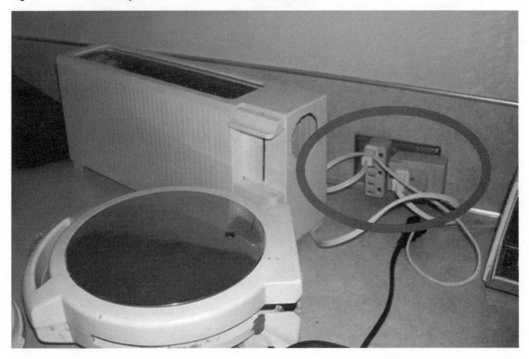

This participant correctly installed a current sensor to monitor the energy use of her toaster.

Figure 10.4 **An Example of a Correct Installation: Refrigerator**

This participant correctly installed a vibration sensor near the compressor of her refrigerator. Notice how she chose to place it to the side, where her young children were less likely to notice it (though it runs the risk of being knocked off when someone tries to access the nearby magazines).

Figure 10.5 **Troubleshooting Installation Challenges**

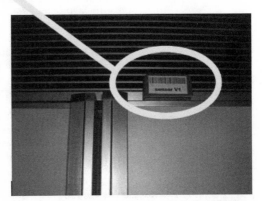

ticipated in our in situ study in summer 2003 (Beckmann, Consolvo, and LaMarca, 2004). They were recruited by a market research agency and each received $75 for participating. Sessions were conducted one participant at a time; each session lasted close to ninety minutes and was conducted in the participant's home. The study employed self-report and in situ task-based techniques. Sessions began by having the participants complete a consent and release form and background questionnaire. Participants then had a few minutes to explore the installation kit that contained the sensor mock-ups, before installing ten sensors (two of each type: current, motion, vibration, image, and sound) throughout their homes. Sessions ended with a semistructured interview about the participants' experiences with the installation tasks and thoughts about the *Home Energy Tutor* in general. Additional details about the *Home Energy Tutor,* the installation kit, and the study are in Beckmann, Consolvo, and LaMarca (2004).

Several of the framework's pervasive computing evaluation areas helped to guide the evaluation. For example, the *Adoption* EA's *Cost* metric (i.e., typical time spent setting up the technology) was one of the prime motivators for the study. That is, the installation kit for the *Home Energy Tutor* was our first attempt to create a system that would be easy for typical homeowners to install. Because we were trying to learn about how easy it *actually* was to install, we conducted the evaluation in the participants' homes. This enabled us to learn about the individual peculiarities of the participants' homes and the concerns that each homeowner had about installing sensors in places that were meaningful to them. The following additional EAs and associated metrics and conceptual measures were addressed in the study:

Adoption

- **Value** (perceived cost/benefit, user sacrifice) and **Cost** (user willingness to use such a technology)

  User sacrifice was measured by observation during the installation tasks and questioning during the end-of-session interview. The *perceived cost/benefit* and *willingness to use such a technology* was addressed in the interview. In general, participants were very positive about the technology, though it was clear that improvements in the installation kit would have to be addressed to make the application a success.

Trust

- **Privacy** (availability of the user's information to third parties) and **Awareness** (user awareness of how recorded data are used; user understanding of inferences that can be drawn about the user by the application)

  While we did not directly address the issue of *third-party access* to the participant's information and the *recording of data,* several participants brought it up during the interview phase. As part of the introduction to the *Home Energy Tutor,* participants were told that the data collected about them during the month-long deployment would never leave their homes and could not be accessed by anyone else including the sponsoring organization that loaned them the kit. Despite these assurances, several participants believed that the sponsoring organization would have access to that information, which made them uncomfortable.

- **Control** (ability of users to manage how and by whom their data are used)

  The notion of *control over data collection* was directly addressed during the interview when participants were asked what they would do if they wanted a sensor to stop collecting data. In most cases, participants understood that if they just removed the sensor from where it was installed, it could no longer collect data for that area of their homes (many suggested that they would return it to the box from which it came originally).

Conceptual models

- **Awareness** of application capabilities (user's understanding of model and actual functionality of system)

  Similar to the notion of control above, participants were asked several questions during the interview about the types of data they thought each sensor would collect and how those data were being used by the system. In some instances, an accurate conceptual model helped participants troubleshoot installation challenges (see Figure 10.5, for example).

Interaction

- **Effectiveness** (correctness of each sensor installation)

  While the correctness of the sensor installations was not shared with participants, for each sensor installed, we determined whether or not it was installed correctly. "Correctness" was based on metrics determined by the sensor hardware engineers we consulted to build the mock-ups.

Impact and side effects

- **Social acceptance** (aesthetic ratings of system components)

  Similar to the issue of third-party access to data mentioned above, several participants brought up the aesthetics (or lack thereof) of the sensors. To facilitate installation, we color coded the sensors so that each sensor type was a different color. While participants mentioned that the color coding made the installation task easier, they thought it made the sensors too obvious (and unattractive).

- **Environment change** (user's willingness to modify his/her environment to accommodate the system)

  In addition to the aesthetic comments mentioned above, participants with pets and small children had concerns about the nonpermanent nature of many of the sensors (which was necessary given the temporary nature of the *Home Energy Tutor;* the sensors had to be easy to install and remove—that is, having to pull out the refrigerator to install a sensor would have been unacceptable). For example, the sensor installed on the refrigerator was attached near the refrigerator's compressor (usually at the bottom of the appliance) via a magnet—some participants were worried that the sensor would be removed by their pets or small children and quickly disappear. Other participants were concerned about using removable adhesives to attach sensors to their walls or furniture.

Despite the early stage of this project, the evaluation framework helped us develop an effective study design and expose several important issues with our sensor installation kit.

FUTURE WORK

The evaluation framework needs to be further refined and populated with contributions from researchers, developers, and evaluators. This chapter presents only our initial definitions. We are interested in refining our metrics and in developing methodologies for evaluation of these metrics. While some measures can be easily obtained, others will require new evaluation methodologies. We are interested in more metrics for evaluating the social computing applications. We will continue to examine the literature on pervasive computing evaluations and to use these to determine which measures and metrics are missing and which onces are not useful. We will also continue to review evaluation methodologies used in pervasive computing evaluations to determine which of the suggested metrics in the framework, particular methodologies, might be applicable.

We are interested in having more researchers attempt to use the framework to evaluate their work. In particular, we are interested in determining which methodologies are more appropriate to use for particular EAs. As more researchers use this framework and share their results, best practices will emerge. This will serve to generate consensus about the metrics and methodologies appropriate for various EAs. As this occurs, more precision about the terminology for each EA will be developed. Eventually, certain groups of EAs might be considered as essential for different classifications of pervasive computing evaluations.

We hope that the case study provided in this chapter will encourage others to use the framework in their evaluations of pervasive computing applications. This will enable us to share results with each other and to advance the field more quickly.

NOTES

1. ISO 9241–11:1998, Ergonomic Requirements for Office Work with Visual Display Terminals (VDTs)—Part 11: Guidance on Usability.

2. Friedman and Kahn discuss the distinction between usability and values (Friedman and Kahn, 2003, 1180–1181).

3. The reference to a commercial product is used for illustration purposes only and does not imply a recommendation by the National Institute of Standards and Technology.

REFERENCES

Abowd, G.D. 1999. Classroom 2000: An experiment with the instrumentation of a living educational environment. *IBM Systems Journal,* 38, 508–530.

Abowd, G.D.; Atkeson, C.G.; Hong, J.; Long, S.; Kooper, R.; and Pinkerton, M. 1997. Cyberguide: A mobile context-aware tour guide. *ACM Wireless Networks,* 5, 421–433.

Arnstein, L.F.; Borriello, G.; Consolvo, S.; Franza, B.R.; Hung, C.; Su, J.; and Zhou, Q.H. 2002. Labscape: Design of a smart environment for the cell biology laboratory. *IEEE Pervasive Computing,* 1, 3, 13–21.

Beckmann, C.S. and Consolvo, S. 2003. Sensor configuration tool for end-users: Low-fidelity prototype evaluation. #1, IRS-TR-03–009, 2003. Available at www.intel-research.net/Publications/Seattle/072520031457_156.pdf (accessed April 22, 2005).

Beckmann, C.; Consolvo, S.; and LaMarca, A. 2004. Some assembly required: Supporting end-user sensor installation in domestic ubiquitous computing environments. In *Proceedings of the Sixth International Conference on Ubiquitous Computing: UbiComp '04.* Nottingham, UK: Springer, 107–124.

Bellotti, V.; Back, M.; Edwards, W.K.; Grinter, R.E.; Henderson, A.; Lopes, C. 2002. Making sense of sensing systems: Five questions for designers and researchers. In *Proceedings of the SIGCHI Conference on Human Factors in Computing Systems: Changing our World, Changing Ourselves.* New York: ACM Press, 415–422.

Brooks, R.A. 1997. The intelligent room project. In *Proceedings of the Second International Cognitive Technology Conference (CT'97).* Los Alamitos, CA: IEEE Computer Society Press, 271–278.

Consolvo, S.; Arnstein, L.; and Franza, B. 2002. User study techniques in the design and evaluation of a Ubicomp environment. In *Proceedings of the Fourth International Conference on Ubiquitous Computing.* Berlin/Heidelberg: Springer, 73–90.

Consolvo, S.; Smith, I.; Matthews, T.; LaMarca, A.; Tabert, J.; and Powledge, P. 2005. Location disclosure to social relations: Why, when, and what people want to share. In *Proceedings of the SIGCHI Conference on Human Factors in Computing Systems: Technology, Safety, Community.* New York: ACM Press, 81–90.

Dahlback, N.; Jonsson, A.; and Ahrenberg, L. 1993. Wizard of Oz studies—Why and how. In *Proceedings of the International Workshop on Intelligent User Interfaces: IUI '93.* New York: ACM Press, 193–200.

Davis, F.D.; Bagozzi, R.P.; and Warshaw, P.R. 1989. User acceptance of computer technology: A comparison of two theoretical models. *Management Science,* 35, 982–1003.

Dey, A. and Mankoff, J. 2005. Designing mediation for context-aware applications. *ACM Transactions on Computer-Human Interaction,* 12, 1, 53–80.

Eagle, N. and Pentland, A. 2005. Social serendipity: Mobilizing social software. *IEEE Pervasive Computing,* 4, 2, 28–34.

Feiner, S.; MacIntyre, B.; Hollerer, T.; Webster, A. 1997. A touring machine: Prototyping 3D mobile augmented reality systems for exploring the urban environment. *Personal Technologies,* 1, 208–217.

Fleck, M.; Frid, M.; Kindberg, T.; O'Brien-Strain, E.; Rajani, R.; and Spasojevic, M. 2002. Rememberer: A tool for capturing museum visits. In *Proceedings of the Fourth International Conference on Ubiquitous Computing.* Berlin/Heidelberg: Springer, 48–55.

Fleck, M.; Frid, M.; Kindberg, T.; Spasojevic, M.; O'Brien-Strain, E.; and Rajani, R. 2002a. From informing to remembering: Deploying a ubiquitous system in an interactive science museum. *IEEE Pervasive Computing,* 1, 2, 13–21.

Friedman, B. and Kahn, P.H. Jr. 2003. Human values, ethics, and design. In *The Human-Computer Interaction Handbook.* Mahwah, NJ: Lawrence Erlbaum, 1177–1201.

Friedman, B.; Kahn, P.H. Jr.; and Borning, A. 2001. Value sensitive design: Theory and methods. *University of Washington Technical Report 02–12–01,* December.

Froehlich, J.; Chen, M.; Consolvo, S.; Harrison, B.; and Landay, J.A. 2007. My Experience: A System for In Situ Tracing and Capturing of User Feedback on Mobile Phones. In *Proceedings of the Fifth International Conference on Mobile Systems, Applications, and Services.* San Juan, Puerto Rico.

Gentner, D. and Stevens, A.L., eds. 1983. *Mental Models.* Mahwah, NJ: Lawrence Erlbaum.

Hauptmann, A.; Gao, J.; Yan, R.; Qi, Y.; Yang, J.; and Wactlar, H. 2004. Automated analysis of nursing home observations. *IEEE Pervasive Computing,* 3, 2, 15–21.

Hsieh, G. and Mankoff, J. 2003. A comparison of two peripheral displays for monitoring email: Measuring usability, awareness, and distraction. Technical Report UCB-CSD-03–1286, Computer Science Division, University of California, Berkeley, 2003.

Hulkko, S.; Mattelmaki, T.; Virtanen, K.; and Keinonen, T. 2004. Mobile probes. In *Proceedings of the Third Nordic Conference on Human-Computer Interaction.* New York: ACM Press, 43–51.

Intille, S.; Rondoni, J.; Kukla, C.; Ancona, I.; and Bao, L. 2003. A context-aware experience sampling tool. In *CHI '03 Extended Abstracts on Human Factors in Computing Systems.* New York: ACM Press, 972–973.

Intille, S.; Tapia, E.; Rondoni, J.; Beaudin, J.; Kukla, C.; Agarwal, S.; Bao, L.; and Larson, K. 2003a. Tools for studying behavior and technology in natural settings. In *Ubicomp 2003: Ubiquitous Computing Fifth International Conference.* Berlin/Heidelberg: Springer, 157–174.

Isomursu, M.; Kuutii, K.; and Vainamo, S. 2004. Experience clip: Method for user participation and evaluation of mobile concepts. In *Proceedings of the Eighth Conference on Participatory Design.* New York: ACM Press, 83–92.

Jameson, A. 2003. Adaptive interfaces and agents. In *The Human-Computer Interaction Handbook.* Mahwah, NJ: Lawrence Erlbaum, 316–318.

Jones, M.; Rieger, R.; Treadsell, P.; and Gay, G. 2000. Live from the stacks: User feedback on mobile computers and wireless tools from library patrons. In *Proceedings of the Fifth ACM Conference on Digital Libraries.* New York: ACM Press, 96–102.

Kelley, J.F. 1984. An iterative design methodology for user-friendly natural language office information applications. *ACM Transactions on Office Information Systems,* 2, 1, 26–41.

Lahlou, S.; Langheinrich, M.; and Rocker, C. 2005. Privacy and trust issues with invisible computing. *Communications of the ACM,* 48, 3, 59–60.

Lee, S.L. and Kiesler, S. 2005. Human mental models of humanoid robots. In *International Conference on Robotics and Automation.* Los Alamitos, CA: IEEE Computer Society Press, 2767–2772.

Lunde, T. and Larsen, A. 2001. KISS the tram: Exploring the PDA as support for everyday activities. In *Proceedings of the Third International Conference on Ubiquitous Computing.* Berlin/Heidelberg: Springer, 232–239.

Mankoff, J.; Dey, A.K.; Hsieh, G.; Kientz, J.; Lederer, S.; and Ames, M. 2003. Heuristic evaluation of ambient displays. In *Proceedings of the Conference on Human Factors in Computing Systems.* New York: ACM Press, 169–176.

Masten, D.L. and Plowman, T. 2003. Digital ethnography: The next wave in understanding the consumer experience. *Design Management Journal* 14, 2, 75–84.

Moran, T. and Dourish, P. 2001. Introduction to this special issue on context–aware computing. *Human-Computer Interaction,* 16, 2–4, 87–97.

Mynatt, E.D.; Rowan, J.; Craighill, S.; and Jacobs, A. 2001. Digital family portraits: Supporting peace of mind for extended family members. In *Proceedings of the SIGCHI Conference on Human Factors in Computing Systems.* New York: ACM Press, 333–340.

Palen, L. and Salzman, M. 2002. Voice-mail diary studies for naturalistic data capture under mobile conditions. In *Proceedings of the 2002 ACM Conference on Computer Supported Cooperative Work.* New York: ACM Press, 87–95.

Petersen, M.G.; Madsen, K.H.; and Kjaer, A. 2002. The usability of everyday technology- emerging and fading opportunities. *ACM Transactions on Computer-Human Interaction,* 9, 2, 74–105.

Philipose, M.; Fishkin, K.; Perkowitz, M.; Patterson, D.; Fox, D.; Kautz, H.; Hähnel, D. 2004. Inferring activities from interactions with objects. *IEEE Pervasive Computing,* October, 50–57.

Proctor, R. and Vu, K. 2003. Human information processing: An overview for human-computer interaction. In *The Human-Computer Interaction Handbook.* Mahwah, NJ: Lawrence Erlbaum, 35–51.

Russell, D.; Streitz, N.A.; and Winograd, T. 2005. Building disappearing computers. *Communications of the ACM,* 48, 42–48.

Salvador, T.; Barile, S.; and Sherry, J. 2004. Ubiquitous computing design principles: supporting human-human and human-computer transactions. In *Extended Abstracts of the 2004 Conference on Human Factors and Computing Systems (CHI).* New York: ACM Press, 1497–1500.

Scholtz, J. and Consolvo, S. 2004. Toward a framework for evaluating ubiquitous computing applications. *Pervasive Computing,* 3, 2, 82–88.

Shafer, S.; Brummitt, B.; and Cadiz, J.J. 2001. Interaction issues in context-aware intelligent environments. *Human-Computer Interaction,* 16, 2–4, 363–378.

Smith, J.; Fishkin, K.; Jiang, B.; Mamishev, A.; Philipose, M.; Rea, A.; Roy, S.; and Sundara-Rajan, K. 2005. RFID: Tagging the world: RFID-based techniques for human-activity detection. *Communications of the ACM,* 48, 9 (September), 39–44.

Theofanos, M. and Scholtz, J. 2005. A diner's guide to evaluating a framework for ubiquitous computing applications. In *Proceedings of the HCI International Conference.* St Louis, MO: MIRA Digital Publishing.

Venkatesh, V. and Davis, F.D. 2000. A theoretical extension of the technology acceptance model: four longitudinal field studies. *Management Science,* 46, 2, 186–204.

Waterson, S.; Landay A.; and Matthews, T. 2002. In the lab and out in the wild: Remote Web usability testing for mobile devices. In *CHI'02 Extended Abstracts on Human Factors in Computing Systems.* New York: ACM Press, 796–797.

Weiser, M. 1991. The computer for the 21st century. *Scientific American,* 265, 94–104.

EDITORS AND CONTRIBUTORS

Gregory Biegel is a consultant with a Dublin-based specialist middleware company. He holds an honors degree in computer science from Rhodes University, South Africa, and an M.Sc. in networks and distributed systems from Trinity College Dublin. He recently completed his Ph.D., within the Distributed Systems Group at Trinity College and has previously held research assistant positions at both Trinity College Dublin and the University of Bristol. His research interests include supporting the development of sentient computing applications, and handling uncertainty within pervasive computing environments.

Vinny Cahill is associate professor of computer science at Trinity College Dublin. He has published over seventy peer-reviewed papers in the general area of distributed systems and is particularly well known for his work in middleware and distributed object computing. His current research addresses middleware and programming language support for dependable sentient computing for applications ranging from intelligent vehicles to outdoor smart spaces. He is a member of the editorial boards of *IEEE Pervasive Computing* and *IEEE DSonline*.

Victor Callaghan, B.Eng. Ph.D., C.Eng., MBCS, MIEE, is professor of computer science, head of the Inhabited Intelligent Environments group and co-director of the Digital Lifestyles Centre. He set up the Essex University robotics, inhabited intelligent environments research and digital lifestyle groups, together with supporting laboratories. Before pursuing a university career he spent twelve years in the avionics industry. He has attracted more than £1 million in research funding and authored more than 100 publications. Among other responsibilities, he is a member of the editorial board of the *International Journal of Pervasive Computing and Communications* (*JPCC*), associate editor of *International Journal of Ubiquitous Computing and Intelligence* (*JUCI*), general co-chair of the IEE Intelligent Environments 2005 and 2006, program co-chair of Ubiquitous Intelligence and Smart Worlds 2005 and 2006, and Program Committee chair of the IEEE International Symposium on Pervasive Computing and Applications 2006.

Jeannette Chin, B.Sc., is a senior research officer at the University of Essex. She has a diploma in civil architecture (building) from the Polytechnique of Ungku Omar, Malaysia, and a first class honors degree in Internet computing from the University of Essex. Currently she is completing a Ph.D. on the development of intuitive end-user interaction methods and interfaces for pervasive computing that are sensitive to the human relationships they mediate.

Graham Clarke has been working in computing since 1970. For some years he has had a strong interest in artificial intelligence (AI) and has participated in a number of research projects, collaborating with Nikola Kasabov on connectionist approaches to classification and with Jim Doran on simulating societies. His first degree was in (building) architecture, and his M.Sc. was in the applications of computing. The combination of computing, AI, and building architecture that inhabited intelligent environments represent provide a good match to his interests and skills. Since 1995 he has been actively working on the underlying science of embedded agents for inhabited intelligent environments. He has recently received a doctorate in psychoanalytic studies, which reflects his commitment to the crucial importance of emotion in all human endeavors.

Sunny Consolvo is a member of the research staff at Intel Research Seattle. Her focus is in applying human-centered design to ubiquitous computing. She is currently working in the areas of fitness and elder care. As part of the Ubiquitous Fitness Influencing Technology (UbiFIT) project, she is investigating how technology can encourage people to increase their levels of physical activity. As part of the Computer-Supported Coordinated Care (CSCC) project, she is investigating how technology can be used to help the many people who provide care to elders. Ms. Consolvo has a strong interest in the privacy implications of these types of technologies. She previously worked in industry in Silicon Valley where her focus was on Web design and usability. Ms. Consolvo studied human–computer interaction in the Reentry Program at the University of California, Berkeley and is currently working on her Ph.D. at the University of Washington's Information School.

Andrew Fano is a senior researcher at Accenture Technology Labs, which he joined in 1996. He has played a leading role in defining Accenture's views on the future of mobile and ubiquitous commerce. Currently, he leads Accenture Technology Lab's information insight initiative research efforts. Research projects he is currently leading include Intelligent Cargo Containers using Mesh Networks. Earlier, he worked at the research lab of the Systems Research and Applications Corporation in Arlington, Virginia, where he helped develop natural language processing systems for defense applications. He received his Ph.D. in computer science specializing in artificial intelligence at Northwestern University, he studied business at Kellogg School of Management, and did his undergraduate work at Vassar College.

Michael Gardner holds a B.Sc. in computer science from Leicester Polytechnic (1984) and a Ph.D. in computing from Loughborough University of Technology Computer-Human Interface Research Centre (1987). He is a director of Chimera, a sociotechnical research institute, and has had work experience within both commercial and academic research environments, and spanning the domains of research, development, and business communities. Prior to joining Chimera, he spent fifteen years in the BT research and development laboratories at Adastral Park. He was also research manager for the Asian Research Centre (ARC) in Kuala Lumpur, Malaysia. His main area of interest is the sociotechnical implications of new multidevice and multinetwork customer solutions. The current research focus is on tools to support the mobility of application sessions across different device types. This includes the ability to move Web and voice sessions between devices and is based on the concept of "always-on" services.

Anatole Gershman is director of research at Accenture Technology Labs. Under his leadership, research at the laboratories is focusing on early identification of potential business opportunities and the design of innovative applications for the home, commerce, and workplace of the future. The laboratories are conducting research in the areas of ubiquitous computing, intelligent objects, human–computer interaction, information access and visualization, intelligent sensor networks, and simulation and modeling. Prior to joining Accenture in 1989, Gershman spent over fifteen years conducting research and building commercial systems based on artificial intelligence and natural language processing technology. He has held R&D positions at Coopers and Lybrand, Cognitive Systems, Inc., Schlumberger, and Bell Laboratories. He studied mathematics and computer science at Moscow State Pedagogical University and received his Ph.D. in computer science from Yale University in 1979.

George M. Giaglis is assistant professor of eBusiness in the Department of Management Science and Technology of Athens University of Economics and Business, Greece. He has also held full-time academic posts in Brunel University (UK) and the University of the Aegean (Greece), and has been a visiting professor at universities including the University of London (UK), Nottingham Trent University (UK), Henley Management College (UK), University of Jyvaskyla (Finland), and the Sydney Institute of Technology (Australia). His main teaching and research interests lie in the areas of eBusiness (emphasizing mobile and wireless applications and services), ubiquitous, pervasive, and wearable information systems, business process modeling and simulation, and information systems evaluation. He has published more than sixty articles in leading journals, including the *Information Systems Journal*, the *International Journal of Electronic Commerce*, and the *International Journal of Information Management*, and international conference proceedings. He is a member of the editorial board of seven journals, including the *International Journal of Mobile Communications* and the *Business Process Management Journal*. He is the permanent secretary of the International Conference on Mobile Business, where he has also served as research chair, and permanent track co-chair for the European Simulation Symposium. He has also served on the organizing committee of more than ten international conferences (including the European Conference on Information Systems Evaluation, the International Conference on Business Process Modelling, and the Hawaiian International Conference on Systems Sciences).

Stathes Hadjiefthymiades received his B.Sc., M.Sc., and Ph.D. degrees in informatics from the Department of Informatics and Telecommunications, University of Athens (UoA). He also received a joint engineering–economics M.Sc. from the National Technical University of Athens. In 1992 he joined the Greek consulting firm Advanced Services Group, Ltd. In 1995 he joined the Communication Networks Laboratory of UoA. During 2001–2, he served as visiting assistant professor at the University of Aegean, Department of Information and Communication Systems Engineering. In the summer of 2002, he joined the faculty of Hellenic Open University, Patras, Greece, as an assistant professor. Since December 2003, he has been a member of the faculty of the Department of Informatics and Telecommunications, University of Athens, where he is presently an assistant professor. He has participated in numerous European Union and national projects. His research interests are in the areas of Web engineering, mobile/pervasive computing, and networked multimedia. He has contributed to over 100 publications in these areas. His work is supported by the PYTHAGORAS programme of the Greek Ministry of National Education and Religious Affairs (University of Athens Research Project No. 70/3/7411).

Panos E. Kourouthanassis is lead project manager and research officer at the ELTRUN/Wireless Research Center (ELTRUN/WRC). He holds a Ph.D. in information systems and an M.Sc. in decision sciences with a specialty in eBusiness. He has extensive research experience. Since 1996, he has been a research officer in ELTRUN research group, which is actively involved in the area of eBusiness. He has previously been involved in numerous leading-edge European research projects as project manager. He has published over fifteen research papers in scientific journals and proceedings of European conferences. His main research interests lie in the areas of eBusiness (emphasizing mobile and wireless applications and services), pervasive and ubiquitous computing, software engineering, and information systems design. He has co-organized dedicated workshops and research tracks on ubiquitous commerce at leading international conferences focused on ubiquitous computing. He received the Gold Award of the Fourth ECR Student Award program for his research on the proposition of innovative wireless information systems for the retail sector that enhance consumers' shopping experience. He is a member of ECR Europe (Academics), the International Society of Logistics (SOLE), and the Association for Information Systems (AIS).

Ilias Maglogiannis received a diploma in electrical and computer engineering in 1996 and a Ph.D. in biomedical engineering from the National Technical University of Athens (NTUA), Greece, 2000. From 1996 until 2000 he worked as a researcher in the Biomedical Engineering Laboratory at NTUA. Since February 2001, he has been a lecturer in the Department of Information and Communication Systems Engineering at the University of the Aegean. He has been a principal investigator in many European and national research programs in biomedical engineering and health telematics. His published scientific work includes one book and five lecture notes (in Greek) on biomedical engineering and multimedia topics, twenty-one journal papers and more than forty international conference papers. He has served on program and organizing committees for national and international conferences and he is a reviewer for several scientific journals. His scientific activities include biomedical engineering, telemedicine and medical informatics, image processing, and multimedia telecommunications. He is a member of IEEE—Societies: Engineering in Medicine and Biology, Computer, Communications, SPIE—International Society for Optical Engineering, ACM, the Technical Chamber of Greece, the Greek Computer Society and the Hellenic Organization of Biomedical Engineering. He is also a national representative for Greece in the IFIP Working Group 12.5 (Artificial Intelligence—Knowledge-Oriented Development of Applications).

Javier Muñoz is a Ph.D. student in the Department of Information Systems and Computation (DISC) at the Technical University of Valencia, Spain. His research interests are model-driven development, pervasive systems, model transformations, and software factories. He is a member of the OO-Method Research Group at the DISC, and his research has been published in the proceedings of international events like CAiSE (Conference on Advanced Information Systems Engineering) and MOMPES (International Workshop on Model-based Methodologies for Pervasive and Embedded Software). His Ph.D. dissertation presents a method based on model-driven architecture and the Software Factories proposals for the development of pervasive systems.

Vicente Pelechano is an associate professor in the Department of Information Systems and Computation (DISC) at the Technical University of Valencia, Spain. His research interests are Web engineering, conceptual modeling, requirements engineering, software patterns, Web services, pervasive systems, and model-driven development. He received his Ph.D. from the Valencia University of Technology in 2001. He currently teaches software engineering, design and implementation of Web services, component-based software development, and design patterns at the Technical University of Valencia. He is a member of the OO-Method Research Group at the DISC. He has published articles in several well-known scientific journals (including *Information Systems, Data & Knowledge Engineering, Information and Software Technology*), and presented papers at international conferences (including ER, CAiSE, WWW, ICWE, DEXA). He is a member of scientific committees for well-known international conferences and workshops such as CAiSE (Conference on Advanced Information Systems Engineering), ICWE (International Conference on Web Engineering), ICEIS(International Conference on Enterprise Information Systems), and IADIS (International Association for Development of the Information Society).

Cliff Randell holds a Ph.D. in Applied Wearable Computing from the University of Bristol. He is a research fellow in the Computer Science Department of the University of Bristol, UK. He specializes in wearable computing and is currently carrying out research as part of the Engineering and Physical Sciences Research Council (EPSRC)-funded Equator IRC in collaboration with the Universities of Sussex and Glasgow, and Central St. Martins College of Art and Design. His wide-ranging interests include positioning technologies; context sensing; the use of audio for mobile applications; and the integration of sensors, wiring, and displays into textiles. He obtained his B.Sc. in electrical engineering and M.Sc. in computer science from the University of Bristol, and is a member of the IEE and IEEE.

Johan Redström is research director of the design studio at the Interactive Institute in Göteborg, Sweden, and visiting associate professor at the Center for Design Research of the Royal Academy of Fine Arts, School of Architecture, in Copenhagen, Denmark. He was formerly a lecturer in interaction design at Chalmers University, Göteborg, Sweden. His educational background is in philosophy, cognitive science, and music, and he received a Ph.D. in informatics from Göteborg University. His research involves combining philosophical and artistic approaches with a focus on experimental interaction design. His main design research projects include "Slow Technology," which involves designing for reflection rather than efficiency in use, "IT+Textiles," on combining traditional design and new technologies, and "Static!" on promoting energy awareness through interaction design.

Jean Scholtz is a computer scientist at the National Institute of Standards and Technology where her research interests are metrics and methodologies for evaluating human interaction with intelligent systems. She currently works in the domains of both human–robot interaction and intelligence analysis. She was a program manager at the Defense Advanced Projects Agency (DARPA) where she managed, among other projects, an effort in ubiquitous computing, including MIT's Oxygen project, Berkeley's Endeavor Project, and CMU's Project Aura. Prior to working at NIST, she worked as a human computer specialist at Intel Corporation and was on the Computer Science Faculty at Portland State University. She has a B.A. in mathematics from the University of Iowa, an M.S. in mathematics from Stevens Institute, and a Ph.D. in computer science from the University of Nebraska.

Anuroop Shahi graduated with a first honors class degree in computer science from the University of the West of England in Bristol. He is interested in mobile devices, such as smart phones, and the ways in which these devices can interact with pervasive computing environments. He has looked at ways in which users can control various devices in a smart space environment, together with personalizing services, by treating existing mobile devices as personal entities, which users carry to/from day-to-day environments. He works on the EPSRC-funded Cityware project at the University of Bath, where he is pursuing a Ph.D. His research focuses on examining trust and privacy in pervasive computing environments.

Mary Theofanos is a computer scientist in the Visualization and Usability Group of the National Institute of Standards and Technology where she is working on the Industry Usability Reporting Project and the Common Industry Format for Usability Test Reports developing standards for usability. Previously, she was the manager of the National Cancer Institute's Communication Technologies Research Center, a state-of-the-art usability testing facility for Web sites, applications, and emerging technologies, where her research focused on the intersection of accessibility and usability. She spent fifteen years as a program manager for software technology at the Oak Ridge National Laboratory complex of the U.S. Department of Energy. She has a B.S. in mathematics from the University of Richmond, an M.S. in computer science from the University of Virginia, and is currently a Ph.D. candidate in software engineering at George Mason University, where she is working on her dissertation.

Victor Zamudio received a B.Sc. in physics from the Autonomous University of San Luis Potosi (Mexico) in 1995, an M.Sc. in computer science from Monterrey Tech (Mexico) in 1998, and a certification in project-oriented learning from Aalborg University, Denmark. He is a member of the ACM. In 1998, he joined the Department of Engineering, Monterrey Tech, as a lecturer. He is presently completing Ph.D. research on task allocation, analysis, and visualization in intelligent environments with the Inhabited Intelligent Environments Group in the Department of Computer Science at the University of Essex.

SERIES EDITOR

Vladimir Zwass is the Distinguished Professor of Computer Science and Management Information Systems at Fairleigh Dickinson University. He holds a Ph.D. in Computer Science from Columbia University. He is the founding editor-in-chief of the *Journal of Management Information Systems,* one of the three top-ranked journals in the field of information systems. He is also the founding editor-in-chief of the *International Journal of Electronic Commerce,* ranked as the top journal in its field. Dr. Zwass is the founding editor-in-chief of the monograph series *Advances in Management Information Systems,* the objective of which is to codify the field's knowledge and research methods. He is the author of six books and several book chapters, including entries in the *Encyclopaedia Britannica,* as well as a number of papers in various journals and conference proceedings. He has received several grants, consulted for a number of major corporations, and is a frequent speaker to national and international audiences. He is a former member of the professional staff of the International Atomic Energy Agency in Vienna, Austria.

INDEX

Page numbers in italic refer to figures and tables.

A

abstract factory design patterns, 115
abstraction models, 104–105
accelerometers, 152
Accenture Technology Labs, 151, 159–160, 161
access devices, 37–41, *45*
Active Badge, 13
ActiveHome Pro, 131
actuation, 35–37, 98–100
ad hoc mobile networking, 9, 89–91, 94–95, 184
adaptability, 40
adaptive system. *See* context awareness
adoption, 214–215, 219, 228
advertising, 53, *56*
aeronautic industry, 170
aesthetics, 197–207, 219
age of end-users, 144, 145–146, 162
agent services, 13, 130, 141–142, 172–173
aging workforce, 162
airplanes, 169
Allia, 40
Ambient Agoras, 64
ambient displays, 38, *39*
analogue signals, 92
analysis in pervasive systems design, 51, 108–109
ANODR, 64
appeal, 219. *See also* aesthetics
appliances, standard, 132
Application Program Set (APS), 98
Application Programming Interface (API), 98
application-oriented design, 70
architecture, 40, *107,* 110, 112–115, 129, 166–168
Aristotle, 202
ASL (action semantic language), 110
assembly, 52
asynchronous communication, 93, *94,* 95
ATMs (automated teller machines), 57
AT&T Laboratories, 12
attention, 214
augmented reality, 12, 172–173
Aura, 46

automatic code generation, 116–120
automatic video analysis, 223–224
autonomous agents. *See* agent services
autostereotropic 3D displays, 38
availability of pervasive middleware, 40
awareness, 216, 228

B

bandwidth, *34*
battery power, 36, 39, 69
BBN Technologies, 32
beauty, 66. *See also* aesthetics
Benetton, 63
binding provider, 110, 113
biosignals, 185–191
Blocker Tag, 64
Bluetooth
   in health care technology, 182–183, 185, 190, 192
   in PS design, 38, 113
   in sensor networks, 153
   specifications of, 9, 32, *34, 183*
body-invasive devices, 171
BodyLAN, 32
Bodymedia, 171
Boeing Company, 169
brain, human, 155
broadband access, 38
business process applications, 53, *55*

C

cable, 38
Cage, John, 207
"calm technology," 12, 61
camera phones, 151
capture of data, 91
car production, 170
Carnegie Mellon University, 46
CCDs (charge-coupled devices), 95
cellular networks. *See* mobile/wireless networks
Chimera, 145
classification of pervasive information systems, 47

click-throughs, 62
cloaking, 62, 64
clothing. *See* fashion
Co, Elise, 173–174
COBRA, 93
collaboration technologies, 158
Columbia University, 172–173
commercial off-the-shelf (COTS) elements, 106, 107, 111–112
communication service, *58*
communications layer, 112–113
communities, 133–134, 137–139, *141*
component functional specification, 110
component structure specification, 110
conceptual models, users', 216, 228
Confab, 64
configuration, 41
connectivity, 33, 38, *44,* 168
conservation, 36
Consumers Against Supermarket Privacy Invasion and Numbering (CASPIAN), 63
context awareness
  applications, 96
  data capture of, 91
  data representation, 93, 97, 99
  defined, 16, 41–42, 66, 87
  design challenges for, *45*
  end users' environment, 41–42
  environmental changes, 35–37
  evaluation of, 212
  experience sampling, 222
  incompleteness of data, 91–92
  inference, 97–98
  management, 43
  middleware for, 87
  and pervasive information systems, 41–43
  and privacy, 62
  sensing devices, 167
  uncertainty of, 91–92
  in wearable computing, 167
Context Toolkit, 88
context widgets, 88
control, 216, 228
controlled environments, 185–186
Cooltown project, 47
CORBA (Common Object Request Broker Architecture), 40
corporate environment, 47, 52–57, *59,* 60, *61,* 176
cost, 227, 228
coverage, *34,* 184
Crossbow Technology, Inc., 37
cultural acceptance of technology, 175–176
culture of end-users, 144, 145, 175–176, 198, 221
customer-relationship management (CRM), 52–53, 54, *56,* 158–160
customization, 9, 218
Cyberjacket, 173

D

daily interactions, 172
DAML-S (OWL-S), 139
data management, 4–5, 93
data range, *183*
DCOM (Distributed Common Object Model), 40
dCOMP, 139–141
DEAPspace, 41
deconstructed functions, 132, 133
DECT, *183*
Dempster-Schafer Theory, 96
design principles
  challenges, *44–45*
  deployment of design, 51–52
  infrastructure layer, 30–44
  physical constraints in, 38–39
  for privacy-aware pervasive systems, 64
  of product lines, 112–115
  services layer, 46–59
  social layer, 60–70
desktop systems, *17,* 37, *39*
device discovery, 41
device types. *See* pervasive access devices
DICOM, 185
diffusion, 62
Diffusion Group, 129
digital displays. *See* visualization technologies
Digital Ethno, 221
digital home, 130
digital signals, from analogue, 92
Directive on Privacy and Electronic Communications, 63
disability and access, 57
disappearing computing systems, 12, 15
disclosure boundary, 65
discovery transactions, 40
distribution, 160–161
DIY in pervasive computing, 131, 147
domain context, 42
domestic environments, 47, 51, *59,* 60, *61*
drivers layer, 112
DSL (digital subscriber line), 38
DSL (domain-specific language), 105, 107–110
DSL Tools, 107
Dust, Inc., 37
DyPERS system, 172

E

EAs (evaluation areas), 214–220
Easy Living (Microsoft), 132
ECG (electrocardiogram), 187
educational service, *58*
EEG (electroencephalogram), 187
effectiveness, 228
EIB, 113

802.11 technologies. *See* IEEE 802.x family
electrocardiogram (ECG), 185
electroencephalogram (EEG), 185–186
emergency services, 170, 171, 189
EMF plug-in, 107
emotions, 67, 200
encryption, *44*
end-users
  aesthetic design, factor in, 199
  age of, 144, 145–146
  behavior, monitoring of, 62–63
  culture of, 144, 145, 175–176, 198, 221
  environment of, 41–42
  familiarity with technology, 57, 68, 135, 145
  in home-automation technology, 130–133
  interaction of, 41, *45,* 66, 175, 211–212
  passive, 65
  programming by, 130–133, 136–141
  uncertainty, 68
energy efficiency, 36, 41, *44,* 69. *See also* power
    management
energy waste, 69
engineering applications, *49*
engineering-oriented design, 70
enterprise resource planning, *55*
entertainment, *49, 50, 58*
Envir021s (E21s), 46
environment change, 219, 228
environment of user, 41–42, 66
environmental challenges, 69
environment-directed systems. *See* context awareness
EPE (Ekahau's Positioning Engine), 184
epistemology, 133
Epsilon Project (SUN), 132
ESM (experience sampling method), 222
Ethernet, 38, 113
ethnography, 221. *See also* culture of end-users
ETSI HiplerLAN, *32*
European Telecommunications Standards Institute, 32
evaluations
  case study of, 215, 224–228
  framework for, 213–220
  methodologies of, 221–223
  need for, 211–213
event fillers, 95
event heap, 136
event notifications, 95
event-based communication, 95
everyday life/objects, 38, *39,* 65–68, 103
execution support layer, 40, 43
Experience Clips, 222
experience sampling method (ESM), 222
experience technologies, 155–158, 222
expressional interaction, 67
extensibility, 94
extraorganizational user, 47

F

fabric area networks, 32
fashion, viii, 173–174, 198
FEDER, 123
feelings, 67
female/male voices, 60
field force automation (FFA), 53–54, *55*
firefighting, 170
5 GHz band, 69
4G networks, 192
F-OWL, 141
framework specifications, 116–120, 205–207, 213–220
FreeMarker, 117–119
frequencies, *183*
furniture, augmented, 51

G

GAIA, 40, 88
gambling, 166
gaming, *58,* 173
garments, viii, 173–174, 198
gateway management and control, 41
GEF plug-in, 107
General Dynamics C4 Systems, 170
gesture recognition, 175
global mobility, 31
GMB Union, 176
GPRS (general packet radio service), *32, 33, 34*
GPS (global positioning system), 95, 152, 167, 172, 173
graph grammars, 116
Ground Soldier, 170
GSM, *32, 183,* 192
GUI (graphical user interface), 98, 197
GUIDE project, 97

H

Handy21s (H21s), 46
haptic interfaces, 167
HAVi, 113
HCI (human-computer interaction), 15, 37–41, 201
head-mounted display. *See* HMD (head-mounted display)
health care applications
  biosignal characteristics, *186*
  challenges of, 191–192
  controlled environments, 185–186
  design for, *49*
  home care applications, 186–187
  mobility of, 184
  monitoring of service personnel, 171
  networking technologies for, 182–184
  nonhospital settings, 186–187
  smart furniture for, 159
  wearable computing, 167, 170–172
Hewlett-Packard (HP) Labs, 47
HiplerLAN ETSI, *32*

HiplerLAN2, 32, *34, 183*
HL7, 185
HMD (head-mounted display), 165, 169, 172, *174*
holographic projections, 38
home care applications, 186–187
Home Energy Tutor, 224–228
home environment, 48, *50,* 159, 224–228
home-automation technology, 130
HomeRF, *183*
hospitals, 185–186. *See also* health care applications
HTTP, 93
human-computer interaction (HCI), 15, 37–41, 201

I

ICD+ jacket, 173
identity boundary, 65
identity theft, 62
iDorm, 134–135
iDorm2, 143–146
IEEE 802.x family, 32–33, 38, 182, *183,* 185, 191
IEEE 802.11a, *183*
IEEE 802.11b, 69, *183*
IEEE 802.11b/a/g, *34*
IEEE 802.11g, 69
IEEE 802.15, 182
IEEE 802.15.4, 182
IEEE 802.16, 33, *34*
IEEE 802.16a, *34*
IEEE 13941, 38, 113
IEEE 1451.4, 35
IETF (Internet Engineering Task Force), 192
Image-Based Experience Sampling, 222
impact of pervasive information systems, 218–219, 228
implementation framework, 113–115
IMT-2000, *183*
incompleteness, 91–92, 96
individual layer, 30
industry environment, 168–170
inference, 97–98, 99
infokiosks, *39*
InfoPad, 13
information systems development, 4–9
information transparency, 162–163
information update, *44*
informational service, *58*
infotainment, *49, 50*
infrastructure context, 42
infrastructure layer, technologies for, 29, *30,* 30–44
infrastructure mobile network model, 89
infrastructure systems, 35
initiatives for pervasive information systems, 46–47
input modes, 167
integrator systems, 105–106
Intel, 129
interaction-oriented design, 70

interactivity
    aesthetics of, 66–68, 203–207
    design of, 203–207
    evaluating, 217–218, 228
    in home environment, 51
    human-computer, 15, 37–41, 201
    layers of, 29–30
    of pervasive devices, *39*
    technologies for, 157–158
    through pervasive access devices, 37–41
    triggered by system, 66
interface, 39–41, 113, 115
Internet, development of, 5–7
intraorganizational users, 47
inventory control, 169
invisible computing systems, 12, 66, 218
IrDA (infrared technology), 32, *34, 183,* 190–191
IrisNet, 37

J

J2EE (Java 2 Enterprise Edition), 40
J2ME (Java 2 Micro Edition), 40

K

Kalman filter, 96
Kant, Immanuel, 202–203, 204
key-value pairs, 97
kinesthetics, 48
Kraftwerk, 205
Kroes, P., 207

L

LAN (Local Area Network), 32–33
Land Warrior program, 170
laptops, *39*
latency, 35, *44*
Lauren Scott California, viii
Le Corbusier, 129
learning time, 65
LFU (Learning from the User), 137
licensing requirements, *34*
lifecycle management, *114,* 115
lifeworld, 64
lighting systems example, 106–111, 120–122
Liveboard, 13
local area networks, *183*
local mobility, 31, 32
location, sensing of, 152–153
location privacy, 64
location-based information, 16
logic layer, 114–115
logic-based approach to context representation, 97
LonWorks, 113
loosely-coupled communication, 94–95, 99

M

machine learning, 98
machinery, 169
maintenance, increased efficiency of, 154, 160, 169
male/female voices, 60
Man Machine, The, 205
MAN (Metropolitan Area Network), *32*
mappings for transformation of models, 105
MAps (Meta-Application-appliances), 131–132, 137–138
Martin, Tom, 174
Massachusetts Institute of Technology (MIT), 46, 172
McCann, Jane, 174
MDA (Model-Driven Architecture), 103–105, 116
MDM (mobile device mediator), 135
meaningful presence, 67
MEC, 123
mechanical vibrations, *44*
M-Echo, 40
MediaBroker, 113
MediaCup, 36, 38
medical applications. *See* health care applications
meeting room services model, 106, *108*
MEMS (microelectromechanical systems), 95, 167, 174
mesh networks. *See* ad hoc mobile networking
methodologies of evaluations, 221–223
Metricom Ricochet, *183*
metrics, 220
metropolitan area networks, *183*
MICA, 40
micro mobility, 32
Microsoft Easy Living, 132
middleware. *See* pervasive middleware
MiddleWhere, 40
military applications, *49,* 170–171
miniaturization, 62, 174–175
MITA, 40
Mix Zones, 64
Mixed Reality Lab, 173
mobile business/m-business, 9
mobile commerce/m-commerce, 9
mobile computing, 8–9, 88–91
mobile devices, 37–38, *39,* 222
mobile/wireless networks, 33, 52, 69, 89–91, *183*
mobility
   in health care applications, 184
   infrastructure for, 31–35
   and personal access devices, 37–38
   of pervasive devices, *39*
model-to-model transformations, 116–120
Modern Movement (architecture), 129
modifiability, 40
MOF language, 116
monomodal sensor fusion, 96
MOTES, 37
MS RADAR, 185
Mukherjee, A, 30–31

multimodal sensor fusion, 96
Mundie, Craig, 129
MUSE, 185
museums, 172
My Experience, 222
MyGROCER, 37–38

N

N21s, 46
Naive Bayes classifier, 98
National University, Singapore, 173
natural settings, testing in, 223–224
Navigator 2, 169
network management, *44*
network partitions, 90–91
network types, 32–33, *34*
networking technologies, 182–184
neural networks, artificial, 98
Nibble, 185
nodes (sensor), *44,* 153
nomadic computing systems, 12, 16
nonhospital settings, 186–187

O

object-oriented approach to context representation, 97
off-body networks, 182–184
office automation and support, *49, 56*
021s, 46
OlivaNova Model Execution System, 123
OMG (Object Management Group), 104, 116
on-body networks, 32, 182–184
one.world, 113
ontology, 133, 139–141, *140*
OO-Method, 123
operating frequencies, *34*
OSGi (Open Service Gateway Initiative), 113–119
output modes
   for wearable computing, 167
OWL-S, 135, 139
Oxygen project, 15, 46

P

package delivery, 160–161
Pacman, 173
Palmtops, *39*
Palpable Computing, 137
PAN (Personal Area Network), 32, 182
Panther Access to Web Services (PAWS) system, 64
paper as user interface, 158
para-functionality, 206
ParcTab, 13
Parkinson's disease, 172
PARREHA, 172
participation components, 41
patient monitoring, 181–182, 185–191

PBE (Programming By Example), 137
PDAs, *39*
performance, 40
personal identification numbers (PINs), 57
personal pervasive information systems, 33, 48, *59, 61*
Personnel Status Monitor, 171
pervasive access devices, 16
pervasive information systems
  building challenges of, 91–94
  defined, 15–17
  defining, 10–13
  similar concepts to, 11–13, *14*
pervasive middleware, 39–41, *44, 45,* 87–88, 94–100, *96*
pervasive network technologies, *31,* 31–35, *44*
pervasive office support (POS), 54
PervML (Pervasive Modeling Language), *105,* 107–110, 114–120
Philips/Levi Strauss, 173
physical context, 42
physiological signals, *186*
PICO, 130
piezo materials, 95
PiP (Pervasive Interactive Programming), 136–141
placement, 52
Platform for Privacy Preferences (P3P), 64
pleasure-based approach, 199
PocketPC devices, 222
pollution, 69
Portolano project, 46–47
positioning technologies, 184–185
post-optimal object, 206
power management, 36, *44,* 69, *174,* 224–228. *See also* energy efficiency
predictability, 154–155, 216
privacy
  cloaking, 62
  diffusion, 62
  evaluation of, 216, 228
  and middleware development, 100
  in pervasive systems design, 30, *45,* 61–65
  in public systems, 57
  storage concerns, 62
  for wearable computing, 175
  in wireless sensor networks, 36
privacy-enabling technologies (PETs), 63
proactive systems, 13
probabilistic networks, 96
processing, 62, 168
product lines for pervasive systems, 111–115
production, 160–161
public pervasive information systems, 47, 57, *58, 59,* 60, *61*
PWT, *183*

Q

QADA, *44*
Quake, 173

quality of service (QoS), 33, 41, *44,* 93
Quantum3D Expedition, 170
QWERTY keyboard, 167, 175, 205

R

RACER, 139
radio frequencies, 32. *See also* BodyLAN
Radio Shack, 130
ReachMedia, 38
Reality Online, 160, 162, 163
recycling, 69
regulations and laws, 63, 70
reinforcement learning, 98
relational database tables, 41
relevancy, 43
Rememberer, 217
Remembrance Agent, 172
reminders of system presence, 66
remote mobility, 32
remote testing, 223
resource description framework (RDF), 97
restrictions, 30
reusability, 94
RFID (radio frequency identification device), viii, 9, *32,* 38, 63–64, 151, 159, 212
RFID-augmented pervasive retail systems, 64
robustness, 220
route anonymity, 64
routing protocols, 91
rule-based systems, 96, 98
rumors, 162

S

Saha, D., 30–31
Sahara, 40
sales force automation (SFA), 54, *55*
satellite-based positioning, 184
SCADDS, 41
scalability, 93, 217
scalable intelligence, 154–155
school environment, 66
security
  in design of pervasive information systems, 33–35, *45, 50,* 61–65
  of pervasive middleware, 40
  in transportation, 161
  for wearable computing, 175
  in wireless sensor networks, 35–36
self-reporting evaluations, 221
sensing, of environmental changes, 35–37
sensor abstraction, 95, 99
sensor data, 96
sensor fusion, 96–97, 99, 154
sensor networks, 35–37, 151–154
sensors, 35–37, 92, 95, 224–228

sentient computing systems, 11, 12
Service UI class, 115
services layer, 30, 46–59, *58,* 113–114, 115
SGML (standard generalized mark-up language), 97
shopping technology, 53, 54, *56, 156,* 173
side effects of personal information systems, 218–219, 228
sketching in PS design, 51–52
sleep mode, 165, 168
smart appliances, 37, 38
Smart Doorplate, 66
smart dust, 37, 153
smart furniture, 158–160
smart home. *See* home environment
smart (intelligent) appliances, *39,* 48, *50,* 51–52, 132–133, 136–141
smart phone, 135
smart shopping cart, *156*
Smart-Its, 36
SmartKG, 66
SmartWear Technologies, viii
Social Contract Core, 64
social layer, 30, 60–70
social responses to technology, 60, 175
social units, 63
social-oriented design, 70
soft appliances/applications, 132, 133
software architecture, 112–115
software factories, 103–105, 116–120
software systems, 105–106
solar power, 36, *44*
soldiers, 171
SOUPA, 139, 141
SPARCLE, 64
special needs, 171–172
speech-based user interface, 46, 60, 167, 175
spontaneous networking, 16
stakeholders, 162–163, 212
standard generalized mark-up language (SGML), 97
STEER (semantic task execution editor), 133, 134
stored information, 62, 162–163
SUN Epsilon Project, 132
supply chain management, *55,* 160–161
support, for application development, 99, 100
surveillance, 62
swarm behavior, 16
synchrony, *44,* 93, *94*
system context, 42
system integration, 175
system management, 41

T

tablet PCs, *39*
tagging, 43, 97
Tangible Computing, 137

task definition, *134*
task discovery, 134–135
task grouping, *134*
task interaction, 135–136, *136*
task-based computing, 133–136
technology acceptance model (TAM), 215
temperature, sensing of, 152
templates, 116–120
temporal boundary, 65
temporal community representation, 142–143
temporary pervasive network, 16
terrestrial-based positioning, 184
Tesco, 63
TETRA (terrestrial trunked radio system), 33, *34*
textiles, 173–174
3G network, 182
time, in programming, 142
TM (task model), 135
TOTA, 40
transactional service, *58*
transformation of models, 105, 116–120
transparencies, 40
triggering of interactions, 66
TriSen, Inc., 169
trust, 215–216, 228
TUIs (tangible user interfaces), 197
Twiddler, 167
2.4 GHz band, 69, 70
2.5G network, 182
TZI—Mobile Research Center of the University of Bremen, 170

U

Ubicomp, 141
ubiquitous computing, 11
UML (unified modeling language), 105
UMTS (universal mobile telecommunications systems), *32,* 33, *34,* 192
UMTS (WCDMA), *34*
uncertainty of sensed information, 35–37, *44,* 91–92, 96
University of Birmingham, 171
University of Bristol, 173
University of California, Santa Barbara, 172
University of Karlsruhe, 36, 38
University of South Australia, 173
University of Wales, 174
University of Washington, 47
Unix Mac OS C (Tiger), 132–133
unpredictable (swarm) behavior, 16, 68
UPnP, 113
U.S. Army, 170
usability, 57, 65–66, 199–200, 213
users. *See* end-users
UWB (ultra wideband networks), 32, 152

V

value, 228
video analysis, 223–224
Virginia Tech, 174
visibility and privacy, 62–63
vision technologies, 46
visualization technologies, 156–158
visually impaired users, 172
vocabulary awareness, 216
voice mail diary, 223
VuMan 3, 169

W

WA (wireless assistant), 131
WAE (Wireless Application Environment), 40
WAN (Wide Area Network), *32,* 33
warehousing, 169
WCDMA, *34*
wearable computing
    applications of, 165–176
    architectures, 166–168
    devices for, 38, *39,* 48, 68
    in fabric, viii
    and patient monitoring, 187–188
Wearable Computing Project, 172
wearIT@work project, 169–170
Weiser, Mark, 8, 12

WEP, *44*
WiFi, *32,* 113. *See also* IEEE 802.x family
WiMAX (IEEE 802.16), 9, *32,* 33, 34
wind power, 36
wireless connectivity, *183*
wireless devices, 37–38
wireless discovery, *45*
wireless hotspots, registration of, 70
wireless networks, 9, 41, *44,* 69
Wizard of Oz techniques, 212
WLAN (wireless local area network), 9, 32–33, 182, 184,
    190–191, 192
WLL (wireless local loop), 38
WMAN (wireless metropolitan area networks), 33
workforce applications, 53–54, *55,* 161–162
World Wide Web, development of, 5–7
WPAN (wireless personal area network), 182
WSN (wireless sensor networks), 35–37. *See also* sensor
    networks

X

X10 home-automation technology, 130
XPref, 64
Xybernaut, 170

Z

ZigBee, 32, *34,* 192